'*Conflict, Security and Justice* is an essential handbook for students and scholars of peace and conflict studies. Not only does it impart knowledge in an accessible way, it also provides its readers with a much-needed understanding of the wider international security landscape by linking theory and practice effectively.'

– **Alp Ozerdem**, *Coventry University, UK*

'Eleanor Gordon's book is an excellent and comprehensive introduction to international approaches to constructing peaceful societies after conflict. Drawing on practical examples from a wide range of contexts, this book provides a critical overview of the various tools used in post-conflict engagement and the challenges that face their implementation. As such it represents a valuable addition to the literature on the practicalities of peacebuilding.'

– **Paul Jackson**, *University of Birmingham, UK*

'This insightful text highlights links between security and justice by showing how and why peacebuilding is required to prevent further conflict and create sustainable peace. Students and practitioners will benefit from the author's extensive experience and the practical examples used.'

– **Elisabeth Porter**, *University of South Australia, Australia*

'By combining a comprehensive and accessible theoretical introduction with chapters covering some of the most important but often overlooked issues today, such as small arms, piracy and explosive remnants of war, Gordon has created an excellent introduction for students of peacebuilding, which will remain relevant for a long time to come.'

– **Tony Ingesson**, *Lund University, Sweden*

'This is an excellent new textbook for advanced courses on processes and programmes for developing security and justice in countries emerging from large-scale conflict. It integrates academic literatures with lessons-learned from practitioners, and is admirably clear and well structured.'

– **Owen Greene**, *University of Bradford, UK*

CONFLICT, SECURITY AND JUSTICE

Practice and Challenges in Peacebuilding

Eleanor Gordon

First published 2019 by
RED GLOBE PRESS

Red Globe Press in the UK is an imprint of Springer Nature Limited, registered in England, company number 785998, of 4 Crinan Street, London, N1 9XW.

Red Globe Press® is a registered trademark in the United States, the United Kingdom, Europe and other countries.

ISBN 978–1–137–61069–0 hardback
ISBN 978–1–137–61068–3 paperback

This book is printed on paper suitable for recycling and made from fully managed and sustained forest sources. Logging, pulping and manufacturing processes are expected to conform to the environmental regulations of the country of origin.

A catalogue record for this book is available from the British Library.

A catalog record for this book is available from the Library of Congress.

Table of Contents

List of Figures and Tables

List of Boxes

Preface

This textbook is designed to develop knowledge and understanding of the practical ways in which security and justice can be developed after conflict, as well as ways in which to address the broader international security risks posed by conflict-affected countries. It is designed specifically for students and scholars of conflict and peace studies as well as broader international relations and international development. It is also hoped that it will be of interest to practitioners and policy-makers and help bridge the gap that often exists between academia and practice – by drawing from practical examples and critically reflecting upon engagement and thereby better understanding and thus being able to better respond to the challenges of conflict and peacebuilding.

This textbook is informed by two decades of working on conflict-related security, justice and human rights issues, including over a decade of working in conflict-affected environments in management and advisory roles with the United Nations (UN) and other organisations and a further ten years of consultancy work with the UN, governments, non-governmental organisations (NGOs) and universities. It is also informed by teaching students, principally practitioners in this field, notably through the MSc course in Security, Conflict and International Development (SCID) that I have developed and delivered for the University of Leicester, and through a subsequent unit on Conflict, Security and Development, I teach as part of the Master's programme in International Development Practice (MIDP) at Monash University. This book responds to a perceived gap in the market for textbooks which bridge theory and practice, and draws directly from practical examples and experience to study aspects of peacebuilding. The motivation behind this textbook, and the teaching that has informed it, is to equip students with the skills and knowledge to progress a career in international development – or its study – and, principally, to better respond to the security and justice challenges facing places as they emerge from conflict. The intention is to enable students to develop the requisite skills and knowledge in an engaging way, drawing on a rich variety of resources and practical examples, and through bridging theory and practice.

This first chapter introduces some of the core concepts commonly used in peacebuilding. It begins by presenting various ways of visualising the different stages of conflict, before reflecting upon the concepts of security and peacebuilding. To provide a context for subsequent chapters, there follow short discussions on the causes of conflict, conflict prevention and broad efforts to rebuild peace after conflict.

The following chapters then consider the activities, actors and challenges involved in a specific programmatic area within the security and justice sector. Chapter 2 provides an overview of the importance of security in building peace and looks at the actors and activities involved in building security in the immediate aftermath of conflict, particularly the role of international military forces in post-conflict recovery. Chapter 3 focusses on ways in which to build the rule of law in post-conflict environments and begins by reflecting upon what is meant by 'the rule of law'. Chapter 4 addresses transitional justice, which is generally considered to be the means whereby post-conflict societies can address atrocities committed in war. This chapter considers the definition, origins, objectives and mechanisms of transitional justice. Chapter 5 focusses on mine action and the control of small arms and light weapons (SALW) in post-conflict environments, beginning with the effect of mines and explosive remnants of war (ERW) as well as SALW on such environments, before providing an overview of activities and actors engaged in these programmatic areas as well as ways in which such activities contribute to the peacebuilding process.

Chapter 6 discusses disarmament, demobilisation and reintegration (DDR) of former combatants, specifically DDR objectives, actors engaged and core recommendations including the importance of attending to the specific needs of children and co-ordinating with other peacebuilding efforts in the security and justice sector, particularly security sector reform (SSR), SALW control and transitional justice. Chapter 7 considers the broad area of security sector reform (SSR), including justice reform, police reform, defence reform, penal reform and security sector governance (SSG). The chapter considers the core features, objectives and principles of SSR, as well as the roles of different actors involved and lessons learnt.

The focus of the book then shifts from specific actors and activities engaged in different programmatic areas in the security and justice sector to consider broader cross-cutting issues, namely human rights and gender. Chapter 8, therefore, considers the relationship between human rights and conflict, first by looking at human rights violations as causes and consequences of armed conflict, alongside the prevalence of human rights violations in conflict-affected environments. This is followed by an overview of human rights work in post-conflict environments, specifically activities and actors engaged in this field and challenges faced. Chapter 9 considers the gender dynamics of conflict and peacebuilding. The first part of this chapter focusses on conflict-related gender-based violence before considering the roles of women and men in peacebuilding, particularly efforts to build security and justice after conflict. Cross-cutting issues – including human rights, gender and also children, non-state actors and various principles of engagement (not least context-specificity and local ownership) – are also mainstreamed throughout the book.

The final chapter then further broadens the focus of attention by considering some of the international security threats perceived to be associated with conflict-affected or conflict-vulnerable environments. It considers the impact of conflict-affected countries on the stability of neighbouring and regional countries, as well as on countries further afield, notably through such phenomena as terrorism, piracy, and cross-border and organised crime. In each case, it looks at the effects of the threats, efforts to overcome them and the links with conflict.

Each chapter, while differing in length depending on the area of focus, is structured similarly, with an overview, learning outcomes, summary of key issues, reflective questions and list of core learning resources. Each chapter also contains diagrams or tables and a number of break-out boxes which elaborate upon a particular issue, concept or case study.

Acknowledgements

I would like to thank Dr David Chuter for all his help and guidance throughout writing this book, for his painstaking review and editing of a first draft, and for giving me permission to draw from our communications in sections of this book. His help and support was invaluable and I am enormously grateful. I would also like to thank Andrew Malvern at Red Globe Press for being such a fantastic editor, providing excellent suggestions, guidance, insights and encouragement. Additionally, I would like to thank the four anonymous reviewers who provided such helpful feedback and suggestions. My heartfelt thanks also go to Monash University and my colleagues, for their support, friendship and inspiration and particularly to Aisha Ismail for helping with the bibliography and proofreading. Most importantly, I would like to thank my family for all their support and my son, Tom, for putting up with late pick-ups, burnt dinners and boring weekends, and more besides, for a very long time while I worked. Finally, for those I lived and worked with in conflict-affected environments, this book is for you, in the hope that it contributes to efforts to build more sustainable, inclusive and equitable peace.

1 Introduction: Concepts of Security, Conflict and Peace

Overview

The opening chapter introduces some of the core concepts commonly used in peacebuilding. It begins by presenting various ways of visualising the different stages of conflict, before reflecting upon the concepts of security and peacebuilding. To provide a context for subsequent chapters, there follows a brief discussion on ways in which to resolve armed conflict and build peace beyond those efforts squarely within the security and justice sector.

Learning Outcomes

- Critically assess the concepts of conflict, security and peacebuilding
- Evaluate the value and limitations of the curve of conflict
- Recognise that core concepts in peacebuilding have policy implications
- Articulate some of the major precursors to effective peacebuilding
- Be familiar with other peacebuilding activities outside the security and justice sector

Part 1 – Core Concepts

A number of key concepts are used throughout this book, relating to phases of conflict and third-party interventions, as well as to the underlying principles and wider theories supporting such interventions. Whilst many of these concepts are understood in broadly the same way within the international community, they have no universally accepted definitions. If conflict prevention, mitigation, termination and recovery efforts are ever to be successful, key concepts need to be unpacked and a shared, sensitive and comprehensive understanding arrived at. Without this shared understanding, it is hard for action to be co-ordinated, coherent, efficient and effective. It is also hard to monitor and evaluate progress, identify and utilise lessons learned and best practice, and ultimately improve efforts to prevent and respond to conflict and its challenges.

    As Chetail (2009) notes, increased peacebuilding activity, perhaps ironically, has led to the term 'peacebuilding' becoming more ambiguous and less sharply defined.

Many different interpretations of this and related terms exist. More problematically, perhaps, many different actors actually involved in post-conflict peacebuilding use different terms to refer to it (Barnett et al., 2007; Chetail, 2009). As Chetail suggests, the use of different terms and the different interpretation of similar terms reflect the different mandates, agendas and interests of the various actors. Not surprisingly, the ambiguity and abundance of related concepts in the field of peacebuilding create some confusion. However, this ambiguity also enables the various actors to work together under the same umbrella without ever having to reach an unlikely consensus on the precise nature of the engagement (for further discussion see Alliance for Peacebuilding, 2019; Barnett et al., 2007; Chetail, 2009).

Given these differences of interpretation, as well as differences (described in the next chapter) over causes and remedies for conflict, there seems little point in devoting this chapter to long and complex arguments about who is right. Those interested can follow the controversies through the references provided. In any event, in this chapter – as throughout the book – the intention is to highlight those interpretations and prescriptions which are politically powerful and which influence the way that governments, international organisations and donors behave in practice.

We will first consider the concept of conflict, before considering the concepts of security and peacebuilding. Other concepts will be addressed later in the book, including justice and the rule of law (Chapter 4), transitional justice (Chapter 5), governance (Chapter 8, when we discuss Security Sector Governance), human rights (Chapter 9), gender (Chapter 10) and terrorism (Chapter 11, when we discuss transnational security threats).

The concept of conflict

Before attempting to address the ambiguity described above, it is first important to understand what we mean by conflict. Conflict, broadly speaking, can mean disagreement, tension or incompatibility between positions, opinions, interests, principles, demands or needs. From this perspective, conflict, of course, can occur anywhere – in the home, at school or the workplace, within social groups and communities, within and between societies, on the global stage. We can see conflict everywhere: it is part of everyday life. Social groups, communities and societies generally have mechanisms to respond to conflict, to manage it and to guard against it becoming violent: rules and compliance mechanisms, norms and social expectations, and structures and processes for grievances to be aired and addressed, for instance. When conflict does become violent it may still not be considered to be armed conflict.

As described in Jackson and Beswick (2018) there are a number of ways in which to measure and categorise armed conflict. One of the most common ways is to count 'battle deaths'. This is problematic in itself, not least in securing reliable data, but in determining which deaths 'count'. For some scholars, when defining armed conflict, 'battle deaths' do not include indirect victims of conflict (those who have died as a result of ill-health or malnutrition as a consequence of the conflict, for instance), or civilian casualties. While there is no agreement among scholars that battle deaths are an appropriate way to measure and categorise conflict, even where battle deaths are used to categorise types of violence, there is no broad agreement on the number of battle deaths that should be the threshold to determine whether or not armed conflict exists. For instance, the University of Uppsala Conflict Data Program (UCDP) (http://ucdp.uu.se) and the Correlates of War Project (www.correlatesofwar.org), which manage the most comprehensive and authoritative databases on armed conflict, have markedly different thresholds. For UCDP (2019), the threshold is 25 battle deaths per year, while for the Correlates of War Project (2019) it is 1,000.

Moving on to considering how armed conflict (hereafter, conflict) can be conceived, one attempt to deal with the ambiguity described above was made by Lund (1996), who introduced the idea of the 'curve of conflict'. As shown in Figure 1.1, the curve of conflict maps the point at which the various phases of conflict occur as well as efforts to prevent, mitigate, terminate or recover from it. As USIP's *Peace Terms Glossary:* puts it:

> The curve of conflict is a conceptual tool that helps illustrate how conflicts tend to evolve over time. The curve helps in visualizing how different phases of conflict relate to one another, as well as to identify kinds of third-party intervention. Practitioners can use this knowledge in the determination of effective strategies for intervention, along with the timing of those strategies. (Snodderly, 2011: 15)

The intensity of the conflict is shown by the vertical axis and the duration of the conflict by the horizontal axis. So, you can see that conflict prevention precedes peace negotiations which, in turn, precede peacekeeping. However, you do not really know how long each of these phases will last and whether one might lead to the next or, if unsuccessful, remain 'stuck' in one phase for a prolonged period of time or even revert to a previous phase. In essence, all phases are about stopping armed conflict – whether its outbreak, escalation, continuance or recurrence. To some extent, therefore, phases often share commonalities, in terms of intent and activities. There are, however, often formal signifiers of a new phase, whether through the outbreak of conflict (leading from conflict prevention to diplomacy, for instance) or the signing

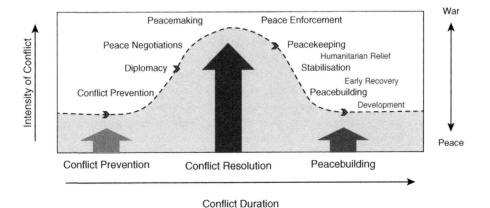

Figure 1.1 The Curve of Conflict (adapted from Lund, 1996)

of a peace agreement (leading to peacekeeping rather than peace enforcement). As the term suggests, on Lund's curve of conflict, peacemaking refers to efforts to make peace when there is none (at the earlier stages of armed conflict), rather than peace-keeping, which refers to efforts to ensure the peace agreement holds. Peacebuilding, as we will soon discuss, tends to be an all-encompassing term referring to a broader range of activities after conflict to build sustainable peace.

It is important to note that the curve does not depict the level of violence that might exist. While armed conflict can formally begin before diplomacy and peace negotiations and end at the signing of a peace agreement (just before peacekeep-ing) – or when there is a truce, defeat, or the successful separation of armed factions (peace enforcement) – armed violence can continue and be prevalent throughout all phases, as will be discussed further shortly. And, of course, conflict can continue; even after the signing of a peace agreement, peacekeepers are needed to ensure the agreement is complied with and lay the groundwork for effective peacebuilding, which should include resolving the causes of the armed conflict and ensuring grievances are addressed and do not lead to conflict recurrence.

To add further nuance, in Figure 1.1, activities beyond those focussed on directly stopping the outbreak, escalation, continuance or recurrence of conflict have been mapped onto the traditional conflict curve. Humanitarian relief, early recovery and development are equally critical to building and sustaining peace (see Kamau, 2018), and tend to take place alongside formal efforts to resolve conflict. Humanitarian relief refers to the provision of life-saving food, water and sanitation, shelter and health services to those within or in the aftermath of conflict or other crisis, such as natural disaster. Development is a more nebulous term which refers to a broad range of activities across the economic, environmental, governance, human rights, health and education sectors undertaken to improve well-being and, in this context, help prevent the outbreak of conflict (recognising the relationship between security and development which will be discussed shortly). Early recovery is a less frequently used concept, which refers to activities which bridge immediate humanitarian assistance and longer-term development, with the aim of augmenting emergency humanitarian assistance and establishing the foundations for longer-term devel-opment. While humanitarian relief tends to begin when there is a modicum of security, and development once there is more stability, in reality both activities can be ongoing throughout all phases other than during heightened insecurity.

Conflict prevention, conflict resolution and, again, peacebuilding are also identified at the horizontal axis. Some analysts distinguish between these three phases of conflict (i.e. before, during and after) although, as we will soon discuss, the lines between these phases are very blurred. Ramsbotham et al. (2016) refer to distinct stages within each of these phases, in order to help identify responses. So, before armed conflict, the trajectory can be seen to move from 'difference' (requiring attending to cultural factors), to 'contradiction' (requiring attending to structural factors), to 'polarisation' (requiring peacemaking), which if unad-dressed leads to violence. After conflict, all being well, the trajectory moves away from conflict, from ceasefire, to 'agreement' (requiring peacemaking), to 'normali-sation' (requiring attending to structural factors) and, finally, to 'reconciliation' (requiring attending to cultural factors). It can be seen from the way Ramsbotham et al. (2016) refer to distinct stages within each of the phases of conflict in order to determine the requisite response, how efforts to build peace are often not too dissimilar to efforts to prevent the outbreak of conflict – we will be looking further into this in the next chapter. We can also use the terms 'escalation' and 'de-escalation' to refer to the way conflict might develop or intensify and end or resolve (see also Jackson and Beswick, 2018).

Distinguishing between the different phases of conflict can be useful in efforts to resolve conflict, to the extent that different strategies or tactics may be more appropriate than others, depending upon the current phase of conflict (or sub-conflict) (see Brahm, 2003). The curve can also be seen as a useful visual tool, in that it can help show common characteristics of different conflicts and, thus, potentially help in efforts to apply lessons learnt from one conflict to another.

It must be remembered, however, that this bell curve hugely simplifies a complex and messy reality. Conflicts do not progress linearly and successively through the various phases: many setbacks may occur, and conflict can repeatedly escalate or re-emerge, for instance. Similarly, efforts to prevent or resolve conflict or make, keep and build peace, will occur at multiple points during the conflict, and often concurrently. This is because the activities associated with these interventions are not exclusive of each other, and anyway there is no consensus around the terms used. Various actors apply different labels to the phases of conflict and related interventions, which further frustrates efforts to simplify. It is also important to realise that different actors and stakeholders, and even parties to the conflict, will perceive the conflict, the stage it is at and how it is developing, differently. There may also be multiple conflicts within one overarching conflict.

It therefore appears increasingly difficult to distinguish between phases of conflict, and third-party intervention, as activities associated with these phases broaden and definitions multiply. The lines between both the theory and the practice of conflict prevention, peacemaking, peacekeeping, peacebuilding and peace enforcement are therefore increasingly blurred.

Thus, the transition from humanitarian action or relief to early recovery to development, for instance, is not as linear and clearly defined as is often implied. Similarly, humanitarian action often continues alongside peacebuilding and state-building efforts and, likewise, development activities often begin during the early recovery stages (and indeed as a conflict prevention measure even before the outbreak of conflict). While a clear understanding of the types of activity required in many post-conflict environments necessitates a delineation of their areas of responsibility, imagining that these activities occur in separate and distinct time frames is not helpful (see Figure 1.2). Recognition of the complexity of recovery efforts does, however, underscore the importance of co-ordination. Whilst co-ordination is widely accepted as a priority among actors involved in facilitating recovery from conflict, divergent and often conflicting or competing priorities, approaches, timeframes, agendas, objectives and perceptions tend to undermine efforts to consolidate a coherent, co-ordinated and effective response.

If we accept that there are inter-dependent relationships between development, security, governance and the protection of human rights, it is perhaps a fallacy to assume that efforts to address insecurity, state fragility and lack of governance,

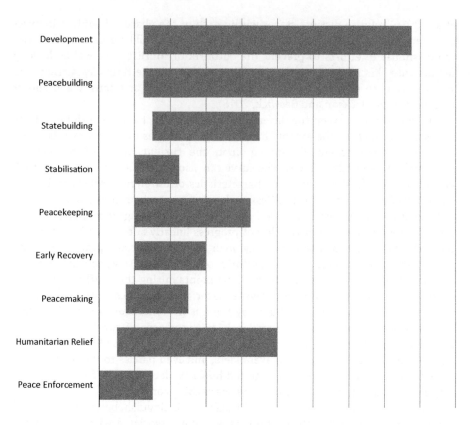

Figure 1.2 The Overlapping Stages of Engagement. (This is just one depiction of how the stages of engagement might be depicted. While this image shows the various stages of engagement are often overlapping, there are rarely definitive start and end dates to each stage as this image might suggest.)

underdevelopment, and violation of human rights can always proceed consecutively in logical order or independently of each other. Efforts – and equally, lack of effort – in one area will always impact another area. The risk of insecurity will be greater, for example, in a country in which some or all of the following are present: high levels of poverty and underdevelopment, weak state institutions, widespread human rights violations and limited justice or confidence in the rule of law. Likewise, the credibility of the state will also be jeopardised where there are prolonged or frequent outbreaks of armed conflict and the state does not enjoy the confidence or support of the majority of the population.

Increasing recognition of the interdependencies between security, governance and development, however, has also caused some concern about the blurring of operationally vital boundaries, not least in the protection of humanitarian space. The 2003 Iraq intervention has rightly been criticised for not paying attention to the subsequent rebuilding of the country and only attending to the security aspects of rebuilding a country. Its proponents assumed that after a short, non-destructive

> ## Box 1.1: Defence, Diplomacy and Development
>
> The type of peacebuilding attempted in, for example, Bosnia and Herzegovina (BiH), Kosovo and Sierra Leone encouraged the belief that there is necessarily a linear transition from war to peace, and that at a certain moment some actors therefore hand over to others. More recent experience in Iraq and Afghanistan has shown that, in practice, military operations, the search for a political solution and development projects may all be taking place at the same time, and impacting upon each other. Even when military operations are effectively concluded, as in BiH, the existence of a sequential plan does not mean it will be implemented automatically. As in BiH, military security can create the conditions for development and a political solution, but it cannot make them happen.
>
> Intervention failures in the last decade, notably in Iraq, have shown military-only solutions to instability to be inherently flawed. Such failures quickly led to a realisation that, without diplomacy or efforts to promote development, military engagement to foster peace will be destined to fail. Moreover, without 'joined-up-thinking' and co-ordination and coherence of efforts, intervention efforts can work against each other. The establishment of the UK Government's Stabilisation Unit – a triumvirate of the Ministry of Defence (MoD), Foreign and Commonwealth Office (FCO) and Department for International Development (DFID) – is an example of commitment to co-ordinated efforts across defence, diplomacy and development. More recently, there has, however, been a shift to 'hard' security as a priority, at the expense of a wider 'whole of government approach'. An increase in military spending and cuts to international aid across many western countries appear to have heralded this return to a focus on military-only or military-led solutions.
>
> Scholars have also underscored the deficiencies of military-only solutions to conflict. Edward Azar (1990), a leading scholar in international relations who developed the theory of protracted social conflict, argued that such conflicts require problem-solving rather than military solutions. Azar contended that conflicts were the results of unmet basic social needs, such as security, acceptance or economic participation and so military solutions which did not address these causes were destined to fail.

war, the recovery and reconstruction phase would be handled by the local population itself, grateful to be free of the yoke of tyranny. This of course did not happen. Some have suggested that the tripartite (security, governance and development) or, rather, 3-D approach (defence, diplomacy and development, as described in Box 1.1) to dealing with conflict and its aftermath that characterised some western approaches in the aftermath of this failure has led to the securitisation of aid (see Box 1.2). There is clearly a need for efforts across the security, governance and development sectors to be co-ordinated, and for there to be supported efforts in these three areas if there is to be sustainable recovery. However, there runs the risk of development aid being used to respond to security concerns and, thus, becoming securitised. This risks undermining the principles, effectiveness and resources available to development programmes. There are also more practical issues to consider in respect of co-ordination and the protection of humanitarian space, such as

Box 1.2: The Securitisation of Aid

The securitisation of aid broadly refers to the use of aid for the security interests of the donor (rather than the recipient). For a discussion on the securitisation of aid see, for example, Saferworld (2011) and Elhawary (2011).

In broader international relations, securitisation theory refers to the process of turning an issue into a matter of security. This, in turn, enables a security response and, often, extraordinary measures to be deployed. Issues that are securitised are not necessarily matters that pose a particular security threat to a state or its people but, rather, those issues which have been successfully categorised by someone as such (see Buzan et al., 1998 – instrumental in introducing securitisation theory to international relations). So, for instance, migration has been securitised and yet communicable diseases and road safety, which pose a direct and significant threat to many people, have not. From this example, it can be seen that the act of securitising is politicised and is often done precisely in order to legitimise certain responses. So, the risk of securitising responses to humanitarian crises or development challenges is that different policy responses are considered to be more acceptable and appropriate. In addition, different actors might become engaged (i.e. security actors), which can undermine humanitarian or development practices or principles, for instance, as well as problematise co-ordination and legitimacy of response.

where humanitarian or development tasks are carried out by the military because the environment is too dangerous for anyone else to operate.

Imagining that the transition from conflict to peace is linear also ignores the prevalence of violence in many allegedly post-conflict environments and many countries ostensibly at peace. Indeed, a high level of violence may historically have been part of the country's culture, and not be greatly affected by the arrival of formal peace. This reminds us that violence, including armed violence, can occur at any stage outside what is formally referred to as armed conflict (see Box 1.3). Violence that occurs in private spaces or against disempowered, marginalised groups can be significant. Violence between or against impoverished male youths is excessive in many countries. Violence and insecurity can, in fact, escalate after the end of armed conflict, due to many factors, including the security vacuum that is often filled by organised criminal groups in the immediate aftermath of conflict. High levels of gender-based violence can also remain after conflict, in the absence of effective security and justice sector institutions, as traumatised combatants return to civilian life, and as gender roles are renegotiated (Grady, 2010; Munala, 2007; Willett, 2010).

It is now generally acknowledged that what were once considered the different stages of conflict are increasingly blurred and overlapping. Indeed, it is better to think of a continuum, with street violence at one end and violent conflict at the other; but even this concept does not account for private violence, structural violence and other harms not so neatly categorised.

As Swanström and Weissmann (2005) point out, the simple bell curve of conflict has received much criticism from academics and policy-makers. They suggest that, in abstract form, conflict may be better represented as a series of irregular

Box 1.3: Armed Violence versus Armed Conflict

Mexico

Criminal gun violence (as in Mexico, for example) can exceed the levels normally associated with armed conflict. The 2013 United Nations (UN) Office on Drugs and Crime (UNODC) Global Study on Homicide identified nearly 450,000 cases of intentional homicide in 2012 (43% of victims were males aged 15–29). Significantly larger numbers were injured or crippled. This excludes suicides and accidents with firearms, which would substantially increase the total. More than a third of the homicides occurred in the Americas, reflecting, among other things, the results of the illegal drugs trade and efforts to suppress it (UNODC, 2013).

Colombia

In the weeks and months following the signing of the peace agreement between the Government of Colombia and the Revolutionary Armed Forces of Colombia – People's Army (Spanish: *Fuerzas Armadas Revolucionarias de Colombia – Ejército del Pueblo*, FARC-EP or FARC), on 24 November 2016, the number of murders by paramilitaries of activists and community leaders and human rights/women's rights advocates escalated as these paramilitary groups try to fill the void left by the demobilised FARC, terrorising communities so they can control territories and drug trafficking routes (see HRW, 2017).

waves, in recognition of the fact that the conflict circle recurs and repeatedly passes through different phases, and that no conflict is like another. Moreover, the curve would be specific to each conflict; the path towards peace no longer represented by a universal, simple trajectory. Protracted conflicts, for instance, may be shown by a curve which extensively oscillates between the higher levels of the curve, or conflicts may repeatedly recur over prolonged periods, or there may simply be no clear delineation between war and peace (see Figure 1.3 for what a path might look like, superimposed onto the traditional curve of conflict to

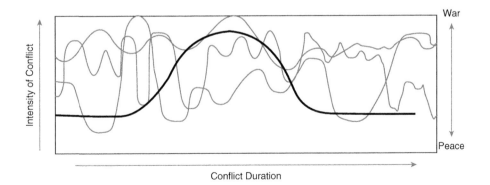

Figure 1.3 How the Curve of Conflict might be More Accurately Portrayed, Overlaid on the Original Curve of Conflict

demonstrate the stark difference often between theory and reality – recognising that even these messy lines cannot capture much either).

For all these reasons, as Swanström and Weissmann (2005) have noted, conflict can never be represented by a single line, not least because each conflict often contains many smaller conflicts, each with its own specific cycle (see Figure 1.3 again for how a conflict with its many smaller conflicts might be mapped). Consequently, different types of intervention may be required simultaneously to respond to different developments and dynamics within a conflict. For example, risk factors from a latent conflict may increase at the point at which armed conflict between two warring factions decreases in intensity, while other sub-conflicts escalate or de-escalate in response to these and other developments.

Whilst visualising or mapping phases of conflict and intervention can be useful, if there is indeed a 'line of conflict', it is not linear or singular: it is multi-faceted, multifarious and dynamic. The complexity of conflict is discussed in the next chapter, when we consider the many and varied causes of conflict as well as the broad range of activities that can constitute effective conflict prevention.

Finally, it is important to remember that the way conflict is defined has a direct impact upon policy and practice. If conflict is perceived as linear, logical and one-dimensional, responses to conflict will seldom be appropriate. If conflict is measured in terms of battle deaths, other insecurities will tend to be overlooked and ignored until they too manifest themselves in terms of fatalities. If conflict is something that occurs between states and/or non-state actors, the blurred lines between the state and non-state will be overlooked, as will the impact of armed violence outside places formally considered to be engaged in armed conflict. If conflict is considered to be something that occurs elsewhere and for purely local reasons, we may continue to overlook the involvement of our governments in conflicts and our own responsibility for insecurities at home and abroad. Of course, there are times when simplification is necessary. Measuring a conflict in terms of battle deaths might be necessary, for instance, to enable large-scale statistical research. But there is a difference between the simplification needed for categorisation, study and analysis, and the need to take complexity into account in order to develop appropriate responses.

The concept of security

In the same way, how we define security determines our thinking about how security is best developed and managed, as well as who or what we believe pose security threats. This, of course, determines how we think we should respond to security threats, as well as who and what we believe are threatened (and who and what are the sources of that threat). The widest definition of security so far offered is that of 'Human Security', usually defined as:

> ... far more than the absence of violent conflict. It encompasses human rights, good governance, access to education and health care and ensuring that each individual has opportunities and resources to fulfil his or her own potential. Every step in this direction is also a step towards reducing poverty, achieving economic growth and preventing conflict. Freedom from want, freedom from fear and the freedom of

future generations to inherit a healthy natural environment – are the interrelated building blocks of human and, therefore, national security. (UN, 2000b: n.p.)

Human security was introduced as a concept by the United Nations Development Programme (UNDP) in its Human Development Report (1994), equating security with people rather than territory and encompassing seven broad areas of threat: economic, health, personal, political, food, environmental and community. Human security moves beyond the narrower national security (which previously tended to focus on territorial security), and this shift was a result of the recognition that security and development are related, as well as recognition of the changing nature of threats: conflicts were increasingly intrastate and threats to security came from environmental degradation, pandemics, poverty, criminality and poor governance and not simply from armies and arms (see Kaldor, 2012). However, it is important to note that traditional security thinking included far more than just 'violent conflict', and many of the problems identified by human security thinking exist in peaceful societies. In addition, many of the human security objectives have been pursued by governments for generations, but without the use of the vocabulary of 'security' and 'threat'.

The concept of human security has, nonetheless, influenced policy-makers and practitioners in the field of security, justice, development and human rights, and efforts to prevent and respond to conflict and crisis have, at least ostensibly, been undertaken in a more holistic and co-ordinated manner. Since it came to prominence in 1994 it has, however, received much criticism, not least because the concept is so broad and, thus, often, vague that it undermines precisely how to conceive of security and ways in which it can be improved (see Paris, 2001).

In practice, in international development, the broadening scope of security is not yet matched by an expanding arena of indigenous security actors. Informal justice and security mechanisms, while often vital in post-conflict and developing states, are only now being given any real attention by international organisations and governments. Additionally, the role of civil society in the security sector is often restricted to pre-implementation outreach and consultation as well as ensuring the accountability of state security actors through specific Civil Society Organisations (CSOs). Moreover, donors have a history of preferring to interact with, and fund, CSOs whose leaders speak western languages and share western ideas. Understandably, perhaps, the focus is generally on how security and justice are delivered, not on how they are received. Donors have their own imperatives, timetables and political limitations, after all.

So, while it is recognised that security is a broad, multifarious and often contested concept, the focus of providing security is very often state-centric and focussed on uniformed state security service providers. This, however, is beginning to change. Consequently, if the Human Security argument is valid, and if it can be made operational, it could be hoped that peacebuilding and statebuilding efforts will be more effective and sustainable, and post-conflict societies will stand a greater chance of not returning to conflict (see Box 1.4 for a definition of statebuilding and its relationship with peacebuilding).

Chapter 3 will further consider the concept of security, and the concept of non-traditional security threats will be considered in Chapter 11.

Box 1.4: Peacebuilding and Statebuilding

Statebuilding refers to '[p]urposeful action to develop the capacity, institutions and legitimacy of the state in relation to an effective political process for negotiating the mutual demands between state and societal groups' (OECD, 2008: 15). While there is an assumption that peacebuilding and statebuilding are mutually support-ive, there can be tension between peacebuilding and statebuilding. While a resilient state may be considered to be a prerequisite for lasting peace, strengthening a state that has been a party to the conflict, is corrupt or is blamed for what it did not do, can increase tension and the propensity for conflict (see Interpeace, 2010). Conversely, peacebuilding can undermine statebuilding efforts. State legitimacy can be undermined, for example, if non-state providers are relied upon to deliver essential goods in the absence of effective state institutions (see Haider, 2010).

Moreover, the specific form of state–societal relations being created – specifically the transformation of war-torn places into liberal market democracies and the forced democratisation that often accompanies such efforts – often under-mines the chances of lasting peace and stability (see Paris, 2004).

The processes of marketisation and democratisation ignore many conflict causal factors and also provide opportunities for those whose interests may be self-serving. In Kosovo and BiH, for instance, these processes tended to further marginalise those who were previously dependent on the land to support them-selves, augment the power of many war opportunists and criminals, and tighten the bonds between organised crime and the political administration (see Bojicic and Kostovicova, 2011, for instance).

The concept of peace

It is worth taking a moment to reflect on what we mean by peace. Is it simply the absence of armed conflict? Certainly, peaceful societies need more than just a guar-antee that there will not be an outbreak of armed violence. Johan Galtung, widely regarded as a leading pioneer of peace studies, was instrumental in drawing a dis-tinction between negative peace (the absence of armed conflict or violence) and positive peace (the presence of all the other factors which contribute to a peaceful society). These other factors would include positive relationships between people, and between people and the state, as well as the presence of co-operation, equity, equality, dialogue and a culture of peace (Galtung, 2013). In the immediate after-math of conflict, in the absence of armed conflict, therefore, there can be a nega-tive peace; the effort, however, will be on building all the structures, processes and relationships which will make the peace sustainable at which point there might be what could be referred to as a positive peace.

The concept of peacebuilding

Fundamentally, security is the core prerequisite of peace, and peacebuilding is gen-erally considered to be the way peace is built after conflict. Peacebuilding has been described as 'a range of measures targeted to reduce the risk of lapsing or relapsing into conflict, to strengthen national capacities at all levels for conflict management, and to lay the foundations for sustainable peace and development' (United Nations Department of Peacekeeping Operations – UNDPKO, 2008: 18). The term has been widely used since the then-UN Secretary-General (UNSG), Boutros Boutros-Ghali, referred to it in his 'Agenda for Peace' in 1992 (UNSG, 1992). It was originally conceived relatively narrowly, but typically for this field, its meanings have expanded enormously (Chetail, 2009; Snodderly, 2011).

Originally the term peacebuilding referred to post-conflict recovery efforts focussed on reconciliation (reconciling formerly warring factions so they can live peacefully together, including through addressing grievances and building trust) and reconstruction (of physical infrastructure, including roads, buildings, transportation and communication systems, and also of state institutions so essential services can be delivered).

Today the term can encompass a wide spectrum of activities. These can include providing humanitarian relief, maintaining security, protecting human rights, facilitating the return of refugees and internally displaced persons (IDPs), aiding reconciliation, supporting the reform of governance structures, and enabling economic recovery and even broader development. The aim is to facilitate sustainable peace, preventing the recurrence of armed conflict and providing mechanisms to enable conflict to be managed without recourse to violence.

In part because the term 'peacebuilding' can be used to cover a huge array of activities, there has been much criticism of its ideological foundations, seen by many as a justification for interventionism, and more to do with promoting domestic interests than protecting the interests of those within countries affected by conflict (see Duffield, 2007). Additionally, as Chetail (2009) points out, high rates of conflict recurrence call into question the effectiveness of peacebuilding activities. Questions about the type of peace being built, the type of activities that should be prioritised, the type of actors who should lead the process, and to whom those involved are ultimately accountable to, need to be critically attended to (see Llamazares, 2005, for instance). There are many examples to show that lack of clarity and shared understanding of the type of peace, and also type of state, being built – and how to do it – have led to peace processes faltering (see Glennie, 2010, for case studies of conflict prevention and peacebuilding interventions in Afghanistan, Kosovo, Bosnia and Herzegovina, and Macedonia). In Bosnia and Herzegovina, for example, particularly in the immediate aftermath of conflict, different international organisations, including the UN and many of its different agencies, had different priorities, depending upon their specific mandate. Within each organisation and agency there were also many different people with different levels of commitment to or understanding of their organisational goals, some of whom were seconded by their government (or another organisation) and so may have had competing aims. Moreover, actively engaged in Bosnia and Herzegovina were many different countries which had different agendas depending upon their often shifting, strategic interests and domestic politics. This not only created confusion, but often competition between individuals and organisations, which undermined prospects for successful cessation of hostilities and sustainable peace and, thus, the prolonged suffering of many people. Returning to the type of peace being built, it is fair to add that the assumptions behind peacebuilding are essentially those of the liberal state, and its effectiveness will therefore inevitably depend, to some extent, on the relevance of these assumptions when applied to other types of societies (see, e.g., Chandler, 2010; Cramer, 2006; Paris, 2010; Richmond, 2009).

The very complexity of peacebuilding and the enormity of its aims – coupled with the delicate balance between providing sufficient and sustained external assistance and ensuring the processes and results are locally owned and supported – are often overlooked, as are the many examples of significant steps taken towards peace in many places.

This is not surprising, since, as Chetail (2009) describes, in addition to the many activities and actors associated with peacekeeping, a triple transition is often involved:

- A security transition, from a situation of open violence to the progressive establishment of sustainable peace
- A socio-economic transition, from conflict economies to a peace economy which is more open to the private sector and to international trade
- A democratic transition, from an authoritarian system to one of representative government (Chetail, 2009: 8 citing David, 1998).

Just one of these transitions could cause much turbulence in any society, let alone in a society just emerging from conflict and also undergoing other transitions. The huge structural shifts, as well as the multiplicity of actors and activities in many sectors at all levels of society, can generate significant potential for tension and renewed conflict, if not managed carefully – that is, if not adequately planned, co-ordinated or communicated – and without sufficient grassroots understanding, involvement and support. Paradoxically, therefore, peacebuilding efforts themselves, unless sensitively handled, can be destabilising.

Part 2 – Building Peace After Conflict

Of course, how we define peace and how we define peacebuilding will have a significant effect upon outcomes for societies that have experienced conflict. It is important to note that, while this book focusses upon formal efforts to build security and justice after conflict, many of the critical peacebuilding efforts are informal – the everyday, local-level initiatives that help build tolerance, raise awareness or increase resilience, for instance.

This chapter has introduced peacebuilding at its broadest; the rest of this book looks at ways in which to build security and justice primarily after conflict, after looking at the causes of conflict and conflict prevention more broadly in the next chapter. Engagement in the security and justice sector does not take place in isolation, of course, and will not be successful unless peacebuilding efforts in other sectors, such as the economy, politics and development, are effective. Such efforts include building a sustainable economy (at the macro and micro levels and, not least, generating employment opportunities), supporting political processes (including electoral processes) and developing good governance, enabling the delivery of essential basic services (including water and sanitation), building the capacity of the health and education sectors, facilitating the return of refugees and displaced persons, promoting the protection of human rights, delivering humanitarian assistance, supporting reconciliation and providing for the development of a robust civil society.

It is important to be aware of the other types of activities involved, not least in order to anticipate the impact that activities in various sectors can have upon each other and to endeavour to ensure coherence of efforts. For example, those engaged in economic reform activities and those engaged in combatant demobilisation programmes or security sector institution rationalisation (often as part of broader Security Sector Reform programmes) should be aware of each other's desired and planned activities in order to ensure that they resonate with each other and, quite simply, are effective (see Box 1.5 on Kosovo for an example of why such co-ordination is important). Those developing programmes for demobilised combatants or those who may lose their jobs in the security sector through rationalisation need to know the opportunities and constraints that exist or will exist in terms of opportunities for employment or training as well as the constraints that might exist in terms of budgets, policy or other factors.

It is also important to remember that, in order for peacebuilding to formally begin, there first needs to be an end to conflict. Despite significant resources and attention given to trying to end conflict, as Kreutz (2010) and Ramsbotham et al. (2016) show, conflicts usually end without decisive conclusions. Consequently, such conflicts are prone to break out again and become protracted, not least because the root causes of the conflict remain unaddressed. A number of methods have been used to resolve conflicts, including not only military means (Flavin, 2003), but also negotiation and mediation (Ramsbotham et al., 2016), and economic pressures such as sanctions (Escribà-Folch, 2010; Gershenson, 2001). As will be mentioned in the next chapter, often the methods used to resolve conflict are quite similar to those used to prevent the outbreak or recurrence of conflict. As will be discussed, however, there are often many more actors involved in conflict resolution and post-conflict peacebuilding, and many more resources and attention given.

As the 2003 Iraq military invasion by the United States, the United Kingdom, Australia and Poland demonstrates, the military can defeat opposing forces, but that in itself may not terminate, let alone resolve conflicts. Indeed, as in the Iraq War, it may simply provoke new conflicts. Often a combination of tools is required, the type and combination of which will need to be revisited regularly. Given the varied tools and many potential actors involved, it is critical that there is an overarching strategy and integral coherence to the interventions, to which all actors are committed.

Box 1.5: Kosovo

In Kosovo, with the planned stand-down of the Kosovo Protection Corps (KPC), it was necessary to know what activities were ongoing or planned in other sectors; were there economic opportunities on the horizon that could be utilised for those in the KPC who would not have a place in the future Kosovo Security Force (KSF); were there budgetary or policy constraints that would impact any planned legislation for veterans?

Various factors can influence whether a conflict recurs: notably, military victories and the deployment of peacekeepers (Fortna, 2004; Kreutz, 2010) are more likely to lead to lasting peace than peace settlements (Licklider, 1995). However, the positive effects of the deployment of peacekeepers may dissipate over time (Sambanis, 2007).

The signing of a peace settlement, significant as it is, is only a step towards lasting peace, which requires a whole series of extra ingredients to be successful. In reality, peace agreements are often not fully implemented and conflict recurs. This may result from lack of commitment, lack of local ownership, omission of wider considerations, deferral of difficult issues and many other factors.

Above all, perhaps, no peace process or agreement can be expected to work unless it reflects a widespread agreement among key indigenous actors that peace is more desirable than continued conflict. Otherwise, only a fragile peace will result. Some have also questioned whether 'peace at any price' is desirable, or even feasible. Others have argued that the cultural context and specificities are often ignored, and reconstruction has sought to impose an alien system on the environment. Others still have argued that peace agreements often do not address power imbalances, oppression or discrimination – and unless they do so, renewed conflict is likely. Certainly, there have been enough failures in peace processes that all of these factors and more can be plausibly blamed. But how to incorporate all these factors into a peace agreement and subsequent peace process – and whether that would provoke new forms of instability and insecurity – is another matter entirely.

Conclusion

This chapter has introduced some of the core concepts commonly used in peace-building, including the concepts of conflict, security and peace. In so doing, it encourages critical reflection upon the concepts that are often taken for granted in practice and sometimes scholarship. We need to question what we mean by peace and security, and whether others share similar views, in order to be able to effectively address or analyse conflict and its causes and manifestations. We also need to question, when considering the broad concept of peacebuilding, whose peace and whose security are we interested in, and who or what are considered to pose threats to peace and security? In so doing, we recognise that these concepts are highly political and often used and misused for strategic gain. Through clarity of concepts, we can aim towards clarity of purpose. More critically, through clarity of concepts, we can also expose those instances where security is not equitable, peace is not meaningful to those beyond dominant or elite groups, and threats to peace are constructed to legitimise otherwise illegitimate interventions or responses.

To provide a context for subsequent chapters, this chapter has also briefly referred to ways in which armed conflict can be resolved and peace – however it is defined – can be built, beyond those efforts squarely within the security and justice sectors, which is the focus of this book. The next chapter provides further context for subsequent chapters by looking at the causes of conflict, recognising that effective peacebuilding needs to be responsive to causes, and conflict prevention, recognising that effective prevention can save countless lives and much of the huge amount of resources that are invested into peacebuilding.

Summary of Key Issues

- The stages of conflict and activities aimed at resolving conflict and building peace are often blurred and overlap.
- Violence, including armed violence, can occur at any stage outside what is formally referred to as armed conflict.
- Whilst visualising or mapping phases of conflict and intervention can be useful, if there is indeed a 'line of conflict', it is not linear or singular: it is multi-faceted, multifarious and dynamic.
- The way conflict is defined has a direct impact upon policy and practice; if conflict is perceived as linear, logical and one-dimensional, responses to conflict will seldom be appropriate.
- How we define security determines how actors think security is best developed and managed, and who or what we believe pose security threats.
- Security is a broad, heterogeneous and often contested concept, while the focus of providing security is very often state-centric and focussed on uniformed state security service providers.
- In part because the term 'peacebuilding' can be used to cover a huge array of activities, there has been much criticism of its ideological foundations.
- Effective peacebuilding requires that conflicts end conclusively and causes are addressed.
- Effective peace processes and agreements need to reflect a widespread agreement among key indigenous actors that peace is more desirable than conflict.
- Engagement in the security and justice sector does not take place in isolation, and will not be successful unless peacebuilding efforts in other sectors, outside the security and justice sector, are effective.

Reflective Question

Consider how to have a shared understanding of peace and how it can be built, while accommodating its subjective, dynamic and complex nature.

List of Core Resources

Concepts

Call, C. (2008) 'The Fallacy of the 'Failed State', *Third World Quarterly*, 29(8): 1491–1507.

Chetail, V. (2009) *'Post-Conflict Peacebuilding – A Lexicon'* (New York: Oxford University Press).

Grimm, S., Lemay-Hébert, N. and Nay, O. (2014) '"Fragile States": Introducing a political concept', *Third World Quarterly*, 35(2): 197–209.

Snodderly, D. (ed.) (2011) *Peace Terms: A Glossary of Terms for Conflict Management and Peacebuilding* (Washington, DC: USIP). Available at www.usip.org/publications/usip-peace-terms-glossary.

Building peace after conflict (key texts relevant also to subsequent chapters)

Alda, E. and Mc Evoy, C. (2017) 'Beyond the Battlefield: Towards a Better Assessment of the Human Cost of Armed Conflict', *Briefing Paper, Geneva: Small Arms Survey*. Available at www.smallarmssurvey.org/fileadmin/docs/T-Briefing-Papers/SAS-BP4-Beyond-battlefield.pdf.

Autesserre, S. (2014) *Peacelands* (New York: Cambridge University Press).

Autesserre, S. (2018) *Peacebuilding in Africa*, Kujenga Amani podcast. Available at http://apnpodcast.libsyn.com/sverine-autesserre.

Centre for Security Governance (CSG) (2016) eSeminar: *Is Peacebuilding Dying?* (video). Available at www.youtube.com/watch?v=_pc2SgTob1g.

Chandler, D. (2017) *Peacebuilding: The Twenty Years' Crisis, 1997–2017* (London: Palgrave Macmillan).

Chuter, D. (2014) 'Fighting for the Toolbox: Why Building Security and Justice Post-Conflict is so Difficult' in E. Gordon (ed.) *Building Security and Justice in Post-Conflict Environments* (Leicester: University of Leicester): 9–25. Available at https://uolscid.files.wordpress.com/2014/08/scid-reader-2014-bookmarked.pdf.

CQ Researcher (ed.) (2011) *Issues in Peace and Conflict Studies: Selections From CQ Researcher* (Washington: Sage).

Crocker, C., Hampson, F. and Aall, P. (eds) (2015) *Managing Conflict in a World Adrift* (Washington, DC: USIP).

Crocker, C., Hampson, F. and Aall, P. (2007) *Leashing the Dogs of War* (Washington, DC: USIP).

Duffield, M. (2007) *Development, Security and Unending War: Governing the World of Peoples* (Cambridge: Polity Press).

Gordon, E. (2014) (ed.) *Building Justice and Security in Post-Conflict Environments: SCID Reader 2014* (Leicester: University of Leicester). Available at https://uolscid.files.wordpress.com/2014/08/scid-reader-2014-bookmarked.pdf.

Haider, H. (2014). *Conflict: Topic Guide*. Revised edition with B. Rohwerder (Birmingham: GSDRC, University of Birmingham).

International Peace Institute (IPI) (2017). *Local Peacebuilding Successes: Lessons for the International Community* (video). Available at www.youtube.com/watch?v=dbmblrAilU0.

ISSAfrica (2016) *Making Peacebuilding More Effective* (video). Available at www.youtube.com/watch?v=a1N9gQTPJCM.

Jackson, P. (2015) *Handbook of International Security and Development* (Cheltenham: Edward Elgar Publishing).

Jackson, P. and Beswick, D. (2018) *Conflict, Security and Development: An Introduction* (3rd edn) (Abingdon: Routledge).

Kaldor, M. (2012) *New and Old Wars: Organized Violence in a Global Era* (Cambridge: Polity Press).

Kamau, M. (2018) *Peacebuilding in Africa*, Kujenga Amani podcast. Available at http://apnpodcast.libsyn.com/episode-1.

Karlsrud, J. (2015) 'The UN at war: examining the consequences of peace-enforcement mandates for the UN peacekeeping operations in the CAR, the DRC and Mali', *Third World Quarterly*, 36(1): 40–54.

London School of Economics (LSE) (2017) *The Human Cost of Conflict: the search for dignity and rights of Palestine refugees*, presentation by Pierre Krähenbühl, UN Relief and Works Agency for Palestine (UNRWA) Commissioner-General. 04 December. Available at www.lse.ac.uk/website-archive/newsAndMedia/videoAndAudio/channels/publicLecturesAndEvents/player.aspx?id=3949.

Mac Ginty, R. (2011) *Peacebuilding by the International Community* (animation). Available at www.youtube.com/watch?v=zN8rIxoXqWo&t=12s.

Mac Ginty, R. and Williams, A. (2016) *Conflict and Development* (2nd edn) (Abingdon: Routledge).

Mason, W. (2014) *A Social Reconstruction Approach to Fostering Security & Justice After Conflict*, University of Leicester (video). Available at www.youtube.com/watch?v=gER3UI8AXaA&list=PLjQX5EXgm57S0L7nT-QMVhQ LKiYNsSPxu&index=3.

Ramsbotham, O., Woodhouse, T. and Miall, H. (2016) *Contemporary Conflict Resolution* (4th edn) (Cambridge: Polity Press).

Richmond, O. (2014) 'The impact of socio-economic inequality on peacebuilding and statebuilding', *Civil Wars*, 16(4): 449–467.

Visoko, G. (2017) Shaping Peace in Kosovo: The Politics of Peacebuilding and State-hood (London: Palgrave Macmillan).

Waterfield, M. (2014) *Conflict Assessments in the Planning of Stabilisation/Conflict Recovery Programmes*, University of Leicester (video). Available at www.youtube.com/watch?v=qXOPxV0FJcE&list=PLjQX5EXgm57S0L7nT-QMVhQLK iYNsSPxu&index=5.

Woodhouse, T., Miall, H., Ramsbotham, O. and Mitchell, C. (2015) *The Contemporary Conflict Resolution Reader* (Cambridge: Polity Press).

2 Causes of Conflict and Conflict Prevention

Overview

This chapter discusses the causes of conflict in recognition of the fact that successful peacebuilding and conflict prevention depend upon acknowledging and addressing perceived causal factors. Various theories of the causes of conflict will be considered and a number of factors presented which can contribute to the outbreak and escalation of conflict. The chapter then considers ways in which to prevent conflict, to avoid the loss of countless lives and huge investment of resources in conflict resolution and peacebuilding. Conflict prevention tools are discussed alongside challenges and limitations that continue to hamper preventive efforts.

Learning Outcomes

- Critically assess some of the key theories of the causes of inter-state conflict
- Articulate the key causes of intrastate conflict
- Recognise the importance of identifying and addressing potential causes of conflict before and after conflict
- Identify sources of information to aid early warning
- Be familiar with conflict prevention tools and actors

Part 1 – Causes of Conflict

We now turn to the question of the causes of conflict, since, without some appreciation of causes, conflicts can neither be prevented nor resolved successfully. A variety of factors are described that have been considered to contribute to the outbreak, escalation or recurrence of intrastate conflict, including economic, social, political, demographic, geographical, geo-political, environmental, security and justice, historical and psychological factors.

Conflicts or outbreaks of armed violence do not come out of nowhere, despite the impression sometimes given by governments and in the media. Often, the risk of a conflict is evident, but the timing, and even the factor that unleashes it, cannot be predicted. As will be explained later, armed violence and conflict can be prevented, but only through an analysis of the potential causes of conflict and, thereafter, gauging appropriate interventions, whether bilateral or multilateral.

Of course, intervention is not the only way to end conflict; defeat or truce definitively end conflict, but this book is focussed on interventions in the aftermath of conflict to build security and justice.

It is also widely recognised that, without addressing the root causes of conflict, conflict is likely to recur. Nonetheless, post-conflict peacebuilding and statebuilding literature often overlooks the fundamental causes or focusses on superficial explanations. Popular explanations of the heightened levels of ethnic violence over the last generation as a result of 'ancient hatreds' between rival ethnic, religious or caste groups (Levy, 2007) are an example of such thinking. However, whilst such tensions and even hatreds certainly exist, and can influence behaviour (Ferro, 2007), these explanations are inadequate when considering some of the conflicts in the Balkans in the 1990s or the Iran–Iraq War (1980–88), for instance. Tension and resentment between Serbs, Muslims and Croats was real enough, but had been contained under Tito by a complicated political balancing act and an efficient secret police organisation. Observers at the time recognised fear, rather than hatred, as the main motivator of conflict, in a terribly confused political environment where all groups saw themselves as threatened minorities. Likewise, relations between Iran and Iraq had always been problematic, even before the 1979 Iranian revolution, and the causes of the conflict were essentially geopolitical and economic (see Levy, 2007). As AlertNet suggests, a 'conflict may erupt over access to scarce resources or political tensions, and polarise along religious or ethnic lines' (AlertNet, 2010: n.p.), and describing conflicts as ethnic or religious wars often ignores the underlying economic, political and social factors.

There is a need to distinguish between underlying causes and the specific circumstances that unleashed conflict. The fact that, one hundred years later, there is no unanimity about the causes of the First World War, or even when it ended, may give us pause for thought against applying superficial analysis to contemporary conflicts. It is also worth remembering that what may be presented as being the root cause of a conflict may, in fact, only be that which is politically expedient to national or international actors. Conflict may also be sought – and with a cause to blame – in a state facing social change or where elites fear the loss of power, for instance. It is also true that causes migrate: 'Sometimes the original grievances that triggered conflicts become lost in time, and wars continue simply because there are enough people making money out of them' (AlertNet, 2010: n.p.).

Conflict can also be welcomed and sustained by other factors unrelated to potential causal factors. Conflict can provide business opportunities for ordinary people that they would not find in peacetime. Armed factions can better exploit natural resources, such as diamonds, and smuggling becomes very profitable in conflict and its immediate aftermath. The presence of an international mission in the country while the conflict is still continuing may be welcomed by many people from government ministers to taxi drivers. Combatants may prefer paid fighting to unemployment, and do not necessarily find conflict a traumatising or even upsetting experience. Some anecdotal evidence suggests that, for young men in particular, facing and overcoming danger together may be a formative and unrepeatable experience in their lives. Some combatants – and sometimes even non-combatants – have looked back on their experiences during war-time with nostalgia (Junger, 2016) or at least drew positive aspects from it; of course, many are severely traumatised for prolonged periods.

If efforts to prevent and recover from conflict are to be successful, they therefore need to be informed by a comprehensive understanding of why and how conflicts erupt or escalate – including possible root causes, triggers and catalysts – recognising, however, that there is little agreement on causal factors, as will shortly be discussed. Without a comprehensive understanding, management of conflicts will be unsuccessful, and conflicts risk escalating, becoming intractable or recurring. The assumption that any peace settlement is better than none is dangerous. The risk of conflicts recurring is also related to the type of settlement arrived at (or sometimes effectively imposed) (Quaskenbush and Venteicher, 2008) and the response of parties to the settlement (whether insincere, disappointed or internally fragmented – see Smith, 2004). The risk of conflicts recurring is also related to post-conflict governance, development and security factors, such as level of state fragility or governance, levels and patterns of poverty, and prevalence of crime and arms, as will be discussed shortly.

Collier et al. (2008) suggest that conflict recurs in 40% of all post-conflict societies and that nearly half of all intrastate conflicts are a result of post-conflict relapses. More recently, Walter (2010) has shown that 57% of countries that experienced some form of civil war between 1945 and 2009 experienced a subsequent return to civil war. This is particularly concerning given that subsequent conflicts are often more severe than previous ones (Quaskenbush and Venteicher, 2008). Analysis conducted by the World Development Report (WDR) team (World Bank, 2011), and drawing on Walter (2010), underscores the cyclical nature of conflict. The analysis suggests that the rate of violent onset in countries that had previously experienced conflict was very high and increasing, to the extent that all civil wars that had occurred since 2003 occurred in countries that had previously experienced civil war. This suggests strongly that many peace settlements fail to resolve the underlying tensions that caused the conflict. It also suggests, more worryingly, that some conflicts are intractable, and may continue whatever the virtues of the settlement.

Causes of conflict

It is important to distinguish between inter-state and intrastate conflict when considering general theories about the causes of conflict. In addition, whilst accepting the value of some general theories, it is also essential to recognise that all explanations must be context-sensitive and reflect the unique circumstances of each conflict. Levy (2007) reminds us that for any theory to be adequate it must account for changes in conflict over time as well as why conflicts occur at one space and time and not another. Given that war is complex and variable, it follows that any theory that is restricted to one static factor – for example, inter-ethnic tension – is inadequate. Any general theory must also account for the fact that most states are at peace with each other and there have been prolonged periods of widespread peace between and within states (Levy, 2007).

Theories of the causes of inter-state conflict

So-called realist theories have traditionally dominated the literature on the causes of inter-state conflict and, broadly, suggest that 'actors behave reasonably rationally to advance their interests, defined primarily in terms of security; that the distribution of power is the primary determinant of international outcomes; and that wars result both as the intended consequence of aggressive states that want war to advance their interests and as the unintended consequence of more defensively motivated behaviour to provide for security' (Levy, 2007: 25).

In an interesting article from 2005, Lieberfeld (2005) also considers general theories of the causes of conflict and considers the implication of the realist approach as an explanation for the US decision to invade Iraq in 2003. From the analytical perspective of realism, Lieberfeld suggests that states go to war because of their 'involuntary participation in eternal quests for power and security due to an international political environment in which each state fears the actual or potential hostility of other states' (Lieberfeld, 2005: n.p.).

Some liberal theories suggest that democracy breeds peace, and that democratic states engage in conflict with non-democratic states because of the fear that the latter can mobilise force without the usual constraints of international law or accountability. Democratic peace theory would posit that democratic states are less likely to go to war than non-democratic states. The assumption is that those states which are democratic are more stable, less autocratic and more responsive to the needs of the people; all of which tend to characterise more peaceful states. The logic is clearly evident in peacebuilding practice, which tends to focus on building a strong, legitimate state with democratic governance under the assumption that this would facilitate the development of a sustainable peace. The logic, however, can be questioned when we consider that many democratic states are, in fact, engaged in conflict or may, in fact, have precipitated the outbreak or escalation of conflict; it may simply be that the conflict is not on their soil or their engagement in the conflict is presented as conflict prevention, humanitarian intervention or peace enforcement.

By way of further contrast to the democratic peace theory of conflict, popular Marxist analyses of the nineteenth and twentieth centuries suggested that economic competition and the desire for elites to maintain and broaden their control of new markets were the ultimate reason for inter-state conflict. Here we might consider conflicts that were borne of powerful states intervening in the affairs of others in an effort to access natural resources or for geo-strategic reasons.

Other economic theories of conflict suggest that, in fact, poor and underdeveloped countries are more likely to go to war. This is because of the link between security and development (see Box 2.1), and the adverse impact on security and stability that poverty and other development challenges can have. At the micro level, when people have no jobs or little to sustain themselves and their families, they are more susceptible to the draw of criminal or armed groups offering meals and subsistence. Likewise, at the macro level, where there are few resources and many development challenges stretching resources further, the state becomes vulnerable to exploitation – corruption and organised criminal activity may gain

Box 2.1: Security-Development Nexus

The security-development nexus refers to the belief that security and development are causally connected: conflict, violence and insecurity hinder progress towards the attainment of Sustainable Development Goals (SDGs) for instance and, conversely, countries which have a low Human Development Index (HDI) are also more prone to conflict, violence and insecurity. This has promoted a more holistic and coherent approach to conflict prevention and recovery.

However, from a critical perspective the concept of the security-development nexus can be seen as securitising development as well as justifying increased intervention in the affairs of others on the grounds of protecting international and national security. Duffield argues that the coupling together of security and development has less to do with providing aid as a means of building peace (in fragile states) and promoting security (at home), and more to do with 'securing the Western way of life' (Duffield, 2007: 2). Under the auspice of helping people in places that pose risks beyond their own borders, people and places are effectively policed and governed. Renewed Western interventionism, far from promoting well-being and international security, Duffield argues, fosters instability and division. In essence, the progressive rhetoric can hide the logic of imperialist intervention in countries at risk of conflict. This highlights the importance of always reflecting upon the policy implications of discourses used; in this case, whether the concept of the security-development nexus is being used to justify intervention, deflect criticism and disguise geo-political motivations. It is also worth asking whose security is improved as a result of development and, indeed, who benefits from development programmes.

Sustainable Development Goals (SDGs)

The SDGs are a set of 17 goals established by the UN in 2015 containing a total of 169 social, economic and development targets. They replace the Millennium Development Goals (MDGs) and are broader in scope and applicability: no longer only pertaining to developing countries but so-called developed ones too. Goal 16 – peace, justice and strong institutions – is one of the more relevant SDGs to the focus of this book on building security and justice after conflict.

Human Development Index (HDI)

The HDI comprises a set of statistics measuring life expectancy, education and per capita income. These are used to rank the development of a country in UNDP's Human Development Reports, emphasising that the development of a country cannot be measured by economic growth alone but should also factor in people's well-being and capabilities. Issues relevant to development such as inequalities and human security are not, however, captured by the HDI (see UNDP, 2019).

a stranglehold, with weak state institutions unable to respond to the threat they pose or prevent their activities.

Similarly, a diversionary theory of war might suggest that certain regimes, particularly illegitimate or revolutionary, find political use/value in external enemies 'and may undertake war as a means of self-legitimization and to create mass consent regarding its policies and to suppress domestic divisions and dissent' (Lieberfeld, 2005: n.p.). A conflict abroad can distract the electorate at home from domestic problems and serve to unite them with a leadership they might otherwise question in the face of an ostensible common enemy, particularly if that enemy is presented as threatening to domestic security, interests or values (see Chomsky, 1994). Consider Russia's engagement in Ukraine and Syria since the price of oil fell in 2014. Consider US intervention in Syria in 2017 at a time when the US Administration was facing unprecedented pressure and criticism. For the UK, the decision to contest the Argentinean occupation of the Falkland Islands in 1982, although probably politically unavoidable, certainly brought British Prime Minister, Margaret Thatcher, renewed popularity at home.

Interstate wars might also be the result of needing an 'exemplary war' to demonstrate domination at home and abroad, through intervening militarily in another country less able to defend itself and call it 'preventive war' (Chomsky, 2006). Interstate wars can also be the result of 'spill-over effects' of civil or intrastate wars, or 'proxy wars' where many states are engaged in a conflict vying for power in the region or demonstrating and reinforcing power. Interstate wars can also result when the 'balance of power' (Waltz, 1979) needs reasserting or adjusting and wars become a means of manoeuvring on the global stage, changing alliances and coalitions, or demonstrating the will to use force. The impulse behind interstate conflicts may be related to a desire on the part of one or more parties to the conflict to gain strategic advantage on the global stage or a particular region for purely economic reasons, as touched upon above (see Bacevich, 2016 for a discussion of US engagement in the Middle East motivated by the region's oil reserves and the increasing reliance of the US on foreign oil imports, a thirst to maintain the privileged position of the US and justify military spending). Lieberfeld (2005) also discusses ideological influences as well as personal and social psychology that have been used as theories of the causes of conflict, and scrutinises them in light of the case study of the invasion of Iraq.

Causes of intrastate conflict

Most conflicts today are intrastate, although invariably countries outside the conflict zone will be involved. Consider, for example, the conflict in Syria: while ostensibly it is a civil war (i.e. an intrastate conflict), many other countries are involved, including Russia, US and Turkey – not to mention the numerous foreign nationals engaged in combat on the ground. Nonetheless, given the proliferation of intrastate conflicts over the last half century, much writing on the causes of conflict have tended to focus on intrastate conflicts. However, many of the causal factors – whether political, economic or developmental in nature, for instance – that are relevant to intrastate conflicts can also be relevant to interstate conflicts.

Almost everything imaginable has been described as a cause or facilitator of conflict at some time or another, and there is considerable disagreement on the importance or even relevance of various factors in respect of the propensity for conflict. To begin to unpack the myriad of possible causes, however, it is useful to distinguish between the different types of risk factors, while recognising that they are often related to and influenced by each other. It is often the existence of multiple factors or stresses, particularly in the context of weak state institutions and poor governance, which dramatically increase the vulnerability to conflict. That is not to say that conflict is mechanistically inevitable, of course: indeed, countries like the Democratic Republic of Congo (DRC) remained stable for improbable lengths of time. Broadly, the categories of risk factors can be divided into:

- *Economic Factors*, including scarcity of resources (which can generate competition over resources) and, conversely, the 'resource curse' (where abundant natural resources encourage predation – see Box 2.2), 'greed vs grievance' (see Box 2.3), unemployment, poverty, and food and water insecurity.
- *Social Factors*, including low levels of education (but also educated young people with no jobs), gender inequality as well as horizontal inequalities.
- *Political Factors*, including fragility, the after-effects of colonialism, stresses caused by democratisation, a weak civil society and the exclusion of some groups from the political process.
- *Demographic Factors*, including large and growing populations, diversity, dominance by one ethnic group, very large numbers of young people and large-scale demographic changes and population movements.
- *Geographical Factors*, including rough terrain, distance from centres of power and the ability of rebels to find foreign sanctuaries.
- *Geopolitical Factors*, whether international (such as economic crises or global efforts to address violent extremism) or regional (such as the spill-over effect, where a conflict can 'spill over' into neighbouring countries).
- *Environmental Factors*, including environmental degradation, climate change and disasters.
- *Security and Justice Factors*, including crime and violence, absence of the rule of law, the tendency of cycles of violence and conflict to be self-reinforcing, organised crime, corruption, the availability of weapons, the militarisation of society and human rights violations.
- *Development Factors*, tying into the theory that development challenges carry security threats and, conversely, improvements in development and security are mutually reinforcing (the security-development nexus)
- *Historical Factors*, including recent exposure to violence, failed or defective peace agreements or peace processes, and memories of past sufferings or humiliations.
- *Psychosocial Factors*, notably to do with attitudes and behaviours.

Reflections on the causes of conflict

As mentioned above, conflicts – whether interstate or intrastate – tend to result from a complex combination of a number of factors, often intimately related to each other. The prominence of one or other cause, or multiple causes, may vary

Box 2.2: The Resource Curse

Where competition over limited resources can increase the risk of conflict, an abundance of natural resources – such as water, diamonds, arable land, gold and especially oil – or economies that depend heavily on natural resources can also instigate armed violence and conflict. It is well known that oil has fuelled conflicts in the Middle East as have so-called 'blood diamonds' in West Africa (see Box 11.3 in Chapter 11). Warring factions may fight over access to resources or resources may help create and sustain them – as occurred in Sierra Leone and the Democratic Republic of Congo (DRC), for instance, with high-value natural resources in effect escalating and prolonging the conflict (see Koning, 2008). A wealth of natural resources can provide both motive and opportunity for conflict. However, resource-rich countries are also some of the more stable countries, which has led some analysts to consider that other factors (such as low resource wealth per capita) need to be in play for resource-rich countries to witness an outbreak of conflict (see Basedau and Lay, 2009).

Box 2.3: Greed versus Grievance

There is much research on whether it is greed or grievance that fuels conflict. Theories of horizontal inequalities suggest that grievance may be more instrumental than greed in precipitating conflict. Stewart (2010) and Stewart and Brown (2007) outline that the differences between access to economic, social and political resources among groups that share a common identity – also referred to as horizontal inequalities – are often a key contributory factor to conflict.

Collier (2007), Collier and Hoeffler (2000), Sriram et al. (2017) and Fearon and Laitin (2003) argue that grievance is an inadequate explanation: 'ethnic antagonisms, nationalist sentiments, and grievances often motivate rebels and their supporters. But such broad factors are too common to distinguish the cases where civil war breaks out' (Fearon and Laitin, 2003: 76). As Collier (2007) and Collier and Hoeffler (2000) have argued, means or opportunity, for example geographic and, particularly, economic viability, are much more credible explanations: whether a rebellion, for example, can access finance or find a safe haven in mountainous terrain are argued to be more crucial in determining the outbreak of conflict than grievances that may motivate those involved.

While the greed versus grievance debate continues, it can be said that neither simply greed nor grievance is a sufficient explanation for the outbreak or escalation of conflict in any one place, let alone as a general theory of conflict.

during the lifespan of a conflict. Initial causes may be lost or forgotten amidst new grievances, dynamics or agendas that form and change throughout conflict. In addition, there may be multiple conflicts within an intrastate conflict, each with its own set of interrelated causes. Moreover, different actors, including parties to the conflict, and different sub-groups therein, may perceive the root causes (and how they should be addressed) differently.

It is also important to recognise that the existence of one or more factors that are generally considered to constitute risk factors, may not necessarily lead to conflict. The abundance of natural resources, for instance, may provide motive and opportunity for conflict (the resource curse) or, conversely, it may in fact contribute to peace, as will be shortly discussed. The balance of factors, context, triggers and the interests and capacity (power, resources and perceived legitimacy or support) of a host of involved or interested actors influence whether or not conflict will break out and to what extent. The uprisings in the Middle East and North Africa (MENA) which began in 2010, originally referred to as the Arab Spring, highlight how decisive are opportunity, ability and will in turning risks into conflict. To generalise, grievance transitioned into protest as a result of various triggers and opportunities, as well as internal, regional and international dynamics and developments. Protests in several countries transitioned into violent conflict as a consequence of disproportionate state and state-sanctioned responses to the protests and, thereafter, into armed conflict as a result of the capacity and will of the state and the protesters/insurgents. The interest and engagement of power-brokers in the International Community also impacted the transitions, as did other internal, regional and international dynamics. The protests and violence in MENA also highlight the importance of distinguishing between factors (or drivers), enablers and triggers, and between different factors, enablers and triggers for each party to the conflict.

To add further complexity, factors which cause conflict are also often a consequence of conflict (for instance, food and water insecurity, or human rights violations). Nonetheless, effective conflict prevention, intervention and response require a rigorous analysis and understanding of the complexity of factors which have influenced, are influencing and are influenced by conflict (not limited to armed conflict) (see Box 2.4 on conflict analysis and conflict mapping). As Haider (2014: 6) states:

> Identifying and understanding the interactions between various causes, dimensions and dynamics of conflict – and the particular contexts in which conflict arises, is essential in determining potential areas of intervention; and designing appropriate approaches and methods for conflict prevention, resolution and transformation.

The sheer number of potential causal factors, their interrelationship and the lack of agreement even on the concept of 'conflict' could reasonably make us hesitate before attempting to produce overarching theories, few of which offer more than partial explanations for the origins of actual conflicts (Cramer, 2006; Reno, 2011). It is important not to assume that there are single or simple causes of a specific conflict; this pertains to interstate conflicts also. It is necessary to address different factors at the local, structural, institutional, regional and international level and recognise that factors – whether social, political or economic – impact each of these levels as well as each other. It is also important to distinguish

---

Box 2.4: Conflict Analysis and Conflict Mapping

Tools such as conflict analysis or conflict mapping can be used to identify (or map) and analyse all the factors relevant to a particular context (such as history, culture, politics, demography, geography, security and of course conflict actors and their motivation and so on) and how they might interact and impact conflict dynamics. Such analyses and mapping are essential prerequisites to the effective study of or engagement in conflict-affected or conflict-vulnerable environments. Today, conflict mapping utilises technological advancements including internet-based and social media information.

John Paul Lederach, a leading pioneer of conflict transformation scholarship and practice, developed a novel approach to conflict mapping by conceptualising conflict transformation as both linked to its current context and to a desired future. This followed from his distinction between conflict resolution (as ending what is undesirable) and conflict transformation (creating what is desirable) (see Lederach, 1997, 2003; Woodhouse et al., 2015).

---

between drivers, enablers and triggers (see Sriram et. al., 2017), and acknowledge that a combination of stresses with adequate means and opportunities provides ripe ground for conflict. If conflict is to be prevented from erupting, escalating or recurring, all of these factors require careful analysis in order to determine the appropriate intervention. Given that there are correlates between the causes, dynamics and consequences of conflict, the policy implications of such an analysis are valid for both conflict prevention and recovery. Dodge's submission to the Iraq Inquiry in the UK (Dodge, 2009) underscores how instrumentally important are explanations of conflict, given that they inform government policy and multi-agency responses.

Part 2 – Conflict Prevention

While there are likely to be multiple and conflicting accounts of the cause of any particular conflict, reflection upon the possible causes of conflict should inform peacebuilding as well as, ideally, enable conflict prevention. Conflict prevention should, thus, address the possible causes of conflict, as well as enablers and triggers (see Ramsbotham et al., 2016). John Burton has coined the term 'conflict provenion' as part of an innovative theory of conflict resolution and conflict prevention, which promotes anticipating and avoiding sources of potential conflict, by addressing the human needs which lead to conflict (such as security, self-esteem, belonging and identity) rather than simply suppressing them. The basis of his argument is drawn from the human needs theory, and like Azar (1990) who coined the term 'protracted social conflict' whom we discussed earlier, he argues that these needs must be addressed to avoid conflict. In other words, society must adapt to humans and address these needs, rather than humans adapt to society and these needs be ignored – with the former necessitating conflict prevention or provention, and the latter necessitating coercive measures of social control (which we have seen are not always, if even often, effective) (see Burton, 1990).

The aim of conflict prevention is, of course, to prevent the escalation of a non-violent or non-armed conflict, disagreement, dispute or grievance into armed conflict. Many international organisations, notably the UN, as well as think tanks and governments, closely monitor global developments to determine where tensions are rising and risk developing into armed conflict. Where tensions are seen to be rising, a number of tools can be deployed in an attempt to prevent conflict, including diplomacy, military intervention and economic sanctions, as will be discussed in the next section. Longer-term efforts to prevent conflict are not dissimilar to comprehensive efforts to build peace after conflict, including as they do efforts to facilitate development, support good governance, and entrench security and the rule of law. Indeed, the recent introduction of the concept of 'sustaining peace' (see Box 2.5) is a response both to the need to attend to building peace before the outbreak of conflict (i.e. invest in conflict prevention) and to the recognition that activities in all phases of the conflict 'cycle' are often not too dissimilar.

Although attempts at conflict prevention between states are as old as history, the modern prominence of the subject, especially for intrastate conflicts, is largely a product of the last generation. From the early 1990s, when the so-called 'CNN effect' was first noticed (see Box 2.6), there has been an increase in the capacity to prevent conflict, but even more in the demand to halt violent conflicts – a public demand and a demand borne of structural factors. Factors include a reduction in

Box 2.5: Sustaining Peace

The concept of sustaining peace is a new concept introduced into the lexicon of conflict prevention and peacebuilding, particularly following the 2016 adoption of identical resolutions on sustaining peace by the UN Security Council and the UN General Assembly (UN Security Council Resolution 2282 and General Assembly Resolution 70/262). The concept marks a shift in the focus of peacebuilding to all stages of a conflict cycle, not just post-conflict; to include conflict prevention, conflict resolution and post-conflict recovery activities. The concept also marks an important ideological shift in focus to peace and not simply conflict. There is concern that it could pave the way for legitimising further intervention in the affairs of others, but there is equal promise that efforts to prevent conflict will be renewed and thus save countless lives and financial resources.

The concept of sustaining peace also underscores the importance of sustaining efforts to build peace beyond a ceasefire, recognising that threats to peace and security are particularly significant in the immediate aftermath of conflict where power dynamics shift and spoilers (those who seek to frustrate efforts to build peace) can mobilise (see UN High-Level Independent Panel on Peace Operations, 2015).

Box 2.6: The CNN Effect and Beyond – Social Media and Information Technology

The CNN effect is a theory that suggests that the development of 24-hour televised news, including CNN, over the last three decades, had a significant impact upon foreign policy, generating foreign policy responses to saturation coverage of certain events (and not others) (see Livingston, 1997). News coverage will guarantee more attention by policy-makers as well as help generate political support for action. The public take much of what they know about political affairs from the media, and will judge governments and organisations on how they respond to events in the media, and, of course, how they are portrayed in the media. In many international organisations, the day begins by reviewing the headlines and determining, in response, what action needs be taken. Former UN Secretary-General of the UN, Boutros Boutros-Ghali, even referred to CNN as the 16th member of the Security Council (Volkmer, 2013). Of course, we can question the extent to which some news media outlets are independent and the extent to which the stories they profile is a result of the influence of powerful elites in government, international organisations and business, for instance (see Herman and Chomsky (1988) for an analysis of how the news media industry in the US protects the interests of government and corporations in order to protect their sources of information, and thus potential sales and profit, and thereby operates as a quasi-propaganda machine, manufacturing public consent for government and corporate policies and activities). Further innovations in information technology and particularly the advent of social media and real-time reportage from people and places that might not have previously generated attention beyond the contours of their experiences, have further impacted foreign policy, as well as the way it is formulated and communicated.

divisions in the UN Security Council in comparison with the Cold War, alarm at the number of violent conflicts in progress, the ambiguous results of previous international interventions, technological advances which have made real-time coverage of fighting available even by mobile telephones, (and by extension easy falsification of images) and continually growing public and media pressure to 'do something' (see Menkhaus, 2004).

Unlike peacebuilding practice, oftentimes, effective conflict prevention tries to comprehensively address the potential causes of conflict, in an effort to prevent it from occurring, escalating or recurring. It is, thus, generally undertaken prior to the outbreak of conflict, whilst peacebuilding often refers to similar activities undertaken post-conflict – although, as mentioned earlier, similar activities may be involved in both conflict prevention and peacebuilding. While it is important to apply lessons from the past or other contexts, it is essential that comprehensive conflict prevention measures address the issues related to the particular context, as well as the potential triggers and opportunities present, and current and anticipated socio-economic and political developments. Consequently, comprehensive conflict analysis and early warning systems are required to ascertain and track the development of key indicators of potential conflict.

There have, however, been some criticisms of the weaknesses and failures in early warning, including the inherently political nature of early warning 'in terms of "who is warning whom and to what end?" and in terms of which warnings are heeded' (Haider, 2014: 50). Aside from these political challenges, there are also financial challenges. Even the largest and most powerful government does not have infinite resources. Western governments followed developments in the former Yugoslavia in 1991 and 1992 with close attention, but were at the same time having to deal with half a dozen other major crises, mostly related to the end of the Cold War, several of which interacted with the emerging crisis in the Balkans in unpredictable ways. The international community does not, after all, possess infinite resources.

Soon after what were frequently described as peacekeeping 'failures' in the 1990s, some writers (e.g. Ackermann, 2003) began to argue that, in fact, a lack of response, rather than limitations in early warning, have resulted in missed opportunities for prevention. The UN High-Level Panel on Threats, Challenges and Change (UNSG, 2004a) made similar arguments. A better understanding of the events of the 1990s, together with discouraging experiences of intervention in more recent years, have modified this approach somewhat, but it remains politically powerful, and morally effective as a political weapon. It can also be said, however, that such an approach tends to marginalise the influence of local actors, and take agency away from them, in favour of an obsessive concentration on the minutiae of manoeuvrings within the international community, which is assumed to have the capability to resolve virtually any conflict. Again, recent disastrous interventions (notably in Libya) have somewhat reduced the force of this argument.

Clearly, prevention is always going to be better than intervention after a conflict, with its inevitable human and economic costs (there has been much research to show that investment in conflict prevention saves many times more the amount that would otherwise be spent on resolving conflict and peacebuilding, up to 16 times according to the most recent research – UN and World Bank, 2018 – which, of course, is inconsequential compared with the many thousands of lives that can also be saved through effective conflict prevention over time). For this reason, since the turn of the millennium, there has been significant investment by major donors in what are described as 'stabilisation' or 'conflict prevention' programmes. It is widely accepted that, given the often cyclical nature of conflict, successful conflict prevention efforts are likely to be more sustainable than efforts to manage or resolve a conflict once it has erupted (see Glennie, 2010). Indeed, as Picciotto says: 'there is little doubt that conflict prevention holds the key to sustainable peace' (Picciotto, 2010: 21). The difficulty remains, of course, that through successive rounds of conflict prevention, one can fall into a policy of 'conflict deferment' where the underlying causes are bound to produce conflict eventually. Burundi is arguable an example of this tendency.

More attention and resources are being dedicated to prevention than ever before, but many argue that more could still be done – and this attention and these resources are far outweighed by the attention focussed on and investment in conflict resolution and post-conflict peacebuilding (Jackson and Beswick, 2018). In his second comprehensive report on the prevention of armed conflict, a decade ago, the UN Secretary-General suggested that a 'culture of prevention' was beginning to take hold at the UN, but there remained an unacceptable gap between rhetoric and reality:

> Too often the international community spends vast sums of money to fight fires that, in hindsight, we might more easily have extinguished with timely preventive action before so many lives were lost or turned upside down. Over the last five years, we have spent over $18 billion on United Nations peacekeeping that was necessary partly because of inadequate preventive measures. A fraction of that investment in preventive action would surely have saved both lives and money. (UN Secretary-General – UNSG, 2006b: 4)

Today, the UN Secretary-General implores the international community 'to make prevention our priority' and urges 'diplomacy for peace' (Lederer, 2018: n.p.). This is in recognition of the many protracted conflicts and the many elusive or short-lived peace agreements. Delegates of the UN General Assembly have also recently called for investment in addressing the root causes of conflict rather than 'bullets and tanks' (Liberia representative speaking at the 2018 UN General Assembly High-Level Debate on Sustaining Peace – UN, 2018b: n.p.).

The difficulty, of course, lies in demonstrating to sceptical publics and parliaments that stabilisation and conflict prevention programmes, often very general and long-term, will actually have the effects that are claimed. It is almost impossible, after all, to prove that a given, well-intentioned project will *not* prevent conflict at some future point. Particularly given the many competing priorities for attention and resources where conflict has already broken out, it can be hard to generate support for conflict prevention. So, while there are a number of examples of successful conflict prevention (including South Africa, Crimea and Macedonia – see Box 2.7), the majority of successful conflict prevention efforts remain unseen. We are also, of course, much more likely to hear on the news about conflict prevention failures, such as occurred in the last decade in Sudan, rather than where conflict has been prevented, such as in Macedonia (see Box 2.7).

Box 2.7: Macedonia

Macedonia in 2001 is often referred to as a conflict prevention success story, particularly in the context of the protracted conflicts that affected other parts of the former Yugoslavia, and scholars have attempted to draw general lessons from it (see Paintin, 2009). However, the basic problem of community division has not been solved and a renewal of violent conflict has seemed likely in the years since (International Crisis Group, 2015). Conflict was avoided in 2001 in part because major international actors were still deeply involved in the Balkans.

Early warning

As mentioned above, early warning is critical to effective conflict prevention. Early warning depends, in the first instance, upon the ability to monitor and gather relevant information which might indicate that tensions are rising or conflict may erupt. Effective early warning does not just depend upon information; we need to know what information to gather, how to analyse the data gathered and what developments might be cause for concern. We also need to know *where* to get the information, and whether it is reliable. Fact-finding missions are often undertaken by the UN and other international organisations to supplement or substantiate information gained from other sources (such as reports from staff on the ground, civil society organisations, media organisations and think tanks).

There have been many models developed to predict the outbreak of conflict, some of which are very elaborate, whilst others focus on one particular factor which is supposed to promote conflict (such as high levels of gender inequality or rising minority rights violations). Ward et al. (2010) found that models that just include simple variables, such as GDP per capita and population, appear to better predict the outbreak of conflict than more elaborate models, while other analysts suggest combining models (especially gathering both quantitative and qualitative data) is more effective (Goldstone, 2008).

There are many datasets (some of which are available online and listed at the end of this chapter), which can be used to monitor risk factors and identify places at risk. It is important, however, to recognise that they can never be entirely objective and value-free, even if accuracy and completeness could ever be assured. As Löwenheim argues, rating the governance capacity of states 'beyond being an analytical tool ... reproduces structures of authority and hierarchy in the international system' (Löwenheim, 2008: 255). As mentioned in the previous section, there is also criticism of who is monitoring who, and for what reason.

Finally, whilst the identification of potential risk factors is relatively easy (e.g., sustained discrimination against a minority group), it remains unclear why some situations end in conflict and others do not, and, for those that do not, whether conflict prevention efforts have actually made the difference. It has also led to an extremely large and disparate number of projects being classified as 'conflict prevention' – not all of which necessarily cause more good than harm.

Of course, early warning is only a step towards effective conflict prevention; there needs to be swift, co-ordinated and well-resourced action in response to any indicators of imminent conflict. There also needs to be effective tools, methods and actors to deploy in order to effectively act upon the warning and prevent conflict.

Tools of conflict prevention

As already indicated, there are many possible ways in which to help guard against the outbreak, escalation or recurrence of conflict. Addressing domestic and global risk factors, including under-development, poverty, state fragility and weak governance, crime and corruption, environmental degradation and human rights violations are chief among these. What are often referred to as structural prevention tools are generally used to address these areas (see Haider, 2014;

Ramsbotham et al., 2016). Structural prevention generally involves long-term efforts to address certain economic, social, political or other factors which are considered to pose a threat to security. So, for instance, development assistance can be seen to be, in large part, investing in conflict prevention, recognising the links between development and security. Likewise, efforts to promote good governance can also impact security dynamics and can, as such, be considered to be a conflict prevention effort in certain circumstances. These are the very type of activities that are often undertaken in the aftermath of conflict in an effort to build a sustainable peace.

Operational conflict prevention tools are those deployed when risk factors suggest an imminent outbreak of conflict (see Haider, 2014; Ramsbotham et al., 2016). Such tools include diplomacy (so-called preventive diplomacy which can include mediation), mediation and facilitating dialogue in order to repair relationships and/or resolve grievances, economic sanctions, and, less frequently, military intervention (including, in some circumstances, humanitarian interventions if there is the risk of the outbreak or recurrence of armed conflict – see Box 2.8 on the Responsibility to Protect).

The UN also refers to systemic prevention (UN and World Bank, 2018) which includes addressing transnational risks that threaten or increase the likelihood of conflict, and which are dealt with by global partnerships. Such risks include organised crime or illicit economies, including trafficking and the illegal arms trade; war crimes and crimes against humanity; pandemics; and climate change.

In terms of actors engaged in conflict prevention, governments are primarily responsible for preventing conflict on their own territory, but the support and engagement of civil society, the private sector and the international community is also often needed (UN and World Bank, 2018). Civil society actors include academia, the media, think tanks, advocacy groups, civil society organisations (CSOs) and the general public. International community actors engaged in conflict prevention include:

- International organisations (including the UN and many of its various departments, offices, agencies, funds and programmes)
- Regional organisations (such as the Economic Community of West African States (ECOWAS), the European Union (EU) and the Organization for Security and Co-operation in Europe (OSCE))
- International financial institutions (IFIs) such as the World Bank (WB), the International Monetary Fund (IMF), the Asian Development Bank (ADB) and the Inter-American Development Bank (IADB)
- Development agencies, including government development agencies such as the Swedish International Development Cooperation Agency (SIDA) and the Japan International Cooperation Agency (JICA)
- International non-governmental or independent organisations such as Saferworld and the Nairobi Peace Initiative Africa (NPI-Africa)
- Other organisations, including think tanks (such as the International Crisis Group), research centres (including universities) and the media can play a significant role in conflict prevention.

Generally, many more than one actor will be engaged in a single area of conflict prevention at any one time. For instance, both the Norwegian and Cuban governments, with the support of the UN, mediated between the Government of Colombia and the Revolutionary Armed Forces of Colombia (FARC) in order to facilitate their recent peace agreement (UN and World Bank, 2018). Of course, more than one conflict prevention activity will often be going on at any one time, cross-cutting political, development, economic and humanitarian sectors. In order to be effective, therefore, there needs to be a holistic and comprehensive conflict strategy incorporating all of these aspects as well as addressing pressing needs and longer-term structural issues.

As mentioned earlier, it is often quite difficult to see conflict prevention successes, and the media often chooses to focus on failures. So, it can be hard to know 'what works'. There are also criticisms that efforts to prevent conflict can have detrimental effects or are simply excuses to meddle in the affairs of others responding to national self-interest and hegemonic impulses (see Whittall, 2010). Others, however, consider that rather than an excuse to interfere and consequently undermining other state's sovereignty, preventive action can reinforce sovereignty rather than, as is often levied at the international community, undermine it – because effective conflict prevention often entails the development of national and local capacity to manage tensions peacefully. It is also suggested that, if successful, preventive action can also help avoid the extensive external intervention that often characterises the later stages of conflict. Moreover, as mentioned earlier, many regard conflict prevention as essential, as the complexity of conflicts increase and resources are stretched.

There have been a number of policy reports elaborating on the criteria which should guide conflict prevention and which can increase the likelihood of success. In the Secretary-General's first comprehensive report on the prevention of armed conflict (UNSG, 2001), the basic premises that were laid out remain relevant today. They include a recognition that conflict prevention is a primary obligation of member states; that the primary responsibility rests with national governments, with support from the UN and other organisations; that the role of civil society is of critical importance; that preventative action should be initiated as early as possible in a conflict cycle; that a fully comprehensive approach is needed, incorporating a wide range of activities and actors; that conflict prevention and equitable development are mutually reinforcing; and that a successful conflict prevention strategy depends on the co-operation of many actors, both within and outside the UN. Others have underscored the critical importance of effective early warning capabilities, swift responses, political will, requisite resources and institutional capacity, and supporting the development of in-country long-term prevention capabilities (see Zartman, 2015; Menkhaus, 2004; Ackermann, 2003).

Despite the many actors and activities involved in conflict prevention, and increased attention and resources dedicated to conflict prevention, there remain continual failures to predict and prevent outbreaks of armed conflict and violence. The uprisings in MENA from late 2010 clearly show there was – and remains – a need to improve early warning – not least through improved information collection, collation and analysis – in order to better predict potential causes and triggers of conflict and events that may rapidly develop into conflict. Similarly, in many of these cases, it is clear there is also a need to develop systems and processes whereby an improvement in early warning is matched by an improvement in early response. However, even with effective early warning and response, conflict prevention remains highly politicised and therefore exponentially more difficult. Solomon and Woocher (2010) argue that it is widely accepted that armed conflict is preventable, but the biggest obstacle to preventing conflict remains lack of political will, due to a number of reasons:

- The cost of preventive action (in relation to visible results)
- Whether or not action might be perceived as infringing state sovereignty
- Political, economic or strategic interests that run counter to preventive action
- Competing priorities
- The interests and level of support of key players, allies or voters
- Whether an unwelcome precedent might be established (Solomon and Woocher, 2010).

However, as Solomon and Woocher (2010) note, the conflict prevention environment is changing, not least given significant technological advancements in respect of the internet and use of social media and the advent of the Responsibility to Protect (R2P) doctrine (see Box 2.8 and Chapter 9).

Box 2.8: Responsibility to Protect (R2P)

As adopted at the 2005 UN World Summit, the responsibility to protect (R2P) mandates that 'each individual State has the responsibility to protect its populations from genocide, war crimes, ethnic cleansing and crimes against humanity' (UN General Assembly – UNGA, 2005a: 31). The international community has a responsibility to assist states in fulfilling this responsibility. Through the UN, the international community also has the responsibility to protect populations through the use of diplomatic, humanitarian and other peaceful means. Where a state reneges on its responsibilities and peaceful means are insufficient, through the Security Council the international community should be prepared to 'take collective action, in a timely and decisive manner' (UNGA, 2005a: 31).

While both R2P and humanitarian intervention can involve the use of military force for humanitarian reasons, they differ in a number of respects. Firstly, R2P emphasises prevention; the use of military force is a last resort, with many other measures employed under R2P to prevent atrocities (although some people also consider that humanitarian intervention also includes more than just the use of military force – see Scheffer (1992). R2P also refers to the responsibility, rather than the right, of states to intevene in the affairs of others in order to protect others. Military force also requires the authorisation of the UN Security Council under the R2P doctrine, while humanitarian intervention allows for the use of force for humanitarian reasons without such authorisation.

(Continued)

Many criticise the R2P doctrine for failing to protect those at risk of genocide, war crimes, ethnic cleansing and crimes against humanity – because of the failed intervention in Libya in 2011 (the only time the R2P doctrine was used to justify military intervention) and because of the failure to intervene where there were mass atrocities (e.g. Syria, Yemen and Myanmar) (Rieff, 2018). However, some argue that the failures in Libya point to poor planning and implementation, rather than failures inherent to the R2P doctrine itself. Moreover, there are many other measures besides military intervention under the R2P doctrine which have contributed to averting crisis (e.g. Kenya in 2007 after the violent national elections) (Rieff, 2018).

See Bellamy (2010) and also Welsh (2010) for discussions on the implications for national sovereignty and the political autonomy of the weak. See also Katz (2011), Luck (2010) and Paris (2014) for discussions on the challenges which continue to characterise implementation of the R2P doctrine including lack of political will, selective application and structural deficiencies. For a discussion on the relationship between R2P and humanitarian intervention see Bellamy (2010).

To prevent conflict, aside from the need to improve the record of early warning and response, there is also a need to attend to the possible adverse impact that preventive action can have. Without a thorough understanding of the context and the ways in which preventive action and actors are perceived domestically, preventive action (such as Quick Impact Projects – QIPs – and democracy promotion – see Evans, 2006) can be counter-productive. Picciotto (2010) also highlights how 'big bang' policy adjustments, to improve efficiency or increase output, for instance, as advised by international financial institutions (IFIs), can often inflame social tensions. Picciotto suggests that a conflict-sensitive approach might instead advocate enhancing horizontal equality and increasing employment, for instance. Continual evaluation of whether conflict prevention initiatives are generating the anticipated and desired outcomes, or whether they might be fuelling further grievances, discontent, corruption or incapacity (see Evans, 2006) is also essential.

Conclusion

To provide a context for subsequent chapters, this chapter has looked at the causes of conflict and at conflict prevention. This chapter has underscored the importance of attending to the potential causes of conflict in order to prevent and resolve conflict as well as build a sustainable peace. It is recognised, however, that there are many different theories on the causes of conflict. Even in a single conflict, there are often multiple and sometimes competing perceived causes. But conflict prevention, conflict resolution and peacebuilding are complex endeavours. Rather than reducing the potential causes of conflict to single factors or simple models, and prioritising one activity or focus above another in efforts to prevent conflict or build peace, it is more important to recognise and respond to the complexity of conflict and of peace. Nonetheless, accepting fully the complexity of conflict risks making the concept of conflict unmanageable and impossible to define – and certainly risks agreement between various actors on its meaning. With no contained definition and shared agreement, this risks undermining efforts to prevent conflict and build peace. A balance is, therefore, needed between avoiding overly simplifying and overlooking significant factors in conflict dynamics and peacebuilding, and indefinitely delaying action until all detail is known, understood and agreed: in other words, a pragmatic approach and common sense are needed.

Summary of Key Issues

- In any one conflict, the causes of conflict are likely to be many, changing over time and different for different actors.
- Lack or abundance of resources can be a critical factor in conflict outbreak, protraction and recurrence – whether there is a lack of resources or an abundance (often referred to as the resource curse).
- There is significant research on whether greed or grievance is the main cause of conflict, while general recognition that neither alone can explain the outbreak or escalation of conflict.
- Development challenges can adversely affect security and increase the likelihood of conflict; investment in development is therefore seen as a way to prevent conflict.
- Conflict analyses and mapping are useful tools to use to identify causal factors and other issues and actors that need to inform peacebuilding, conflict prevention or other engagement in conflict-affected environments.
- If efforts to prevent and recover from conflict are to be successful, they need to be informed by a comprehensive understanding of why and how conflicts can occur – including possible root causes, triggers and catalysts.
- Effective early warning and early response systems are required for effective conflict prevention.
- It is difficult to demonstrate successful conflict prevention, which makes it hard to effectively lobby for the requisite investment in conflict prevention.
- Failure to prevent conflict as well as the potentially politicised nature of early warning and response further complicates efforts to garner the necessary political and financial support for conflict prevention.
- The new concept of sustaining peace aims to shift the focus of peacebuilding to all stages of a conflict cycle, to include conflict-prevention as well as post-conflict peacebuilding.

Reflective Question

Reflect on what you consider to be the main causes of conflict today and, then, what preventative action could be taken to stop such potential causal factors resulting in conflict.

Barometers, Watch Lists and Datasets

The International Crisis Group's (ICG) monthly 'Crisis Watch' – www.crisisgroup.org/crisiswatch.

Heidelberg Institute's Annual 'Conflict Barometer' – http://hiik.de/en/konfliktbarometer.

Vision of Humanity's 'Global Peace Index' (and other peace indexes) – http://visionofhumanity.org/reports.

State Fragility Index of the Center for Systemic Peace – www.systemicpeace.org/.

The World Bank's Worldwide Governance Indicators – http://data.worldbank.org/data-catalog/worldwide-governance-indicators.

The Fund for Peace's Failed States Index – http://fundforpeace.org/fsi.

The UN Development Programme's (UNDP) Human Development Index (HDI) – http://hdr.undp.org/en/statistics.

The biennial publication of the Center for International Development and Conflict Management (CIDCM) of the University of Maryland, 'Peace and Conflict' – https://cidcm.umd.edu/publications/academic-books.

The Minorities at Risk (MAR) project at the University of Maryland's CIDCM – www.mar.umd.edu.

Datasets of the Uppsala Conflict Data Project (UCDP) of the Department of Peace and Conflict Research of Uppsala University – http://ucdp.uu.se.

Stockholm International Peace Research Institute's (SIPRI) datasets – www.sipri.org/databases.

Correlates of War – www.correlatesofwar.org.

The Organization for Economic Cooperation and Development's (OECD) Country Risk Classification – www.oecd.org/trade/xcred/crc.htm.

The Cingranelli-Richards (CIRI) Human Rights Dataset – www.humanrightsdata.com.

The University of North Carolina's Political Terror Scale – www.politicalterrorscale.org.

University of Edinburgh's Women and Peace Agreements Database (PA-X Women) – www.peaceagreements.org.

Armed conflict dataset of the Uppsala Conflict Data Program (UCDP) and the Peace Research Institute Oslo (PRIO) – www.prio.org/Data/Armed-Conflict/UCDP-PRIO.

List of Core Resources

Causes

Collier, P. and Hoeffler, A. (2000) *Greed and Grievance in Civil War*, World Bank Policy Research Working Paper (Washington DC: World Bank). Available at http://documents.worldbank.org/curated/en/359271468739530199/pdf/multi-page.pdf.

Global Development (2015) *What causes conflict and how it can be resolved, The Guardian's* Global Development podcast (2015). Available at www.theguardian. com/global-development/audio/2015/may/17/conflict-resolution.

Levy, J. (2007) 'International sources of interstate and intrastate war', in C. Crocker, F. Hampson and P. Aall (eds), *Leashing the Dogs of War* (Washington: USIP): 17–38.

Rupesinghe, K. Sciarone, P. van de Goor, L. (eds) (2016) *Between Development and Destruction: An Enquiry into the Causes of Conflict* (Basingstoke and London: Palgrave Macmillan).

Stewart, F. (2010) *Horizontal Inequalities as a Cause of Conflict: A Review of CRISE Findings,* World Development Report 2011 Background Paper, Washington: World Bank. Available at http://siteresources.worldbank.org/EXTWDR2011/ Resources/6406082-1283882418764/WDR_Background_Paper_Stewart.pdf.

Prevention

Lund, M. (2009) 'Conflict prevention: Theory in pursuit of policy and practice' in J. Bercovitch, V. Kremenyuk, and I. Zartman (eds), *The SAGE Handbook of Conflict Resolution*, London: Sage, 287–308. Available at www.wilsoncenter.org/sites/ default/files/Conflict%20Prevention-%20Theory%20in%20Pursuit%20of%20 Policy%20and%20Practice.pdf.

SIPRI (2017) *Where do we go from here? Conflict prevention and new multilateralism,* video of panel discussion hosted by SIPRI. Available at www.youtube.com/ watch?v=vSYCdp3jPIc.

UN and World Bank (2018) *Pathways for Peace: Inclusive Approaches to Preventing Violent Conflict* (Washington DC: World Bank). Available at https:// openknowledge.worldbank.org/handle/10986/28337.

3 Building a Safe and Secure Environment

Overview

This chapter initially considers the importance of security in building peace. It looks specifically at the task of creating and maintaining a safe and secure environment, without which all the other tasks required to build a sustainable peace will be more difficult, if not actually impossible. The chapter provides an overview of the, predominantly, international military actors and activities involved in building security in the immediate aftermath of conflict, and the role of international military forces in post-conflict recovery. The chapter concludes by identifying some of the challenges in the way of building security after conflict, and discussing whether, and if so how, such challenges may be satisfactorily addressed.

Learning Outcomes

- Identify some of the key post-conflict security challenges
- Be familiar with the history of the engagement of international military forces in building a safe and secure environment, and the problems encountered
- Critically reflect upon what constitutes a safe and secure environment and how it can be developed
- Understand the value and limitations of international military forces in post-conflict environments
- Articulate some of the challenges and lessons learned associated with different types of interventions

Part 1 – Why Security is Important

Chapter 1 has already discussed the concept of security, which is as contested and ambiguous as the other concepts that this book deals with. Nonetheless, large-scale, long-term and complex international missions have regularly been undertaken over the past generation to provide a 'secure environment'. So, what did the originators of these missions think they were trying to achieve?

This question requires us to understand the importance of security, and what it is. As we have seen, the definition of security and the components of it, are fiercely contested. It is frequently described in sweeping and very general terms. As you will recall from Chapter 1, security in its broadest sense refers to human security, that is security from threats from environmental degradation, pandemics, poverty, criminality and poor governance and not simply from armies and arms. Often, however, when talking about security, we refer to the basic security a state needs to provide, without which it will be unable to fulfil its other core tasks, command the loyalty of the citizenry or, consequently, be seen as legitimate (Chuter, 2017).

If a state is to achieve acceptance for its control of security, the minimal pre-requisite is that it protects its citizens better than they could do themselves. The basic method of ensuring this is what has been called, since Max Weber in 1918, the 'monopoly of the legitimate use of force' (Waters and Waters 2015: 136). Weber saw this monopoly (including the ability to delegate the right to others) as the irreducible minimum qualification for a modern, developed state. The point remains valid today, as the OECD has noted: 'A state that cannot achieve a legiti-mate monopoly over the means of, at least, large-scale violence will not be able to preside over almost anything else' (OECD, 2010: 88). It is critical to note that 'legitimacy' is fundamental here; a state may not monopolise all forms of violence, of course – there may be insurgent groups and organised criminal groups – but it is the only actor legitimately able to use force (to punish, or to defend).

Consequently, after conflict, re-establishing security is key to a state regaining legitimacy (see Putzel, 2007). It is also of critical importance that the people of the state are confident that they will be protected by the security and justice sec-tor institutions (see DFID, 2010). This has obvious political consequences when it is not the state itself, but an international actor, that secures this monopoly. Likewise, in accepting the importance of security, we should not forget that secu-rity is a contested concept and often located within discourses of the powerful: those who can define what constitutes security and what and who is deemed to threaten it (see Luckham, 2010).

Nonetheless, the establishment of physical security after armed conflict is an immediate priority, without which attempts at peacebuilding, statebuilding and development are destined to fail. Additionally, improving security is the most obvious signal to people who have suffered the effects of armed conflict that they can begin to have confidence in the future of their country and begin to rebuild their lives. It is also an important signal to the wider international com-munity, to the business community and also, critically, to potential spoilers (see Box 3.1).

Box 3.1: Spoilers

'Spoilers' is defined in the USIP Glossary as – 'Anyone who seeks to block or sabo-tage a peace process or the implementation of an agreement, usually because it threatens their power and interests' (Snodderly, 2011: 48).

(Continued)

In any place emerging from conflict, it is critical that the threat to a fragile peace posed by potential spoilers is addressed. Potential spoilers can include those whose grievances have not been addressed, those for whom the peace process does not respond to their needs or wants, and those who either do not benefit (perhaps just as much as others) from the peace or might benefit more from instability. Spoilers are often considered to be those who would take up arms, or otherwise cause instability, during peacebuilding. They can include demobilised combatants, political actors who find themselves without adequate access to power, or members of organised criminal groups, for instance.

Because of the threat posed by spoilers, oftentimes those engaged in peacebuilding pay more attention to the needs and demands of potential spoilers of peace rather than those who may pose no threat but whose needs may be greater. Consequently, vulnerable or marginalised groups are often sidelined during peace processes and peacebuilding – the irony being that those who may have particularly suffered during conflict and who remain vulnerable to insecurity and injustice after conflict are ignored. While these groups may not take up arms – in fact, they might – there cannot be said to be a meaningful or comprehensive peace if the dividends of peace are only enjoyed by those who wield the greatest power and those perceived to pose a threat. Moreover, unless the peace process has the confidence of a broad cross-section of the people, it is unlikely to succeed. For, while focussing exclusively on the needs of potential spoilers, those who may be better advocates for peace are being ignored – and, thus, the potential for peace is undermined.

Part 2 – A Safe and Secure Environment

Some very broad and ambitious definitions of a secure environment have been produced. For example, the USIP/US Army Peacekeeping and Stability Operations Institute states:

> A safe and secure environment is one in which the population has the freedom to pursue daily activities without fear of politically motivated, persistent, or large-scale violence. Such an environment is characterized by an end to large-scale fighting; an adequate level of public order; the subordination of accountable security forces to legitimate state authority; the protection of key individuals, communities, sites, and infrastructure; and the freedom for people and goods to move about the country and across borders without fear of undue harm to life and limb. (USIP/US Army Peacekeeping and Stability Operations Institute, 2009: 38)

However, it is important to be realistic about the type and level of security that can be provided in the immediate aftermath of conflict. Oftentimes, the expectations of the international community and commentators can be unrealistic. Security is also, of course, a relative concept, and it is well known that people will often move to a region or town where, although there is still insecurity, it is less than the insecurity they knew. During the height of the Darfur crisis, for example, ethnic Fur fleeing the fighting settled in Khartoum, where the situation, though far from perfect, was better than the one they had left behind.

Establishing a safe and secure environment

Fundamentally, what is required to establish a safe and secure environment after conflict is to stop large-scale violence, including separating warring factions and managing spoilers; remove significant threats to physical security for all people and provide for territorial security, including managing state borders; enable the development of the rule of law (as will be discussed in Chapter 4); and facilitate the development of the state's monopoly of the legitimate use of force, including through the development of professional state security institutions and the demobilisation of non-state armed groups (as will be discussed later) (see USIP/US Army Peacekeeping and Stability Operations Institute, 2009).

International military actors are generally responsible for a safe and secure environment in post-conflict environments, but they often work alongside civilian actors on many of the tasks required to build a safe and secure environment (as will be discussed later). Military troops are often mandated to provide security, protect people and property, monitor compliance with the peace agreement (such as ensuring there remains a ceasefire), as well as engage in other security tasks (as will be discussed later).

The establishment of basic security needs to be done swiftly so that the potential for vengeance attacks is reduced, and so that organised crime or insurgent groups do not proliferate and take advantage of the 'security vacuum' (see Box 3.2) that is often present in the immediate aftermath of conflict. The security vacuum is a result of the devastation, confusion and vulnerability left by conflict, when institutions that should provide security and maintain the rule of law are incapable of doing so or may no longer exist or be trusted. The widespread presence of landmines, small arms and former combatants in society after some conflicts also create insecurity and tension. Sexual and gender-based violence (SGBV) is also often prevalent in the immediate aftermath of conflict – as it often is during conflict – 'as a means of reinforcing or reasserting lost power or 'glory' of the perpetrator' (Munala, 2007: 36). There may, therefore, be a high level of violence and insecurity prevalent in post-conflict societies: the immediate aftermath of conflict does not necessarily signal the end of violence, merely the beginning of the process towards potentially securing sustainable peace. In terms of establishing security swiftly, there is a window of opportunity after conflict or crisis where recovery and prevention can be seized. Jones, Wilson, Rathmell and Riley (2005) refer to a 'golden hour' during which establishing security should be the top priority after the cessation of armed conflict (see also the 'Report of the Secretary-General on peacebuilding in the immediate aftermath of conflict' – UNSG, 2009). This 'golden hour', of course, can take many months; the term often refers to the period of time in which emergency treatment after traumatic injury is most effective and most likely to prevent death.

Box 3.2: The Security Vacuum

The term 'security vacuum' generally refers to an absence of security provision (often by the state); so, organised crime and insurgent groups can both conduct clandestine affairs without fear of punishment, and can provide security to those in need and, in turn, extend their control, power and profit.

Stabilisation

Sometimes, the response to the immediate security challenges in post-conflict recovery is referred to as 'stabilisation', particularly if involving military tasks – although increasingly not necessarily so – and political aims (see Box 3.3 for a definition of stabilisation). As described by the Stabilisation Unit of the UK Government, the term 'stabilisation' can be used to describe efforts to stabilise insecure environments (some of which may be experiencing conflict, others which are conflict-vulnerable and/or have just experienced conflict) to the extent required to reach a political agreement or establish a sustainable, legitimate government. Unlike similar terms, such as post-conflict reconstruction or peace-building, its overarching aims tend to be predominantly political. The most recent guidance for policy makers and practitioners from the UK's Stabilisation Unit is that the priority in any stabilisation intervention should be 'to address any immediate security deficit to build space for peaceful political processes and – in time – support the restoration of long-term security, the rule of law and access to justice' (Stabilisation Unit, 2018: 10).

The term 'stabilisation' remains contentious, however. Part of the problem is that, given the vast range of factors identified as making conflict more likely, almost any initiative can be presented as 'stabilising'. Indeed, even the invasion, destruction and occupation of nations can be presented as stabilising and intended to create a secure environment.

There is also a concern that the concept of stabilisation – and also a multi-dimensional approach to conflict and insecurity (combining diplomacy, defence and development approaches) – constitutes a securitisation or militarisation of aid, as touched upon in the last chapter. As already stressed, it is naïve to suppose that purely military solutions to conflict and insecurity are sufficient, as the intervention in Iraq in 2003 most clearly highlights. However, some have argued that 3-D or tripartite approaches (combining diplomacy, defence and development) to similar environments gives military intervention a new moral legitimacy and does little, in reality, to protect the vulnerable, either in the short- or long-term (see Collinson et al., 2010; Elhawary, 2011; Saferworld, 2011). As we have seen, there are major limitations on what the military can be expected to do. Many also argue that 3-D responses also threaten humanitarian space – notably the humanitarian principles of independence and neutrality – and, with it, the security of humanitarian personnel (see Tennant, Doyle and Mazou, 2010) (see Box 3.4 for a definition of humanitarian space).

Box 3.3: Stabilisation

An early definition provided by the UK's Stabilisation Unit referred to stabilisa-tion as 'the process of establishing peace and security in countries affected by conflict and instability. It is the promotion of a peaceful political settlement to produce a legitimate indigenous government, which can better serve its peo-ple. Stabilisation often requires external joint military and civilian support to perform some or all of the following tasks: prevent or reduce violence, protect people and key institutions, promote political processes and prepare for longer-term development' (Stabilisation Unit, 2011: n.p.).

The term 'stabilisation' has developed rapidly since this early definition, although it is still an ambiguous and often contested term (Stabilisation Unit, 2018). While early definitions focussed on the use of military force to combat insurgent groups, coupled with building local governance institutions and the capacity to deliver basic services, today military force is not a prerequisite. There is also an under-standing that stabilisation interventions will not all be the same, given the need for interventions to be context specific (Stabilisation Unit, 2018).

While there is a move away from a single, fixed definition of stabilisation, there are common aims and approaches. For instance, in the latest guidance from the UK's Stabilisation Unit, stabilisation interventions are intended to '**protect** the means of survival and restore basic security, **promote** and support a political pro-cess to reduce violence as well as **prepare** a foundation for longer term stability' (Stabilisation Unit, 2018: 6). (Also see the website of the UK Stabilisation Unit at www.stabilisationunit.gov.uk.)

Peace enforcement, peacemaking, peacekeeping and peacebuilding

While activities undertaken by international military actors to establish and maintain a safe and secure environment after conflict are generally considered to be part of peacekeeping, they can continue throughout the peacebuilding phase. Indeed, as was discussed in Chapter 1, it is generally very hard to distinguish between the different phases of conflict, with activities and actors engaged in each phase overlapping as they do. International military actors may also be con-ducting activities similar to those conducted during peace operations (as part of peacekeeping or peacebuilding), amidst conflict (as part of peacemaking or peace enforcement).

Box 3.4: Humanitarian Space

Humanitarian space can be considered to be the space which allows for humani-tarian aid to be delivered to those in need and humanitarian actors to assess and respond to that need.

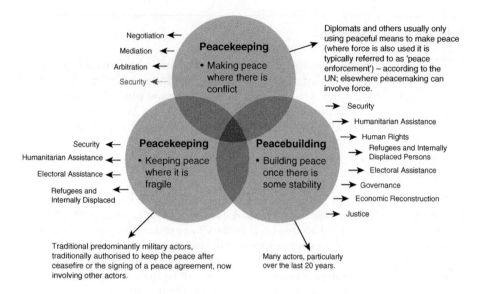

Figure 3.1 Overlapping Activities

So, generally it is understood that peacemaking refers to efforts to make peace when there is none (at the earlier stages of armed conflict), peacekeeping refers to efforts to ensure the peace agreement holds, and peacebuilding refers to a broader range of activities after conflict to build sustainable peace. However, in actuality, activities undertaken at each phase are very similar, and it is also very difficult to identify whether, in fact, these activities are intended to make peace where there is conflict (peacemaking), keep peace where it is fragile (peacekeeping), or build peace once there is a modicum of security and stability (peacebuilding) (see Figure 3.1).

It is important to recognise these blurred boundaries, as they impact legitimacy and shared understandings of what is being undertaken and why.

To add further complexity, while peacemaking (making peace where there is conflict) is regarded by many as including the use of force, for the UN the term peacemaking only includes peaceful measures, while peace enforcement refers to the use of force to make peace where there is conflict (and no ceasefire or peace agreement) and requires UN Security Council authorisation under Chapter 7 of the UN Charter (while other peace operations require authorisation under Chapter 6). Under Chapter 6, the use of force can only be used in defence (of themselves and others).

Part 3 – International Military Actors

UN peacekeepers

As mentioned in the previous section, international military actors are generally responsible for establishing and maintaining a safe and secure environment after conflict. Generally, they are deployed as part of a peacekeeping mission. The UN provides the most peacekeeping troops, although it does not have its own standing army; these troops remain part of their respective armed forces while under the operational control of the UN when deployed on peace operations.

The UN has been deploying military personnel in peace operations since 1948 and today has 124 countries contributing uniformed personnel to peace operations. UN peacekeepers are sometimes referred to as the Blue Helmets or, less frequently, Blue Berets because of their blue helmets or berets. Today, the UN also deploys police and civilian peacekeepers on peace operations. There have been 71 peace operations since 1948 and today there are 14 across four continents, the oldest being the UN Truce Supervision Organization (UNTSO) which began in 1948 and the most recent being the UN Mission for Justice Support in Haiti (MINUJUSTH) which began in October 2017 (as at early 2019 – see the UN website for a list and details of current operations and information on TCNs: https://peacekeeping.un.org).

The UN Security Council authorises peace operations, requiring a majority vote and no veto from its five Permanent Members (UK, US, France, China and Russia). The UN Security Council can also authorise a peace operation to be undertaken by regional organisations or country coalitions.

Regional organisations

In recent years, many other organisations, besides the UN, have become engaged in peacekeeping. For instance, regional organisations – including the North Atlantic Treaty Organization (NATO), the European Union (EU) and the African Union (AU) – are increasingly responsible for the military component of peace missions.

NATO

NATO was, of course, originally a war-fighting alliance, and its involvement in international operations has been part of a wider attempt to ensure its continued relevance. Its elaborate and complicated command structure, headed by a commander reporting directly to Washington, has not always made this easy. Its increased use in the last stages of the Bosnian conflict and in Kosovo and Afghanistan was partly the result of a search for continued relevance, but partly also because no other suitable command structure existed. Aspiring NATO members, and those who wanted good relationships with the West, deployed contingents to these forces.

European Union

In contrast, deployments by European Union forces since 2003 have largely been intended to progressively construct precisely the kind of independent European military capability previously lacking (Chuter, 2017). Under the EU's Common Security and Defence Policy (CSDP), the EU deploys on military operations (for peacekeeping and other tasks) and civilian missions. The establishment of the CSDP followed the Balkans conflicts in the 1990s, which prompted the EU to decide it wanted to be able to plan and conduct its own operations (EU, 2019). The first mission was launched in 2003 with a military operation in the Former Yugoslav Republic of Macedonia, alongside a policing mission in Bosnia and Herzegovina (BiH). Since its inauguration, there have been 34 missions and operations, 11 of which have been military. Today (early 2019), there are 6 military operations and a further 10 civilian operations under CSDP (Austrian Embassy, 2019; EU, 2019).

African Union

Another relative newcomer to military deployments to peace operations is the African Union (AU). The AU, established in 2002, succeeded the Organisation of African Unity (OAU). Its first peacekeeping mission was to Burundi in 2003. AU troops have also been deployed in a peacekeeping capacity to Sudan and Somalia. It was hoped that responsibility for multinational peace missions in Africa could be increasingly entrusted to the AU's African Standby Force (ASF). The ASF is intended to demonstrate and allow the AU to be a lead player in peace operations in Africa. This Force was originally intended to reach full operational capability in 2010, although that date was postponed several times. The ASF was declared fully operational in 2016 but by the beginning of 2019 had yet to be deployed in its originally-envisaged form, not due to lack of need but rather the influence of the Regional Economic Communities/Regional Mechanisms (RECs/RMs), which are Africa's sub-regional security structures (Darwka, 2017). Many other obstacles have stalled its progress, to date, including lack of adequate resources, insufficient political will and a mandate that needs to be updated to enable the ASF to respond to current and future challenges (see ISS, 2017).

Co-ordination between actors

Oftentimes, military deployments in peace operations will be multinational, so troops from a number of different countries will be working alongside each other. This can pose challenges, as will shortly be described. When the UN, NATO, AU and EU, for instance, deploy peacekeeping troops, these can be from a large number of countries. Additionally, transfer of authority for the military component of a peace operation is also not uncommon. For example, in Bosnia and Herzegovina (BiH), the EU took over responsibility for the military component from NATO, which in turn succeeded a UN-led mission. In addition to the sequential deployment of troops, there is also increasingly parallel and integrated deployment of troops by these international organisations (IOs), which is driven in part by a desire to pool resources and risks as well as the emergence of shared normative values (see Brosig, 2010). All of these factors highlight the demand for good co-ordination and communication.

The issue of co-ordination does not only pertain to military actors; the military also needs to work closely alongside non-military actors in peace operations. While originally peacekeeping was just undertaken by the military, today there are many civilian peacekeepers responsible for tasks beyond the immediate establishment of security. So, multinational organisations (or international organisations – IOs) often work together with the military in the same mission. For example, NATO provided the military component in Kosovo (Kosovo Force – KFOR) and Afghanistan (International Security Assistance Force – ISAF), working alongside the EU and UN civilian components. International military actors also, of course, need to work alongside civilian actors at other stages of the conflict 'cycle', when they are deployed (civil–military co-operation is often referred to by the acronym CIMIC by military actors).

Challenges facing military actors in UN peace operations

Multinational operations are always difficult – exponentially more so as the number of nations increases. Basic requirements generally include commonality of doctrine and training, a single language of command, experience of working together and a common strategic vision for the operation. For this reason, to facilitate co-ordination, it can be useful to identify a framework nation, which would be the single nation responsible for providing the functional or institutional framework, which other participating nations would work to; there would, thus, be different roles and responsibilities between framework nations and non-framework nations, but no difference in status (Palmer, 2017). NATO adopted the Framework Nation Concept (FNC) in 2014 in recognition of the advantages of structured co-operation in today's often complex and dynamic missions. This is not possible for the UN for political reasons; it would be hard to secure agreement to an effective lead nation among other Troop Contributing Nations (TCNs) (i.e. those countries which contribute troops to UN peace operations) and countries of the territory on which peacekeepers were deployed. Nonetheless, in many peace operations, particular nations are, in effect, given lead roles, by allocating command positions to those nations. However, there still remain co-ordination problems on the ground and in pre-deployment training.

There are a host of practical problems in trying to put together multinational forces: different equipment, different procedures, different structures, different languages, different doctrines, even different diets. One of the most difficult set of issues relates to the use of force. Not only may nations want to put limitations on the Rules of Engagement (RoE) of their own contingents for political reasons, they may also seek to influence the RoE for the mission as a whole (Chuter, 2017). The motives of TCNs vary also, which can impact coherence of efforts. For some, it is a way of earning money; for others, a way of providing their troops with operational experience; for others, a way of increasing their political profile in the region or internationally. But few send troops to fight and die for somebody else's country.

In respect of UN peace operations, there are specific criticisms that can be made related to decision-making within the UN system. The most important is that mandates are decided by negotiations between members of the Security Council (SC), often in secret, but are implemented by the UN bureaucracy and by TCNs who have no influence over the process. Mandates can thus be seen as political compromise documents, drafted by nations who may not have to contribute forces to implement them. This puts non-permanent members of the SC in a powerful position to pursue political objectives, since everything proceeds by consensus (for an insider's account of UNSC discussions on intervention, see Puri, 2016). In addition, the classic disciplines of Force Generation and Force Balancing are difficult to pursue, and command positions are generally allocated for political reasons, not necessarily on the basis of ability. The classic instance of this problem was the UN Protection Force (UNPROFOR) in BiH, where a relatively simple initial mandate underwent multiple transformations for political reasons, resulting in overlapping and contradictory instructions which left both headquarters staff in New York, and commanders in the field, unclear what it was they were supposed to be doing (Chuter, 2017). A further political dimension of UN peacekeeping which poses operational and ethical challenges concerns the gap between the Global South and the Global North; increasing numbers of troops deployed from the Global South in peace operations can be regarded as bridging the epistemic gap between those deployed on peace operations and ostensible beneficiaries, or could be regarded as legitimising business as usual with the added benefit of reducing risk to troops from the Global North.

Many of these problems have been recognised in the Brahimi Report, less commonly known as the Report of the Panel on United Nations Peace Operations (UN, 2000) and more recently in the 2015 report of the High-Level Independent Panel on Peace Operations (HIPPO) (see Box 3.5). The Brahimi

---

Box 3.5: The Brahimi Report and the 2015 HIPPO Report

The Brahimi Report made a large number of comprehensive recommendations, including the need for:

- Robust doctrine and realistic mandates
- Improved information management and strategic analysis
- Improved mission guidance and leadership
- Rapid deployment standards and 'on-call' expertise
- Enhanced HQ capacity to plan and support peace operations
- Establishment of Integrated Mission Task Forces for mission planning and support
- Adaption of peace operations to the information age
- Strategy and support to build peace and prevent conflict
- Peacekeeping being an appropriate option and its mandate achievable
- Peacekeeping being part of a comprehensive approach to resolving conflict by addressing root causes, regional dimensions and issues outside the security sector, including political, economic, developmental, humanitarian and human rights issues (UN, 2000a).

The 2015 report of the High-Level Independent Panel on Peace Operations (HIPPO) underscores the need for four strategic shifts if peace operations are to be more successful:

- First, politics must drive the design and implementation of peace operations ...
- Second, the full spectrum of UN peace operations must be used more flexibly to respond to changing needs on the ground...
- Third, a stronger, more inclusive peace and security partnership is needed for the future ...
- Fourth, the UN Secretariat must become more field-focused and UN peace operations must be more people-centered. (UN HIPPO, 2015: viii)

Report was the first of a number of comprehensive efforts by the UN to respond to criticism of the effectiveness and professionalism of its peacekeeping troops and its peace operations. The Panel on United Nations Peace Operations, chaired by Lakhdar Brahimi, was tasked by the UN Secretary-General to thoroughly review UN peace and security activities with a view to providing recommendations for improvements. The High-Level Independent Panel on Peace Operations was similarly convened by the UN Secretary-General to review UN peace operations and provide recommendations on how peace operations can better respond to the need to build sustainable peace, protect civilians and prevent conflict.

A considerable amount of work has gone on over the last 15–20 years to identify problems related to peace operations and seek to remedy them. The International Forum for the Challenges of Peace Operations, in existence since 1996, brings together the P5 nations and the major troop contributors for conferences and workshops in this regard (see International Forum for the Challenges of Peace Operations, 2017). It should not be forgotten that other international organisations, not least NATO (see, for example, Gheciu, 2011; Williams, 2011), have also come in for criticism: NATO almost came apart politically during the 1999 Kosovo crisis, for example, and its mission in Afghanistan is considered by many to be a failure (Chuter, 2017).

Other military actors

Finally, it should be added that sometimes both local security actors and private security companies (PSCs) – or private military and security companies (PMSCs) – assume some of the functions required to establish a safe and secure environment. Indeed, in both Iraq and Afghanistan, rebuilding local forces has been the greatest priority, with the hope of increased mission legitimacy if local security forces are utilised. However, issues of capability, trust and co-ordination may also arise.

PSCs are often contracted by governments, international organisations and NGOs to deploy former military personnel to provide security for people (staff, visitors, VIPs) and buildings (offices, embassies, sensitive buildings). The explosive growth of such companies has caused worries about quality and standards (not least from within the industry itself) and over fifty nations have now signed the 2008 Montreux Document, intended to regularise such activities. There are also other concerns surrounding issues of legitimacy, co-ordination and accountability (see Inclusive Security and DCAF, 2017; Pascucci, 2008; Spearin, 2011). However, for governments and organisations, the value of PSCs is considerable, not least in terms of the security expertise many former military personnel will have – there can also sometimes be financial and political advantages for certain governments and organisations.

Other non-state actors can also provide security in conflict-affected environments, which is often overlooked by major external actors. There are, of course, issues of accountability, capability and trust (see Box 3.6 for a broader discussion of non-state actors, including on how they can provide security as well as undermine it).

Box 3.6: Non-State Actors

For the purpose of this book, non-state actors are not confined to armed non-state actors (insurgents, vigilantes, local militias, paramilitaries, terrorists or PSCs – see Holmqvist, 2005; Clapham, 2017), as is increasingly typical in the peacebuilding literature, but also encompass all those who are not representatives of the state e.g. NGOs, CSOs, media organisations, academic institutions and think tanks, local communities, the private sector, and international and regional organisations. Crucially, the term non-state actors generally refers to those who have influence. Non-state actors can often have substantial influence, particularly if they wield financial or political power. It is also worth emphasising that in many times in many places, non-state actors are the norm because there is little if any state.

Of course, the relationship between the state and the non-state is often ambiguous, complex and dynamic, and an actor can be both non-state and state, or be in alliance with other state and non-state actors. Moreover, as Clapham (2017) describes, the non-state means different things to different people in different times and places; it is a subjective and expansive term. Further, to define something in terms of what it is not is rarely helpful. However, in peacebuilding discourse and practice it does remind us that peacebuilding cannot be reducible to statebuilding and that inclusive approaches to peacebuilding that go beyond dominant or elite groups who tend to represent the state (or at least their interests are often protected by those representatives) often result in more comprehensive and sustainable peace. As conflict-affected environments contain and are impacted by a complexity of actors, it makes sense, of course, that efforts to build peace engage with that complexity.

Nonetheless, efforts to engage the 'non-state' can be problematic with such a broad and fluid term; engaging the 'non-state' can become almost meaningless when everything but the state and its representatives is contained within its definition. Reluctance to engage the 'non-state' relates in part to the term's ambiguity, but also concerns that legitimacy is conferred and power divested through such engagement; where the international system remains state-centric, genuine and comprehensive efforts to engage the 'non-state' are unsurprisingly unforthcoming (see Clapham, 2017).

Nonetheless, when we consider how to build security and justice after conflict we must not overlook the capabilities and knowledge that exist beyond the state, nor assume a strong state necessarily leads to increased security and justice. Additionally, non-state actors often play a key role in meeting security, development and other needs of people where the state is weak or lacks public confidence and legitimacy, which is often the case in conflict-affected environments. Often in conflict-affected environments, there are non-state as well as state security providers; this is what Donais (2017: 2) refers to as 'hybrid forms of security provision'. While non-state, informal or customary security and justice providers can be affordable, accessible and efficient, they can also reflect and reinforce dominant power relations, evade accountability and create new injustices or harms and be open to abuse.

(Continued)

> Similarly, we must not assume that threats to peace and security come just from non-state actors. While the shift in attention of the international community to the threat posed by non-state actors and weak rather than strong states shifted after 9/11, at the start of 2018, in presenting the latest national defence strategy, the US Defence Secretary said that 'great power competition, not terrorism, is now the primary focus of US national security', pointing fingers at China and Russia (Liang, 2018). (For more on the role of non-state actors in peacebuilding see Baker, 2010; Clapham, 2017; McCullough, 2015.)

Part 4 – Activities of International Military Actors

The military come in standard-sized units (often very unlike other types of actors engaged in peacebuilding), are generally trained and disciplined to work together, and have various technical capabilities. They can be ordered into dangerous situations, and know how to survive and protect themselves once there. This special status leads to their use – and sometimes misuse – in a variety of non-traditional functions. So, in addition to establishing a safe and secure environment, military actors perform a number of other security tasks, humanitarian and reconstruction tasks, and law enforcement tasks, and are often asked by civilian actors to assist in the fulfilment of their tasks, where security or logistics support is required, for instance.

Security tasks

So, in addition to being responsible for establishing and maintaining a safe and secure environment, international military forces and personnel are also often engaged in the Disarmament, Demobilisation and Reintegration (DDR) of combatants, the control of Small Arms and Light Weapons (SALW), as well as Security Sector Reform (SSR), particularly Defence Reform, which will be considered in detail in later chapters (where we will also look at other actors engaged in these activities).

Humanitarian and reconstruction tasks

More speculatively, international military forces can also be engaged in humanitarian and reconstruction tasks, particularly when conditions are too dangerous for civilian actors. Some relevant specialist military technical capabilities can be called on, and military engagement in these tasks can help meet humanitarian needs and also potentially strategic political goals – for example, building support for the political process and those who are leading it (see Brett, 2009). This can both stretch the resources of the military and divert their attention from strategic goals, as well as potentially undermine the humanitarian principles (such as neutrality and independence) that particularly guide humanitarian actors. The use of the military in such tasks has been criticised as much from within the military themselves as by humanitarian and development actors (for discussion on the relationship between military and civilian actors in the immediate aftermath of conflict, see Brett, 2009). Nonetheless, it is widely recognised that oftentimes the active engagement of the military in humanitarian and development tasks is instrumental.

Law enforcement tasks

Finally, international military forces may be used in certain law enforcement tasks. Whilst the military's prime function is ensuring a secure environment at the strategic level, they may also be sometimes drawn into public order duties when limited capacity exists elsewhere. During the NATO-led mission in Bosnia and Herzegovina (BiH) after 1995, a Multinational Specialised Unit (MSU) was formed, from gendarmerie units of different nations, and was effective in containing political violence. But trying to use the military in more traditional police functions is seldom advisable. The military have no powers of arrest, and lack the training and specialised knowledge of the police, and their habit of acting individually or in small groups (Chuter, 2017). Attempts to use the military in this way have evoked criticism on many grounds (see Friesendorf and Penksa, 2008). For this reason, since the deployment of the UN Interim Administration Mission in Kosovo (UNMIK) in 1999, the international community has preferred to use Formed Police Units, typically some 140-strong, for this task (see UN Police, 2019).

Part 5 – Challenges and Lessons Learned

It is clear from the foregoing that there are a number of practical difficulties in endeavouring to establish and maintain a safe and secure environment, especially with international forces, as is now the custom. Moreover, these practical difficulties are compounded by the number of other tasks international military actors engaged in post-conflict environments often have to fulfil, as outlined above. There are also more fundamental challenges associated with what are often referred to as the duration and footprint dilemmas, time pressures, blurred boundaries, co-ordination and managing expectations, as will now be discussed.

The duration and footprint dilemmas

Of course, the post-conflict environment itself poses a number of challenges to those mandated to build and maintain a safe and secure environment. Not least among these challenges are pervasive insecurity, continued threats to public order, the presence of armed criminal gangs and, perhaps, aggrieved former combatants, the prevalence of small arms and light weapons as well as mines and explosive remnants of war (ERW) (see Chapter 6).

Outside the security challenges associated with countries emerging from conflict, the very presence of international military forces endeavouring to secure peace and stability can present its own difficulties, especially from the unconsidered use of force. International military forces may be exploited by one or more sides and may also be physically attacked. Additionally, there are often compromises to be reached between short-term security and stabilisation goals, and longer-term development or governance goals or even principles of justice. For example, short-term security may warrant dealing with people who played a key part in the conflict, which can compromise justice and longer-term stability if it is seen that a culture of impunity is allowed to continue.

Paris and Sisk (2009) examine two of the fundamental dilemmas associated with the type of military interventions we are discussing here: the often inverse relationship between the length of time military forces remain actively engaged and the support that such engagement usually engenders (the duration dilemma), and the size and intrusiveness of such engagement, which can risk alienation and resistance or inability to maintain security if the balance is not found (the footprint dilemma). The level of local support and mission legitimacy are critical to the success of such interventions, which is often significantly impacted by the duration and extent of the intervention, particularly if it results in a prolonged suspension of the ability of host nations to control their own affairs, which it often does. On the other hand, without a significant presence, military forces may be unable to maintain security (see Box 3.7 on the concept of escalation dominance) – the footprint dilemma. Likewise, leaving early can equally compromise success, as has been a criticism of the UN in the past, especially when effective exit strategies have not been developed or implemented – the duration dilemma.

Box 3.7: Escalation Dominance – The Case of Bosnia and Herzegovina (BiH)

The difference between the UN Protection Force (UNPROFOR) in Bosnia and Herzegovina (BiH) and Croatia, and the subsequent NATO-led Implementation Force (IFOR) and later Stabilization Force (SFOR), both in BiH, is an instructive example of the need for military forces to have the ability to defeat potential challenges at any level – what the military call 'escalation dominance'.

UNPROFOR was the first UN peacekeeping force deployed to BiH and Croatia during the conflicts in the Balkans. It was established in February 1992 and restructured in March 1995 into the UN Confidence Restoration Operation in Croatia (UNCRO) and UN Preventive Deployment Force (UNPREDEP) in Macedonia, while continuing operations in BiH. In BiH, UNPROFOR was principally mandated to protect the delivery of humanitarian aid and safe areas. In December 1995 UNPROFOR was succeeded by the NATO-led SFOR, mandated to implement the military annexes of the General Framework Agreement for Peace (GFAP, more commonly known as the Dayton Peace Agreement) signed earlier that month.

Although UNPROFOR at its maximum had, in theory, a strength of more than 35,000 soldiers in Bosnia and Croatia, the number of troops usable in combat in Bosnia never exceeded 5,000 (which is quite normal in terms of the balance

(Continued)

between combat and support elements). By contrast, there were some 100,000 combatants from the different warring factions, often heavily armed and motivated to fight. Likewise, in 1994 the UN Assistance Mission for Rwanda (UNAMIR) was lightly armed and often poorly equipped, and faced perhaps twenty times as many well-armed and experienced combatants in the government and rebel forces. Such forces could scarcely hope to influence, let alone control, the security situation.

In comparison, when the NATO-led IFOR in BiH replaced UNPROFOR in December 1995, it had a strength of 50,000 well-armed and well-trained troops, (although again, only a small proportion of these would be combat troops), who also brought with them heavy arms and equipment, had an effective command and intelligence infrastructure, and more robust rules of engagement. Consequently, the exhausted combatants were completely dominated. This enabled IFOR, and its successor SFOR, whose mandate began a year later in December 1996, to control the situation.

Time pressures

If interventions are to be successful, adequate preparation is needed, including full consideration of exit strategies. Such preparation should also include addressing risks and opportunities and developing a number of contingency plans, with a comprehensive understanding of the historical, political, geographical, economic, social and cultural dimensions of the specific conflict.

The uniqueness of conflicts needs to be remembered. An understanding of the context needs to inform every decision, without compromising the need for decisions to be swift and different perspectives to be integrated. Without such awareness, the root causes of the conflict will not be able to be effectively addressed, and the opportunities and risks that are present in each society emerging from conflict will not be recognised. An understanding of the context is, of course, an ongoing process.

The difficulty, of course, is the limited time on the part of those who make the decisions, which can compromise efforts to understand the specific context in depth and comprehensively plan. In practice, there is only limited time in which to deploy troops after the decision has been reached to do so. Further, actions are often taken 'without weighing the pros and cons, or understanding the underlying social and cultural forces and political dynamics at work' (Puri, 2016: 5). After all, decision-making in governments and international organisations often takes place at a swift pace, which limits the extent to which those making decisions can have an in-depth understanding of context and the root causes of a specific conflict, for instance.

Likewise, time pressures can thwart efforts to promote local ownership, even if it is recognised that it is critical to success. So, it should be recognised that local actors and local institutions are key to building sustainable peace: security is never something that can be imposed, at least not for very long. Engaging local actors, developing mutual trust and confidence, building local institutions and govern-ance, ensuring local ownership of the peace process and the peace being built are of fundamental importance to an effective peace process. However, engaging local actors is costly and time-consuming and local actors may, of course, speak different languages and not share the same principles and priorities as their international counterparts (as will be discussed later, particularly when we consider SSR in Chapter 8).

The furious pace at which decisions about intervention have to be made encour-ages the use of pre-existing models of intervention because there is no time, and often no appetite, for detailed analysis, even if information is available (see Paris, 2002). It is often unusual for decision-makers, or those who brief them, to have any personal knowledge of the country or the crisis. Thus, the UN hastened to send a force (UNAMIR) to Rwanda in 1993, assuming that its mission would be one of traditional cease-fire monitoring. A proper analysis – the aftermath of a brutal civil war between heavily armed and mutually distrustful groups, neither of which was committed to a ceasefire imposed by outsiders – might have produced a different solution and prevented the escalation of violence and the subsequent genocide. However, it might also have led to a decision not to deploy a UN mis-sion, which would have been politically unacceptable and may also have resulted in further violence and atrocities. Much the same might be said of BiH, where UN Security Council resolutions and mandates arguably bore little relationship to the actual situation on the ground. Modern theories of intervention owe much to the reaction to the failings of these two episodes on the part of the international community.

Blurred boundaries

Returning to the issue of blurred boundaries between the stages of a conflict and responses to it, the increasing lack of distinction between peacekeeping and peace-building, for example, in effect extending the presence and engagement of interna-tional military actors, risks further compromising effectiveness. This is especially if it affects clarity of purpose, availability of resources and transfer of responsibility for security to the in-country government and security institutions. The increas-ing number of tasks of military actors in conflict-affected environments also risks compromising clarity of purpose, spreading the military too thinly across many tasks, and blurring of boundaries between the responsibilities of different actors engaged in conflict-affected environments. This boundary blurring can com-promise effectiveness, particularly if co-ordination and coherence of efforts are adversely affected (and, as discussed earlier, can lead to the duration and footprint dilemmas). This is often the case if different actors speak different languages, have different aims or adhere to different principles.

Increasing attention paid to the security-development nexus (as discussed in Chapter 2) and the recognition that development and security are mutually supporting, have led to increased contact between military and civilian actors in post-conflict environments, if not a complete blurring of lines between the responsibility of military and civilian actors. While principles of co-ordination are ostensibly adhered to and arrangements to formalise such principles often exist, actual co-ordination on the ground is often ad hoc, notably between NGOs and military organisations. This is particularly because of differences in their structures, cultures, capacity, objectives and perceptions of each other's objectives and cultures (see Brett, 2009; Gheciu, 2011).

Co-ordination

In terms of challenges, there is also the question of sequencing. Published guidance on post-conflict reconstruction, as well as internal planning documents for individual missions, show a sequence of events, typically beginning with the end of conflict, establishing a secure environment, moving to the reintegration of former combatants, reform or reconstruction of police and justice systems, creation of a new national army, a political settlement, elections and so forth (we will be discussing many of these undertakings in depth in future chapters). The problem is that, whilst these phases theoretically follow each other, there is no necessary causative relationship between them. A secure environment may facilitate political progress, but does not guarantee it. BiH, for example, has been peaceful for more than 20 years, and the environment is safe and secure. However, political progress has been slow – and may even have been compromised because of the heavy-handedness of the international community in creating an environment it considered to be peaceful, discouraging engagement of the citizenry in the political process, for instance.

In other words, you cannot build peace simply by stopping violence and improving security. In Chapter 2, we considered the many possible causes of conflict, which indicate the breadth of issues that may need to be addressed in order to build sustainable peace. Few would dispute that peacekeeping and peacebuilding cannot be reduced to efforts in just the security sector or, indeed, any other sector (whether governance, development or humanitarian relief, for instance). Comprehensive, co-ordinated and coherent efforts across all of these sectors are required if sustainable peace is to be achieved. Governance and development will not occur spontaneously after a military victory, as failures in Iraq and Afghanistan attest. Nor does negative peace (the absence of violence) guarantee lasting peace. To develop what Galtung refers to as positive peace (as discussed in Chapter 1), there is a need to attend to developmental, humanitarian, justice, human rights and other needs as well as the root causes of conflict (see Figure 3.2 for a depiction of how a negative peace might follow conflict, if basic security has been achieved, but this needs to lead to efforts in other sectors, to achieve positive peace, if sustainable peace is to be secured). The synergies between the different sectors also need to be acknowledged along with the fact that development in one area impacts another.

While 'better co-ordination' is a theme of many studies of international intervention, that co-ordination will only be of value if the underlying political problems actually have a solution. In the case of BiH, as well as of Iraq and Afghanistan, it may be the case that they do not. Much the same could be said of Lebanon, where the 1991 Taef Accords stopped the disastrous civil war, but introduced a political system so elaborate and complex that it has itself been a cause of endemic political instability ever since (Habib, 2009). However, the international community wants

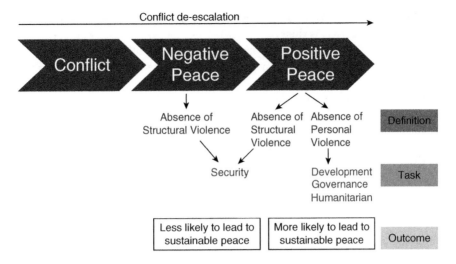

Figure 3.2 Positive and Negative Peace

progress, as measured by significant events. As a result, there is a tendency for all of the stages described above to be carried out, by different actors, more or less simultaneously. Elections may be held in the middle of a war, for example.

Managing expectations

There is now substantial literature on actual attempts to build safe and secure environments, much of which is discouraging. It ranges from general studies (Pouligny, 2004; Chesterman, 2004) to more recent accounts of specific interventions, often by first-hand observers (Ledwidge, 2011; Tarif and Virculon, 2016; Trefon, 2011; Van Buren, 2012). Wider studies have suggested that the international community fails to understand the causes and nature of conflict, especially in Africa (Cramer, 2006; Keen, 2012; Reno, 2011), or indeed the way that politics functions elsewhere (Chabal, 2009; Herbst, 2000). Finally, much has been written about the perils of attempts at the wholesale export of western political structures, processes and ideas, particularly when at odds with the local context and when ignoring local knowledge and capacity (Chandler, 2010; Cramer, 2006; Gheciu and Paris, 2011; Mac Ginty and Richmond, 2013; Paris, 2010; Richmond, 2009). As many have argued, efforts to build security which do not resonate with local needs or are resisted by local actors will be destined to fail (Gordon, 2014a, 2014b). There have also been many criticisms that the complexity of building safe and secure environments, and the time it takes for such efforts to lead to lasting peace, are often overlooked.

Many of these criticisms would be, at least privately, accepted as valid by many of those engaged in peacebuilding within the international community. Nonetheless, missions are dispatched to provide a secure environment, and subsequently to transform security and political systems, with just as much enthusiasm. Lessons are learned – or at least identified – and technical changes are made, but the overall approach has survived any number of disappointments and dubious qualified successes. Why is this?

Clearly, the individuals involved are intelligent and well meaning. Indeed, that may be part of the problem. To say, in the words of the title of Van Buren's book (2012) *We Meant Well* is for many people a justification in itself. Many arguments about intervention are couched in normative, moralistic terms, assuming that once something called 'intervention' has been decided upon, a moral duty has been accomplished. If the actual intervention proves counter-productive, or even disastrous, no blame attaches, since 'we meant well', and it was obviously the execution that was at fault. This helps in part to explain the persistence of the desire to intervene. This is linked to the so-called 'CNN effect' (as discussed in Chapter 2), and the need to be seen to be doing something, even if the deployment of peacekeeping forces is considered to be futile or premature – as was argued by many European governments during debates over whether to deploy troops to Bosnia from 1992; ultimately the pressure to do something outweighed technical advice and concerns about whether engagement would have the desired impact. The significant role of politicians and civil society in decisions about whether to intervene, who may not have substantial experience in the security or defence sector, may have also led to unrealistic expectations about what the military can actually achieve.

In reality, even very large military forces cannot do more than create the strategic security that enables the rebuilding of security in everyday life. After all, no victory could have been more complete than that of the Allies over Nazi Germany in 1945. Yet, in spite of the presence of millions of disciplined and heavily armed troops, as well as large and elaborate civilian administrations, the allies were unable to prevent widespread lawlessness and violence, hundreds of thousands of deaths and millions of refugees expelled between 1945 and 1948 (Lowe, 2012).

Of course, there are criticisms that military interventions, whether as part of a peace operation or a preventive deployment, are often self-serving and frequently further undermine the security and wellbeing of those intended, at least ostensibly, to be its beneficiaries. Duffield (2007), for instance, questions whether current western intervention sustains insecurity and the divide between the rich and poor, rather than bridging it and stabilising countries and regions; from this perspective, intervention can be seen as little more than part of the continuum of the colonial endeavour. Gleditsch et al. (2007) suggest that intervention tends to occur in poor or resource-dependent countries in non-democratic regions. Some suggest that protracted or recurrent conflicts are fuelled by the characteristics of the conflict zone itself – and given that intervention generally occurs in such places, it is unsurprising that even with prolonged engagement during and after conflict, a higher propensity to conflict remains. Others, however, suggest that intervention can itself fuel violence (see Rosen and Theros, 2011) and efforts to reach and implement peace agreements can entrench power relations which sustain insecurity (see Bojicic and Kostovicova, 2011).

Despite these criticisms, many of the studies that have identified the shortcomings of peace operations, as mentioned earlier, have also provided a number of recommendations on how practice can better respond to the challenges of building security after conflict and how, in turn, the record of peacekeeping and peacebuilding can be improved. A number of core principles tend to feature among the recommendations contained both in recent critical scholarship and policy guidance. Such principles include the need:

- For every intervention to be adequately planned, for all outcomes to be prepared for and for an exit plan to be developed prior to engagement, but continuously reviewed (*well-planned*)
- To respond to the specific context (*context-specific*)
- To recognise that any intervention will not succeed without the will of the people in the country and their eventual (ideally swift) ownership of the peacebuilding process (*local ownership*)
- To engage and respond to the needs of all stakeholders, not least those who may be marginalised or particularly vulnerable in a given society (*inclusion*)
- To recognise that longer-term peacebuilding and the principles of context-specificity, inclusion and local ownership cannot be adequately attended to with an exclusive focus on state-level structures and dominant or elite groups (for literature on bottom-up or hybrid approaches to building security after conflict, see for example Mac Ginty, 2010; Babayoko, 2017; Autesserre, 2018).

Recommendations beyond the core principles are invariably context-specific, recognising that each context is unique and what works in one place or at one time may not work in another. There have also been lessons identified and guidance provided by governments, military organisations and other organisations engaged in building security after conflict, from the experiences of the last 25 years, and some improvements made. A representative example is NATO's *Allied Joint Doctrine for the Military Contribution to Peace Support* (2014). This document provides comprehensive guidance to NATO-led forces engaged in stabilisation or post-conflict reconstruction missions, and also identifies the principles which should guide military engagement in peace support operations:

- *Political Primacy* – supporting the achievement of a political settlement (recognising that lasting peace comes from political solutions and not just efforts in the security sector)
- *Strategic Consent of the Main Parties* – this consent likely reflects general acceptance of external engagement
- *Impartiality* (as distinguisged from neutrality) – which distinguishes engagement in peacekeeping or peacebuilding from war-making.

NATO's *Allied Joint Doctrine for the Military Contribution to Stabilisation and Reconstruction* (2015) identifies a number of other principles which guide this later stage of peacebuilding:

- *Focus on the Population* – the needs of the population must be met
- *Understand the Context* – including understanding sources of instability, who benefits from them and capacities which can help mitigate risks
- *Foster Host Nation Governance and Capacity* – in order to secure enduring stability
- *Window of Opportunity* – act swiftly to take advantage of the initial response period in which external militaries may be viewed more favourably
- *Manage Efforts Over Time* – continuously adapt to provide long-term security, while also being able to respond quickly to unanticipated threats or opportunities

- *Adhere to OECD Principles for Good International Engagement in Fragile States and Situations* (2007b), including adhering to principles of doing no harm, non-discrimination, promoting local ownership and co-ordination.

It may be hard to argue with any of this in principle: the difficulty lies, as always, in the execution. Attempts to bring a secure and stable environment to Burundi or Haiti for over 20 years have floundered on the inability to turn principles into action. The general belief remains, however, that with better co-ordination, improved understanding and genuine adherence to the principles of local ownership and context specificity, the task is actually feasible.

Conclusion

This chapter has reflected on the importance of security in building peace, before reflecting upon the actors and activities oftentimes engaged in building security in the aftermath of conflict. Particular attention has been given to international military actors, who are often responsible for building and maintaining what is often referred to as 'a safe and secure environment' (the acronym SASE is often used by military actors). As this chapter has highlighted, the task of building and maintaining a safe and secure environment, as well as other tasks assigned to international military actors, is beset with many challenges. Not least among these are the characteristics of the conflict-affected environment, of course, with its many security and political challenges, damaged infrastructure, prevalence of landmines and small arms, presence of former combatants and organised criminal groups, high levels of distrust and trauma, and large displaced populations. These challenges are compounded by the increasing number of tasks international military actors are assigned, as well as the blurred lines between organisational mandates and the stages of conflict. This can complicate efforts to ensure unity of focus, coherence of efforts and co-ordination between all actors engaged in building security and peace after conflict. There are also more fundamental challenges associated with what are often referred to as the duration and footprint dilemmas, time pressures and managing expectations. While there have been a number of criticisms levied at efforts to build security after conflict, as has just been discussed, there remain some fundamental principles which many agree should guide engagement and are likely to lead to a more sustainable peace. Core among these principles are context-specificity, local ownership and inclusion.

Summary of Key Issues

- Security is a relative concept as well as a contested concept and is often located within discourses of the powerful: those who can define what constitutes security and what or who is deemed to threaten it.

- The establishment of physical security after armed conflict is an immediate priority, without which attempts at peacebuilding, statebuilding and development are destined to fail.
- The establishment of security needs to be done swiftly to fill the security vacuum that is often present in the immediate aftermath of conflict.
- The immediate aftermath of conflict does not necessarily signal the end of violence, merely the beginning of the process towards potentially securing sustainable peace.
- Military actors are principally responsible for establishing and maintaining a safe and secure environment after conflict; they are also engaged in other activities which can sometimes overlap with the responsibilities of other actors.
- If interventions are to be successful, it is necessary to address underlying political problems in conflict-affected environments and ensure interventions are context-specific and are informed by the needs of the population.
- Purely military solutions to conflict and insecurity are insufficient; there is also a need to engage in other sectors (notably diplomacy and development).
- Stabilisation is an ambiguous and contested term, but often refers to efforts to address security obstacles that obstruct peaceful political processes.
- Efforts to establish a safe and secure environment can be counterproductive, without sufficient planning or consultation, for instance, or because they might compromise efforts to promote justice or longer-term peace.
- Peacekeeping and peacebuilding cannot be reduced to efforts in just the security, governance, development or humanitarian relief sectors; comprehensive, co-ordinated and coherent efforts across all of these sectors are required if sustainable peace is to be achieved.

Reflective Question

Consider the rationale behind military interventions to prevent conflict, stabilise conflict-affected or conflict-vulnerable environments and build security in the aftermath of conflict, in spite of the large number of places where conflict has recurred, continued or escalated after such interventions.

List of Core Resources

Beban, P. (2010) Can the UN Keep the Peace? (video). Available at https://vimeo.com/9157432.

Bellamy, A. and Williams, P. (2010) *Understanding Peacekeeping* (Cambridge: Polity Press).

Call, C. (2007) (ed.) *Constructing Justice and Security after War* (Washington: USIP).

Chiyuki, A., de Coning, C. and Karlsrud (2017) 'Introduction: Addressing the emerging gap between concepts, doctrine, and practice in UN peacekeeping operations' in C. de Coning, C. Aoi and J. Karlsrud (eds) *UN Peacekeeping Doctrine in a New Era* (Abingdon and New York: Routledge).

de Coning, C. and Stamnes, E. (eds) (2016) *UN Peacebuilding Architecture: The First 10 Years* (Abingdon: Routledge).

GSDRC (2016) *Security and justice – Paul Jackson* (video). Available at www.youtube.com/watch?v=hwPYqmswbYg.

Jackson, P. and Beswick, D. (2018) (3rd edn) *Conflict, Security and Development: An Introduction* (Abingdon: Routledge) (particularly Chapters 1, 6 and 9).

Kaldor, M. and Selchow, S. (2015) 'From Military to "Security Interventions": An Alternative Approach to Contemporary Interventions', *Stability: International Journal of Security and Development* 4(1): 32, 1–12.

Keen, D. (2012) *Useful Enemies: When Waging Wars is More Important than Winning Them* (New Haven: Yale University Press).

Melander, E., Pettersson, T. and Themnér, L. (2016) 'Organized violence, 1989–2015', *Journal of Peace Research* 53(5): 727–42.

Paris, R. and Sisk, T. (eds) (2009) *The Dilemmas of Statebuilding: Confronting the Contradictions of Postwar Peace Operations* (Abingdon: Routledge).

Saferworld (2014) *Community Security: A Vehicle for Peacebuilding and Statebuilding,* Briefing (London: Saferworld). Available at www.saferworld.org.uk/resources/publications/833-community-security-a-vehicle-for-peacebuilding-and-statebuilding.

Sharwood-Smith, C. (2014) *The Structure and Activities of the UN Police Division,* (University of Leicester) (video). Available at www.youtube.com/watch?v=dYeGNmoO6oI&index=8&list=PLjQX5EXgm57S0L7nT-QMVhQLKiYNsSPxu

Stamnes, E. and Psland, K. (2016) 'Synthesis Report: Reviewing UN Peace Operations, the UN Peacebuilding Architecture and the Implementation of UNSCR 1325', Report No. 2 (Oslo: Norwegian Institute of International Affairs). Available at www.un.org/pga/70/wp-content/uploads/sites/10/2016/01/NUPI_Report_2_16_Stamnes_Osland.pdf.

UN High-Level Independent Panel on Peace Operations (HIPPO) (2015) 'Uniting Our Strengths for Peace: Politics, Partnership and People', Report of the UN High-Level Independent Panel on Peace Operations, 16 June. Available at http://peaceoperationsreview.org/wp-content/uploads/2015/08/HIPPO_Report_1_June_2015.pdf.

USIP (2015) *The Future of U.N. Peace Operations* (video). Available at www.youtube.com/watch?v=qZPqYNqsWNk.

USIP/US Army Peacekeeping and Stability Operations Institute (2009) *Guiding Principles for Stabilization and Reconstruction,* Washington: USIP (Section 6 – 'Safe and Secure Environment', pages 37–61), Available at www.usip.org/sites/default/files/guiding_principles_full.pdf.

Weiss, T. (2012) *What's Wrong with the United Nations and How to Fix it* (Cambridge: Polity Press).

Wilton Park (2014) *The UN in some of the toughest places in the world* (podcast). Available at www.wiltonpark.org.uk/podcast/the-un-in-some-of-the-toughest-places-in-the-world/.

4 Promoting the Rule of Law

Overview

This chapter discusses the importance generally accorded to establishing the rule of law in places emerging from conflict, and examines the relationship between security and the rule of law. It also discusses some of the actors typically seen as advancing the rule of law in post-conflict environments, including the UN Police, and domestic security and justice actors, including state and non-state actors and mechanisms. The chapter concludes by reflecting upon challenges faced and recommendations for improving the record of rule of law initiatives in post-conflict environments. Later chapters will consider the reform of security and justice sector institutions and transitional justice. More than most of the concepts discussed in this book, the rule of law is contested in its definitions, and even its very utility as a concept. The chapter begins, therefore, with a discussion of the concept of 'the rule of law' and how it is understood by some of the actors engaged in this field.

Learning Outcomes

- Articulate the meaning and importance often accorded to the rule of law in post-conflict environments, and what it is expected to achieve
- Be familiar with some of the actors and activities involved in attempts to advance the rule of law in post-conflict environments
- Articulate some of the challenges and weaknesses prevalent in the field of post-conflict rule of law efforts and assess ways in which they could be overcome
- Have an understanding of the relationship between security and the rule of law

Part 1 – The Rule of Law

Security and the rule of law are often presented as essential preconditions for stability, sustainable peace and long-term development, and as causally linked to each other. Efforts to improve security and the rule of law have accordingly become a central feature of post-conflict recovery, and activities and actors in this field have multiplied. Additionally, the increasing support for integrated approaches – which is predicated upon the assumed interdependence between security, the rule of law, governance, development and human rights – now expands the involvement of actors and issues outside the security sector. While many might agree with Tamanaha (2004: 4) that the rule of law is '*the* pre-eminent legitimating political idea in the world today' (emphasis in original), there remains little agreement on what the rule of law actually means. Nonetheless, this uncertainty about what the concept means has not prevented an explosive growth of attempts to implement whatever it is.

What is the rule of law?

The rule of law is an abstract concept and there is no agreed universal definition. However, there is general agreement that the rule of law is an important ideal and necessary in any peaceful society. A fundamental principle inherent to the rule of law is that of equality. In other words, everyone needs to adhere to the law and it is applied equally. As the government is also bound by law, rule of law as a system can be seen to be in contrast with rule by power free from political constraints. A broader definition also holds that the rule of law embraces human rights standards (and so it is not enough that the law is applied equally; the substance of the law matters too).

One way to begin to consider what the rule of law means is through the concept of 'justice'. As the UN has observed:

> The concept of rule of law is deeply linked to the principle of justice, involving an ideal of accountability and fairness in the protection and vindication of rights and the prevention and punishment of wrongs. (UN Rule of Law, 2013: n.p.)

However, we must not make the mistake of equating 'justice' with 'criminal justice', still less with a 'justice system' along western lines. The essential question of justice concerns what is the right thing to do (Sandel, 2009). Justice, therefore, is a subset of practical ethics, and many important works have been written about aspects such as distributive justice, which have nothing to do with crime or police. 'Justice' is essentially how we feel that people, including ourselves, should be treated. A justice system, then, is a mechanism for codifying and enforcing these norms, and a justice sector is responsible for practical enforcement (a justice sector includes all actors engaged in the provision, management and oversight of justice – see DCAF, 2015a). Justice is therefore distinct from law, and from legal codes, codes of conduct and regulations of all kinds (Chuter, 2017). From this perspective, it can be seen that justice and the law can be in conflict with each other, just as order and security can.

Early concepts of law have little to do with how the western establishments generally conceive of the law today. Greek words for 'law' (notably *nomos*) actually mean something closer to 'custom', and virtue and justice were about respect for traditional norms with justice being about restoring 'the natural order of things' (Lane, 2014: 31). This concept of justice still influences many cultures today. It can also be said that what many people want after war is not the introduction of a new technical legal system, but the natural order of things restored. Thus, as Mani argues, 'For ordinary people, restoring the rule of law will be meaningful only if it is synonymous with justice, with protecting their rights and dignity so that they can live safe from humiliation and fear' (Mani, 2002: 85).

Many people therefore want justice, which is to say the enforcement of norms of treatment of themselves and others. Earlier and smaller societies generally managed themselves, and many still do to some extent. Societal organisations from sports clubs to university departments function as much according to unwritten rules and understanding as to formalised regulations. Procedures that are arrived at by negotiation and discussion, and enshrined in tradition, may have various defects, but they are seldom arbitrary. As societies become larger and more complex, however, and political power becomes more distant from the ruled, the possibility of arbitrary power arises: the risk of power being indiscriminately and unsystematically abused. Most people do not want to live in a society characterised by arbitrary power, and, to the extent that the rule of law has an origin, we can perhaps locate it there (Chuter, 2017).

Constraining arbitrary power can be done in a number of ways. These can include setting up countervailing powers, obliging a ruler to be subject to laws, setting up an extensive legal framework to cover every eventuality, and so on. Different traditions have tried to constrain the potential for arbitrary power in different ways: separation of powers between regions and levels of government, involvement of courts and parliaments, elaboration of highly complex legal systems outside which power cannot be exercised, recourses of various types for citizens and so forth. All have very specific origins. For example, the rule of law tradition as it is generally understood has its origins in Anglo-Saxon practices, of liberal distrust of the strong state, a tradition of powerful parliaments controlling public finance, local and regional power, and a respect for tradition and precedent (see Bassu, 2008). Clearly, not many countries in which rule of law initiatives are introduced today will have all these characteristics, and some will have none at all. Conversely, the Roman Law tradition, common in Europe and Latin America and with analogies elsewhere, constrains arbitrary power by a highly complex legal framework, where powers of various authorities are exhaustively defined, and may not be exceeded. Documents are more important than precedents, and parliament often plays a subordinate role (Chuter, 2017).

The interaction and confusion of these traditions, and the use of the term 'rule of law' to cover both, as well as their respective developments in recent decades, have contributed to confusion surrounding what is meant by 'the rule of law'. This confusion has been further entrenched as a result of many recent rule of law initiatives not seeking to limit the power of governments but quite the opposite. Recognising threats to individuals often come not from governments but from elsewhere, and governments in conflict-affected environments are often weak rather than strong, rule of law initiatives can often include statebuilding aspects, building the capacity of state institutions to develop and enforce the law, for instance. Rather than the 'rule of law', this may be better described as 'rule by law', where the monopoly of law-making is established, where procedures are fair and honest and where laws are openly promulgated and fairly enforced. The rule of law and rule by law are not necessarily mutually exclusive (Gowlland-Debbas and Pergantis, 2009). However, simply enabling the government to have a monopoly of law-making and law enforcement without providing for the checks and balances against arbitrary power, could equip the government with tools to suppress, exploit and thus undermine the rule of law.

When building the rule of law after conflict, therefore, it is not sufficient to reform the law and build the capacity of the agencies of the criminal justice system, for instance; it is also necessary to ensure that there are checks and balances on the use of government power; for example, by ensuring the independence of the judiciary, and establishing and/or strengthening other oversight bodies. Rule of law, rather than rule by law, is broadly considered to be intrinsic to peace and stability. Having recourse to the law to resolve grievances, and a belief that everyone is equal before the law, can guard against resolving grievances through violent means (or seeking revenge in post-conflict environments – see Mihr and Sriram, 2018). Moreover, if recourse to violence is to be guarded against, it is important that the substance of the law itself does not favour one group or groups above others.

Many also agree that, fundamentally, it is important that human rights are protected in law to guard against the use of violence to address grievances. The preamble of the Universal Declaration of Human Rights (UN, 1948) states that 'it is essential, if man is not to be compelled to have recourse, as a last resort, to rebellion against tyranny and oppression, that human rights should be protected by the rule of law'. Many international organisations engaged in rule of law initiatives in post-conflict environments also refer to the mutually reinforcing relationship between security, the rule of law and human rights (Gowlland-Debbas and Pergantis, 2009; Hurwitz, 2008; Sriram et al., 2017) (see Box 4.1 on the UN's definition of the rule of law). The assumption that the rule of law and human rights are mutually reinforcing should not be taken for granted, not least because both categories of the 'rule of law' and 'human rights' are often vague and contested. Moreover, this assumption overlooks the fact that laws can reflect and protect the interests of those who have power in a society, because of who writes the law or is more able to influence its development. However, unless the law is broadly regarded as protecting all equally, in its substance as well as in the way it is applied, those without power are more likely to resort to violence to challenge the distribution of power. We also need to critically engage with assumptions often contained in the policy discourse of international actors that the 'rule of law' paves the way for security and development; we should ask 'whose security?', 'whose development' and 'in whose interests?' Assumptions that the 'rule of law' and 'security' are homogenous and equally enjoyed by all should be avoided. However, while the rule of law does not automatically lead to security or the protection of human rights, the alternative is certainly not better. So, in short, it can be said that the rule of law is a necessary but not wholly sufficient precondition for security and human rights protection. Indeed, it can be seen that a strong rule of law – with predictable laws and institutions able to enforce them, and where everyone is equally subject to the law and has equal access to justice – provides a possible mechanism for the peaceful resolution of conflicts and protection against violations of human rights, if the necessary political consensus exists. Security and the rule of law can, thus, be seen to be mutually reinforcing.

> ## Box 4.1: The UN's Definition of the 'Rule of Law'
>
> ... a principle of governance in which all persons, institutions and entities, public and private, including the State itself, are accountable to laws that are publicly promulgated, equally enforced and independently adjudicated, and which are consistent with international human rights norms and standards. It requires, as well, measures to ensure adherence to the principles of supremacy of law, equality before the law, accountability to the law, fairness in the application of the law, separation of powers, participation in decision-making, legal certainty, avoidance of arbitrariness and procedural and legal transparency. (UNSG, 2004, 46)
>
> As described by Sriram (2008: 74), this is 'an extremely procedurally focussed definition of the rule of law', which emphasises the need for 'appropriately constituted authorities, public creation of laws, and accountability of state apparatuses' (Sriram, 2008: 75) rather than focusses on the concept of justice and what that might entail. This definition also demonstrates the breadth of many definitions of the rule of law and how elements cross over, or are confused, with other areas of policy and practice, notably the protection of human rights, transitional justice and Security Sector Reform (SSR).

Part 2 – Rule of Law Activities and Actors

Rule of law activities

Because of the perceived interdependence of security, the rule of law and human rights, resulting in the increasing centrality of the rule of law to peacebuilding, there are an increasing number of actors engaged in post-conflict rule of law activities. Further, given the lack of consensus on what the 'rule of law' means, it is not surprising that there are different understandings of what rule of law activities involve on the ground by external actors engaged in such activities (as described in the next section). Activities stemming from a belief that the rule of law concerns checking arbitrary power and limiting the power of governments will clearly be very different to activities stemming from the notion that the rule of law requires a strong state able to provide security and dispense justice. These activities may not necessarily conflict with each other although, given the multiplicity of actors, it is common to find parallel projects at cross-purposes. Nonetheless, there tends to be a shared understanding of the broad range of activities involved in building the rule of law after conflict. Foremost amongst these is the need to develop professional, effective and responsive security and, particularly, justice sector institutions.

Conflicts can produce a breakdown in the rule of law and security (and indeed can, in part, be the result of such a breakdown), and restoring them in post-conflict environments is often a priority. Depending on the context, security and justice sector institutions may be weak or non-existent: where they exist, they may be corrupt or dysfunctional. Their problems may include simple lack of capacity, confidence, trust and/or legitimacy. This could be described as a 'rule of law vacuum' and in such vacuums, organised crime can flourish and insecurity and human rights violations escalate.

In practice, therefore, most international interventions under the label of the 'rule of law' seek to address perceived lack of institutional capacity through organisational restructuring, vetting and recruitment, training, legislative and policy development, securing additional material resources (equipment, buildings, transport, telecommunications and so on) and other measures. It is held that undertaking these measures in a transparent manner, creating professional and accountable institutions that are responsive to the needs and fears of the people, and addressing war-time and post-conflict abuses and atrocities, will help build trust and legitimacy where it is lacking.

Access to justice

In addition to institutional capacity building, a number of other rule of law activities are commonplace, not least efforts to facilitate equal access to justice. Access to justice is recognised in international human rights law as a basic human right and as a means to protect other human rights. In any society, those who are marginalised or dispossessed may have limited access to justice. This is likely to be particularly pronounced in conflict-affected societies, where there is limited institutional capacity and competing priorities. In conflict-affected societies, the effects of limited access to justice are also likely to be more severe. So, those who may be particularly vulnerable to insecurity and threat in post-conflict environments (e.g. women, ethnic or religious minorities and children) are also often likely to have limited access to justice. In order to improve access to justice and ensure that everyone has access to justice, a number of measures can be taken. These include awareness-raising (for all members of the community as well as security and justice service providers) of the importance of equality of access to justice, including tangibly how that justice can be accessed. Liaison with informal justice providers, and capacity building and support of civil society organisations can also help enable access to justice for women and marginalised groups. Law reform, training of police and judicial practitioners, investment in infrastructure (to build police stations in remote or under-serviced areas, or create mobile services – see Box 4.2), and investment in services (to provide legal aid or extend the services available – see Box 4.3 on the Saturday Courts, for example) can also increase equitable access to justice. Moreover, there may be structural, financial, cultural and psychological barriers in the way of accessing justice which need to be addressed. For instance, gender norms in any given society can often limit the extent to which women and girls can access justice.

Women's access to justice

Women's access to justice is often compromised as a result of a number of barriers. These barriers include discriminatory laws, lack of awareness among women about their rights and how to exercise them, lack of knowledge of the justice system and

Box 4.2: Access to Justice for Survivors of SGBV in Iraq

In 2012, UNDP with three NGO implementing partners – Harika, Public Aid Organization (PAO); Democracy and Human Rights Development Organization (DHRD); and Independent Board of Human Rights (IBHR) – began supporting legal aid service delivery to displaced (both refugee and internally displaced persons – IDPs) survivors/victims of SGBV in the Kurdistan Region of Iraq (KRI), where the majority of IDPs and refugees were located. Previously, these survivors/victims had been unable to access justice. Legal Aid Centres were established inside the main IDP and refugee camps in the three KRI Governorates: one in Sulaymaniya inside the Ashti IDPs camp, two in Erbil inside the Baharka (IDP) and Kawrgosk (refugee) camps, and three in Duhok, – two inside Shariya (IDP) camp and one in Domiz (refugee) camp. A mobile legal team was also created, to provide legal advice and support for IDPs and refugees outside camps, particularly those displaced from Mosul, including those unable to travel or who lack the financial resources to otherwise access justice. Combined, these Centres have served many tens of thousands of displaced survivors/victims of SGBV.

The Centres provide other services (including psychosocial, welfare, health services and livelihood programmes) and referrals to other services, in addition to legal aid. They thus provide a 'one-stop-shop' for those in need, recognising the limited freedom of movement and access to help among displaced persons.

UNDP's programme also incorporated awareness-raising activities which also facilitated access to justice. Awareness-raising of SGBV in communities has helped this form of violence not be regarded as such a taboo subject, which it was previously. Awareness-raising activities also provided communities with information on how to help prevent SGBV and where help can be found. Among service-providers, activities helped raise awareness of the importance of acknowledging and addressing SGBV and ways in which this can best be done in order to improve access to justice and contribute to prevention.

From 2016 to 2017, this programme was delivered jointly with UN Women, and in 2017, UNDP also initiated a gradual transitioning of overall management of the legal aid centres to their government counterpart, the Directorate of Combatting Violence Against Women (DCVAW) of the Kurdish Regional Government. UNDP also undertook capacity building of DCVAW as part of the programme, which has ensured the sustainability of efforts to increase access to justice for survivors of SGBV.

how it works, and gender bias operating in the justice system. Discriminatory laws can include family law which give wives few social and economic rights, or criminal law which recognises property crime but not domestic violence, for instance. Lack of awareness among women of their rights and how to exercise them can be a result of their limited access to education and resultant limited knowledge and/or literacy, as well as the fact that justice sector institutions often do not reach out to women. This can hinder women's knowledge of their legal rights and how they

Box 4.3: The Saturday Courts

In Sierra Leone, access to justice has been compromised as a result of limited resources, which has resulted in considerable backlogs of cases and congestion of courts. Survivors/victims of SGBV are particularly affected by such congestion, not least because it also compromises privacy, which is very important with such sensitive cases. To help clear the massive backlog of cases involving SGBV and increase access to justice for those who are survivors of SGBV, the Saturday Courts were established in 2011.

The Saturday Courts were held in Freetown and in regional headquarter cities (Bo, Kenema, Kono and Makeni) and involved opening existing courts on Saturdays for the hearing of SGBV cases. Simultaneously, UNDP and others trained judicial staff and police, and provided logistical support, in order to improve the manner in which SGBV cases were dealt with, including better treatment of survivors/victims and witnesses.

The Saturday Courts not only facilitated increased access to justice for women and children survivors of SGBV, clearing a backlog of SGBV cases and expediting new ones (hearing over 630 cases in the first year of operation), but also provided a sensitive and protective setting for women and children in SGBV cases. The Saturday Courts also provided the privacy needed for witnesses to provide sensitive testimonies. Further, the Saturday Courts had a significant impact on attitudes towards SGBV – that such crimes are unacceptable and there will no longer be impunity – which contributed to increasing women's and children's access to justice as well as increasing their security.

The Saturday Courts were a relatively inexpensive method of increasing access to justice and addressing impunity for SGBV crimes – inexpensive because the infrastructure already existed and only a few staff were required. Nonetheless, political will has hampered efforts to sustain the support required to retain the Saturday Courts.

can assert these rights to get redress for criminal and civil wrongs. Gender bias operating in the justice system is often implicit and the result of cultural norms and gender stereotypes. Gender bias influences judicial decision-making and can result in women's testimonies not being taken as seriously or men's mitigating circumstances in the case of violence against women (VAW) being readily accepted. In turn, gender bias can perpetuate women's marginalisation and the gendered inequalities that contribute to insecurity and violence.

Other obstacles in the way of accessing justice include fear – both of treatment by police and judicial practitioners and the stigma associated with certain crimes (particularly those involving sexual and gender-based violence (SGBV). There is also often tangible fear of physical violence in justice systems where there are not effective witness protection mechanisms, protective orders are not issued, or anonymity is not assured, which is commonplace in conflict-affected environments. Societal attitudes that certain crimes are not serious or the victim is to blame for certain crimes, as is often the case with SGBV, can also deter women from accessing justice (it can also deter men and LGBTIQ people from accessing justice when victims of such crimes, particularly when men feel obliged to live up to hypermasculine ideals which do not include vulnerability or in societies which outlaw homosexuality).

Difficulties accessing childcare can also problematise women's access to justice (and that of other sole or primary carers), particularly when the justice system is not efficient or the nearest court is very far away.

Structural inequalities often mean that women are socio-economically disadvantaged. Because they may be poor, women can often not afford justice (the cost of hiring a lawyer, travelling to court, paying for childcare or bribing a court official in societies where corruption is rampant). If women are also poor or otherwise marginalised (if they are from an ethnic or religious minority, displaced, disabled etc.) barriers to accessing justice are likely to be compounded.

To address these obstacles in the way of access to justice, there are a number of measures that can be and often are undertaken in post-conflict – and other – environments. For instance, paralegals can be employed to build legal literacy of the general population through teaching people how to access the justice system, what their legal rights are and how to utilise available legal resources. Innovative methods to reach out to women and other marginalised groups can be employed, including mobile courts (as in Kurdistan, Iraq, described in Box 4.2), Saturday Courts (in Sierra Leone, see Box 4.3) and new technologies (in Sierra Leone a justice app has been developed, for instance, that has helped build people's awareness of the law). Legal aid can also be provided to impoverished and marginalised populations, including women, ensuring that women are not disadvantaged in accessing legal aid if it is means-tested based upon household income. Additionally, law reform, institutional reform and training of members of the criminal justice system can increase confidence and trust among the people in the system, which would lead to greater access to justice and use of the services that are available. As will be discussed further in Chapter 8, reform of the criminal justice system to ensure that it is responsive and representative of the demographic it services is crucial to enabling equal access to justice.

General Recommendation No. 33 on women's access to justice of the UN Committee on the Elimination of Discrimination against Women (CEDAW Committee) recognises the impact of discrimination, inequalities, stereotypes and gender bias in the justice system as impeding women's access to justice. It recommends that States Parties take 'measures, including awareness-raising and capacity-building programmes for all justice system personnel and law students, to eliminate gender stereotyping and incorporate a gender perspective into all aspects of the justice system' (para 29 (a)). It also urges a gender-sensitive approach to handling cases in the justice sector and removal of other obstacles in the way of access to justice, including guarding against stigmatisation and secondary victimisation of women in their interactions with judicial authorities.

CEDAW's General Recommendation No. 30 also urges 'the provision of legal aid and the establishment of specialised courts, such as domestic violence and family courts, providing mobile courts for camps and settlement settings and for remote areas, and ensuring adequate protection measures for victims and witnesses, including non-disclosure of identity and the provision of shelters' (para 81(k)). It also contains provisions to guard against gender bias and re-traumatisation, stipulating that 'equal weight is given to the testimony of women and girls as to that of men' (para 81(h)). General Recommendation No. 30 also encourages direct engagement with informal justice mechanisms to encourage compliance with human rights standards, including gender equality.

CEDAW's General Recommendation No. 35 on gender-based violence against women also urges 'an effective and accessible legal and legal services framework in place to address all forms of gender-based violence against women' (para. 22) and 'mandatory, recurrent and effective capacity-building, education and training for the judiciary, lawyers and law enforcement officers' (para. 30 (e)).

Other Rule of Law Activities

Aside from developing effective, efficient and responsive security and justice sector institutions, and enabling equitable access to justice, rule of law activities also include efforts to reform the law itself (endeavouring to ensure it is fair and equitable), improve oversight of state institutions (to guard against abuse of authority), and promote the engagement of civil society (not least to help hold those in power to account and raise awareness of rights and duties). Additionally, while transitional justice is a distinct area of activity (see Chapter 5), sometimes there is not a clear distinction between efforts to promote accountability in order to build the rule of law and efforts to address wartime atrocities in order for society to move forward. It is generally accepted that society needs to address war crimes and other serious crimes committed during conflict if it is to move forward. Equally, accountability for crimes, particularly serious crimes, and other wrongdoing or harm is critical to the rule of law, not least to guard against others transgressing the law and to guard against grievances turning into vengeance.

Table 4.1 maps the broad range of activities that are often undertaken under the umbrella of developing the rule of law in conflict-affected environments. This table maps these activities against the intended aim of the activity. These intended aims are what are considered to be the various prerequisites to the rule of law (see also Jackson and Beswick, 2018; Mihr and Sriram, 2018; UN, 2008b; USIP/US Army Peacekeeping and Stability Operations Institute, 2009). These preconditions constitute an ideal-type scenario and cannot be regarded as a coherent panacea for establishing the rule of law, however it is conceived, but they are valuable in ensuring activities are determined based upon the intended outcome or aim. While the types of rule of law activities that occur in post-conflict environments tend to be similar, it is very important that that activities are determined based upon aims and objectives, rather than simply because it is what may have been done elsewhere or before. This is particularly important given that each context is unique.

In post-conflict environments, rule of law activities also often include providing assistance on housing, land and property issues relating to refugees and internally displaced persons, combating organised crime, promoting gender equality, attending to juvenile justice and broader human rights protection.

Table 4.1   Rule of law prerequisites and associated activities

Aim	Effect	Indicative Task
Equal access to justice	Everyone has equal access to remedies, and the law is applied fairly, equally, effectively and transparently.	Constructing police stations in remote areas; translating laws into different local languages; recruiting women and ethnic minorities into the criminal justice system; establishing legal aid systems; supporting alternative dispute resolution or informal justice mechanisms (see police and judicial reform activities in Chapter 8).
A just legal framework	Including a constitution or its equivalent, in which laws are equitable, responsive to the needs of all people in a society, are legally certain and transparent, and generally adhere to international human rights norms.	Drafting or amending a constitution and a country's laws (see law reform in Chapter 8).
Public order	The rights of individuals are protected, and crime and violence are at manageably low levels.	The police are professionalised and their capacity developed, through training, equipping, mentoring, engendering sufficient political and financial support, improving co-ordination with other agencies in the criminal justice system and drafting/amending internal and external policies (see police reform activities in Chapter 8).
An electoral system	The people are allowed to vote for their political representatives and thereby contribute to holding them to account.	Electoral processes are developed.
Functioning security, justice, governance and human rights institutions	These institutions are effective, efficient and responsive to the needs of all people.	Security Sector Reform (SSR) activities to improve the effectiveness, efficiency and responsiveness of security and justice sector institutions, including their management and oversight bodies (see Chapter 8) as well as the establishment or development of human rights institutions and efforts to promote good governance across state institutions. These activities can include vetting or lustration to remove from these institutions those responsible for alleged war crimes, for instance (see Chapter 5 on transitional justice).

Aim	Effect	Indicative Task
Engaged public and civil society	This engagement can empower the citizenry, raise awareness, and promote transparency and accountability.	Awareness-raising and outreach; public information campaigns; facilitating communication between state institutions and civil society; civil society capacity building; developing an enabling environment for civil society actors to engage (e.g. removing political constraints and addressing security concerns).
Effective oversight mechanisms	These mechanisms can limit the abuse of authority and further promote accountability.	Establishing or developing oversight bodies, including parliamentary committees, ombudsperson organisations and civil society actors; promoting an independent media and an independent and professional judiciary.
Accountability and transitional justice mechanisms	These mechanisms include the existence of an independent judiciary which is free from political influence.	Taking action to guard against political interference in the judiciary; establishing or developing efforts to promote individual accountability through prosecutions and other measures, including for crimes committed during the conflict (see Chapter 5 on transitional justice)

The activities outlined in Table 4.1 clearly overlap with those sometimes undertaken as part of Security Sector Reform (SSR) (see Chapter 8); notably, law reform and efforts to reform and develop the justice sector (including the judiciary, police and prison system). Similarly, as identified in Table 4.1, rule of law activities are also sometimes considered to include transitional justice measures (see Chapter 5), although there can be tension between their aims and objectives. There are also synergies (and sometimes tension) between rule of law activities and human rights work, particularly when developing legislation to promote a just legal framework or developing mechanisms to promote accountability and address war-time atrocities.

Before moving on to looking at some of the lead actors engaged in rule of law activities in post-conflict environments, it is worth highlighting that there are a number of shared principles which tend to inform the work of those engaged in rule of law activities. The Secretary-General's Guidance Note 'UN Approach to Rule of law Assistance' (UNSG, 2008b), for instance, outlines eight guiding principles for UN rule of law activities:

1. Base assistance on international norms and standards.
2. Take account of the political context.
3. Base assistance on the unique country context.

4. Advance human rights and gender justice.
5. Ensure national ownership.
6. Support national reform constituencies.
7. Ensure a coherent and comprehensive strategic approach.
8. Engage in effective coordination and partnerships (UNSG, 2008b: 1).

Rule of law actors

As the number of rule of law activities undertaken in post-conflict environments has multiplied, so too has the number of actors engaged. Rule of law activities are now a central feature of peace operations. This stems from an increasing recognition of the importance of the rule of law in peacemaking and peacebuilding. As a result, a multitude of international actors are involved, often working alongside or building the capacity of their national counterparts in conflict-affected environments. International actors include international and regional organisations and alliances, government agencies, donor agencies, NGOs and others who are actively engaged in providing technical and advisory support (and sometimes have executive authority). The media, academia and think tanks can also play a role in setting the agenda in terms of rule of law tasks and priorities and their fulfilment. The most critical actors, of course, remain, various stakeholders in the host country: their leadership and support of rule of law initiatives and programmes is crucial to their success.

The UN is a major actor in this field. The instrumental Brahimi Report (UN, 2000a) emphasised the importance of establishing the rule of law in post-conflict environments and paved the way for formal rule of law components to be integrated into UN peacekeeping operations. A key recommendation was to institute 'a doctrinal shift in the use of civilian police, other rule of law elements and human rights experts in complex peace operations to reflect an increased focus on strengthening rule of law institutions and improving respect for human rights in post-conflict environments' (UN, 2000a: 8).

Today, the UN regards the rule of law as lying at the heart of its mission (UN, 2011). The UN is involved in many capacities and in a wide variety of areas to promote the rule of law, including most peacekeeping operations and special political missions mandated by the UN Security Council (see Box 4.4 on the UN Mission for Justice Support in Haiti).

Box 4.4: United Nations Mission for Justice Support in Haiti (MINUJUSTH)

MINUJUSTH is a unique UN peacekeeping mission in that it is focussed exclusively on the rule of law. Its mandate is to support the Government of Haiti in further developing the Haitian National Police (HNP) as well as strengthen other criminal justice institutions, including the judiciary and prison system. It is also mandated to support the government in the promotion and protection of human

---

(Continued)

rights. MINUJUSTH was established pursuant to UN Security Council Resolution 2350 (April 2017) and was given an initial mandate of six months (October 2017– April 2018). MINUJUSTH succeeded the previous UN Stabilization Mission in Haiti (MINUSTAH), which began its mandate in 2004. MINUJUSTH has a much lighter footprint, and is composed of both police and civilians.

Some critics have suggested that this is an attempt at rebranding on the part of the UN, having been responsible for a cholera outbreak in 2010 that caused the death of 10,000 Haitians and infected 800,000 more, and been the subject of many scandals concerning the sexual exploitation and abuse of Haitians (Danticat, 2017; Persio, 2017). The response of the UN to these crimes is widely considered by Haitians to be lacklustre; initially it refused to investigate the cause of the cholera outbreak and often ignored or did not robustly respond to claims of sexual exploitation and abuse (Danticat, 2017; Persio, 2017). The same critics argue that if the UN wanted to promote the rule of law and human rights in Haiti 'it would wind down its presence in the country by having *minujusth* also investigate the damage done to both individuals and entire communities by *minustah*' (Danticat, 2017: n.p.).

The Office of Rule of Law and Security Institutions (OROLSI) in the UN Department of Peacekeeping Operations (DPKO), established in 2007, supports rule of law components in peacekeeping operations and special political missions. OROLSI encompasses the following:

- *Police Division (PD)* – develops policy and guidance, defines the parameters of international police peacekeeping, supports police components of peace operations, and facilitates efforts to recruit and deploy mission staff
- *Justice and Corrections Service (JSC)* – formerly known as the Criminal Law and Judicial Advisory Service (CLJAS) – addresses issues related to justice and corrections in post-conflict environments, and supports UN staff and national authorities in these environments working in the justice and corrections sector
- *Disarmament, demobilisation and Reintegration (DDR) Section* – supports DDR programmes and community violence reduction in peace operations
- *Security Sector Reform Unit (SSRU)* – provides assistance to peace operations engaged in SSR efforts, develops partnerships to facilitate SSR work, and develops and communicates SSR guidance and norms
- *United Nations Mine Action Service (UNMAS)* – leads, co-ordinates and implements United Nations efforts to eliminate landmines and explosive hazards and to mitigate their impact on people's lives.

The Police Division supports the deployment of thousands of police officers (seconded by individual countries) as part of UN Police. Oftentimes in peace operations, UN Police are the most visible face of the international community's efforts to establish and support the development of the rule of law in post-conflict environments. The UN Police generally support, mentor, train and develop the in-country police service. The size and complexity of police components in peacekeeping operations have grown considerably over the last decade and their role has greatly expanded. In some missions, for instance in Kosovo (UNMIK) and Timor-Leste (UNMIT), the UN Police were given an executive mandate to protect law and order while also building up a national police capacity.

In future chapters, we will discuss the work that comes under the remit of JSC and SSRU (when we discuss SSR in Chapter 8), the DDR Section (in Chapter 7) and UNMAS (in Chapter 6, when mine action is discussed). Many other UN agencies and departments are engaged in these and other rule of law activities, including the UN Office on Drugs and Crime (UNODC) (focussing on combatting illicit drugs, terrorism and crime), UN Development Programme (UNDP) (focussing upon building justice institutions as a way to build sustainable development and alleviate poverty), UN Women (promoting gender equality including equal access to justice, the engagement of women in peacebuilding, including building the rule of law after conflict, and the protection of women and girls against violence, including conflict-related sexual violence) and the UN Children's Fund (UNICEF) (including promoting justice for children, protecting children against violations of international law and supporting the development of legal frameworks which protect child rights).

Other international actors are increasingly involved in rule of law activities in conflict-affected environments. The European Union (EU, 2019: n.p.) sees the rule of law as 'one of the founding principles stemming from the common constitutional traditions of all Member States, and one of the fundamental values upon which the European Union is based'. It has carried out a number of rule of law missions, of which the most important, in Kosovo, involved at one point some 800 personnel. The EU also deploys international police and has done so in Macedonia and BiH (replacing the UN International Police Task Force – IPTF).

Individual nations have occasionally managed the police components of peace operations and other interventions, such as the US in Haiti in 1994 before transitioning responsibility to the UN six months later (Dobbins et al., 2007).

Other organisations are also engaged in efforts to professionalise the police in conflict-affected environments, such as the Organization for Security and Cooperation in Europe (OSCE), which established a police training school in Kosovo (now called the Kosovo Centre for Public Safety Education and Development – KCPSED).

The increasing perceived importance of the rule of law has resulted in an increase in the number of actors involved in rule of law assistance. Beyond international and regional organisations and alliances, government agencies, donor agencies, NGOs and others are actively engaged in providing technical and advisory support. For example, in Indonesia, the Australian Government's Department of Foreign Affairs and Trade (DFAT) collaborates with a number of Indonesian NGOs in working with representatives of the judiciary and the Government in an effort to address gender bias and improve access to justice for all. The media, academia and think tanks can also play a role in setting the peacebuilding agenda in the security and justice sectors. For example, the American Bar Association's Europe and Eurasia division of the Rule of Law Initiative (ABA-CEELI) worked in BiH for 12 years, since 1996, providing training to prosecutors, defence lawyers and judges, as well as engaging in criminal law reform work, building the capacity of criminal justice institutions, promoting alternative dispute resolution, and supporting access to justice through supporting free access to information (ABA, 2019). Also in BiH, the Geneva Centre for the Democratic Control of the Armed Forces (DCAF) and BiH's Atlantic Initiative implemented a number of programmes aimed at building the capacity, professionalism and efficiency of the jusitice system. Their work has included building the capacity of judicial staff to more effectively integrate gender awareness into the procedures and practices of the judiciary. The aim of this project was to improve the judicial response to domestic violence and to gender-based harassment and violence, and to be more cognisant of gender bias within the judiciary, in order to strengthen the justice system's delivery of non-discriminatory services as well as support the role of women in the justice sector (DCAF/Atlantic Initiative, 2017; Galic and Huhtanen, 2014; Halilovic, 2015; Halilovic and Huhtanen, 2014).

The most critical actors, of course, remain various stakeholders in the host country, including government, justice sector and civil society actors: their engagement and support of rule of law initiatives and programmes is crucial to success and to the sustainability of peace and security.

Part 3 – Challenges and Recommendations

Conceptual challenges

There are a number of challenges that may confront attempts to implement rule of law programmes in post-conflict environments. The first, and probably the most important, challenge is conceptual. It is difficult for scholars to agree on what the 'rule of law' means. It should therefore be of little surprise that such an ambiguous and often contested concept poses challenges for those involved in implementing 'rule of law' programmes. This is particularly the case when such programmes may be implemented by a heterogeneous group of internationals from different legal traditions and cultures in a country that perhaps few of them have visited before.

In addition, many of the often-cited components of the rule of law – equality before the law, for example – are abstract and declarative in nature. As Proudhon and Marx pointed out long ago, such rights are meaningless in practice without the ability to enjoy them. Actual equality before the law would require equality of wealth and power, which is unlikely any time soon. Ironically, clan-based societies, where even the humblest clan member has the right to seek justice from its head, may actually provide more equality before the law than a modern complex western system, most useful to those who can afford expensive lawyers (Chuter, 2017).

Because of the very abstract nature of such principles as equality before the law, a further challenge is to translate them into tangible projects which can be implemented in a (frequently) short timeframe. Moreover, demonstrating that such projects positively impact the rule of law can be challenging, particularly where there is no agreed definition of the rule of law. Evaluating projects is often focussed on tangible, quantitative outputs (new laws or codes of conduct, the number of police officers trained and so on), rather than outcomes (how new laws, codes and training impact the rule of law).

Contextual challenges

More obvious challenges concern the environment in which rule of law programmes are implemented. Conflict may have led to the criminalisation of state institutions, including state security and justice sector institutions. The capacity of such institutions may be limited, or they may be corrupt or otherwise lack public trust and confidence. Infrastructure (courts, police stations, prisons and so on) may be damaged or destroyed, staff (members of the judiciary, police officers, prison staff and so on) may have fled the country during the conflict or may have participated in the conflict, and material resources may have been lost or destroyed.

While such challenges may be prevalent in post-conflict environments, it is important not to generalise, of course – or to assume that such challenges are the result of the conflict or are not also faced in countries that may have not recently experienced armed conflict. It may be true that prisons 'are overcrowded, unhealthy places where brutality has reigned and people have languished for years without charge or trial' (OHCHR, 2006: 5) but they may have been so before the conflict and so are many in countries not afflicted by conflict. Before the conflict, security and justice sector institutions may have been corrupt, 'been used only as a tool of powerful elites or criminal power structures' (USIP/US Army Peacekeeping and Stability Operations Institute, 2009: 64), had limited capacity or otherwise lacked public trust and confidence – as is often the case in post-conflict environments.

Other challenges are common to many peacebuilding projects: an insecure environment with potentially high levels of violence and widespread organised crime; tension or mistrust between groups; easy access to small arms; prevalence of landmines and other explosive remnants of war (ERW); a devastated economy and unmet humanitarian needs. Additionally, rule of law projects may threaten the interests of powerful groups and potential spoilers 'bent on taking advantage of a period of flux to consolidate their authority' (Bull, 2007: 6). Other challenges concern the tension that can be perceived as existing between short-term stabilisation goals and longer-term justice and governance goals (see Carter and Clark, 2010). This will be returned to in the next chapter when discussing the so-called 'justice versus security' dilemma. Similarly, stretched resources, co-ordination challenges born of a multiplicity of actors, competing agendas and lack of political will are also challenges that are commonplace to programmes in post-conflict environments.

Shortcomings in implementation

Common shortcomings (and principles which are often compromised) in the implementation of rule of law programmes include:

- application of formulaic or culturally alien programmes (the principle of context- specificity)

- limited accountability of those implementing rule of law programmes (the principle of accountability)
- lack of lessons shared and learned within and between organisations and with local counterparts (the principle of reflection and learning)
- limited engagement and leadership of local actors in the development and implementation of rule of law programmes (the principle of local ownership)
- programmes which do not adequately respond to the needs of all groups or overlook bottom-up or community-based approaches to delivering justice (the principle of inclusion).

Context-specificity

Despite all the attention and resources aimed at establishing and promoting the rule of law in post-conflict environments, and the increasing number of actors involved, success has often proved elusive. Hurwitz (2008) suggests that this could be, in part, due to lack of integration of conflict analyses into programme design and implementation, in favour of 'template' strategies and technical solutions reproduced with insufficient consideration of the local context. The situation seems hardly to have improved in the last decade.

Because rule of law initiatives can take a 'toolbox' approach (even if the tools are sometimes hard to identify) local populations may be confronted with an entirely new set of concepts, processes, policies and structures that may not resonate with the local context. Belief in an imported system that can ultimately protect rights equally and fully is likely to be limited.

Mani (2008) emphasises the importance of rule of law programmes responding to a country's needs, culture and context and involving the active participation of the people of that country, as well as being more realistic and not promising to deliver more than is possible. Awareness of the political dimensions of the rule of law and the local context is obviously necessary, alongside knowledge of other actors engaged in rule of law and related programming, in order to ensure co-ordination and coherence of efforts, and avoid gaps and duplication (and thus wasted resources and confusion). In short, we 'must be guided in our rule of law work by a sense of accountability to post-conflict populations – to protect them the best we can, without promising what we can't deliver' (Mani, 2008: 40). With respect to co-ordination, it is also vital that there is co-ordination between the activities and aims involved in related fields, notably transitional justice, SSR and DDR – recognising overlaps between and interdependencies across these fields.

Accountability

One of the most significant obstacles in the implementation of rule of law programmes concerns the lack of effective accountability mechanisms and limits to the authority of international organisations mandated to implement rule of law programmes. Abuse of power and limited means to hold to account international actors for violations of human rights or administrative misconduct can undermine the legitimacy of rule of law initiatives introduced by these organisations (see Box 4.5 on accountability and the Office of the High Representative of Bosnia and Herzegovina).

Box 4.5: Accountability of International Organisations and the Case of BiH

The High Representative of Bosnia and Herzegovina (BiH) had considerable powers (the so-called *Bonn powers*, granted by the Peace Implementation Council at its meeting in 1997 in Bonn). The excessive use of these powers received considerable criticism, not least given they were subject to little accountability or challenge. These powers included the ability to unilaterally dissolve political parties and overturn decisions taken by local elected representatives. Ironically, reflecting upon his role as High Representative, Paddy Ashdown has said:

> In hindsight, we should have put the establishment of the rule of law first, for everything else depends on it: a functioning economy, a free and fair political system, the development of civil society, public confidence in police and the courts. (Ashdown, 2002: n.p.)

Ashdown was known for being more vigorous and aggressive in his job than any other incumbent and here he indicates that he should have been more vigorous in imposing the dominance of the international community on the country, and tolerated less opposition; ironically quite the opposite to most understandings of the rule of law.

This issue of accountability and the lack of effective mechanisms that can hold the UN and other international organisations to account are highlighted as key challenges by Gowlland-Debbas and Pergantis (2009), who suggest that:

> Double standards and absence of control render rule of law precepts dead letter and de-legitimizes the work of the UN and other IOs in the field. (Gowlland-Debbas and Pergantis, 2009: 331)

Learning lessons

Another common shortcoming is the limited utilisation of institutional knowledge and successful experiences, both within and between organisations, regionally and globally. There is little systematic promotion of lessons learned and best practices in the field, although this is beginning to slowly change. Similarly, the knowledge, perceptions and understanding of local counterparts in the field are often ignored or considered not to be objective and thus not of value. To ignore local knowledge is to under-utilise the most valuable resource of any post-conflict recovery effort.

Local ownership

Whilst local ownership is unarguably vital to the success of most post-conflict recovery efforts, as described by Gowlland-Debbas and Pergantis (2009), securing it comes with its own challenges. Norms and values of international organisations may be at odds with the wishes and needs articulated by local stakeholders or with local cultures and practices. Identifying a reliable and capable local counterpart or institution to develop and implement programmes may be difficult. There will also be different local stakeholders with different needs, wishes and possibly agendas, some of which may be at odds with each other and/or the peace process.

Inclusion

Additionally, the voices of those who may be the most vulnerable or insecure may be precisely those voices that are not heard or championed by more powerful local groups or representatives. It is essential that efforts to establish and promote the rule of law take into account the needs and concerns of the most vulnerable members of society, as they are often the most at risk from violence and crime and the least able to access protection and justice. This is particularly true when it comes to children (see Box 4.6). If the rule of law is to mean anything in any society, it is that no one is above the law and everyone, particularly the most vulnerable, is protected by the law. Similarly, it is also necessary that rule of law programmes mainstream gender; the limited number of women that continue to be represented in rule of law programmes and, for instance, the UN Police, speaks to the needs to improve efforts in this regard (see Box 4.7).

Programmes which do not adequately respond to the needs of all groups will not be responsive to their needs, and thus the principle of equality which underpins the rule of law will be undermined. Similarly, programmes which overlook bottom-up or community-based approaches to delivering justice can have similar shortcomings. Rule of law activities often overlook traditional community-based or informal justice mechanisms that have existed for a long time, focussing instead upon top-down or state-centred approaches, although this is beginning to change to some extent. This reflects the confusion about what the rule of law is. Even for everyday public safety, there is a tendency to overlook what communities do for themselves, because it is often informal and unstructured. As a classic study of collective life in cities observed:

> ... the public peace – the sidewalk and street peace – of cities ... is kept by an intricate, almost unconscious network of voluntary controls and standards among the people themselves, and enforced by the people themselves. (Jacobs, 1961: 31–32)

Box 4.6: Children and Access to Justice

Children's access to justice in conflict and post-conflict environments 'is hampered by the fact that the infrastructure of judicial systems is often inadequate or non-existent' (UN General Assembly – UNGA, 2011: 6). Children and other disadvantaged or vulnerable groups may also lack the knowledge and support they need in accessing justice. They may be illiterate or may lack the financial resources to travel to police stations or pay any bribes expected to file a case, or the institutions that exist may be corrupt or discriminatory. To help protect children's rights, it is essential that they have access to justice (see UNDP, 2005b).

Box 4.7: UN Police

A criticism that is often levied specifically at the UN Police is the limited representation of women, although the record is slowly improving (with the goal of reaching 20% by 2020 – UN Police, 2019). Other concerns raised with regard to the UN Police have included disparities in the level of training, motivation and professionalism of police officers deployed on peace operations; abuse of authority and lack of accountability; limited transferral of lessons learnt to replacement police contingents; sub-optimal co-ordination between mission components and with other actors; inadequate pre-deployment training on the context in which they will work and also on gender and human rights issues; and mandates which are sometimes vague and result in confusion and mission creep (see Mobekk, 2005; Sanchez, 2018; Sharwood-Smith, 2014, 2015 – balance – mention achievements also).

Informal justice mechanisms (also often referred to as non-state, customary, traditional, community-based justice mechanisms or providers) may be preferred by the majority of the population. Indeed, there are estimates that 80% of the world's population access security and justice through informal or non-state providers (UN Rule of Law, 2019). Rule of law programmes, particularly those developed and implemented by external actors, may not resonate with this fact or may be completely oblivious to it.

The fact that members of international organisations themselves often come from societies where this kind of community has largely disappeared, as well as the practical invisibility of much of the local process, means that elaborate and complex structures may be introduced which just duplicate existing informal ones. So, it is important to remember that in security, as elsewhere,

> Formal order … is always and to some considerable degree parasitic on informal processes, which the formal scheme does not recognise, without which it could not exist, and which it alone cannot create or maintain. (Scott, 1998: 310)

Over the last decade or so, these concerns have begun to be acknowledged by international organisations engaged in rule of law activities. Related to these concerns is the issue of sustainability of efforts; while many rule of law activities may be instrumental in facilitating the transition to peace, the results of those programmes developed and often led by international actors, falter or unravel once these actors depart. This is particularly the case if programmes have not built requisite capacity or were not developed and 'owned' by local actors.

Of course, informal justice mechanisms are not without their shortcomings. As will be discussed further in Chapter 8 (see Box 8.17), informal justice mechanisms may often be more accessible, cheaper and quicker in some societies than formal mechanisms, but they can also be unaccountable, corrupt and discriminatory, particularly against women and marginalised groups – as can state institutions – reinforcing power relations and exclusion, and perpetuating human rights violations. They might be the preferred choice for many, but this may be simply due to lack of alternatives. Nonetheless, the fact that they are so widely prevalent and used by people in many societies should warrant engagement with them by external actors in efforts to promote access to justice and the rule of law. In some countries, a hybrid legal system exists, incorporating both state and non-state justice providers, with non-state providers potentially granted power to administer justice in civil law cases.

Lessons learnt/recommendations

There are a number of lessons that can be learnt from past practice in order to help overcome some of the challenges and shortcomings just referred to. Fundamentally, there is a need to conduct an in-depth context analysis of the political culture, history and structures of the country or region concerned (see Box 2.4 in Chapter 2). This can help contribute to ensuring that programmes are context-specific. It also can help avoid assumptions about conflict-affected environments and prerequisites for peace that cannot be generalised but often are in practice, which leads to processes and structures being rejected or otherwise failing. In this regard, it is also necessary to understand customary, traditional or informal justice mechanisms, and how they fit into the wider political culture, and appreciate that such mechanisms vary from place to place and are often the preferred choice for many people.

Further, it needs to be fully acknowledged that 'the law' is man-made, not God-given nor static; it is of its time and often reflects and protects the interests of the powerful and is, thus, political. This understanding needs to inform rule of law efforts so that there is critical reflection upon aims, outputs and outcomes, and methods of evaluation; assessing progress through public opinion surveys and qualitative research rather than only on the number of laws passed or police trained and other easily measurable outputs, for instance. More broadly, the rule of law is about politics and power; it can never be considered to be simply a technical exercise.

Additionally, sharing of knowledge between international organisations, civil society and academia could provide valuable perspective and test assumptions that have, as yet, received little rigorous academic consideration. For instance, institution building is prioritised based upon the assumption that a strong state is more resistant to conflict. But research into what ordinary people feel about security is limited and could yield useful insights; the types of population surveys conducted by Saferworld and their national partners, for example, are invaluable resources to inform policy and practice, not least because they often challenge untested assumptions about public perceptions of security and security and justice sector institutions.

Moreover, while blind application of foreign templates is not a good idea, learning lessons from elsewhere or the past is always valuable. Ironically, while rule of law initiatives in post-conflict environments are dominated by western theoretical norms, western historical experience is largely ignored; not least the fact that the construction of the rule of law took a very long time and is arguably not yet

> **Box 4.8: Context-specificity and Local Ownership**
>
> Context-specificity and local ownership can be facilitated, in part, by ensuring that local actors, including and beyond elite actors, are meaningfully and actively included throughout project planning, implementation and evaluation. In other words, local actors, representing a broad cross-section of society (particularly marginalised groups who might otherwise not have their needs articulated nor inform project plans), need to be engaged in large numbers (not just tokenistic representation) and in decision-making roles (not without influence) from the outset of the planning process. This may require additional time (identifying which local actors to engage with) and investment in co-ordination (not least because of the number of additional actors and potentially competing agendas involved), but equally provides opportunities to capitalise upon local knowledge and initiatives already underway to build the rule of law, as well as develop rule of law initiatives that are more likely to be directly responsive to local needs and thus more likely to be successful.

complete (if we consider, for example, increasing state powers and curtailment of civil liberties for citizens in various western countries in recent years – Chuter, 2017). In this regard, humility is useful and realistic expectations about what can be achieved in the short timeframes that donors and governments like. Humility is also necessary in recognising that legitimate or valid knowledge is not the sole recourse of external 'experts' in building the rule of law after conflict; context-specificity and local ownership are generally integral to successful projects and thus local engagement and local knowledge should be privileged (see Box 4.8 on how to facilitate context-specificity and local ownership).

What, therefore, can be tangibly undertaken to help establish and promote the rule of law in post-conflict environments? Some of the answers are essentially practical as outlined in Table 4.2:

Table 4.2   Rule of law activities – recommendations and associated principles

Principle	Recommendation	Task
Planning	Recognise scope and complexity	Acknowledge that rule of law goes well beyond effective law enforcement.
	Comprehensively plan	Ensure rule of law mission components and programmes are meticulously planned.
	Prioritise and sequence tasks	Give due consideration to the prioritisation and sequencing of tasks.
	Conduct conflict analyses	Conduct a comprehensive context analysis of the political culture, history and structures of the country or region concerned.

Principle	Recommendation	Task
Co-ordination and Communication	Ensure co-ordination and coherence	Introduce mechanisms and processes to promote co-ordination and coherence at all stages between all elements and actors engaged in rule of law activities and related fields (transitional justice, SSR, DRR etc.).
	Attend to interdependencies and tensions	Seek coherence between short- and long-term goals and be aware of the impact of efforts in one area on another area.
	Manage expectations	Ensure programme aims are not over-ambitious and expectations are managed.
Local Ownership and Inclusion	Engage communities and civil society	Ensure civil society and communities are represented in rule of law intervention planning and decision-making, recognising that our concept of 'civil society' may not correspond to local realities and that 'expertise' of the context is to be found among those from the specific environment.
	Support not replace ownership of programmes	Promote local ownership of programmes, recognising that without it, outputs are less likely to respond to local needs, enjoy public support and thus be sustainable.
	Address the needs of marginalised groups	Ensure the needs and concerns of the vulnerable and marginalised are able to be articulated and are responded to.
	Promote a gender-responsive and human rights approach	Promote a gender-sensitive approach and mainstream human rights, to help meet the needs of those who may otherwise be marginalised and to address some of the causal factors of injustices and inequalities which compromise rule of law efforts, while recognising there may be tension with other principles, including that of local ownership.
	Engage informal security and justice mechanisms	Utilise the strengths and opportunities presented by informal security and justice mechanisms in advancing the rule of law, whilst not ignoring the problems.

Principle	Recommendation	Task
Context-specificity	Ensure programmes and activities are context-specific	Recognise that programmes and activities need to be informed by an understanding of the unique context if they are to be successful and sustainable.
	Remain flexible and responsive	Be flexible to changing dynamics and developments.
Learning Lessons	Share knowledge and best practice	Utilise and share institutional knowledge and the results of successful programmes, with a comprehensive understanding of the local context and an integration of conflict analyses into programme development and implementation.

Conclusion

This chapter has discussed challenges associated with rule of law initiatives in post-conflict environments. Chief among these, as highlighted, is the fact that there is little consensus on what 'the rule of law' means and that, fundamentally, it is a highly political concept, concerning the relationship between the citizen and the state, and the rights and obligations of each. Nonetheless, there is broad agreement that establishing the rule of law in places emerging from conflict is of fundamental importance. Operationally, there are also a number of tangible, if broad, recommendations based upon recent rule of law initiatives, which could improve the effectiveness of similar interventions and contribute to peacebuilding, even if there remain multiple and sometimes competing understandings of what the rule of law is and, thus, how it should be developed. These recommendations include adhering to and promoting the principles which should generally guide peacebuilding interventions, namely the principles of inclusive local ownership, gender equality and context specificity, and that interventions are evidence-based and comprehensively planned, co-ordinated and coherent with other efforts, adequately resourced and effectively communicated.

Summary of Key Issues

- The 'rule of law' is an abstract concept and while it is a widely contested term, it is generally considered to be critical to peaceful societies.
- The rule of law is political, concerning as it does the relationship between the citizen and the state, and the rights and obligations of each.
- The increasing recognition of the interdependence of security, the rule of law, governance, development and human rights has expanded the involvement of actors and issues outside the security and justice sector in rule of law activities.

- Given the lack of consensus on what the 'rule of law' means, it is not surprising that there are different understandings of what rule of law activities involve on the ground.
- Rule of law activities often involve legal reform and reforming or reconstructing the criminal justice system, including oversight bodies that play a role in maintaining the rule of law and holding public officials and institutions to account.
- While contentious, rule of law activities can also include building the capacity and professionalism of other security sector institutions; transitional justice measures; and efforts with regard to gender justice, juvenile justice, property and land rights, and broader human rights protection.
- Many consider preconditions for the rule of law include equal access to justice, a just legal framework and public order where crime and violence are minimal and the rights of individuals are protected; these preconditions or prerequisites tend to inform the type of rule of law activity undertaken.
- The 2000 Brahimi Report emphasised the importance of establishing the rule of law in post-conflict environments and paved the way for formal rule of law components to be integrated into UN peacekeeping operations.
- There are a number of challenges that frustrate efforts to implement rule of law programmes, including those of a conceptual, security, political, financial and practical nature.
- Rule of law initiatives should generally be context-specific, well-planned and co-ordinated, locally owned, inclusive, responsive to the needs of marginalised and vulnerable groups, gender responsive, flexible, and cognisant of informal security and justice mechanisms as well as best practice.

Reflective Question

How can informal justice mechanisms be incorporated into rule of law activities in post-conflict environments without compromising the reason why they may enjoy the trust and confidence of the people (as a result, for example, of drawing them into external programmes or formal structures)?

List of Core Resources

Baker, B. (2017) 'Policing for conflict zones: What have local policing groups taught us?, *Stability: International Journal of Security and Development*, 6(1): 9, 1–16.

Batesmith, A. (2015) *How 'International' Lawyers can Work More Effectively with their National Counterparts*, (University of Leicester) (video). Available at www.youtube.com/watch?v=ZwgZLSt8x_w&index=14&list=PLjQX5EX gm57STSvD19VcobrSyhF5pey-U.

Bellamy, A. and Williams, P. (2010) 'Policing', Chapter 17, *Understanding Peacekeeping*, (Cambridge: Polity Press): 377–96.

Centre for International Governance Innovation (CIGI) (2010) *Rule of Law and Justice Development in Post-Conflict with Jasteena Dhillon* (video). Available at www.youtube.com/watch?v=oAVcOua17S8.

Chuter, D. (2015) *The Security Sector in a Law-based State: A Short Guide for Practitioners and Others*, pre-publication draft (may be cited). Available at www.davidchuter.com/Texts/ChuterROLBook.pdf.

Delcourt, B. (2016) 'The Rule of Law as a Vehicle for Intervention', *Journal of Intervention and Statebuilding*, 9(4): 471–94.

Donais, T., (2017). 'Engaging Non-State Security Providers: Whither the rule of law?', *Stability: International Journal of Security and Development*, 6(1): 7, 1–13.

Geneva Centre for the Democratic Control of Armed Forces (DCAF) (2015a) *The Justice Sector*, SSR Backgrounder Series (Geneva: DCAF). Available at www.dcaf.ch/sites/default/files/publications/documents/DCAF_BG_6_The%20 Justice%20Sector.11.15.pdf.

Global Policy (2013) *Chandra Lekha Sriram – Justice Programming in Conflict Affected and Transitioning Countries* (video). Available at www.youtube.com/watch?v=pvB4jXnDIX8.

Hills, A. (2009) *Policing Post-Conflict Cities* (London and New York: Zed Books).

International Security Sector Advisory Team (ISSAT) (2015) *Piet Biesheuvel on police and justice* (video). Available at www.youtube.com/watch?v=bLL0MAjZnLo.

Luccaro, T. (2016) *Customary Justice: An Introduction to Basic Concepts, Strengths, and Weaknesses*, International Network to Promote the Rule of Law (INPROL) Practitioner's Guide, September 2016. Available at www.inprol.org/publications/15761/customary-justice-an-introduction-to-basic-concepts-strengths-and-weaknesses.

O'Connor, V. (2015) *Defining the Rule of Law and Related Concepts*, INPROL Practitioner's Guide. Available at www.inprol.org/publications/14549/defining-the-rule-of-law-and-related-concepts.

O'Connor, V. (2015) *Mapping the Justice System and Legal Framework in a Conflict-Affected Country*, INPROL Practitioner's Guide. Available at www.inprol.org/publications/14887/mapping-the-justice-system-and-legal-framework-in-a-conflict-affected-country.

O'Connor, V. (2015) *Understanding the International Rule of Law Community, Its History, and Its Practice*, INPROL Practitioner's Guide. Available at www.inprol.org/publications/14886/understanding-the-international-rule-of-law-community-its-history-and-its.

Rule of Law Legal Studies (2012) *Video 1 – The Rule of Law* (video). Available at www.youtube.com/watch?v=0Hubr8mZlIc.

Sharwood-Smith, C. (2015) Preparing Police Peacekeepers, (University of Leicester) (video). Available at www.youtube.com/watch?v=YVZz6o9XUdU.

United States Institute of Peace (USIP)/US Army Peacekeeping and Stability Operations Institute (2009), 'Rule of Law', Section 7, *Guiding Principles for Stabilization and Reconstruction* (Washington: USIP): 63–96. Available at www.usip.org/sites/default/files/guiding_principles_full.pdf.

UNOHCHR (2016) *Human Rights and Traditional Justice Systems in Africa* (New York: UN). Available at www.ohchr.org/Documents/Publications/HR_PUB_16_2_HR_and_Traditional_Justice_Systems_in_Africa.pdf.

5 Transitional Justice

Overview

The concept usually known as 'transitional justice' has arisen, slowly and erratically, over the last quarter of a century, to find now a prominent place in post-conflict transformation. It is often presented as a means whereby post-conflict societies can address atrocities committed in war. This chapter considers the definition of transitional justice and its historical origins. It addresses the advertised objectives of transitional justice and outlines the key transitional justice mechanisms that are available, including truth-seeking processes, prosecution initiatives, reparations, institutional reform and memorialisation. The concluding section details some of the challenges and dilemmas in the field of transitional justice, with specific reference to what is often called the 'peace versus justice' debate.

Learning Outcomes

- Articulate the declared key objectives of transitional justice
- Be familiar with the key transitional justice mechanisms, as well as their particular strengths and weaknesses
- Identify some of the challenges and dilemmas in the field of transitional justice
- Propose ways in which some of the identified challenges and dilemmas can be addressed

Part 1 – Historical Context

Transitional justice is about addressing atrocities committed during conflict in order to be able to move forward and build peace. The need to acknowledge atrocities, redress impunity and respond to the needs of the victims is necessary if grievances and fears are to be addressed, if justice and the rule of law are to be meaningful, and if further atrocities are to be prevented. Without addressing grievances or instilling the rule of law, for instance, sustainable peace is unlikely. Indeed, some people consider that the Balkans conflicts erupted 50 years after the end of World War II precisely because crimes were left unaddressed and led to grievances and memories of atrocities feeding discourses of victimisation and nationalism (Ostojić, 2014). While conflict is inherently violent and destructive, there are parameters within which parties to the conflict should act; there are limits to the violence that can be inflicted. How these legal parameters came about will now be discussed.

Warfare has always been immensely destructive. During the Hundred Years' War between England and France (roughly 1300–1450), the population of France was reduced by half, because of the interrelated scourges of war, famine and the Black Death. The 30 Years' War (1618–48), arguably the most destructive war in European history, is estimated to have caused eight million deaths – proportionate to the population, this is a much higher death rate than that of the same area in World War II (Chuter, 2017; Wilson, 2009).

International codification of the rules of war – formally known as international humanitarian law – to control and limit war's brutality, began with the original Geneva Convention of 1864, entitled the Geneva Convention for the Amelioration of the Condition of the Wounded in Armies in the Field. As the title suggests, it was concerned only with protecting the provision of medical assistance to the wounded on the battlefield regardless of their nationality and protecting medical personnel by recognising their neutrality (ICRC, 2019). The Geneva Convention was spearheaded by a man called Henry Dunant, motivated by what he had witnessed during the Battle of Solferino in 1859 (part of the Second War for Italian Independence). His lobbying efforts also resulted in the establishment of the International Committee of the Red Cross (ICRC, 2019). The original Geneva Convention was expanded in 1906 and greatly expanded in the four Conventions of 1949. Two Additional Protocols were negotiated in 1977 (ICRC, 2019) (see Box 5.1).

This tradition, to do with treatment of non-combatants or those no longer taking part in hostilities (if they are wounded or taken as prisoner, for instance), is sometimes referred to as the 'Geneva' tradition and coexists with the so-called 'Hague' tradition, designed to make war more humane, and to ban or restrict certain weapons (see Box 5.2). They were effectively brought together by the 1998 Rome Statute of the International Criminal Court (ICC), hereafter referred to

---

Box 5.1: The Geneva Conventions (1949) and the Two Additional Protocols (1977)

- The Geneva Convention (I) for the Amelioration of the Condition of the Wounded and Sick in Armed Forces in the Field
- The Geneva Convention (II) for the Amelioration of the Condition of Wounded, Sick and Shipwrecked Members of Armed Forces at Sea
- The Geneva Convention (III) relative to the Treatment of Prisoners of War
- The Geneva Convention (IV) relative to the Protection of Civilian Persons in Time of War
- The Protocol Additional to the Geneva Conventions and relating to the Protection of Victims of International Armed Conflicts (Protocol I)
- The Protocol Additional to the Geneva Conventions and relating to the Protection of Victims of Non-International Armed Conflicts (Protocol II).

Box 5.2: The Hague Conventions

The Hague Conventions of 1899 and 1907 bring together a number of international treaties and declarations, including the Convention with respect to the Laws and Customs of War on Land, the Declaration concerning the Prohibition of the Use of Projectiles with the Sole Object to Spread Asphyxiating Poisonous Gases, and the Declaration Prohibiting the Discharge of Projectiles and Explosives from Balloons.

The Hague Conventions and the Geneva Conventions are among the first formal statements concerning the laws of war established in the body of international law.

---

as the Rome Statute, establishing the ICC, which entered into force in 2002 (UN, 2002). The Statute, as often with legal texts, reproduced wholesale much of the language of earlier treaties and stands as a useful summary of the law of armed conflict as it now exists (Chuter, 2017; ICC, 2019; ICRC, 2008).

The first treaties were signed at a time of optimism when it was hoped that war was becoming obsolete, if only because it was so expensive and destructive, and that it could be made more humane. Yet, in a kind of overture to the First World War (WWI), the two Balkan Wars of 1912–13, first against the Ottomans and then among the victorious states, were fought with unparalleled brutality (Evans, 2016). In WWI, the level of barbarity of Russian forces in particular towards the civilian population between 1915 and 1917 helps to explain the ease with which Nazi policies in the area were accepted a generation later (Watson, 2014). The post-war chaos in the region was, if anything, more brutal still (Chuter, 2017; Gerwarth, 2016).

There were several reasons why civilians were increasingly becoming, not just collateral damage, but actual targets. These wars were mainly among multi-ethnic states created from the ruins of the Hapsburg and Ottoman Empires, and largely fought to create a new type of ethno-nationalist entity, in which someone of another ethnicity was automatically an existential threat. This encouraged what would later be called 'ethnic cleansing', sometimes on a massive scale, with the murder and expulsion of hundreds of thousands of Armenians from Turkey in 1915, and the 'population exchanges' between Greece and Turkey that followed the war of 1919–22 (Chuter, 2017).

To this must be added the vague but highly influential concept of Social Darwinism, which foresaw competition between 'races', to the point of extermination. The nadir was no doubt World War II (WWII), especially on the Eastern Front, where the German High Command gave written orders that Soviet prisoners were not entitled to the protection of the Geneva Conventions; over 3.3 million were subsequently executed, worked to death in concentration camps, or just left to die of hunger and cold (Niewyk and Nicosia, 2000).

Civilians were treated even worse, if that is possible. Those viewed as racially inferior and, indeed, sub-human by the Nazis were enslaved, expelled or killed, leading to the partial destruction of the Jewish, Roma, Slavic peoples in Europe and others considered to be 'undesirable' or 'inferior'. Seventeen million people were killed in the Holocaust, including 6 million Jews (about two-thirds of their population in Europe at that time), up to half a million Roma (about half of their population in Europe at that time), Polish citizens (including approximately 1.9 million non-Jewish Poles and 3 million Jewish Poles), other Slavic groups, prisoners-of-war (including over 3.3 million Russian POWs referred to above), Soviet citizens, homosexuals, black people, Jehovah's Witnesses, disabled people and political opponents, overall including 1.5 million children (Niewyk and Nicosia, 2000; United States Holocaust Memorial Museum, 2018).

By this stage, the Geneva Conventions were already a century old. However, the immense destruction of WWII created a favourable opportunity for the International Committee of the Red Cross (ICRC), which had been working on drafts for some years, to present ambitious proposals for updating and extending them. After long negotiations, principally involving the victorious allied powers, four much longer and more complex texts were agreed in 1949. As with all treaties, there were lacunae, compromises and contradictions – the British, for example, could hardly accept the criminalisation of the indiscriminate bombing of civilians, since they had been doing precisely that since 1941 (Best, 1994). Thus, it can be seen that the process by which criminality, and even moral responsibility, is determined is dependent upon exactly how the balance of political forces results in the drafting of a particular technical provision (Chuter, 2017).

The 1949 Geneva Conventions entered into force once the Cold War was underway, but it was not until the early 1990s that there was a renewed focus on holding to account those responsible for atrocities. This is, in part, because of the brutality and proximity (to Western Europe, at least) of the Balkans conflicts in the 1990s. There were also technological developments which enabled real-time footage of the war to be brought home to the desks of policy-makers and living rooms of electorates. The constraints and practices of news media outlets tended to result in over-simplified, partial portrayals of what was going on; supposedly easily identifiable aggressors and victims also lent credence to renewed focus on transitional justice. This also relates to the 'CNN effect', as discussed in Chapter 2, which put enormous pressure on governments to step in and act in order to prevent human rights violations.

In respect of the Balkans conflicts, for instance, reports of mass atrocities led to the UN establishing a Commission of Experts in 1992 to investigate on the ground. This Commission reported numerous violations of international humanitarian law, including grave breaches of the Geneva Conventions (ICTY, 2019). In response, the UN Security Council established the International Criminal Tribunal for the former Yugoslavia (ICTY) in 1993. It was hoped that threat of retribution would help to end the fighting, as diplomatic efforts were failing and military intervention was unsupported. The ICTY was the first war crimes court the UN had established. It was followed the next year by the establishment of the International Criminal Tribunal for Rwanda (ICTR). The ICTR was established a few months after the Rwandan genocide which killed over 800,000 ethnic Tutsi and politically moderate Hutu earlier in the year. It was established in light of the failure of the international community to take effective action to prevent and respond to the genocide, including the failure of the UN Assistance Mission for Rwanda (UNAMIR) to effectively respond to the violence, in part due to the limitations of its mandate, and the refusal on the part of major powers to even acknowledge that a genocide had occurred (for doing so would have warranted robust action in the form of deploying troops, for instance) (Dallaire, 2003; Winfield, 1999).

Part 2 – Objectives, Measures and Processes

The preamble of the Rome Statute draws attention to the crimes that transitional justice seeks to address:

> ... during this century, millions of children, women and men have been victims of unimaginable atrocities that deeply shock the conscience of humanity. (UN, 2002: preamble)

War is defined by extreme aggression and mass casualties. Combatants, but also innocent civilians, may be harmed or killed. All of this can be, but is not always, quite legal. Unlike a domestic jurisdiction, where a body riddled with bullets is a good indication of a crime, the law of armed conflict regulates the circumstances under which such acts are legal or not. A distinction also needs to be drawn between suffering and crime; while there is much suffering in conflict, not all of it constitutes a crime. Skills of investigators and forensic scientists can determine, for instance, whether those killed were engaged in combat at the time of their death, which would ultimately help determine whether or not a crime was committed. For instance, the massacre of more than 8,000 Bosnian Muslims in and around the town of Srebrenica, Bosnia and Herzegovina (BiH), in July 1995, was defended at the trial of General Krstić as a result of fierce fighting that accompanied the 28th Division's attempt to escape to Tuzla. The fact that the executions were with automatic weapons against standing victims, meant that the wounds could, in theory, have been inflicted during legal combat. What showed the incident to be a crime, however, was evidence that at least some of the victims had their hands fastened with ligatures, and so could not have been engaged in combat at the time. Other war crimes are more obvious; Lt. Gen. Romeo Dallaire, Force Commander of the UN Assistance Mission to Rwanda (UNAMIR), 1993–94, wrote of the atrocities committed during the Rwandan genocide in which hundreds of thousands of Tutsi and moderate Hutu were killed in 100 days between April and July 1994 – his reflections also provide a vivid account of the magnitude and scale of the atrocities that transitional justice aims to address:

> ... if you looked, you could see the evidence, even in the whitened skeletons. The legs bent and apart. A broken bottle, a rough branch, even a knife between them. Where the bodies were fresh, we saw what must have been semen pooled on and near the dead women and girls. There was always a lot of blood. Some male corpses had their genitals cut off, but many women and young girls had their breasts chopped off and their genitals crudely cut apart. They died in a

position of total vulnerability, flat on their backs, with their legs bent and knees wide apart. It was the expressions on their dead faces that assaulted me the most, a frieze of shock, pain and humiliation. (Dallaire, 2003: 430)

Crimes addressed by transitional justice

Today, transitional justice is generally perceived as a means whereby, predominantly, post-conflict societies can address genocide, war crimes, crimes against humanity and other gross violations of human rights:

- **Genocide** – refers to acts intending to 'destroy, in whole or in part, a national, ethnical, racial or religious group' (see Box 5.3)
- **Crimes Against Humanity** – refer to serious crimes knowingly committed 'as part of a widespread or systematic attack directed against any civilian population' (see Box 5.4)
- **War Crimes** – refer to serious crimes which violate the Geneva Conventions (see Box 5.5).

The UN Secretary-General has defined transitional justice as 'the full range of processes and mechanisms associated with a society's attempts to come to terms with a legacy of large-scale past abuses, in order to ensure accountability, serve justice and achieve reconciliation' (UNSG, 2010: 2). Broader conceptions of transitional justice also include addressing structural inequalities and other harms (see Mihr and Sriram, 2018), many of which have, in part, contributed to the outbreak of conflict or the serious violations of international law committed during the conflict.

Aims and objectives

It is argued that societies must address large-scale wartime abuses if reconciliation and peace are to be secured. It is often important for those who have been victims. It is often hard for people to let go of the past and begin healing until their suffering has at least been acknowledged; the same can be said of communities and

---

Box 5.3: Genocide

The Rome Statute (Art 6) defines genocide as 'any of the following acts committed with intent to destroy, in whole or in part, a national, ethnical, racial or religious group, as such:

(a) Killing members of the group.
(b) Causing serious bodily or mental harm to members of the group.
(c) Deliberately inflicting on the group conditions of life calculated to bring about its physical destruction in whole or in part.
(d) Imposing measures intended to prevent births within the group.
(e) Forcibly transferring children of the group to another group'.

Box 5.4: Crimes Against Humanity

The Rome Statute (Article 7) defines crimes against humanity as 'any of the following acts when committed as part of a widespread or systematic attack directed against any civilian population, with knowledge of the attack:

(a) Murder.
(b) Extermination.
(c) Enslavement.
(d) Deportation or forcible transfer of population.
(e) Imprisonment or other severe deprivation of physical liberty in violation of fundamental rules of international law.
(f) Torture.
(g) Rape, sexual slavery, enforced prostitution, forced pregnancy, enforced sterilization, or any other form of sexual violence of comparable gravity.
(h) Persecution against any identifiable group or collectivity on political, racial, national, ethnic, cultural, religious, gender as defined in Paragraph 3, or other grounds that are universally recognised as impermissible under international law, in connection with any act referred to in this paragraph or any crime within the jurisdiction of the Court.
(i) Enforced disappearance of persons.
(j) The crime of apartheid.
(k) Other inhumane acts of a similar character intentionally causing great suffering, or serious injury to body or to mental or physical health.'

nations. There is a need for grievances to be addressed and trust to be built, not least to avoid a recurrence of conflict. It is also argued that a message that there will not be impunity for crimes committed during conflict helps promote a rule of law climate whereby people begin to feel they need to rely less on arms and violence to seek justice or protection. Some also argue that efforts to ensure accountability for the most serious crimes committed will act as a form of deterrent for future times or other places. Pursuing transitional justice can also be an effective signalling mechanism that can be used to show governments are breaking away from past practices and promoting accountability, which can help break cycles of violence (see ICTJ, 2019; Greiff, 2010).

The goals of transitional justice have thus been argued to include:

* Addressing, and attempting to heal, divisions in society that arise as a result of human rights violations
* Bringing closure and healing the wounds of individuals and society, particularly through 'truth telling'
* Providing justice to victims and accountability for perpetrators
* Creating an accurate historical record for society
* Restoring the rule of law

> ### Box 5.5: War Crimes
>
> The Rome Statute (Article 8) defines war crimes as grave breaches of the Geneva Conventions, and other serious violations of the laws and customs applicable in armed conflict (including wilful killing, torture or inhuman treatment, intentionally directing attacks against civilians, committing rape).

- Reforming institutions to promote democratisation and human rights
- Ensuring that human rights violations are not repeated
- Promoting co-existence and sustainable peace (Anderlini, Conaway and Kays, 2007: 1).

The UN (UNSG, 2010) has outlined the principles that should guide transitional justice work as including context-specificity, gender sensitivity, incorporating a child-sensitive approach, aiming to enhance national capacity, ensuring the centrality of victims throughout the design and implementation of programmes or initiatives, endeavouring to address root causes, and promoting a co-ordinated approach among all actors engaged across all transitional justice and rule of law activities. Ideally, decisions about transitional justice measures and processes should be informed by consultation with members of the post-conflict society, particularly victims. Outreach activities are generally essential to any transitional justice programme in order to consult, engage and inform all stakeholders, as well as raise awareness and remove suspicion, doubt or confusion which can result in significant obstacles for the realisation of the aims of transitional justice (see Ramírez-Barat, 2014). Generally, national actors and institutions should lead the process where possible (and, of course, this is not always the case), in order to promote sustainability, relevance and the rule of law. However, there may be times when national capacity and a conducive environment first need to be built, which often entails institutional reform and taking steps towards improved security and reconciliation. Timing and sequencing are also of fundamental importance; rushing decisions can compromise context-specificity and the requisite buy-in and can also be potentially destabilising.

Measures and processes

Since the early 1990s, transitional justice has become an increasingly integral part of peacebuilding efforts. With the growth in transitional justice, an increasing number of judicial and non-judicial means to address past crimes have become available, including prosecution initiatives, truth-seeking processes, memorialisation, reparations programmes and institutional reform. Amnesties are another such means, but are inconsistent with international law and UN policy (UN Office of the High Commissioner for Human Rights – UNOHCHR, 2009). Traditional processes are another means, which can often address some of the challenges posed by more formal means but, as we will see, carry their own challenges too.

Prosecution initiatives

The investigation and prosecution of those alleged to have committed serious violations of international humanitarian law or gross violations of human rights are a key part of transitional justice. Prosecutions are often regarded as being an effective means of delivering justice and sending a message that there will not be impunity for such crimes and thus an effective means of contributing to promoting the rule of law and security and preventing such crimes from recurring. Given the large number of crimes often committed during conflict, and in order to send a strong signal that such crimes will not be tolerated, high-level leaders, whether political or military (those with command responsibility) tend to be prosecuted above others. As will now be discussed in turn, prosecutions can be conducted in-country or by third-party national courts as well as international or hybrid (or mixed national and international) courts. International courts include ad hoc courts (such as the ICTY and ICTR) and the ICC.

Domestic and third-party prosecutions

In-country prosecutions are generally considered to be the most effective in terms of promoting justice, reconciliation and sustainable recovery from conflict. Often, however, particularly in the immediate aftermath of conflict, the requisite in-country capacity and political will is absent. Where domestic courts are unable or unwilling to address past abuses, third party national courts have done so under the principle of universal jurisdiction, which concerns those crimes that are so serious that all countries have an interest in prosecuting them and include war crimes, crimes against humanity and genocide (see Sriram et al., 2017).

International and hybrid criminal tribunals

Over the last quarter century, the UN has established a number of international and hybrid criminal tribunals, including the International Criminal Tribunal for the former Yugoslavia (ICTY), the International Criminal Tribunal for Rwanda (ICTR) and mixed tribunals for Sierra Leone, Cambodia, Kosovo, Bosnia and Herzegovina (in the form of a Special Chamber in the State Court of Bosnia and Herzegovina) and, more recently, the Central African Republic (CAR). While expensive and doing relatively little to build domestic judicial capacity, these international and hybrid criminal tribunals were deemed to have 'enhanced the global character of the rule of law' (UNSG, 2004b: 14). They have also helped enable public denunciation of criminal acts, victims reclaim dignity, and the removal of the most serious offenders from political life and public office. They have also promoted accountability, countered impunity and increased public confidence in the state's ability and willingness to abide by and enforce the law (UNSG, 2004b).

The ad hoc International Tribunal for the Prosecution of Persons Responsible for Serious Violations of International Humanitarian Law Committed in the Territory of the Former Yugoslavia since 1991, commonly referred to as the International Criminal Tribunal for the former Yugoslavia (ICTY), was established in 1993, pursuant to UN Security Council Resolution (UNSCR) 827. It was established to judge those allegedly responsible for grave breaches of the Geneva Conventions, violations of the laws or customs of war, genocide and crimes against humanity committed during the Balkans conflicts since 1991. It was considered necessary to establish because, like the ICTR that followed it, there was insufficient domestic capacity or political will to prosecute those responsible; given the serious nature and extent of the crimes involved it was considered necessary for prosecutions to address wrongs, signal the end of impunity and help contribute to reconciliation – as well as serve as a deterrent for other places and other times.

The ICTY comprised the Chambers (three trial chambers and one appeals chamber, which included 86 judges from 52 UN Member States over the lifetime of the ICTY), the Registry (responsible for the administration of the Court and the Detention Unit for indictees while on trial) and the Office of the Prosecutor (the OTP, which was responsible for investigating and prosecuting individuals). In total, 161 people were indicted by the ICTY, of whom 89 were sentenced (see Figure 5.1). After sentencing, those convicted were transferred to one of the many countries which had signed agreements with the UN to carry out custodial sentences. Many of those indicted held senior positions in the military, police force and government, including Slobodan Milošević, who was the first sitting head of state indicted for war crimes. The final indictments were issued in 2004 and the last judgement was issued in November 2017, a month before the Tribunal ceased to exist (December 2017). The Mechanism for International Criminal Tribunals (MICT) was established by the UN Security Council in 2010 to perform any residual functions of the ICTY and ICTR, including overseeing sentences and hearing any outstanding appeals.

The International Criminal Tribunal for Rwanda (ICTR) was established in 1994, pursuant to UNSCR 955 to judge those allegedly responsible for the 1994 Rwandan genocide, as well as other serious violations of international law on the territory of Rwanda or neighbouring territories in 1994. The Rwandan genocide involved the killing of over 800,000 ethnic Tutsi and politically moderate Hutu over approximately 100 days in 1994 (April to July), directed by the Hutu-majority government. The Tribunal was located in Arusha in 1995, pursuant to UNSCR 977 and was officially closed on 31 December 2015. Like the ICTY, the ICTR was comprised of the Chambers (three trial chambers and one appeals chamber), the Registry (responsible for the administration of the Court) and the Office of the Prosecutor (the OTP, which was responsible for investigating and prosecuting individuals). In total, 93 people were indicted by the court, of whom 61 were convicted and sentenced, 14 acquitted, 3 died before judgement, 2 had their charges withdrawn, 5 were referred to national jurisdictions for trial and 8 remain at large (ICTR, 2018).

The ICTY and ICTR have been repeatedly criticised for being costly, slow and, as a consequence, relatively ineffective. Both courts have had annual budgets in the millions of US dollars and only a small number of indictments and sentences (see Sriram et al., 2017). Each case has required a huge number of testimonies and evidence. For the 161 ICTY indictees there were 4,650 witnesses, for instance. The number of testimonies required also increases the time and cost involved in each case, which can be perceived to further hinder justice (see Figure 5.1 for a comparative overview of the number of indictments, sentences, witnesses and financial cost).

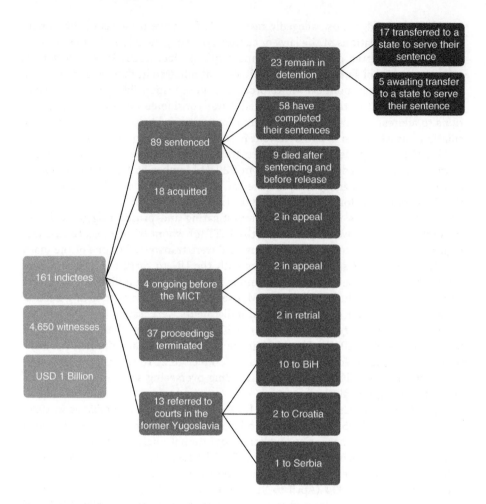

Figure 5.1 ICTY Figures (ICTY, 2017, 2019)

The harm caused by testifying – as a result of reliving traumatic experiences and facing alleged perpetrators – is also a cost that needs be borne in mind (although some witnesses have attested to the psychological benefit of testifying – see ICTY, 2019). While the harm caused by testifying and the financial cost of running the international tribunals can be considered to outweigh the benefit of prosecuting and sentencing a handful of those responsible for the most serious crimes during the conflicts, it should also be remembered that each case often involves thousands of victims. For instance, crimes related to the genocide in and around Srebrenica involved 20 indictees, 1,000 witnesses and 8,000 victims. The benefits also extend beyond justice for many thousands of victims to an important declaration that impunity will no longer be tolerated and a message of deterrence to other would-be violators.

These courts have also been criticised for limited engagement with local populations and doing little to build domestic judicial capacity. Steps were taken, however, by both courts to build domestic capacity, reach out to domestic and other audiences, and expedite cases. The courts have also done much to advance the understanding of gender crimes – since the trial of Kunarac, Kovač and Vuković in the ICTY it is clear that rape can be a war crime (see Box 5.6) – and to provide many lessons learned for the International Criminal Court (ICC) and hybrid tribunals. Additionally, the message that those who are indicted will not escape the reach of the law – as indicated, for instance, by the arrest and extradition in 2011 of Ratko Mladić to the ICTY, nearly 16 years after having been indicted for genocide, war

---

Box 5.6: Rape as a War Crime, a Crime Against Humanity and Genocide

As will be discussed further in Chapter 10, conflict-related sexual violence (CRSV) is widely prevalent in many conflicts; this involves rape, sexual slavery and other forms of sexual violence, sometimes used as a military strategy or tactic to terrorise communities and sometimes as an opportunistic practice that forms part of the continuum of violence against women and girls (see Wood, 2014).

In prosecutions, crimes involving sexual violence against women have tended not to be regarded with the same seriousness as other war crimes or crimes against humanity. Indeed, while rape, for example, has been prohibited under the Geneva Conventions (article 27 of the 4th Geneva Convention) since 1949, particularly until recently it has rarely been prosecuted.

However, the ICTY advanced international gender justice through a number of landmark judgements, by enabling the prosecution of sexual violence including rape as a war crime, a crime against humanity and genocide. These judgements have raised the profile of crimes of sexual violence in conflict and helped show that such crimes can be 'a powerful tool of war, used to intimidate, persecute and terrorise the enemy' rather than simply 'the unrestrained sexual behaviour of individuals' (ICTY, 2019). Crucially, they have 'paved the way for more robust adjudication of such crimes worldwide' (ICTY, 2019).

While crimes of sexual violence were prohibited in the Geneva Conventions, it was not until the ICTY and ICTR that such crimes were prosecuted as a crime against humanity. Landmark cases at the ICTY include the first international war crimes trial which involved charges of sexual violence, which was also the first-ever trial for sexual violence against men (the trial of Duško Tadić, who was sentenced in 2000 to 20 years' imprisonment). In a subsequent trial (concerning crimes committed in the Čelebići prison camp), rape was deemed to be a form of torture for the first time in any judgement by an international criminal tribunal. In the first ICTY case focussed entirely on charges of sexual violence (against Anto Furundžija, local commander of a special unit of the military police of the Croatian Defence Council (HVO)), rape was widened from potentially constituting a crime against humanity to also a grave breach of the Geneva Conventions and a violation of the

(Continued)

laws and customs of war. In the second ICTY trial to focus solely on charges of sexual violence, the judgement included sexual enslavement for the first time as a crime against humanity, and the three accused (Kunarac, Vuković and Kovač) were the first to be convicted by the ICTY of rape as a crime against humanity (following the precedent set by the ICTR in the Akayesu case). A later trial against Krstić established a link for the first time between rape and ethnic cleansing, deemed to be linked to genocide with regard to the crimes committed in Srebrenica in 1995 (ICTY, 2019).

While these are substantial successes, there have been criticisms levied against ICTY and ICTR that more could have been done, particularly with regard to the minimal sentences given to some found guilty of such crimes, the limited number of convictions due to deficiencies in investigations or lack of evidence, and the charges of rape in some instances being dropped in exchange for admitting guilt to other crimes (Crider, 2012).

Improvements have been made with the International Criminal Court (ICC), learning from the errors of the ICTY and ICTR and responding to sustained and significant pressure by civil society women's organisations. There was pressure, for instance, for the ICC to recognise and engage gender expertise, including expertise on SGBV. Hitherto, testimonies provided by women in international courts were not taken as seriously, excuses were made that evidence of crimes involving SGBV was too hard to gather, and the burden of proof was much more significant for such cases than others (see Chappell, 2016).

However, there remain many shortcomings with cases incolving SGBV at the ICC. For instance, there have been cases where charges of SGBV have not been added to other charges (Lubanga), where the accused has been convicted of all crimes except SGBV crimes (Katanga), and where the accused has been found guilty of crimes against humanity and war crimes involving SGBV only to have been acquitted on appeal (Bemba); in all cases victims/survivors of SGBV have not received justice or reparations (Chappell, 2018).

crimes and crimes against humanity committed in the Srebrenica genocide and siege of Sarajevo (he was eventually convicted and given a life sentence in 2017) – is an important message to send to would-be violators of international humanitarian law and international human rights law.

Some of the other challenges faced by the ad hoc tribunals, which also apply to the ICC (see Chuter, 2012 and 2003), include that the legal texts (notably the Geneva Conventions) had never been intended as a basis for prosecutions (the Geneva Conventions, for instance compelled criminal legislation to be enacted regarding grave breaches of the Convention, and also did not even compel prosecution for intrastate or non-international conflicts – see Wouters, 2005), and the meaning of even the most elementary terms was often disputed. Fundamental legal questions had to be decided in the first trials. Further, prosecutors and investigators came from a variety of different legal traditions, where court procedures, standards of proof, rules of evidence, treatment of witnesses and legal definitions vary widely. This added value at times, but could cause confusion and cost time at others. Additionally, judges are appointed by governments and, combined with the perception that trials were used by the international community for political purposes, this caused some concern (see Voeten, 2009; Ford, 2013). Other obstacles concerned obstruction of investigations by local communities, tension between different elements of the UN system (notably the ICTY and UNMIK – see UN, 2006) and, particularly in the early days, weaknesses in witness protection.

It was partly the challenges faced by the ad hoc tribunals that encouraged the development of hybrid or mixed tribunals, often using international and national law as well as international and national judges, and usually based in the post-conflict state. They are less costly than international courts – although they are not entitled to compulsory contributions from UN Member States and have no powers to demand extradition of suspects from other territories. They can also be more effective at building the capacity of the domestic justice sector as well as public confidence in state institutions, which is instrumental to sustainable peace and security (see Sriram et al., 2017).

There have been hybrid or mixed tribunals in a number of countries, including Sierra Leone, Cambodia, Kosovo, Bosnia and Herzegovina (BiH) and the Central African Republic (CAR). In Kosovo, for instance, in part because the ICTY had limited capacity to try many cases, and in part because there were serious concerns about the capacity of courts in Kosovo and the ability to try such cases without bias, the international community agreed to the appointment of international judges and prosecutors to oversee the administration of justice (Sriram et al., 2017). These international judges and prosecutors presided over a number of cases, including war crimes cases. While these mixed courts enabled a backlog of war crimes cases to be heard and guarded against bias and intimidation, there were a number of concerns voiced about the independence of the judges (from the UN Interim Administration Mission in Kosovo – UNMIK), due process (given that defence lawyers were not as adequately resourced as international prosecutors), and the limited focus on war crimes after 2002 (with only six cases opened between 2002 and 2007) (Sriram et al. 2017). As with other hybrid or mixed courts, questions around the issue of accountability – with such courts often regarded as foreign courts – risk undermining the potential that such courts have of promoting justice while building national capacity and ownership.

International Criminal Court

The International Criminal Court (ICC) is 'the first permanent, treaty based, international criminal court established to help end impunity for the perpetrators of the most serious crimes of concern to the international community' (ICC, 2019: n.p.). It was established by the 1998 Rome Statute on 1 July 2002. It was greeted by the UN Secretary-General, as 'the most significant recent development in the international community's long struggle to advance the cause of justice and rule of law' (UNSG, 2004b: 16). It investigates and prosecutes individuals responsible for genocide, war crimes and crimes against humanity committed since 1 July 2002 where countries are unable or unwilling to do so. There are, however, two important caveats: national courts retain priority and the Statute is only bind-ing on signatories, unless the UN Security Council chooses to intervene.

By the end of 2018 there were 123 States Parties to the Statute of the Court (ICC, 2019). Burundi was also a State Party, but withdrew in October 2017. A further 31 countries have signed but not ratified the Rome Statute, four of which (US, Israel, Sudan and Russia) have since effectively unsigned it, having informed the UN Secretary General that they do not intend to become State Parties and thus are no longer obliged to refrain from acts which would defeat the object and purpose of the treaty. As at 2018, a further 41 UN Member States have neither signed nor acceded to the treaty. Those countries that have not ratified the Rome Statute can only be investigated by the ICC if referred by the UN Security Council (ICC, 2019).

Like the ICTY and ICTR, the ICC can only handle a small number of cases because of the time and cost involved in each individual case, and it is located in Europe. Unlike them, it is a permanent organisation, and so must continually justify its existence and costs. Its first prosecutor was strongly criticised for what appeared to be poorly conceived and politically motivated investigations and indictments intended to keep the organisation in the public eye (Flint and De Waal, 2009). It has also been criticised, as have the ICTY and ICTR, for adversely affect-ing efforts to resolve or prevent a recurrence of conflict. In Uganda, for instance, the leader of the Lord's Resistance Army (LRA), Joseph Kony, refused to sign a peace accord in April 2008 unless ICC arrest warrants for LRA members were removed (Sriram et al., 2017). More generally, the court's exclusive focus on Africa has angered many states in the region and led a number to withdraw, and a threat-ened mass withdrawal of African Union members in 2017 (Rieff, 2018), thinking it wrong for a Security Council whose permanent members are lukewarm or hostile to the Court to use it as a political weapon. There has been particular anger at what African states see as the cynical employment of the ICC as a device to get rid of President Bashir of Sudan, thus frustrating their attempts at a peaceful settlement. But this should have come as no surprise: western states, sure that their own pro-cedures were sufficient, saw the Court essentially as a new tool for crisis resolu-tion, especially in Africa. As the then-British Foreign Secretary Robin Cook assured Parliament, there was no question of western leaders being indicted for episodes such as the just-concluded Kosovo crisis (Bosco, 2014: 66). In addition, the pattern of signatures, and the ability of large states to protect their allies, resulted in the concern that, in practice, only small weak states would ever be investigated anyway (Chuter, 2012).

Truth-seeking processes

Prosecutions are limited in the effect they can have, not least because costs, case-loads and politics ensure that only a fraction of those who have committed past abuses will ever be tried. Other transitional justice measures can help overcome the limitations of prosecutions, particularly in terms of providing a record of what hap-pened in the conflict.

Truth-seeking processes – such as truth and reconciliation commissions (or truth commissions), freedom of information legislation, investigations into missing persons and the declassification of archives – can be effective in documenting and demonstrating acknowledgement of abuses (ICTJ, 2019). Truth and reconciliation commissions involve the collection of evidence – from official sources, victims and others – and the publication of reports and recommendations (see Box 5.7 on the South African Truth and Reconciliation Commission; see also USIP's Truth Commission Digital Collection (USIP, 2011) for a wealth of information on truth commissions). There have been over 20 truth commissions over the last two decades, generally pursued by local actors (Jackson and Beswick, 2018). They are non-judicial inquiries to establish an accepted historical record and recognise the suffering caused, through documented interviews with victims and individuals responsible for violations of international law.

Truth-seeking processes are generally short-term – often lasting between six months and two years – and often result in the publication of a report of findings and recommendations, which should, ideally, be widely disseminated (see Dobbins, Seth, Keith and DeGrasse, 2007). In principle, more than prosecutions, truth-seeking processes can focus on wider issues than single criminal culpability, including structural factors which may have led to the crimes (see La Rosa and Philippe, 2009). While the intention is that such commissions can contribute to personal and societal healing and reconciliation processes as well as help prevent recurrence of such abuses, their actual impact is, inevitably, impossible to measure.

Like trials, they originated more or less by accident, in Latin America in the 1980s, with the departure of military regimes. The new civilian regimes wanted to deal with the question of political dissidents who had been murdered by their

---

Box 5.7: The South African Truth and Reconciliation Commission

After the end of apartheid in South Africa, the African National Congress (ANC) and other members of the struggle for liberation wanted trials of those apartheid leaders responsible for serious crimes committed during the apartheid period, whereas many of those leaders sought a blanket amnesty – as is often the case, of course, to evade punishment. The compromise between prosecution and amnesty was a Truth and Reconciliation Commission (TRC) (see Asmal et al., 1997; Garkawe, 2003). This compromise was inspired by Latin American examples (such as truth commissions in Argentina and Chile), where disagreements over whether or not there should be amnesties for serious violations of international law had arisen before. The compromise in South Africa, however, had the addition of a 'reconciliation' element in order to legitimise a peaceful transfer of power. This compromise arose after an unprecedented, extensive public consultation process and a year-long debate on the legislation establishing the Commission (Garkawe, 2003). The TRC was successful in that civil war was averted, which was really its purpose. But in spite of the high moral tone of the proceedings, it was fundamentally a pragmatic political deal to avert conflict. Moreover, because it dealt only with symptoms, the deeper underlying questions of apartheid and political and economic power were not addressed (Chuter, 2017; Wilson, 2001).

predecessors. Prosecutions were not politically feasible, not only because of the residual power of the military, but also because the societies were still very divided, with important sections of the population supporting the military governments. All that was possible was to discover the 'truth' about those who had disappeared during the dictatorships and, to an extent, this was achieved (Chuter, 2017).

Where such commissions have existed as an alternative to prosecutions, as in the case of South Africa, criticisms have been raised that reconciliation cannot occur without justice. On the other hand, where prosecutions have existed in parallel, as in Sierra Leone, for instance, confusion and tension can arise because of conflicting objectives – for instance, when it comes to exposing the truth versus protecting potential evidence. The 'justice versus truth' debate has received less attention in scholarship and practice than the 'justice versus peace' debate, as will shortly be discussed. The debate was prominent in the 1990s in part due to the establishment of the South African TRC at roughly the same time as the ICTY. As Fischer (2011) explains, truth-seeking and truth-telling are essential in light of the role that historical distortion and nationalist myth-making has had in fuelling and sustaining conflicts. There are, however, challenges associated with truth commissions, which have led at times to disillusionment and fixation on the assumed dichotomy between justice and truth (Fischer, 2011). Of course, the dichotomy has been oversimplified, and societies emerging from conflict need to address wrongdoings committed during war-time in a comprehensive, multifaceted way. Boraine (2006), for instance, suggests that both retributive and restorative justice are needed based upon truth, accountability, reparations, reconciliation and institutional reform (see Fischer, 2011).

Memorialisation

Memorialisation refers to an object or event used to remember the suffering of victims of war crimes and other violations of international law, as well as more broadly the victims of conflict. The erection of memorials or museums and other symbolic initiatives to promote memorialisation has occurred in many post-conflict countries (Bickford, 2014; ICTJ, 2019). This is not new and can be itself a source of conflict, as well as a means of promoting understanding and reconciliation. For instance, memorials to wartime resistance heroes in France are still regularly defaced with anti-communist slogans. This is because 'the truth' is a highly ambiguous and partial concept, as historians and lawyers would be the first to acknowledge, and the selection of one 'truth' implicitly excludes all others (Chuter, 2017, 2003) (Figure 5.2).

Reparations

Reparations include material aspects (including financial compensation or the provision of health services) and symbolic aspects (including public apologies or the establishment of a day of remembrance) (ICTJ, 2019). While they constitute a form of acknowledgement and can help victims meet some of the financial costs that they may have incurred, criticism has been levied at reparations that without the

Figure 5.2   Memorialisation – Graffiti in Bogota, Colombia

use of other transitional justice methods – such as prosecutions – reparations can equate to an attempt to buy victims' silence (ICTJ, 2019).

Institutional reform

As will be discussed in more detail later in Chapter 8, the reform and reconstruction of security and justice sector institutions after conflict is often considered an integral part of formal peacebuilding processes. There is a need to build public trust and confidence in these institutions and, particularly in places where they may have been directly involved in war-time atrocities, take steps to guard against the recurrence of such abuses. Reform can include the complete dismantling and reconstruction of these institutions and will often involve the vetting and (re-) recruitment of staff, staff professionalisation and human rights training, the establishment and strengthening of oversight bodies, and legislative reform.

Traditional procedures

Some of the challenges and weaknesses of formal transitional justice measures and processes, which will be discussed further shortly, pose the question of whether traditional justice and reconciliation processes can positively contribute to peacebuilding and be an effective means of processing an enormous number of cases within an acceptable time frame. Examples of such traditional processes include the *gacaca* courts in Rwanda, *magamba* spirits in Mozambique and the *bashingantahe* institution in Burundi (see Huyse and Salter, 2008). The *gacaca* courts in

Rwanda were informal and participatory processes which addressed over 100,000 cases concerning crimes committed during the 1994 genocide, helping to clear a huge backlog of cases and enable access to justice for many thousands of people (see Mihr and Sriram, 2018). Such traditional processes have been criticised for not fulfilling due process rights of defendants and even for weakening justice and the rule of law (see IRIN, 2006; Moore, 2011). Ingelaere (2009) has also argued that *gacaca* courts, for instance, have become a tool of the entrenched elites (see also Mihr and Sriram, 2018). Brouneus (2008) also found that many of the women who have testified before *gacaca* courts were threatened before, during and after the process and remained unconvinced that attitudes of the perpetrators had changed.

When considering traditional procedures, we can also look at attitudes to war and conflict generally in such societies. Although there are cultures that glorify war, many in Africa, for example, see violence and killing as inherently evil, without the technical legal qualifications that westerners employ. Returning combatants must therefore often undergo purification rituals, which wipe away the evil they have done, before being allowed back into the community. These traditions are not unknown in western history, either. The medieval *horror sanguinis*, the shame of the warrior at spilling blood even in a just cause, had to be expiated by penance and reconciliation. This was not a question of guilt based on fear of reprisal, but rather disquiet about what one has done or been obliged to do (Chuter, 2017; Verkamp, 2006).

Part 3 – Challenges and Recommendations

As outlined above, there are a number of transitional justice measures and processes. These different measures and processes are sometimes used in combination, supported by different donors, and can be (as in Sierra Leone) in conflict with each other. The approach taken should ideally be specific to each context. However, with a multiplicity of possible approaches, drawn from many very different situations, and promoted by various internal and external interest groups, choosing what, if any, measure to adopt is extremely difficult. The circumstances following an ethnic conflict are different from those after a political civil war, from those following the overthrow of a dictatorship, from those of an authoritarian government giving way to a democracy, and from those at the end of a contentious, but popular, campaign against separatists or terrorists. Inasmuch as the political objective should be stability – without which no other form of progress is possible – the measures chosen, if any, will be very different in each case. As Andrieu argues (2010: 24), 'there is no turnkey solution for dealing with past abuses. What works in one country might not work in another, depending on numerous political, economic and cultural factors... expressions such as "mass violence" or "mass atrocities" actually hide a wide range of different abuses calling for different forms of justice'. Different cultures will also have affinities with different methods and approaches, whether seeking to punish or forgive, for instance, underscoring the need to ensure that approaches are context-specific (see Andrieu, 2010; Garland, 1990).

Today, there is much enthusiasm for transitional justice programmes in conflict-affected environments because of assumptions that justice, accountability and reconciliation contribute to building the rule of law, peace and stability. However, it is hard to measure whether specific initiatives have contributed to peacebuilding in these ways, not least because such effects take a long time to materialise, are hard to measure and are, in any regard, subjective. Nonetheless, given the time many of these transitional justice measures and processes have been implemented, some evaluation or assessment of their impact is not unreasonable, not least to justify continued and substantial resources. There is, as yet, however, little substantive empirical evidence to show that transitional justice has either a positive or a negative impact on societies (Haider, 2016; Thoms et al., 2010).

As well as being subjective, concepts such as 'truth' and 'justice' are highly politically and emotionally charged. Few alleged perpetrators of war crimes and atrocities, whether before courts or truth commissions, for instance, admit their guilt, or they might provide justification ('I was protecting my people' or 'they would have done the same thing to us'). Individuals, groups and states also deny that atrocities happened (see Cohen's *States of Denial*, 2001). Moreover, it could be asked to what extent transitional justice mechanisms can reveal 'the truth'. For instance, prosecutions are limited in their scope and focus, verdicts are limited to what can be proved, and if the evidence is not available 'the truth' may never be known. Some of the major actors in the fighting in the former Yugoslavia, such as Tudjman, the Croatian leader and Izetbegovic, the leader of the Bosnian Muslims, died before they could be indicted. We may never know what they knew. It is legitimate to ask, therefore, how far the discourse of truth or, indeed, that of reconciliation can take us in such circumstances. Such ethical challenges, often rooted in simplistic binaries which distinguish between victims and perpetrators, are explored further in Box 5.8.

Box 5.8: Beyond Good Versus Evil

Simple binaries of victim/perpetrator and good/evil rarely capture the complexity of warfare. However, many scholars have referred to the construction of a victim/perpetrator dichotomy as defining the recent, dominant model of transitional justice located in a normative liberal framework, which tends to be based in western dominant notions of peace, conflict and security (Shaw and Waldorf, 2010; Hourmat, 2016). Some scholars have argued that the construction of a victim/perpetrator dichotomy demonstrates the political nature and limits of mainstream transitional justice mechanisms, with the victim/perpetrator dichotomy located in the political process of constructing simplified post-conflict narratives and dominant discourses on victimhood (Hourmat, 2016; Kaulemu, 2012). These narratives remove the complexity of warfare and, indeed, social life, and instead construct narratives located in dichotomies and binary oppositions, underpinned by a basic opposition of good versus evil (Hourmat, 2016; Kaulemu, 2012; Turner, 2013).

(Continued)

As Hourmat (2016: 43) argues: 'Settling for a single conflict story and defining a rigid victim-perpetrator dichotomy can be profoundly excluding and limited in capturing the diversity of victimhood and perpetration experiences, memories and perceptions; and can also (re)produce former and new unequal relations of power.'

Prosecutions, in particular, which distinguish between victim and perpetrator, can be disrupted when a victim is not simply a victim or when a perpetrator can also be seen to have been victimised (see Murphy, 2017, for instance). An example which exemplifies the problem with the simple victim/perpetrator binary that is often reified in prosecutions is the case of Dominic Ongwen. The 2005 ICC arrest order of Ugandan Dominic Ongwen highlighted a dilemma that has yet to be resolved: that of crimes against humanity committed by those who have been the victim of the same crimes. Ongwen was forcibly recruited to the Lord's Resistance Army (LRA) at the age of 10 and subsequently served 18 years, rising to command-level positions, and is accused of crimes against humanity. Charges include recruiting other children to the LRA and other crimes alleged to have been committed when he was an adult. He is the first person accused by the ICC of the same crimes of which he was also a victim (see Escola de Cultura de Pau, 2009). His trial began on 6 December 2016, with the defence starting the presentation of its evidence on 27 September 2018 (see ICC, 2019). Child Soldiers International (2019), an international human rights organisation, argues that his experience of having been abducted and recruited as a child to the LRA will have had a significant impact upon him and should be taken into consideration when sentencing, should he be found guilty, but should not absolve him of his responsibility or be used to evade justice. Some scholars argue that 'only by moving beyond the binary distinction between victim-and perpetrator-hood, the complexity of childhood soldiering can be grasped' (Derluyn et al., 2015: n.p.).

The value of truth commissions (while, as we have discussed, there may be no single truth) is that the complexity of conflict can sometimes be better captured, in part because culpability is not always the focus and because many more people can be involved. For instance, Gibson (2004: 76) has suggested that the South African Truth and Reconciliation Commission has resulted in it now being 'difficult for South Africans to characterise the struggle in terms of absolute good vs absolute evil' with a complex but broadly agreed common understanding of the past having been achieved.

More broadly, with respect to the concepts of 'good' and 'evil', as Nietzsche (2000) has elaborated in *On the Genealogy of Morality: A Polemic*, building upon *Beyond Good and Evil: Prelude to a Philosophy of the Future*, what is perceived as good and what are signs of possessing what is good differ between people. Moreover, what is 'good' is generally determined by 'good' (i.e. powerful) people. The law and its institutions are also man-made, of course. So, we need to be careful when assigning labels of 'good' and 'evil' and assuming that conflicts comprise distinct categories of perpetrators and victims.

Bauman (in *Modernity and the Holocaust*, 1989) and Arendt (in *Eichmann in Jerusalem: A Report on the Banality of Evil*, 2006) have explained that events considered 'evil' are not so unusual, abnormal or anomalous to the everyday as is often portrayed. Assigning the label of 'evil' can in fact be dangerous, in overlooking the dynamics and processes which led to and characterise the event and which, if left unchecked or escape attention, could lead to a similar recurrence.

This is further underscored because of the political underpinnings of transitional justice measures and processes (see Moore, 2011). The decision about which transitional justice processes should be progressed, which cases should be pursued, and so on, are imbued with the political agendas of those who have the power to make or influence such decisions (see Vinjamuri and Snyder, 2015). A related common criticism of war crimes prosecutions, in particular, as referred to earlier, is that it can constitute a victor's justice and is disproportionately influenced by powerful nations, such as the US and Russia who are not States Parties to the Rome Statute and have veto powers in the UN Security Council. Given the political nature of transitional justice mechanisms and processes, people often regard specific processes and mechanisms as partial or biased, which can further undermine the extent to which they can contribute to reconciliation or broader peacebuilding.

There are also, of course, more practical challenges facing many transitional justice mechanisms, aside from the conceptual, ethical and political challenges noted above and the challenges posed by the assumed tension between justice and peace that can sometimes occur after conflict, as discussed below. These tangible challenges include difficulties securing evidence for prosecutions, for instance.

Other challenges include the large number of resources required for many transitional justice mechanisms, if they are to be comprehensive and effective. Securing evidence also poses problems. Physical and documentary evidence is often limited and so witness testimony becomes essential (Walling, 2018). However, prospective witnesses may have been killed, may be too traumatised to testify and may be threatened against giving evidence (underscoring the need for robust victim and witness protection mechanisms).

Limited political will also undermines efforts in particular to hold those who have committed serious violations of international law to account. Even where individual countries resist prosecutions (or simply lack capacity), limited political will (as well as resources and, in some cases, jurisdiction) also means that international mechanisms such as the ICC may not be able to fill the gap (Sriram et al., 2017). Referrals of cases to the ICC depend upon political will and are already highly contentious, demonstrated by the withdrawal of a number of African countries from the ICC claiming the Court is biased against them (Gumede, 2018). Where domestic courts and the ICC cannot take action, ad hoc or hybrid courts can be established, or domestic courts in other countries can be used. Again, however, all of these options depend upon there being sufficient political will; the challenges faced by ad hoc and hybrid courts outlined earlier will impact political will, and few countries are willing to hear cases involving serious crimes committed in another country, given that it is highly politically contentious (Sriram et al., 2017). Of course, the biggest challenge in the way of transitional justice – which intersects political and practical challenges – is the resistance on the part of those who may be held to account for serious crimes committed during conflict.

Peace versus justice

The 'peace versus justice' debate concerns how societies transition from conflict and violence and specifically how atrocities committed should be addressed: at its most simplistic, whether those who have committed the gravest crimes should be prosecuted or whether, in the interests of ending conflict and securing peace, amnesties should be granted.

One of the main criticisms often levied against efforts to hold alleged war criminals to account is that, in seeking justice, security can be undermined and with it prospects for sustainable peace. When, for example, in July 2008 the Sudanese President Omar al-Bashir was indicted by the ICC for genocide, crimes against humanity and war crimes in Darfur, much concern was voiced that this would undermine efforts to resume peace talks and would also incite retaliation, which could include attacks on humanitarian aid workers (see HRW, 2009). Similar criticisms were raised when indictments were brought against members of the LRA in Uganda (see Sriram et al., 2017). Likewise, tension between ICTY and the UN Interim Administration Mission in Kosovo (UNMIK) grew with the indictment of Ramush Haradinaj who was seen as key to the peacebuilding process by some within UNMIK and the wider international community: as highlighted by Lyck (2007).

While war crimes prosecutions can heighten tension and trigger outbreaks of violence, recently, there has been an increasingly widespread understanding that without 'justice' there can be no 'peace'. Immunity from prosecution for those responsible for war crimes and crimes against humanity may only provide short-term and superficial stability, while compromising efforts to secure longer-term peace. The International Centre for Transitional Justice (ICTJ, 2011: n.p.) has, for example, stated that where such 'crimes are not addressed, when the root causes of conflict are not sought out and removed, when victims' calls for justice are not heard, the danger of violence recurring remains high'.

Sierra Leone, Angola and Sudan suggest that peace built on impunity is not sustainable and may, in fact, encourage further atrocities to be carried out. Likewise, the inclusion of suspected or alleged war criminals into government in order to consolidate peace can backfire, as has been seen in the DRC and Afghanistan, for instance, with heightened insecurity, violence and criminality. Moreover, the distrust and desire for revenge that can result, in particular, in post-conflict environments where accountability for atrocities committed during conflict has not been pursued can threaten a fragile peace, as has been seen in Burundi, for example. It has also been suggested that the Rwandan genocide, in part, resulted from 'the willingness of influential governments to overlook crimes that predated the genocide' (HRW, 2009: 7). On the other hand, peace negotiations were not scuttled in BiH or Uganda when, respectively, Slobodan Milošević was indicted or when justice provisions were included in negotiations as a result of the ICC's pursuit of a number of LRA leaders.

Of course, as Sriram (2009) has emphasised, the peace versus justice dilemma is often hugely over-simplified. As was discussed earlier, there is no agreement on the meaning of either concept, which means that in many ways the peace versus justice debate is a futile one: what we perceive as 'justice' is seldom perceived as such by communities on the ground. This is less of a problem when the violence is small-scale and local, and where, as in Kenya after the post-election violence of 2007-8, involvement by an outside party can be useful, with 'any desire for revenge being channelled through legitimate institutions' (Grono, 2009: n.p.). Where an international institution is respected and regarded as objective, and where there is a general consensus in favour of prosecutions, the ICC or similar institutions can be effective, but these conditions are not often met.

Conclusion

There are many transitional justice mechanisms – from truth-seeking processes, prosecution initiatives, reparations, institutional reform and memorialisation – which have been used in post-conflict environments to address atrocities committed in war as a means of securing long-term peace. This chapter has provided an overview of some of these mechanisms as well as some of the challenges facing transitional justice today and ways in which these challenges can be addressed. To begin with, the number of mechanisms and actors often involved in any one place, speaks to the need for effective communication, co-ordination, complementarity between concurrent or consecutive processes, timing and sequencing of efforts. Requisite political and financial support, and adherence to the principles of local ownership, context-specificity, inclusion and gender sensitivity are important, as they are to all peacebuilding endeavours, as well as sensitivity to the needs of victims, vulnerable groups and children. Recognising tension that can exist between different principles, different activities, short- and long-term aims and sometimes between different actors is necessary in order to mitigate the risks that such tension can pose. Operationally, comprehensive planning, informed by contextual knowledge, best practice and conflict analysis, is vital. Conceptually, an awareness that terms such as 'truth', 'justice' and 'fairness' are subjective and highly political needs to inform efforts to address past atrocities as part of the peacebuilding process. In conclusion, in referring to the tension that can sometimes be perceived to exist between 'peace' and 'justice', this chapter underscores the need to attend to past injustices if longer-term peace is to be secured. Moreover, this chapter emphasises the need to recognise the complexity of conflict and, thus, the necessary complexity of efforts required to address the causes and consequences of conflict and build peace.

Summary of Key Issues

- Today, transitional justice is generally perceived as a means whereby, predominantly, post-conflict societies can address genocide, war crimes, crimes against humanity and other gross violations of human rights.
- It is widely held that societies must address large-scale wartime abuses if reconciliation and peace are to be secured.
- The principles that should guide transitional justice work include local ownership, context-specificity, gender and child sensitivity, the centrality of the needs and voices of victims, and co-ordination of efforts.

- There are many transitional justice mechanisms, including truth-seeking processes, prosecution initiatives, reparations, institutional reform, memorialisation and traditional procedures.
- Prosecutions are often regarded as being an effective means of delivering justice, challenging impunity and thus promoting the rule of law, and deterring similar crimes from recurring.
- Where domestic courts are unable or unwilling to address past abuses, third party national courts, international and hybrid criminal tribunals have done so.
- Truth-seeking processes can be effective in documenting and demonstrating acknowledgement of abuses.
- Traditional justice and reconciliation procedures are often overlooked but can positively contribute to peacebuilding.
- Concepts such as 'truth' and 'justice' are subjective, highly political and emotionally charged.
- The 'peace versus justice' debate concerns the tension that can be perceived to exist between efforts to hold to account perpetrators of war-time atrocities and build security in places where peace is fragile.

Reflective Question

Can you have peace without justice?

List of Core Resources

ANU College of Law (2015) 'Professor Gerry Simpson, The Annual Kirby Lecture on International Law 2015' (video). Available at www.youtube.com/watch?v=bxzJK0nlNrY.

Arnould, V. (2016) 'Transitional Justice in Peacebuilding: Dynamics of Contestation in the DRC', *Journal of Intervention and Statebuilding*, 10(3): 321–38.

Baker, C. and Obradovic-Wochnik, J. (2016), 'Mapping the Nexus of Transitional Justice and Peacebuilding', *Journal Of Intervention And Statebuilding*, 10(3): 281–301. Available at www.tandfonline.com/doi/full/10.1080/17502977.2016.1199476.

BBC (1999) *A Cry from the Grave* (video). Available at www.youtube.com/watch?v=Fliw801iX84 (MySrebrenica, 2011).

Chandra, S. (2017) 'Beyond Transitional Justice: Peace, Governance, and Rule of Law', *International Studies Review*, 19(1): 53–69.

Chuter, D. (2012) 'The ICC: A Place for Africans or Africans in Their Place?' in V. Nmehielle (ed.) *Africa and the Future of International Criminal Justice* (The Hague: Eleven International Publishing): 161–184.

Cohen, S. (2001) *States of Denial: Knowing About Atrocities and Suffering* (Cambridge: Polity Press).

Cubbon, J. (2014) *International Criminal Justice in the Context of Conflict Prevention and the Promotion of Peace – John Cubbon* (University of Leicester) (video). Available at www.youtube.com/watch?v=1Wz4P_KH_No&index=2&list=PLjQX5EXgm57S0L7nT-QMVhQLKiYNsSPxu

ELAC, University of Oxford (2012) *The ICC at 10*, Panel Discussion (podcast). Available at https://podcasts.ox.ac.uk/icc-10.

Gordon, E. (2017) 'Crimes of the Powerful in Conflict-Affected Environments: False Positives, Transitional Justice and the Prospects for Peace in Colombia', *State Crime Journal* 6(1): 132–55.

Haider, H. (2016) *Transitional justice: Topic guide*, Birmingham, UK: GSDRC, University of Birmingham. Available at www.gsdrc.org/wp-content/uploads/2016/08/TransitionalJustice_GSDRC.pdf.

ICC (2014) *International Criminal Court (ICC-CPI) – Institutional Video* (video). Available at www.youtube.com/watch?v=1K4Y8iqLzxQ.

ICC (2017) *Remarks of ICC Prosecutor on future of international criminal justice* (video). Available at www.youtube.com/watch?v=hhBm_CftY7o.

ICTJ (2011) *Peace and Justice* (video). Available at www.youtube.com/watch?v=PWFpngEfu84.

ICTJVideo (2017) *I Am Not Who They Think I Am | ICTJ* (video). Available at www.youtube.com/watch?list=PLP8pOH5Q3gXU8a4qF6K9DuR9gGMy5tQi6&time_continue=54&v=GZz9TUVvnVk.

ICTR-TPIR (2014) *20 Years Challenging Impunity – United Nations International Criminal Tribunal for Rwanda* (video). Available at www.youtube.com/watch?v=Q6nGK4A1UJ4.

ICTY (2010) *Voice of the Victims: Witness DD in the Krstić case* (video). Available at www.youtube.com/watch?v=ZHnydxCvjKw.

ICTY (2012) *Sexual Violence and the Triumph of Justice* (video). Available at www.youtube.com/watch?time_continue=4&v=HZ4EM6iiq0k.

International Civil Society Action Network – ICAN (2017) *ICAN's Gendered Transitional Justice Video* (video). Available at www.youtube.com/watch?v=nAmWHdH0Doo.

Jackson, P. and Beswick, D. (2018) (3rd edn) 'Truth, memory and peacebuilding' (Chapter 11) in *Conflict, Security and Development: An Introduction* (Abingdon: Routledge).

Labuda, P. (2017) 'The Special Criminal Court in the Central African Republic: Failure or Vindication of Complementarity?' *Journal of International Criminal Justice*, 15(1): 175–206.

Mihr, A. Sriram, C. (2018) 'Rule of Law, Security, and Transitional Justice in Fragile and Conflict-affected Societies' in W. Durch, J. Larik, and R. Ponzio (eds) *Just Security in an Undergoverned World* (Oxford: Oxford University Press).

Ministry of Foregn Affairs, Sri Lanka (2017) *Lecture on Transitional Justice by UN Special Rapporteur Pablo de Greiff* (video). Available at www.youtube.com/watch?v=wHcb0wzCm1g.

O'Reilly, M. (2016) 'Peace and Justice through a Feminist Lens: Gender Justice and the Women's Court for the Former Yugoslavia', *Journal of Intervention and Statebuilding*, 10:3, 419–45.

Oxford Institute for Ethics, Law and Armed Conflict (ELAC), University of Oxford (2013), *Order and the International Criminal Court: The Society of States and 'Humanitarian Pluralism'*, lecture by Dr Matthew Killingsworth (podcast). Available on iTunes.

Sriram, C. (2009) 'Justice as Peace? Liberal Peacebuilding and Strategies of Transitional Justice', *Global Society* 21(4): 579–91.

USIP (2014) *Preventing and Mitigating Conflicts: Role of the International Courts* (video). Available at www.youtube.com/watch?v=gz9zTbo_QI4.

Voice of the Tribunal: UNICTR (2017) *Symposium: Looking Back to Move Forward: Final Reflections on the ICTY* (video). Available at www.youtube.com/watch?v=2tdKBHbZCnc.

6 Mine Action and the Control of Small Arms and Light Weapons

Overview

In post-conflict environments, the prevalence of mines and explosive remnants of war (ERW) as well as the widespread availability and misuse of small arms and light weapons (SALW) pose many security risks and can hinder efforts to build a meaningful and lasting peace. This chapter considers the challenges presented by the prevalence of mines and ERW as well as SALW, and ways in which these challenges can be addressed. The first part of this chapter considers mines and ERW, beginning with the nature and extent of their threat and the wider impact on post-conflict recovery and development. The chapter then looks at the actors and activities involved in mine action, including mine clearance (or demining), mine risk education, victim assistance, advocacy and stockpile destruction. The international legal tools will also be reviewed before considering ways to address the challenges posed by mines and ERW. The second part of this chapter considers the ways in which the presence of SALW in post-conflict environments undermines security and the rule of law, as well as ways in which to promote reconciliation, protect human rights, and facilitate good governance and socio-economic development. After exploring the threat of SALW, the chapter looks at some of the fundamental developments in SALW control as well as some of the key components and principles of SALW control programmes, concluding by considering ways in which to address the challenges posed by SALW in post-conflict environments.

Learning Outcomes

- Understand the impact of mines and explosive remnants of war (ERW) on civilians, communities and the wider post-conflict environment
- Be familiar with some of the actors and activities involved in mine action as well as the relevant international legal instruments
- Be familiar with the key components and principles of SALW control programmes
- Identify the need for SALW control programmes to be integrated with other peacebuilding efforts
- Evaluate the role of mine action and SALW control in post-conflict peacebuilding and development

- Identify some of the challenges in the field of mine action and SALW control in post-conflict environments, as well as ways in which these challenges can be addressed

Part 1 – Mine Action

The effects of conflict far outlast the conflict itself. Nowhere is this more evident than with the existence of anti-personnel and anti-tank landmines (hereafter mines) and other explosive remnants of war (ERW), including unexploded ordnance (UXO) and abandoned explosive ordnance (AXO), which can remain in many post-conflict environments for many years. For instance, ERW (notably WWI-era shells in Belgium and WWII-era bombs in Germany) even continue to pose problems in Western Europe, demonstrating the long-term challenge posed even to wealthy countries.

Of all ERW, cluster munitions are especially pernicious as each munition can contain hundreds of sub-munitions, the area contaminated can be very wide and they are prone to failure. In theory, records should be kept of where land mines have been sown and attempts made to clear them at the end of hostilities. However, this has not always happened, even in the two World Wars, and few insurgent forces have kept records of where they placed minefields.

Historically, mobility has been a major asset in conflict. An aggressor wants to move as fast and as freely as possible. A defender, or a weaker party, wants to slow down an attacker and if possible keep them out of certain areas. The use of land mines for defence is probably as old as history but really began on a large scale during the positional warfare of World War 1. Their purpose was less to destroy and kill than to obstruct and delay, forcing attackers to go more carefully and to stop periodically to deal with the wounded. The Soviet victory at the climactic Battle of Kursk in 1943 was partly due to the laying of some 400,000 mines to slow the German advance. During the Cold War, mines were widely used by liberation movements and rebel organisations against superior government forces. This was especially the case in Africa, where mines became such a threat that the apartheid regime in South Africa was forced eventually to develop a special mine-proof vehicle, the Casspir – still in use today with demining experts.

Simple and cheap to manufacture and easy to deploy, the mine was pre-eminently the weapon of the weak against the strong or against the attacker. After the Cold War, and the end of anti-colonial and post-colonial wars in Africa, advanced western nations saw no need to retain stocks of such weapons that, indeed, could prejudice their own interests. Apart from the United States, therefore, which had minefields in place in Korea to defend against an attack from the North, they generally saw advantage in signing the Mine Ban Convention. Nonetheless, mines and other explosive devices continue to be used in conflict-affected environments today, including post-conflict environments, predominantly by non-state armed groups to control territory, inflict terror or destabilise political environments.

Extent of the problem

By the end of 2017, 61 states and areas were reported as contaminated by mines, of which 10 (Afghanistan, Angola, Azerbaijan, Bosnia and Herzegovina, Cambodia, Chad, Croatia, Iraq, Thailand and Turkey) have contamination at the level of 100 per square kilometre (ICBL-CMC, 2017b).

According to the International Campaign to Ban Landmines – Cluster Munition Coalition (ICBL-CMC), 100,000 casualties were recorded over the previous 17 years, of which about one third were fatal (ICBL-CMC, 2016b). In 2017, ICBL-CMC reported that 2016 was the second year in a row 'with exceptionally high numbers of people recorded as killed or injured by landmines'. These included victims of improvised mines, cluster munition remnants and other ERW. In 2016, there were 8,605 such victims, including at least 2,089 of whom were killed as a result. According to ICBL-CMC (2017b), this constitutes the highest casualty rate since 1999, as well as the most child casualties ever recorded (constituting 42% of victims where their age was known), and the highest number of victims of improvised mines (ICBL-CMC, 2017b). It is likely that these increases are the result of an increase of victims of mines and ERW in conflict-affected environments although, of course, gathering data from such environments is problematic (ICBL-CMC, 2017b). Nonetheless, after a long period of decline in the number of victims, reported casualties increased significantly from 3,695 in 2014 to 6,461 in 2015, then 8,605 in 2016. Since 1999, ICBL-CMC (2017b) has recorded more than 110,000 victims of mines and ERW. The proportion of reported victims who are civilians is very high, at 78% in 2016. It has been a similar proportion in the previous three years (ICBL-CMC, 2017b). Among civilians, it is often children who are most vulnerable to risk (see Box 6.1 and Figure 6.1 – note the figure shows recorded incidents only, not estimates and is therefore unlikely to reflect the full extent of the casualties resulting from mines and ERW).

The impact of mines and other ERW on survivors is not limited to the physical and mental trauma that results. The effects on individuals and families, who are often the rural poor, can include further impoverishment (due to the medical costs incurred and loss of income) and further marginalisation and exclusion, because of discrimination of and attitudes towards disabled people (see the Geneva International Centre for Humanitarian Demining (GICHD), 2011).

Box 6.1: Children and Mines

Children are particularly at risk from mines and other ERW because they are often outside playing, have a natural curiosity and may pick up objects to look at them, and because they sometimes cannot read landmine warning signs. Additionally, as many mines are designed to maim adults, they are likely to kill children. Furthermore, child survivors can particularly suffer due to a lack of child-focussed victim assistance and medical care and difficulties in continuing their education. (UN Educational, Scientific and Cultural Organization – UNESCO, 2010).

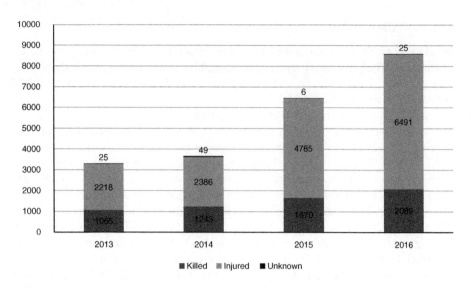

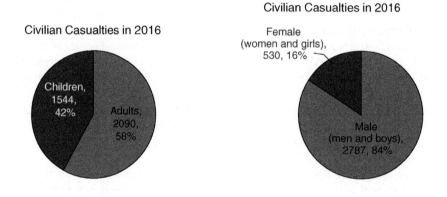

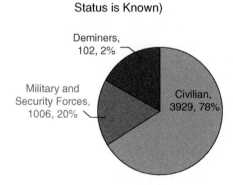

Figure 6.1 Recorded Mine Incidents (data drawn from ICBL-CMC)

The impact of ERW is not limited to direct human casualties, but has many far-reaching effects on post-conflict societies. Recall that the purpose of mines (and an incidental effect of other ERW) is to cause fear and uncertainty, and to discourage access into certain areas. It is easy to see how this can play out once the conflict is over, in inhibitions on freedom of movement, economic recovery, return of refugees and internally displaced persons (IDPs), with much land made inaccessible. It also impedes humanitarian efforts, peacebuilding and post-conflict reconstruction:

> These weapons instill fear in communities, whose citizens often know they are walking in mined areas, but have no possibility to farm other land, or take another route to school. When land cannot be cultivated, when medical systems are drained by the cost of attending to landmine/ERW casualties, and when countries must spend money clearing mines rather than paying for education, it is clear that these weapons not only cause appalling human suffering, they are also a lethal barrier to development and post-conflict reconstruction. (International Campaign to Ban Landmines (ICBL), 2010: Preface)

Financial cost

Aside from the direct harm suffered by casualties, their families and communities, there is also the financial cost of ERW, including providing medical and psychosocial care, other forms of assistance to victims, mine risk education, and clearing land of mines and other ERW. Individuals, families and communities also suffer because agricultural land may be no longer accessible. As mentioned above, individuals and families of casualties also suffer financially because of the medical costs, because one member of their family may be no longer able to work, and because their land may no longer be able to be farmed. While the international community may provide resources, a significant financial burden is frequently borne by the population of places affected by conflict, often individuals and their families, and often the rural poor. The result is likely further impoverishment and exclusion of these groups.

Mine action activities

The definition of mine action has changed over time, alongside activities associated with mine action (see Orifici and Damman, 2009). The definition of mine action provided by the UN in the International Mine Action Standards (IMAS) refers to 'activities which aim to reduce the social, economic and environmental impact of mines, ERW and unexploded sub-munitions' (IMAS, 2003: 23), so that 'people can live safely; in which economic, social and health development can occur free from the constraints imposed by landmine and ERW contamination' (IMAS, 2003: 33). Consequently, mine action includes:

- *Mine Risk Education (MRE)* – informing people of the risks of mines and ERW and how to avoid those risks, through public information campaigns, education and training, to reduce the risk of injury and death from mines and

ERW. For example, in Afghanistan, more than 25 million individual mine and explosive hazard risk education sessions have been delivered by humanitarian mine action actors.

- *Demining or Mine Clearance* – mapping and marking minefields, removing and destroying mines and ERW. In South Sudan, the UN Mine Action Service (UNMAS) has surveyed, cleared and released over one billion square metres of land back to the people of South Sudan.
- *Victim Assistance* – providing medical help, psychosocial care and rehabilitation support, including training and job opportunities, to victims. In Syria, victim assistance services, from medical referrals to prosthetics and rehabilitation support, have been provided to to 2,456 people, but services remain severely underfunded to meet the need.
- *Advocacy* – encouraging states to become signatories to international treaties and conventions banning the production, trade and use of mines, as well as encouraging states and others to protect the rights of those with disabilities or otherwise affected by mines and ERW. UNMAS coordinates global UN advocacy in support of legal instruments related to mines and ERW, and in support of the rights of people affected by such devices.
- *Stockpile Destruction* – supporting states destroy their stockpiles of mines (UNMAS, 2019). In Côte d'Ivoire, all known stockpiles of anti-personnel mines and cluster bombs have been destroyed.

Mine action actors

Due to the extent of the mine problem and the number of activities involved in mine action, a number of actors, both military and civilian, are involved. NGOs tend to do much of the work, with military and commercial organisations engaged in certain situations. The UN has the primary responsibility for co-ordinating mine action globally and for supporting the development of national capacity (often found wanting in the aftermath of conflict when, of course, the need is most acute). There are 12 UN departments, agencies, funds and programmes involved in mine action. The UN Mine Action Service (UNMAS), within the UN Department of Peacekeeping Operations (UNDPKO), is the focal point in the UN system for mine action. It is also responsible for setting the International Mine Action Standards (IMAS) used by UN agencies, governments and NGOs. IMAS are a set of comprehensive standards governing every aspect of mine action (see www.mineactionstandards.org). The development and review of these standards is managed by the Geneva International Centre for Humanitarian Demining (GICHD) on behalf of UNMAS (see more in the UN Mine Action gateway: www.mineaction.org).

Actors may work at the international, state or community level. At the international level, they include the UN agencies mentioned above, but also the World Bank (WB), the World Food Programme (WFP), the World Health Organisation (WHO) and the Food and Agriculture Organisation (FAO). Individual donor states, the International Committee of the Red Cross (ICRC) and the GICHD are also involved, as well as various NGOs. Regional organisations such as the Organization of American States (OAS) and the European Union (EU) also play a role. At the state level, governments and the military are often involved in developing and implementing mine action policies and, respectively, mine clearance and stockpile destruction; at the sub-state level, communities, civil society organisations and the media can also play a key role in mine action (see Bryden, 2005) (see Box 6.2 for an overview of mine action actors and their work in Cambodia).

Legal instruments

As explained in the previous chapter, there is a long tradition of agreements to try to make warfare more humane. The *Convention on Certain Conventional Weapons* (more formally known as the Convention on Prohibitions or Restrictions on the Use of Certain Conventional Weapons Which May Be Deemed to Be Excessively Injurious or to Have Indiscriminate Effects) entered into force on 02 December 1983 (reviewed in 1996 and 2001). This Convention bans or restricts the use of various types of weapons that are deemed to cause unnecessary suffering or affect either soldiers or civilians indiscriminately. These weapons include weapons that leave undetectable fragments in the body (Protocol I), mines, booby-traps and other devices (Protocol II, amended in 1996), incendiary weapons (Protocol III), blinding laser weapons (Protocol IV) and explosive remnants of war (Protocol V) (GICHD, 2019). By 2018, there were 125 States Parties to the Convention, with a further five having signed but not yet ratified (UN Office for Disarmament Affairs – UNODA, 2019).

Box 6.2: Mine Action in Cambodia

Cambodia is one of the most mine-/ERW-contaminated countries in the world, resulting from conflicts from the mid 1960s until the late 1990s, notably the Vietnam War when the US dropped 2.75 million cluster munition bombs (GICHD, 2019). This has resulted in over 60,000 victims of mines and other ERW since 1979, approximately 30% of whom were killed (GICHD, 2019). The mine action programme in Cambodia is one of the oldest in the world, established in 1993 with the assistance of the UN and the broader international community. Many Cambodian and international organisations have been engaged in mine action, including the Cambodian Mine Action Centre (CMAC), the National Centre for Peacekeeping Mine and ERW Clearance (NPMEC), Mine Advisory Group (MAG), The HALO Trust (HALO) and Norwegian People's Aid (NPA) (GICHD, 2019). A national mine action authority was established in Cambodia in 2000. In the same year, further demonstrating Cambodia's commitment to mine action, Cambodia became a State Party to the Mine Ban Treaty. Given the extent of the mine contamination problem in Cambodia, the country has an extended period of time in which to clear land. There has been significant progress in land clearance (i.e. surveying and, where needed, clearing land) since 2009 when more effective and efficient methods were adopted. Nonetheless, it is anticipated that Cambodia will still not be able to clear all mined areas by the deadline of 2020 (GICHD, 2019).

The *Mine Ban Convention* entered into force on 1 March 1999. The Mine Ban Convention is more formally referred to as the Convention on the Prohibition of the Use, Stockpiling, Production and Transfer of Anti-Personnel Mines and on Their Destruction, also known as the Anti-Personnel Mine Ban Treaty or Ottawa Convention. By the end of 2018, 164 states had signed and ratified the Convention, while a further 30 had acceded. There are 33 states that are not party to the Convention (including the United States, China, India and the Russian Federation), including one state (the Marshall Islands) which has signed but not yet ratified the Convention (ICBL-CMC, 2017b). Nonetheless, many of the states not party to the Treaty abide by its key provisions (ICBL-CMC, 2017b). The Convention bans the use, stockpiling, production and transfer of anti-personnel mines. It also obliges those states that accede to the Convention to destroy stockpiled and emplaced anti-personnel mines and assist the victims of mines. State Parties must destroy stockpiled mines within four years of entry into force of the Convention (two States Parties have missed this deadline – Greece and Ukraine – HRW, 2018). Of those 61 states and areas which were reported as contaminated by mines in ICBL-CMC's 2017 annual report, 24 states are not party to the Mine Ban Treaty, while 33 are party to the Treaty and there are four other areas. Since the Treaty entered force in 1999, 28 States Parties, one state which is not a party to the Treaty, and one other area have completed clearance of all mined areas under their jurisdiction (ICBL-CMC, 2017b).

The *Convention on Cluster Munitions* entered into force on 1 August 2010, after 30 states ratified it. It prohibits all use, stockpiling, production and transfer of cluster munitions. It also establishes strict deadlines for clearing contaminated land and for destroying stockpiles of cluster munitions. In addition, the Convention includes provisions for assistance to the victims of cluster munitions, including efforts to facilitate their socio-economic inclusion, and affected communities. By mid-2018, 120 countries have signed or ratified the Convention (ICBL-CMC, 2018). Demonstrating support for the Convention even among non-signatories, on 5 December 2016, 141 states voted in favour of adoption of the second UN General Assembly resolution supporting the Convention; only Russia and Zimbabwe voted against the resolution (ICBL-CMC, 2017a). While there have been no confirmed reports of use of cluster munitions by State Parties since the Convention was adopted in May 2008, there has been documented use by states not party to the Convention. For instance, in 2017, government forces in Syria have consistently used cluster munitions with the support of Russia, and cluster munitions have been used by a Saudi Arabia-led coalition of states in Yemen (ICBL-CMC, 2018).

Mines and ERW can adversely impact the exercise of economic, social, political, civil and cultural rights, including the right to life, freedom of movement and the right to education. Consequently, international human rights law is directly relevant, not least the most recent human rights treaty; the *Convention on the Rights of Persons with Disabilities*, which came into force on 3 May 2008. International Humanitarian Law (IHL), notably the Geneva Conventions and their Additional Protocols, provides the legal framework for limiting the most deleterious effects of war and protecting those who are not participating in hostilities.

Refugee law, notably the Convention relating to the Status of Refugees, signed on 28 July 1951, is also relevant, not least given that refugees and internally displaced persons (IDPs) are particularly vulnerable to the threat of mines and ERW, particularly given that they are often mobile (UN Office at Geneva – UNOG, 2018).

Continuing threat

While mine action continues to clear land, destroy stockpiles, educate people about the risk of mines and provide assistance to victims, the threat of mines and ERW continues – both the residual threat from mines and ERW already deployed as well as their continued use by armed groups. ICBL-CMC (2017b) has reported that mines and improvised explosive devices (IEDs) continue to be used in conflicts; in 2017, they were used in Syria and Myanmar by government forces and they were also used by non-state armed groups in at least nine countries. Notably, 2017 was the first year there was no use of mines by non-state armed groups in Colombia, following the ratification of the peace agreement between the Government of Colombia and the Revolutionary Armed Forces of Colombia – People's Army (Spanish: *Fuerzas Armadas Revolucionarias de Colombia – Ejército del Pueblo*, FARC-EP or FARC). There has, however, been extensive use of IEDs by Islamic State (IS) throughout 2017. Indeed, the significantly increased and systematic use of IEDs, including a large proportion of victim-operated IEDs, by armed groups contribute 'to a new landmine emergency' (Rhodes, 2017: 4). As mentioned above, there has also been new use of cluster munitions in Syria and Yemen (ICBL-CMC, 2018, 2017a).

Challenges and recommendations

Mine action is one of a series of humanitarian issues that have arisen over the last generation, and that compete for international attention, funding and a place in post-conflict planning. For all governments and international organisations, there is a limited amount of political space available in any area of policy, and the problems of progress and funding described below result essentially from this competition.

Fundamentally, demining remains under-resourced, dangerous and time-consuming. Donor fatigue and the competition for funding led to a significant decline in funding for mine clearance until 2016, which saw a notable increase in international support. After a decrease of $139 million USD (23%) in 2015 from 2014 (ICBL-CMC, 2016b), there was an overall increase of $39.3 million (7%) in 2016 (this incorporates a significant increase of $85.5 million or 22% from donors, but a decrease from affected states of $46.2 or 35%, since the previous year). The US, EU, Japan, Germany and Norway are the top five mine action donors, contributing 70% of all international funding (ICBL-CMC, 2017b). It is necessary, of course, for mine action to receive sufficient funding and support from the international community if it is to be able to fulfil its potential to contribute to building peace and security, including through facilitating the return of refugees and IDPs, economic recovery and reconciliation.

Perhaps because of funding constraints, and in response to the comparatively large number of people killed as a result of lethal violence (perhaps as many as 400 times as many each year), mine action organisations have expanded their area of activity into broader armed violence reduction (AVR) programmes in recent years (Naidoo, 2013).

Outside funding, a fundamental challenge in mine action work is to reach those groups who may otherwise not benefit from mine action because security conditions may be too difficult to reach them, or because they do not have access to formal channels of information through which MRE might be delivered (see UNMAS, 2019). The fact that it is often the rural poor, displaced persons and children that are affected by mines and other ERW poses the additional challenge in ensuring that survivors are not further marginalised as a result of being a victim or losing a family member.

Other challenges relate to the need to have reliable information for demining activities. Limited trust between communities often frustrates efforts to obtain accurate information required for such activities, including information on contaminated areas and on victims. However, efforts to secure this information do have the potential of contributing to confidence-building and reconciliation between former adversaries through sustaining their interaction (see Peace Building Initiative, 2009).

Another challenge concerns the prevalent reluctance to fully promote national ownership and build national capacity for mine action, and implement the principles of national ownership in the legislation. There is still a long way to go before mine action is managed by the countries affected. Again, as is not unusual, there can be competing agendas between different demining groups, including where the military, NGOs and commercial enterprises are engaged in mine action work (Peace Building Initiative, 2009). As is the case in other peacebuilding endeavours, there is scope to promote co-ordination and coherence between actors and activities. This relates to another challenge in mine action: the fact that issues of security are often politicised, particularly when money is involved. Additionally, security issues are traditionally considered to be issues to be addressed by men; it is of the utmost importance, however, that women and children also feed into mine action planning, and are consulted on the location of mines and priorities for clearance, as well as specifically targeted through MRE and victim assistance.

Part 2 – The Control of Small Arms and Light Weapons

The second half of this chapter looks at the control of Small Arms and Light Weapons (SALW) in post-conflict environments, beginning by considering what SALW are and the threat they pose. The chapter then considers the activities and actors engaged in SALW control, and ends by reflecting upon some of the challenges in this field.

What are small arms and light weapons?

Small arms (weapons carried by one person) include revolvers and self-loading pistols, rifles and carbines, sub-machine-guns, assault rifles and light machine-guns, while light weapons (those weapons which require two or more people to operate and are often vehicle-mounted) are less easily defined, but can include heavy machine-guns, hand-held under-barrel and mounted grenade launchers, portable anti-aircraft guns, portable anti-tank guns, recoilless rifles, portable launchers of anti-tank missile and rocket systems, portable launchers of anti-aircraft missile systems, and mortars of less than 100 mm (UN, 1997b).

The threat of SALW

Given that many small arms and light weapons (SALW) are portable, concealable and often widely available, low cost and durable, the impact on conflict-affected environments can be considerable. Because many people in post-conflict environments often have little confidence in the peace process, at least in the early days, opposing parties will often want to retain their weapons as an insurance policy. It should be recognised that most conflicts recur; the Peace Research Institute Oslo (PRIO) estimates that 60% of conflicts recur and the average length of post-conflict peace lasts seven years (Nygård and Trappeniers, 2016). Even where there are peace agreements, the recurrence rate of conflict is high, although not as high as where there are no agreements; as Westendorf points out, although statistical analyses of the success and failure rate of peace agreements vary in terms of coding, parameters and timeframes, all agree there is a high failure rate (of between approximately a third and a half of all cases, Westendorf, 2015). So, it is unsurprising that many people may want to keep their weapons as an insurance policy. Many people may also have more confidence in small arms to defend themselves, particularly in the immediate aftermath of conflict where there is heightened insecurity, and state security and justice institutions lack capacity and/or legitimacy. So, there can be a high prevalence of SALW in post-conflict environments as well as conflict zones. It should also be stressed that the durability and mobility of SALW also makes the problem they pose long-term and unpredictable. For instance, weapons which proliferated during the Vietnam War have made their way from South East Asia to Mexico, where today they are used in drug wars. Likewise, many weapons were stolen in the early 1990s from Russian stockpiles and found their way to conflicts in the Balkans; after the end of the conflicts, these and other weapons were trafficked to other conflict zones as well as criminal and terrorist groups. Moreover, as Kaldor (2012) describes, efforts to control SALW, and thereby improve security, can never keep pace with the production and distribution of SALW because they are so mobile and easy to replicate.

It is argued in the 'Report of the Panel of Governmental Experts on Small Arms' that, while the availability of SALW may not directly cause armed conflict, it does contribute 'towards exacerbating conflicts by increasing the lethality and duration of violence in various ways, by encouraging a violent rather than a peaceful resolution of differences, and by generating a vicious circle of a greater sense of insecurity, which in turn leads to a greater demand for, and use of, such weapons' (UN, 1997b: 10). This is tautologically true in the sense that, as Clausewitz was the first to point out, it takes two sides to make a war. Thus, liberation struggles in countries like Algeria, Angola and Rhodesia/Zimbabwe were only possible at all because of the willingness of the Soviet Bloc and China to supply SALW. But SALW do not 'contribute' anything by themselves. In the cases cited, their supply was part of a wider policy of equipping, organising and training groups which one of the major powers sympathised with. In the case of Angola, this went as far as the deployment of Soviet and East German advisers, and entire Cuban combat units. For much the same reasons, western powers organised, armed and trained Islamic fighters during the war against the Soviet Union in Afghanistan.

It is also tautologically true that the 'small arms and light weapons have been ... a primary cause of casualties in almost all modern conflicts, and especially civilian fatalities (particularly among women and children)' (Security Council Report, 2011: 15). But this is because the definition is so wide that it includes virtually all weapons other than sophisticated and highly expensive heavy artillery, tanks, armoured vehicles helicopters and aircraft. Indeed, SALW would make up the vast majority of the firepower of a battalion from a sophisticated western nation deployed on peace operations, for example.

Moreover, if SALW are *a* primary cause of death in conflicts, they are certainly not the only one. Advanced weapons used by the West and its allies in Iraq, Afghanistan, Libya, Syria and Yemen have been responsible for many deaths as well. Further, direct casualties caused by weapons are dwarfed by indirect casualties of conflict. It need also be remembered that a significant proportion of deaths by SALW each year occur in so-called peaceful states. To demonstrate the impact of small arms beyond the battlefield: in 2016, 210,000 people were killed by firearms (totalling 38% of all victims of lethal violence that year), while only about 15% of these died as a direct result of armed conflict (81% were homicide victims) (Mc Evoy and Hideg, 2017).

Nonetheless, the presence of SALW in post-conflict environments can undermine security by fuelling crime, undermining the rule of law, compromising reconciliation efforts and hindering development notably by discouraging external investment (IDDRS, 2006; Stohl and Hogendoorn, 2010). Economic activity and daily routines can also be adversely impacted by the presence and use of SALW. All of this can contribute to undermining confidence in state security institutions as well as the peacebuilding process. In post-conflict environments, the legal and social control of weapons, which is often more instrumental to reducing violence than simply reducing the presence of weapons, breaks down. In such circumstances, if weapons are available, they are likely to find their way into the hands of militias or organised criminal groups (where there is a difference). The effect is to further undermine the authority of the state and the force of the law.

SALW can also 'have a transformative or multiplier effect on coercion and violence' (Frey, 2004: 45). Nonetheless, if SALW control programmes are to be effective, there needs to be a specific, contextualised understanding of SALW. Moreover, it could be argued that a category (SALW), which extends from homemade guns, bombs and mortars, through pistols and heavy machine guns, to sophisticated modern anti-tank weapons, is of limited use in post-conflict planning. Effectively it could be replaced with the word 'weapons'. For that reason, whilst some weapons can be 'tools used to violate human rights' (Frey, 2004: 45) and have the potential to undermine peace and security, this applies more in some cases than others. Unsurprisingly, perhaps, very generic and situation-independent analysis of this type leads to equally generic assumptions about how to tackle the problem of SALW.

The raised profile of SALW

Most of the SALW used in contemporary conflicts were supplied in the Cold War, as the superpowers encouraged or opposed different political movements in numerous intrastate conflicts, and sometimes in interstate conflicts as well. Arms supplies were also used as a source of political influence (e.g. Soviet supplies to a number of key states in the Middle East). Most of these Cold War conflicts involved irregular combatants (such as guerrilla forces) and SALW were the natural choice of weapons in such cases: easy to carry and easy to use.

During the Cold War, proliferation of SALW was, in effect, official policy. However, this calculation changed after 1989, as the loss of bipolar control after the Cold War coupled with recently opened borders, huge arms surpluses and the expansion of free trade resulted in increased trade and transfer of SALW (see Lumpe et al., 2000; Peace Building Initiative, 2009). The nature of the game had changed and, if countries still saw arms supplies as an important political tool, there was an increased focus within the international community in the 1990s on SALW and how to control them.

One result was the International Action Network on Small Arms (IANSA) established in 1998 (see www.iansa.org) and an international conference in 2001 that agreed a (politically binding) Programme of Action to Prevent, Combat and Eradicate the Illicit Trade in Small Arms and Light Weapons in All Its Aspects – referred to simply as the Programme of Action, or PoA. Through the PoA, states committed themselves to strengthening agreed norms and measures to combat the *illicit* trade in SALW and to mobilise the requisite political will and resources to prevent the *illicit* transfer, manufacture, export and import of SALW (IDDRS, 2006).

In 2005, another politically binding document, the International Tracing Instrument (ITI), was adopted (technically referred to as the International Instrument to Enable States to Identify and Trace, in a Timely and Reliable Manner, Illicit Small Arms and Light Weapons). Also in 2005, the legally binding UN Firearms Protocol (more formally referred to as the International Instrument to Enable States to Identify and Trace, in a Timely and Reliable Manner, Illicit Small Arms and Light Weapons) entered into force. Another significant development was the establishment of International Small Arms Control Standards (ISACS) by the United Nations Coordinating Action on Small Arms (CASA), launched in 2012, which provides detailed guidance on all aspects of SALW control to policy-makers and practitioners (and is publicly available; see www.smallarmsstandards.org). CASA is a small arms co-ordination mechanism within the UN, which draws from expertise on small arms across the UN, and engages in fact-finding missions, capacity-building and technical assistance as well as leads in the UN on developing the international standards on small arms control.

The fundamental distinction in these and other policy documents is between licit small arms required by states in order to maintain security and uphold the law, and the spread and use of illicit SALW. This has led to considerable resources being devoted to SALW control and to important progress since the late 1990s at the policy and programmatic levels in controlling and reducing the availability of SALW.

Increased attention and resources allocated by the international community since the 1990s have resulted in structures and frameworks that, if adhered to, could significantly impact the proliferation and misuse of SALW. A significant development occurred on 2 April 2013 when, after 20 years of lobbying by civil society (Saferworld, 2013), the landmark Arms Trade Treaty (ATT), which regulates the international trade in conventional weapons, including small arms and light weapons, was adopted by the UN General Assembly and entered into force on 24 December 2014. This is the first Treaty to provide global, legally binding and comprehensive standards on the trade and transfer of conventional arms. Additionally, the somewhat vague language of the PoA has begun to be translated into more specific prescriptions and processes. The year 2013 also witnessed the first UN Security Council Resolution on SALW (UNSCR, 2117), urging states to be committed to SALW control and observe embargoes.

SALW control in post-conflict environments

The objective of SALW control programmes in a post-conflict environment is 'to secure a safer environment and control small arms and light weapons within society in order to promote the conditions that will encourage the continued return of the region to normalisation' (IDDRS, 2006: n.p.). SALW control includes a wide range of activities, including:

- Developing legislation and administrative procedures
- Building or reforming institutional structures
- Collecting and destroying surplus weaponry and munitions
- Managing stockpiles
- Controlling the manufacture, movement, security and possession of SALW
- Conducting surveys, and gathering and managing SALW-related information
- Developing and delivering public awareness campaigns
- Promoting international co-operation.

SALW control is, thus, a very complex process, typically consisting of many components, including practical, political and legal measures. In a post-conflict situation, many of these measures will be a part of a DDR programme (see IDDRS, 2006 for a discussion of each of these components).

Wider considerations

SALW control post-conflict is not, of course, just a technical matter. As with all peacebuilding efforts, it is important to consider the context and, in this case, why SALW might be readily available and the attitudes to SALW of people in post-conflict environments. In the security vacuum that often characterises post-conflict environments, organised criminal groups may take advantage of weak SALW control and individuals may also keep arms to be used, if necessary, as a means of self-defence. Thus:

> While the aim should always be to remove or legally register all weapons in society, the reality of a gun culture and the desire for self-protection should always be recognised. In many societies, gun ownership has always been acceptable within the community, therefore perhaps a more realistic aim could be to

recover the military-style weapons that create an imbalance with neighbouring communities, or those that could be used for trade. (IDDRS, 2006: n.p.)

It is important to address the fundamental reasons why people procure and (mis) use SALW as well as tackle the symptoms of SALW proliferation and use. In other words, from a programmatic perspective, it is important to work bottom-up as well as top-down and consider how to build community safety as well as how to build the security of the state in post-conflict countries. Working from the bottom-up would require addressing the reasons why people possess weapons, building security, taking steps to increase confidence in the peace process (through 'quick wins', outreach and communication initiatives), improving trust and confidence in security providers and – oftentimes – the state, and developing reconciliation and trust between groups. Such bottom-up initiatives would help address the demand side of the equation, while more top-down initiatives and formal security programmes can help to address supply. Likewise, as emphasised by the Norwegian Initiative on Small Arms Transfers (NISAT), 'reducing the number of arms is a means to an end rather than an end in itself – *the real objective is not just fewer guns but safer people*' (Hubert, 2001) (see Box 6.3 for an overview of SALW control activities and challenges in Kosovo).

Box 6.3: SALW Control in Kosovo

SALW control efforts in many post-conflict environments have been hampered because of cultural attitudes about gun ownership, because of security fears and lack of confidence in security providers, and because of the need for 'insurance' should the peace process fall apart. These factors impacted SALW control efforts in Kosovo, for instance. Where gun ownership was intrinsically linked to ideas of masculinity and, for many, was important for reasons of pride as well as security, SALW control programmes that did not resonate with these cultural aspects were doomed to fail. Nonetheless, assumptions about attachments to weapons should not be made; a 2003 public opinion survey, for instance, found that most Kosovans would not choose to own a gun even if it was legal and that most people thought people in their neighbourhood would surrender their weapons in exchange for investment in the community (Khakee and Florquin, 2003). A later survey conducted by Saferworld and the Forum for Civic Initiatives (SEESAC, 2006) showed that the majority of those who said they have or would acquire a weapon would do so for reasons of protection, and many people agreed that weapon ownership in rural and border areas was legitimate due to increased insecurity in these areas. The prevalence of SALW in Kosovo was also shown to be linked to high unemployment, weaknesses and lack of confidence in the Criminal Justice System, uncertainty regarding the future of Kosovo and whether it would become independent, and organised crime, as well as rivalries between political and ethnic groups – or at least, these were factors which increased insecurity and potentially impacted choices people made about owning or perhaps using weapons (SEESAC, 2006). There were also broader concerns among some Kosovo Serbs and Kosovo Albanians that the other was armed and there was, therefore, a need to retain arms to 'sustain a balance of fear' (Saferworld, 2007: 5).

SALW control actors

While national governments should take the primary responsibility to control SALW – through raising awareness, identifying the scope of the problem, and developing and implementing policy and programmes – in the aftermath of conflict not only is the problem of SALW proliferation likely to be more acute, but the capacity to address the problem is likely to be severely limited. Consequently, a number of external actors are often engaged, including other states and international organisations, such as the UN, the International Criminal Police Organization (ICPO, otherwise known as INTERPOL), the World Customs Organization (WCO), International Civil Aviation Organization (ICAO) and the International Maritime Organization (IMO). In addition, many regional organisations are also involved in SALW control, including the North Atlantic Treaty Organization (NATO), the Economic Community of West African States (ECOWAS), the Organization for Security and Co-operation in Europe (OSCE) and the European Union (EU). In addition, a broad range of civil society actors are engaged in SALW control, including NGOs, the media, academia, research organisations and think tanks, communities and others both within and outside the country of concern. The private sector or business community is also often engaged. Clearly, the number of different actors and different activities involved in SALW control necessitates co-ordination (see Box 6.4 for an overview of some of the actors engaged in SALW control in Libya, as an example). Of course, SALW

Box 6.4: SALW Control in Libya

The 2011 Libyan revolution and its aftermath led to the proliferation and widespread use of SALW, with state military stockpiles raided and a thriving illicit arms industry developing. Light weapons became widely available to non-state armed actors and individuals, many improvised weapons were developed, and weapons were stored unsafely or abandoned in areas where the war spread, further enabling the easy accessibility of weapons and spreading the threat they posed (Alusala, 2016; Small Arms Survey, 2016).

In response to the illicit arms flows and threats posed by SALW, a number of external actors supported and delivered SALW control programmes in Libya, including risk education, research and building the capacity of national institutions. These actors included UN Mine Action Service (UNMAS), EU Non-proliferation Consortium, DanChurchAid (DCA), the Danish Refugee Council (DRC), the German Federal Foreign Office, Small Arms Survey, GICHD and Handicap Initiative (Alusala, 2016; UNMAS, 2019). Given the threat posed and the number of actors involved, there was clearly a need for co-ordination to avoid duplication of efforts and minimise gaps. Some programmes were postponed due to deteriorating security conditions, and limited resources meant that programmes could not match need (as demand outweighed control efforts) (UNMAS, 2019). Today, the widespread use and illicit trade of SALW remains of serious concern for the security of Libya as well as other countries, with reports that Libya has become a hub for the illicit trade of SALW (Small Arms Survey, 2016).

proliferation and use is a transnational problem and so there needs to be co-ordinated efforts at regional and international levels also.

On the ground, many of these organisations can be involved in any number of SALW control activities, as outlined above. The overarching aim will be to address both demand and supply, that is, both the driving factors which compel people to arm themselves with weapons, as well as the illicit economy which sustains criminal groups and perpetuates insecurity. Some organisations will, therefore, focus on attending to community security needs in an effort to find ways in which to address those needs in ways beyond the possession of personal weapons for defence, for instance. Other organisations will be focussed upon the more formal security tasks of collecting and destroying weapons and managing stockpiles. Of course, these efforts will be limited in their success unless action is taken against groups which profit from the illicit trade in SALW and unless there is a con-certed and co-ordinated international approach to controlling the manufacture and movement of such weapons.

Challenges and recommendations

Despite progress at the policy and programmatic level, and the considerable resources directed into SALW since the late 1990s, efforts have been hampered by lack of agreement on what the SALW problem is (Krause, 2007). This is in part due to the differing impact of the presence of SALW in different contexts and due to different perceptions of the level and scope of external control required and desired (the strong US gun lobby feared that the advent of the Arms Trade Treaty in 2013 could have undermined the constitutional right to bear arms, for instance). It can even be asked whether SALW control is actually a post-conflict problem (and even just one problem), or is it really more to do with domestic and transnational crime and interpersonal violence. It is also evident that SALW cannot simply be banned, unlike mines. In addition, even in post-conflict environments, much depends on the perspective of the actor defining the problem and how the problem is framed – whether as a human rights, crime, peacebuilding, development or security issue. As we have seen, this naturally follows from the very different situations in different countries.

Additionally, there is a lack of commitment on the part of many states to the Programme of Action (PoA) and the International Tracing Instrument (ITI), and it remains unclear whether much has changed since their adoption in terms of concrete implementation (Small Arms Survey, 2011). However, the entry into force of the ATT in 2014 reinvigorated focus on the PoA and ITI. This was compounded by a renewed focus on the need to control SALW resulting from a number of crises seen to have been fuelled by the illicit trade in SALW, notably in the Sahel where insurgent groups in Mali and Nigeria benefitted from weap-ons looted from stockpiles in Libya (Bromley, 2016). Further, the 2016 Biennial Meeting of States (BMS) to consider implementation of the PoA and ITI resulted in a powerful outcome document which has the potential to improve implemen-tation of the PoA and ITI (Bromley, 2016). Of particular note in the outcome document is reference to Sustainable Development Goal 16, principally Target

16.4 requiring states to reduce illicit arms flows, and calling on states to develop national-level indicators based upon the PoA and ITT in order to measure progress (Bromley, 2016).

Nonetheless, limited information and independent assessment of implementation make it hard to fully ascertain the extent of the gaps or weaknesses in implementation, and thus thwart efforts to address any such gaps and weaknesses. Moreover, SALW control is a complex issue that has not been sufficiently studied and which is also often obscured by more newsworthy issues, such as weapons of mass destruction (WMD). Progress in adopting multilateral agreements on SALW has been slow and painstaking due to the consensus required, with certain countries – including the US, Russia and China – having consistently blocked efforts to regulate weapons that they see as an indispensable right and of central importance to maintaining national security.

At the policy-making and implementation levels, as is often the case with peacebuilding efforts, coherence of efforts and co-ordination could be improved. For example, Bourne (2018) refers to a fragmented and fragile global SALW control regime, which protects sovereignty more than individuals against violence. Different attitudes to SALW and different understandings of what the problem is and how it should be addressed make any effective practical measures problematic. There also tends to be an excessive focus on generic approaches, rather than understanding the specific context. There is a need, in other words, to address the demand as well as supply side of the equation – recognising that the SALW trade is big business, with transactions amounting to estimates of USD70 billion per annum (Luban, 2014) – and to address the causes of insecurity, socio-economic and political exclusion, and criminality if possession of arms by those who seek self-defence, empowerment or criminal gain, for instance, is to be addressed.

SALW control programmes, therefore, must take into account governance, as well as community safety, law enforcement and economic development. They must also promote local ownership as well as inclusion of all stakeholders, and be prepared to respect local people's views. People need to have confidence that the state will protect them, and pursue and punish violent criminals. Good governance and easing of tensions between communities are also indispensable if SALW control efforts are to be effective. Otherwise the proliferation and misuse of SALW will further undermine these very socio-economic, security and political conditions.

It is also important to recognise the effect of SALW control programmes on local conflict dynamics and other peacebuilding efforts – and vice versa. However, SALW control programmes are often not fully integrated into the political logic of broader peacebuilding efforts and are often seen simply as technical projects which, while important, lack resonance with these wider efforts (see Box 6.5 on how SALW control and SSR are linked and thus need to be co-ordinated).

Other issues that hamper effectiveness in this field include financial and programmatic constraints, as well as a lack of agreed and actionable norms and standards, and mechanisms to disseminate such norms and standards. However, as indicated earlier, the development of International Small Arms Control Standards (ISACS) by the UN Coordinating Action on Small Arms (CASA) is a positive development, which provides much-needed guidance. National legislation regulating

---

Box 6.5: SALW Control and Security Sector Reform (SSR)

SALW control and SSR are clearly linked. Unless efforts to control SALW are successful, efforts to create effective security sector institutions will be hampered. For, poor SALW control undermines the rule of law and wider security. It also means that much of the work of security sector institutions and broader government will need to be squarely focussed on combatting the threats posed by organised criminal groups and other threats associated with SALW, to the detriment of providing other forms of security and justice for the people. Similarly, unless there are effective security sector institutions, individuals may want to keep their weapons for self-protection, and armed organised criminal groups and militia may continue to operate. This will of course hinder any SALW control efforts. While the integral relationship between SALW control and SSR is acknowledged in policy, in practice two distinct sets of actors are engaged in respective programmes, and co-ordination and coherence of efforts have tended to be wanting. There are clearly other obvious synergies and interdependencies between SALW control and SSR with mine action and Disarmament, Demobilisation and Reintegration (DDR) programmes, which demand co-ordination in the field as well as recognition in policy and guidance (see GICHD and DCAF, 2017; IDDRS, 2006; Sedra and Burt, 2016; von Dyck, 2016).

SALW is also weak in many countries and – where it is not – commitment to the implementation of such legislation is sometimes not evident.

The fact that SALW control requires cross-border and transnational efforts adds further complication and difficulties, particularly given disparities in legislation, political will and cultural attitudes to SALW control. This is especially the case where those involved include organised criminal groups, insurgent and terrorist groups, states and other powerful actors with vested interests in the illicit trade of SALW. As was seen in Liberia, SALW control efforts in 2005 were hampered by similar efforts in neighbouring Côte d'Ivoire where it was perceived that there was higher compensation for handing over weapons. Consequently, many weapons were trafficked from Liberia to Côte d'Ivoire. A regional approach to SALW control could have improved the effectiveness of SALW control programmes, not least by avoiding false expectations and the establishment of false economies (OECD, 2007a). But this, in turn, requires that the political situation, attitudes to guns and commitment, if any, to control, should be at least approximately the same.[1]

Conclusion

This chapter has provided an overview of the impact of mines and other ERW as well as the presence of SALW in conflict-affected environments, and described why mine action and SALW control are fundamental to successful peacebuilding efforts. This chapter has also returned to the political issue of definitions. Oftentimes, there is no universally agreed definition of issues that need to be dealt with in the post-conflict environment. However, without an agreed understanding of what is being talked about and, more importantly, without specificity and a context-specific approach to such issues, efforts aimed at addressing them will be hampered.

This chapter has also underscored the importance of co-ordination in the field, given the number of activities and actors involved, as well as the interlinkages with other peacebuilding programmes, notably DDR (Chapter 7) and SSR (Chapter 8). The absence of requisite political will and financial support for efforts to minimise the threats posed by mines and SALW in post-conflict environments has also been referred to. The longevity of the threats posed by mines and SALW is compounded by their continued widespread manufacture and use, necessitating that action be taken to address both the supply and demand sides of the equation. In this regard, with respect to SALW, for instance, there is a need to attend to reasons why SALW remain desirable in post-conflict environments (including lack of confidence in the peace process and/or security providers), as well as to take action to inhibit the operation of organised criminal and other groups engaged in the illicit trade of SALW (recognising that there is often a blurred line between the licit and illicit trade in SALW – see Luban, 2014). For even after a formal end to armed conflict, the proliferation of SALW, as well as mines and other ERW, undermines prospects for meaningful security and sustainable peace within the post-conflict environment. Given their mobility, the security threat posed by SALW also extends far beyond the post-conflict environment to other societies, not least those particularly vulnerable to conflict, organised crime and other forms of insecurity.

Summary of Key Issues

- Mines can remain in conflict-affected environments for decades after the end of the conflict and have far-reaching effects on individuals, families, communities and societies beyond physical and mental trauma.
- Children are particularly at risk from mines and other ERW, and child survivors can particularly suffer from lack of bespoke victim assistance.
- Mine action refers to activities which aim to reduce the impact of mines and ERW on individuals, communities and societies as well as on the environment.
- Mine action includes Mine Risk Education (MRE), demining or mine clearance, victim assistance, advocacy and stockpile destruction.
- Demining remains under-resourced, dangerous and time-consuming.
- SALW control includes developing legislation and administrative procedures, building or reforming institutional structures, collecting and destroying surplus weaponry and munitions, managing stockpiles, developing and delivering public awareness campaigns, and promoting international co-operation to control SALW and promote safer societies.

- In the security vacuum that often characterises post-conflict environments, organised criminal groups can take advantage of weak SALW control, and individuals also often retain small arms as a means of self-defence.
- The presence of SALW in post-conflict environments can undermine security by fuelling crime, damaging the rule of law, compromising reconciliation efforts and hindering development notably by discouraging external investment.
- Increased attention and resources allocated by the international community since the 1990s have resulted in structures and frameworks that, if adhered to, could significantly reduce the proliferation and misuse of SALW.
- However, a lack of commitment on the part of many states to realise their commitments has hampered progress to control SALW.

Reflective Question

Can the world be mine-free? If not, how can the world be mine risk-free?

List of Core Resources

Mine action

Bryden, A. (2005) 'Optimising Mine Action Policies and Practices', in A. Bryden and H. Hänggi (eds), *Security Governance in Post-Conflict Peacebuilding* (Münster: LIT Verlag).

GICHD and DCAF (2017) *Seeking more coherent implementation in post-conflict security: Can we better align SSR, DDR, SALW and Mine Action?*, Event Report (Geneva: GICHD and DCAF). Available at www.gichd.org/fileadmin/GICHD-resources/rec-documents/GICHD-DCAF-event-report-2017-05.pdf.

Hofmann, H., Maspoli, G., Massleberg, A. and Rapillard, P. (2016) *Linking Mine Action and SSR through Human Security*, SSR Paper 15 (Geneva: DCAF). Available at www.dcaf.ch/sites/default/files/publications/documents/ONLINE-DCAF-SSR-15-2016-06-16.pdf.

International Campaign to Ban Landmines – Cluster Munition Coalition (ICBL-CMC) (2016c) *The Impact of Mines/ERW on Children*. Available at www.the-monitor.org/media/2389719/MinesChildren2016Final.pdf.

Kiener, R. (2011) 'Dangerous War Debris: Who Should Clean Up After Conflicts End?' in CQ Researcher (ed.), *Issues in Peace and Conflict Studies: Selections From CQ Researcher* (Washington: Sage): 341–367.

Laws, E. (2017) *The impact of mines and explosive remnants of war on gender groups*, K4D Helpdesk Report (Brighton, UK: Institute of Development Studies). Available at https://assets.publishing.service.gov.uk/media/59844e0c40f0b6 1e4b00005c/149-the-impact-of-mines-and-explosive-remnants-of-war-on-gender-groups__1_.pdf.

Naidoo, S. (2013) 'Mission creep or responding to wider security needs? The evolving role of mine action organisations in Armed Violence Reduction', *Stability: International Journal of Security and Development* 2(1): 11, 1–8.

UN (2010) *Gender Guidelines for Mine Action Programmes* (New York: UN). Available at https://unmas.org/sites/default/files/ma-guidelines_0.pdf.

UN (2016b) *The United Nations Policy on Victim Assistance in Mine Action* (New York: UN). Available at www.mineactionstandards.org/fileadmin/user_upload/images/publications/16-06-09_FINAL_UN_Policy_on_Victim_Assistance_in_Mine_Action.pdf.

UNMAS (2010) *UN Mine Action Service (UNMAS)* (video). Available at www.youtube.com/watch?v=qkCBfrTAT0Y.

UNMAS (2016) *World Humanitarian Summit Opening Ceremony* (video). Available at www.youtube.com/watch?v=ahgrJ7ram8M.

USIP (2017) *Demining War Zones: Opening Space for Building Peace* (video). Available at www.youtube.com/watch?v=Y-UuIYgwctg.

Vice News (2014) *After the Flood: Mines and Mass Graves in Bosnia* (video). Available at: www.youtube.com/watch?reload=9&v=Gy5hX267fi0.

Wilton Park (2017) *Effective IED clearance* (video). Available at www.youtube.com/watch?v=gu-aqikxZ84.

For further information and current statistics see the websites of UNMAS www.mineaction.org), Landmine and Cluster Munition Monitor (www.the-monitor.org), Mine Action Review (www.mineactionreview.org), the Geneva International Centre for Humanitarian Demining (www.gichd.org) as well as the website of its AP Mine Ban Convention Implementation Support Unit (www.apminebanconvention.org).

SALW control

BICC (2008) *A Gun in Every Home* (video). Available at www.youtube.com/watch?v=fUflPzT_QkY.

BICC (2017) *Keep The Safety On* (video). Available at www.youtube.com/watch?v=gMKQWMLdcgg.

Božanić, D. (2016) *Gender and SALW in South East Europe* (Belgrade: South Eastern and Eastern Europe Clearinghouse for the Control of Small Arms and Light Weapons (SEESAC)). Available at www.seesac.org/f/docs/Armed-Violence/Gender_and_SALW_publication_eng-web.pdf.

Garcia, D. (2014) 'Global Norms on Arms: The Significance of the Arms Trade Treaty for Global Security in World Politics', *Global Policy* 5(4): 425–32.

Greene, O. and Marsh, N. (2013) *Small Arms, Crime and Conflict: Global Governance and the Threat of Armed Violence* (London: Routledge).

Krause, K. (2007) *Small Arms and Light Weapons: Towards Global Public Policy*, Coping with Crisis Working Paper Series (New York: International Peace Academy) (now International Peace Institute). Available at www.files.ethz.ch/isn/126967/small_arms_light_weapons_03_2007.pdf.

Muggah, R. (2010) 'Rethinking small arms control in Africa: it is time to set an armed violence reduction agenda', *Conflict, Security and Development*, 10(2): 217–38.

Saferworld (2015) *Saving lives: Improving community security through arms control in Kenya* (video). Available at www.youtube.com/watch?v=Z6Jpq5N3N3U.

Sedra, M. and Burt, G. (2016) *Integrating SSR and SALW Programming* SSR Paper 16 (Geneva: DCAF). Available at www.dcaf.ch/sites/default/files/publications/documents/ONLINE-DCAF-SSR-16-2016-06-16.pdf.

Small Arms Survey (2014), *Small Arms Survey 2014: Women and Guns* (Geneva: Small Arms Survey. Available at www.smallarmssurvey.org/publications/by-type/yearbook/small-arms-survey-2014.html.

Small Arms Survey (2011), *Small Arms Survey 2011: States of Security*, Geneva: Small Arms Survey). Available at www.smallarmssurvey.org/publications/by-type/yearbook/small-arms-survey-2011.html.

Soysa, I., Jackson, T. and Ormhaug, C. (2010) 'Tools of the torturer? Small arms imports and repression of human rights, 1992–2004', *The International Journal of Human Rights*, 14(3): 378–93.

Oxford Academic (2017) *What is the Arms Trade Treaty?* (video). Available at www.youtube.com/watch?v=wasPiNwe6hQ.

Note

[1]For more information on SALW control and related issues, see the following websites: Control Arms (www.controlarms.org); International Action Network on Small Arms (IANSA) (www.iansa.org); Small Arms Survey – www.smallarmssurvey.org); South Eastern and Eastern Europe Clearinghouse for the Control of Small Arms and Light Weapons (SEESAC) (www.seesac.org); UN Office for Disarmament Affairs (UNODA) (www.un.org/disarmament); International Small Arms Control Standards (ISACS) (www.smallarmsstandards.org); Norwegian Initiative on Small Arms Transfers (NISAT) (http://nisat.prio.org); Saferworld (www.saferworld.org.uk/effective-arms-control).

7 Disarmament, Demobilisation and Reintegration

Overview

Disarmament, Demobilisation and Reintegration (DDR) of former combatants is an increasingly key feature of peacebuilding efforts, the success of which depends upon whether DDR efforts are effective and their results sustainable. This chapter considers the concept of DDR and ways in which DDR has changed over recent years. DDR objectives and key actors will also be looked at, before considering some fundamental issues – including the importance of attending to the specific needs of children, women and other vulnerable groups, and the importance of integrating DDR programmes with other peacebuilding efforts, particularly Security Sector Reform (SSR), Small Arms and Light Weapons (SALW) control, community safety, transitional justice and reconciliation. The chapter concludes by considering some of the overarching challenges in the field of DDR and recommendations to overcome some of these challenges.

Learning Outcomes

- Be familiar with the key elements and objectives of DDR programmes
- Articulate ways in which DDR programmes should respond to the specific needs of women, children and other vulnerable groups
- Identify ways in which DDR programmes could be integrated with other peace-building efforts
- Identify some of the challenges in the field of DDR in post-conflict environments
- Assess ways in which some of the identified challenges and weaknesses can be overcome

Part 1 – Defining DDR

The history and concept of DDR

The issues covered by DDR programmes are not new and have been addressed with greater or lesser success for most of human history (see Box 7.1, for instance, for an overview of DDR after the First and Second World Wars). What has changed is the insertion of these issues into large and ambitious peacebuilding programmes

> **Box 7.1: DDR after WWI and WWII**
>
> As long as there have been conflicts, the problem has arisen of how to treat the combatants once the fighting is over. The demobilisation of the huge forces that fought the First World War (WWI) was very clumsily handled, especially among the defeated nations and empires, and the states created from the wreckage. The economies of most of the defeated parties were devastated, and in Germany, for example, groups of unemployed ex-servicemen, many of extreme nationalist beliefs, banded together to form roving militias, the *Freikorps*. Friederich Ebert, the Socialist who became the first Chancellor of post-war Germany was obliged to turn to the *Freikorps* for protection against the left-wing revolutions that convulsed Germany. Many of the *Freikorps* alumni went on to join extreme nationalist paramilitary groups, including the Nazi Party. Conscious of these problems, the victorious powers after 1945 (and WWII) handled what we would now call a DDR programme much better. Worried about suddenly dumping millions of newly demobilised soldiers into the economy, they adopted a staged and very deliberate approach, as well as managing the economy in such a way that there were jobs for everybody (Chuter, 2017).

led by international organisations and donors, as well as attempts to develop a consistent set of generic DDR principles. This change also reflects the increasing involvement from the 1990s of development ministries as well as donors and NGOs from outside the security sector, and the increasing weight given to the security–development paradigm, where development and security are seen as mutually reinforcing (Berdal, 2009; Muggah, 2010a). Today, DDR is seen as an increasingly key feature of peacebuilding efforts, with most of the recent UN peacekeeping operations including DDR responsibilities in their mandate. The UN has also supported DDR programmes in many other countries when there is not a UN peacekeeping operation.

The UN Integrated DDR Standards (IDDRS) are a comprehensive set of consolidated DDR policies, guidelines, procedures and best practices, providing a UN integrated approach to DDR – available on the UN DDR website (www.iddrtg. org). As stated in IDDRS, the UN 'uses the concept and abbreviation "DDR" as an all-inclusive term that includes related activities, such as repatriation, rehabilitation and reconciliation, that aim to achieve sustainable reintegration' (UN IDDRS, 2006: n.p.). DDR is also intended to contribute to reconciliation and the building of trust between former conflicting groups.

The UN definitions of DDR and its primary components are:

- *DDR* – A process that contributes to security and stability in a post-conflict recovery context by removing weapons from the hands of combatants, taking the combatants out of military structures and helping them to integrate socially and economically into society by finding civilian livelihoods.
- *Disarmament* – Disarmament is the collection, documentation, control and disposal of small arms, ammunition, explosives and light and

heavy weapons of combatants and often also of the civilian population. Disarmament also includes the development of responsible arms management programmes (Secretary-General, note to the General Assembly, A/C.5/59/31, May 2005).

• *Demobilisation* – Demobilisation is the formal and controlled discharge of active combatants from armed forces or other armed groups. The first stage of demobilisation may extend from the processing of individual combatants in temporary centres to the massing of troops in camps designated for this purpose (cantonment sites, encampments, assembly areas or barracks). The second stage of demobilisation encompasses the support package provided to the demobilised, which is called reinsertion (Secretary-General, note to the General Assembly, A/C.5/59/31, May 2005).

• *Reintegration* – Reintegration is the process by which ex-combatants acquire civilian status and gain sustainable employment and income. Reintegration is essentially a social and economic process with an open time-frame, primarily taking place in communities at the local level. It is part of the general development of a country and a national responsibility, and often necessitates long-term external assistance (Secretary-General, note to the General Assembly, A/C.5/59/31, May 2005) (UN IDDRS, 2006 citing UNGA, 2005b: 1) (see Figure 7.1).

These definitions raise a number of questions. We have already seen that there is no agreed understanding of the concept of security, nor what armed conflict is, why it happens and how it ends. It is equally unclear what the concept of reconciliation is, or whether there are cases where it has actually occurred. There is also no agreement on the way in which disarmament impacts conflict dynamics. More generally, we have seen that all of these concepts are highly context-dependent, interdependent and, often, subjective. It would therefore be helpful to have a set of clear definitions and criteria for DDR. Unfortunately, given the increasing focus on DDR activities in peacekeeping and peacebuilding operations and the associated increase in DDR activities and actors, there is in reality a wide array of definitions.

It should be noted that there are also a number of related terms used interchangeably. In particular, reinsertion, rehabilitation, repatriation and/or resettlement might be used instead of, or as well as, the term reintegration. As often, it is not clear whether these terms are being used in a way that makes it possible to distinguish them clearly from each other.

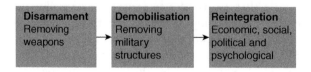

Figure 7.1 DDR Process

For the purpose of this chapter, the concept 'disarmament, demobilisation and reintegration' (DDR) will be used. It is, however, worthwhile defining 'reinsertion' as this is a concept commonly used in the DDR process. Reinsertion generally refers to the short-term material and/or financial assistance offered to ex-combatants during demobilisation, prior to the longer-term process of reintegration, and can help cover the costs of food, shelter and medical assistance, as well as short-term education or training and employment.

Objectives and principles

As we have seen, the objectives of DDR are manifold and ambitious, with the ultimate aim of contributing to security and stability in immediate post-conflict environments, so that recovery and development can commence and the risks of a return to violent conflict are reduced (see Stabilisation Unit, 2010). In essence, DDR constitutes a structured approach to removing arms, dismantling military structures and providing former combatants with the ability and the will not to take up arms again, or to lead a life of criminality and violence, by economically, socially and politically reintegrating them into society. Specifically, with respect to reintegration:

> The key objective of reintegration is to enhance national and community security and recovery by supporting ex-combatants in their efforts to find a new role in society and the economy, through sustainable, peaceful livelihoods for them and their families. Reintegration opportunities should not be considered as an entitlement for ex-combatants but as an opportunity to facilitate their transition to civilian life. (UNDP, 2005a: 50)

Of all of the components of DDR, reintegration is generally recognised as being the most difficult, as well as the least under the control of international missions. Effectively, reintegration requires something to reintegrate into, and social and economic structures capable of managing the process. We have seen that conflict frequently arises in times of economic failure or decline, and that conflict further damages the economy.

The era that saw the development of DDR was also the period of the triumph of neoliberal economic policies (which is no coincidence). Earlier development theory, inspired by the success of countries like Singapore and South Korea, saw a substantial role for the state (as indeed had been the case with 'DDR'-style activities after the Second World War). Neoliberal thinking, by contrast, saw the rebirth of post-conflict economies through minimal government involvement and Foreign Direct Investment; the latter to be facilitated by a 'business-friendly' climate with limited social and economic protection for the population. The result has been post-conflict economies that have largely stagnated. Whilst, as we have seen, security is a necessary condition for economic development, it is not a sufficient one, and much of the growth in post-conflict economies has been based on foreign aid and the presence of large international forces. After conflict, few individuals are keen to invest for the long term, not least in case conflict recurs, as it often does. In turn, reintegration policy is linked with current beliefs that training and education will themselves naturally produce economic growth; something that has no empirical support (Chang, 2010; Wolf, 2002). Training programmes, even if they are well targeted, often simply produce a better-trained population of unemployed youth. When unemployment may itself have been a factor in unleashing conflict, this can be unhelpful.

In addition, social factors often underlie conflicts. The explosive growth in the under-25 population in Africa, for example, is itself a source of stress and a reason why some young people, no longer feeling at home in traditional societies, have opted to join in military adventures. For some of these young former combatants, it is not clear that sending them back to their villages, to take on social roles they had previously rejected, is good for stability in the long term. In many ways, therefore, DDR programmes are a gesture of faith, in that they rely for ultimate success on things that the international community cannot control, or necessarily even influence.

Today, DDR will usually (and ideally – although not always) be agreed to and defined within a comprehensive peace accord, ceasefire or cessation of hostilities. As will soon be discussed, however, the DDR of children should happen immediately and not await a peace agreement. The whole DDR process will thereafter often extend well beyond immediate post-conflict stabilisation, particularly if the reintegration phase (and thus the whole DDR process) is to be successful; without the investment of considerable time as well as financial resources, the socio-economic reintegration of former combatants into society can be unsustainable, as we have seen.

Preparations for DDR processes often begin before any peace agreement and should include efforts to build trust and awareness, and secure financial and political support. Plans also need to include identification of risk factors, contingency plans and exit strategies. Aside from the need for in-depth advance planning, other principles, also endorsed within the IDDRS, include the need to be:

- *Context-specific*: being familiar with and responsive to the specific context in which the DDR process is being planned for or implemented, and sufficiently flexible in order to be able to respond to changing dynamics
- *Nationally and Locally Owned*: identifying and building capacity, ensuring the active engagement of local communities and authorities to ensure that plans are relevant, and thereby increasing the likelihood of sustainability
- *People-centred*: focussing upon the needs of individuals (rather than, for instance, just focussing upon technical aspects such as the collection of weapons), particularly women and children and other vulnerable groups (such as abductees and disabled people), ensuring non-discrimination and fair and equitable treatment, and adhering to human rights and humanitarian law and principles
- *Co-ordinated and Integrated*: ensuring co-ordination and unity of effort between national and international stakeholders from the outset and throughout planning and implementation, in order to ensure clarity, focus and success – and ensuring that DDR is co-ordinated with other peacebuilding efforts, notably SSR and economic regeneration programmes
- *Accountable*: prioritising accountability and transparency throughout the DDR process in order to build confidence in the process and, thus, the likelihood of success.

Part 2 – DDR Actors and Issues

DDR actors

As stated in UN IDDRS (2006), all key stakeholders in the political process to build peace and the wider peace process should be involved in the development of DDR policy and institutions. This is so trust can be built, which is instrumental to the success of any DDR effort. Stakeholders include those who have not participated in the armed conflict, not least prospective receiving communities and those who have suffered as a result of the activities of the armed forces or groups. National NGOs and CSOs, government and political party representatives, military authorities, community representatives, media representatives, the private sector and members of think tanks will all have a role to play in DDR planning. Their support throughout implementation will also be crucial. International actors include:

- International organisations, particularly the UN and its various entities engaged in the UN Inter-Agency Working Group on DDR, established in 2005 and co-chaired by the Department of Peacekeeping Operations (DPKO) and the UN Development Programme (UNDP)
- Regional organisations
- Development banks (particularly the World Bank)
- Bilateral and multilateral donors and agencies
- NGOs (for implementing DDR components, particularly development and humanitarian components).

DDR and children

In accordance with the 2007 Principles and Guidelines on Children Associated with Armed Forces or Armed Groups (known more commonly as the Paris Principles), a child soldier is a boy or girl under the age of 18 recruited, conscripted or used by an armed force or armed group for any purpose, including support functions and other capacities (such as for sexual exploitation) as well as combat roles. Article 8 of the Rome Statute defines 'conscripting or enlisting children under the age of fifteen into armed forces or groups or using them to participate actively in hostilities as a war crime'. As such, the reintegration of children into civilian life has been deemed not to be a part of the DDR process, but an endeavour to prevent or redress a violation of the human rights of the children (UN IDDRS, 2006). Consequently, the process and its requirements are separate and distinct from the process of reintegrating adult former combatants. Specific attention is usually given to the psychosocial and socio-economic aspects of reintegration, including facilitating access to education and a livelihood, and the funding of child protection agencies and programmes to ensure long-term support.

It has generally been argued that child DDR should not await a peace agreement or the launch of adult DDR programmes, but that efforts to reintegrate and prevent the recruitment of child soldiers should be continuous. Thus, the rights of children 'should be identified as an explicit priority in peacemaking, peace-building and conflict resolution processes, both in the peace agreement and in DDR plans' (UN IDDRS, 2006: n.p.). Additionally, it is argued that peace agreements should articulate a commitment to release children from and stop recruiting children to armed forces and groups, with specific attention given to girls (UN IDDRS, 2006). Child DDR should be guided by the Paris Principles, which can be found at www.unicef.org/emerg/files/ParisPrinciples310107English.pdf, and the Optional Protocol on the involvement of children in armed conflict to the Convention on the Rights of the Child (2002), which can be found at https://childrenandarmedconflict.un.org/mandate/optional-protocol/.

However, it can often be difficult to identify who is a child combatant. In some conflict areas, not even the combatants may know their age. It is usually impossible to prove or disprove the age of a given combatant, pretending to be or denying being, a child. It can be hard to prove that a child was conscripted or recruited and that the perpetrator either knew or should have known their age. Additionally, children may be recruited in support functions as well as in combat roles, which further problematises the concept of child soldier. Further challenges arise when those recruited to armed groups as children then commit war crimes and other serious violations of international law (refer back to Box 5.8 in Chapter 5 for a discussion of Lord's Resistance Army (LRA) Commander Dominic Ongwen who was abducted and recruited at the age of 10 and faces 70 charges of war crimes before the International Criminal Court).

Oftentimes, children are abducted and forcibly recruited to armed forces and groups, in particular because they are often more easily indoctrinated and are more economically efficient option than using adult combatants (UN Special Representative of the Secretary-General for Children and Armed Conflict, 2012). Sometimes children 'voluntarily' join armed forces or groups for economic, ideological or security reasons; they can offer children escape from poverty and mass unemployment; provide protection, a means of survival and a sense of belonging or purpose; and offer opportunities for revenge or liberation – a means of empowerment or a way to satisfy a desire to strike back against oppression, corruption or violence (ACCORD, 2016; UN Special Representative of the Secretary-General for Children and Armed Conflict, 2012). This is consistent with what we know about why young people have gone to fight in the past, and broadly correlates with the reasons why others join armed groups and armed forces. Many young people joined the FARC in Colombia, for example, partly because of 'poverty, unemployment, vengeance, avoiding violence from the rival group, and the allure of the military life' (Sanin, 2010: 137).

Consequently, DDR programmes that simply try to reinsert children (by now adults, perhaps) in a society from which they fled, fought and/or which offers them nothing, can only fail. A DDR programme which does not recognise that children have agency and may have similar motivations for engaging in combat as adults, but rather considers children only to be passive victims, will equally not be able to respond to the specific needs of former child combatants in a way that will facilitate their effective reintegration into civilian life (see Brocklehurst, 2008; Harris, 2015).

DDR and women

It is widely argued that unless gender is mainstreamed into peacebuilding efforts – with both men and women engaged in decision-making, and which is also informed by and responsive to their specific needs – such efforts will be largely unsuccessful. Nonetheless, women are infrequently engaged in the planning and implementation of DDR programmes. This can impact the extent to which the needs of women are addressed in DDR programmes, as will be discussed in more detail in Chapter 10.

DDR programmes often overlook the specific needs of women, often because programme developers or implementers wrongly assume that active combatants were only male (Houngbedji et al., 2012; Sjoberg and Gentry, 2007). DDR in Liberia, for instance, overlooked women other than as victims of conflict or as secondary to the real purpose of reintegration (Jennings, 2009). Women have also self-demobilised, removing themselves from DDR programmes. This has happened where they have not been provided with crèche facilities, training that meets their specific needs, or psychosocial support to respond to the fact that they may be further stigmatised once they return to their communities for being combatants and having transgressed gender norms (Avoine and Tillman, 2015; Colekessian, 2010; MacKenzie, 2009; Saferworld, 2010). Where programmes are intended to target the specific needs of women, they can reinforce gender stereotypes (see Box 7.2). DDR programmes also face gender-related challenges because programmes often fail to unpick militarised masculinities which often reinforce the link between masculinity and violence and thereby compromise DDR success (see Mazurana et al., 2018).

Box 7.2: DDR and Women in Colombia

DDR programmes infrequently respond to the specific needs of women. Where they do, they can reinforce gender stereotypes – for instance by providing gender-specific training such as hairdressing for women and plumbing for men. This happened in Nepal (Goswami, 2015), Sierra Leone (MacKenzie, 2009) and Sri Lanka (Martin, 2017). Ní Aoláin (2016, 34) argues that DDR can involve 'a complex recalibration of masculine identity and status in any society emerging from conflict' for men, but for women it often involves a disappearing through ostracism or 'return to normal' where women are marginalised.

This is illustrated by an example from Colombia when in 2012 the government-hired PR company developed a public service campaign for the DDR programme, which read '*Guerrillera*, feel like a woman again. Demobilize.' (Alpert, 2016, n.p.). It featured lipstick colours with the names 'freedom', 'love', 'happiness' and 'tranquility', and encouraged women to 'smile and become the mother [they've] always dreamed of being'. (Alpert, 2016, n.p.). Evidence from the current DDR process in Colombia, however, suggests that it is inclusive of women and does not reinforce traditional gender stereotypes, with 32% of those in demobilised

---

(Continued)

zones being women and with women attending demining training, for instance (Henshaw, 2017b). This is most likely due to women playing a much more significant role in the peace negotiations and thus influencing the DDR programme (Bouvier, 2016).

Gender-responsive DDR could not only better respond to the needs of both women and men, but could also contribute to unpicking gender norms and stereotypes that reinforce gendered power relations and support structural inequalities and violence. As Flisi (2017, n.p.) suggests, in her discussion of the recent gender strategy of the Colombian Agency for Reintegration, a gender-responsive DDR can include 'initiatives to promote the role of men as care givers, equal redistribution of the childcare responsibilities and women's economic and political empowerment'. Unpicking militarised masculine identities through gender-responsive DDR and SSR could ultimately contribute to a more sustainable peace, and one which is meaningful beyond dominant and elite groups (Cockburn, 2010; Enloe, 2000; Flisi, 2017).

It should be emphasised that if DDR is to be successful, it needs to respond to the specific needs of beneficiaries and stakeholders, both men and women, as well as the specific context – and the context as it is now or is anticipated to be in the near future, not necessarily how it was before the war; it is no good training people for jobs that no longer exist or expecting former combatants to return to villages they no longer feel are home.

The political economy of DDR

As discussed, the reintegration part of DDR is often perceived to be the most difficult. It is certainly often the lengthiest phase, the most costly and the most complex in terms of requiring the engagement of many different actors. In some respect, while DDR programmes typically last 3–4 years, reintegration takes place during the many years after the formal end of any DDR programme (Özerdem, 2015). The post-conflict context also poses further challenges to successful reintegration: communities may be vengeful, traumatised or fearful, as can former combatants; the economy is likely to be heavily damaged and there are few prospects of jobs for many people. In terms of social and economic reintegration, prospective jobs for former combatants need to be meaningful if they are to do the job of preventing former combatants from taking up arms again, whether through necessity (if they cannot sustain themselves or their families they may be easily lured by militant or organised criminal groups at the prospect of an income), or grievance (if self-pride or high regard from others has been lost, for instance), or hopelessness (if they have little stake in the future). Meaningful employment helps avoid turning former combatants into prospective spoilers of the peace process and helps increase the likelihood of averting future conflict and instability.

It is therefore important that in-depth analysis of the socio-economic context and prospective beneficiaries' needs, expectations and skill-sets is undertaken during the development of reintegration programmes. This is to ensure that prospective economic opportunities are identified, which should be based upon the likelihood that they would suit prospective beneficiaries and be viable options in the specific context (and, importantly, viable options for a considerable period of time). The diverse needs of former combatants also require consideration. In other words, a reintegration package or prospective job that suits one former combatant need not suit another, whether because they have a different set of skills, interests and aspirations, or because they live in different geographical areas, for instance. Similarly, as just discussed, reintegration should not sideline women or seek to reaffirm gendered stereotypes; however, DDR programmes often do privilege male entry into the labour market, while encouraging women to return to the home or service-providing, low-paid employment. The assumption often is that reintegration efforts need to attend to the needs of young, male former combatants as a priority, assuming that they are potential spoilers who may pose more of a threat to a fragile peace than their female (or older or disabled) counterparts. However, securitising male unemployment and reaffirming gendered socio-economic inequalities does little to contribute to meaningful, sustainable peace. As Jennings (2009) makes clear, the threat of the 'idle young man' which seems to inform many DDR programmes, is narrow-minded and overlooks both women's and men's multidimensionality. It also conflicts with the slow pace of progress often seen in DDR programmes, where former combatants can be on cantonment sites for many years before effective reintegration. Moreover, despite much scholarship that considers that greed plays a key role in conflict (Collier, 2000), there remains little empirical evidence on the causal link between unemployment or underemployment and armed conflict (Munive, 2014). Further, focussing on the potential threat posed by men overlooks the threats to security posed by a reaffirmation of gender stereotypes, gendered socio-economic and power inequalities, and the violence which is sustained by and sustains such inequalities – as the links between gender inequality, violence against women and propensity to armed conflict suggest (Avoine and Tillman, 2015; Cockburn, 2010; Enloe, 2000; Mazurana and Proctor, 2013).

Many scholars also consider DDR programmes to be informed by neoliberal economic theory, which elevates the economic reintegration of former combatants above all other efforts, and focusses attention on the private sector for their economic reintegration, with limited attention given to how the economy operates in post-conflict environments. As Munive (2014) explores with regard to DDR in South Sudan, for instance, entrepreneurship and self-employment tend to be prioritised in economic reintegration programmes, in line with a neoliberal economic and political model which reduces the role of the state in the economy. There is, though, an inherent paradox, given that much peacebuilding seeks to strengthen the capacity and role of the state, assuming that a strong state is more likely to be a peaceful one. Of course, this is not always true, but the focus on building state institutions after conflict suggests that this assumption enjoys widespread support. Of more concern is the fact that entrepreneurship and self-employment may not suit many former combatants and may not provide access to sustainable employment in the post-conflict context.

When we consider the political economy of DDR, we must also remember that the trade in used weapons is big business. When a conflict ends, weapons are often retained for self-protection or other motivations, or can be sold to criminal, insurgent and other armed groups. An effective DDR programme will reduce the number of illicit weapons in circulation and will ensure that weapons are collected, securely stored and then destroyed – often as a symbolic, public ritual to mark the end of armed hostilities. However, because weapons are valuable, DDR and SALW control programmes (see Chapter 6) face significant challenges.

DDR and health

Those who have been seriously injured or disabled during the conflict or suffer from serious ill health also require special attention and specific provisions. Many DDR programmes are linked to SSR programmes which are reconstructing or establishing state security institutions; those with disabilities or chronic illness will most likely not have a place in these institutions. It is argued that specialist reintegration assistance for these former combatants – as well as those with substance addiction – will need to be provided, to include medical and psychosocial support as well as vocational training (UN IDDRS, 2006). Whilst there has been a significant decrease in the number of people dying from HIV-related causes (World Health Organisation, 2019), it is argued that there remains a need to address the subject in DDR programmes 'in the interests of the individuals concerned, the sustainability of reintegration efforts and general post-conflict recovery' (UN IDDRS, 2006: n.p.). Most DDR programmes do not, however, address the needs of those who are terminally ill or physically disabled (see Lord and Stein, 2015, for instance). Even the many former combatants who have been traumatised rarely receive the support that they need and that is required in any post-conflict environment if people are to recover and peace is to be sustainable. These facts further underscore how economic reintegration is privileged above all forms of reintegration; there is, for instance, little regard for the social or psychosocial reintegration of disabled former combatants despite a rhetorical commitment in all reintegration programmes to social and psychosocial reintegration.

Co-ordination with other peacebuilding programmes

There has been a tendency in recent years to link, at least conceptually, DDR and SSR on the basis that both can be seen as having the purpose of restoring or establishing the state's monopoly of the legitimate use of force after conflict (see McFate, 2010; von Dyck, 2016) and to link DDR to development or reform activities in other sectors. It is argued that, for example, decisions and activities concerning the integration of former combatants into the security sector need to be considered with an awareness of prospective structural reform of security providers and vice versa, and that both DDR and SSR 'are often best considered together as part of a comprehensive security and justice development program' (OECD, 2007a: 105).

Integrating former combatants into state security institutions can help rebuild trust between formerly warring parties. It can also help dis-incentivise potential spoilers by enabling them to have a stake in the state security structures, in effect in the provision of security for the people of the state, as well as giving them access to prospective long-term employment (Ansorg and Gordon, 2019; McFate, 2010). From this perspective, DDR and SSR can be seen to be mutually reinforcing, but also both are potentially compromised if the other faces challenges (see Knight, 2008). Of course, both DDR and SSR are also highly political exercises, involving the redistribution of power and broadly aiming to re-establish the state's monopoly of the legitimate use of force. The challenges to both programmes, as such, are significant, and compounded when they rely on each other.

The reintegration of former combatants should also be addressed in the context of broader development and economic reform activities, including economic regeneration and job creation programmes. The key stakeholders and decision-makers in SSR, economic reform and broader development need to be aware of the requirements of the reintegration process in order that it receives the support required, and in order to capitalise upon opportunities and avoid misunderstandings and programmatic tensions or conflicts.

DDR should also take account of any processes of transitional justice and reconciliation as well as SALW control programmes. As with SALW, DDR is also related to issues of perceptions of security and community safety. It is, therefore, insufficient to address DDR as a technical process and, as with all peacebuilding efforts, the specific context and conflict dynamics need to be considered prior to and throughout any engagement. For instance, it is insufficient just to focus on collecting weapons; there is a need to address why individuals may want to keep their weapons, what can be done to allay security fears, what future assurances can be given, how former combatants might be perceived by returning communities and others and so on. This requires building trust, developing in-depth knowledge of the context and prospective participants of the programmes, as well as detailed planning, including identification of interdependencies and contingency plans.

Interactions between DDR and other peacebuilding programmes are difficult enough by themselves, but DDR may also take place at a time when building a new national military is underway, or at least plans have been developed. Often these processes are managed by different actors, often with different aims and objectives, and the needs of the various programmes are often in conflict.

Part 3 – Challenges and Recommendations

As we touched upon at the beginning of this chapter, DDR is not a new problem, but one that has been grappled with, often on a very large scale, for hundreds of years. In 1945, for example, the provisional French government, amidst political and economic chaos, still managed to repatriate and reintegrate more than a million prisoners of war from Germany. From the 1940s to the 1970s, millions of young French, British and Portuguese conscripts fought in colonial wars and then returned to civilian life. These examples can be broadly regarded as successful, in contrast to many of today's DDR programmes which frequently fail. Of course, there is a huge difference between reintegrating former combatants in their own country by their own government and DDR programmes targeting former combatants associated with an organisation hostile to the government. The challenges facing today's DDR programmes are often much more complex, with competing demands from external actors and interest groups, and limitations in the extent to which programmes may be locally or even nationally owned.

Whilst everyone accepts, at least in theory, that the DDR process should be responsive, flexible and context-related, and that lessons learnt from elsewhere should be considered, in practice this does not always happen. Examples from elsewhere are either ignored or blindly applied and a one-size-fits-all approach is often adopted, rather than a nuanced and flexible approach to the specific context. Likewise, it is widely accepted that planning and decision-making should be preceded by comprehensive conflict, security, socio-economic and political analyses – as well as a comprehensive needs analysis; and such analyses should be continually undertaken throughout the process to inform decision-making. Additionally, as the context and conflict dynamics change, the DDR programme should be sufficiently flexible to be able to respond to the challenges and opportunities that may be presented. Again, however, inflexible doctrine tends to be the norm.

Ensuring that programmes are context-specific and responsive to changing dynamics takes time and resources; where resources and time are limited, and actors engaged in DDR are often experts of DDR rather than the specific context, and those with context-specific knowledge are often treated with suspicion, it is easy to see how the principles which are deemed to inform successful DDR programmes are not adhered to.

Other reasons for the high rate of failure of today's DDR programmes also include their scope and ambition, in contrast to the early examples of DDR given above. Reintegration today ostensibly must attend to the needs of all vulnerable groups, including children, women, disabled people, those who are chronically ill, as well as combatants' dependents who may have depended on a military salary. Reintegration must also be attentive to the social tensions that may arise as a result of a perception that combatants are being rewarded or compensated, rather than civilians who did not take up arms and may have disproportionately suffered the effects of the conflict. In addition to economic reintegration, the social, psychological and political aspects of reintegration are, in principle at least, given equal importance today. In other words, DDR programmes today are much more than a technical exercise, focussed on efforts to transform post-conflict societies in an effort to develop comprehensive security and stability.

Related to the broad scope of activities and ambition of DDR programmes today are the other challenges of co-ordination and resources, given the multiplicity of actors engaged and the significant amount of time and financial resources required to fully implement such programmes. Without co-ordination, however, gaps and duplication undermine effectiveness and efficiency (see, for example, Lamb and Stainer, 2018, on the adverse impact on DDR in South Sudan as a result of inflexible organisational structures of international and national actors, which led to poor co-ordination). The breadth and ambition of DDR programmes also compromises the extent to which the principles deemed to be inherent to DDR are adhered to: aside from complicating co-ordination efforts, the expanse of issues and actors can also undermine the extent to which DDR is locally owned and context-specific; it may be considered hard enough to share information and consult with the actors directly engaged in DDR programmes, let alone other stakeholders or potential beneficiaries and receiving communities.

Good communication is key to effective co-ordination with and support from key stakeholders, to avoid misunderstanding, misinformation and disinformation, which can undermine DDR efforts. It is important that key stakeholders and, particularly, former combatants and receiving communities, have trust and confidence in the DDR programme. Implementing public information and outreach campaigns, and also establishing effective communication channels to receive and impart information and ask questions, can help build trust and confidence as well as manage expectations. It is also important that particular attention is given to what key messages should be disseminated and which language should be used; given the sensitivity of DDR programmes, progress can be stalled and instability arise through insufficient attention given to ensuring that messages respond to the concerns of stakeholders and the language used is sensitive to their concerns. For example, mismanaging expectations and poor communication led to rioting in Liberia after three times the number of anticipated participants demanded reintegration benefits and were turned away (Muggah, 2005) (also see Box 7.3 on communications and DDR in Kosovo, and Figure 7.2 as an example of the public information campaigns used in Kosovo to disseminate a message that the Kosovo Protection Corps (KPC) was striving to be a multi-ethnic organisation).

Figure 7.2 KPC Public Information (2005)

Box 7.3: DDR and Communications – in Kosovo

Communicating a Separation with the Past

The Kosovo Protection Corps (KPC) was a civil emergency organisation established in September 1999 pursuant to Regulation 1999/8 of the UN Interim Administration Mission (UNMIK) subsequent to the signing of the Undertaking for Demilitarisation and Transformation three months earlier. It was comprised primarily of demobilised members of the Kosovo Liberation Army (KLA). The lack of a clear distinction between the KPC and the KLA caused political problems, including potentially jeopardising the political future of Kosovo, and undermined efforts to create a more multi-ethnic organisation. This led to a more robust approach to the demobilisation of the KPC once preparations for the Future Status of Kosovo were underway. The KPC was stood down in June 2009 and today, the Kosovo Security Force (KSF) is responsible for the civil emergency tasks previously fulfilled by the KPC (see Figure 7.2 for the public information poster, in the three languages used in Kosovo – Albanian, Serbian and English – which was developed by the KPC and erected around Kosovo in an effort to encourage Kosovo Serbs to join the Kosovo Albanian-dominated organisation).

The Use of Language

Decisions made in the planning and implementation of DDR programmes should include the use of language. This is because there can be unintended connotations and consequences with certain terms. The use of the language used in DDR programmes, if not the DDR process itself, is often interpreted by combatants as them having failed or been dismissed (see Stabilisation Unit, 2010). For instance, in Kosovo, the term 'dissolution' of the Kosovo Protection Corps (KPC) was used rather than the terms 'demobilisation' or 'disbandment', which were regarded less favourably and would have compromised efforts to dissolve the KPC as well as broader peacebuilding efforts, including the establishment of other security sector institutions.

Likewise, 'development' rather than 'reform' is often used in SSR to avoid unnecessarily insulting host nations, and thus compromising 'reform' and broader peacebuilding efforts, because of the assumption that dysfunctional security systems need reforming whereas 'development' can suggest simply further improvement. While of course it may be true that armed groups are being 'demobilised' and security sector institutions are being 'reformed', host governments and other in-country actors have a reputation to manage with their own stakeholders and, in any respect, are likely to be more co-operative with those external actors who are responsive to these demands and cognisant of their perspective.

Particular challenges occur when DDR programmes tie into SSR programmes. As already mentioned, both programmes involve the redistribution of power which can be destabilising, especially in the aftermath of conflict. Furthermore, where former warring factions are brought together through a reintegration programme which incorporates former combatants from non-state armed groups into state security institutions, there are inevitable tensions (see Box 7.4 on the integration process of former combatants in the People's Liberation Army (PLA) of Nepal into the Nepal Army).

Other challenges are associated with weaknesses of economic reintegration programmes. Often, they are limited in scope and funding, and expectations of them are too high. There is often insufficient analysis of the current and prospective economy, and subsequent identification of skills to be developed that will be competitive or appropriate to context. This can limit the prospects of finding employment, let alone sustainable employment (Munive, 2014). There may also be lack of commitment to the programmes among former combatants, which can compromise success.

Box 7.4: Nepal

The Nepal Civil War (1996–2006) ended with the signing of the Comprehensive Peace Agreement (CPA) in November 2006. It took many more years, however, for political consensus to be achieved on key issues contained within the CPA, including the rehabilitation of former combatants with Nepal's People's Liberation Army (PLA) into civilian life and/or integration into state security agencies. Internal disputes between political parties and different interpretations of the CPA contributed to these significant delays. This was alongside reluctance on the part of the Nepal Army to welcome former PLA combatants, believing they had neither the skills nor the correct aptitude or motivation. Eventually, and after a new Chief of Staff of the Nepal Army was appointed, the Army regarded itself as being the only institution able to control the former combatants and considered that the potential problems caused by integration (particularly the potential adverse effect on troop morale) could be avoided if the number to be integrated was not too high – as it was, by this stage in 2011, many had self-demobilised or sought voluntary retirement (Bogati, 2014). In fact, while the majority of the former combatants had intended to be part of the Army, 80% chose voluntary retirement, in part because of fears of discrimination and distrust of the integration programme because of the exclusion of a number of commanders on the grounds of insufficient education (Bogati, 2014).

In essence, former PLA combatants spent many years on cantonments while politicians stalled and grappled with the thorny issue of integrating some of them into the Nepal Army, thus compromising peacebuilding efforts. Cantonments were closed in 2012 almost six years after the CPA was signed.

Limited socio-economic profiling and local and national labour market analyses also undermined the confidence of former Maoist Army combatants in the process and the possibility of successful reintegration. Many female former combatants did not benefit at all from any DDR programme, often having chosen to informally demobilise due to caring responsibilities and lack of healthcare facilities and poor conditions on cantonment sites, or because they feared stigmatisation from their communities if they participated in a DDR programme (see Colekessian, 2010; Saferworld, 2010).

Other challenges include the presence of criminal groups, which often characterise post-conflict environments and can attract former combatants for economic, social, psychological or ideological reasons (see Jennings, 2008; Kaplan and Nussio, 2018; Mashike, 2007). Indeed, many scholars have conducted research demonstrating how former combatants have subsequently engaged in criminal activity, including in Colombia (see Kaplan and Nussio, 2018) and Bosnia and Herzegovina (Moratti and Sabic-El-Rayess, 2009). Former combatants may be motivated by money or lack viable alternatives for economic sustenance, may be pressured into engaging in criminal activities, may feel aggrieved or think they lack the status or prestige they once had, may feel disaffected or frustrated with the reintegration programme, or may face other security threats which might compel association with a criminal group (see Jennings, 2008; Kaplan and Nussio, 2018). This latter point signals the security dilemma that can exist in DDR programmes, which aim to address security by reducing the perceived threat posed by former combatants, but often do not address the security concerns of former combatants (many of whom may have joined armed groups due to perceived security threats and may still be inclined to join criminal or belligerent groups for similar reasons) (see Bøas and Hatløy, 2008; Kalyvas and Kocher, 2007; Kaplan and Nussio, 2018).

Kaplan and Nussio (2018) also find that those former combatants with weak family ties, antisocial personality traits and strong motives for having originally joined the armed group are also warning signs that a former combatant may be more at risk of joining criminal or belligerent groups after reintegration. Not having children, not completing basic education and being in the vicinity of criminal groups also increased the likelihood of engagement in criminal or belligerent activity (Kaplan and Nussio, 2018). The factors identified by Kaplan and Nussio (2018) and others show that there is, in fact, only so much a DDR programme can do to remove the potential threat to security and stability posed by former combatants. However, they also show that there is much a DDR programme can do – including increasing access to education and the prospects of meaningful, sustainable employment – including beyond economic reintegration, not least in terms of social and psychological reintegration.

Specht (2010) recommends that the youth (combatants being predominantly young males) feel they have a stake in the peace being built so they do not undermine it, and that demobilised combatants are supported long after the formal end of a DDR programme to ensure their long-term, successful reintegration. If this were regularly implemented, it might well be valuable. Likewise, it is sensible for communities – especially receiving communities – to be engaged in the development and implementation of DDR programmes (Willems, Verkoren and Derks et al., 2009). The wider implications of DDR programmes on the rest of the community should be considered also – there is frequently the perception that combatants are unfairly privileged, because they are singled out for financial reward. This can cause resentment and unrest if not properly managed.

Consequently, engaging communities and other stakeholders in the development and implementation of DDR programmes is critical to success, as are – as always – political will and sufficient resources. Without the requisite support from the government and donors, it is unlikely that armed groups or forces will demobilise, given that there will be little incentive to relinquish weapons, as well as little means of securing societal status, power and/or income. Indeed, even if armed groups and forces agree or are obliged to demobilise, they may still keep some weapons hidden and some soldiers available particularly as an insurance policy in case the peace process falters. In this scenario, DDR – like other peace-building interventions – could be regarded more as a political symbol of trust and the end of conflict than a contribution to either.

The recurrence of conflict and uncertainty of conflict outcomes contribute to the likelihood of such insurance policies and, more fundamentally, the failure of DDR programmes. This is in contrast to the historical examples provided at the start of this section, when the political and security situation was usually clear and unambiguous. Either the war itself, or the term of service of the individual, was over, and so the objective of returning combatants to civilian life could be planned within a fixed and known context. In contrast, DDR programmes today sometimes take place even while conflict is ongoing or where the outcome of the conflict is less clear. In the historical examples given, DDR (by force if necessary) was generally an inevitable consequence of the situation, not something that had to be negotiated, even if some groups resisted. So-called second-generation DDR programmes refer to the more recent programmes developed to address situations still in conflict or where a peace agreement is absent or ineffective, and where there are often a number of diverse armed groups and the line between combatant and civilian is not clear (Idris, 2016). Muggah and O'Donnell (2015) refer to 'next generation DDR' which is broader, more flexible and more responsive to the specific context than first- and second-generation DDR programmes in order to respond to some of the challenges noted above.

The most important question, already touched on but worth repeating, is that reintegration does not happen automatically or magically. Reintegration is, of course, crucial and without it the DDR process is undermined and thus the whole peace process is at risk. In respect of economic reintegration, it is important to know what economic opportunities exist and what avenues are feasible. This can be done through socio-economic profiling, labour-market analysis and mapping opportunities. This would avoid, for example, training vehicle mechanics in an area where spare parts for vehicles are not available, or providing livestock to former combatants who have no experience of or wish to return to farming or in places where sustenance farming is not or is no longer viable. Poorly targeted or inappropriate economic reintegration packages are a common failing of DDR programmes. Even with the best of efforts, however, nothing will work unless there is a healthy economy for ex-combatants to reintegrate into, which is not generated by DDR programmes or even broader peacebuilding efforts.

In the absence of such reintegration, threats to security remain. There is little evidence that ex-combatants themselves will try to restart conflicts (more usually they turn to crime), but where DDR fails (as notably in Angola in 1991), a ready pool of frustrated ex-combatants is available to follow their leaders once more.

In summary, perhaps the main DDR challenge is that a relatively simple concept (demobilising forces and collecting weapons) has acquired a large number of extra dimensions and many new actors each with their own agenda, sometimes competing (as is common in peacebuilding interventions). DDR is now massively more ambitious and wide-ranging than in the past, as are many other peacebuilding efforts, notably efforts to build the rule of law, discussed earlier, and SSR, discussed in the next chapter. It has increasingly expanded from programmes whose success in principle can be measured (collection of weapons, for example) towards highly ambitious objectives such as facilitating reconciliation, where success is almost impossible to measure – even if monitoring and evaluation of DDR programmes actually take place to the extent that they should. Like many other peacebuilding measures, it is based on a hypothesis (attempts to demobilise and disarm forces will lead to peace and reconciliation), which is difficult to objectively test and which, therefore, must be taken on trust. The assumption that providing some (it can never be all) former combatants with the prospect of alternative livelihoods (despite policy guidance, reintegration still tends to focus on economic reintegration and ignores social, psychosocial and political reintegration) overlooks the fact that prospects are not always realised (in other words, training will not necessarily result in employment). Even if opportunities for alternative livelihoods are realised, reintegration tends not to address the reasons why people may have taken up arms in the first place nor address the reasons why they might do so again. Nor does reintegration effectively address the adverse security effects that DDR can have: potentially destabilising, or exposing to harm, receiving communities, families and institutions. DDR also potentially risks upsetting the balance of power between competing forces, which can also be destabilising.

Conclusion

DDR is a complex, challenging, costly, long-term process, and if it is ever to succeed it requires an inclusive and holistic approach as well as the active engagement and support of all key stakeholders. It carries risks, particularly if insufficient time, resources and planning have been invested, and former combatants who have retained their weapons, with few employment prospects, remain real threats to security. Widespread violence and criminality become more likely in such conditions (see Child Soldiers International, 2019; UNDDR, 2019). There are other challenges associated with DDR, not least because of its highly political nature, involving as it does the redistribution of power. As this chapter has touched upon, there are also limitations to traditional DDR programmes, particularly in terms of reinforcing a neoliberal economic theory, prioritising the economic reintegration of former combatants above all other reintegration efforts, and focussing attention on the private sector for their economic reintegration, even though this may be inappropriate particularly in post-conflict environments and may not yield sustainable or even actual employment. Limitations in terms of addressing the needs of female former combatants as well as the needs of those who are disabled, also compromise the extent to which DDR programmes contribute to meaningful and long-term peace where the dividends of peace are enjoyed by all. These common limitations speak to the need to ensure that DDR programmes are inclusive and context-specific in order that they respond to the needs of all stakeholders as well as the particular context.

Summary of Key Issues

- DDR constitutes a structured approach to removing arms, dismantling military structures and providing former combatants with the ability and the will not to take up arms again, or lead a life of criminality and violence, by economically, socially and politically reintegrating them into society.
- Of all of the components of DDR, reintegration is generally recognised as being the most challenging, costly and time-consuming.
- DDR will usually (and ideally) be agreed to and defined within a comprehensive peace accord, ceasefire or cessation of hostilities.
- DDR principles include that DDR programmes should be context-specific, nationally and locally owned, people-centred, co-ordinated and integrated with other peacebuilding efforts, and accountable.
- Reintegration must be attentive to the social tensions that may arise as a result of a perception that combatants are being rewarded or compensated, rather than civilians who did not take up arms and may have disproportionately suffered the effects of the conflict.
- If DDR is to be successful it needs to respond to the specific needs of beneficiaries and stakeholders, including both women and men and those with diverse gender identities; all these stakeholders also need to actively engage in DDR planning and implementation.
- Those who have been seriously injured or disabled during the conflict, or who suffer from serious ill health, also require special attention and specific provisions within DDR programmes.
- The DDR of children should happen immediately and not await a peace agreement; it should not be a part of the formal DDR programme but be regarded as an endeavour to prevent or redress violations of the children's human rights.
- There is a high rate of failure of today's DDR programmes, partly the result of their scope and ambition.
- Even if armed groups and forces agree or are obliged to demobilise, they may still keep some weapons hidden and some soldiers available particularly as an insurance policy in case the peace process falters, thus undermining the potential success of any DDR programme.

Reflective Question

How can reintegration assistance be successful without being seen as rewarding combatants for their role in the conflict?

List of Core Resources

Al Jazeera (2017) *Inside Story – What happens to child soldiers when war ends?* (video) Available at www.youtube.com/watch?v=9FISTRzjqXU.

Cockayne, J. and O'Neil, S. (eds) (2015) *UN DDR in an era of violent extremism: Is it fit for purpose?* (Tokyo: UNU-CPR). Available at https://peacekeeping.un.org/sites/default/files/un_ddr_in_an_era_of_violent_extremism.pdf.

Coventry University (2012) *Reintegrating ex-combatants into civilian life: how not to do it! – Professorial Lecture: Alpaslan Özerdem* (video). Available at www.youtube.com/watch?v=EE0FJNxMh0o.

Dudenhoefer, A.-L. (2016) 'Understanding the Recruitment of Child Soldiers in Africa', *Conflict Trends*, 16 August, African Centre for the Constructive Resolution of Disputes (ACCORD). Available at www.accord.org.za/conflict-trends/understanding-recruitment-child-soldiers-africa.

Dyke, C. (2016) *DDR and SSR in War-to-Peace Transition* SSR Paper 14 (Geneva: DCAF). Available at www.dcaf.ch/sites/default/files/publications/documents/ONLINE-DCAF-SSR-14-2016-12-21.pdf.

Idris, I. (2016) *Lessons from DDR programmes*, GSDRC Helpdesk Research Report 1368 (Birmingham, UK: GSDRC, University of Birmingham). Available at www.gsdrc.org/wp-content/uploads/2016/06/HDQ1368.pdf.

International Labour Organization (ILO) (2006) *Red Shoes: Experiences of girl-combatants in Liberia* (Geneva: ILO). Available at www.ilo.org/wcmsp5/groups/public/---ed_emp/---emp_ent/---ifp_crisis/documents/publication/wcms_116435.pdf.

Muggah, R. and O'Donnell, C. (2015). 'Next Generation Disarmament, Demobilisation and Reintegration', *Stability: International Journal of Security & Development* 4(1): 30, 1–12.

Munive, J. and Stepputat, F., (2015) 'Rethinking Disarmament, Demobilization and Reintegration Programs', *Stability: International Journal of Security and Development* 4(1): 48, 1–13.

Özerdem, A. (2015) 'Disarmament, demobilization and reintegration (DDR) of ex-combatants and development with a specific reference to the reintegration of the Taliban in Afghanistan' in P. Jackson (ed.) *Handbook of international security and development* (Cheltenham: Edward Elgar): 452–446.

USIP (2014) *Female Soldiers and DDR: Sierra Leone, Nepal, and Colombia* (video). Available at www.youtube.com/watch?v=exlyTT3t7lo.

Zena, P. (2013) *The Lessons and Limits of DDR in Africa*, Africa Security Brief: A Publication Of The Africa Center For Strategic Studies, No. 24. Available at www.files.ethz.ch/isn/158581/AfricaBriefFinal_24.pdf.

8 Security Sector Reform

Overview

It is frequently argued that key to securing peace, stability and development is an effective, efficient and fair security and justice sector. In recognition of this, comprehensive Security Sector Reform (SSR) programmes are often implemented in post-conflict societies where some or all these characteristics are considered to be missing. This chapter, which covers a number of related subjects and is necessarily relatively lengthy, takes an in-depth look at the core features of SSR, alongside the roles of the different actors involved and challenges faced. The chapter will provide brief overviews of Justice Sector Reform, Police Reform, Penal Reform and Defence Reform, before discussing Security Sector Governance (SSG), which lies at the heart of SSR. A discussion of challenges, lessons learnt and best practices will conclude the chapter.

Learning Outcomes

- Define Security Sector Reform (SSR), its aims, principles and methods
- Identify the actors and activities involved in SSR in post-conflict environments
- Articulate the aims of Security Sector Governance (SSG) and how they can be reached
- Explain the common challenges encountered by SSR programmes and various ways in which they can be overcome
- Critically evaluate the success of SSR programmes in achieving sustainable solutions to post-conflict security and justice challenges

Part 1 – Security Sector Reform – Overview

Introduction

Policy makers, practitioners and many scholars have come to appreciate in recent years that security and justice are prerequisites to sustainable peace and development (OECD, 2007a, 2009; UNSG, 2008a). In the absence of functioning security and justice sector institutions, they argue that stability, the rule of law, security and human rights are threatened. This in turn adversely impacts the prospects for peace and prosperity. Threats to regional stability and international security are also likely consequences. Consequently, the reform or (re)construction of security and justice sector institutions in post-conflict and post-crisis environments has become an increasingly significant feature of peacebuilding and recovery efforts (Sedra, 2010; UNSG, 2013, 2008a).

The concept of security sector reform (SSR)

The term Security Sector Reform (SSR) began to be widely used in the mid-1990s, although activities to reform security sectors in transitional and post-conflict states were common for many decades beforehand. This continued from colonial times, with the organisation of indigenous militias, through the formation of European-style armies by departing colonial powers, through training and organisation of government and rebel forces by different sides during independence wars, and during the many intrastate conflicts of the Cold War.

What changed in the mid-1990s was the increased involvement of the development community in the security sector, with objectives that were largely normative rather than focused on technical improvements (Chuter, 2006). This shift was in response to a recognition of the interdependence of security and development (the security–development nexus) and the increasing importance of the concept of human security (moving away from the traditional concept of state-centric security) (Law, 2006). No longer was security seen as just about the state – the security of the people equally matters. And no longer is security understood purely in military terms – economic, environmental, political and social security matter just as much as territorial security. Demand for SSR subsequently increased in line with the argument that there are links between sustainable peace and an effective and efficient security sector that operates under democratic control.

Development agencies (notably the Organisation for Economic Co-operation and Development – OECD) often refer to the term 'security system reform', while some refer to the term 'Security and Justice Sector Reform' (SJSR) or similar terms, underscoring the perceived interrelationships between justice and security institutions. Oftentimes, it would be more appropriate to use the term 'reconstruction' rather than 'reform' given the wholesale institution-building that often occurs after conflict (see DCAF, 2009). As mentioned in the previous chapter, it is also important to remember that the terms 'reform' or 'reconstruction' may be resisted in some countries because of the implication that current security structures are inadequate; while they may well be, it can be more sensitive and appropriate to use the term 'development'. Other words in the lexicon of SSR may have similar pejorative overtones in certain places or among certain groups, and it is important to be aware of and responsive to these if reform efforts are to be successful and sustainable.

Despite widespread use of the term SSR and the increasing prevalence of SSR activities, especially in post-conflict environments, there is no single universal definition of SSR. It is, however, generally understood that SSR refers to the reform or (re)construction of the security sector, including its institutions, policy and processes, as well as the establishment or strengthening of democratic governance of the security sector, in order to ensure the effective, efficient and equitable delivery of security and justice for all the people of a state.

The security sector

As defined by the Geneva Centre for the Democratic Control of Armed Forces (DCAF, 2009: 2), the security sector is argued to consist of 'all organised groups in society that are capable of using force, as well as the institutions and actors that manage, direct, oversee and monitor them, and otherwise play a role in the development of a country's security policy and the provision of its security'. The security sector can be defined as security sector providers, justice sector institutions, non-statutory security forces, and management and oversight bodies, as shown in Figure 8.1.

It is important, of course, to distinguish between organisations that have a constitutionally or legally defined function and those that do not. The media and NGOs, for example, can perform effective oversight functions but are not legally mandated to hold security providers to account, unlike parliamentary committees or human rights commissions, for instance. The same applies even more to militia and terrorist groups – by analogy, nobody would class drug traffickers as part of the health sector – they are, nonetheless, security actors, albeit not formal nor, in most people's eyes, legitimate. Furthermore, different institutions have different and separate constitutional functions, which should not be confused (see Chuter, 2011).

Common features of effective and accountable security sectors

As highlighted in the 2008 report of the UN Secretary-General on SSR (UNSG, 2008a), while no single model of a security sector exists and states define security according to their specific contexts, security sectors that are considered by the population to be effective and accountable do share a number of common features:

(a) A legal and/or constitutional framework providing for the legitimate and accountable use of force ...;
(b) An institutionalized system of governance and management ...;
(c) Capacities: structures, personnel, equipment and resources to provide effective security;
(d) Mechanisms for interaction among security actors ...;
(e) Culture of service: promoting unity, integrity, discipline, impartiality and respect for human rights among security actors and shaping the manner in which they carry out their duties (UNSG, 2008a: 6).

SSR aims and principles

The aim of SSR is to create a professional, effective, efficient, inclusive, representative, affordable and accountable security sector, responsive to the needs of all the people under its jurisdiction, with adherence to the rule of law and international human rights standards. In short, SSR programmes should create operationally effective institutions that also guard against abuses of power and ensure respect for human rights. The overarching goal is to ensure the effective, efficient and

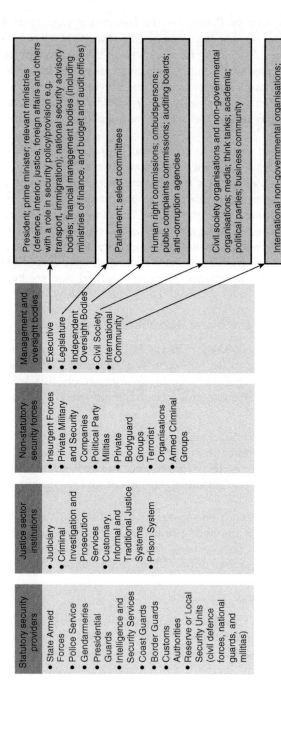

Figure 8.1 The Security Sector (DCAF, 2009; OECD, 2007a)

equitable delivery of security and justice and, in post-conflict environments, ultimately to contribute to building sustainable peace.

Most policy documents on SSR agree that it should adhere to the following principles, even if not always feasible in practice:

- *Holistic* – attend to the interdependencies between the different parts of the security and justice sector as well as other parallel peacebuilding efforts.
- *Context-specific* – tailored to the particular needs of the country or region, avoiding blind application of foreign templates or best practice from elsewhere.
- *Locally Owned and People-centred* – with national authorities leading reform efforts and the active engagement of communities throughout the process, including marginalised groups, in order that their needs are attended to when defining security needs and requirements.
- *Gender-sensitive* – attentive to the particular needs of men and women, inclusive of them throughout the process, including in decision-making roles, and responsive to the need to develop security sector institutions that are gender-responsive and inclusive.
- *Planned and Sequenced* – where comprehensive planning begins early and is continuously reviewed, with a clearly defined and communicated strategy; co-ordinates with the various parts of the security sector and other peacebuilding efforts; identifies relevant and lead actors; has agreed priorities and timelines; and includes exit strategies if external actors are engaged.
- *Co-ordinated* – particularly important given the large number of activities and actors often engaged in SSR and related activities.
- *Affordable and Sustainable* – where plans for the security sector are not disproportionate to requirements or resources, and there are sufficient resources for planned reform outputs to be able to be maintained after the departure of any external actors (see DCAF, 2009; Hänggi, 2009; OECD, 2007a; Sedra, 2010a).

It is also widely argued that SSR should promote the rule of law and democratic accountability, and should prioritise good governance and civilian oversight (see also OECD, 2007a; UNSG, 2008a). It should be noted that, while not necessarily as explicit, these principles should also guide other core peacebuilding interventions. In particular, all interventions should be context-specific if they are to be responsive to the particular context and thus effective. It also goes without saying that all peacebuilding interventions should be affordable and sustainable. Further, it is broadly agreed that interventions should be locally owned if they are to be sustainable beyond the departure of external actors, and gender-sensitive if they are to equally respond to the needs of both women and men, as well as people of diverse sexual orientation and gender identity and expression (SOGIE). In SSR programmes, however, there is often an increased need to articulate the importance of planning, sequencing and co-ordination because of the wide number of actors and activities involved. Nonetheless, it should go without saying that, again, all interventions should follow careful, comprehensive planning with due regard to interdependencies and co-ordination of actors, activities and policies.

SSR programmes and activities

In conflict-affected environments, security and justice sector institutions have often been partially or fully destroyed or are non-existent. Where they exist, they are also likely to lack sufficiently trained staff; lack public trust and confidence; lack effective management or oversight; be under-resourced or oversized; be perceived as illegitimate; and not be representative or responsive to the needs of all groups in society (see Lidauer and Ngapna, 2009).

Because security and justice are seen as critical to peace, SSR has increasingly become a distinct feature of post-conflict recovery and peacebuilding efforts – including in Bosnia and Herzegovina (Box 8.3 and 8.4), Sierra Leone (Box 8.8) Kosovo (Box 8.9, 8.11, 8.13 and 8.15), Nepal (Box 8.10) and Afghanistan (Box 8.12). It is also increasingly regarded as a stabilisation device to prevent conflict, and has been widely attempted in the Middle East, the Maghreb and other parts of Africa.

While SSR is a central feature of most peacebuilding endeavours today, it needs to be remembered that each conflict-affected environment is different, of course. Consequently, SSR interventions should follow comprehensive context and conflict analyses and assessment of needs, which should inform project design and be continuous. The assessment should cover physical (e.g. buildings) and human capacity (e.g. staff); mandates, policies and procedures (that regulate the powers and responsibilities of the security and justice sector institutions) and budgetary support (see UNODC and USIP, 2011). Ideally, the assessment of needs should be a consultative process with all stakeholders, in order to ascertain the security needs and concerns of a wide cross-section of society and thus help ensure that future security structures and policies are able to be responsive to them. Current capabilities of security and justice sector institutions, including management and oversight bodies, also need to be assessed in order to identify gaps and determine where capabilities do not meet priority needs.

Following assessment of needs, institutions, processes, and the legislative and policy frameworks are reformed, constructed or reconstructed, or developed. This often involves vetting and recruiting staff; training and equipping institutions; drafting or amending legislation and standard operating procedures (SOPs); and building public trust and confidence through various confidence-building measures, outreach activities and communication strategies. The latter is particularly important if efforts are to be successful and sustainable; it can also be the most challenging aspect of SSR, particularly in post-conflict environments where security actors may be accused of war-time atrocities or otherwise be seen as illegitimate or ineffective by parts of the population.

Key SSR actors in post-conflict environments

Key actors involved in SSR include national governments; international organisations (IOs); non-governmental organisations (NGOs) and civil society organisations (CSOs); private military and security companies; and security services (see DCAF, 2009).

Whilst much of the effort continues to come from individual donors (including governments and NGOs), the UN (including UNDP and UNDPKO) and other international organisations (such as OSCE, EU, CoE, ECOWAS, AU, NATO, WB,

IMF, OECD) are increasingly involved in a broad range of SSR activities in post-conflict environments from policy development to capacity building and technical assistance (DCAF, 2009). Oftentimes, the UN is the lead agency in post-conflict environments, but it can be a regional organisation (such as the EU in Bosnia and Herzegovina) or a single state (such as the UK in Sierra Leone).

In line with the whole-of-government approach being advocated by development agencies (believing that the co-ordinated engagement of diverse ministries is required for effective action in development and peacebuilding), international and domestic bodies engaged in other sectors are also being drawn into the planning and implementation of SSR programmes. Moreover, the cornerstone of SSR is a people-centred, locally owned philosophy – albeit in practice often state-centric (top-down rather than bottom-up or hybrid) – the aim of which is to ensure that people can be protected by, participate in and hold accountable security and justice sector institutions. Consequently, the general public can (and should) be directly engaged in SSR.

Part 2 – Reform of Justice and Security Sector Institutions

While there are a wide variety of state and non-state actors in the security sector, core institutions targeted by SSR programmes in post-conflict environments tend to be the police, courts, prisons and defence forces. The following parts of this chapter will separately focus on these institutions before looking at the issue of democratic control and oversight, and finally reflecting on challenges and lessons learned. For details on SSR and intelligence and the security services, integrated border management, private security and military companies, and civil society see OECD (2007a) and DCAF's website for a wealth of relevant resources (www.dcaf.ch).

Across all areas of reform, a number of key activities often involve:

- Legislative and policy reform and development
- Institutional restructuring and capacity building, including restructuring or creating organisations and organisational units
- Addressing infrastructure and equipment needs
- Developing and managing processes for selection, vetting and recruitment
- Introducing policies and procedures to improve the representation of women and other under-represented groups, and promote non-discrimination and equality
- Building effective management and administrative tools, structures and processes
- Training, mentoring and guidance
- Raising awareness (within the institutions and among the public) of human rights and the principles of equality, access to justice and accountability
- Generating political and financial support for reform
- Building effective management and oversight bodies, including relevant ministries and parliamentary committees, and oversight mechanisms
- Introducing codes of conduct, internal oversight mechanisms, and disciplinary policies and procedures to promote compliance and accountability
- Introducing or strengthening fiscal controls, not least in order to counter corruption

- Promoting co-ordination between different security and justice sector institutions, and other organisations, including government bodies and civil society organisations that provide welfare services or oversight, for instance
- Attending to the role played by informal security and justice providers.

Sector specific activities, alongside core aims, processes and challenges are addressed below.

Justice reform

Justice reform includes reforming or drafting laws (law reform) as well as the development or establishment of policies, procedures, structures and mechanisms that allow for the practical implementation of laws and equal access to justice (justice sector reform). The aim of justice reform is to improve the efficiency, fairness, accountability, impartiality and independence of justice institutions – and ensure that laws are fair and applied equally to all. It is also to contribute to good governance in the security sector and, ultimately, promote the rule of law.

The main focus of much justice reform is criminal justice. However, civil justice, property law and commercial law are often considered in the reform process, not least because they impact human security (see OECD, 2007a).

In addition to the general reform activities listed above, key activities often involve:

- Reviewing, drafting or amending laws, including the Constitution, ensuring that they are consistent with international legal norms and standards, protect human rights and provide for effective redress
- Awareness-raising among judicial and administrative actors as well as the general public of such issues as the importance of the independence of the judiciary, equal access to justice and the protection of human rights
- Providing advice, mentoring and oversight, and sometimes residing over sensitive and serious cases, such as war crimes, where domestic capacity is severely lacking in the immediate aftermath of conflict
- Scoping ways in which to try sensitive and serious crimes cases, which can include designing and establishing special jurisdictions.

Box 8.1: Rebuilding the Capacity of a Post-Conflict Justice System

In post-conflict environments, a justice system's physical infrastructure, including courts, can be severely damaged or destroyed and many judicial staff may have fled or been killed during the conflict. Of course, this can seriously undermine the capacity of a justice system.

In the immediate aftermath of conflict, Timor-Leste, for instance, had very few courts – most having been destroyed during the conflict – and very few judges, prosecutors, lawyers and support staff – most having fled the country during the conflict. Similarly, after the conflict in Liberia, there were very few trained personnel and infrastructure was destroyed with no courts, prisons or police stations in many parts of the country.

Effective justice reform demands collaboration among the various stakeholders, both international or external actors and national stakeholders, including:

- The judiciary and its oversight mechanisms, including the executive, legislature, civil society organisations and law schools
- Traditional and customary justice systems
- Lawyers associations
- Legal aid mechanisms
- Other elements of the criminal justice system, including prosecution services, the police and other investigative authorities, and the prison system – to ensure coherence of efforts and effectiveness.

While generally, judicial reforms take longer to implement than police reforms, not least because of the length of professional training, it is essential that reforms are co-ordinated, integrated and holistic in approach, recognising the interdependence between the many areas of the security and justice sector. However, in SSR the police often receive significantly more attention than the other core components of the criminal justice system, namely the judiciary and prisons. Often the justice sector receives less attention because it is sometimes regarded as a more closed institution and sometimes as more elitist, and thus not tax-payer friendly to invest in. Moreover, the international community tends to focus on core security tasks in the aftermath of conflict, neglecting the importance – and thereby undermining the likely success – of justice reform (see Box 8.2).

Aside from the challenges generic to SSR – including widespread insecurity and corruption as well as a lack of resources and infrastructure – justice reform can be hampered by the existence of competing legal systems, including both formal and

---

Box 8.2: The Need for Coherence of Efforts across Criminal Justice Sector Institutions

SSR efforts in post-conflict environments tend to focus on the police, recognising the importance of an effective police service in maintaining order and thus contributing to peacebuilding. Disproportionate attention given to police reform is also the result of the police being the most visible institution in the criminal justice system. However, a professional police service will achieve little in the way of establishing and maintaining law and order, if the judiciary and prison systems are corrupt, weak or otherwise dysfunctional, as has been seen in many post-conflict environments where reform of the police service took precedence over other aspects of the criminal justice system. If the prison system cannot effectively detain suspects or convicts, or the court system cannot adequately or fully administer justice, efforts to build an effective police service will often be futile. In some places, this leads to vigilantism or extrajudicial executions where the police might feel justice will not otherwise be served. It has also led to attempts to frustrate police reform efforts given the perceived futility of such efforts.

informal or traditional, as well as reform efforts informed by external legal systems at odds with in-country legal systems (legal systems can be based on civil law, common law, statutory law or religious law systems, or a combination of these, and are also uniquely shaped by a country's unique history and culture). The time required for reform efforts can also undermine people's confidence in the justice sector. Ignoring the role of informal justice mechanisms, particularly as a means of enabling access to justice for many communities, can also undermine reform efforts, as can the assumption that informal or community-based justice mechanisms are, by definition, inclusive of or responsive to the needs of all those at the community-level (Box 8.17).

Police reform

Police reform is often perceived as being central to SSR efforts, and the overarching objective of establishing the rule of law, building security and, as a result, long-term peace and stability after conflict (see DCAF, 2009; OECD, 2007a; Jeong, 2005; UNOHCHR, 2006; RUSI and FPRI, 2009). The police service is often viewed as an indicator of the government's intention and ability to enforce law and order and ensure that security and justice are fairly and equitably provided. In essence, the police service can be the most credible manifestation of the government's authority and legitimacy (see OSCE, 2008). The police service is also often the security sector institution that most directly impacts upon people's lives (see OECD, 2007a).

The focus is often on professionalising and restructuring the police, including democratisation and demilitarisation where relevant, or creating new police institutions. The aim is to improve the effectiveness and efficiency of the police, and ensure that it is humane, responsive and inclusive, complies with the law, respects human rights, and is publicly accountable.

Police reform also often involves clearly delineating between the roles of the police, gendarmerie (where relevant) and military; developing effective democratic control and oversight, while ensuring sufficient operational independence; and removing undue political influence over the police or engagement in political affairs of the police and its staff.

In addition to the general reform activities listed above, police reform may include some or all of the following, depending on the context:

- Training police services and their management and oversight bodies, on the principles of democratic policing and human rights as well as technical competencies
- Developing strategies, legislation and policies that facilitate the work of a professional police service, and ensuring that they are coherent and linked to a national security or policing strategy or policy
- Reviewing salaries and benefits as well as incentives and rewards to discourage corruption (by ensuring adequate compensation) and improve performance
- Co-ordinating the work of the police with other relevant agencies and building partnerships to improve internal security, including the prevention and detection of crime

- Improving internal and external communications, in order to improve performance, efficiency and accountability; build public trust and confidence; and secure the engagement of the public in building security by encouraging them to report crimes, comply with the law and stay safe, as well as informing them of what they can expect from the police.

Oftentimes, in post-conflict environments, foreign police officers are engaged in police reform programmes, due to the assumption that police officers are more likely to listen to the advice of other police officers when it comes to police business, and they are more likely to speak the same language, articulating the aims of the reform programme into meaningful and relevant objectives (see Marenin, 2005). However, the choice of foreign police officers is key (Box 8.3 highlights the type of harm that can arise without due regard to the calibre of officers seconded), and they must be knowledgeable of the country and the culture concerned.

There are many challenges inherent to police reform, of which the most common are limited public trust and confidence, as a result of police inefficiency, corruption or engagement in criminal activities, including war crimes (as was the case in BiH and Rwanda, for instance – see Box 8.4 for an indication of how these challenges manifested themselves in BiH). These challenges can be more difficult in post-conflict environments, where there is a need to maintain internal security while reforming the police, which often requires external actors to provide security functions. As with other SSR efforts, police reform is highly political and will significantly impact in-country power relations. As with defence reform, discussed later in this chapter, integration of former combatants or adversaries or other groups under-represented in the police can cause significant tension and threaten the peace process; this happened with the police force in Timor-Leste

---

Box 8.3: Bosnia and Herzegovina

Although the police in Bosnia and Herzegovina (BiH) were well trained by western standards, reform efforts were hampered by a heritage of the political use of the police in the Communist era, the disintegration into three separate ethnically based police services after 1992, continuing high levels of politicisation of the police services, resistance to co-operation and reform efforts, and the involvement of police personnel in war crimes and in organised criminal networks and corruption (see DCAF, 2009). While the understanding and respect that is often shared between police personnel from different countries often aids reform through the existence of effective partnerships, it can also hamper reform efforts if those mandated to mentor, advise and monitor are more attentive to the needs of the local police than the needs of the overarching peacekeeping mission and the citizens of the conflict-affected country. This happened in BiH, evidenced when efforts to curtail human trafficking and forced prostitution were hampered by parts of the UN Mission in Bosnia and Herzegovina (UNMIBH), the organisation principally responsible for such efforts.

Box 8.4: Police Vetting and Bosnia and Herzegovina

While police reform and particularly vetting procedures can be destabilising, without removing from positions of authority those who may have committed serious crimes against civilians, including war crimes, police reform and broader peace-building efforts will be unsuccessful. In Bosnia and Herzegovina, for instance, post-conflict recovery and stabilisation were seriously undermined for many years by the continued occupation of posts within the police, as well as other security institutions and government structures, of those who had committed war-time atrocities (see, for example, ICG, 2000).

and defence forces in the Democratic Republic of the Congo (DRC) and South Africa (see Peace Building Initiative, 2009). Low police morale, which can result from lack of public trust and confidence as well as poor salaries or inadequate training and support, for instance, can also present significant challenges to the reform process.

Other challenges include lack of agreement on best practice; whether, for instance, training should be all-encompassing or target senior management and future leaders, be intensive but enable the swift deployment of police, or target skills or belief systems. Co-ordination, as often, can be a problem. Moreover, much police reform – as with broader SSR and peacebuilding – is based upon unsubstantiated assumptions. As Hills (2009) details, there is an assumption that improved policing improves state resilience and development, but little has been done to test or question such assumptions.

For instance, having created a police service that is deemed to be effective and efficient, it would be useful to ask whether the perceived and actual security of the people has improved, whether people's confidence in the state and state institutions has risen, and whether investment and employment have increased. Further analysis would then unpack the relationship between security, state resilience and development, and investigate, as Hills (2009) does, how order is perceived and policed and how it re-emerges. It is, furthermore, necessary to question whether the way 'democratic policing' is popularly conceived in reform programmes is context-relevant, or whether it is another example of western models and ideas being applied to conflict-affected environments with little regard for relevance or the challenges which can compromise success. In this regard, it should be asked whether there are risks that police reform, by responding to the interests of donor states and, also, through so doing, potentially reinforcing power relations and benefiting dominant and elite groups, in fact compromise the ostensible aim of police reform which is to improve security for all:

The imposition of democratic policing models may, for example, contribute to dependency and underdevelopment through imposing or advocating inappropriate or unsustainable schemes. Or it may constitute 'a new form of exploitative, entrepreneurial neo-colonialism' (Murphy, 2005: 143) structuring change and assistance programmes in ways that are favourable to the geostrategic interests of key western states such as the USA and EU members (Huggins, 1998; Ioannides, 2007). Such moves may benefit ruling elites in recipient cities and the senior officers sent on study visits to the USA or UK, but they rarely improve the lot of ordinary officers, let alone that of inhabitants in the longer term. (Hills, 2009: 76)

Penal reform

Penal reform aims to improve the effectiveness and efficiency of the penal system, including prisons, but also alternatives to custody (such as community service), related institutions (such as probationary services) and traditional or informal sanctions systems (see Bastick, 2010). In many developing countries, there are few alternatives to custodial sanctions and many of those who are ordered to pay fines are incarcerated because they are poor. Indeed, incarceration for non-payment of fines happens in many countries, including rich countries. In Australia, for example, Aboriginal and Torres Straits women are over-represented in prisons because they are poor and therefore disproportionately affected by imprisonment due to unpaid fines. In 2017, the UN Special Rapporteur on Violence Against Women, its Causes and Consequences, Dubravka Šimonović, urged the Government 'to review a policy of incarceration for unpaid fines, which has a disproportionate effect on the rates of incarceration of Aboriginal women because of the economic and social disadvantage that they face' (UNOHCHR, 2017). Incarceration for unpaid fines effectively operates as a policy of the criminalisation of poverty.

Consequently, because incarceration is overused, coupled with the potential for abuse and torture (International Centre for Prison Studies, 2008), much penal reform focuses on prisons. Nonetheless, it is often argued that penal reform work should help establish non-custodial alternatives.

A penal system should pursue several objectives: retribution or punishment, deterrence, rehabilitation and protection of the community through isolation or exclusion of offenders, ultimately aiming to contribute to a just, safe and peaceful society (see ICCLR, 2001). This is particularly important in post-conflict environments where the re-establishment of the rule of law is a priority. A penal system should also operate transparently and adhere to international standards, not least ensuring that those incarcerated are not deprived of their fundamental human rights and are free from cruel, inhumane or degrading treatment. This is not only a legal and moral obligation, but helps avoid building grievances and tension and is, crucially, an effective crime prevention strategy. In this regard, prisoners should not be tortured or exposed to threat. They should also have access to food and clean water, and children should not be incarcerated with adults, nor women with men. Furthermore, punishment should be fair, non-discriminatory and proportionate to the crime (see World Prison Brief, 2017, for comprehensive guidance on prison reform).

Of course, in reality, many prisons in many countries are places where the human rights of those who are incarcerated are violated and they are exposed to cruel, inhumane or degrading treatment, including torture. This is not just the case in places affected by conflict. Even rich countries where challenges associated with lack of resources need not arise, such as the United States (American Friends Service Committee, 2014), Australia (Royal Commission into the Protection and Detention of Children in the Northern Territory, 2017), the UK (Fenton, 2017) and Russia (Carroll, 2018), torture and abuse of prisoners are commonplace (see also Penal Reform International, 2019). The fact that torture and abuse – including physical, sexual and psychological abuse; withdrawal of medicine, water and food; and solitary confinement of people with mental health problems and children – occur in countries where the challenges of conflict are not prevalent (including minimal resources, few trained staff, poor facilities and infrastructure, and height-ened security fears) indicates the difficulties that are involved in compelling prison authorities in conflict-affected environments to comply with international law that prohibits torture and other forms of abuse in prisons.

Violations of the rights of prisoners are often much more prevalent and acute in conflict-affected environments for a number of reasons. Arbitrary detention and subsequent torture can be widely prevalent and often used as a strategy to defeat opponents or intimidate communities (see Penal Reform International, 2018). Amnesty International (2017a) has reported that almost 18,000 people died in government custody in Syria between 2011 and 2015. Additionally, in many post-conflict environments, prisons can be in a derelict condition, overcrowded, unsanitary, lacking water and electricity, lacking adequate medical care, without sewage systems, with insufficient food and water for prisoners, and without reha-bilitation support (see Box 8.5 for an overview of how poor prison conditions and security can lead to prison escapes in conflict-affected and conflict-vulnerable envi-ronments and, as a result, adversely impact internal security). Men, women and children can be detained together, and those on pre-trial detention can be held for prolonged periods of time (as a result of deficiencies in the justice system), which can significantly contribute to problems of overcrowding. Prisons in post-conflict environments can also be without adequate policy frameworks, sufficient numbers of staff, effective oversight and co-ordination with the other criminal justice insti-tutions (ICRC, 2005a; UNDPKO, 2011; UNODC, 2010b).

Box 8.5: Prison Escapes in Conflict-affected Environments

Poor prison conditions and security have led to mass escapes in Burundi, Chad, Côte d'Ivoire, DRC, Haiti and Liberia. Approximately 60% of prisoners in Haiti escaped during and immediately after the 2010 earthquake – 5,138 of a total of 8,535 prisoners escaped, including all 4,000+ prisoners from the national peniten-tiary and an estimated 300–500 members of armed gangs (see Fortin, 2011; ICG, 2010). More recently, 100 prisoners escaped from Côte d'Ivoire, in part because of severe overcrowding, contributing to increased insecurity (Adele, 2017). Detainees elsewhere – such as Bosnia during the conflict – have also been released by those who saw the potential resource in large numbers of (often) young, violent men with little to lose. These scenarios have a potentially huge impact on internal security.

Penal reform has only very recently been recognised as an important part of SSR and of building peace in post-conflict environments (see UNDPKO, 2011). Key UN actors involved in penal reform include DPKO, UNODC and OHCHR, with the World Health Organization (WHO), UN Women, UNICEF and others also actively engaged. UN work to address prison conditions in post-conflict settings is led by DPKO through the Justice and Corrections Service (JSC) of the Office of Rule of Law and Security Institutions (OROLSI) (see Chapter 4).

International NGOs also play a key role, as do national NGOs and CSOs, particularly in respect of needs assessments, awareness raising, outreach and advocacy. ICRC plays a particularly important role in visiting prisoners, particularly during armed conflict, to ensure that they are treated in accordance with international standards and norms (see ICRC, 2010b). IFIs, such as the World Bank, and specialist organisations, such as the International Corrections and Prisons Association (ICPA), can also play a role in prison reform.

In addition to the general reform activities listed above, penal reform activities can include improving prison security, management and administration, including official data collection. Improving governance and oversight is particularly important in prison reform because of the closed nature of the prison system, which can hinder efforts to enhance accountability (see International Centre for Prison Studies, 2008). Oversight and accountability will be discussed further shortly, when we consider Security Sector Governance (SSG). Other activities might include advocating for or establishing programmes which support the rehabilitation of prisoners and their social reintegration upon release. Activities promoting alternatives to incarceration might also be part of penal reform work. More immediate needs can also be addressed through prison reform work, including activities to ensure that prisoners receive food, water, appropriate sanitary facilities and medical care.

Particular attention is often given to the needs of vulnerable prisoners and those with special needs, who include children, women, those with mental healthcare needs and those who are HIV-positive (see UNODC and USIP, 2011; UNODC, 2010b, 2009, 2008a, 2008b). Other efforts include encouraging prison to be used as a last resort through the introduction of non-custodial punishments for minor offenders (see OECD, 2007a).

The establishment of secure, legitimate facilities to detain those charged with war crimes and other serious crimes is particularly important in conflict-affected environments, to instil public confidence in the peace process and to help stabilise the immediate post-conflict environment.

Aside from generic challenges to SSR, such as inadequate facilities and resources, specific challenges include securing adequate political and financial support for penal reform programmes, which are rarely as popular as defence or police reform programmes (see Bastick, 2010). Penal reform may be regarded as less of a priority in the aftermath of conflict and may therefore generate less attention. As mentioned earlier, efforts to reform the police or the judiciary without attention given to penal reform will suffer – as has been seen in Afghanistan, Haiti and Liberia – if the prison system does not rehabilitate detainees, arbitrarily releases detainees, or does not improve prison security to prevent escapes or curtail organised crime and violence (see Bastick, 2010; UNDPKO, 2009). Similarly, if penal reform is addressed without proper attention given to the other agencies beyond the prison system, prisons may continue to be used as dumping grounds for the poor and marginalised, those deemed to be undesirable, political opponents or anyone who happens to be in the wrong place at the wrong time (for further information on penal reform see World Prison Brief, 2019; Penal Reform, 2019).

Defence reform

Bilateral defence assistance has been provided in some form or other for many decades, primarily in the form of the provision of training and equipment, although in some cases with the wholesale imposition of foreign models of organisation. However, in the context of SSR and a comprehensive approach to reform of defence capabilities in post-conflict or transitional countries, institutional defence reform is a relatively recent phenomenon.

Defence reform is a process designed to improve the effectiveness and efficiency of a state's armed forces and the making and implementation of defence policy, and to promote democratic control of the armed forces. As part of this process, defence reform also aims to ensure that the armed forces adhere to the rule of law, are accountable through democratic structures, and provide services that are affordable and appropriate to the determined security needs of the state and its people.

In essence, the aim of defence reform is to improve the professionalism, accountability, effectiveness and efficiency of a state's armed forces. It seeks to achieve this through a process of building or reforming structures and processes, developing policies and procedures, equipping and training, and building good relationships with other stakeholders and partners, including other security institutions at home and abroad. It also includes work to develop effective management, budget and defence planning systems, not least to ensure that investments in training and equipment are not wasted. Defence reform may also involve mentoring in order to inculcate a change in attitudes, beliefs or perceptions; often central to defence reform success, but particularly time-consuming, challenging and subjective for reform efforts.

Part of the reform process will be to strive towards capabilities matching requirements, and for the armed forces to meet the security needs of a country. This should mean that defence reform emanates from a coherent process, which may include a formal defence review, and in turn helps to implement a national strategy or policy, resulting from a higher-level national security review and the definition of a national security strategy or policy. Missions for the defence forces, including responses to threats, are then deduced from this intellectual framework. Moreover, capabilities required, including the size and structure of defence institutions, should be determined after this process has identified the requirements, including through a threat assessment (regularly undertaken to ensure that capabilities remain relevant to the changing environment).

Part of the overarching objective of improving the effectiveness of the defence sector is that it will enjoy public trust and confidence. This could be facilitated by locating defence reform firmly in the context of a legitimate, inclusively developed national security strategy or policy, and also by ensuring that the defence sector is representative of the people it serves as well as responsive to their needs and concerns. Promoting effective democratic control and oversight is also central to defence reform and directly impacts performance, efficiency, and public trust and confidence. The aim is also to create an armed force that is effectively managed, flexible and able to respond to a range of potential threats, and that adheres to international humanitarian law and human rights standards (see DCAF, 2009). The challenges of doing this, particularly after conflict or major political transition, should not be under-estimated.

It is important that the armed forces are well-trained, and sufficiently manned and equipped to fulfil their responsibilities. Equally, it is important that investment in the armed forces does not result in taking away resources from other essential peacebuilding efforts or state functions, or contribute to sustained militarisation of post-conflict environments. Since armed forces always reduce in size after conflicts anyway, it is necessary to ensure that those who do not go forward into the new or reformed structures have opportunities to secure other employment and do not become spoilers in the peace process. Downsizing and demobilisation can both be highly sensitive and potentially destabilising (see Chapter 7); programmes to mini-mise the extent of these effects can also be very expensive.

Similarly, the process of demobilising non-state armed groups and, in some cases, integrating them into formal defence and other security structures can be potentially destabilising to the reform process and broader peacebuilding efforts, although it is frequently included in peace agreements: hence the need to co-ordinate DDR and SSR efforts, as we discussed in the last chapter (see Box 8.6 for an overview of the integration of armed groups into a new National Defence Force in South Africa).

Box 8.6: South Africa

There were seven statutory and non-statutory armed groups at the time of the political transition in South Africa in 1994, from which it was agreed that a new National Defence Force (NDF) would be created. It was decided early on that those who wanted to integrate could remain in the military, since large numbers of demo-bilised combatants would be extremely dangerous for the stability of the country – although this did lead to an inflated structure and thus the need to downsize or rationalise the NDF (Mortimer, 1995). South Africa had a sophisticated military machine. Experienced officers had to be persuaded to stay, and officers and soldiers from rival political traditions, many of whom had no command experience, had to be trained for future more senior positions. The political leadership had aban-doned security policy to the military (the Ministry of Defence had been abolished in 1967). Consequently, new defence structures had to be created and staffed by competent individuals. South Africa faced no threats in the new strategic environ-ment, but was still seen as a threat by its neighbours. It was therefore necessary to design a policy that would be effective but non-aggressive. It was estimated that it would take 25 years to fully implement these changes. This transformation process is unusual in that it was driven from the very beginning by South Africans them-selves, and the process enjoyed a high level of public support (Chuter, 2017).

Plans for the integration of former non-state combatants should take into consideration the appropriate force size and structure of a defence force. Of course, what is deemed to be the appropriate size of a defence force may require that the force downsizes even without taking into account the number of additional members that may come from non-state armed groups. Integrating former enemy combatants and members of non-state armed groups is challenging enough at the best of times, without also needing to downsize and, in effect, demobilise existing personnel of the defence force who have recently fought against those who might be perceived to be assuming their positions.

The development of the armed forces is ultimately linked to the formation of the state (ISSAT, 2010); hence the added difficulty when integrating members of non-state armed groups (see Box 8. 7). While recognising that states can and do exist without militaries (albeit rarely), the military is often the most symbolic manifestation of the power of a state; it is the means by which it can defend itself and is often perceived as the very embodiment of the power of a state. Defence reform in post-conflict environments can therefore often be seen to be a crucial aspect of statebuilding and peacebuilding. It is also, fundamentally, about changing power relations; not least limiting the power of the armed forces and ensuring that they operate under the control of democratically elected leaders, taking power away

---

Box 8.7: Integrating Members of Non-State Armed Groups into Armed Forces

The process of integrating into state armed forces those who may have been fighting against the state previously – and often perceived as terrorists and/or violent criminals by the state – is highly sensitive. Guerrilla fighters often have little formal training or education, and their integration into state armed forces often meets much resistance. Much depends on whether the process is one of amalgamation (where former non-state combatants are brought together into a new defence force, as in the South African case) or assimilation (where former non-state combatants are brought into an existing defence force, as in Nepal).

In Nepal, for instance, reluctance to integrate former PLA combatants into the Nepal Army undermined the DDR process and risked jeopardising the peace process, with many former combatants remaining in cantonments for many years after the signing of the Comprehensive Peace Accord (CPA) in 2006, which explicitly referred to the need to monitor, integrate and rehabilitate these former combatants. There is also often resistance to improving the ethnic and religious representation of armed forces or integrating armed forces, often because of issues of trust, grievance and perceived inability. In Kosovo, efforts to increase the representation of Kosovo Serbs and other ethnic minorities in the predominantly Kosovo Albanian Kosovo Protection Corps (KPC) – the antecedent of the Kosovo Security Force (KSF) – were mobilised in large part due to the recognition that in so doing, certain standards established by the UN and regional organisations would be met. Meeting these standards was perceived as a precursor to favourable political talks to determine Kosovo's status and, subsequently, integration into Euro-Atlantic structures (EU and NATO).

from powerful actors for whom the armed forces may have been a tool for influence, and ensuring that they are more inclusive and representative of the broader societal demographic, even integrating those they may have previously fought against. It therefore carries a high risk of destabilisation.

Much work on defence reform is done bilaterally – and indeed multilateral assistance can be very complicated to organise. There is therefore an increasing tendency for 'South–South' arrangements, sometimes sponsored by an outside power (e.g. Jordan in Yemen, South Africa in Sierra Leone and the Central African Republic in Burundi). Regional and international organisations have also engaged in defence reform, including NATO, UN, EU, ECOWAS, OSCE, OECD and the World Bank. The UN and NATO are probably the most well-known and experienced actors in defence reform and often work together in post-conflict defence reform programmes (NATO, 2018). Where such organisations are military or engage military staff to deliver defence reform programmes, the effect can be positive in that defence organisations are more likely to listen to those in the defence sector when advocating for defence reform activities; the relatively high turnover of military staff is, however, a hindrance to effective reform programmes.

Many NGOs, learning institutions and international foundations are also often engaged in defence reform. DCAF, for instance, has engaged with many post-conflict and transitional countries, providing assistance to defence organisations and democratic institutions responsible for their oversight. The frequent engagement of many actors underscores the importance of co-ordination, communication and coherence of efforts (see Box 8.8 for an example of where defence

---

Box 8.8: Sierra Leone

Defence Reform in Sierra Leone is widely regarded as being among the more successful defence reform programmes, at least in the early years, because a single actor (UK) led the external engagement in supporting national authorities. This resulted in avoiding the challenges posed by co-ordinating between many different actors that characterises many other SSR interventions. The Defence Reform process is widely considered to have been a success because of the effective co-ordination of activities, singularity and clarity of purpose, as well as focus on security priorities. It is also considered to be successful because of well-planned and -resourced downsizing, and because of a delineation of security responsibilities between security actors. Furthermore, success has been credited to the establishment of the Office of National Security responsible for co-ordinating the efforts of the national security institutions and facilitating a bottom-up and consultative approach to identifying security issues of concern to the population. A focus on building understanding and awareness, rather than simply training and equipping security institutions, is also considered to be key to success (see DCAF, 2009; UK MoD, 2009).

However, even in this example of a successful defence reform programme, there were limitations. While co-ordinated external engagement contributed to building peace at the local level, it failed to impact power dynamics between national political elites and local chiefs, and this posed a potentially significant threat to governance and, thus, stability (Ansorg and Gordon, 2019; Nickson and Cutting, 2016).

reform has been widely considered to be successful, at least in part because of a single-actor lead and thus effective co-ordination).

A wide range of national actors are engaged in defence reform, including the head of state; representatives of the national security council or similar decision-making body; the ministry of defence; the armed forces; other security institutions that work with the armed forces, including gendarmerie, customs and border guards, intelligence services, and police; parliamentary defence and security committees; criminal justice institutions, including the judiciary and corrections; and non-state actors who work with or for the armed forces, including private military and security companies (PMSCs) and suppliers (see DCAF, 2009). Civil society actors are also key players in defence reform, particularly in respect of performing oversight functions.

While consultation and communication are key to defence reform success, particularly where downsizing or the integration of former enemy combatants is concerned, total consensus will seldom be possible, so there is a need to manage expectations and minimise risks. Resistance may come from concerns about loss of power or influence, loss of employment and means of sustenance, lack of trust or confidence in those who may lead the reform process, disagreement that reform or aspects of it are necessary or desirable, or fear of the unknown. Change itself is also potentially very destabilising for any organisation, and managing change is always difficult; in the case of the armed forces, this potential instability has far-reaching effects. Maintaining capabilities during the reform or (re)construction process can therefore be particularly difficult.

External communications are necessary to address public fear and hostility, or general lack of confidence and trust, which can be prevalent in the aftermath of conflict and can significantly undermine reform efforts and the extent to which any security institution can be effective. If security sector institutions played a role in the conflict there may be a need to implement and communicate a break with the past when it comes to proposed future security structures. For instance, post-WWII defence sector reform in West Germany created the *Bundeswehr* in 1955, which had the specific goal of creating a completely new, democratic institution free from influence from and association with its predecessors, either Hitler's *Wehrmacht* (1935–46) or the Weimar Republic's *Reichswehr* (1921–35). The concept of the *Staatsbürger in Uniform* (Citizen in Uniform), central to the mission statement of the *Bundeswehr*, is still relevant today as an example of successful SSR (see Searle, 2003). Also, see Box 8.9 for an overview of the need to communicate a break with the past in establishing the Kosovo Security Force (KSF) and, thus, disbanding the Kosovo Protection Corps (KPC).

External communications are also needed to raise public awareness of the defence and wider security sector, to enhance oversight and engagement. Part of this process will also address the common assumption that only the military can understand military matters, and that democratic control and civilian oversight benefit both the armed forces and the society they serve.

Establishing or reinforcing democratic control of the armed forces can be a particularly challenging part of any defence reform programme. There can

Box 8.9: Establishing the Kosovo Security Force (KSF) and Disbanding the Kosovo Protection Corps (KPC)

While recognising the interdependencies between SSR and DDR, it is important to be familiar with the specific context which may demand that the processes are separated to a notable degree. In Kosovo, for instance, many of those former combatants of the Kosovo Liberation Army (KLA) found a place in the post-conflict Kosovo Protection Corps (KPC), a civilian emergency organisation, while others were integrated into the Kosovo Police Service (KPS). Recognising that the links between the KLA and KPC were still seen by many, whether favourably or unfavourably, and realising that any future armed force for Kosovo had to disassociate itself from the KLA (in order to be perceived as being legitimate by all stakeholders) the process of demobilising or, rather, disbanding the KPC had to be independent of the process of establishing the Kosovo Security Force (KSF) – an organisation that was envisaged to be the embryonic armed force of a future independent Kosovo (see Box 7.3 in Chapter 7 on DDR and communications in Kosovo). Prior to the declaration of independence, some feared that integrating the processes could have jeopardised discussions to resolve Kosovo's status and harmed the peace process, as well as hampered efforts to recruit a workforce that was younger and more representative of the social demographic in Kosovo. The processes were closely co-ordinated but the linkages were specific to the context and, here, that meant co-ordinating the activities – to ensure that capabilities continued – but separating the processes, while also being attentive to the level of discord that such an approach would have among those who saw they had a rightful place in the future army of Kosovo.

be reluctance on the part of the military to accept that civilians can speak authoritatively on defence matters; this can be compounded because there is often a lack of civilian capacity to provide effective oversight or perform the functions required of a ministry, for instance. Because many armed forces have a history of political interference and exploitation by civilian leaders, there is often a reluctance to support democratic or civilian control, particularly where the distinction between being responsive to democratically elected leaders and political interference is not clear. This was initially the case in post-conflict Nepal, for example: the Ministry of Defence lacked capacity, while the armed forces, based upon previous experience, feared that efforts to build this capacity would increase political interference and undermine operational capabilities (see Box 8.10).

Part of the problem lies in the misuse of terms by SSR practitioners and the subsequent misconception that what is being advocated is subordination of the armed forces to civilians. In essence, there is no reason to pursue civilian control as an objective in itself, of course, and indeed it frequently leads to corruption and politicisation. Most really bad national leaders have been civilians. What needs pursuing is control of the armed forces by democratically elected leaders in the executive and legislative branches of government to ensure that the armed forces are not misused. As Blair (2016: n.p.) has said, democratic control 'is achieved not by certain officials wearing suits rather than uniforms, it is assured by constitutional and legal processes ensuring that elected leaders in the executive and legislative branches have the ultimate authority over how the power of the armed forces is used.' In essence, when we talk about democratic control or something similar, we simply mean that the security sector functions in the same way and according to the same norms and rules as any other sector of government in a democracy.

Part 3 – Security Sector Governance

Since around the turn of the millennium, governance is a term so widely used in international development by practitioners, scholars and policy-makers alike that its precise meaning is often unclear, although it is often associated with a set of political values, albeit often obscured or denied (Frederickson, 2005). As Jenkins and Plowden (2006: 1) have argued, the concept of governance, like many other generic terms used in international development, has 'a deceptive simplicity' concealing 'wide disagreement' about what it actually means. In a subject as complex and important as security, it is essential therefore that we are clear about its meaning.

Security Sector Governance (SSG) specifically refers to the processes, actors and structures that shape decisions about security; in essence, the way in which various actors exercise power over the provision of security (see DCAF, 2015b). The ultimate aim of SSR has always been to promote good SSG and, through so doing, improve the effective, efficient, equitable and accountable delivery of security. Ways in which SSG can be achieved include efforts to build the capacity of management and oversight bodies, notably ministries and parliamentary committees in the security sector, as well as efforts to facilitate the establishment or development of other oversight mechanisms, which will be discussed shortly.

Despite the centrality of SSG to SSR, in practice the focus of many actors engaged in SSR is often on the operational effectiveness of security providers, rather than on improving the effectiveness of oversight and management bodies (Ansorg and Gordon, 2019; Jackson, 2018; Sedra, 2018). Considerably fewer resources, for instance, are given to building the capacity of parliamentary security and defence committees than to building the capacity of the police and the armed forces. The focus has often been on performance rather than governance, and training and resource requirements rather than less tangible requirements such as accountability and transparency. This has tended to undermine the sustainability of reform and broader peacebuilding efforts. SSR should be about rebuilding the relationship between the state and its security institutions with the people, rather than simply being about rebuilding the security institutions; without a focus on governance, effectiveness and accountability will be hindered, and public trust and confidence will be less likely to grow.

The importance of security sector governance

It is widely accepted that, like all executive agencies of government, security institutions need to be accountable to democratically elected representatives and ultimately the general population, and to be under the control of the state. Democratic oversight and control is widely regarded as an essential part of an effective security sector and is, ultimately, indispensable to security, stability, democracy and development (DCAF, 2008, 2009; Inter-Parliamentary Union (IPU)-DCAF, 2003; OECD, 2005b, 2007a; OSCE, 1994; Parliamentary Assembly of the Council of Europe, 2005; UNSG, 2008a; UNDP, 2002; UNDP/DCAF, 2006; Venice Commission, 2008). It is argued that democratic oversight and control provides for checks and balances to prevent abuses of power and ensures that security sector institutions operate effectively and efficiently within the confines of the law. It also protects against misallocation or misuse of financial resources, the politicisation of the security sector (neither misused for political purposes nor interfering in domestic politics), human rights abuses and impunity (see DCAF, 2008). Ultimately, it is argued, democratic oversight and control ensures transparency, accountability and responsibility. It helps ensure that security providers serve the interests of the public, enjoy their support and are regarded as legitimate. It is also important to note that through democratic oversight and control, the rights and interests of those employed in the security sector are also protected.

Simply put, as security institutions are provided with special powers to intrude into people's lives, curtailing their freedoms and rights, and they ultimately have the power to undermine the will or interests of the public, safeguards and oversight are required. The interests of security providers must be subordinate to the interests of a democratic society, particularly in view of the potential for the power of security providers to affect democracy and its values (see the Venice Commission, 2008). Moreover, because security is of fundamental importance to people and their well-being (see IPU-DCAF, 2003) and is funded by the public purse, the public have a right to influence decisions about security, just as every other sector of government, through elected representatives and through its own capacity to oversee the work of the security sector.

In essence, oversight limits the power, not the effectiveness, of the security sector. In fact, democratic governance is necessary for both an effective security sector (one that is responsive, accountable, transparent, representative and fair) as well as comprehensive, long-term security. History has shown that where there is limited accountability and democratic oversight, security institutions can be used to oppress, abuse and harm the people they ostensibly serve.

Actors engaged in security sector governance

Comprehensive oversight of the security sector is ensured by the engagement of many actors, including the security providers themselves (internal oversight or control), each having distinct but often related functions or mechanisms. These actors are the legislative (parliament), executive (government, including line ministries), judiciary, civil society, independent oversight bodies (such as national human rights institutions) and, increasingly, international organisations, which can monitor, advise, influence and, in some instances, instruct and enforce. Taken together, the multiple levels or layers of oversight contribute to full democratic accountability and thus the protection of the interests and will of the people. In practice, the co-ordinating and reporting responsibilities need to be defined, understood and, together with the broader oversight responsibilities, expressed in binding policy documents or law.

Principal among the primary oversight bodies is the legislative, which can ostensibly represent the wider public, being the democratically elected representatives of the people. The executive is obliged to reveal, explain and justify to parliament what is done (policy accountability) and what is spent (financial accountability), as with every other sector of government, as well as to ensure the transparency that is required for broader civil society oversight to be effective (see Van Eekelen, 2006; see also UNDP/DCAF, 2006).

The executive includes line ministries, which are responsible for establishing basic security and defence policy, and managing or exercising control over the security providers. Ministries should ensure that the security providers have the tools required to fulfil their mandates, not, as is often feared, interfere in the ability of the security providers to do their job.

Engaging civil society in the oversight of the security sector can promote accountability, provide a very useful indicator of public contentment with the security sector and the performance of security institutions, and can enable the voices of marginalised groups to be heard and thus enhance the responsiveness of security institutions to a wider cross-section of society (see Caparini and Cole, 2008). Moreover, in many societies, it has only been civil society actors that have endeavoured to hold the security sector and other branches of government to account. Civil society is, however, often hampered in its efforts to exercise oversight, not least because of a perception amongst those directly involved in the security sector that engagement and comment should be reserved for the 'experts' – that is, those directly involved in the security sector themselves.

Developing effective democratic oversight and control

Effective security governance depends, as in all areas of government, on the existence of responsible and capable institutions, an enabling legislative framework, and formalised and accepted principles. Institutional capacity also depends upon will, knowledge, resources and level of support. In addition, appropriate structures and processes are required. In respect of parliamentary oversight, for instance, there would be specialist committees and regular public inquiries (see Van Eekelen, 2006).

In countries that may not have a long tradition of democratic oversight, oversight bodies can lack the necessary knowledge and expertise to be able to fulfil their responsibilities. They may also lack sufficient resources, the necessary legal basis, or the support that might come from a general awareness and acceptance of the legitimacy of the principles of democratic oversight. Often, lack of information and transparency are not the result of deceit, but can be due to the reluctance of security providers to engage with or inform those it believes not to have sufficient expertise. However, this creates a vicious circle, whereby those with perceived or real lack of knowledge and expertise are denied knowledge and prevented from developing their awareness and expertise – or even just doing their job. As a result, security providers become less and less accountable to the public.

Security providers, particularly defence and intelligence organisations, are of necessity closed institutions, predicated upon a culture of operational security, and with a 'need to know' rule even for their own members. This can seem at odds with democratic control, the purpose of which is to facilitate transparency and accountability. Democratic control is not, however, at odds with operational security. Indeed, a high level of confidentiality can co-exist with accountability as long as there is openness about what is held in confidence and why, and the reasons for withholding information are legitimate and tightly defined (see UNDP/ DCAF, 2008).

Critical to SSG is therefore development of awareness of and support for the principles of SSG within the security sector as well as among other stakeholders, including the general public. This requires training, awareness-raising and confidence-building programmes. Also, fundamental to SSG and requiring significant investments of time and money, are public trust and confidence in security sector institutions, trust between security sector institutions including between security providers and oversight bodies, and the development of a service culture. A free press, independent judiciary and other oversight bodies, promotion of freedom of information, and a robust civil society are also critical to SSG. As with all aspects of peacebuilding, programmes aimed at developing good SSG will also need to be informed by comprehensive planning rooted in a deep understanding of the context, local ownership, and co-ordination and coherence of efforts.

SSG challenges and recommendations

There can be much reluctance to promote democratic control and oversight, often emanating from a lack of understanding of what is involved as well as, often, a long history of excessive political interference in the security sector. In actual fact, oversight and control mechanisms are there to guard against undue interference, but this does little to allay the fears of those who have experienced the consequences of strong alliances between political elites and security sector institutions. It can also be the result of the potential impact on power relations, an assumption that more control and oversight would limit the power of the security institutions, including the ability to do their job where civilians are perceived as not having the necessary expertise, as just discussed (see Box 8.10 on how these concerns manifested themselves in Nepal).

> **Box 8.10: Nepal**
>
> In Nepal, for instance, after the conflict many members of the armed forces believed that civilians did not possess the necessary knowledge and skills to be able to make decisions that would not harm the performance and operational capability of the armed forces. This assessment may be correct, given that the Ministry was bypassed by the Palace, which managed the armed forces before the conflict and the overthrow of the monarchy. However, rather than recognising the evident need to build the capacity of the Ministry, particularly through training civilian staff, a resistance to change where change is not seen as necessary can become rooted. This is often informed and compounded by the political dimensions of SSR and SSG, where relinquishing control and power can be fiercely resisted. As Hills suggests: 'most political elites regard any control other than their own as dangerous; knowledge is power, and political patronage, cronyism, and corruption are a way of life' (Hills, 2007: 98).

It is also important to mention that it is not just the security sector institutions that should be accountable, but those engaged in SSR as well – not just the end results of SSR but also the SSR process. While it is of the utmost importance that decisions can be informed by and are accountable to the people those decisions will most directly affect, external interventions in particular remain lacking in terms of democratic accountability (see Brzoska, 2009), instead remaining primarily accountable to external governments and donor agencies.

Another concern, as Hills (2007) has highlighted, is that democratic control is often seen as an end in itself, or as synonymous with accountability and transparency, without addressing how accountability can be assured and how those responsible for democratic control can be held to account. Consequently, the goal of instituting democratic control can often be reduced to technical, institution-building projects, often imitating western models. This risks undermining the very principles of democratic control, as its success or otherwise is measured upon whether a functioning ministry, for instance, has been established rather than on less tangible results, such as increased accountability or improved security. It also ignores the huge element of unspoken norms and unwritten procedures in any organisation, which make the difference between success and failure (see Hall, 1977).

Part 4 – Challenges and Lessons Learned

SSR risks

SSR success, where programmes are externally driven, is generally dependent upon effective leadership, appropriate organisational approaches, sufficient resources, strategic planning and perceived legitimacy by the host nation

(Law, 2006). However, aside from cases where SSR is poorly co-ordinated, insufficiently planned or deficient in other areas, SSR carries a particular risk of destabilising a fragile peace. This is because of the power that is associated with the security sector and especially certain positions within the sector. This is the main reason why key power brokers (political parties) were given a share of the Iraqi Ministry of Interior, for example – in order to prevent the Ministry becoming 'an armed wing of any one party' (Stabilisation Unit, 2010: 6). Focussing on the technical aspects of SSR, rather than recognising its political nature, can undermine the extent to which substantial and sustainable reform can be achieved. As articulated by the OHCHR in its *Rule of Law Tools for Post-Conflict States*:

> Those used to controlling the police and using it to enforce their will, control the population or steal property will see reform as a threat. So will those who have used the courts to ensure their economic or political dominance. (UNOHCHR, 2006a: 3)

Significant risks can also be presented by the nature of many post-conflict security sectors, which can be characterised by a culture of corruption, militarisation, ethnicisation or exclusionary practices, and politicisation or undue influence over politics (see Brzoska, 2009). Widespread insecurity, the legacies of conflict, the presence of non-state armed groups, and the prevalence of mines and explosive remnants of war (ERW) and small arms and light weapons (SALW), as was discussed in Chapter 6, also contribute to the enormity of challenges facing SSR programs in the aftermath of conflict. Inadequate human and financial resources, infrastructure, equipment (including transport and communications) and trained and skilled personnel can also combine to present significant challenges for SSR (see OECD, 2007a). These risks can be compounded with the possible involvement of security sector personnel in war-time and post-conflict atrocities and abuses of power. The very existence of SSR programmes themselves also creates opportunities for corruption and political manipulation.

The need for security functions to be performed while the security sector is undergoing reform can also pose serious threats to the reform process as well as the wider peace process (see Box 8.11 for an overview of prudent planning and co-ordination of reforms in Kosovo, in advance of anticipated independence). There is a need to balance the longer-term goals of building professional security and justice sector institutions with the short-term goals of maintaining basic security, which can prove difficult. This is why co-ordination and a holistic approach to SSR is so important, for instance co-ordinating SSR with DDR and transitional justice programmes. Without good co-ordination, duplication and gaps arise, programmes become less cost-efficient, misunderstandings and false expectations can arise, and efforts to address cross-cutting issues – such as gender and human rights – become piecemeal. Recent efforts in Mali, for example, have resulted in an impressive number of laws and bureaucratic innovations aimed at the longer term, but at the expense of any real improvement in security in a country that is effectively at war.

Box 8.11: Kosovo

Prudent Planning

SSR programmes take a long time to plan, if they are to be effective. In particular, a lot of work is needed to develop co-ordination mechanisms, identify priorities and lead actors, and secure the necessary political and financial support. The timeframe for doing this can be cut dramatically short in the aftermath of conflict where immediate steps to reform security structures are often required. In the case of Kosovo, prudent planning had to commence prior to the determination of its status in order that the foundations were laid for the development of democratic security structures in the event that Kosovo became independent. Such prudent planning was very sensitive and, if misinterpreted, had the potential to derail the talks that were intended to determine Kosovo's future status.

Co-ordination of Reforms in the Security Sector

In Kosovo, plans for the establishment of the Kosovo Security Force (KSF) as well as the reform of other parts of the security sector were co-ordinated with the planned stand-down of the Kosovo Protection Corps (KPC), as previously the establishment of the KPC had been co-ordinated with the demobilisation of the Kosovo Liberation Army (KLA). It was necessary that there was no security vacuum or gap in the civil emergency capabilities of the KPC/KSF as a result of poor planning or errors in timing. It was also essential that co-ordination extended beyond the security sector and actors engaged in it. The planned stand-down of the KPC also included discussions with actors engaged in economic reform, to best prepare for those KPC officers who might not find a place in the future security structures. Moreover, there was centralised co-ordination with donors engaged in Kosovo and with Government counterparts responsible for budgeting, legislative development, physical infastructure (buildings) and logistics.

As has already been stressed, reform of one security sector institution cannot be effective without considering the whole security sector. Thus:

> ... efforts to reform the police without engaging the justice and corrections sectors will be met with only limited success. Likewise, improving the effectiveness and accountability of the police requires engaging with a range of other actors such as the military (to delineate roles and responsibilities) the parliament (to improve oversight) the finance ministry (to improve financial accountability) the ministry of interior (to improve governance, and the policy framework) as well as civil society (to benefit from research expertise, or to get insight into public issues of concern). (DCAF/ISSAT, 2011: 11–12)

Recognising the holistic nature of SSR does not mean that everything should be undertaken simultaneously, even if that were possible. Appreciating the interdependencies within and beyond the security sector means that planning

> ## Box 8.12: Afghanistan
>
> In Afghanistan, responsibility for areas of the security sector was divided between the key donors, as is often the case: the Americans were responsible for the army, the Germans for the police, the Italians for the justice system and the British for counter-narcotics. As Grono (2009) has described, this resulted in poor co-ordination, large differences in resources, limited attention paid to the executive and oversight bodies, and significant philosophical differences in respect of training, engagement and goals. Of course, the effects significantly hampered efforts to improve security and the rule of law in Afghanistan, and in later years, the arrangements became more flexible.

should be comprehensive and consultative. It also means acknowledging and responding to the ways in which reform in one area can impact developments in another. This was particularly problematic in Afghanistan where different actors were responsible for reform efforts in different parts of the security sector (see Box 8.12).

Moreover, it is important to recognise that building professional security and justice sector institutions takes a lot of time: training staff, equipping institutions, developing processes, drafting legislation can take years, notwithstanding the much longer amount of time it can take to secure agreement on security priorities, capability gaps, resource requirements, key appointments and so on. Moreover, it can take very many years for fully trained and fully resourced institutions with a solid legal framework to become effective, efficient and responsive to the needs of all people, and enjoy broad-based public confidence and trust, especially where new institutional or political cultures have been introduced (see Samuels, 2005). Consequently, an important part of SSR is expectation management and ensuring that programmes are sufficiently long-term; a necessity often compromised by the desire for short-term wins, donor budgetary cycles and the rotation of international staff in missions.

Disparity between principles and practice

Policy-makers and scholars have increasingly cited the lack of SSR success stories and often blamed the disparity between the principles and practice of SSR, with particular reference to the principles of local ownership, context-specificity, gender equality and being holistic and comprehensive (see Bryden and Olonisakin, 2010; Donais, 2018; Schnabel and Born, 2011; Sedra, 2018, 2010b; Zyck, 2009).

Local ownership

The principle of local ownership is widely considered to be the main prerequisite of successful SSR (Donais, 2009; Mobekk, 2010b; OECD, 2007a; Oosterveld and Galand, 2012). Local ownership is seen as instrumental to the success of SSR because security sector institutions, processes and policy must respond to local needs if they are to be effective. If local security needs are largely unmet, trust and confidence in the state and its security institutions will be limited (see Gordon, 2014a, 2014b; Gordon, Sharma, Forbes and Cave, 2011; Jaye, 2006; UNSG, 2013). This will result in the relationship between the state and its people being weak and people feeling divorced from the decisions that affect their security and their futures. If the new or reformed security structures are at odds with local customs, traditions and practices, it is likely that they will be rejected after the departure of the international community (Nathan, 2007; Scheye and Peake, 2005; Smith-Höhn, 2010). However, donors themselves are often limited by what their governments and parliaments will accept, and are sometimes obliged to ignore local customs and popular pressures, because they cannot easily be reconciled with the norms that donors work to and encourage. This places very severe limits on 'ownership'.

However, an approach that marginalises the engagement of local actors is likely to result in their 'resentment, resistance and inertia' (Nathan, 2007: 3). This, in turn, would compromise the peacebuilding process, increasing frustration among local actors and dependence on external assistance (Narten, 2009), which can lead to increased spoiler activity and, as a consequence, further dependency. Ironically, this can further increase the inclination of international actors away from meaningfully engaging local actors and simultaneously undermine prospects of sustainable peace.

While local ownership remains part of the 'contemporary commonsense' of SSR (Donais 2009: 119), there remains, therefore, a significant gap between policy and practice (Donais, 2009; Gordon, 2014a, 2014b; Nathan, 2007; Sedra, 2010a), with external actors frequently imposing 'their models and programmes on local actors' (Nathan, 2007: 7). Some reasons for this gap have already been mentioned, but others can include:

- Concerns about limited capacity and lack of expertise of local counterparts, as well as their credibility and commitment
- Concerns that other principles inherent to SSR might be compromised, or it would take too long to get local counterparts on board with these principles and favoured norms or plans
- The time and cost constraints already mentioned, which limit the extent to which it is feasible to engage many others in the planning process
- The allure of quantifiable results and quick wins, with programmes that are seen to respond to developments quickly and implement change rapidly often regarded as more effective and efficient
- The fact that it is easier to consult with fewer people, especially if they are located in the capital or speak the same language.

Even with recent improvements in promoting local ownership, the concept remains vague and generally narrowly interpreted – both in terms of what ownership constitutes and who the locals are (see Box 8.13, taking Kosovo as an example, of the limitations of local ownership in SSR programmes).

Box 8.13: SSR and Local Ownership in Kosovo

The planning for the establishment of the Kosovo Security Force (KSF) and its Ministry was driven by the international community, for political and practical reasons. Discussions with Kosovan stakeholders regarding the size, structure, mandate and authority of the KSF and other security institutions generally involved a process of getting Kosovan stakeholders on board in respect of decisions that, to a large extent, had been reached within the international community. Moreover, the Kosovan stakeholders were predominantly government representatives and, while democratically elected, this effectively translated local ownership into quasi-ownership by an elite.

Likewise, The National Security Strategy (NSS) developed in Kosovo in 2009–10 was 'quietly dropped from view by the Kosovo authorities and never implemented' (Blease and Qehaja, 2013: 16) because the International Civilian Office (ICO) had undermined local ownership by drafting it, rather than building the capacity of the national authorities to develop it themselves. This left Kosovo 'without a realistic or realisable security strategy for some four years' (Blease and Qehaja, 2013: 16) and without a solid basis for further reform.

Despite the challenges, without fully considering the specific needs of local actors – and not just central-level representatives but members of all communities – security structures will not be effective, responsive or sustainable, primarily because they will not be relevant to the context or have the trust and confidence of the people. Local actors need to participate in the decision-making and implementation processes, even if this causes what may at first appear to be less optimum decisions and results. It is important that SSR processes are inclusive – not just engaging elites or those who speak the same language or have the same ideas – in order that the security sector not just respond to the needs of elites but to all people. In particular, SSR processes should ensure that those whose voices are often ignored, and whose security is often most threatened, are able to inform decisions about future security structures, policies and priorities. There are many ways in which to promote local ownership of SSR programmes and ensure voices of ordinary people feed into plans and implementation, including so-called hybrid approaches to SSR which incorporate bottom-up as well as top-down approaches to SSR (see Box 8.14), widely consulting with the population before the development of plans (see Box 8.15 for an overview of Kosovo's Internal Security Sector Review as an example), and conducting public opinion surveys to inform plans (see Box 8.16).

Context specificity

Another core principle that underpins SSR is context-specificity. The application of good practice and lessons learned from elsewhere must be relevant and adapted to the current context: what works in one context may not, of course, work in another. For example, the culture, history, conflict dynamics, socio-economic conditions, political regime, legislative traditions, security risks and expectations

Box 8.14: Hybrid Approaches to SSR

There are many ways in which to facilitate a more inclusive and responsive SSR. One way is to incorporate community safety structures in SSR programmes. This would enable the concerns of those at the community level to feed into SSR planning; communicate information on SSR and security policy to those at the community level; and help build trust and confidence in the process and in representatives of the state (given that community safety structures or similar often include the participation of the local security providers and representatives of the local administration). In some circumstances, it can also help build trust and reconciliation between different groups at the community level, as well as address concerns or grievances before they develop into potential causes of conflict.

Community safety structures exist in many post-conflict countries and are sometimes referred to as district or provincial security committees, community safety councils, local security forums or citizen security councils (Bastick and Whitman, 2013; Gordon, 2014b; van Tongeren, 2013). Examples include local security committees established by women's community support organisations in Haiti (Bastick and Whitman, 2013), Local Security Councils in Colombia and Guatemala (Barnes and Albrecht, 2008) and community-based approaches to building safety and security developed by Saferworld in the Balkans, Nepal, South Sudan and Kenya (Donnelly et al., 2013; Gordon, 2014b).

are markedly different between Nepal and Kosovo, although lessons relevant to Nepal could have been drawn from experience in Kosovo in respect of whether and how to integrate demobilised non-state former combatants into state security structures, for instance. The gap between policy and practice in respect of the principle of local ownership also adversely impacts the extent to which SSR programs

Box 8.15: Kosovo – Internal Security Sector Review (ISSR)

In Kosovo, an Internal Security Sector Review (ISSR) was conducted, based upon a comprehensive process prepared by the British Security Sector Development Advisory Team (SSDAT) in 2005, at the request of the Special Representative of the UN Secretary-General (SRSG). The Review was intended to identify the needs of the security sector in Kosovo and prepare a development plan which would outline how those needs could be met. The ISSR provided solid ground for the subsequent developments in the security sector, informed by extensive public consultation (see ISSR, 2006). There were, however, criticisms that ISSR did not go far enough and that public consultation, while Kosovo-wide and at the early stages of SSR and even though more comprehensive than had been the case elsewhere, did not inform key decisions and was not as broad nor as lengthy as it could have been (Gordon, 2014a, 2014b).

Box 8.16: Public Opinion Surveys

Public opinion surveys of perceptions of security and security providers, as those conducted by Saferworld, for instance, are an invaluable source of information that can feed into the planning and implementation phases of SSR programmmes as well as inform monitoring and evaluation. See Saferworld's website – www. saferworld.org.uk – for many reports presenting and analysing the findings of such surveys in post-conflict and conflict-vulnerable environments.

---

are context-specific; oftentimes, models, structures and laws are replicated from elsewhere rather than organically developed by local actors with the support of external actors. When it comes to externally driven SSR programmes, the difficulty lies in finding SSR experts who are familiar with different cultures and political systems, and ideally speak several languages.

Gender equality

Another core and related principle is gender equality and the need for SSR to be inclusive of and responsive to the needs of both women and men, as well as people of diverse SOGIE. A security sector which is representative of the people it serves and responsive to their needs is more likely to be accountable to the people and considered to be legitimate. A security sector which is representative and responsive is also more likely to enjoy broad-based public trust and confidence. Fundamentally, this will help determine whether security sector institutions are effective and whether people have confidence in security and the rule of law. In turn, this directly contributes to whether people might take the law into their own hands, rely on insurgent or criminal groups to provide security, or address grievances through illegitimate means. In essence, then, the extent to which the security sector is inclusive, responsive and legitimate directly informs whether peacebuilding efforts will be successful and their results sustainable.

Gender equality in the security sector is often advocated for on the grounds of increased operational effectiveness – for instance, women should be recruited because women victims of crime might be better responded to or more likely to have confidence in a female security or justice provider (especially if the case is of a sensitive nature such as involving SGBV), or because women have special access to certain places or people, or possess unique skills (perhaps they are more diplomatic). This is an essentialist or instrumentalist argument, and often overlooks basic arguments of equality.

While it may well be true that women (and men) are more likely to report crimes involving SGBV if they regard the security and justice institutions that would handle the cases as not being overly male-dominated or machismo in character (Dharmapuri, 2011; Gordon, Sharma, Forbes and Cave, 2011; Khattab and Myrttinen, 2014), there are limitations to the essentialist or instrumentalist argument. Such arguments often fail to recognise that neither men nor women are homogenous groups, and that gender identities and assumptions about skillsets are socially constructed. Moreover, such arguments tend to result in tokenistic recruitment (Baaz and Utas, 2012; Dharmapuri, 2011) without considering whether or not those recruited have influence (are appointed to positions of authority, are listened to, are protected) (Diaz and Tordjman, 2012) or are recruited in sufficient numbers – the 'critical mass' argument (Salahub and Nerland, 2010: 272). Such arguments also often overlook the structural, cultural and institutional barriers to engagement, influence and the potential to effect transformational change; oftentimes tokenistic recruitment of women co-opts feminist arguments of equality and simply reaffirms and legitimises patriarchal structures, reinforces gendered inequalities and prolongs the violence which sustains and is sustained by those inequalities (Cockburn, 2010; Cohn, 2013; Enloe, 2000).

Normative arguments – advocating for gender equality as a principle, for instance – are often discredited as being culturally specific. Advocating for gender equality is sometimes argued to be advocating for a principle which is culturally alien in certain societies and its imposition would, thus, compromise local ownership (so essential to successful interventions). This is even though it tends to be predominantly male elites in such places who are consulted on whether or not gender equality is a principle they would advocate, rather than women and other marginalised groups (see Chapter 10 where mainstreaming gender in SSR programmes is discussed in more detail).

Holistic and comprehensive

Another principle inherent to SSR is the need for it to be holistic and comprehensive, and attendant to the interdependencies of different institutions within the security and justice sector as well as different peacebuilding efforts outside SSR, notably transitional justice, DDR, mine action and SALW control. However, reform efforts in one part of the security sector are often not fully co-ordinated with efforts in another part; different actors tend to work on police reform from those on defence reform, for instance, and planning and implementation often occur in silos. Moreover, the focus of SSR tends to be on the police, judiciary and armed forces, where the need to reform the penal system or management and oversight mechanisms often receives less attention. This is in spite of general awareness that reform in one area affects reform in another, as discussed earlier. Lack of co-ordination and lack of focus on all aspects of the security sector undermine the effectiveness of any reform effort and often result in duplication, gaps and inefficiency as well as confusion and wasted resources, all of which adversely impact intended results.

Given the very large number of actors and possible tasks, co-ordination is enormously difficult, and a truly holistic and comprehensive approach is impracticable in all but the most simple or narrow of programmes. No donor government or NGO, after all, can be prevented from launching its own SSR programme, even if it duplicates, or conflicts with, an already existing one. Police reform challenges in

Afghanistan, for instance, were compounded by a proliferation of bilateral police assistance programmes that were often not co-ordinated and, at times, advocated competing approaches and principles.

Co-ordination can be particularly problematic, but particularly necessary, between actors from very different fields brought together under the broad umbrella of SSR: different actors who might not otherwise work together and who might have very different priorities, operating procedures and ways of communicating. It should also be noted that different actors engaged in the same field may have different approaches. For instance, Ghimire (2018) has investigated how the UK, China and India demonstrated very different security approaches to reform efforts in Nepal, with different successes and challenges.

Where there are many actors engaged in SSR programmes, standardisation policies are desirable to ensure interoperability and to ensure that equipment is not provided which cannot be used (because it is too expensive to maintain, or staff have not been trained on how to use it). Likewise, training provided, perhaps by different providers, should be coherent with a long-term training plan, which should be developed as part of the reform process. This would avoid confusion and the resultant adverse impact on performance, as well as wasted investment. The provision of training and equipment is not, in itself, a good thing if the end result creates confusion or additional costs.

SSR as state-centric

SSR has also often been criticised for focussing on building or strengthening state institutions, rather than the relationship between the state and its people (the social contract). The assumption is that a strong state is a peaceful one, with the security sector as 'the defining element of modern statehood' (Benedix and Stanley, 2008: 97).

The capacity of state security and justice institutions may therefore be improved but state legitimacy and, thus, the effectiveness of state institutions, is left wanting. Efforts have therefore often been on training and equipping state institutions rather than building good governance; developing awareness of security issues at the community level and of community-level security needs at the state level; addressing ways in which to build public trust and confidence in state institutions; enabling those at the community-level to engage in SSR and inform security policy and priorities; and supporting the development of informal security and justice providers. Many academics and practitioners see SSR as part of the wider neoliberal statebuilding project, which reinforces dominant power relations, further disempowers the marginalised and undermines the likelihood of sustainable peace (see Albrecht and Jackson, 2014; Ansorg and Gordon, 2019; Donais, 2018; Jackson, 2018, 2010). Consequently, the specific needs of communities can be overlooked, as can the importance of informal security and justice mechanisms for many people in post-conflict or transitioning states (see Box 8.17). The irony is that state-centric SSR programmes continue to dominate even though the record of success is questionable (Jackson, 2018; Jackson and Bakrania, 2018; Sedra, 2018).

Box 8.17: Informal Security and Justice Providers

Approximately 80% of the world's population access security and justice through informal, that is non-state, providers or customary or traditional security and justice systems (UN Rule of Law, 2019). This is particularly the case in conflict-affected and developing countries (see Baker, 2010) and particularly where state institutions lack capacity or credibility, or access to them is problematic. The urban poor and people in rural areas are particularly likely to access informal security and justice mechanisms.

Informal security and justice mechanisms can be unaccountable, corrupt and discriminatory, particularly against women and marginalised groups – as can state institutions – reinforcing social structures and exclusion and perpetuating human rights violations. Nonetheless, they can be more responsive to the needs of people, cheaper, quicker, fairer, more understandable and, as such, can contribute significantly to providing access to justice, particularly to the poorer and more vulnerable members of society.

Despite this, very few donors and external actors engage with these informal security and justice providers – although things are beginning to improve. This may be in part because of lack of knowledge of these providers, language barriers, logistical and security challenges which problematise access, or simply fear, suspicion or disregard of informal security and justice providers. It is also, of course, often easier for external actors to engage state representatives who are more familiar, more reachable and who may also share similar views or speak the same language. It can be perceived to be quicker and cheaper to engage with actors and institutions at the state-level; time and cost constraints can inhibit engagement with actors at the sub-state level.

In developing and delivering SSR programmes, there is a need to acknowledge the role that informal security and justice providers can play in delivering security and justice, and the public confidence and trust they may enjoy – as well as weaknesses or limitations they may have. It is not sufficient simply to integrate such informal providers into SSR without due regard to the benefit and harm they may have. Similarly, incorporation of informal providers and mechanisms may compromise their value and legitimacy, and the public trust they enjoy. Disregarding the role they play can undermine their effectiveness, and thus compromise security and justice provision for people in a society, by building or strengthening processes, policies and institutions which, perhaps inadvertently, harm their effectiveness and reach (see Ansorg and Gordon, 2019; Gordon, 2014a, 2014b). Disregarding their role can also turn them into potential 'spoilers' (see Meharg and Arnusch, 2010).

Measuring success

A recurring challenge in SSR implementation is how to measure success (see DCAF, 2009; OECD, 2007a; Sedra, 2010c). The focus on training and equipping institutions rather than addressing less tangible aspects of building legitimacy, good governance, and public trust and confidence, is related in part to an assumption that strong state institutions build a strong state which is central to state resilience and, ultimately, peace. It is also related to the fact that measuring quantifiable results – such as the number of cars provided or people trained – is much easier than ascertaining the impact of interventions on people's security, public trust and confidence in security providers, and changes in attitudes or behaviours. It is therefore much harder for donor organisations to show results and impact if less tangible criteria are assessed. Utilising victim surveys or security perception surveys conducted by NGOs such as Saferworld and their national counterparts is a good step in the right direction. This would help encourage a focus on results or outcomes rather than simply outputs (whether more facilities and vehicles, for instance, do result in better access to security and justice), and ideally feed into programme development through monitoring and evaluation processes. Of course, perceptions of security are not always aligned to actual security, and so caution is advised when translating survey results into policy, even with in-depth knowledge of the context.

Conclusion

This chapter has provided an overview of SSR including key actors and activities, aims and guiding principles, challenges and critiques, and lessons learned and recommendations. Fundamentally, this chapter has demonstrated that SSR is a highly complex, sensitive, political process that requires significant investment of resources and time if efforts are to be successful. Adherence to the related principles of inclusion, local ownership, gender equality and accountability are key to success, not least in ensuring that outputs are responsive to actual needs and that the needs of the more marginalised are factored into decisions about security. The latter is necessary if reformed security structures are to be responsive to the needs of the population they serve, rather than just elite or dominant groups, and thus contribute to building meaningful and sustainable peace; for where the security and justice needs of the more marginalised are not attended to, and the peace dividends are enjoyed only by a few, peace cannot be said to be meaningful. However, as we have seen, while these principles are widely considered to be the bedrock of SSR, recognising that they are critical to successful SSR programmes and thus peacebuilding, there is often a gap between principles and practice. There are many reasons for this, some of which are related to the complexity of SSR programmes, not least the tension that can exist between principles and between short and long-term aims.

To help bridge the gap that can exist between SSR principles and practice, the complexity of SSR and the long-term nature of building inclusive security should be acknowledged rather than avoided, and SSR regarded as a process rather than a means to an end. In other words, the aim is to build effective security sector institutions which are responsive, accountable and enjoy broad-based public trust and confidence – not simply to build well-equipped, trained and resourced institutions. In recognition of this, the complexity of SSR programmes – not least in terms of the number of issues that can be addressed and actors engaged – provides an opportunity to identify and discuss the many security needs there might be in a post-conflict environment, and potentially arrive at a shared understanding of needs and a vision of security. This can contribute to creating policies, mechanisms and institutions able to respond to the diversity of needs under a single shared vision. This process can also help build relationships between different stakeholders and notably help build trust and confidence in the state and its institutions, where a diverse range of civil society actors and state representatives are engaged in SSR discussions and decision-making.

Summary of Key Issues

- The reform or (re)construction of security and justice sector institutions in post-conflict environments remains a significant feature of peacebuilding on the basis of the broad agreement that security and justice are prerequisites to sustainable peace and development.
- It is generally understood that SSR refers to the reform or (re)construction of the security sector, including its institutions, policy and processes, as well as the establishment or strengthening of democratic governance of the security sector.
- The aim of SSR is to promote SSG and create an accountable, professional, effective and efficient security sector, responsive to the needs of all the people under its jurisdiction, with adherence to the rule of law and international human rights standards, and which ultimately contributes to building sustainable peace.
- Most policy documents are agreed that SSR should be holistic, context-specific, locally owned and people-centred, gender-sensitive, well-planned and sequenced, co-ordinated, affordable and sustainable; however, there is often a disparity between SSR principles and practice.
- While there are a wide variety of state and non-state actors in the security sector, core institutions targeted by SSR programmes in post-conflict environments tend to be the police, courts, prisons and defence forces; the focus also tends to be on the operational effectiveness of security providers, rather than on improving the effectiveness of oversight and management bodies.
- Justice reform includes reforming or drafting laws as well as the development or establishment of policies, procedures, structures and mechanisms that allow for the practical implementation of laws and equal access to justice.
- Police reform is often perceived as being central to SSR efforts and the overarching objective of establishing the rule of law, building security and, as a result, long-term peace and stability after conflict.

- Penal reform aims to improve the effectiveness and efficiency of the penal system, including prisons, but also alternatives to custody (such as community service), related institutions (such as probationary services) and traditional or informal sanctions systems.
- Defence reform is a process designed to improve the effectiveness and efficiency of a state's armed forces and the making and implementation of defence policy, as well as to promote democratic control of the armed forces.
- SSR is a highly complex, sensitive, political process that requires significant investment of resources and time if efforts are to be successful.

Reflective Question

Is disparity inevitable between SSR principles and practice?

List of Core Resources

Albrecht, P. and Jackson, P. (2014) 'State-building through security sector reform: the UK intervention in Sierra Leone', *Peacebuilding*, 2(1): 83–99

Baker, B (2010) 'The Future is Non-State' in M. Sedra (ed.) The *Future of Security Sector Reform*. Waterloo: Centre for International Governance Innovation: 208–228. Available at www.cigionline.org/sites/default/files/the_future_of_security_sector_reform.pdf.

Bastick, M. (2017) 'Gender, Militaries and Security Sector Reform' in *The Palgrave International Handbook of Gender and the Military*, edited by R. Woodward and C. Duncanson, 387–402 (London: Palgrave).

Bastick, M. and Valasek, K. (Eds.) (2008) *Gender and Security Sector Reform Toolkit*, Geneva: DCAF, OSCE/ODIHR, UN-INSTRAW. Available at www.dcaf.ch/gender-security-sector-reform-toolkit.

Bastick, M. and Whitman, T. (2013) *A Women's Guide to Security Sector Reform* (Geneva: DCAF). Available at www.inclusivesecurity.org/wp-content/uploads/2013/02/WGTSSR-Web.pdf.

Burt, G. (2016) 'Security Sector Reform, Legitimate Politics and SDG 16', SSR 2.0 Brief, Issue No. 5 (Ontario: Centre for Security Governance). Available at http://secgovcentre.org/wp-content/uploads/2016/11/SSR-2.0-Brief-5_-_Burt_-_July_2016.pdf.

Centre for Security Governance (CSG) (2016) 'eSeminar: New Frontiers in Security Sector Reform' (video). Available at www.youtube.com/watch?v=flqINeGsZBs.

Chuter, D. (2011) *Governing and Managing the Defence Sector* (Pretoria: Institute for Security Studies). Available at www.files.ethz.ch/isn/127832/GovManDefSec.pdf.

Chuter, D. (2018) 'African Solutions to Western Problems: Western-sponsored Training Programmes for African Militaries: impact on Peace and Democratic Consolidation' in D. Francis (ed.) *African Peace Militaries: War, Peace and Democratic Governance* (Abingdon: Routledge): 103–120.

Geneva Centre for the Democratic Control of Armed Forces (DCAF) (2015) *Gender Equality and Security Sector Reform*, SSR Backgrounder Series (Geneva: DCAF). Available at www.dcaf.ch/sites/default/files/publications/documents/DCAF_BG_5_Gender%20Equality%20and%20SSR.11.15.pdf.

Geneva Centre for the Democratic Control of Armed Forces (DCAF) (2015) *The Security Sector,* SSR Backgrounder Series (Geneva: DCAF). Available at www.dcaf.ch/sites/default/files/publications/documents/DCAF_BG_3_The%20Security%20Sector.11.15.pdf.

Geneva Centre for the Democratic Control of Armed Forces (DCAF) (2015) *Security Sector Governance*, SSR Backgrounder Series (Geneva: DCAF). Available at www.dcaf.ch/sites/default/files/publications/documents/DCAF_BG_1_Security_Sector_Governance_EN.pdf.

Gordon, E. (2014) 'Security Sector Reform, Statebuilding and Local Ownership: Securing the State or its People?' *Journal of Intervention and Statebuilding* 8(2–3): 126–48.

Gordon, E. (2019) 'Gender and Defence Reform: Problematising the Place of Women in Conflict-Affected Environments', *Journal of Intervention and Statebuilding*, 13(1): 75–94.

Gordon, E., Welch, A. and Roos, E. (2015) 'Security Sector Reform and the Paradoxical Tension between Local Ownership and Gender Equality', *Stability: Journal of Security and Development*, 4(1): 53, 1–23.

Hills, A. (2009) *Policing Post-Conflict Cities* (London and New York: Zed Books).

Hills, A. (2014) 'Security Sector or Security Arena? The Evidence from Somalia', *International Peacekeeping*, 21(2): 165–80.

Inclusive Security and DCAF (2017) *A Women's Guide to Security Sector Reform: Training Curriculum* (Washington, DC: Inclusive Security and DCAF). Available at www.dcaf.ch/womens-guide-security-sector-reform-training-curriculum.

International Security Sector Advisory Team (ISSAT) (2015) *Alwin van den Boogaard: Security Sector Development and Lessons from Burundi* (video). Available at www.youtube.com/watch?v=t_EENdRB-1Q&list=PLVtNme7lSHM27k0-nvMKde7NBUBTCiyKt&index=3.

International Security Sector Advisory Team (ISSAT) (2015) *Nicole Ball on democratic governance and SSR* (video). Available at www.youtube.com/watch?v=P6rA4x-XFTg&list=PLVtNme7lSHM27k0-nvMKde7NBUBTCiyKt.

International Security Sector Advisory Team (ISSAT) (2015) *Richard Monk on Police Reform and UN peacekeeping* (video). Available at www.youtube.com/watch?v=kbQF5d7hxHI&list=PLVtNme7lSHM27k0-nvMKde7NBUBTCiyKt&index=5.

International Security Sector Advisory Team (ISSAT) (2015) *When Everything is Broken – SSR in Libya: John Durance, former Director of the Security Sector Advisory and Coordination Division, UN Support Mission in Libya (UNSMIL)* (video). Available at www.youtube.com/watch?v=V7jKtwfV8Fg.

ISSAT (2015) *Reforming Security Sectors in Africa – Lessons from Burundi – Nicole Ball* (video). Available at www.youtube.com/watch?v=_0-t5rhWGFU.

Jackson, P. (2018) 'Introduction: Second-Generation Security Sector Reform', *Journal of Intervention and Statebuilding* 12(1): 1–10.

Lawrence, M. (2012) *Towards a Non-State Security Sector Reform Strategy*, SSR Issue Paper No. 8 (Waterloo: Centre for International Governance Innovation (CIGI)). Available at www.cigionline.org/sites/default/files/ssr_no_8_0.pdf.

OECD (2007a) OECD DAC *Handbook on Security System Reform – Supporting Security and Justice* (Paris: OECD).

Reed, P. (2015) *Creating Strategies for Security Sector Reform in VUCA Operating Environments* (University of Leicester) (video). Available at www.youtube.com/watch?v=L25OBjhWscs&list=PLjQX5EXgm57STSvD19VcobrSyhF5pey-U&index=4.

Sedra, M. (ed.) (2010) *The Future of Security Sector Reform* (Waterloo: The Centre for International Governance Innovation (CIGI)). Available at www.cigionline.org/sites/default/files/the_future_of_security_sector_reform.pdf.

Sedra, M. (2014) 'An Uncertain Future for Afghanistan's Security Sector', *Stability: International Journal of Security and Development*, 3(1): 1–16

Sedra, M. (2017) *Security Sector Reform in Conflict-Affected Countries: The Evolution of a Model* (Abingdon: Routledge).

Uesugi, Y. (2014) *Peacebuilding and Security Sector Governance in Asia* (Münster: LIT Verlag). Available at www.dcaf.ch/sites/default/files/publications/documents/FINAL_Pcbldng_SSG_Asia.pdf.

UNODC and USIP (2011) *Criminal justice reform in post-conflict States: A guide for practitioners* (New York: UN). Available at www.unodc.org/documents/justice-and-prison-reform/11-83015_Ebook.pdf.

Welch, A. (2014) *Security Sector Management/Development, Security and Local Ownership* (University of Leicester) (video). Available at www.youtube.com/watch?v=C-ydEU2E6p8.

Useful websites include: Centre for Security Governance (CSG) (http://secgovcentre.org); Centre for International Governance Innovation (CIGI) (www.cigionline.org); Geneva Centre for the Democratic Control of Armed Forces (DCAF) (http://dcaf.ch/) and DCAF's International Security Sector Advisory Team (ISSAT) (https://dcaf.ch/issat/cat8). Other useful webpages include UNDPKO's SSR page (https://peacekeeping.un.org/en/security-sector-reform); the UN's Rule of Law website (www.un.org/ruleoflaw); and the International Network to Promote the Rule of Law (INPROL) (www.inprol.org).

9 Human Rights, Security and Justice

Overview

This chapter considers the often complex relationship between human rights and armed conflict, looking at human rights violations as causes and consequences of armed conflict, alongside the prevalence of human rights violations in conflict-affected environments. The chapter opens by critically engaging with the concept of human rights. The next part looks more closely at human rights work in post-conflict environments, by providing a brief overview of the relevant activities and actors. The section concludes by referring to some of the challenges faced in this field and ways in which they might be overcome. The final part of the chapter briefly reflects upon which groups of people may be more vulnerable to human rights violations, with a particular focus on children.

Learning Outcomes

- Describe the nature and extent of conflict-related human rights violations
- Analyse the relationship between human rights and conflict
- Identify the principles that guide human rights work and be familiar with the legal framework
- Be familiar with the activities of and actors engaged in human rights work in post-conflict environments
- Critically evaluate the role of the international community in protecting and promoting human rights in conflict-affected environments
- Identify challenges in the field of human rights work in post-conflict environments, as well as ways in which they could be overcome

Part 1 – International Human Rights

Discussions of human rights usually begin with reference to various legal and political documents of relatively recent origin. This is not wrong, but it is incomplete, unless we understand that practically all societies in history have had, and many retain, their own mechanisms for avoiding conflict and establishing the rights and duties of individuals (see Box 9.1).

> ## Box 9.1: Human Rights before 'Human Rights'
>
> As we noted in our discussion of the rule of law in Chapter 4, few people or socie-ties have ever voluntarily chosen to live under arbitrary or unaccountable rule. Virtually all societies (including those that later developed 'human rights' in its current form) had long-established and often very complex arrangements for bal-ancing and limiting powers, such that individuals at all levels of society, including their leaders, lived in a complex pattern of rights and responsibilities. This was (and sometimes still is) seen as the only protection against uncontrollable violence developing in the community (Girard, 1972). In their current form, 'human rights' are a product of liberal political theory, which began to develop in the eighteenth century, and emphasised, as might be expected, the maximisation of individual autonomy through explicit written contract law-style arrangements with govern-ments. Societies elsewhere in the world had often developed highly sophisticated models of rights and accountability themselves, but, because they were often not written down, they were 'invisible' to westerners, whose own concept of rights, in turn, was regarded as bizarre and often simplistic by locals. These attitudes still have influence, and part of the purpose of this chapter is to warn against the twin risks of assuming either that "human rights" in their modern form are part of a colonial endeavour, or that by contrast they are self-evidently universal, and only evil authoritarian leaders stand in the way of their joyful adoption (Chuter, 2017).

Universal Declaration of Human Rights

Traditionally, rights had been specific to places and times, and often to groups. This began to change under the universalising influence of liberal thought. The preamble to the American Declaration of Independence famously identified 'life, liberty and the pursuit of happiness' as 'inalienable' rights, which had been granted to all human beings by God. A few years later, the two Declarations of the Rights of Man and the Citizen, of 1789 and 1793, also sought to establish univer-salising principles, to be spread – by force if necessary – to less fortunate nations.

However, the 1948 Universal Declaration of Human Rights (UDHR) was the first attempt to establish rights in an international forum, through a political declaration. It asserted that the 'recognition of the inherent dignity and of the equal and inalienable rights of all members of the human family is the foundation of freedom, justice and peace in the world' (UN, 1948: preamble). The UDHR was adopted by the UN General Assembly on 10 December 1948 in the aftermath of World War II, when the international community was motivated to take steps to prevent atrocities recurring which had been seen during war-time. The UDHR enu-merated fundamental human rights which are to be universally protected, meaning that all should enjoy these rights, regardless of race, ethnicity, colour, gender, age, geographical location and so on. The UDHR enumerates civil, cultural, political, social and economic rights, not least the right to life and the prohibition of tor-ture, slavery, genocide and crimes against humanity. The Declaration, although

non-binding, has led to the establishment of international human rights standards, laws, institutions and organisations in succeeding decades.

The concept of human rights

As we have seen, the concept of rights existed prior to the UDHR. However, the
concept of equality of rights, whereby everyone is entitled to the same set of human
rights, is a relatively modern phenomenon. Today, human rights are generally perceived as inalienable rights to which every person is inherently entitled because he
or she is a human being. In this concept, people are seen as autonomous individuals,
rather than members of groups or communities, with inalienable fundamental rights
(see Box 9.2) which should be safeguarded by the state. Moreover, it was only the adoption of the UDHR that ended 'the traditional view that states have full liberty to decide
the treatment of their own citizens' (Icelandic Human Rights Centre, 2019: n.p.).

   Today's discourse sees human rights as inherent in all human beings (you are
born with them and cannot lose them) and universal (equally applicable to everyone, everywhere). They are also considered to be inalienable, in that that they cannot be given away or taken away. This is even though they are are often *taken away*,
even in democracies, although under specific circumstances and in accordance with
due process (UNOHCHR, 2019). For example, the right to liberty can be restricted
if a person is found guilty of a crime by a court of law. It is also common for some
rights to be limited or suspended (derogated) in times of national emergency, as has
happened in most western countries today. There are certain human rights that, in
principle, can never be suspended. These are referred to as non-derogable human
rights and include the right to life; the prohibition of torture or cruel, inhuman
or degrading treatment or punishment; the prohibition of slavery and servitude;
the prohibition of retroactive criminal laws; and the right to freedom of thought,

---

Box 9.2: Distinguishing between Human Rights

Aside from distinguishing between rights that are fundamental and those that are
not, some scholars and legal practitioners (following Vasak, 1977) also distinguish
between different 'generations' of rights:

- First generation (generally civil and political rights, including the right to live,
  equality before the law, right to free speech)
- Second generation (generally economic, social and cultural rights including
  rights to food, housing and safe employment)
- Third generation (largely unofficial and aspirational, including the right to participate in cultural heritage and the right to a healthy environment).

There is also a distinction between positive and negative rights, whereby the latter
generally correlates with first generation rights and refers to that which must not
be done, to protect against the excesses of the state, for instance. For instance, the
right to life is a negative right. Positive rights, on the other hand, refer to those
rights which require action – what must be done – and generally include economic,
social and cultural rights such as the right to education or the right to healthcare.

conscience and religion (ICRC, 2010a, 2003). In legal terms these rights are also referred to as peremptory norms of international law or *jus cogens* norms. In practice, however, governments largely decide for themselves what these rights consist of; the United States Government, for example, has defined 'torture' in such a way as to exclude its own (often brutal) methods of interrogation (Basolglu, 2017).

Rights as universal or culturally relative

While human rights are presented as universal, there is a considerable debate about their nature, and whether they have always existed and apply to all people regardless of who they are or where they are, or whether human rights are socially constructed and shaped by socio-political and cultural contexts. Those who advocate the latter, often referred to as cultural relativists, argue for the acceptance of different cultures and, thus, possibly, practices that may contravene currently dominant concepts of human rights. They might view the imposition of human rights norms and standards as a form of western imperialism. Opponents (universalists) have suggested that this argument can be very useful to authoritarians and can undermine the security of the individual and leave vulnerable groups, in particular, susceptible to threats from the state and other powerful structures and groups. It has been argued, for instance, that '(r)elativism is the invariable alibi of tyranny' (Ignatieff, 2000: 335), and that the claim that human rights are not universal is often used by repressive regimes in order to justify their repression (Shestack, 1998: 230–231). Both, of course, may be true. It is clear that authoritarian regimes may make use of cultural relativism in their own defence, just as it is clear that 'human rights' can also be used as a political weapon by western and other governments.

Pragmatically, universalists argue, correctly, that the modern concept of human rights is new to all cultures and has been incorporated into domestic legislation across the world. Ratification of four or more of the core human rights treaties by 80% of states 'gives concrete expression to universality' (UNOHCHR, 2019), as does universal protection by customary international law of some fundamental human rights 'across all boundaries and civilizations' (UNOHCHR, 2019). Because, for historical reasons, the western individualist concept of rights has become very powerful, it has resulted in many texts that have been widely signed, and is the vision of social order that informs interventions in conflict-affected and other countries. This can be at odds and cause disharmony with those societies that have retained traditional concepts of social harmony and collective rights. Liberal ideas of the supremacy of the autonomous individual are part of the broader logic of liberal peacebuilding, as its critics have highlighted; imposing culturally alien principles and practices does not lend itself well to peacebuilding interventions that are accepted by and responsive to the context or, ultimately, that are successful (see Newman et al., 2009).

Human rights principles

As we have seen, UDHR and subsequent human rights instruments are grounded in certain principles, including universality and inalienability. Other principles also include those of equality and non-discrimination, in the sense that all people are equal and that all people, regardless of who they are (in respect of a person's race, gender or age, for instance) and where they are, are entitled to human rights. Human rights are also generally recognised as being interdependent and interconnected, with enjoyment of one right often dependent upon the enjoyment of other rights. Human rights are also broadly considered to be indivisible, in the sense that no right is more important than another.

However, western agencies and organisations have been criticised for stressing civil and political rights over and above economic, social and cultural rights, which are often considered to be of equal if not greater importance by communities in conflict-affected and other countries (see, Cahill-Ripley, 2016, for instance). In many post-conflict environments, while it might seem logical that the overriding concern of communities is security and justice, the priority for many people is securing sufficient means to sustain themselves and their families. In Kosovo, for instance, community safety structures have revealed that safety and security concerns are predominantly socio-economic in nature (such as concerns about poor infrastructure and unemployment) (see Saferworld, 2019). It is also clear that addressing socio-economic rights is just as important as addressing civil and political rights when it comes to promoting stability and security in post-conflict environments. Many would agree with Brecht: *Erst kommt das Fressen, dann kommt die Moral* – roughly, 'when your belly is full, you can start thinking about ethics' (Brecht, 1928; Chuter, 2017).

Conflicting rights

Not only is there disagreement about the nature of human rights and the principles upon which they are based, people also disagree on which rights are more valid or important than others. This is particularly the case when it comes to competing rights where protection of one right threatens another.

As Ignatieff argues:

> The idea of rights as trumps implies that when rights are introduced into a political discussion, they serve to resolve the discussion. In fact, the opposite is the case. When political demands are turned into rights claims, there is a real risk that the issue at stake will become irreconcilable, since calling a claim a right is to call it non-negotiable, at least in popular parlance. (Ignatieff, 2000: 300)

There has also been significant debate about which (or whose) rights should take precedence in other circumstances. For example, freedom of movement is often curtailed when it is perceived that others' right to life may be threatened (as in the case of the SARS epidemic which broke out in China in 2002 and led to many countries imposing quarantines, for instance, see Xu, 2007). As Xu (2007) explains, there may also be a conflict of the same right between different right-holders. For example, when life-saving resources, such as medical facilities, are inadequate to respond to the needs of all those facing the threat of death, decisions need to be made regarding whose right to life takes precedence over another's. There may also be conflict of rights experienced by one rights-holder: Xu (2007) suggests that euthanasia, for instance, may present this dilemma.

As more and more rights are recognised, there has been pressure to distinguish 'fundamental' human rights from the broader category of human rights. Fundamental human rights include the right to life and the inviolability of the person. Fundamental human rights are also sometimes referred to as 'elementary', 'essential' or 'core' human rights. Given the focus on conflict and peacebuilding, this chapter generally refers to those human rights which are considered to be 'fundamental' or 'basic'. It should be mentioned, however, that the broader category of human rights is also relevant to conflict resolution and peacebuilding work. For instance, economic, social and cultural rights are key to peace and their violation often spurs conflict. However, in the immediate aftermath of conflict, the focus of much human rights work is on fundamental rights.

This naturally leads to the debate about how to react when these 'fundamental' rights are violated, thought to be violated, or alleged to be violated, and how this discourse has been used and misused, notably in the doctrine of the 'responsibility to protect' (R2P) and, more broadly, the discourse of humanitarian intervention over the last few decades. In Chapter 2 (Box 2.8), R2P was discussed in the context of preventing conflict. In effect, the R2P mandate obliges the international community to assist states in fulfilling their responsibilities to protect their populations from genocide, war crimes, ethnic cleansing and crimes against humanity and take active measures to protect these populations when a state fails in its responsibilities. These measures include diplomatic, humanitarian and other peaceful means, and military interventions – through the UN Security Council – when peaceful means are unsuccessful.

Early enthusiasm for robust military interventions to prevent or punish those responsible for serious human rights violations has given way in recent years to a more nuanced view. Some argue that intervention itself is inhumane, results itself in human rights violations, or simply utilises the human rights discourse to legitimise intervention motivated by other reasons. Many have argued that military interventions, whether as part of a peace operation or a preventive deployment, are often self-serving and frequently further undermine the security and wellbeing of those intended, at least ostensibly, to be its beneficiaries. Duffield (2007), for instance, questions whether interventions sustain insecurity and inequalities rather than address them, and, similarly, Rosen and Theros (2011) ask whether interventions fuel violence rather than reduce it. Harding (2011) also draws attention to the neo-colonial implications of military interventions on the grounds of humanitarian or human rights reasons. Others, however, argue that sovereignty is a responsibility rather than a right: it should no longer be seen as absolute, but conditional upon the responsibility of the state to protect the human rights of its citizens (see Badescu, 2011). Therefore, if a state does not fulfil its responsibility to protect its citizens, other members of the international community have a responsibility to do so and, as a last resort, use military force to do so (as articulated in the R2P doctrine). However, the inconsistency in respect of intervention on the basis of alleged human rights violations, as well as the relative lack of success of such interventions, has undermined rather than reinforced the legitimacy of the human rights discourse – it has also led many to question whether political and economic motives, rather than humanitarian ones, drive humanitarian interventions. See Frei, Stahl and Weinke (2017) and Weiss and Collins (2018) on humanitarian intervention. Also see Aydin (2010), Bellamy (2010), Ignatieff (2000, 2001),

Katz (2011), Luck (2010), Paris (2014) and Reiff (2018) particularly on the challenges which continue to characterise implementation of the R2P doctrine including lack of political will, selective application and structural deficiencies.

Box 9.3: International Humanitarian Law (IHL) and International Human Rights Law (IHRL)

We were introduced to international humanitarian law (IHL), otherwise known as the law of war or armed conflict, in Chapter 5 when discussing violation of international law in war-time and post-conflict transitional justice mechanisms to address those violations in order for societies to move forward and build peace. Aside from IHL, international human rights law (IHRL) can also be used to address serious human rights violations. As we saw in Chapter 5, the main IHL treaty sources applicable in armed conflict are the Geneva Conventions and their Additional Protocols. The Hague Conventions also contain regulations on the conduct of armed hostilities and other international treaties which regulate armed hostilities by addressing the production, use and stockpiling of certain weapons (such as the Convention on Cluster Munitions) can also be considered to be part of IHL.

At the international level, the IHRL main treaty sources are the International Covenants on Civil and Political Rights and on Economic, Social and Cultural Rights (1966), as well as the Conventions on Genocide (1948), Racial Discrimination (1965), Discrimination Against Women (1979), Torture (1984) and Rights of the Child (1989) (ICRC, 2003). As ICRC (2003) explains, while IHL and IHRL have developed separately, some recent treaties draw from both bodies of law (such as the Convention on the Rights of the Child and the Rome Statute of the ICC).

IHL and IHRL are different in their origin, scope, aim and formulation. While both these branches of law protect human rights, the aim of IHL is to regulate armed conflict rather than protect human rights, seeking to limit the effect of armed conflict for humanitarian reasons (ICRC, 2005b; Sriram et al., 2017). IHL applies only in armed conflict, while it is now generally agreed that IHRL applies in both times of peace and armed conflict (see Happold, 2013). In terms of substance, the main distinction is that IHL distinguishes between civilians and combatants, which IHRL does not; IHL protects those who are not, or no longer, participants in the conflict – it also aims to limit the effects of armed conflict on active participants by restricting the means and methods of warfare (UNOHCHR, 2011). In terms of applicability, it is generally considered that IHRL addresses only states. While IHL contains provisions that protect a number of human rights – including the right to life, the right to food, the right to health – it only protects some rights 'and only to the extent that they are particularly endangered by armed conflicts, and is not, as such, incompatible with the very existence of an armed conflict' (UNOHCHR, 2011: 16).

The relationship between these branches of law in times of armed conflict is complex (see Ohlin, 2016). There are, for instance, increasingly blurred distinctions between civilian and combatants and the changing nature of conflict, which have created confusion about the applicability of IHL. The biggest challenge, however, remains widespread non-compliance. This is not least because there are often limited consequences to non-compliance.

Part 2 – Human Rights and Conflict

Irrespective of the precise wording of human rights law or how rights are differently perceived in different cultures, people have grievances and expectations related to concepts such as fairness and justice, which have to be seriously addressed if peace is to be maintained.

As we have seen, it is widely argued that peace, security, development and human rights are interdependent, and that it is difficult to have one without the other. Without the protection of human rights, it is suggested, security, justice and development are jeopardised. Similarly, when security and justice are absent and development is poor, human rights violations are likely to be widespread. The UN has made this argument on many occasions, for example in the Secretary-General's report *In Larger Freedom*:

> ... we will not enjoy development without security, we will not enjoy security without development, and we will not enjoy either without respect for human rights. Unless all these causes are advanced, none will succeed. (UN General Assembly – UNGA, 2005a: 6)

The UN Charter itself outlines one of the purposes of the UN to be to encourage respect for human rights and, in so doing, acknowledges the connection between security and human rights:

> In setting out to save succeeding generations from the scourge of war, they understood that this enterprise could not succeed if it was narrowly based. They therefore decided to create an organization to ensure respect for fundamental human rights, establish conditions under which justice and the rule of law could be maintained, and "promote social progress and better standards of life in larger freedom". (UN General Assembly – UNGA, 2005a: 5)

Human rights violations are widely held to be both a symptom of conflict and a cause of conflict; they can also contribute to the escalation of conflict as well as undermine efforts to build a sustainable peace (see Mertus and Helsing, 2006; Parlevliet, 2010; Peace Building Initiative, 2009; Rost, 2011; Sriram et al., 2017). It is often difficult to distinguish between the causes and consequences of conflict, particularly when it comes to human rights violations, as increasing violations and violence descend into armed conflict, and as grievances multiply and cycles of revenge can become entangled with other motives that incite or prolong conflict. As Rost (2011) has highlighted, human rights violations are both part of the escalating conflict that can lead to internal armed conflict and a cause of armed conflict. Consequently, the exact causal nature between conflict and human rights violations is hard to determine (Rost, 2011; Thoms and Ron, 2007). It is also important to reiterate, as was discussed in the second chapter, that there is no single factor that can be attributed to causing conflict: conflict dynamics are complex and each conflict has unique and evolving causal factors.

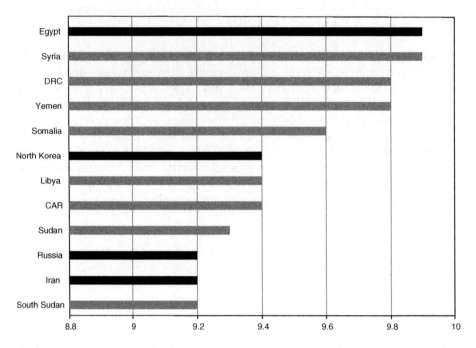

Figure 9.1 Human Rights and Rules of Law Rating (Fragile States Index, 2019) and Correlation with Armed Conflict (UCDP, 2019)

For an indication of the correlation between human rights violations and armed conflict, see Figure 9.1. This figure lists the countries with the lowest ranking of human rights and rule of law (the higher the number, the worse the record) and identifies which of these countries have experienced armed conflict in 2018 (by highlighting in black), using UCDP's definition of 1,000 battle field deaths in a year. Even Russia and Egypt have witnessed conflict during 2018 resulting in fewer battle deaths than 1,000 as a result of the insurgencies in the North Caucasus (ICG CrisisWatch, 2018) and in Egypt (ACLED, 2019). The remaining two countries, North Korea and Iran, are also not without concern when it comes to matters of international peace and security, of course (see ICG CrisisWatch, 2018).

Human rights violations as causes of conflict

In Chapter 2, the causes of conflict were considered. A key causal factor is widespread human rights violations. Countries where human rights are routinely and systematically violated appear to be more prone to conflict, where violations can contribute to the outbreak, escalation or recurrence of conflict. This is most likely due to a combination of the grievances that result (Thoms and Ron, 2007), a signal that the state is unable or unwilling to protect its citizens (Walter, 2010), and the increase in violence and instability with civilians left feeling that, in order to protect themselves and their families and communities, the best option is to join or support opposition or rebel groups (see Rost, 2011). As forewarned by Mertus and Helsing:

> States that neglect human rights do so at their own peril...The daily abuses that are part of systematic government oppression may initially leave citizens feeling insecure and powerless, but at some point those same citizens may conclude that the only possible response to a violent system is violence. (Mertus and Helsing, 2006: 5)

Similarly, Mertus and Helsing (2006) point out that human rights violations cause the fear that can lead to conflict. This fear is manipulated by political and military leaders for their own ends and creates 'cycles of dehumanization based on fear' (Mertus and Helsing, 2006: 4). Systematic violations of fundamental human rights, particularly in weak states (see Rost, 2011; Mertus and Helsing, 2006), can therefore constitute an important early warning of potential conflict; likewise, rights-based approaches to conflict resolution can be fruitful (see Thoms and Ron, 2007). When combined with significant socio-economic inequalities and division of political power along ethnic or religious lines, the likelihood of conflict can increase (see O'Neill, 2008).

Thoms and Ron (2007: 674) suggest that different types of human rights violations impact conflict dynamics differently. So, while violations of social and economic rights tend to constitute underlying causes of conflict ('creating the deep grievances and group identities that may, under some circumstances, motivate collective violence'), violations of civil and political rights are generally direct conflict triggers.

Kaldor (2012) has argued that after the end of the Cold War a new form of organised violence has developed, christened 'new wars', which tend to be intrastate and differ from 'old wars' not least because of the blurred distinction between armed conflict, organised crime and large-scale human rights violations. Indeed, these 'new wars' witness civilian casualties at an increasingly high rate and also target civilians with 'atrocities against non-combatants, sieges, destruction of historic monuments, etc., now [constituting] an essential component of the strategies of the new mode of warfare' (Kaldor, 2012: 9).

It is important to note that human rights and their violation may be perceived differently by different groups. Indeed, both sides in a conflict may say that their rights have been violated and may justify their actions on this basis (see Avruch, 2006; Lund, 2006; Lutz, 2006). Serious human rights violations are also often cited as one of the reasons for humanitarian intervention, as is pre-emptive war, which can, in turn, also result in claims that the rights of others have been violated.

Similarly, addressing often-competing human rights demands in post-conflict environments may itself raise tensions, which can threaten a fragile peace. Whilst it may be accepted that respect for human rights underpins security and stability, some practitioners have argued for human rights work to be 'conflict-sensitive': to make informed decisions about any action (or non-action) that might be taken in order to minimise negative impacts and maximise positive ones (see Peace Building Initiative, 2009).

Human rights violations as consequences of conflict

It is widely acknowledged that internal conflicts often entail a heightened level of human rights violations, including indiscriminate attacks on civilians, sexual violence, torture, genocide, arbitrary imprisonment, execution of prisoners, limited access to life-saving resources, and attacks on aid workers, schools and hospitals (see Parlevliet, 2002; Peace Building Initiative, 2009; Rost, 2011). As outlined by Mertus and Helsing, human rights violations are 'both a common by-product of the violence and a component of wartime strategy' (Mertus and Helsing, 2006: 20); in effect both a cause and consequence, resulting from conflict and contributing to its escalation and thus helping to create a vicious circle. The murder and torture of civilians, rape and forced displacement have been widely used as tools of war by state and non-state armed groups in many conflicts. Such violations of human rights against non-combatants can terrorise communities, intimidate armed groups and, thereby, help to gain control of land and power. These violations can also include crimes against humanity, genocide and war crimes, as we saw in Chapter 5 (see Box 9.4 for examples of human rights violations as part of military strategies during armed conflict).

Box 9.4: Human Rights Violations as Part of Military Strategies During Armed Conflict – Bosnia and Herzegovina (BiH) and South Sudan

The massacre of more than 8,000 Bosnian Muslims in and near Srebrenica in Bosnia and Herzegovina (BiH) in July 1995, was ostensibly aimed at military-aged men although it included many boys and elderly men. It was part of a Serbian war strategy in the Balkan conflict to control areas in the Republika Srpska in BiH. Similar patterns occurred elsewhere during the conflict, with Serb forces controlling areas then burning properties belonging to Bosniaks (Bosnian Muslims), rounding up civilians and detaining and/or torturing them, often separating men and women and often killing men and boys. Serious human rights violations were also committed by Bosnian and Croat forces (see ICTY, 2019). One witness, who lost two young sons and her husband during the Srebrenica genocide, testified during the trial against Krstić in 2000 and described the moment her 14-year-old son was taken away from her by Serb forces:

> I grabbed him by his hand and I – he kept repeating, "I was born in 1981. What will you do with me? What do you want me to do?" And then I begged them, I pleaded with them. Why are you taking him? He was born in 1981. But he repeated his order, and he threw the boy's bag on a pile nearby. Witness DD remembers that, while the Serb soldier was dragging her son away, she heard the boy's voice for the last time: "And he turned around, and then he told me, "Mommy, please, can you get that bag for me? Could you please get it for me?"... "How is it possible that a human being could do something like this, could destroy everything, could kill so many people. Just imagine this youngest boy

(Continued)

I had, those little hands of his. How could they be dead. I imagine those hands picking strawberries, reading books, going to school, going on excursions. Every morning I wake up, I cover my eyes not to look at other children going to school, husbands going to work, holding hands ... (ICTY, 2019: n.p.)

More recently, in South Sudan, human rights violations have been committed by the Government's Sudan People's Liberation Army (SPLA) and the Sudan People's Liberation Movement/Army in Opposition (SPLM/A-IO), their affiliated armed groups, and other armed actors with the direct targeting of civilians along ethnic lines. Documented crimes since 2016 include mass murder and rape as well as forced displacement, arbitrary arrest and forced disappearance of civilians (Beaumont, 2018; UN Office of the High Commissioner for Human Rights (UNOHCHR) and UN Mission in South Sudan (UNMISS), 2017, 2018). Villages and towns were often set ablaze and civilians were killed, which often meant those unable to flee – children, the elderly, the disabled and the sick. When villages and towns were controlled by armed groups, civilians who did not comply with demands for money were beaten or hanged to terrorise others into compliance (UNOHCHR and UNMISS, 2018). From late February 2018, government-aligned forces attempted to clear the presence of the opposition in multiple areas and deliberately targeted civilians:

The modus operandi of SPLA and associated forces clearly indicates that they deliberately targeted civilians. According to witness accounts, they stormed into villages, early morning, or around dawn catching civilians unaware. They would surround the village, then start shooting at fleeing villagers ... Others were allegedly summarily executed after being found in their hideouts ... women were killed when they sought to resist being raped. (UNOHCHR and UNMISS, 2018: 6–7)

Such violations of human rights can also be the result of the pursuit of precious natural resources, such as the conflicts in DRC, Sierra Leone and Liberia which have witnessed widespread killing and displacement of civilians (see Sriram et al., 2017). Those who witness or are the victims of such violations are often intimidated into silence, and human rights defenders are often intimidated or murdered (see Front Line Defenders, 2019). As Amnesty International wrote in 1993, conflict contexts also facilitate the violation of human rights in other ways:

A war mentality sets in, where loyalty to one side or another dulls the public perception of the need to respect human rights. Those who question any official action are branded as traitors, and important sectors of public opinion are willing to accept the perpetration of gross violations of human rights as normal acts of war. The conflict becomes both a pretext and a disguise for human rights violations as these are passed off as the result of armed conflict or as the work of the opposing party. Opposition groups likewise use the atmosphere of armed conflict as a rationale or a disguise for similar abhorrent acts committed by them. (Amnesty International, 1993: 2)

Forced displacement is also a common result of conflict, with millions of people being forced to leave their homes due to conflict, particularly over the last few years.

The widespread destruction of homes, infrastructure and institutions also hinders the ability to access a wide variety of civil, economic, political and social rights.

It is also important to note that a prevalence of human rights violations continues in the aftermath of conflict. This is particularly while there remain:

- Absent, weak or corrupt state institutions
- Widespread fear and/or distrust between groups and/or of the state and its institutions
- A culture of impunity and little regard for the rule of law
- Unaddressed grievances and trauma
- Infrastructural and economic devastation.

Such violations can hinder the recovery process, reinforce or create new grievances, and incite renewed violence and conflict. Protecting people from human rights abuses as well as addressing structural conditions and root causes is, therefore, a key aspect of peacekeeping and peacebuilding: helping societies recover from conflict and preventing a return to it.

Human rights, and conflict prevention and resolution

As highlighted by Parlevliet (2002), institutionalised respect for human rights, as well as structural accommodation of diversity, can be an effective means of preventing the occurrence or reoccurrence of conflict. As Parlevliet (2002) notes, the protection of human rights as an effective means of conflict prevention was recognised in the UDHR: 'it is essential, if man is not to be compelled to have recourse, as a last resort, to rebellion against tyranny and oppression, that human rights should be protected by the rule of law' (UN, 1948: preamble). Once conflict has erupted, to avoid a recurrence, efforts to build peace must address the root causes of conflict, including human rights violations (see Bell, 2006; Sriram et al., 2017, for instance). Addressing human rights violations that contributed to the cause of conflict and occurred during and in the immediate aftermath of the conflict, while a very sensitive endeavour, can also help build trust and reconciliation as well as rebuild confidence in the rule of law, justice and peace. As detailed by Sriram et al. (2017), however, questions over human rights protection and accountability for human rights violations can often cause difficulties during peace negotiations and peacebuilding. This can be because of a proliferation of violations where all belligerents feel aggrieved, because of competing claims for the realisation of certain rights (such as property or land rights), or because those in a position to negotiate peace are not willing to address such questions (particularly if they fear they might be held accountable for their actions during the conflict).

Part 3 – Human Rights Work in Post-Conflict Environments

Addressing human rights in post-conflict environments entails more than dealing with wartime atrocities, discussed in Chapter 5 when we considered transitional justice. It also involves an effort to build a culture that promotes and respects human rights and thus, it is argued, one that will be less susceptible to further outbreaks of conflict.

There are a number of principles that should guide all human rights work, which include non-discrimination, universality, inclusion and accountability. In recognition of the importance of human rights, the integral relationship between human rights and security, and the need to address human rights in all peacebuilding areas, the concept of human rights mainstreaming is promoted within the UN and wider international community in conflict-affected environments.

To build a culture of human rights protection and promotion, it is important to address political, legislative, institutional and attitudinal requirements. Activities often include:

- *Monitoring* – gathering and analysing data over time to ensure compliance with international human rights standards (to inform further action in respect of any violation, including political or economic sanctions or, as a last resort, humanitarian intervention i.e. military action).
- *Advocacy and Lobbying* – disseminating information and lobbying to encourage support for human rights promotion and protection (including the ratification of international human rights instruments) among decision-makers and key actors (which specific actors will depend upon the specific right or set of rights being advocated and the individual or group being advocated for), as well as the broader public and wider international community (as their lobbying power can be influential).
- *Awareness Raising and Reporting* – disseminating information to encourage compliance and encourage others to assist in improving compliance, whether through support or sanctions.
- *Capacity and Institution Building* – building the capacity of key actors engaged in protecting and promoting human rights through restructuring; legislative and policy development; enhancing co-ordination mechanisms; and addressing resource requirements, including financial and political support, training requirements and equipment needs.
- *Human Rights Education, Training and Mentoring* – enhancing understanding and awareness of international human rights law as well as international human rights standards and norms among duty-bearers and right-holders.

There are many actors engaged in activities to promote and protect human rights in conflict-affected environments. These include (Figure 9.2):

- *The State and its Institutions* – the state has ultimate legal responsibility for ensuring the protection of human rights of everyone on its territory – relevant actors include the executive, the legislative, the judiciary and law enforcement agencies
- *National Human Rights Institutions* – including human rights commissions and ombudspersons, which are independent bodies established by a national government
- *Civil Society* – including national and international human rights organisations, NGOs and civil society organisations, community groups and individuals, the media and academia
- *International and Regional Organisations* – including the UN, OSCE, EU, AU, OAS and the Association of Southeast Asian Nations (ASEAN).

Principles	• Non-discrimination • Universality • Inclusion • Accountability
Activities	• Monitoring • Advocacy • Awareness Raising • Capacity Building • Education and Mentoring
Actors	• State and its institutions • National Human Rights Institutions • Civil Society • International and regional organisations

Figure 9.2 Human Rights Work: Guiding Principles, Key Activities and Core Actors

Human rights challenges – security, priorities and justifications

There are many challenges facing those engaged in human rights work in post-conflict environments, notably the security conditions they often work in. Many actors engaged in human rights work often work in NGOs and other civil society organisations, which seldom have the security provisions that can be found in international organisations and military structures, although this is starting to change.

Their work can also sometimes be undervalued, particularly in the immediate aftermath of conflict where security and then governance, economic and development factors are generally prioritised. In order to effect lasting change, those engaged in human rights work need to be able to influence those with political and economic power, which can be difficult if human rights issues are not considered to be a priority. Those who are subject to human rights violations are often among the more vulnerable and marginalised in society. These groups of people are often overlooked in the peacebuilding process, not least because they are perceived to pose no threat to it. This can also contribute towards human rights work being sidelined. In some places, even the very term 'human rights' can create hostility and suspicion, and has sometimes been replaced by such terms as 'good governance' or 'the rule of law' (see Bell and Coicaud, 2006).

In a country, certain types of human rights limitations (such as strict controls on freedom of expression) may be accepted or justified as the way things are done (and external actors may view such violations as cultural) or as an unpleasant truth that accompanies countries in transition or recovering from conflict and other forms of crisis. There are explanations for heightened domestic violence, firearms use and violent criminality in the aftermath of conflict. Some of these explanations include the trauma suffered during war and post-conflict depression amidst high levels of unemployment and poverty; the proliferation of small arms and the belief that they provide better defence than the state security agencies; a spate of revenge or grievance attacks; and the rule of law vacuum that can lead to high levels of organised crime and the violent criminality that can accompany it. However, these explanations do not mean that violence and other forms of human rights violations are inevitable. And, as such, swift action should be taken to ensure that people are protected from human rights violations (in other words, in all these instances, they are protected from violence).

Some of those involved in post-conflict work might fear that protection of human rights could take away effort from peacebuilding. Indeed, there are times in the aftermath of conflict where the protection and promotion of human rights are viewed as potentially destabilising and, thus, not to be pursued. The Stabilisation Unit (2010), for example, notes that at times the objectives of human rights and stabilising countries in the immediate aftermath of conflict (stabilisation) can diverge. For instance, this can occur when those alleged to be responsible for having committed atrocities are included in the political process in order to promote a political solution, at least in the short term. Human rights actors would argue, on the other hand, that long-term, sustainable peace is untenable without the bedrock of the rule of law and respect for human rights (see Box 9.5 on how the sidelining of human rights in the aftermath of conflict can compromise peacebuilding efforts, and see Human Rights Watch, 2009, for example). This means that justice for human rights violations is a priority, as are the establishment of norms and mechanisms which protect and promote human rights for all. Such an approach would generate the confidence in state institutions that is required for societies to be peaceful, and help address and avoid some of the grievances that can lead to conflict. However, those who argue against human rights concerns trumping all others, suggest that without the absence of conflict the protection and promotion of human rights are virtually impossible. Others suggest that a balanced, conflict-sensitive and context-driven approach is required, albeit difficult in practice, and that the question should not be whether to pursue the protection and promotion of human rights and justice, but when and how.

Box 9.5: Sidelining Human Rights and Compromising Peace

Approaching peacebuilding from a human rights perspective can lead to a more just and lasting peace. Oftentimes, however, the priority is to secure a political agreement and address immediate security concerns. This can sideline, and sometimes compromise, efforts to address human rights issues, where it is considered that human rights issues should be addressed once hostilities have ended (see Kaldor, 2012; Mertus and Helsing, 2006). In Bosnia and Herzegovina, for example, the priority was to stop the fighting. This led to engaging those alleged to have committed war-time atrocities in the peace process. This approach resulted in difficulties in removing nationalists, alleged war criminals and those engaged in organised crime from positions of power. This has, in turn, compromised long-term security and stability.

Human rights challenges – power, evidence and context

Whilst the UDHR lists rights that could be violated by non-state actors (e.g. employers), more serious violations are typically the responsibility of the authorities in a country (see Jeong, 2005 and 2017). In conflict-affected environments, state security forces may be responsible for violations of human rights against political opponents – including torture, unlawful detention and murder – and for not taking appropriate action when others violate rights. Here too the judiciary may be culpable. There can be complex and often unhealthy relationships between government, security and justice sector institutions, and organised criminal networks. In post-conflict environments, much therefore needs to be done to rebuild the confidence of the public in the rule of law and the legitimacy of state institutions.

A related problem is that there is often insufficient evidence to advocate for action. People may simply 'disappear', and the activities of some of the security forces may be unknown except to a very small circle of political and security leaders. Official statistics may be impossible to establish, even after political transitions (e.g. in South Africa). Moreover, some researchers also suggest that human rights advocacy does not always influence state governments in desired or expected ways (see Hafner-Burton and Ron, 2007). Hafner-Burton (2008), for instance, suggests that governments do not always respond in anticipated ways to the naming and shaming strategy because they have different capacities to improve their human rights record and may have specific strategic aims in sustaining violations.

The nature and extent of the challenges depend, of course, on the context and the human rights issue being addressed, as well as the human rights actor. Human rights NGOs, for instance, may face different challenges from those experienced by UN agencies such as the Office of the High Commissioner for Human Rights (OHCHR), as indicated above. Bell and Coicaud (2006), for example, highlight the challenge of unequal power between international NGOs based in the Global North, which dominate the field, and those in the South. This not only creates ethical dilemmas, but can also limit the extent to which interventions are successful, where intimate knowledge of culture, history and language may be lacking. Similarly, the agenda, principles, priorities and discourse of international NGOs may influence or dominate national and local NGOs and other civil society organisations in places recovering from conflict.

Human rights challenges – resources, co-ordination and cultures

As with all peacebuilding efforts, limited funding and competing priorities pose challenges for those working in the field of human rights. The funding secured (not least from governments) may also influence the human rights issues investigated (or ignored) (Bell and Coicaud, 2006) or the human rights NGOs supported (or ostracised) (Muižnieks, 2017). Similarly, international human rights NGOs working in specific countries may recognise that publicising allegations may make further work in the same country much more difficult, thus undermining the extent to which that NGO can address this and other human rights issues in that country. For instance, a report published by an international NGO highlighting the levels of extrajudicial killing that have been reached in a post-conflict country may result in the relevant authorities not allowing access to the state security services in the future or, indeed, a legitimate presence in the country. Few governments respond favourably to public condemnation. Indeed, countries emerging from conflict rarely have functioning state institutions that are needed to protect and promote human rights domestically. In such contexts, a better approach could be to work with the authorities to address human rights concerns, rather than 'naming and shaming' those alleged to be responsible, for instance. Such an approach would also increase the likelihood of more sustainable reform than more divisive and less locally owned approaches (Peace Building Initiative, 2009).

The size and complexity of human rights issues, the number of actors, different perceptions of human rights and different human rights priorities – between different geographic areas, different peacebuilding actors and, indeed, different human rights actors – can also create significant challenges, not least in terms of co-ordination, communication, and an efficient and effective use of limited resources. So, for example, until the global North prioritises economic, social and cultural rights alongside civil and political rights, actors in the Global South may be less receptive to efforts by the North to improve the rights record in places recovering from conflict (see Council on Foreign Relations, 2012). Likewise, until the focus of all peacebuilding actors rests equally upon their own conduct and respect for human rights, their efforts – and the efforts of the broader international community – to ensure that others promote and protect the human rights will be ineffective (Deen, 2018; Uddin, 2014).

There are also co-ordination difficulties between human rights and other actors, in spite of the widespread conviction that human rights, security, justice and development are mutually supportive. Indeed, there is often a strict division between them, limiting the possibility for a coherent, integrated approach to building peace, whereby different intervention efforts across the human rights, humanitarian, security, political and development sectors are integrated in order to promote greater coherence of efforts and, thus, greater effectiveness and greater likelihood of building sustainable peace. Poor contact between those engaged in different fields, combined with individual agendas and activities, further limits effectiveness and awareness of how their work impacts upon that of others and vice versa. It also hinders understanding of the complexity of conflict and post-conflict recovery, and helps to encourage unhelpful generalisations about the motives and abilities of those engaged in other fields of activity. So, for example, security actors might have little contact with human rights actors and, consequently, have little understanding or little respect for their work, perhaps seeing it at odds with their own or of lesser importance. Likewise, human rights actors may also have little understanding or regard for the work of security actors, perhaps regarding their work as undermining their own. Lack of contact, lack of a shared language and stereotypes about each other feed themselves, and often prevent human rights and security actors from seeing that they are often working on the same issues, for the same ends and with the same overarching purpose and motivation (see Winslow, 2018, for a discussion on the differences and tension between military actors, and human rights actors as well as other civilian actors in humanitarian crises).

Whilst integrated missions are an attempt to consolidate resources and promote interconnectedness within missions in order to improve coherence of efforts and co-ordination, they are not without their difficulties. For instance, aside from tension between security and justice (should those accused of atrocities be engaged in the peace process), humanitarian space can be threatened when all those engaged in integrated missions are not seen as impartial, due to their involvement in the political process to establish peace (see Eide et al., 2005; Oxfam, 2014; Tennant et al., 2010). Likewise, there is a concern that an integrated or multi-dimensional approach to building peace results in the blurring of operationally vital boundaries, which can threaten the principles upon which human rights and humanitarian work are based. This can, in turn, threaten the security of humanitarian personnel (see Cornish, 2007). And rather than promoting coherence and co-ordination for the ultimate benefit of all whose aim is the establishment of sustainable peace, an integrated approach to building peace can co-opt the resources and moral currency invested in one field of activity to another. As some have suggested, it can lead to the securitisation of aid whereby humanitarian and developmental needs are subjugated to security, or rather, political agendas (see Collinson et al., 2010; Elhawary, 2011; Saferworld, 2011). Indeed, part of the criticisms levied at human rights discourse may not be because the concept of human rights is potentially destructive in that it justifies intervention, imperialism and oppression and ignores cultural specificity, but because (western) intervention is justified and legitimised with recourse to the human rights discourse, in effect consuming and undermining the very principles inherent to the concept of human rights.

As we discussed earlier, cultural relativists regard the supposed universality of human rights as a part of the logic of interventionist western imperialism. Intervention on humanitarian grounds has been seen to respond to the geopolitical interests of the interveners and not always the humanitarian needs of those in the country in question. As Chandler notes: 'human rights intervention can easily become a dehumanizing project of bombing and sanctions in the cause of great power interests' (Chandler, 2002: 15). Using human rights discourse to intervene is also of concern to human rights and humanitarian actors (see Box 9.6), as their work and their aims can be co-opted and undermined by close association with political and security actors who may have different overarching aims, practices and principles.

In essence, there are a number of criticisms levied against human rights as a discourse, including human rights being informed by a western perspective and trumping state sovereignty (as in the case of intervention in another country on humanitarian grounds). There are also feminist critiques which question the universal nature of human rights, including the way human rights can maintain inequalities, by not distinguishing between the ways certain rights might be differently enjoyed by men and women. For instance, equal access to employment can sustain unequal power relations unless a more transformative approach to the care economy is taken (which enables men and women to equally enjoy access to employment and takes into account the disproportionate amount of unpaid labour

> **Box 9.6: Human Rights and Humanitarian Actors**
>
> Human rights and humanitarian actors often work on the same issues in con-flict-affected environments and increasingly their work overlaps, particularly as humanitarian work is increasingly addressing people's rights as well as their needs (see Duffield, 2001 discussing the 'new humanitarianism' and see DuBois, 2018 on 'new humanitarian basics'). Humanitarian work is generally focussed on alleviating and reducing human suffering, while human rights work can be said to be focussed on justice and addressing root causes. So, humanitarian actors might be engaged in delivering food supplies or medical assistance to those in conflict-affected environments, while human rights actors might be endeavouring to hold those to account who have violated the rights of others. However, the nor-mative principles and priorities of human rights and humanitarian actors might not always align. As Darcy (2004) describes, the core principles guiding human rights and humanitarian work tend to be those contained in the bodies of inter-national human rights and humanitarian law respectively. Principles which guide humanitarian work tend to be humanity, impartiality, neutrality and independ-ence. While human rights work also tends to adhere to principles of humanity and independence, it often is not regarded as neutral or impartial, particularly if the human rights actor focusses upon the actions of one specific actor or set of actors. So, there is some convergence in terms of goals and principles, and also often in terms of mode of operating, although, as Darcy (2004) explains, humanitarian actors would tend to refrain from naming and shaming, as discussed earlier, in order to adhere to the core principles of humanitarian work and, thus, ensure that they are able to maintain their presence and continue addressing humanitarian needs.
>
> There is a further distinction that needs to be reiterated: humanitarian action is very different to humanitarian intervention, which is generally the use of mili-tary force to intervene in another country on humanitarian grounds (it sometimes means use of non-military forms of intervention including delivery of humanitar-ian aid).

women often undertake in looking after children and other dependents as well as household labour – see The Open University, 2016).

Recommendations

Some of the recommendations for improving the effectiveness of human rights work are implicit in the challenges noted above. To generalise, the lack of formal structures, shared norms and secure funding constitute challenges but they also, importantly, create freedoms for organisations working in the human rights field that may be absent for many organisations working in the security and govern-ance sectors, for instance. Likewise, competing human rights priorities may always exist, and efforts to harmonise or compromise or broaden the scope of activities for many organisations, whilst valuable, risk further undermining the credibility with which the sector is regarded by outsiders. There may be value in further restructuring or reforming the global human rights architecture, including the Human Rights Council, as well as bolstering the role of regional human rights organisations. However, some argue that reform efforts could undermine the significant strides that have been made recently, not least in establishing the Human Rights Council (see Council on Foreign Relations, 2012). It could also focus attention on structures rather than practices, although, of course, the two are interrelated. Others recommend specific improvements in, for instance, the work of the Human Rights Council, rather than wholescale reform (Universal Rights Group, 2017).

A note on vulnerable groups

So-called vulnerable groups can suffer disproportionately during conflict and continue to suffer violence and abuse in the transition from armed conflict. They are also often denied the protection and access to justice they require. Discrimination and unequal access to resources (including education, employment, housing, financial resources, political power and media coverage) tend to compound the level of harm such vulnerable groups suffer. Moreover, their specific security needs are often overlooked in mission and programme planning and implementation by the international community, which often focusses its attention on elite groups and potential spoilers. This is despite repeated calls for their inclusion in such programmes. Any peace will be shallow and short-lived, however, if many people remain vulnerable to human rights violations and violence; peace will be superficial if only elite or dominant groups enjoy its benefits. We have seen that human rights violations are an indication of insecurity and a causal factor in conflict. Unless everyone's human rights matter, then human rights do not matter in a society and, moreover, that society will be vulnerable to violence and armed conflict. Even in a society ostensibly at peace, it is pretty meaningless if widespread and serious violations of human rights against certain sections of the population are ongoing.

Vulnerable groups are often considered to include:

- Women, particularly single parents
- Children, particularly orphans
- The elderly
- Stateless people
- Prisoners and detainees
- People living with HIV/AIDS
- People with disabilities
- Nomadic communities
- Indigenous people
- Homeless people
- The very poor
- Indigenous, ethnic, religious minorities
- Migrants, refugees and internally displaced persons (IDPs)
- People of diverse sexual orientation and gender identity and expression (SOGIE).

People can, of course, belong to more than one vulnerable group; and of course, such a list of potential vulnerable groups demonstrates that the majority of people in a conflict-affected environment may, in fact, be considered to be vulnerable. Vulnerable groups may bear the brunt of revenge attacks and scapegoating, or may lack the necessary protection of effective and legitimate security sector institutions. In an environment where violence is often prevalent long after the end of armed conflict and where competition for scarce resources is rife, vulnerable groups can also be the target or unintended victim of abuse and discrimination. The focus of many peacebuilders on the potential spoilers of a fragile peace may unintentionally heighten the invisibility and thus the vulnerability of such groups. Nonetheless, as many human rights defenders and advocates would claim, without protecting and promoting the human rights of vulnerable groups, the protection and promotion of human rights will be meaningless – and without the protection and promotion of human rights in post-conflict environments, violence and insecurity will remain and, as such, so will the likelihood of a renewed outbreak of armed conflict.

A note on the special case of children

Despite recent increased attention on the plight of children in conflict-affected environments, children continue to be severely and often disproportionately affected by armed conflict and to have their basic rights violated. The conflict in Syria has highlighted to the international community the extent to which children are affected by conflict and indeed targeted by armed forces and groups. Among many other international governmental and non-governmental organizations, the websites of the UN Special Representative of the Secretary-General for Children and Armed Conflict (www.un.org/children/conflict/english/index.html), Human Rights Watch (www.hrw.org) and Amnesty International (www.amnesty.org) refer to documented evidence of the deliberate killing and torture of children (particularly those children in detention, and including those killed to punish their parents), the disproportionate killing of children in massacres, as well as the use of children as human shields. Children in conflict-affected environments are also often the victims of sexual violence, trafficking and forced recruitment into armed groups. The 2017 Report of the Secretary-General on Children and Conflict noted particular concern in Afghanistan, the Democratic Republic of the Congo (DRC), Iraq, Somalia, South Sudan, Syria and Yemen; it also drew attention to the denial of humanitarian access by armed forces and armed groups, and the use of children as human bombs by armed terrorist groups such as Al-Shabaab, Boko Haram and the Islamic State (IS) (UN Special Representative of the Secretary-General for Children and Armed Conflict, 2017). The following year, the UN Special Representative of the Secretary-General for Children and Armed Conflict (2018) noted a large increase in the number of violations since the previous year, with over 6,000 verified violations by government forces and more than 15,000 by non-state armed groups. This included an increase in many conflict zones in the recruitment and use of child soldiers (notably DRC and the Central African Republic – CAR), the killing and maiming of children, and the use of children as suicide bombers (by Boko Haram in Nigeria). Children in conflict-affected environments are also often deprived of education and healthcare, and have little access to security and justice. Oftentimes, schools and hospitals are directly targeted in conflict, which can directly affect children and deny them access to basic rights. As we have discussed in Chapter 6, children are also often particularly at risk from mines and ERW, during and after conflict, because they are smaller and thus more vulnerable, often play outside and can mistake ERW for toys. In 2016, 42% of civilian casualties where the age was known were children (International Campaign to Ban Landmines – Cluster Munition Coalition, 2017). Children are also often displaced as a result of conflict; UNICEF (2016) estimates that more than half of the world's refugees are children.

Adherence to IHL and IHRL during times of armed conflict is particularly important when it comes to children who often have no means to defend themselves against violations. While the full range of children's economic, social and cultural as well as political and civil rights should be protected and promoted, the UN Security Council has identified six categories of violations that demand priority attention. These Six Grave Violations against children during armed conflict are:

1. Killing or maiming of children
2. Recruitment or use of child soldiers
3. Rape and other forms of sexual violence against children
4. Abduction of children
5. Attacks against schools or hospitals
6. Denial of humanitarian access to children (for further detail, see the website of the UN Special Representative of the Secretary-General for Children and Armed Conflict: www.un.org/children/conflict/english/index.html).

It is important to note that there can be a continuum of violence between conflict and its aftermath, particularly for the more vulnerable members of society. Not only do the consequences of violence continue into peacetime – with children living with trauma, injuries, having lost parents, or witnessed atrocities – but children can remain vulnerable to renewed forms of violence, exploitation and abuse. Some evidence, for instance, suggests that there is a strong correlation between armed conflict and post-war domestic violence, including that inflicted on children (Catani et al., 2008). Where violence against vulnerable members of society rarely threatens to destabilise a burgeoning social order, domestic violence and child abuse tend to be issues left to specific agencies and civil society – often severely weakened if not destroyed by the conflict – rather than as a fundamental issue for peacebuilding, for instance. Moreover, psychosocial support in post-conflict societies is often not considered to be a priority when institutions need to be built, laws drafted and immediate threats to peace countered; crime and the propensity for violence and conflict are often controlled in a reactive way and root causes, let alone the intangible psychological state of a country's inhabitants, are often only paid cursory attention at best.

The security and justice needs of children should be attended to as a priority in the aftermath of conflict, and children need to be engaged in peacebuilding efforts (see Box 9.7). This need extends to those who are incarcerated, particularly because children may suffer disproportionately from the breakdown of the prison system and wider criminal justice system. Whilst detention of children should be in line with the UN Standards on Minimum Rules for the Administration of Juvenile Justice (1985, also known as the Beijing Rules – www.un.org/documents/ga/res/40/a40r033.htm), this is very often not the case in the aftermath of conflict, with children incarcerated with adults, for instance (see Box 9.8).

Box 9.7: Engaging Children in Peacebuilding

As children are often marginalised in peacebuilding efforts – neither considered to be crucial to it, nor potential spoilers of peace – their security can continue to be undermined. They are rarely engaged in peacebuilding efforts, which limits the extent to which these efforts will respond to their specific needs and concerns. A peacebuilding process inclusive of children and responsive to their needs will also enable those who have little political power or access to it to have a voice, utilise their skills and vision, and increase the prospects of building a sustainable peace, given that children – and their experiences – will determine what future there is.

Therefore, in SSR, DDR, transitional justice and other peacebuilding processes, the specific needs of children need to be addressed *and* children need to be actively engaged in these processes to both inform and be informed by them. These processes also need to remain attentive to children's special needs and afford them the protection and support they require (see Machel, 2010; Nosworthy, 2010). Importantly, children should not only be seen as passive victims, but as potential active agents of their own security (see Lee-Koo, 2018).

In short, engaging, supporting and protecting those who could be tomorrow's combatants or tomorrow's leaders is one of the best ways to ensure against future conflict.

Box 9.8: Juvenile Justice

Children are often the subject of arbitrary arrest and detention in conflict and post-conflict environments, sometimes for alleged association with armed groups (whether voluntarily or forcibly, or association of one of their relatives). This, of course, is a violation of their human rights. In detention, children often suffer inhumane conditions and violent abuse, again in violation of their human rights (UNICEF, 2019). In Burundi, for instance, prolonged conflict and adverse poverty have resulted in lack of viable alternatives to detention for children as well as periods of pre-trial detention for children which can last years, during which a child can suffer sustained human rights violations, including torture (Children's Legal Centre, 2011).

The detention of children should be in line with the UN Standards on Minimum Rules for the Administration of Juvenile Justice (1985, also known as the Beijing Rules – www.un.org/documents/ga/res/40/a40r033.htm). This means that specific age-related protection should be given to the child and access should be granted to child protection agencies, appropriate legal counsel and psychosocial support. Most importantly, the focus of juvenile justice should be on their future reintegration into society. In conflict and post-conflict environments, however, the international standards for juvenile justice are often contravened; there is often over-crowding, ill-treatment, torture and sexual violence. Not least because of these factors and to avoid violation of their human rights, alternatives to prison for children should always be sought.

Aside from attending to security issues, a human rights priority in the aftermath of conflict is to enable access to education and, thus, rebuild and reopen schools. Another critical factor in building a sustainable peace is providing jobs to adolescent children, not only as part of their development, but also because educated but unemployed youth are widely considered to be a classic contributing factor to resumption of conflict.

Box 9.9: Convention on the Rights of the Child

The UDHR contains both general protections that include children (e.g. the right to life) and specific provisions (e.g. on education) that concern children directly. In addition, there is a complete treaty (the 1989 Convention on the Rights of the Child) now signed by every country in the world except the United States and implemented by most, although with reservations in many cases.

Conclusion

While there remain fundamental, practical issues that need to be addressed, not least in respect of co-ordination and the protection of humanitarian space, there is an increasing recognition that peace is predicated upon respect for human rights – as well as the rule of law, good governance and development – and this necessitates a coherent, co-ordinated approach to building peace. This recognition of the interconnectedness of security, justice, human rights and development has improved prospects for sustainable conflict recovery as well as, potentially, effective conflict prevention. Given the current confluence of armed conflict, organised crime and large-scale human rights violations, effective peacekeeping and peacebuilding should be premised on a co-ordinated approach to building the rule of law, which would include security, justice, political, economic and human rights components, and be firmly located in a framework of international law based upon international humanitarian law and international human rights law.

Despite the widespread recognition that human rights are of fundamental importance to peace and vice versa, the human rights record remains poor and conflict continues to affect many places and many millions of people. The paradox is that today, human rights have never been regarded by so many as so important. Part of the reason for this can be in the selective utilisation of the human rights discourse by self-interested powerful groups, in the utility of human rights violations for military and political strategic aims, and in the lack of political will on the part of governments and other powerful groups to defend and protect the rights of marginalised or minority groups. Reasons can also be found in the tension or clash between rights as well as in the often limited number of avenues for recourse when rights are violated, perhaps leading to grievance, fear, revenge attacks, and other forms and manifestations of insecurity. In the last few years, nationalist and populist discourses have also been increasingly and extensively used in many countries for political and self-serving purposes, and have directly contributed to increased and widespread violations of the human rights of marginalised and vulnerable groups, as well as the erosion of the legitimacy of rights and protection mechanisms (Rodríguez-Garavito and Gomez, 2018; Roth, 2017). What is needed beyond broad-based support for the promotion and protection of fundamental human rights – and a recognition that violations lead to insecurity, violence and conflict – is leadership, resources and commitment to human rights even when it might not align with geopolitical interests or profit. Moreover, to withstand the challenges posed by rising populist nationalism, civil society actors – including NGOs, media organisations, universities and think tanks, and individual citizens – have an increasingly important role to play in advocating for the protection and promotion of human rights, raising awareness of violations and demanding the accountability of state and other powerful actors.

Summary of Key Issues

- The 1948 Universal Declaration of Human Rights (UDHR) was the first attempt to establish rights in an international forum.
- Human rights are commonly perceived as universal, inalienable and indivisible; in practice, however, there is much debate.
- Both international humanitarian law (IHL) and international human rights law (IHRL) seek to protect human rights but are different in their origin, scope, aim and formulation.
- Human rights violations are a cause and consequence of armed conflict.
- Peace is predicated upon respect for human rights.
- The principles of non-discrimination, universality, inclusion and accountability should guide human rights work.
- Human rights activities include monitoring; advocacy and lobbying; awareness raising and reporting; capacity and institution building; and human rights education, training and mentoring.
- Co-ordination, security, protection of humanitarian space and securing sufficient resources and support are among the biggest challenges facing those engaged in human rights work.
- Vulnerable groups can suffer disproportionately during conflict and its aftermath.
- Children continue to be severely and often disproportionately affected by armed conflict and to have their basic rights violated.

Reflective Question

Do you agree with Thoms and Ron (2007) that violations of social and economic rights tend to constitute underlying causes of conflict, whereas violations of civil and political rights are generally direct conflict triggers? Think of examples that might support or challenge their argument.

List of Core Resources

Human rights and conflict

Dudouet, V. and Schmelzle, B. (2010) (eds) *Human Rights and Conflict Transformation: The Challenges of Just Peace* (Berlin: Berghof Conflict Research).

Gearty, C. (2014) 'The State of Human Rights', *Global Policy* 5(4): 391–400.

LSE (2010) *Human Rights in 21st Century*, lecture by Professor Noam Chomsky, MIT (video). Available at www.youtube.com/watch?v=_AS34drNiOo.

LSE (2012) *The Burning Issue: The DNA of Human Rights*, lecture by Professor Conor Gearty, LSE (video). Available at www.youtube.com/watch?v=U88_GY7uQwg.

LSE (2013) *Sri Lanka and the culture of impunity: human rights challenges in a post-war and post-conflict environment*, panel discussion by Dr Paikiasothy Saravanamuttu, Dr Asanga Welikala and Uvindu Kurukulasuriya (Chair: Professor Chetan Bhatt) (audio). Available at www.lse.ac.uk/website-archive/newsAndMedia/videoAndAudio/channels/publicLecturesAndEvents/player.aspx?id=1937.

Meernik, J. (2015) 'The International Criminal Court and the Deterrence of Human Rights Atrocities', *Civil Wars* 17(3): 318–39.

Mertus, J. and Helsing, J. (2006) (eds) *Human Rights and Conflict: Exploring the Links between Rights, Law, and Peacebuilding* (Washington: USIP).

Sriram, C. (2015) *Seminar on Mass Atrocities* (GSDRC podcast). Available at www.gsdrc.org/professional-dev/mass-atrocities/.

Sriram, C., Martin-Ortega, O. and Herman, J. (2017) *War, Conflict and Human Rights: Theory and Practice* (3rd edn.) (Abingdon: Routledge).

Stanford Center on Democracy, Development, and The Rule of Law (CDDRL) (2015) *Conflict and Crisis: Implications of Ongoing Human Rights Violations in Syria* (video) (Stanford: Stanford) CDDRL. Available at www.youtube.com/watch?v=XTF4sgIqc8I.

TEDx Talks (2017) *White Helmets: the power of trained volunteers* (video). Available at www.youtube.com/watch?v=dpuny2eynIM.

Thoms, O. and Ron, J. (2007) 'Do Human Rights Violations Cause Internal Conflict?', *Human Rights Quarterly*, 29 (3): 674–705.

UNOHCHR (2012) *The United Nations Human Rights Treaty System*, (New York: UN). Available at www.ohchr.org/Documents/Publications/FactSheet30Rev1.pdf.

Children

Annual Report of the Special Representative of the Secretary-General for Children and Armed Conflict (New York: UN). Available at https://childrenandarmedconflict.un.org/virtual-library/documents/reports/.

Conflict Dynamics International (2015) *Children in Armed Conflict Accountability Framework: A Framework for Advancing Accountability for Serious Violations against Children in Armed Conflict* (Cambridge: Conflict Dynamics International). Available at www.cdint.org/documents/CAC_Accountability_Framework-1.pdf.

International Peace Institute (IPI) (2017) *Peacemaking and Child Protection* (video). Available at www.youtube.com/watch?v=E7Mj4dl6Vcg.

Lee-Koo, K. (2018) '"The intolerable impact of armed conflict on children": The united nations security council and the protection of children in armed conflict', *Global Responsibility to Protect* 10(1–2): 57–74.

Lee-Koo, K., D'Costa, B. and Huynh, K. (2015) *Children and Global Conflict* (Cambridge: Cambridge University Press).

LSE (2017) *Protecting Children in War and Conflict: European and global implications for child rights*, lecture by Helle Thorning-Schmidt, Save the Children CEO, at the LSE, 12 January 2017 (London: LSE) (audio). Available at www.lse.ac.uk/website-archive/newsAndMedia/videoAndAudio/channels/publicLecturesAndEvents/player.aspx?id=3689.

Save The Children (2017) *Invisible Wounds: The impact of six years of war on the mental health of Syria's children* (London: Save The Children). Available at www.savethechildren.org/atf/cf/%7B9def2ebe-10ae-432c-9bd0-df91d2eba74a%7D/INVISIBLE%20WOUNDS%20FINAL%20020317.PDF.

UN (2017) *Twenty Years for Children* (New York: UN) (video). Available at https://childrenandarmedconflict.un.org/video/twenty-years-for-children/.

You may also want to look at the UNOHCHR Universal Human Rights Index database (http://uhri.ohchr.org) where you can retrieve individual recommendations and full documents from the UN human rights treaty bodies, the special procedures and the Universal Periodic Review (UPR).

10 Gender, Security and Justice

Overview

This chapter considers the gender dynamics of conflict and peacebuilding, particularly efforts to rebuild security and justice after conflict. Of course, it has been recognised that the involvement of women and men in conflict and its effects on them are different, but this chapter explains why the subject has recently assumed a much higher profile and how in turn this has translated into doctrine and practice of post-conflict operations.

The first part of the chapter provides an overview of the links between violence against women and armed conflict, and considers violence against women as an indicator of impending conflict. Violence against women during and after conflict, and efforts to address this violence, are then considered. The subsequent discussion of the gender dynamics of peacebuilding focusses on the role of women in building peace, particularly their engagement in efforts to build security and justice. However, this is not a chapter just about the experiences of women. Rather, the discussion is then broadened to consider different forms of conflict-related gender-based violence which, among other things, might challenge the stereotypes of the vulnerable or peaceful woman and the protective or aggressive man. The final section then builds upon the distinction between sex (as biological difference) and gender (as norms and behaviours commonly associated with being male or female), by reflecting upon the construction of stereotypical assumptions of what constitutes 'a good woman' or 'a real man', for instance, and how gender norms, gender power relations and gender inequalities can sustain and, in turn, be sustained by violence, in both private and public domains.

Learning Outcomes

- Be familiar with some examples of gender-based violence in conflict-affected environments, and responses to it
- Analyse the complexities of the relationship between gender and conflict
- Define gender mainstreaming and describe what it might entail in the context of post-conflict programming or policy development
- Provide an overview of the Women, Peace and Security Agenda
- Assess the level of participation of women in post-conflict peacebuilding and the impact this might have on conflict dynamics

Part 1 – Violence Against Women

It is increasingly argued that there are strong links between violence against women and armed conflict, where violence against women is a key indicator of conflict, causes and exacerbates conflict, and undermines efforts to build a lasting and meaningful peace. This argument takes various forms. Anderlini (2011), for instance, emphasises the connections between public and private violence, and argues that gender inequality and domestic violence are indicators of public violence. Hudson et al. (2009) maintain that the physical security of women is a key indicator of the peacefulness of states. Schmeidl and Piza-Lopez (2002) propose that increased discrimination against women and violations of their human rights could be direct precursors of armed conflict. Others suggest that gender inequality increases the risk of internal armed conflict (Caprioli, 2003; Greenberg and Zuckerman, 2009), while some argue that 'more democratic societies are more peaceful only if there have been moves to gender equality' (Bjarnegård and Melander, 2011: 139). Other research has shown that where women are included in political life or have a relatively high status in society, there is less political violence (Melander, 2005) or peacebuilding is more likely to be successful (Gizelis, 2011), particularly if women participate in peace negotiations (Krause et al., 2018) or if women participate in peacebuilding and peace agreements are gender-sensitive (True and Riveros-Morales, 2019). Others (Enloe, 2000; Cockburn, 2010; Mazurana and Proctor, 2013) argue that patriarchal gender relations, which marginalise and disempower women, also perpetuate armed conflict, suggesting that masculinities, militarisation and the acceptance of violence as a political tool are mutually reinforcing.

Violence against women in conflict

Many argue that the nature of war has changed since the end of the Cold War; today, conflicts are predominantly, albeit often only ostensibly, intrastate rather than interstate; small arms and light weapons are easily available and cheap; non-state armed groups have proliferated; and civilians are deliberately targeted as an effective tool in warfare (Kaldor, 2012). This has contributed to blurring the boundaries between the battlefield and the home front, and has resulted in civilians, often women, increasingly becoming the victims of conflict (Holt, 2014; Kaldor 2012; UN Women, 2019). As stated by Margot Wallström, UN Special Representative of the Secretary-General (SRSG) on Sexual Violence in Conflict, when presenting her third annual report on sexual violence in conflict to the Security Council in 2012:

> In contemporary wars, it has become more dangerous to be a woman fetching water or collecting firewood, than to be a fighter on the frontline. Wars have entered the marketplaces where women trade; they follow children en route to school; and haunt the prison cells where political activists are detained. (UN, 2012: n.p.)

Although some research has shown that increasingly women are more likely than before to die as a direct consequence of conflict (Kuehnast et al., 2011), men remain more likely to be direct casualties of armed conflict because they are much more likely to be directly engaged. However, research has also suggested that the majority of deaths in conflicts today are the indirect result rather than direct consequences of conflict (Kuehnast et al., 2011; Ormhaug et al., 2009), although of course this is a complex issue and it is hard to establish 'excess mortality', that is, distinguish between indirect victims of conflict and those who might have died anyway. It has been argued that women are more likely to be these indirect victims of conflict: dying because of limited access to food, water, healthcare and poor sanitation; being exposed to risks related to displacement; suffering illness and being exposed to contagious diseases; and suffering domestic violence and conflict-related sexual violence (Mazurana and Proctor, 2013; Plumber and Neumayer, 2006; UN Women, 2019).

In particular women may be subject to what the UNSG (2018: 1) describes as conflict-related sexual violence (CRSV): 'rape, sexual slavery, forced prostitution, forced pregnancy, forced abortion, enforced sterilization, forced marriage, and any other form of sexual violence of comparable gravity perpetrated against women, men, girls or boys that is directly or indirectly linked to a conflict' – also sometimes referred to as sexual violence in armed conflict (SVAC). The current UN Secretary General (UNSG), António Guterres, has said that 'sexual violence is a brutal form of physical and psychological warfare rooted in the gender inequality' (UNSG, 2017b: 2). CRSV can oftentimes be seen to be used as a military tactic, aimed to punish, humiliate or terrorise the enemy, and displace or destroy communities. Indeed, conflict-related sexual violence is often the weapon of choice, the UN SRSG on Sexual Violence in Conflict has said, because it is 'cheap, silent and effective' (Berger, 2010). As stated in the 2018 report of the Secretary-General on conflict-related sexual violence (UNSG, 2018: 4):

> Wars are still being fought on and over the bodies of women, to control their production and reproduction by force. Across regions, sexual violence has been perpetrated in public or witnessed by loved ones, to terrorize communities and fracture families through the violation of taboos, signifying that nothing is sacred and no one is safe.

Recently, it can be seen to be used as a tactic of terrorism, with non-state violent extremist groups and criminal-terrorist networks using 'the bodies of women and girls as a form of currency in the political economy of war' (UNSG, 2017b: 3), through sex trafficking and sexual slavery, and also committing CRSV to terrorise, displace and impose an ideology which suppresses the rights of women (UNSG, 2017a). This has been seen in CAR, Cote d'Ivoire, Mali, Iraq, Somalia, Sudan, South Sudan, DRC and Syria (UNSG, 2017a). In CAR, for instance, as conflict spread in 2017 to parts of Eastern DRC previously unscathed, sexual violence increased in severity and scale, with numerous cases recorded, including where men and boys were the victim (UNSG, 2018). This violence has prevented women in particular from participating in vital economic and livelihood activities, has forced the displacement of many people, and has led to high rates of maternal mortality as a result of unsafe abortions (in societies in which children conceived through rape are often ostracised) (UNSG, 2018). In Iraq, in places under the control of the Islamic State (IS), people were often subject to rape including for disobeying IS rules. Women and girls from minority religious and ethnic groups were particularly targeted, but others, including men and boys, also suffered (UNSG, 2018). In Nigeria, Boko Haram insurgents have abducted, raped and forcibly married thousands of women and girls. Many of these victims/survivors are further victimised when they return to their own communities, as a result of social stigma partly resulting from suspicions that they are Boko Haram sympathisers (UNSG, 2018). Some have also been subject to further sexual violence by the Nigerian military and other actors claiming to be rescuing them and sometimes in exchange for food (Amnesty International, 2018).

Cohen et al. (2013) and Wood (2014) guard against CRSV only being seen as a military strategy or tactic; sometimes it is rather an opportunistic practice – and tolerated rather than ordered by commanders – and part of the continuum of violence against women and girls. They also remind us that not all armed groups inflict sexual violence and, if efforts to counter and prevent CRSV are to be effective, it is important to understand the various ways in which sexual violence is and is not employed during conflict. While it is generally regarded that the prevalence and scale of CRSV is very high, there are still a lot of unknowns, particularly regarding the patterns of CRSV. This is not least because it tends to be massively underreported by victims. While reliable statistics are rare, to give an indication of the scope of CRSV, some estimates include 40,000–60,000 rape cases in Bosnia during the conflict, 500,000 rape cases during the Rwandan genocide and 200,000 survivors of rape in the Democratic Republic of Congo (DRC) (Anderlini, 2011; Nobel Women's Initiative, 2012). Of course, these numbers should not detract from the harm that is caused by a single act.

The magnitude of the harm caused by CRSV is captured, in part, by the words of Elisabeth Rehn and Ellen Johnson Sirleaf, who were commissioned by UNIFEM at the turn of the millennium to conduct an independent assessment of women, war and peace. As former Defence and Finance Ministers with first-hand experience of war, they still found themselves unprepared for the scale and the nature of the violence against women in conflict that they uncovered:

> Violence against women in conflict is one of history's great silences. We were completely unprepared for the searing magnitude of what we saw and heard in the conflict and post-conflict areas we visited. We knew the data. We knew that 94 per cent of displaced households surveyed in Sierra Leone had experienced sexual assaults, including rape, torture and sexual slavery. That at least 250,000 – perhaps as many as 500,000 – women were raped during the 1994 genocide in Rwanda. We read reports of sexual violence in the ongoing hostilities in Algeria, Myanmar, Southern Sudan and Uganda. We learned of the dramatic increase in domestic violence in war zones, and of the growing numbers of women trafficked out of war zones to become forced labourers and forced sex workers.
>
> But knowing all this did not prepare us for the horrors women described. Wombs punctured with guns. Women raped and tortured in front of their husbands and children. Rifles forced into vaginas. Pregnant women beaten to

induce miscarriages. Foetuses ripped from wombs. Women kidnapped, blind-folded and beaten on their way to work or school. We saw the scars, the pain and the humiliation. We heard accounts of gang rapes, rape camps and mutilation. Of murder and sexual slavery. We saw the scars of brutality so extreme that survival seemed for some a worse fate than death.

On every continent we visited, in refugee camps, bars, brothels, prisons and shantytowns, women survivors shared their stories with us. They told us about their struggles to heal from the physical violence and the enduring psychological pain. And with each survivor whom we met, the numbers simply could not begin to capture the anguish that permeated their lives. (Rehn and Sirleaf, 2002: 9)

Recently, CRSV has received significant attention, particularly among policy-makers, and there is also an increasing awareness that CRSV is not an inevitable by-product of war, but preventable and a key factor in causing further insecurity (see, for example, Cohen et al., 2013; Nordås, 2011a, 2011b). Various efforts aimed at preventing and responding to conflict-related sexual violence have included the adoption of a number of UN Security Council Resolutions – UNSCR 1325 (2000) and subsequent Resolutions on Women, Peace and Security, specifically UNSCRs 1820 (2008), 1888 (2009), 1960 (2010) and 2106 (2013) (see Box 10.1) – the appointment of a UN Special Representative on Sexual Violence in Conflict in 2010, the 2014 Global Summit to End Sexual Violence in Conflict (FCO, 2014), and a number of tools to prevent and prosecute perpetrators of crimes of CRSV, including publicly naming and shaming those armed forces and groups who are alleged to be the worst offenders of CRSV (UNSG, 2012a). Other measures aimed at preventing CRSV include further research on the patterns of CRSV in order to inform where and how preventive measures should be targeted, as well as learning from places where sexual violence has not been widely prevalent, perhaps communicating where, how and why commanders of certain armed groups have not tolerated sexual violence (see Cohen et al., 2013). Nonetheless, CRSV remains widespread and prolific and continues to be significantly underreported, in part due to fear of reprisals, social stigma, perceived futility of reporting and lack of available support

---

Box 10.1: UNSCRs on Women, Peace and Security

To date (early 2019), there have been 8 UN Security Council Resolutions (UNSCRs) adopted on Women, Peace and Security:

1325 (2000) – a landmark resolution in which the Security Council addresses for the first time the unique impact conflict has on women, and the necessary but under-utilised contribution of women to peacebuilding as well as conflict prevention and resolution. This Resolution paves the way for subsequent resolutions which comprise the Women, Peace and Security (WPS) Agenda, and constitutes the first time there was broad agreement at the policy level that women and men have different conflict-related experiences, perspectives and needs.

(Continued)

1820 (2008) – recognises sexual violence as a tactical weapon of war, calls for increased training of peacekeepers and deployment of women, and reiterates that sexual violence can be a war crime, crime against humanity and part of genocide. Reiterates the importance of women's full and active participation in all aspects of prevention, resolving conflict and building peace, including at decision-making levels.

1888 (2009) – states that sexual violence can undermine peacebuilding efforts and intensify conflict, and calls both for leadership and for deployment of experts to address sexual violence in conflict-affected environments, as well as further deployment of women military and police for peacekeeping operations.

1889 (2009) – calls for the full participation of women in all phases of the peace process, including conflict prevention and resolution, recognising the important role they play, and expresses concern at their continued marginalisation in this regard. Also underscores the importance of empowering women and addressing their needs and priorities in post-conflict programmes.

1960 (2010) – reiterates the need for complete cessation of conflict-related sexual violence (CRSV); calls for the UN to establish monitory, analysis and reporting arrangements on CRSV; encourages reports of the UN Secretary-General to identify parties to the conflict suspected of having committed sexual violence (as a preventive measure); and urges commitment of the UN to zero tolerance of sexual violence by UN personnel.

2106 (2013) – reiterates the harm caused by sexual violence to peace and security; urges commitment to addressing impunity for crimes involving sexual violence; underlines the need for women to participate meaningfully in all aspects of the peace process, including combatting sexual violence; and underscores the importance of a comprehensive approach to transitional justice.

2122 (2013) – underlines the importance of women's leadership and participation in all aspects of conflict resolution and peacebuilding, including DDR, SSR, SALW control, and electoral and other political processes; draws attention to the need for information and analysis on the gendered impact of conflict as well as the gendered nature of peace processes, conflict resolution and peacebuilding; reiterates the commitment of the Security Council to include provisions on gender equality and empowerment in mission mandates; emphasises the importance of the Security Council interacting with civil society organisations, including women's organisations; and underlines the importance of attending to obstacles in the way of women's access to justice in conflict-affected environments.

2242 (2015) – underlines the importance of women's leadership and participation in countering terrorism and violent extremism as well as in peace negotiations and peacekeeping; calls for increased funding for gender-responsive training, analysis and programmes; emphasises the importance of civil society organisations being engaged in ensuring that gender considerations are integrated into programming; reiterates the importance of enabling women's access to justice in conflict-affected environments; and expresses concern at the continuing sexual exploitation by UN peacekeepers and others, and in this regard urges further training and robust response to any allegations, including thorough investigations and prosecutions (see PeaceWomen, 2018; UN Women, 2019).

See Davies and True (2019) for a comprehensive overview of the WPS Agenda today.

(Saferworld, 2010; UNSG, 2017a; UNSG, 2012a; see also True and Davies, 2015, on structural gender equality as a causal factor in CRSV).

Despite increased attention, there also continues to be widespread impunity, compounded by a lack of capacity and expertise in most countries to investigate and prosecute the perpetrators of CRSV. Moreover, CRSV often exposes victim-survivors to further violence and insecurity, because of the shame that being raped brings to families and communities. Victim-survivors might be attacked or ostracised by families and communities, leading to homelessness and destitution; the fact that children conceived through rape are rarely accepted by societies in CAR leads many women to seek unsafe abortions, which is the leading cause of maternal mortality in the country (UNSG, 2017a). Pregnancy outside marriage is a crime in certain countries and has led to victim-survivors of rape being arrested – in Darfur, for instance (Ward and Marsh, 2006). Boesten and Fisher (2012) argue that gender inequality in post-conflict Peru also subjected victim-survivors to further violence and marginalisation.

It is not just a heightened risk of sexual violence that women face in conflict. Women and children are also more likely to be displaced as a result of conflict (in part, of course, because men are more likely to be engaged in combat), which further heightens their vulnerability to risk, including of forced recruitment into armed groups, forced prostitution and trafficking, often for the purpose of sexual exploitation (Jackson and Beswick, 2018; UNSG, 2017a; UN Women, 2019; UNODC, 2016, 2014; UNHCR, 2019). In camps for displaced persons, during and after conflict, they can be more vulnerable to sexual violence and exploited by those mandated to protect them (Ferris, 2007; Jackson and Beswick, 2018; Laville, 2015; Save the Children UK, 2009; UN OCHA/IRIN, 2005). The 2018 report of the Secretary-General on conflict-related sexual violence (UNSG, 2018) highlighted that many women and girls in such camps continue to be subject to sexual violence in exchange for goods or services from camp officials or migrant smugglers. Domestic violence can also escalate in camps and other situations of displacement – as well as across society during times of conflict and its aftermath – where the pressures associated with conflict and displacement are severe (see Jackson and Beswick, 2018; Gomez and Christensen, 2010).

Violence against women after conflict

For women, the threat of violence can continue after the end of hostilities, not least because, as Grady (2010) has said, many of the same structures, dynamics and attitudes that operate during conflict continue past the formal cessation of hostilities. Moreover, impunity is rife; domestic security and justice sector institutions are destroyed, weak or dangerous; and the rule of law is absent. These factors leave women open to renewed threats of violence and also often unable to secure the support required to recover from war-time violations and abuse (whether in the form of seeking justice, healthcare or securing psychosocial support, for instance). Research by PRIO has suggested that women die more frequently than men in post-conflict environments, while during conflict more men tend to die than women (Ormhaug et al., 2009; see also Mazurana and Proctor, 2013; Kuehnast et al., 2011). Although accurate, comprehensive data on deaths in conflict-related environments is difficult to secure. Research by Ormhaug et. al. (2009), using different datasets referring to different conflict settings, does indicate, however, that women are more likely to die from the indirect results of conflict after conflict. This is a reversal of the normal rule of thumb that women live longer than men, and, whilst the statistics and possible causes are unclear, the authors suggest it may be partly related to illness in pregnancy and childbirth (with conflict-affected environments exacerbating poor health conditions and dilapidated healthcare systems ill-equipped to respond to healthcare needs). Indirect deaths can also be caused by the effects of conflict on health, healthcare provision, living conditions and sanitation (which can be especially dire as a result of displacement and/ or poverty), nutrition (with severe malnutrition resulting from lack of food) and intentional self-harm (resulting from trauma and mental illness). It is also important to note that in many conflicts, indirect conflict deaths – principally resulting from disease and malnutrition – far outweigh conflict deaths. To take a particularly extreme example, in Ethiopia, less than 2% of deaths between 1976 and 1991 were a direct result of the conflict; although the comparative rate vastly differs between conflicts – in Mozambique up to 29% of conflict-related deaths may have been directly rather than indirectly related to the conflict (Ormhaug et al., 2009, drawing from Lacina and Gleditsch, 2005).

After conflict, risks associated with displacement continue. Human trafficking and forced prostitution can also increase in the aftermath of conflict where there are security vacuums, no rule of law and dire economic conditions. Sexual exploitation and abuse (SEA) of the vulnerable and those in need, including through trafficking and forced prostitution or in return for food and other essential goods, by those in positions of power – including UN peacekeepers and others mandated to protect, as mentioned above – can also often persist in post-conflict environments (Bolkovac, 2011; Dharmapuri, 2011; Ferstman, 2013; Simić, 2010; UNSG, 2017a). Indeed, despite recurrent cases of SEA and the subsequent attention paid to such abuses and efforts on the part of the UN, there continue to be scandals involving UN peacekeepers and those employed by international humanitarian aid agencies. A recent report by the UK House of Commons International Development Committee (2018) pointed to cases of SEA being perpetrated across different countries and organisations for a long time. It also suggested that the extent of the abuses that are publicly known is probably the tip of the iceberg, given the underreporting of such crimes and impunity that perpetrators are often afforded. The report was the result of an inquiry into abuse in the aid sector after scandals involving Oxfam and Save the Children emerged in early 2018.

It has also been argued that sexual and gender-based violence (SGBV), or CRSV, may also be used after conflict 'as a means of reinforcing or reasserting lost power or "glory" of the perpetrator' (Munala, 2007: 36). Willett (2010), citing Anderson (2008), suggests that SGBV often becomes 'socially normalised' after the cessation of armed hostilities: 'It exists on such a widespread and systematic scale that it constitutes a major characteristic of the post-conflict era' (Willett, 2010: 154). Citing Pankhurst (2007), Willett suggests that SGBV may even expand in post-conflict environments as part of a back-lash 'against women's newly assumed rights and behaviour' (Willett, 2010: 156). Low levels of reporting and frequent impunity for such crimes also allow SGBV to continue in peacetime.

Research has suggested that domestic violence against women and girls can often be prevalent in post-conflict societies for similar reasons: the psychosocial impact of the conflict, challenges to traditional gender roles (if women assumed traditional male roles during the conflict), and lack of economic opportunities, as well as weaknesses in the security and justice sector (Munala, 2007; Saferworld and the Nepal Institute for Policy Studies, 2010; Vlachova and Biason, 2005).

Part 2 – The Gender Dynamics of Peacebuilding

Politics, including the politics of conflict, has traditionally been largely the preserve of men, although conflict itself affects all parts of society. In recent years, however, the international community has increasingly called for greater representation of women in peace processes and peacebuilding, not least in response to a recognition that sustainable peace requires inclusive peacebuilding. Nonetheless, despite such calls, women continue to be marginalised, which has adverse impacts on the extent to which women's security and justice needs are addressed after conflict as well as broader peacebuilding efforts.

The marginalisation of women from formal efforts to rebuild security and justice after conflict stems from women's marginalisation in formal peace processes which often set the parameters for peacebuilding. Between 1992 and 2011, women comprised only 2% of chief mediators, 4% of witnesses and signatories, and 9% of negotiators (Diaz and Tordjman, 2012). Leaders of parties to the conflict, predominantly male, are invited to the peace table, and agreements are reached which tend not to resonate with the needs of others, particularly if marginalised or dispossessed. Key decisions reached during negotiations on SSR, DDR and transitional justice therefore often overlook gender dynamics, creating frameworks which do not respond to the specific needs of women and which thereby serve to further marginalise.

In recent years, however, through high-level lobbying and advocacy, an increasing number of peace agreements include reference to women: 7 out of 10 agreements in 2015 compared with 73 out of 664 (11%) between 1990 and 2000, before the advent of UNSCR 1325 and 138 out of 504 (27%) between 2000 and 2014 (UN Women, 2019). Whether or not this translates to increased responsiveness and representation of women in peacebuilding is, of course, another matter. There have also been positive developments in respect of women's participation in peace negotiations (recent peace negotiations between the Government of Colombia and Fuerzas Armadas Revolucionarias de Colombia-Ejército del Pueblo (FARC-EP) are a notable example – see Box 10.2). Again, whether this positive development is sustainable is yet to be seen.

Another reason for the marginalisation of women from formal efforts to rebuild security and justice after conflict relates to the fact that the international community, especially at the higher echelons and within the security sector, is male-dominated. For instance, only 15–25% of field missions since 2010 have been headed by women (UNSG, 2015), there has yet to be a female UN

Box 10.2: Colombia

During peace negotiations between the Government of Colombia and FARC-EP (Revolutionary Armed Forces of Colombia – People's Army, in English) the significant participation of women and the focus on women's rights issues was unprecedented. Women comprised a third of participants at the peace negotiations and more than 60% of delegations of victims called to present evidence at the negotiations. Gender experts were also invited to the negotiations, from various women's organisations, to present proposals for peace and peacebuilding. A unique Gender Sub-Committee was also established in 2014, which was mandated to ensure that gender is mainstreamed and women's rights are attended to in all aspects of the agreement (UN Women, 2019), which was ratified by the Government in November 2016. However, whether this will translate into women meaningfully and comprehensively participating in the peacebuilding process and their specific needs being addressed is another matter. By mid-2017, there were already concerns with lack of gender parity in the Peace Monitoring Committees, with women comprising only 13% of members appointed (Reuters, 2017).

Secretary-General, and only about 3–4% of UN military peacekeepers are women – although there is a greater percentage of female police peacekeepers at 9–10% and civilians in peacekeeping missions at approximately 22% (Ghittoni et al., 2018; UNDPKO, 2018). The reasons are manifold and include barriers to deployment (such as family responsibilities and societal expectations) as well as low numbers of female military and police personnel in the troop contribution nations (TCNs). In a recent baseline study on female peacekeepers, Ghittoni et al. (2018) identify these and other barriers as well as ways in which they can be removed. Efforts to improve the gender balance could include identifying and taking action against discriminatory treatment as well as providing support to enable those with caring responsibilities to take advantage of opportunities, among many other efforts that could be taken if there was genuine commitment to improving gender equality.

Consequently, gender issues may not be prioritised, particularly in the face of pressing security threats or challenges (Gordon et al., 2015). Moreover, members of the international community are more likely to engage members of the male-dominated, central-level political and security elite in formal peacebuilding processes, in part because they too are male but predominantly because they are easier to reach and often speak the same language – and because that is where the power is seen to lie. The security agenda is thus generally set by men, which can result in efforts to build security and justice after conflict not responding to the specific needs of women. As a result, women's insecurity can often be further reinforced. Oftentimes, it is only those with the power to use violence or threaten peace who are included to any significant degree in formal peace negotiations (Gordon, 2014a). This is even though more inclusive peace processes and peacebuilding endeavours are widely considered to be more likely to enjoy more broad-based support, be responsive to the needs of a wider constituent of people and be more successful. For instance, research has suggested that where women are included in peace processes, there is a greater likelihood that the agreement will be sustainable: a 20% increase in the likelihood of the agreement lasting more than two years and a 35% increase in the agreement lasting more than 15 years (O'Reilly et al., 2015; see also Paffenholz et al., 2016; True and Riveros-Morales, 2019; UN Women, 2019). This may well be, in part, because agreements reached between warring factions are more responsive to their need to protect their interests and maintain power than to the requirements of a sustainable peace. Indeed, UNSCR 2242 (2015) underscored the need to train mediators on the positive impact of inclusive peace processes on sustainable peace agreements and how inclusion can be achieved.

While parties to the conflict need to agree to end hostilities if there is to be peace, it is ironic that often those who had dominant roles in the conflict are those who then have the key positions in building peace, 'even as they very often lack the skills, temperament or even will to do so' (Mazurana and Proctor, 2013: 20). Moreover, as Norville (2010) argues, meaningful peace is unattainable with half the population disengaged from the formal process of building peace and those very people remaining vulnerable to the threat of violence, insecurity and injustice.

It is a peculiar paradox that women are marginalised from formal peacebuilding efforts, particularly in respect of building security and justice after conflict, given that women's security and access to justice generally continue to suffer beyond the immediate aftermath of conflict. The marginalisation serves to further reinforce gendered power relations. It also serves to limit the effectiveness of efforts to build security and justice, given that the outputs tend not to be responsive to and representative of the broader demographic. Combined, reinforced gendered power relations and ineffective security and justice sector institutions further expose women to insecurity and further undermine prospects for sustainable peace.

Women, Peace and Security Agenda

The arguments sketched out above have acquired considerable international support in recent years, and have led to a number of institutional and political initiatives. For example, in 2000, the groundbreaking UN Security Council Resolution (UNSCR) 1325 was adopted (refer back to Box 10.1). This was the first time at the policy level that there was broad agreement that women and men (and girls and boys) have different experiences in conflict, have different needs after conflict, have different perspectives on the causes and outcomes of conflict, and have different things to bring to the peacebuilding process.

Subsequently, there have been a further seven Resolutions adopted which comprise the Women, Peace and Security (WPS) Agenda: 1820 (2008), 1888 (2009), 1889 (2009), 1960 (2010), 2106 (2013), 2122 (2013) and 2242 (2015). The goals of the WPS Agenda are to:

- Promote gender equality and strengthen the participation of women in decision-making in all aspects of conflict prevention, peace processes, peace operations and peacebuilding
- Improve the protection of women in conflict-affected environments, and end conflict-related sexual violence and impunity for these crimes

- Ensure that engagement in conflict-affected environments addresses the specific needs of women and improves the protection of women's rights.

Despite a comprehensive normative framework (see Box 10.3), implementation has been slow, particularly in respect of engaging women in formal peace processes and peacebuilding. Furthermore, action on CRSV is still sub-optimal among key actors in the international community, and funding to address the requirements of the WPS Agenda is severely wanting (Tryggestad, 2016). In part to bolster efforts to promote gender equality and implementation of the WPS Agenda, UN Women was established in 2010 (see Box 10.4). However, challenges remain within the UN, not least in terms of co-ordination within and beyond the UN and encouraging gender mainstreaming where the existence of a UN entity dedicated to this might suggest that work on gender issues outside this entity is not required.

Box 10.3: Legal and Normative Framework on Non-Discrimination and Gender Equality

There is a broad legal framework obliging states to protect the rights of all regardless of gender, guard against violence and discrimination, and promote equality. Key, relevant international laws and instruments include:

- **Universal Declaration of Human Rights (1948)**, which refers to the entitlement of each individual to enjoy their rights and freedoms '...without distinction of any kind, such as race, colour, sex, language, religion, political or other opinion, national or social origin, property, birth or other status' (Art. 2). Article 3 further states: 'Everyone has the right to life, liberty and security of person'.
- **International Covenant on Civil and Political Rights (1966)** which states: 'All persons are equal before the law and are entitled without any discrimination to the equal protection of the law.' (Art. 26)
- **Convention on the Elimination of all Forms of Discrimination against Women (CEDAW) (1979)** seeks to end discrimination against women and holds States Parties responsible for adopting appropriate legislation and other measures to prohibit discrimination against women and establish legal protection of the equal rights of women, including abolishing discriminatory laws.
- **Declaration on the Elimination of Violence against Women (1993)** calls on states to refrain from engaging in violence against women and to exercise due diligence to prevent, investigate and punish acts of violence against women. It also urges states to take action against those responsible for violence against women (VAW) as well as enable access to victims/survivors.
- **UN General Assembly Resolutions, Rules and Protocols:** UN General Assembly instruments, in addition to those mentioned above, include Resolutions and Protocols which address violence against women and girls (including against migrant workers, including domestic violence, and including criminal justice measures to help eliminate violence), treatment of women

---

(Continued)

prisoners (and alternatives to imprisonment), trafficking in persons and, more recently (2017 – under Resolution 71/278), UN action on sexual exploitation and abuse (SEA).

- **UN Security Council Resolutions:** In addition to the eight UN Security Council Resolutions comprising the WPS Agenda, UN Security Council Resolution (UNSCR) 2272 addresses the under-reporting of SEA by UN and non-UN personnel engaged in peacebuilding efforts, and urges action to be taken to prevent and robustly respond to cases involving SEA.
- **UN Human Rights Council (HRC):** The HRC has issued a number of resolutions on accelerating efforts to eliminate all forms of violence against women, including sexual violence and domestic violence, eliminating discrimination against women and girls, and promoting a human rights-based approach to combatting trafficking in persons.
- **UN Committee on the Elimination of Discrimination against Women (CEDAW Committee):** The CEDAW Committee has issued a number of General Recommendations on violence against women (no. 19 and no. 35), on women migrant workers (no. 26), on women in conflict prevention, conflict and post-conflict situations (no. 30), and women's access to justice (no. 33). General Recommendation no. 30 underscores the importance of 'advancing substantive gender equality before, during and after conflict and ensuring that women's diverse experiences are fully integrated into all peacebuilding, peacemaking and reconstruction' (para. 2).
- **Fourth World Conference on Women (1995):** the Beijing Declaration and Platform for Action calls on governments to review all national laws to ensure non-discrimination and adherence to international human rights standards and instruments.
- **Regional Instruments:** There are also a number of regional laws and other instruments which oblige states to promote non-discrimination and gender equality.

Gender mainstreaming

Gender mainstreaming is a policy within the UN and wider international community of addressing gender issues in all areas of activity; notably ensuring the different needs of women and men – and people of diverse sexual orientation and gender

Box 10.4: UN Women

In 2010, as part of the UN Reform Agenda, the UN General Assembly adopted a resolution creating a new UN body – UN Entity for Gender Equality and the Empowerment of Women, better known as UN Women – merging the four UN agencies and offices responsible for gender issues: Division for the Advancement of Women (DAW); International Research and Training Institute for the Advancement of Women (INSTRAW); Office of the Special Adviser on Gender Issues and Advancement of Women (OSAGI); and United Nations Development Fund for Women (UNIFEM).

identity and expression (SOGIE) – are attended to throughout decision-making, and the meaningful participation of women and men in decision-making and all areas of activity. It is intended to address the marginalisation of women and their specific needs. It is often misunderstood as simply addressing the needs of women in interventions, policies or programmes; including a few more women into activities, programmes or structures; or positively discriminating in favour of women to the detriment of men. Put simply, gender is not just about women, and mainstreaming cannot be reduced to adding a few women, or tagging on a gender-specific task or unit.

The Economic and Social Council agreed that conclusions of 1997 define gender mainstreaming as:

> ... the process of assessing the implications for women and men of any planned action, including legislation, policies or programmes, in all areas and at all levels. It is a strategy for making women's as well as men's concerns and experiences an integral dimension of the design, implementation, monitoring and evaluation of policies and programmes in all political, economic and societal spheres so that women and men benefit equally and inequality is not perpetuated. The ultimate goal is to achieve gender equality. (UN, 1997a: I.A.)

Ultimately, gender mainstreaming is about promoting gender equality (see Box 10.5) and encompasses much more than simply representation of women (see Box 10.6 for an overview of what gender mainstreaming might include in post-conflict rule of law and security activities).

Box 10.5: Gender Equality

Gender equality is an international norm that stipulates the equal right of women and men to opportunities and resources irrespective of their gender or the sex with which they were born. Gender is often reduced to women and gender equality is sometimes assumed to be positive discrimination for women and curtailment of rights for men; it is not, but gender equality is about a redistribution of power and therefore is likely to generate resistance from those who yield power.

Gender inequality remains pervasive and systemic in most societies today, although efforts have been made in recent years to reduce inequalities and their effects. Gender inequality sustains and is sustained by violent practices, including SGBV. Underscoring the importance of justice to many women's lives across the world, Brigid Inder, OBE, Executive Director of the Women's Initiatives for Gender Justice (WIGJ), has said:

> Whether in family courts, or seeking the right to inherit property, advocating for attitudinal changes to protect women from harmful practices or enforcing laws which prohibit violence and sexual harassment, all of these efforts are to establish the central truth of gender equality. For women living in countries with armed conflicts, the basis for many of the forms of gender-based violence are similar to those expressed in peaceful countries, however they become exaggerated in scale and brutality during war. (Coalition of the ICC, 2018: n.p.)

> ## Box 10.6: Requirements of Gender Mainstreaming in Rule of Law and Security Activities
>
> - The gender implications of all decisions in the security and justice sector, including reform activities (planning, implementation, and monitoring and evaluation), being considered and attended to – with respect to both service delivery (e.g. how legislation, policies, programmes or operations might differently impact women and men) and internal organisation (e.g. how internal policies and practices, such as personnel policies or training, might differently impact women and men)
> - Security and justice actors, both women and men – and other stakeholders in the security and justice sector or engaged in reform activities – being sensitised to gender issues
> - Women, as well as men, actively participating in decision-making in the security and justice sector and related reform programmes, including the development of policy
> - Security and justice sector institutions being representative of the social demographic they serve (rather than often almost exclusively male and from the dominant social, racial, ethnic and religious groups) and meaningfully representative (not just in certain sectors or at lower ranks, for instance)
> - Security and justice sector institutions being responsive to the different needs of all social groups, including both women and men
> - Security and justice being accessible to all social groups, including both women and men.

Gender, however, can often become just be a 'box to be ticked, a meeting to be had, a paragraph to be written' (Anderlini, 2007: 230 cited in Kuehnast et al., 2011: 13). While things have improved in the last few years and increasingly gender mainstreaming is regarded as critical to peacebuilding success, often efforts are ad hoc, piecemeal or superficial. Addressing gender issues can be regarded as less of a priority where there are immediate concerns about political violence and stability; the fact that both can be addressed simultaneously or that not addressing gender issues leaves women, in particular, vulnerable to insecurity and threat can be overlooked. Where gender is addressed, it can often not move beyond tokenistic gestures that rarely address the structural factors that perpetuate inequalities and insecurity. The odd appointment, new policy, or report does not directly correlate with the specific needs of women and men being addressed, or women and men having equal opportunity to engage in decision-making. In fact, gender mainstreaming, if reduced to quantifiable targets, can often disguise the fact that nothing much has changed and the status quo remains relatively intact – if not all the more secure now that it has renewed legitimacy.

Gender and Security Sector Reform (SSR)

As we saw in Chapter 8, effective security sector institutions are widely considered to be those that are responsive to the needs of a broad demographic as well as representative of that demographic. Gender-responsive Security Sector Reform (SSR) speaks to the need to develop institutions that are responsive to the security needs of both women and men, and more equally representative of them. Given that women and men can experience conflict differently and can have different security concerns during and after conflict – that is, conflict and security are gendered – security and justice sector institutions need to attend to these concerns.

There are core policy guidance resources on SSR which guide many practitioners in this field. These include the *Handbook on Security System Reform* by the Organisation for Economic Co-operation and Development's Development Assistance Committee (OECD, 2007a); the resources on gender and SSR by the Geneva Centre for the Democratic Control of the Armed Forces (DCAF), notably the *Gender and Security Sector Reform* Toolkit (Bastick and Valasek, 2008, with a new Toolkit forthcoming in 2019); and the reports of the UN Secretary-General on SSR, notably *Securing Peace and Development: The Role of the United Nations in Supporting Security Sector Reform* (UNSG, 2008a) and *Securing States and Societies: Strengthening the United Nations Comprehensive Support to Security Sector Reform* (UNSG, 2013). As outlined in these policy documents, integrating gender issues into SSR is now broadly recognised as being instrumental to operational effectiveness, responsiveness, local ownership, public trust and confidence, and strengthened oversight and, consequently, effective peacebuilding. Gender-sensitive SSR entails addressing the gender implications of all decisions, ensuring that the specific security and justice concerns of women and men are addressed, and ensuring the meaningful inclusion of both women and men throughout the process and in its outputs (the post-reform security sector). With regard to the latter, it is important to acknowledge that women engaged in SSR processes may not be representative of especially vulnerable women and that particular concerns may not be articulated or heard. Consequently, it is important not to reduce gender-sensitive SSR to just including (often token) women in the process, as is often the case (Baaz and Utas, 2012; Hendricks, 2012; Mobekk, 2010). With this in mind, it is also important to ensure that women are included throughout the SSR process and at decision-making levels and that there is the opportunity for gender issues to be addressed. For instance, attention should be given to the structure of meetings and the processes of decision-making, to ensure that they do not disadvantage women, by privileging the voices of men (there is much research in management studies and other social sciences to suggest that men feel more comfortable airing their views and are more likely to be listened to in formal meetings, for instance). Not only does there need to be an opportunity to address gender issues, there needs to be an acceptance that gender issues need to be addressed (all the structures and processes will not mean much if the political will is not there). Equally, it is necessary that consultation with others, particularly at the community level, attends to the barriers that may privilege or disadvantage men, women and different social groups, in order that the security needs of a representative cross-section of society are able to find expression and be heard.

Beyond this, it is important that gender issues are addressed and that the gendered implications of each decision are considered in the subsequent security structures – and that preparations for this is made during the SSR process. There need to be policies and processes in place which will foster a culture of gender equality both within security sector institutions and in the services they provide (Gordon et al., 2015). In addition to facilitating the meaningful engagement of women, tangible tasks in a gender-sensitive SSR programme often include delivering gender-sensitive training and education to security sector staff; developing ways to improve the recruitment, retention and promotion of women; strengthening the capacity of civil society and parliamentary oversight; and promoting zero tolerance for discrimination and sexual and gender-based violence (see Figure 10.1, and also see Hendricks and Hutton, 2008).

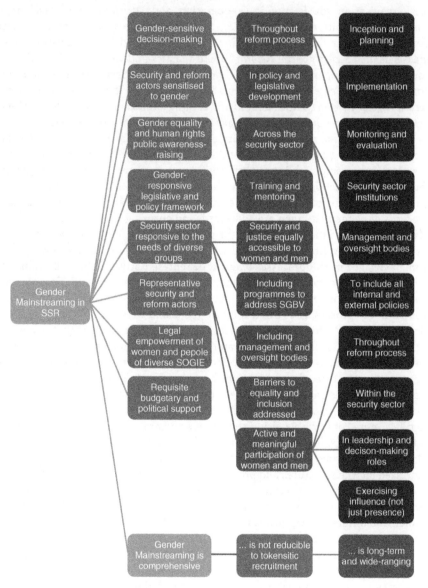

Figure 10.1 Gender Mainstreaming in Security Sector Reform

A gender-sensitive approach can help ensure that the specific security concerns of women are addressed in the reform or reconstruction of security sector institutions and the development of security policy. It can also build security sector institutions that are inclusive of and responsive to the specific needs of both women and men. While gender-responsive SSR is not reducible to simply increasing the representation of women in the security sector, this can help in enhancing women's security because, for example, female security sector personnel may be more approachable to women (and others) especially if reporting incidents of a sensitive nature such as sexual violence, for example (Gordon et al., 2011). It can thus help build trust and confidence in security sector institutions among women and others, as well as increase the ability of these institutions to respond to women's security and justice needs (thus improving effectiveness and, as a consequence, security more broadly). A more responsive security sector that enjoys broad-based public confidence and trust is also more likely to be successful, which has obvious consequences for peacebuilding.

Aside from these utilitarian reasons, centred around the notion of operational effectiveness, there are also normative reasons, centred around the notion of equality. Utilitarian reasons are often referred to as essentialist or instrumentalist arguments, which tend to homogenise women and men, as well as overlook the fact that gender identities and assumptions about skillsets are socially constructed. Normative arguments, on the other hand, are sometimes discredited as being culturally specific. For instance, as was mentioned in Chapter 8, the principle of gender equality is sometimes regarded as being at odds with the principle of local ownership and thus should not be advocated in environments where the principle of gender equality might not resonate. However, such arguments do tend to assume that dominant norms and values are shared by all; that is, few ask whether gender equality would be anathema to those beyond the male-dominated elite groups who occupy formal political and security structures (see Box 10.7).

Aside from utilitarian and normative reasons, there are also obligations to adhere to international instruments (the UN Security Council Resolutions that comprise the WPS Agenda and the broader legal framework which includes the Convention on the Elimination of All Forms of Violence against Women, CEDAW – see Box 10.1 and Box 10.3).

Despite these utilitarian, normative and legally binding reasons for SSR to be gender-responsive, there often remains a gap between policy and practice. While policy advocates for increased representation of women and responsiveness to their specific needs, in practice women continue to be marginalised in peacebuilding, particularly in the security sector. This is in part because, historically, security has been seen as a male domain and thus the security sector remains dominated by men, particularly at the decision-making levels. SSR practitioners are predominantly male, as are their interlocutors in security and political structures in recipient countries. Many consider that women do not have the requisite knowledge, skills or experience to engage in the security sector or participate in SSR, particularly when it comes to the defence sector (see Box 10.8 on the marginalisation of women from the post-conflict defence sector in Nepal and also see Gordon, 2019). The fact

Box 10.7: Gender Equality and Local Ownership

While gender equality and local ownership are integrally related, there is often a paradoxical tension between the two principles, where it is considered that the principle of gender equality is not accepted by the local population. In these circumstances, it can be argued that promoting gender equality would undermine the principle of local ownership, which would undermine the success of SSR and sustainability of any outputs. However, this position belies the fact that the principle of local ownership is often disregarded, that 'locals' do not constitute a homogenous whole with shared values (including the dominant values of patriarchal societies), and that women are infrequently consulted on whether a more gender-equitable security sector and reform process would be amenable to them. It is often wrongly assumed that the principle of gender equality is antithetical to certain countries; it is often SSR practitioners (predominantly male) making this assumption, consulting with (predominantly male) members of the security and political elite in a country. It is also ironic that in those countries where gender equality may be the most wanting (where women are marginalised, discriminated against and especially insecure), it is argued that it should be the least advocated, for fear of jeopardising local support for reform efforts. In other words, not promoting gender equality for fear of undermining local ownership risks uncritically accepting and reinforcing the status quo, disguising the power relations at play in conflict-affected environments and further undermining the security of women (Gordon et al., 2015).

that many women do have the requisite knowledge, skills and experience – or the fact that a wide range of knowledge, skills and experiences is required among those engaged in the security sector and reform activities (beyond archetypally masculine attributes such as brute strength) – does not appear to challenge the logic which continues to marginalise women from this sector.

In practice, where gender-responsive or gender-sensitive SSR is promoted, it is often reduced, as indicated above, to tokenistic recruitment of women to post-reform structures. There is also often little consideration of the need to meaningfully engage women (beyond tokenistic representation) and enable women to inform decision-making throughout the reform process (see Baaz and Utas, 2012; Hendricks, 2012; Mobekk, 2010). Moreover, little is often done to address the structural and institutional barriers to women's participation in SSR and in the security sector. SSR and the subsequent security structures thus tend to remain unrepresentative, unresponsive and discriminatory. Focussing on recruitment without addressing structural and institutional factors can sometimes be counterproductive; recruiting a small number of women to security sector institutions can expose them to risk (Barr, 2013) and can lead to gender issues not being addressed because of an assumption that by simply recruiting some women, that task has been ticked off. There is a related assumption that those few women who are recruited are inclined to (or are in a position to)

Box 10.8: Nepal – Integration of Former Female Combatants into the Nepal Army: the Gap Between Gender-Responsive DDR and SSR Policy and Practice

Despite policy that advocates for gender-responsive and inclusive DDR and SSR programmes, women continue to be marginalised. This is particularly the case with the defence sector and defence sector reform. This is in part because women are often considered to not have the correct aptitude, skills or inclination to work in the defence sector. This is in spite of their engagement in large numbers in many insurgent forces during the conflict in many of these places where they are subsequently marginalised.

In Nepal, for example, during the People's War (1996–2006), 20% of combatants registered by the UN were women (3,846 of 19,692), while estimates of the number of female members of the PLA are as high as 30–50% (Yadav, 2016; Goswami, 2015). Of those 20% of female combatants registered by the UN, only 3% (104) chose integration into the security sector, as opposed to voluntary redundancy and social reintegration, compared with 1,318 men (Bhandari, 2015; Goswami, 2015). Today women comprise only 4% of the Nepal Army and predominantly at the lower ranks – only reaching the rank of Major, for instance, for the first time in 2016 (Pariyar, 2016).

There are a number of reasons for the small number of female former PLA combatants in the Nepal Army. Many women did not meet the eligibility criteria for integration (Goswami, 2015; Thapa and Canyon, 2017). Most registered female combatants choose not to integrate into the Nepal Army, in large part because of concerns about security and childcare responsibilities (Saferworld, 2010). If there had been female participation in negotiating the peace agreement, these issues might have been addressed and the DDR and SSR processes may have had somewhat different outcomes (Colekessian, 2010).

---

promote gender issues, where the opposite may be the case (see Gordon et al., 2015; Hudson 2012).

Given that power dynamics are embroiled in gender relations and the security sector, promoting gender-sensitive SSR can carry risks both to the individuals involved and to general post-conflict stability. There can be a reluctance to share power and expose power relations within structures and institutions that have hitherto been disguised or appeared as natural or just. Shifting power relations, including gender relations, can provoke hostility and violence in the aftermath of conflict, in as much the same way as shifting power relations in the reform of the security sector. There are, however, security risks associated with not promoting gender equality; without attending to the specific security needs of women, women's security more broadly will continue to suffer. Waiting to address gender issues until there is a modicum of stability might avoid some immediate risks, but it would miss the opportunity to promote gender equality and women's security – which is more difficult once structures and power bases have been consolidated.

Ultimately, gender-sensitive SSR responds to the fundamental objective of SSR, which is to develop security institutions which respond to the security and justice needs of the people these institutions serve, and not those of just elite or dominant groups.

Gender and Disarmament, Demobilisation and Reintegration (DDR)

Similarly, while a gender-sensitive approach to Disarmament, Demobilisation and Reintegration (DDR) is important, DDR planning and implementation often overlook the needs of women, although they are often quite distinct from the needs of male former combatants or members of receiving communities. For instance, DDR programmes rarely include the provision of reproductive health services or crèche facilities, without which significant barriers to effective reintegration for many women can remain.

As discussed in Chapter 7, women have been marginalised from DDR programmes because they had – or were wrongly assumed to have – support rather than combat roles (Sjoberg and Gentry, 2007) or did not have their own gun, shared it or had it taken away (MacKenzie, 2009; Henshaw, 2017). They have also been marginalised by insurgent leaders, predominantly male, especially where reintegration assistance has been limited (Ortega, 2015). Further, they have been considered not to pose a threat to burgeoning peace and therefore not a priority for assistance (de Watteville, 2002). In addition, many female former combatants have disengaged from the process for fear of stigmatisation because they were seen to have transgressed traditional gender roles by engaging in combat (Avoine and Tillman, 2015; MacKenzie, 2009). Many also informally demobilised because of caring responsibilities (Colekessian, 2010; Saferworld, 2010).

Where DDR programmes have included women they often reinforce gender stereotypes, as happened in Nepal (Goswami, 2015), Sierra Leone (MacKenzie, 2009) and Sri Lanka (Martin, 2017). In Sri Lanka, for instance, only female former combatants with the Tamil Tigers (the Liberation Tigers of Tamil Eelam – LTTE) were offered training in bridal dressing, hairdressing and makeup, while only male former combatants were offered training in plumbing and welding (Bureau of Commissioner General of Rehabilitation, 2018). As Ní Aoláin (2016, 34) has argued, 'reintegration is conceptually gendered – organically connected to the social, political and legal status of women in the conflicted society before the outbreak of hostilities'; this has often resulted in women assuming traditional roles and marginalised status as part of wider efforts to 'return to normal' (MacKenzie, 2009) and the imagined pre-war social order, at least insofar as gender relations and patriarchy are concerned. In other circumstances, including women in DDR programmes can play into biases in the local context, as the example from South Sudan below shows (Box 10.9).

Another frequent gendered critique of DDR programmes is that they can also be deficient and face challenges as a result of not unpicking gendered norms and, specifically, militarised masculinities. As briefly mentioned in Chapter 7, these

Box 10.9: South Sudan

The 2009–11 DDR programme in South Sudan, designed and supported by UNDP and co-ordinated by the National DDR Commission, is widely recognised as being unsuccessful. In response to resistance from the Sudan People's Liberation Army (SPLA) to demobilise able-bodied men, the programme was redesigned to focus on women, as well as the disabled and the elderly. This was received well by the SPLA who now saw the programme as a means of getting rid of women from the payroll and not demobilising many able-bodied, young men. As a result, women comprised approximately half of those participating in the DDR programme despite only constituting approximately 2% of the SPLA before conflict broke out in 2013. The irony is that a DDR programme designed to support women and be inclusive of them served to disenfranchise them by taking them out of the SPLA, which offered one of the few sources of income in South Sudan. The DDR programme was therefore only superficially responsive to the needs of women; it was not attentive to societal gender dynamics or the broader context, and neither did it fulfil the purpose of the DDR programme (Gordon et al., 2015).

militarised masculinities often reinforce the link between masculinity and violence and can compromise DDR and broader peacebuilding success (see Mazurana et al., 2018).

Where women have joined armed groups and armed forces to escape forced marriage (such as with Boko Haram) or fight for women's liberation (such as with the People's Liberation Army (PLA) of Nepal or the Sri Lankan Tamil Tigers (LTTE)), reintegration can be particularly difficult; how do women reintegrate back into the societies they rejected or tried to change? The same of course is true of men; it is difficult to reintegrate those who took up arms as a result of grievances or lack of opportunities if these issues have not been addressed, and equally difficult to persuade communities to receive former combatants if they have recently been the source of considerable threat to those communities. But if women do not receive the same reintegration assistance, women are more likely to be ostracised from communities and forced into destitution or illicit activities (Cheldelin and Eliatamby, 2011) – the successful reintegration of women therefore can have broader security and development implications.

The specific needs of women must therefore be attended to, but it must also be recognised that the female population is not a homogenous whole and the specific needs of former combatants, supporters, dependents and others need to be considered. Likewise, when considering the needs of male combatants, it is important to remain attentive to the specific context and, to as great an extent as possible, the individual requirements to best ensure the success of any DDR programme.

In practice, the kind of nuanced research and planning described above is seldom even considered, let alone attempted, and DDR programmes tend to have pre-determined components aimed at female former combatants. Thus, UN Security Council

Resolution 1325 explicitly encourages those involved in planning DDR programmes 'to consider the different needs of female and male ex-combatants and to take into account the needs of their dependants' (UNSC, 2000: 3).

Gender and transitional justice

Women are poorly represented in peace talks when key decisions are made about transitional justice, accountability, and post-conflict security and justice. This contributes to the specific needs of women often being overlooked in subsequent peacebuilding efforts, including transitional justice programmes. For instance, peace agreements can contain amnesties which deny a victim justice and expose that victim to more insecurity, or, as Steinberg puts it: 'too often, peace agreements provide blanket amnesties in which men with guns forgive other men with guns committed against women and children' (Steinberg, 2010). As was discussed in Chapter 5, in prosecutions, crimes involving sexual violence against women have not been regarded with the same seriousness as other war crimes or crimes against humanity. So, for example, while rape has been prohibited under the Geneva Conventions (article 27 of the 4th Geneva Convention) since 1949, it has rarely been prosecuted, particularly until recently.

It is important that the specific needs of women and men are attended to in war crimes prosecutions, as well as other transitional justice mechanisms, including reparations, truth and reconciliation commissions, memorialisation and, of course, institutional reform. For instance, judicial practitioners and others coming into contact with victims/survivors need expertise in interviewing victims/survivors and witnesses without causing them further harm. For their needs to be attended to, it is essential that women are actively engaged in designing and implementing transitional justice mechanisms after conflict (see ICTJ).

General Recommendation no. 30 on women in conflict prevention, conflict and post-conflict situations of the UN Committee on the Elimination of Discrimination against Women (CEDAW Committee) obliges States Parties to secure women's access to justice, including by ensuring that transitional justice mechanisms are gender-sensitive, promote women's rights, address all gender-based violations (rejecting amnesties and ensuring compliance with decisions) and involve women in their design, operation and monitoring at all levels (as well as the design of all reparations programmes).

Gender, mine action and SALW control

As was mentioned in Chapter 6, mine action should also address the needs of women. For instance, mine risk education (MRE) needs to ensure that all groups at risk have access to information. Demining activities need to ensure that women, men and children are consulted on the location of mines and other explosive remnants of war (ERW). Likewise, the prioritising of areas for clearance needs to take into account the needs of women and children, as well as men, which has not always been the case (see Steinberg, 2011). Victim assistance also needs to be gender-sensitive, ensuring that medical care, psychosocial support and vocational training, for instance, are available to and target the specific needs of all victims (UNMAS, 2019). It is particularly important that victim assistance addresses the fact that female victims can face heightened discrimination, including abandonment (in places such as the DRC and Uganda) and isolation (disabled girls can be hidden away from sight in places such as Iraq and Afghanistan), and given limited access to medical services (Laws, 2017).

Likewise, SALW control programmes need to be gender-sensitive, recognising that SALW can increase the insecurity of women as well as men, including in the home. Programmes also need to recognise that it is not only men who possess, use or are knowledgeable about SALW. Recognising the need for SALW control programmes to be gender-inclusive and to contribute to empowering women, UNMAS has implemented a programme in Libya empowering women to deliver SALW risk awareness training, recognising the role women can and do play in building security in their communities (UNMAS, 2019; CASA, 2017).

Part 3 – Gender Stereotypes, Conflict and Peacebuilding

When attending to the gender-dynamics of conflict or peacebuilding, it is important not to reduce 'gender' to 'women': conflict affects women and men differently and it is important to attend to these differences if conflict is to be understood and effectively responded to. Likewise, the different experiences and needs of both women and men need to be attended to in peacebuilding, if peacebuilding efforts are to be responsive to those different needs and, thus, effective. Moreover, while 'gender' should not be reduced to 'women', women – or men – should equally not be considered to be a homogenous group; they do not all share the same experiences, needs or values. How gender intersects with race, class, age, ethnicity, religion and other demographic identifiers, in different places and in different times, also needs to inform any gender analysis. These differences between different women and men also need to be attended to if responses to conflict and peacebuilding are to be effective. If all women are considered to be passive victims in need of protection, and all men as either protectors or perpetrators of violence, responses to insecurity and violence will only ever be superficial and, as a result, ineffective.

For example, it is important to observe that CRSV or broader GBSV is not always committed by combatants or males (Cohen et al., 2013). It must be also mentioned that that recent focus of attention on CRSV against women and girls has tended to eclipse male victims of such crimes (Carpenter, 2006; Dharmapuri, 2011; IRIN, 2011), as well as the other harms suffered by women and girls during conflict (Swaine, 2018). While much-needed attention has eventually been given to CRSV and the civilian fatalities of conflicts today, this should not, of course, detract attention from or diminish the significance of the large number of male direct and indirect victims of conflict.

The binary stereotypes which cast men as protectors or perpetrators tend to diminish the suffering that men face during and after conflict: their exposure to violence and the traumatic effect of combat that continues to impact men and the societies in which they live for many years after the end of war. While violence against women can increase during and after conflict, men are much more likely to be directly killed in conflict and civilian men are also much more likely to be the targets of mass killings: for instance, 90% of all the dead in the war in Bosnia between 1992 and 1995 were adult males (Nettlefield, 2010). Men are often coerced into joining armed groups, whereas in the literature, coercion into such groups is often only referred to when we speak of female or child combatants. Likewise, fear experienced by soldiers on the battlefield tends to be overlooked in popular discourse and academic literature. Men are also more likely to be the victims of public violence (violence in public spaces whether in the context of armed conflict or not), because they often occupy public spaces more than women and because cultural norms often encourage male-on-male violence (see Saferworld, 2014). Additionally, suicides also tend to increase during and after wars and, as is true in peacetime, the majority of the victims are male (see for example Selakovic-Bursic et al., 2006).

Equally, while victims are not just women, women are not *solely* victims. Many thousands of women have directly engaged in armed combat in many countries across the globe, although their role as combatants is often overlooked (Sjoberg, 2014) or assumed to be the result of coercion (Puechguirbal, 2012). Mazurana and Proctor (2013) list 59 countries in which women have been combatants in non-state armed groups or insurgencies between 1990 and 2013 (see Box 10.10).

Likewise, men are not the only aggressors. Women have also engaged in wartime atrocities committed against civilians. For instance, women in armed forces in DRC engaged in violence against civilians, including sexual violence, but this has been generally overlooked in academia and policy circles (Baaz and Stern,

---

Box 10.10: Women Combatants

Mazurana and Proctor (2013) have identified 59 countries in which women have been combatants in non-state armed groups or insurgencies between 1990 and 2013. These include Iraq, Syria, Sudan, DRC, Colombia, Haiti, Nepal, Timor-Leste and countries of the former Yugoslavia. In Nepal, Sri Lanka, El Salvador, Nicaragua, Colombia, Syria and Eritrea, women constituted more than 30% of combatants in the Nepalese People's Liberation Army (PLA), the Sri Lankan Tamil Tigers (the Liberation Tigers of Tamil Eelam – LTTE), Farabundo Marti National Liberation Front (FMLN) in El Salvador, Sandinista National Liberation Front (FSLN) in Nicaragua, Revolutionary Armed Forces of Colombia (FARC), the People's Protection Unit (YPG) in the form of the Women's Protection Unit (YPJ) in Syria, and the Eritrean People's Liberation Front (EPLA) (Eliatamby, 2011; Henshaw, 2017; Ortega 2015).

2013a, 2013b). As Sjoberg (2016) argues, while women who commit acts of sexual violence are in the minority, by ignoring them our gendered assumptions about sexual violence limits our understanding and thus ability to prevent such crimes. Women have also been engaged in terrorism, notably suicide terrorism: consider, for example, the involvement of the Chechen Black Widows in the infamous Beslan school massacre and Moscow theatre bombing, and the involvement of the Black Tigresses of Death in Sri Lanka in almost 40% of all suicide missions conducted between 1980 and 2008 in Sri Lanka (see Eliatamby and Romanova, 2011).

When we talk about female victims of conflict-related crimes and harms, their agency is often overlooked – beyond being victims, however, they have often survived the atrocities they suffered. They may have also survived the conflict and helped their family and community survive also. Conversely, where men are victims or otherwise do not comply with the hypermasculinised ideals cherished in many conflict-affected environments, they can be marginalised or ridiculed. This is part of the reason why men can be criticised for not taking up arms in conflict, why male politicians in conflict-affected environments can be criticised for not being sufficiently aggressive, why few societies have specific referral systems or support mechanisms for male victims of SGBV, and why post-traumatic stress disorder among members of the armed forces can be overlooked (see Khattab et. al., 2014; Whitworth, 2008). These gendered stereotypes, which reinforce the passivity of women and the aggressiveness of men, do little to contribute towards effective peacebuilding.

Moreover, focussing only on specific types of harm against women (such as CRSV) also tends to avoid the more systemic and structural violence, which enables such harms to continue. As Swaine (2018) has argued, there is a need for a deeper transformational change to effect the structural change required to address drivers of gendered violence and reduce gendered harms. This transformational change must come through a comprehensive approach to building peace after conflict which ensures that all peacebuilding interventions (to include efforts across the security, economic and governance sectors) are comprehensively gender-responsive from the outset.

It must also be remembered that gendered harms can be intensely suffered by members of the lesbian, gay, bisexual, transgender, intersex and queer (LGBTIQ) community or people of diverse SOGIE (see Box 10.11). Gendered harms can also be intensified when systems of patriarchy intersect with other discriminatory systems, such as racism or economic deprivation (as described in Box 10.12 on intersectionality).

Ultimately, it can be seen that gendered stereotypes feed into insecurity and undermine prospects for peace. In patriarchal systems, women are marginalised from formal peacebuilding processes and their agency denied during and after conflict, while men can be denied the assistance they often need, can feel compelled to fulfil roles that are ultimately unsatisfying and can suffer if they do not conform to dominant masculinities (see Box 10.13). Such binary stereotypes also reinforce structural inequalities and perpetuate violence (in both public and private spaces), including gender-based violence against both women and men. Militarised masculinities, the conflation of masculinity and violence, and structural inequalities and

Box 10.11: Violence and Discrimination against Members of the LGBTIQ Community and People of Diverse SOGIE

People who are lesbian, gay, bisexual, transgender, intersex and queer (LGBTIQ) or people of diverse sexual orientation and gender identity and expression (SOGIE) are often more likely to suffer violence and discrimination in conflict-affected environments, as they are in most other environments. While more likely to suffer violence and other harms, they are often simultaneously less likely to be able to access security and justice. In many countries, people of diverse SOGIE are criminalised and hate crimes against them go unpunished. In many countries, the perpetrators of violence against those who are of diverse SOGIE are state representatives, and such violence has included torture and arbitrary, summary and extrajudicial executions (Knight and Wilson, 2016; UNSG, 2015).

In countries where homosexuality is criminalised, people of diverse SOGIE who are victims of rape and other forms of SGBV may be reluctant to report such crimes and seek justice. And while people of diverse SOGIE have tended to be particularly vulnerable to atrocities committed during armed conflict, transitional justice mechanisms have generally ignored their experiences to date (Daigle and Myrttinen, 2018). Notable exceptions are in Peru and Colombia where the experience of diverse SOGIE groups were addressed in Peru's Truth and Reconciliation Commission and by Colombia's National Centre for Historical Memory (Daigle and Myrttinen, 2018).

While international standards do not specifically refer to LGTBIQ or people of diverse SOGIE, the inherent principles of equal access to justice, non-discrimination, victim safety, empowerment and offender accountability remain relevant.

cultural norms which privilege the hypermasculine also increase the likelihood of conflict. This is because violent or hard security solutions to challenges are often elevated above other options. The use of violence as a political tool also reinforces structural inequalities and inequitable power relations, which further feed into the war machine.

Box 10.12: Intersectionality

There is a need to attend to connections between gender, race, ethnicity, indigeneity, class, age, sexual orientation, age, disability and other demographic characteristics, as the dynamics of exclusion, inequality and violence are often intensified when more than one discriminatory system interact (such as patriarchy, racism or economic deprivation): for instance, when a woman is also socioeconomically marginalised and/or a member of an indigenous community or ethnic minority group, when a girl is displaced and/or of diverse SOGIE, when a boy is disabled and/or an orphan, or a gay man is also a member of an ethnic minority. An intersectional approach can accommodate multiple identities and remain attentive to the way in which these multiple identities can further oppress and marginalise.

Box 10.13: Masculinities

In any society, there are assumptions about how women and men, girls and boys should behave; what constitutes 'a good woman' or 'a real man', for instance. Socially constructed gender norms shape the way people act, think and treat each other. These norms change over time and place, but oftentimes masculinities and femininities conform to a gendered binary framework, which positions men as strong, active and aggressive or protective, and women as vulnerable, passive and in need of protection.

Societal attitudes about what constitutes 'a good woman' or 'a real man' can expose to harm those who do not fit these gendered stereotypes, or serve to constrain the behaviour and life-choices of men and women. They can also encourage harmful practices by those seeking to fit in. While patriarchal gender norms disadvantage, dispossess and harm women and girls, men and boys can also suffer where they feel compelled to conform to masculine ideals and practices which demonstrate their masculinity. Such practices might include adolescent boys cattle raiding in South Sudan (Wright, 2010) or involvement in criminal activity (JURIST, 2018), which can expose them to harm and cause wider societal harms.

In most societies, the way in which 'real men' should behave is associated with notions of physical strength, courage and dominance. Masculinity is, therefore, often associated with violence and militarism. Consequently, dominant masculinities can be used to mobilise men into armed groups and armed forces and thus contribute to the escalation of insecurity and conflict.

While there are multiple masculinities (from patriarchal to transformative), hegemonic, militarised and violent masculinities dominate in most societies, and the gendered binary distinction between men as the aggressors or protectors and women as the victims and protected often informs peacebuilding practice. Hence, the frequent focus on protection of women above participation of women and above protection of men.

Conclusion

This chapter has provided an overview of the policy discourse on gender mainstreaming in peacebuilding, and the increasing recognition that there needs to be a greater representation of women in peace processes and peacebuilding if such efforts are to be inclusive, responsive and, ultimately, successful. The chapter has also provided an overview of the gap between policy and practice, as yet, in this regard, with women continuing to be marginalised in formal peace processes and peacebuilding. Since women often have different experiences during conflict and its immediate aftermath, and have different security and justice needs, it is particularly important that efforts to rebuild security and justice after conflict engage women and are responsive to their specific needs. The chapter concludes by reminding us that neither women nor men are homogenous groups, and that assumptions about experiences, needs, skillsets, demands and knowledge based upon a person's gender are unproductive.

Moreover, continuing to view peace and security in a gendered binary way (where men are aggressors, protectors and leaders, and women are vulnerable victims in need of protection) can undermine peacebuilding efforts. In contrast, a more nuanced understanding of the gender dynamics of conflict and a gender-sensitive approach to peacebuilding can help build a more lasting peace and more equitable peace dividends. A 'gender lens' (or a 'gender perspective') can help reveal the complexities of conflict: that women are combatants; that men are victims; that armed conflict extends beyond the battleground into the private sphere; and that peace co-exists with conflict in examples of protecting families and building bridges between communities amidst conflict without resorting to violence. Ultimately, an understanding of the complexities of conflict and the gendered nature of conflict can better equip those committed to resolving conflict and building sustainable peace.

Summary of Key Issues

- There are strong links between violence against women and armed conflict, where violence against women is a key indicator of conflict, causes and exacerbates conflict, and undermines efforts to build a lasting and meaningful peace.
- CRSV is not an inevitable by-product of war, but preventable and a key factor in causing further insecurity.
- For women, the threat of violence can continue after the end of hostilities.
- Men can be victims of CRSV and other threats during and after conflict, and are more likely than women to be direct casualties of armed conflict because they are much more likely to be directly engaged.
- UNSCR 1325 represents the first time there was broad agreement at the policy level that women and men have different experiences in conflict, different needs after conflict, different perspectives on the causes and outcomes of conflict, and different things to bring to the peacebuilding process.
- Women are poorly represented in peace talks when key decisions are made about transitional justice, DDR, SSR and other peacebuilding programmes.
- Gender-responsive SSR speaks to the need to develop institutions that are responsive to the security needs of both women and men, and more equally representative of them.
- DDR programmes rarely include the provision of reproductive health services or crèche facilities, without which significant barriers to effective reintegration for many female former combatants can remain.
- SALW control and mine action programmes need to recognise that it is not only men who have security-related knowledge or whose security is undermined due to the presence of SALW and mines and other ERW.

- Responses to insecurity and violence will be ineffective if all women are considered to be passive victims in need of protection, and all perpetrators of violence are considered to be men.

Reflective Question

Beyond ensuring the active engagement of both women and men in the planning, design and implementation of peacebuilding efforts, how can the specific security and justice needs of both women and men be addressed in post-conflict environments?

Useful Datasets

Council for Foreign Relations (CFR) *Women's Participation in Peace Processes* – www.cfr.org/interactive/womens-participation-in-peace-processes.

Georgetown Institute for Women, Peace and Security (GIWPS) and Peace Research Institute of Oslo (PRIO) *Women, Peace and Security (WPS) Index* – https://giwps.georgetown.edu/the-index.

Monash Gender, Peace and Security (GPS) *Towards Inclusive Peace: Mapping Gender Provisions in Peace Agreements* – http://mappingpeace.monashgps.org.

List of Core Resources

Baaz, M. and Utas, M. (2012). 'Beyond "Gender and Stir"' in Baaz, M and Utas, M (eds) *Beyond 'Gender and Stir': Reflections on gender and SSR in the aftermath of African conflicts*. (Uppsala: The Nordic Africa Institute): 5–10. Available at http://nai.diva-portal.org/smash/get/diva2:570724/FULLTEXT01.pdf.

Bastick, M. and Valasek, K. (eds) (2008) *Gender and SSR Toolkit*. (Geneva: DCAF, OSCE, ODIHR, UN–INSTRAW). Available at www.dcaf.ch/gender-security-sector-reform-toolkit.

CASA (2017) 'Women, men and the gendered nature of small arms and light weapons', *International Small Arms Control Standard* 06.10. Available at www.smallarmsstandards.org/isacs/0610-en.pdf.

Cockburn, C. (2010) 'Gender Relations as Causal in Militarization and War: A Feminist Standpoint', *International Feminist Journal of Politics*, 12(2): 139–57.

Cohen, D., Green, A., and Wood, E. (2013) '*Wartime Sexual Violence: Misconceptions, Implications, and Ways Forward*', USIP Special Report, (Washington: USIP). Available at www.usip.org/files/resources/SR323.pdf.

Davies, S. and True, J. (2017) 'When there is no justice: gendered violence and harm in post-conflict Sri Lanka', *The International Journal of Human Rights* 21(9): 1320–36.

Enloe, C. (2000). *Maneuvers: The International Politics of Militarizing Women's Lives* (Berkeley: University of California Press).

Henshaw, A. (2016) 'Where Women Rebel: Patterns of Women's Participation in Armed Rebel Groups 1990–2008', *International Feminist Journal of Politics* 18(1): 39–60.

HRW (2017) *Central African Republic: Sexual Violence as Weapon of War* (New York: HRW) (video). Available at www.hrw.org/video-photos/video/2017/10/04/central-african-republic-sexual-violence-weapon-war.

Kaufman, J. and Williams, K. (eds) (2016) *Women, Gender Equality, and Post-Conflict Transformation: Lessons Learned, Implications for the Future* (Abingdon: Taylor and Francis).

Lee-Koo, K (2002) 'Confronting a Disciplinary Blindness: Women, War and Rape in the International Politics of Security', *Australian Journal of Political Science* 37(3): 525–36.

LSE (2011) *Peace Vs. Women's Rights in Afghanistan: Compatible or Contradicting Concepts?* Presentation by Zainab Salbi, founder and CEO of Women for Women International (video). Available at www.youtube.com/watch?v=F3PA0gjnChU.

LSE (2017) *Women, Peace and Security in the Global Arena*, Panel Discussion hosted by the LSE, London, 5 June. (London: LSE) (video). Available at www.lse.ac.uk/website-archive/newsAndMedia/videoAndAudio/channels/publicLecturesAndEvents/player.aspx?id=3833.

Mazurana, D. and Proctor, K. (2013) *Gender, Conflict and Peace* (Massachusetts: World Peace Foundation). Available at https://sites.tufts.edu/wpf/files/2017/04/Gender-Conflict-and-Peace.pdf.

Mobekk, E. (2010) 'Gender, Women and Security Sector Reform', *International Peacekeeping* 17(2): 278–91.

Paffenholz, T., Ross, N., Dixon, S., Schluchter, A.-L. and True, J. (2016) *Making Women Count – Not Just Counting Women: Assessing Women's Inclusion and Influence on Peace Negotiations* (Geneva: Inclusive Peace and Transition Initiative (The Graduate Institute of International and Development Studies) and UN Women). Available at www.inclusivepeace.org/sites/default/files/IPTI-UN-Women-Report-Making-Women-Count-60-Pages.pdf.

Pruitt, L. (2016) *The Women in Blue Helmets: Gender, Policing, and the UN's First All-Female Peacekeeping Unit* (Berkeley: University of California Press).

Saferworld (2014) *Women and Security in Yemen* (video). Available at www.youtube.com/watch?v=nPjclFe5Zsc.

Sjoberg, L. (2014) *Gender, War, and Conflict* (Cambridge: Polity Press).

Small Arms Survey (2014) *Women and Guns* (Geneva: Small Arms Survey). Available at www.smallarmssurvey.org/fileadmin/docs/A-Yearbook/2014/en/Small-Arms-Survey-2014-Highlights-EN.pdf.

True, J. (2015) 'Winning the Battle but Losing the War on Violence: A Feminist Perspective on the Declining Global Violence Thesis', *International Feminist Journal of Politics* 17(4): 554–72.

UN Women (2017a) *Colombian women play central role in peace process*, UN Women video, 18 January. Available at www.youtube.com/watch?v=jhoYzh–tVw.

UN Women (2017b) *Feminism in Times of War and Peace* (video). Available at www. youtube.com/watch?v=mIP8XHi9938.

UNSG (2017a) *Report of the Secretary-General on Conflict-Related Sexual Violence, S/2017/249*, 15 April. (New York: UN). Available at www.un.org/en/events/ elimination-of-sexual-violence-in-conflict/pdf/1494280398.pdf.

USIP (2013) *Men, Peace, and Security Symposium: Agents of Change – The Changing Nature of Conflict* (video). Available at www.youtube.com/ watch?v=LEAYxr8Xo7I.

USIP (2017) *When Women in War Aren't Victims: A Security Blindspot* (video). Available at www.youtube.com/watch?v=snXKuley0L4.

Wright, H. (2010) *Masculinities, Conflict and Peacebuilding: Perspectives on Men Through a Gender Lens* (London: Saferworld). Available at www.saferworld.org. uk/resources/publications/862-masculinities-conflict-and-peacebuilding-perspectives-on-men-through-a-gender-lens.

11 Countering Transnational Security Threats: Terrorism, Piracy and Organised Crime

Overview

This chapter addresses some of the international security threats perceived to be associated with conflict-affected or conflict-vulnerable countries. It considers the impact of conflict-affected countries on the stability of neighbouring and regional countries, as well as on countries further afield, notably through such phenomena as terrorism, piracy, and cross-border and organised crime. In each case, it looks at the effects of the threats, efforts to overcome them and the links with conflict.

The Terrorism part of the chapter begins by considering the definition of terrorism, before looking at some alleged causes, its changing nature, the legal dimension and possible improvements in efforts to counter it. The Piracy part of the chapter looks at twenty-first century piracy, focussing in particular on Somali piracy. It begins by providing an overview of the definition, character, location and prevalence of piracy, before discussing the economic and human costs of piracy, its causes, and some of the wider security, economic, geostrategic and political issues involved. The Organised Crime part of the chapter focusses in particular on transnational organised crime and its relationship with armed conflict. It will consider the definition of organised crime, its causes and effects, as well as wider security, economic, developmental and governance threats associated with organised crime. To provide a context to discussion of these three transnational security threats, the chapter opens with a broader discussion of the types of security threats typically associated with conflict-affected environments.

Learning Outcomes

- Critically evaluate the nature and extent of international security risks posed by conflict-affected and conflict-vulnerable states and their effect on regional stability
- Articulate the complex relationship between conflict and crime, particularly cross-border and organised crime
- Understand the problems associated with attempts to define terrorism and some alleged causes or explanations
- Identify key international legal instruments and measures to counter threats posed by terrorism, piracy and organised crime

- Analyse the broad relationship between armed conflict and political violence
- Provide an overview of modern-day piracy, including economic and human costs, as well as wider security, economic and developmental dimensions
- Provide an overview of the definition and types of organised crime and its effects
- Analyse the threats posed by organised crime to countries emerging from conflict and to wider international security

Part 1 – Conflict and Global Risks

Patrick (2011b, 2006) and Jackson and Beswick (2018) note the common perception – at least in the West – that the global risks posed by countries in conflict, or at least vulnerable to it, are greater than the threats posed by stable countries. Prior to 9/11, threats to security were perceived to emanate primarily from powerful countries. A renewed interest in conflict-vulnerable or fragile states came about after 9/11 as part of the argument about the potential security threats they were alleged to pose (see Patrick, 2011b, 2006; Schreier, 2010, for instance). The US National Security Strategy of 2002, for example, claims that 'America is now threatened less by conquering states than we are by failing ones' (US Government, 2002: 1). Similarly, it is argued not so much that such states are themselves threats, but that '(f)ailed and fragile states increase the risk of instability and conflict... [with many, for instance, lacking] the capacity and, in some cases, the will adequately to address terrorism and organised crime' (UK Cabinet Office, 2008, cited in Jackson and Beswick, 2018: 10). Western governments in particular also refer to the increasing interconnectedness of the world which means that the threats such states pose have far-reaching implications:

> One of the defining challenges in our world, now and for many years to come, will be to deal with weak and poorly governed states... where violence and oppression can spread; where arms traffickers and other transnational criminals can operate with impunity; and where terrorists and extremists can gather, and plot, and train to kill the innocent. In a world as increasingly connected as ours, the international state system is only as strong as its weakest links. (Condoleezza Rice, the then-US Secretary of State, 2008, cited in Patrick, 2011b: 3)

As we will shortly discuss, the discourse of the substantial and far-reaching threat has policy implications and justifies, as we have seen over the last two decades, for instance, further engagement in the affairs of others.

Consequences of conflict at the national level

If some of the consequences of conflict far away have now started to come home to more stable or stronger states, it is nonetheless vital to remember that those who are most affected by conflict are still those in the midst of it. Even in the aftermath of conflict, people suffer the consequences of high levels of violence and other forms of insecurity, limited access to essential services and goods (shelter, water, food, healthcare, education, security), and damaged or destroyed economy and physical infrastructure.

As we have seen, damage to the state infrastructure, the economy and development, and security and the rule of law, increases the vulnerability of the state to renewed outbreaks of armed conflict. It also exposes the state to other vulnerabilities, including decreased resilience in the face of threats such as natural disasters or the presence of organised criminal networks, which can further undermine the resilience of the state. Post-conflict states may be more attractive to organised criminal networks and tend to have a surfeit of small arms and other weapons (see DCAF, 2007, Patrick, 2006; Mbadlanyana and Onuoha, 2009). A vicious circle can thus ensue with each crisis or threat increasing the chances of another, and certain places can become increasingly vulnerable to (and a source of) insecurity and conflict.

Consequences of conflict at the regional level

However, as Patrick (2011b) notes, the consequences of conflict are also borne by neighbouring states. This is because 'violent conflict, refugee flows, arms trafficking, and disease are rarely contained within national borders' (Patrick, 2011a). There is much evidence to show how the effects of conflict or crisis 'spill over' the borders of a state and potentially create regional instability (as well as hinder growth).

Refugee flows can cause instability in receiving countries. The trafficking of arms, drugs, people and other commodities that often accompanies conflict can also cause regional instability (see Marc, Willman, Aslam, Rebosio with Balasuriya, 2013; OECD, 2005b). The economy of neighbouring countries can also be severely harmed. Kaldor (2012), for instance, highlights the negative impact on trade and GDP in places such as Malawi and Zimbabwe as a result of the conflict in Mozambique.

The adverse economic, political, security and psychological impacts on neighbouring and regional states create conditions conducive to conflict or humanitarian crisis. Particularly if neighbouring or regional states also possess some of the characteristics of a fragile state, violence can erupt or spill over (see Iqbal and Starr, 2008). In the words of the former President of the World Bank, Robert B. Zoellick: 'fragile states can create fragile regions [a]nd fragile regions can become global threats' (Zoellick, 2009: 2).

Because warring groups are seldom neatly contained within national borders, conflict can also spread to neighbouring countries, particularly where borders are contested or have little historical significance. Neighbouring countries may also become directly involved in the conflict, choosing to provide safe havens or other forms of support to armed groups, for instance. For example, support has been provided to the Free Syrian Army by Turkey, as well as Qatar and Saudi Arabia (New York Times, 2019), which led to border skirmishes between Syria and Turkey in 2012. The bloody conflict in the DRC (1996–2000) began with an invasion by Rwanda and Uganda to place a compliant ally in power and exploit the country's mineral resources. It subsequently involved intervention by other states including, in different degrees, Sudan (and Sudanese rebels), Zimbabwe, Zambia, Namibia,

Burundi and Angola (BBC, 2012). The DRC, however, may be better understood as a country that has suffered years of intensive conflict due to the vested interests of outside actors, which have exploited it for generations and continue to do so, through militias sponsored by its neighbours. Thus, it is perhaps easy to blame conflict states for increased risks to regional and even global security, whereas a more nuanced analysis might show that these risks (and even the conflict itself) are exacerbated and even caused by external actors or dynamics.

Consequences of conflict at the international level

As well as the risks to conflict-affected countries, and their immediate neighbours and other countries in the region, there can also be consequences for wider international peace and security, from factors including:

- Terrorism
- Piracy
- Trafficking and other forms of organised crime
- Mass movement of peoples and the risks that this can entail
- Easy availability of weapons and the risks posed by weapons of mass destruction (WMD)
- Disruption of international trade and investment
- Environmental degradation
- Increased energy, food and water insecurity (see Patrick, 2011b, 2006; Schreier, 2010; Steinberg, 2008; Zoellick, 2009).

Importantly, transnational threats are widely considered – and articulated by policy-makers – to be, in large part, a consequence of the lack of governance, security and the rule of law in conflict-affected, conflict-vulnerable or otherwise 'weak' or 'fragile' states (see Patrick, 2011b). While conflicts do have consequences for the wider global community, as we shall see, assigning blame for transnational threats to these states facing crises is also a very effective way of fulfilling a number of functions at home and abroad.

This discourse removes the focus from outside (especially western) governments, and their foreign and economic policies, which could be otherwise seen as contributory factors in conflict. It also legitimises involvement in the affairs of other countries and intervention in conflict-vulnerable or 'fragile' states, allegedly to prevent threats to international peace and security, against potential accusations of interference or neo-colonialism. Likewise, it legitimises policies advertised as protecting national security, but which compromise the protection of human rights and obligations under IHL. Finally, it provides a rationale for legitimising increased interference by the state in the private lives of its citizens, as well as increased and more pervasive forms of social control. Electorates are naturally most conscious of direct threats that they may face: fear has always been an effective means of control.

More generally, this discourse simplifies the relationship between geopolitical risk factors and conflict, blaming 'fragile' or 'weak' states themselves for transnational threats rather than those threats on the fragility of states. It also facilitates

International Community Transnational Threats	• Terrorism and piracy • Trafficking and other forms of organised crime • Mass movement of peoples and associated risks • Easy availability of weapons and the risks posed by WMD • Disruption of international trade and investment • Environmental degradation • Increased energy, food and water insecurity
Neighbours and Region Instability and Insecurity	• Spillover of conflict • Refugee flows • Arms trafficking • Adverse economic, political, security and psychological impacts • Increased vulnerability to conflict and humanitarian crises • Exploitation by militia groups
Conflict Zone Direct Harm	• High levels of violence and insecurity • Lack of essential services and goods • Economic devastation and severe development challenges • Damaged physical infrastructure and state institutions • Weapons profileration and presence of mines and ERW • Vulnerability to organised crime, renewed conflict and the effects of disasters

Figure 11.1 The Effects of Conflict at the National, Regional and International Levels

arguments for simple responses to address those threats, and provides a political hierarchy for the ranking of threats. In reality, it is obvious that climate change poses a greater threat to international peace than terrorism, and also that so-called 'fragile' states are the least responsible for that threat and the most at risk from it.

We will now look at three examples of transnational security threats which are most commonly associated with conflict-affected or conflict-vulnerable environments (Figure 11.1).

Part 2 – Terrorism

Defining terrorism

Whilst we may all be familiar with the use of the word 'terrorism', the term is widely contested and there is no generally accepted definition (see Martin, 2017; Schmid, 2012). Because it is often used to discredit opponents, particularly in the context of asymmetric warfare, and because recourse to arms against a state is considered (at least by some) to be legitimate on occasions, endeavouring to find an agreed definition of terrorism within the international community has become a highly politicised and relatively unfruitful activity. Lauderdale and Oliverio (2005), for instance, argue that it is very hard to define given its many diverse manifestations and its integral relationship with war-making and state-making. Without defining what we are talking about, however, discussion becomes highly problematic.

Governments and sympathetic scholars often argue that terrorism involves the illegal use of force, is politically motivated, is aimed at influencing (or terrorising) an audience (not necessarily the immediate target) and often has civilian (or passive military) targets (see Martin, 2017, for further discussion). More recently, it has also been widely argued that an extremism of intolerance and moral absolutes underpins terrorist acts (Martin, 2017; Martin and Prager, 2019; see also Shanahan, 2016). Clearly, this definition would exclude 'traditional' terrorist organisations like the Basque ETA (*Euskadi Ta Askatasuna*, a Basque separatist group), the Irish Republican Army (IRA) or the Sri Lankan Tamil Tigers (the Liberation Tigers of Tamil Eelam, LTTE). More recently still, cyber-terrorism has come in to the lexicon, which includes use of computers and information technology to facilitate terrorist activity and, more broadly, for politically motivated reasons to instil fear and cause harm to critical infrastructure (including efforts to influence elections and destabilise governments) and to persons (through violence) (see Hardy and Williams, 2014).

No modern militant armed organisation has ever described itself as a 'terrorist' group, though almost all such organisations (including the French Resistance and the African National Congress) have been so described by their detractors. Indeed, the term has only ever been deliberately used by states – from the French Revolution to the dictatorships of the twentieth century – to describe a political strategy to instil fear in populations to control them. In general, 'terrorist' groups do not seek to cause terror as an end in itself, but to exert political pressure on governments.

Lauderdale and Oliverio (2005) suggest that the state has a key role in defining 'terrorists' and 'terrorist activity' and indeed has the ability to disguise it, present it as legitimate (even as counter-terrorism efforts) or even sponsor it. It is, therefore, useful to look at the context in which something is defined as 'terrorism' and the agenda of those who make the judgements. In this regard, it is helpful to look to where groups are simultaneously seen as terrorist groups by some and not by others (e.g., the Kosovo Liberation Army (KLA), Sri Lankan Tamil Tigers (LTTE) and Nepal's People's Liberation Army (PLA)). Similarly, it is important to consider why incidents that look like similar acts are treated very differently by the mass media. It is also useful to consider whether acts of terrorism should be distinguished from acts of war or criminal acts, and who decides (see Duff, 2005). It is also helpful to ask how terrorism might be differentiated from similar terms, such as violent extremism, extremism and intolerance.

The terrorist threat

In its *Global Terrorism Index 2018*, the Institute for Economics & Peace (IEP) (2018) noted that terrorist-related fatalities decreased in 2017 by 27% since 2016. This is the third year that terrorist-related fatalities have decreased, since the peak of deaths from terrorism in 2014. Much of the decline in 2017 is due to significant decreases in the number of fatalities in Iraq and Syria (primarily due to the continuing decline of the Islamic State (IS) – see Box 11.1) and due to reinforced counter-terrorism efforts since 2018 which has led to 94 countries recording a decline in the number of fatalities in 2017 (compared with 46 that recorded an increase) (IEP, 2018).

The number of terrorist-related fatalities in 2017, however, remains substantial at 18,814. The primary driver of terrorism appears to be conflict, with the 10 countries most affected by terrorism being engaged in conflict (with 8 of the 10 being in a state of war) – and these 10 countries accounting for 84% of all terrorism-related deaths in 2017. The five countries with the most terrorism-related deaths are all in conflict, and conflict-related deaths in these five countries alone far outnumber terrorism-related deaths for all other countries combined (see Table 3). This demonstrates that, while often overlooked in popular discourse and media reportage, the victims of terrorism are much more likely to be those within conflict-affected environments.

In many places (including Afghanistan, Iraq and Nigeria) battle deaths also move in tandem with the number of terrorism-related deaths. Furthermore, more people are likely to die in a terrorist attack in a conflict-affected environment than an attack in a country not affected by conflict; in conflict-affected environments,

Box 11.1: The Islamic State (IS)

The Islamic State (IS) is also known as the Islamic State of Iraq and the Levant (ISIL), the Islamic State of Iraq and Syria (ISIS) and *Daesh* (the Arabic language acronym). It is a Salafi Jihadist militant group, recognised as a terrorist organisation by the UN and many countries. IS began in 1999 as *Jama'at al-Tawhid wal-Jihad*, pledging allegiance to al-Qaeda, but gained prominence in 2014 when it drove Iraqi forces out of key cities in Iraq. This is around the time when it began referring to itself as the Islamic State and proclaimed a worldwide caliphate. The magnitude of the atrocities committed by IS against civilians and captives also contributed to its raised profile (see Amnesty International, 2014). IS has also been active in many other countries, notably Syria where it has attacked both government and opposition forces. Since 2014, IS has lost much of the land it controlled: over 100,000 square metres across Iraq and Syria, resulting in the liberation from IS of 4.5 million people in Iraq and 3.2 million people in Syria. In December 2017, Iraq was widely declared to be fully liberated from IS control.

As territory was recaptured from IS control by the Global Coalition against Daesh, IS increased its terrorist activities, evidenced by a significant increase in terrorist activity, primarily attributable to IS, in 2016 (IEP, 2017; The Global Coalition Against Daesh, 2018). The Global Coalition against Daesh was formed in September 2014 after massive gains in the control of territory by IS, widely publicised atrocities and concern about the spread of IS in the region. The coalition includes 79 countries, committed to 'the military campaign in Iraq and Syria [as well as] tackling *Daesh*'s financing and economic infrastructure; preventing the flow of foreign terrorist fighters across borders; supporting stabilisation and the restoration of essential public services to areas liberated from *Daesh*; and countering the group's propaganda' (The Global Coalition Against Daesh, 2018).

terrorist attacks kill 2.4 people on average per attack, compared to 0.84 people per attack in countries not directly affected by conflict.

With the decline of IS, terrorist attacks in Iraq declined by 56% in 2017 (from 9,783 in 2016 to 4,271 in 2017). In Syria, there were over 1,000 fewer terrorism-related deaths in 2017 than in 2016. Of course, with the decline of IS in Iraq and Syria, the group's activities have moved elsewhere, which has seen a growth of IS-related activity in the Maghreb and Sahel regions (particularly Libya, Niger and Mali) and Southeast Asia (notably the Philippines) (IEP, 2018). For current terrorism data and trends see the Institute for Economics and Peace's Global Terrorism Index (http://visionofhumanity.org/indexes/terrorism-index/) (see Figure 11.2).

Terrorism has the potential not only to cause loss of life but to threaten development, stability and peace. It can harm socio-economic development, contribute to undermining human rights and civil liberties, challenge the rule of law, and destabilise fragile places and delicate diplomatic relationships (IPI, 2009 and UNODC, 2010c). It helps to maintain and create distrust and fear, can have strong links with organised crime networks, contributes to the flow SALW and other weapons, and can misdirect focus and resources away from other security threats.

Causes of terrorism – or why people engage in political violence

Whatever we call it, throughout history some people have taken up arms for political reasons. There are many reasons why. These can be categorised as psychological, ideological and structural (see USIP, 2001). Martin (2017) underscores the importance of looking at the individual, as well as group dynamics and socio-political environments. From a sociological perspective, structural theory might suggest that causes can lie in popular discontent, the alienation of elites or a pervasive crisis, while relative deprivation theory would look more to horizontal inequalities to explain the cause of some types of terrorism. From a psychological perspective, psychopathic individuals and group dynamics where political violence

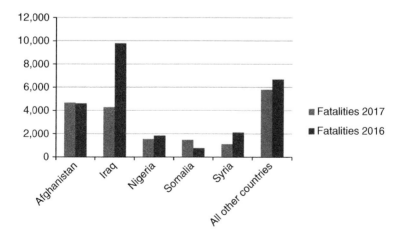

Figure 11.2 Global Terrorism Deaths (IEP, 2018)

is common and the desire to belong to a group is strong, are among some of the causes that have been investigated (see Martin, 2017 for further discussion). Each perspective has its value and policy implications.

As Martin (2017) emphasises, analysis of causes must be context-specific: explanations are not readily transferable across geographic or temporal boundaries. We should also not assume that causal factors or motivations are the same for every member of a particular terrorist or violent extremist group; causes are multiple and complex, and the fact that the various ways in which women are involved in violent extremist groups have until recently been widely overlooked, suggests that such groups are often treated as homogenous and unidimensional (see True and Eddyono, 2017). Similarly, it is important to recognise that causal explanations themselves are influenced by their socio-political origin. Consequently, as Lauderdale and Oliverio (2005) emphasise, it is important to acknowledge the role of the state in the construction of terrorism and terrorists, for instance.

It is also important to distinguish between causes, intentions, motives and explanations. Motives may be criminal, religious, political or emanate from a sense of injustice, and may be quite different from a set of complex causes that can also change over time. The intent of acts of terrorism may be to terrorise, coerce or intimidate with the purpose of soliciting money, securing publicity or, ultimately, affecting a change in policy, for instance (see Schmid, 2012). It is also important to look for triggers as well as enablers, when analysing the causes of a specific conflict.

Burgoon (2006), Rogers (2009) and others draw attention to the politico-economic roots of some types of terrorism, which implies addressing these causes rather than just the symptoms, which much counter-terrorism focusses upon. Others, however, argue that this approach might play into the hands of those motivated more by criminal interests than ideological ones. It is popularly thought that being 'soft' on terrorism encourages more of it and that democratic societies are accordingly more vulnerable to terrorist attacks. However, others argue that democracies are less vulnerable, partly because there may be fewer grievances and also partly because there are non-violent options if aggrieved (see Crenshaw, 2007 and Li, 2005). Li (2005), for example, sampled 119 countries from 1975 to 1997 and showed that democratic states (particularly those with political systems of proportional representation) are less susceptible to international or transnational terrorist attack. Since then, however, most attacks in democratic states have been related to their policies abroad, and it is unclear how far this judgement would still be true today.

Counter-terrorism

Because terrorism is widely held to be a key threat to international peace and security, counter-terrorism is important for national governments, and regional and international organisations (Crenshaw, 2007; IPI, 2009; Martin, 2017; Patrick, 2011b; UNSC, 2010; UN Office of Counter Terrorism, 2019). As a subject, though, counter-terrorism is not new, and current discourse and methods recall those used in Algeria in the 1950s, or in the later campaigns against the IRA and the Corsican separatists.

Martin (2017) outlines a number of types of responses to terrorism, ranging from counter-terrorism measures (which aim to eliminate terrorist activities and groups), anti-terrorism measures (which aim to defend potential targets from attack) and other defensive measures (which aim to deter or prevent attacks). He outlines a number of types of counter-terrorist responses including diplomacy, financial controls, military force, covert action, repressive and conciliatory responses, as well as targeted and untargeted prevention.

At the global level there is a comprehensive network of actors, structures and legal instruments intended to counter and prevent terrorism and violent extremism, including many UN Security Council Resolutions (the website of the UN Security Council Counter Terrorism Committee (CTC) – www.un.org/sc/ctc/ - has an updated list), 19 international legal instruments, a UN Global Counter Terrorism Strategy, a Counter Terrorism Implementation Task Force (CTITF) established by the UN Secretary-General in 2005 and endorsed by the General Assembly the following year, the UN Counter Terrorism Centre (UNCCT) established in 2011 and the UN Office of Counter Terrorism established in 2017 (UN Office of Counter Terrorism, 2019).

Improvements in international co-operation and capacity-building at the national level have also been urged (UNSG, 2012c). While it has largely been recognised in the last few years that military-only (or even security-only) solutions to security threats are insufficient, non-military options still warrant further attention. Yet without any agreement on why terrorism happens, or even what it is, this a challenging task. Likewise, improved co-ordination and communication in conflict-affected environments, and interstate co-operation and joined-up law enforcement efforts to prevent terrorist attacks are essential. However, the collection and analysis of intelligence, being covert, does not lend itself to absolute co-operation and co-ordination (Martin, 2017; Rosendorff and Sandler, 2005).

The link between terrorism and conflict

It is widely held that conflict-affected and conflict-vulnerable environments are conducive to terrorism (see Patrick, 2011b). It is easy to see that terrorist groups may be attracted to countries with little rule of law, heightened insecurity, poor governance, weak state institutions, widespread poverty and unemployment, prevailing violence and criminality, unprotected borders, abundant weapons, and limited economic and employment prospects. It is also easy to see how terrorist groups may grow amidst the trauma and grievance resulting from the armed conflict, especially if its causes of conflict have not been addressed. Conflict zones can provide access to new recruits, sanctuaries, bases, weapons, financing, transit routes and conflict experience (Patrick, 2011b).

Terrorist groups are also motivated by the grievances which led to the conflict (such as inequalities or injustices) or, indeed, the grievances due to the conflict (as in the case of Iraq, Afghanistan or the Palestine–Israeli conflict, for instance) (see Box 11.2). So, they may be attracted to conflict-affected countries out of conviction

> **Box 11.2: The Blurred Line Between Terrorists, Militants and Insurgents**
>
> The politicised, subjective nature of the concept of terrorism problematises efforts to theorise about its causes and relationship with conflict. If terrorism is simply the use of violence to inflict terror for a political end, it can be seen as a tool of insurgent forces and states. Without taking a partial approach, it is often hard to distinguish between terrorism and conflict, and between cause and effect. We need only look to the Middle East or Afghanistan to see the messiness between what is deemed to be legitimate violence in the eyes of the international community and what is deemed to be terrorism. For instance, violent oppression has led to the birth of many groups at least at one time popularly considered to be terrorist groups (such as the KLA, LTTE or PLA). The Russian military invasion of Afghanistan and the support given to the mujahideen by Pakistan, United States and Saudi Arabia can be seen to have lead to the birth of the Taliban (Hillenbrand, 2015; Martin, 2017). Evidence from the Chilcot report (the 2016 report of a British public inquiry into the invasion of Iraq) suggests that the invasion of Iraq spawned the birth of Islamic State (IS) and increased the terrorist threat at home (Wintour, 2016). Some scholars and commentators also consider that the so-called 'War on Terror' has increased the threat posed by terrorism as well as other security threats, which are being overlooked and/or exacerbated by directing most resources towards counter-terrorism (see Kaldor and Beebe, 2010; Zala and Rogers, 2009; Zeigler and Smith, 2017).

or in order to take advantage of economic, political and strategic opportunities. There is a close – sometimes indistinguishable – relationship between terrorism and insurgency, both of which are often considered to involve the weaker party engaging in political violence to achieve the greatest effect with limited means. As mentioned above, insurgents have themselves often been simultaneously regarded by different audiences as liberation fighters and terrorists – for example, the Kosovo Liberation Army (KLA), Sri Lankan Tamil Tigers (LTTE) and Nepal's People's Liberation Army (PLA) (see Box 11.3).

There is also ambiguity in the definition of those individuals and groups that travel to a conflict environment to engage in the conflict. If they are private individuals or groups motivated by ideological or political reasons, they are today considered to be terrorists. Indeed, in much western counter-terrorism legislation, freedom fighters are today synonymous with terrorists. It was not always so, of course (see Box 11.4 on the engagement of British citizens in the Spanish Civil War).

As mentioned earlier, many of the countries most impacted by terrorism are affected by conflict (IEP, 218). IEP (2017) also describes armed conflict as facilitating and leading to an increase in terrorism. IEP's research has also shown that 99% of all terrorist-related fatalities over the last 17 years have been in conflict-affected countries or places where there are high levels of 'political terror', what IEP refers to as 'extra-judicial killings, torture and imprisonment without trial'

Box 11.3: Insurgents or Terrorists – the Kosovo Liberation Army

The Kosovo Liberation Army (KLA) has been simultaneously regarded as both an insurgent force and a terrorist group. For example, the administration of the United States (US) initially regarded the Kosovo Liberation Army (KLA) as a terrorist organisation, only to intervene in the conflict in Kosovo in 1999 effectively on the side of the KLA. Some analysts consider that part of the US's reluctance to officially deem the KLA a terrorist organisation from 1998 stems from a reticence to condone Serbian declarations that they were fighting a terrorist organisation and, in so doing, encourage further excessive violence against civilians in Kosovo (see Crawford, 2001).

After the conflict, the legacy of the KLA harmed the reputation of its successor organisation, the Kosovo Protection Corps (KPC). Parts of the international community continued to regard those who fought in the KLA as terrorists and thus regarded the KPC, which predominantly comprised former KLA combatants, as having links with terrorism. Other members of the international community and the Kosovo Albanian majority of Kosovo, however, instead regarded the Serb regime as having committed acts which were terrorist in nature and intent (see Martin, 2017).

Full confidence in the KLA as a legitimate organisation was never, however, openly forthcoming and acknowledgement of the perceived associations of the KLA (and its successor organisation, the KPC) with terrorist activity held by some impacted decisions about future security structures for Kosovo. Of course, the complexity of such groups as the KLA, with internal power struggles and competing agendas as well as dynamics that change over time, often problematises any serious attempt at categorisation.

(IEP, 2017: 3). The link between conflict and terrorism is underscored by a strong correlation between conflict intensity (indicated by the number of battle deaths) and high levels of terrorist activity (indicated by the number of fatalities from terrorism); Syria, Iraq, Afghanistan and Yemen have among the highest number of battle deaths as well as the highest fatality rates from terrorism since 2012 (IEP, 2017).

However, not all conflict-affected places experience high levels of terrorist activity or become sanctuaries for terrorist groups, and many attacks have been planned from wealthy and stable countries. Indeed, the resources that terrorist groups require are much more likely to be found in wealthier countries (Patrick, 2011b). In conflict environments, the operational security required by terrorist groups is absent, as is the semblance of governance that might minimise the likelihood of intervention by the international community (Patrick, 2011b). The transport and communication networks and banking services are also more favourable to terrorist activity in places that have not suffered armed conflict (Martin, 2017; Patrick, 2011b). Patrick (2011b) concludes that while a state's weakness can attract and sustain terrorist groups, it is a state's ability and willingness to support (or turn a blind eye to) terrorist groups that is the key factor.

Box 11.4: British Foreign Fighters in the Spanish Civil War

British foreign fighters who fought against the Franco regime during the Spanish Civil War in the 1930s, for instance, while they transgressed the British Government's policy of non-intervention and could have been prosecuted under the 1870 Foreign Enlistment Act, have mostly been lionised in history and popular discourse and in the form of memorials across the UK (see Baxell, 2012; Monbiot, 2014; Stewart, 2018). Interestingly, those engaged in conflicts in other countries motivated by money rather than political or ideological reasons, such as mercenaries, are likely to be able to evade being labelled and targeted as terrorists (Monbiot, 2014). This might not be surprising in today's political economy which simultaneously depoliticises and lends moral gravity to economic relations: that is, those who are economically disadvantaged are often presented as being so because of their moral deprivation – they are the undeserving poor – rather than socio-political inequities, which justifies the unequal distribution of wealth and power (see Gordon, 2017).

Also, while there are many conflicts and millions of people are affected, terrorism itself remains relatively rare (Crenshaw, 2007; Zeigler and Smith, 2017). Armed conflict may present opportunities to terrorist groups which would exist anyway, but it can reflect or result in factors that contribute to causing terrorist activities. It could also be argued that some terrorist groups (and organised criminal networks) may have a vested interest in sustaining a conflict (for economic, political or strategic aims) and thus it is the prospect of peace that precipitates or feeds into terrorism.

Counter-terrorism and other threats to international security

Zala and Rogers (2011) argue that the focus on countering the threat of terrorism since 9/11 has led to the neglect of key security challenges of socio-economic divisions and climate change. Indeed, they and others (such as Kaldor and Beebe, 2010) suggest that the 'War on Terror' has perhaps counter-intuitively caused more insecurity than the threat it was designed to mitigate (see also Rogers, 2009 and Hurwitz, 2008). A focus on terrorism and the application of primarily military means to fight it have thus been both counterproductive and have resulted in resources being directed away from issues that warrant more attention (see also Zeigler and Smith, 2017). Zala and Rogers (2011) and Rogers (2009) suggest that, by addressing the challenges of increasing socio-economic divisions and climate change, the factors that cause and exacerbate conflict can be better dealt with. Indeed, poverty, under-development and exploitation, particularly in respect of the process of marginalisation, can be important driving factors for terrorism as well as insurgency and organised crime (Zala and Rogers, 2011).

Crenshaw (2007) notes that terrorism has nonetheless remained a top concern for many intergovernmental organisations and states due to its unpredictable nature and the fact that, consequently, it reminds us of our vulnerability. The media also plays a pivotal role in magnifying this threat (Crenshaw, 2007) thus, ironically, often playing into the hands of terrorists who may seek to publicise their cause and extend the reach of their terror. The picture many receive of terrorist activity is, however, a partial picture and one that often excludes state terrorism committed by domestic or friendly states and one that often overlooks victims of terrorism from conflict-vulnerable or conflict-affected environments. In order to maintain mass media exposure and evade detection by law enforcement agencies, terrorist groups do often seek more innovative and shocking means of attack. However, despite terrorism continuing to constitute a threat to international peace and security, it is imperative, of course, that the cure does not feed the illness.

Part 3 – Piracy

Defining piracy

Unlike terrorism, piracy has a long-standing and generally accepted definition. Article 101 of the United Nations Convention on the Law of the Sea (UNCLOS) defines piracy as an illegal act 'of violence or detention, or any act of depredation, committed for private ends by the crew or the passengers of a private ship or a private aircraft' directed against another ship or aircraft, or its passengers, on the high seas or outside the jurisdiction of any state. According to UNCLOS, piracy must occur on the high seas and so excludes any act that occurs within territorial boundaries (which is often referred to as armed robbery at sea or armed robbery against ships).

Pirates today generally try to extort ransom by hijacking vessels and kidnapping the crew. Once hijacked, the vessel is usually taken to a pirate-friendly port and the hostages are taken ashore until the ransom is paid (BBC, 2011a; Hannan, 2012). Attacks are becoming more sophisticated, particularly with the success of pirate attacks in recent years and the increased ransom sums being demanded and paid and reinvested into piracy (Binkley and Smith, 2012; Bridger, 2011; Hannan, 2012).

The effects of piracy

Piracy has a long history, at least since the time of the Romans (Bellamy, 2011), but was always considered a small-scale problem (see Bridger, 2011; Department for Transport, UK Government, 2012; Patrick, 2011b). Yet today, it is widely asserted to be a significant threat to international peace and security (see, for example UNSCR 2039, 2012, on piracy in the Gulf of Guinea). Is this justified? In financial terms, it is estimated that piracy costs the international economy US $7bn per year (Department for Transport, UK Government, 2012) although estimates vary depending upon what factors are taken into account. Somalia and neighbouring countries have suffered from the inflated cost of basic goods. Regional coastal countries have also reported losses in tourism revenue, fishing profits and docking fees (Bridger, 2011). Humanitarian aid has also been prevented from reaching those in need in Somalia (see Beri, 2011; CQ Researcher, 2011). Yet others warn against exaggerating the threat posed by piracy, particularly when annual global maritime commerce amounts to trillions of US dollars (see, for instance, Hanson, 2009; Murphy, 2007).

Given the importance of maritime commerce and the number of nations potentially affected, it is unsurprising that the subject has a high profile internationally. The first UN Security Council debate on global piracy, held on 19 November 2012, underscored the threat that piracy posed to international peace and security, and the importance of continuing the counter-piracy measures. These measures have led to a dramatic decrease in the number of global attacks (UNSC, 2012b).

The current threat of piracy

Since 2010, piracy incidents have declined: 2017 saw the lowest number of incidents over the previous five years: 180 compared with 191 in 2016, 246 in 2015, 245 in 2014 and 264 in 2013 compared with 445 in 2010, when modern piracy was at its peak (ICC IMB PRC, 2019, 2017). In 2018, however, the number of incidents increased to 201, compared with 180 in 2017 (ICC IMB PRC, 2019). The International Maritime Organisation (IMB) Piracy Reporting Centre (PRC) of the International Chamber of Commerce (ICC) also considers that about half of all attacks go unreported, so the figures will be much higher (MAREX, 2019). Of the incidents that occurred in 2018, only six ships were hijacked; the remaining were attempting hijackings or attempted attacks (143 ships were attacked and boarded, but only 6 of these successfully hijacked) (ICC IMB PRC, 2019). No crew members were killed in 2018, compared with 3 the previous year (ICC IMB PRC, 2019). Others, however, died as a result of malnutrition or disease while in captivity and during rescue or escape attempts (OBP, 2019). Nonetheless, there is a decline in crew members killed in hijackings or attempted hijackings (with a total of seven crew members killed from January 2013 until September 2017) compared with a few years earlier (ICC IMB PRC, 2019, 2017).

There are many reasons for the very recent decline in the incidence of piracy, bearing in mind that not all incidents are reported. There has been considerable investment in protective measures, including armed guards, water cannons and razor wire around the vessels, as well as increased pre-emptive interception of pirate boats by international naval forces (BBC, 2011b; ICC IMB PRC, 2019), improved co-ordination and information sharing, and capacity building for security and criminal justice sectors of the countries involved (UNSC, 2012b). There have also been initiatives to discourage young men from becoming pirates, especially in Somalia. But often the effect of such measures is to move the problem elsewhere. For example, piracy has been increasing off Indonesia; see the IMB Piracy Reporting Centre (PRC) website (ICC IMB PRC, 2019) for current information, as well as the live piracy and armed robbery report and map (www.icc-ccs.org/piracy-reporting-centre.

Fighting piracy

There are a number of different ways that are currently used to combat piracy, including on-board deterrents, naval deployments, new laws, better law enforcement and judicial measures, and addressing governance and underdevelopment, as well as addressing root causes and actual or perceived grievances. The ways in which piracy is combatted can be quite similar to the efforts to resolve conflict and build peace: quite simply, military or hard security solutions alone are insufficient – what are required are also efforts to address weaknesses in governance and development challenges. Of course, these challenges – which are perceived to allow piracy to thrive – are also typical of conflict-affected or conflict-vulnerable environments, as we will discuss shortly. As will be discussed shortly, grievances which can lead to conflict can also be seen to have contributed to the development and escalation of piracy in some areas (notably off the coast of Somalia – see Box 11.5).

Returning to ways in which to combat piracy, onboard deterrents can include protecting vessels with barbed wire or water cannons and by carrying armed guards. With regard to naval deployments, many countries (including the UK, US, India, Pakistan, Japan, Malaysia, Singapore, China, Russia and France) sent warships to the Gulf of Aden to prevent pirate attacks (Beri, 2011; Hanson, 2009). The EU and NATO have also been involved (see Bridger, 2011; Hanson, 2009).

However, beyond defensive and military efforts alone being insufficient, they may even cause the situation to escalate, becoming more violent or widespread (see Bridger, 2011; ICC IMB PRC, 2019). Navies cannot patrol the entire ocean, and even if there were no other factors to address – such as causal factors or perceived grievances, and weaknesses in the legal framework or judicial capabilities, for instance – pirates will continue to find novel ways of overcoming detection and defensive measures. Thus, it is now widely acknowledged that a 'land-based solution' to piracy is required (see CQ Researcher, 2011; Hanson, 2009; House of Commons Foreign Affairs Committee, 2011; Menkhaus, 2009; Murphy, 2011; Ramsey, 2011; Shortland, 2012; UNODC, 2019). A land-based solution is required, not least because piracy needs a land base (to secure ransoms, return captured ships to port and hold hostages), because different sectors of the population may support or have a vested interest in piracy (particularly because of the reinvestment of funds – see Binkley and Smith, 2012; CQ Researcher, 2011) and because of the perceived link between conflict, insecurity and piracy.

Outside defensive and military efforts, there is a need for a coherent, comprehensive body of piracy law at the international level, and for the legal framework to enable action in response to those acts of armed robbery at sea that occur within territorial waters. There is also the need for a co-ordinated effort on the part of the international community, with agreement, for instance, on whether or not ransoms should be paid.

Above and beyond what the international community can do, of particular importance is the need for effective prosecutorial systems and political will in those countries where piracy has developed. So, for example, the UN Security Council Resolution 2383 of 2017 underscores the responsibility of Somali authorities and urges the continued development of a comprehensive set of anti-piracy and maritime laws, and effective and responsive security and justice sector organisations.

Clearly, it is also necessary to address some of the real and perceived grievances as well as respond to other potential causes or enablers, including limited economic opportunities. Piracy must begin to be seen as a less attractive option in terms of the potential rewards and in terms of the likelihood of success (low reward/high risk rather than the high reward/low risk that has existed). Pervasive weaknesses in governance and state security structures need to be addressed, along with the prevalence of organised criminal networks and weapons.

Many international and regional organisations are engaged in efforts to combat piracy, including the UN, notably the UN Office on Drugs and Crime (UNODC) and International Maritime Organization (IMO), INTERPOL, EU, AU and NATO, as well as various maritime and seafarer organisations.

However, all these activities notwithstanding, piracy may continue to flourish, not least because of the influence of those who may have a vested interest in it. As *The Economist* put it in 2011:

> Unfortunately, too many people like things as they are. Pirates gain wealth, excitement and glamour. Marine insurers, which last month extended the sea area deemed to be at threat from Somali pirates, are making good money from the business that piracy generates. At least for the time being, shipowners are willing to take the calculated risk of sailing in pirate-infested waters; so long as everyone bears his part of the extra $600m a year in premiums, they can pass the bill on to their customers. Patrolling foreign navies can demonstrate their usefulness to their sometimes sceptical political masters, while countries such as China and Russia are strengthening their operational experience. (*The Economist*, 2011: 62)

Piracy, conflict and insecurity

Many argue that piracy flourishes in so-called 'uncontrolled space' (Bellamy, 2011, for instance) or, rather, space that is not controlled by legitimate governing structures. In other words, it is commonly assumed that conflict-affected and conflict-vulnerable environments where there is limited state capacity provide an enabling environment for piracy. Nonetheless, many places affected by conflict (or even lack of functioning governments) do not pose serious threats of piracy. It could be argued that structures that are receptive to (or ignore) piracy are more important than a lack of governing structures themselves (see Patrick, 2011b). However, a country's level of security could be the most relevant factor. For example, conflict-affected Somalia and Nigeria both witnessed surges in piracy off their coasts, and insurgents were also engaged in piracy (Patrick, 2011b). Of course, Somalia's strategic position, with an extensive coastline providing easy access to many of the most important global commercial transit routes is also key (see Holzer, 2008). It is clear, however, that piracy is much more likely to flourish where the will or ability to prevent or prosecute pirates is absent: the difficulty in dealing with Somali piracy lies in the relative impunity of pirates who mainly operate in Somalia's territorial waters (see Bento, 2011, for instance).

Box 11.5: Somali Piracy

For many years, notably between 2003 and 2010, Somali pirates were responsible for the majority of attacks globally. Some commentators looked to the underdevelopment and weak governance of Somalia, as a result of years of civil conflict, to explain the phenomenon (see Bellamy, 2011; Beri, 2011; Binkley and Smith, 2012; Hannan, 2012; Holzer, 2008). Initially, many Somali pirates were fishermen who were angry at the extensive illegal fishing by foreign ships and the dumping of toxic waste (including nuclear and other hazardous waste) in Somali waters – a result of a state weakened from conflict with no effective coastguard or means of protecting its interests (see Beri, 2011). These grievances fuelled the development and escalation of piracy off the coast of Somalia. So, we can see that there is a relationship between conflict and piracy here, but it is the weakness of the state that allowed its waters to be plundered and led to grievances which resulted in the escalation of piracy – rather than the weaknesses of a conflict-ridden state per se that attracted pirates and allowed piracy to flourish.

Aggrieved fishermen therefore sought to extract 'licence fees' from international fishermen and others, and presented themselves as 'the coastguards of Somalia' (see Beri, 2011; Binkley and Smith, 2012; Holzer, 2008). Others lacked other viable opportunities to provide for themselves and their families, amidst widespread poverty and unemployment combined with weak governance and limited rule of law (see Hannan, 2012). The economic opportunities that piracy presented soon encouraged people to engage in piracy beyond any concern about protecting their fishing industry, motivated solely by profit and keen to retain instability in Somalia in order to maintain their illegal operations.

Piracy rapidly grew in this area for a number of reasons: a number of successful attacks and the significant ransoms that could be secured, which in turn could be invested in more advanced operations and equipment (Binkley and Smith, 2012). Busy international shipping lanes in the Gulf of Aden also presented many opportunities.

Reasons for the explosion of Somali piracy can also be found in conflict and the effect it has had on Somali society: weak governance creates space for organised criminal networks and militia groups, encourages corruption, and does little to assuage public grievances and disquiet; security sector structures lacking capacity undermine efforts to enforce the law and bring perpetrators to justice; underdevelopment and particularly high levels of unemployment results in swathes of new recruits and community support for pirates; the widespread availability of small arms and light weapons and the large number of conflict-experienced men fortify piracy.

Some scholars consider that there are other conflict-related factors which can help to explain the rise of Somali piracy. Beri (2011), for instance, refers to the hostility between Eritrea and Ethiopia which was being played out in proxy wars in Somalia and elsewhere, the US securitisation of Somalia as result of the 'war on terror' and the lack of resources to support the African Union Mission in Somalia (AMISOM).

(Continued)

Between 2010 and 2016, Somali piracy decreased dramatically, as a result of concerted efforts on the part of the international community, including the deployment of navies and military efforts. However, Somali piracy made a resurgence in 2017 with double the number of attacks as the previous year and the first successful hijack of a commercial ship in five years in March 2017 (ICC IMB PRC, 2019). The resurgence was partly due to the decrease in the number of counter-piracy patrols as well as well as less rigid enforcement of self-protection measures due to complacency assuming that the threat from piracy in the region was declining (Dahir, 2018). Significantly, it must also be said that some of the root causes and enablers of piracy have yet to be addressed; initial grievances have yet to be addressed and unemployment remains rampant. The recent and sudden increase in Somali piracy after a significant time during which it was in decline, underscores the importance of taking a comprehensive approach to dealing with the threat it poses; military and hard security responses to piracy will be insufficient, at least in the medium and long term, unless efforts to address prospective causes and enablers are also taken. Ironically, the success of military responses to piracy off the coast of Somalia led to the proposed land-based solutions being overlooked and underfunded by the international community (Shortland, 2018). The recent resurgence in Somali piracy underscores the need for a land-based solution if successes are to be sustainable.

A piracy–conflict nexus?

While armed conflict may play a role in the development of piracy in some places, it is also clear that piracy can feed into disorder and insecurity, undermining efforts to improve governance, the rule of law and socio-economic development. For instance, UNSCR 1816 suggested that that 'the incidents of piracy and armed robbery against vessels in the territorial waters of Somalia and the high seas off the coast of Somalia exacerbate the situation in Somalia' (UNSCR, 2008: 2).

Aside from increasing the risk of conflict, there are also fears that piracy can increase the risk of terrorism (see House of Commons Foreign Affairs Committee, 2011). The distinction between piracy and terrorism is sometimes vague, although most distinguish between the economic motives of pirates and the political motives of terrorists (Chalk, 2008; Hanson, 2009). There has been, nonetheless, fear that terrorists may be able to access funding through piracy, as well as target commercial traffic and so harm western interests. For example, there were concerns about links between Somali pirates and the terrorist group al-Shabab (Bento, 2011; IISS, 2011).

Effective counter-piracy measures require a multi-faceted and co-ordinated approach that address a range of issues and a range of actors. It is also important that root causes are addressed and national and regional actors take the lead in determining and implementing responses. It is equally important that the cure does not exacerbate the symptoms or feed into other threats, and that the strategic and geopolitical dimensions of piracy and counter-piracy are recognised. We might consider, for instance, the role that counter-terrorism has in the exercise of power on the international stage (see Willett, 2011). Equally, we might ask whether the focus of the international community on the security and governance needs of the Somali people resulted in part from concerns about individual national security, economic and strategic interests (see Stroehlein and Kroslak, 2008).

Part 4 – Organised Crime

Defining organised crime

The United Nations Convention Against Transnational Organised Crime does not define transnational organised crime (TOC) as such, but does define organised criminal groups; as a structured group of people acting together with the aim of committing serious crimes to benefit themselves financially or materially. This lack of definition of organised crime was intended to allow for a broad applicability to the new types of crime that continuously emerge (UNODC, 2019). Nonetheless, based upon the definition of organised criminal groups, it can be read that organised crime encompasses profit-motivated serious crime and, where it is transnational organised crime, has international implications (UNODC, 2019).

Defining organised crime is, however, a subjective and often political activity. There is no universally agreed definition, and it remains a label that is traditionally applied by the state. In the context of conflict-affected environments in particular, where the legitimacy of the state is often questioned, the state's view of what constitutes organised crime may not always be shared by the people affected by or, unsurprisingly, participating in it, and the term may not capture the complex interpenetration of the legitimate and the illegitimate, the state and crime, that is part of the lived experience of many populations in weak states and conflict-affected areas (Cockayne and Pfister, 2008: 13).

As Cockayne and Pfister (2008) suggest, labelling something as organised crime has policy implications and promotes law enforcement responses over political, economic and social ones. In conflict-affected environments, the distinction between organised criminal groups and state structures also often becomes blurred, where they resemble each other in terms of the functions or services they provide, and where government officials can form part of the complex organised criminal networks. Consequently, use of the term 'organised crime', particularly in conflict-affected environments, requires sensitivity to the context-specific interpretations and connotations of the term.

Without a shared understanding of the term 'organised crime', as we discussed earlier with regard to terrorism, effective and coherent efforts to fight it are problematised 'because how the problem of organised crime is defined goes a long way toward determining how laws are framed, how investigations and prosecutions are conducted, how research studies are done and, increasingly, how mutual legal assistance across national borders is or is not rendered' (Finckenauer, 2005: 68). For an indication of the lack of universal agreement of the term organised crime, see Klaus von Lampe's collection of over 200 definitions of the term (on his website at: www.organized-crime.de/index.html).

Types of organised crime

Until recently, organised crime was largely a threat contained within individual nations. However, globalisation has resulted in organised crime becoming increasingly transnational, with organised criminal groups exploiting the structural changes and technological advancements associated with globalisation (see Worcester, 2007). Consequently, organised crime is becoming an increasingly powerful international threat (see Shaw, 2011; UNODC, 2010c, 2012, 2019).

The 2010 UNODC Report *The Globalization of Crime* (UNODC, 2010c) provides one of the first attempts at a comprehensive assessment of the global organised crime market, looking at the threat of transnational organised crime, which includes the smuggling of people, drugs, weapons and illicit resources as well as cybercrime, piracy and environmental crime. The report discusses the nature and extent of firearms smuggling, which supplies markets where people seek weapons for criminal purposes (the flow from US to Mexico, for instance) and where they seek weapons for political purposes (the flow from Eastern Europe to Africa, for instance). With respect to arms smuggling for political purposes, UNODC details how the process is often different to other forms of smuggling, which are entirely clandestine, as it often takes place under a veneer of legality, depending on corrupt officials.

The report also looks at the production, transit and consumption of illicit drugs, focussing in particular on the transnational flows of heroin and cocaine. Most of the world's heroin comes from Afghanistan, and many of the profits fund organised criminal groups, terrorist groups and insurgent groups (UNODC, 2019). UNODC (2017) estimates that in 2016, non-state armed groups raised USD150million from the opiate trade. Elsewhere, the drug trade supports non-state armed groups and contributes to sustained insecurity. In Colombia, for instance, while FARC-EP (Fuerzas Armadas Revolucionarias de Colombia-Ejército del Pueblo, in English – Revolutionary Armed Forces of Colombia – People's Army) pledged to disengage from the drug trade as part of their commitments under the 2016 peace agreement, other non-state armed groups, notably BACRIM (*bandas criminales emergentes*, in English – emerging criminal bands), are taking control of territories and businesses previously controlled by FARC. This example shows the way in which organised crime can fuel and be fuelled by armed conflict, and the frequent lack of clear distinction between insurgent, terrorist and organised criminal groups (see Box 11.6). We earlier discussed the blurred line between terrorist and insurgent groups – the line is also blurred with organised criminal groups, particularly where insurgent groups employ terrorist methods and rely on profits from organised crime to sustain themselves.

Organised criminal groups are also involved in the illicit trade of other goods, outside weapons and drugs, including the trade in endangered species (as has occurred in Somalia and Sudan, for instance) and natural resources (such as the trade in diamonds from conflict zones in Sierra Leone, Ivory Coast, Liberia, Democratic Republic of the Congo (DRC) and Angola – see Box 11.7). Environmental organised crime has fuelled many conflicts, with profits funding government armed forces and insurgent groups.

Box 11.6: Crime and Conflict in Colombia

In Colombia, crime is inextricably linked with conflict. The production and traf-ficking of drugs has sustained and intensified the armed conflict (Sánchez et al., 2005). Insurgent and criminal groups use extortion and kidnapping as a source of funds, and to pacify communities and control territories (Abierta, 2016; Colak and Pearce, 2015; FIP, 2016; Sánchez et al., 2005). A vicious circle has ensued whereby political and criminal violence are often indistinguishable, and the crimi-nality resulting from conflict has enabled the escalation of the conflict (Sánchez et al., 2005). The opportunities offered by the drugs trade, and the many other illicit economies that exist in Colombia, have attracted paramilitary, criminal and guerrilla groups and others, including officials in the state security sector and administration. There are alliances between these groups and an illicit order has been created, in part due to the absence of the state in many parts of the territory, which appear to have assumed a stranglehold on Colombia beyond the logic and the lifetime of the conflict (Abierta, 2016; FIP, 2016). The penetration of organised crime into the fabric of Colombian society is unlikely to be easily addressed in the aftermath of armed conflict and will continue to pose threats to security and the longer-term peace process.

The trafficking of people is also a hugely lucrative illicit business. The traffick-ing of people is often for sexual exploitation. The 2016 UNODC *Global Report on Trafficking in Persons* reported that between 2012 and 2014, 54% of trafficking victims detected were trafficked for the purpose of sexual exploitation, with a further 38% trafficked for forced labour (UNODC, 2016). In 2014, there were 17,752 victims of trafficking detected in 85 countries. In this year, 51% of traf-ficking victims detected were women, 28% children and the remaining 21% men. Females (girls and women) comprised 70% of victims of trafficking detected in 2014 (UNODC, 2016). Since 2014, the number of victims of trafficking reported and the number of perpetrators convicted has significantly increased. For instance, the number of people convicted of trafficking of people increased by 30% in 2015 upon the previous year and by 67% in 2016 in comparison with 2015. However, it is unclear whether this is because trafficking is increasing or detection is improving (UNODC, 2018).

As described by UNODC (2016, 2018), conflict can fuel the trafficking of per-sons because conditions can be more favourable to traffickers (where there is limited rule of law, and state security and justice sector institutions are weak) and because people fleeing conflict may be more desperate (facing dire circumstances, with immediate needs and few legitimate channels for regular migration). Family ties, community support mechanisms and other networks and forms of support also often break during conflict, particularly as a result of displacement; this can further increase the likelihood of exploitation by traffickers. Armed groups can also engage in trafficking, for forced labour, forced mobilisation or for sexual exploitation (UNODC, 2016, 2018). For the same reasons which make conflict zones conducive for trafficking, post-conflict environments also present favourable

Box 11.7: Blood Diamonds

Earlier we discussed the causes of conflict and considered the resource curse, where a surfeit of natural resources can instigate or fuel conflict. We also looked at the greed versus grievance debate when considering how conflicts begin and are sustained.

Blood diamonds, also referred to as conflict or war diamonds, are diamonds mined in conflict zones, whose trade supports the conflict by financing insurgent groups and others. The diamond trade has supported conflicts in Sierra Leone, Ivory Coast, Liberia, DRC, Angola and elsewhere.

The Kimberly Process Certification Scheme, established in 2002 to curtail the flow of diamonds from conflict zones in part by certifying 'conflict-free' diamonds, has not been wholly successful (see DeWaal, 2013).

However, while exploitation of an abundance of natural resources has fuelled many conflicts, there are many resource-rich countries which are stable. Some scholars have suggested that an abundance of natural resources needs to coexist with other factors to increase the likelihood of conflict. For instance, Basedau and Lay (2009) suggest that resource dependence in conjunction with low resource wealth per capita might create instability, whereas countries that use revenue from resources for large-scale distribution and investment in the security sector are more likely to be stable. Koning (2008) suggests that weak governance and lack of credibility as a result of government mismanagement and corruption in non-renewable resource sectors contributed to the resource-driven conflicts of Sierra Leone and DRC, as did the revenues from easily extractable, high-value natural resources that helped sustain armed groups. Labour exploitation and unequal distribution of wealth also helped fuel the dynamics that sustained conflict in these two countries.

We also need to consider the role that rich, stable countries have played in fuelling the illicit trade in blood diamonds and other natural resources; the market, of course, depends as much on demand as it does on supply.

conditions for traffickers. Indeed, those mandated to protect and facilitate peacebuilding can present opportunities for traffickers, particularly for the purpose of sexual exploitation (UNODC, 2016) and are sometimes engaged in such activities themselves. (Jackson and Beswick, 2018; UN Women, 2019).

The threat of organised crime

The threat from organised crime is not merely economic, but it is also strategic. Organised criminal groups buy power by paying people in government and state security structures, for instance, and by influencing elections. The consequences are severe, threatening security and stability, particularly in conflict-affected environments and places afflicted by disasters or development challenges. Aside from economic and strategic threats, organised crime undermines security, development, governance and the rule of law: it fuels corruption, criminality and insecurity, and it undermines socio-economic growth and stability (see UNODC, 2019).

In human terms, many tens of thousands of people each year die from illicit drug-related deaths. HIV epidemics have been caused by injecting drug-use and the illicit drug trade has fuelled violence, crime and insurgency (see UNODC, 2019). With respect to other forms of organised crime, many people also lose their lives as a result of firearms or because they have been a victim of trafficking or migrant smuggling (see UNODC, 2019).

The fight against organised crime

Much has been done to attempt to combat organised crime over the last quarter century or so, beginning in particular with the World Ministerial Conference on Organized Transnational Crime in 1994. This Conference ultimately led to the UN Convention against Transnational Organized Crime (the Palermo Convention), which came into force in 2003. This Convention is the primary international instrument against organised crime with three supplementary protocols: to Prevent, Suppress and Punish Trafficking in Persons, especially Women and Children (Trafficking in Persons Protocol); against the Smuggling of Migrants by Land, Sea and Air (Smuggling of Migrants Protocol); and against the Illicit Manufacturing of and Trafficking in Firearms, their Parts and Components and Ammunition (Firearms Protocol). The UN Office on Drugs and Crime (UNODC) is the guardian of the Convention and its Protocols, and plays a key role in helping states combat organised crime.

This treaty reflects the fact that, in order to effectively combat organised crime, which is increasingly transnational, it is vital that the approach is also global. This means that state responses to organised crime need to be co-ordinated with each other and contribute to a coherent and comprehensive strategy. Given that organised crime can overwhelm conflict-affected or poor countries, which do not have the capacity and resources to effectively fight it, it is particularly important that international support is forthcoming. It is also vital that – as with any economic activity – the supply and demand ends of the chains are addressed, since 'strategies aimed at the groups will not stop the illicit activities if the dynamics of the market remain unaddressed' (UNODC, 2010c: v), because other groups and individuals will take the place of any who have been disrupted or uprooted. Moreover, as noted in the case of trafficking, it is also important that accurate data on global organised crime is obtained and analysed in order to inform appropriate strategies. Similarly, Cockayne and Pfister (2008) argue that lack of knowledge about the relationship between organised crime and conflict in the international community and academia hampers the extent to which responses to both can be effective (see UNODC, 2018 for data on and analysis of the relationship between organised crime and armed conflict).

McMullin (2009: 97) also emphasises the importance of not exclusively relying on law enforcement approaches to deal with organised crime, advocating a multi-pronged approach, since 'there are no simple solutions to the dependence of some individuals on organised criminality for their livelihoods'. Addressing organised crime also needs to be context-specific and informed by an in-depth conflict analysis, as with all interventions in conflict and post-conflict environments. Stepanova

(2010) also underscores the importance of building the capacity of the state in post-conflict environments, not least the ability to provide minimal law and order, if organised crime is to be effectively addressed. For peace operations, Cockayne (2011) emphasises the importance of developing a more strategic approach and recognising that organised crime constitutes a strategy of governance. Organised crime is thus a strategy 'used by business, military and political entrepreneurs to gain, hold and wield power within a violent political economy' (Cockayne, 2011: 10).

Links between conflict and organised crime

In 2004 at a meeting of the UN High-level Panel on Threats, Challenges and Change, transnational organised crime was identified as one of 'six clusters of threats with which the world must be concerned now and in the decades ahead' (UNSG, 2004a: 12) alongside social and economic threats (including poverty, environmental degradation and infectious diseases) conflict, terrorism and WMD. Organised crime can affect security, stability, governance and development in countries where weaknesses in these areas – which are prevalent in conflict-affected countries – may facilitate its dominance. Links between conflict-affected or conflict-vulnerable states and organised crime have also been regularly referred to or implied in political discourse and, as outlined by Patrick (2011b), form part of popular mythology.

In investigating the link between organised crime and conflict, a number of avenues could be looked at, including:

- The vulnerability of conflict-affected countries to organised crime
- The impact of organised crime on conflict and post-conflict countries, increasing the risks of protracted or recurrent conflicts
- The destabilising effect of organised crime on countries where governance is weak and development challenges are severe, thus increasing the likelihood of the outbreak of conflict
- The profit-seeking motive of those engaged in organised crime that can help explain the causes of conflict.

Countries in conflict or in its immediate aftermath are vulnerable to organised crime because state institutions are weak, illegitimate and/or corrupt (or corruptible). There is little will or capacity within the criminal justice system to address organised crime, governance is poor and development challenges are often severe. The risks are thus limited and the rewards comparatively large. In these circumstances, organised crime can take root, with governance and security being further undermined to the extent that conflicts can become protracted or can recur, particularly given that those involved in organised crime (as well as insurgent or armed opposition groups, who can rely on the funds accrued from organised crime) have a vested interest in undermining stability and ensuring that the state and its institutions remain weak and ineffective (see McMullin, 2009; Shaw, 2011; UNODC, 2010a, 2010c). Conflicts have to be financed and, although the exact relationship between crime and conflict in different cases remains controversial, 'drugs pay for bullets and provide a lifestyle to combatants that makes them less likely to come to the negotiating table' (UNODC, 2010c: 221). Looking at Afghanistan, almost all the opium produced there came from the provinces in the south and west where governmental control was weakest. Here, as in other conflict-affected places, both insurgents and those involved with organised crime can have a vested interest in maintaining instability and often work together to maintain the status quo (see UNODC, 2010c). Ultimately, a vicious circle can thus ensue, with organised crime exacerbating the very conditions that are conducive to it (Figure 11.3).

A number of studies have raised concerns about the compartmentalisation of security issues and actors as a contributory factor to the lack of progress in dealing effectively with organised crime:

> Security challenges tend to be categorized and compartmentalized rather than connected. The "space between" is ignored – that is, the connections between trafficking in different commodities or between different kinds of actors. (IPI, 2009: 32)

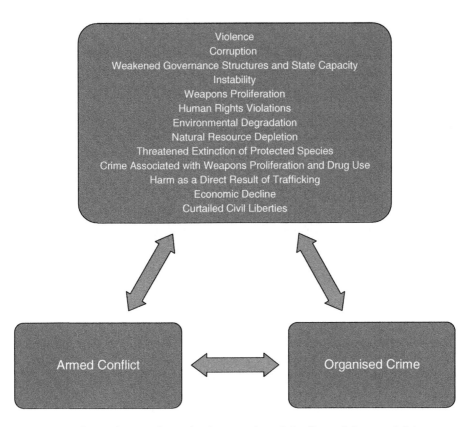

Figure 11.3 The Symbiotic Relationship between Armed Conflict and Organised Crime

Boussiouni (CFR, 2010) refers to the many resolutions dealing with separate aspects of terrorism and also separate issues related to drugs, while no comprehensive resolution addresses all aspects, let alone connects the aspects to broader issues concerning organised crime and conflict. And as mentioned earlier, when looking at effective ways in which to combat organised crime, it is important to reflect upon how the label is used (and not used), who has the power to use that label and what policy-implications certain terms may have (see Cockayne and Pfister, 2008).

Indeed some (such as Ruggiero, 2007) suggest that in fact war is an extension of crimes of the powerful. Insofar as it may be motivated by profit, be particularly devastating in its effects and involve a structured group of people acting in concert, 'war-making' (see Tilly, 1985) could be deemed to be a form of organised crime. Indeed, Tilly argues that war-making and state-making are interdependent and the processes of both, 'when less successful and smaller in scale', are called organised crime (Tilly, 1985: 170).

Returning to the link between conflict and organised crime, McMullin (2009) describes how the demand for weapons by insurgent groups increases the level of organised criminal activity to meet this demand. However, the existence of organised crime in conflict-affected or conflict-vulnerable environments cannot be explained simply by organised criminal groups taking advantage of the weaknesses in these environments. This ignores the demand side of the equation and encourages an exclusively law enforcement-response to a problem that is much more complex, since conflict also stimulates a demand both for protection from violence and for goods and services which have been made scarce by the fighting and cannot be provided by the state. As McMullin (2009) explains, therefore, it is not simply that organised criminal groups simply step in to take advantage of conflict, but that the demands produced by conflict-affected environments lead to the engagement of criminal and other groups to meet those demands.

An effective response to organised crime in post-conflict environments, for instance, can thus not be limited to the role of law enforcement. Weaknesses in governance and underdevelopment need to be addressed, as do factors related to demand as well as supply. Similarly, while there is undoubtedly a relationship between conflict and organised crime (see Steenkamp, 2017; UNODC, 2018), the biggest market for illicit goods are still the richest countries, which is where transnational organised crime is strongest (UNODC, 2010c). Thus, an approach to organised crime that focuses or places the blame solely upon conflict-affected or conflict-vulnerable countries will remain ineffective. Patrick (2011b) argues that geographic location and proximity to global markets is a key factor in determining the prevalence of certain organised criminal activity. Additionally, conflict-affected or conflict-vulnerable environments can be detrimental to all business, including organised crime, with the lack of security and limited access to infrastructure and modern financial services that it often entails. However, whether or not transnational organised crime targets places affected by conflict and other weak states, it makes states weaker (Patrick, 2011b: 163).

Organised crime and the causes of conflict

Where organised crime can increase the risk of protracted or recurrent conflicts, it can also increase instability, insecurity and the risk of conflict in other places where governance is weak and development challenges are severe (such as parts of Central America and West Africa).

With regard to the profit-seeking motive of those engaged in organised crime contributing to the cause of conflict, we have considered the validity of greed as a causal factor of conflict in Chapter 2 (see particularly Collier, 2007). McMullin (2009) suggests that organised crime in vulnerable states has contributed to conflict, but there are generally other socio-political factors involved, notably the political power associated with resource ownership and control that motivates resource extraction and smuggling in such conflicts as the DRC, Sierra Leone, Liberia and Angola. There is often a need, of course, to sustain insurgencies, which is where organised crime can play a key role in the transition to armed conflict; insurgent groups need to secure weapons, arms and sustenance for combatants, hence the engagement in organised crime and/or involvement of organised criminal groups to supply these requirements (see Boer and Bosetti, 2015).

Organised crime and peace processes

The evidence suggests that organised crime often flourishes better immediately after conflicts than during them, where lack of stability and predictability can discourage organised criminal activity (Berdal, 2009; Boer and Bosetti, 2015; Cheng, 2012). Organised criminal groups can also provide 'a restored sense of masculinity for ex-male combatants who might feel as though they lost power and status by surrendering their weapons and position' (Boer and Bosetti, 2015: 12). Furthermore, peace operations can lead to other factors that can increase the prevalence of organised criminal activities. For instance, peace operations can lead to an increased demand for illicit goods (such as pirated DVDs or commercial sex) as well as be a potential source of supply (with the theft of humanitarian aid being commonplace, for instance) (Cockayne and Pfister, 2008; see also van der Lijn, 2018). Occasionally, those working for peace operations can also sometimes be directly involved in organised crime:

> Examples to date include the alleged role of Ukrainian contingents in trafficking fuel in Bosnia during the 1990s, the alleged involvement of peace operations in the Middle East in trafficking in cigarettes and vehicles, the alleged involvement of contingents in Africa in smuggling diamonds, gold and arms, and the role of peace operations personnel in numerous locations in organised sexual exploitation and abuse. (Cockayne and Pfister, 2008: 26)

Peace operations and other international interventions can also affect a range of socio-economic and structural factors that can increase the prevalence of organised criminal activity. Conversely, while the prevalence of organised crime can undermine efforts to consolidate peace, it can also sometimes reinforce peace processes where 'new opportunities for organised crime during conflict can create new stakeholders in peace, with an interest in investing into post-conflict reconstruction' (Cockayne and Pfister, 2008: 29). Given that organised crime can also often fill security gaps and respond to other unmet needs in conflict-affected environments, it could be argued that, in certain circumstances, focussing the efforts of the international community on managing potential spoilers of the peace process rather than combating the wide and complex spectrum of organised crime might prove more effective in the short term (Cockayne and Pfister, 2008).

Combatting organised crime in conflict-affected environments

To conclude, conflict and organised crime can be seen to be integrally related, with one often leading to the other where '[transnational] organised crime is both a symptom and a cause of instability in a diverse range of regions around the world' (UNODC, 2010c: 272). However, while conflict and organised crime are symbiotically related, as McMullin (2009) highlights, conflict is not a sufficient explanation for organised crime and nor is organised crime a sufficient explanation for conflict. Nonetheless, both can be said to facilitate each other, with organised crime increasing the likelihood, protraction or recurrence of conflict and, conversely, conflict increasingly the likelihood of organised crime taking root and constituting a more serious threat to security and stability. While a vicious circle can thus ensue with conflict and organised crime becoming ever more deeply entrenched, opportunities are also presented: efforts to combat transnational organised crime, which need not and should not be made exclusively in the conflict-affected environment, can carry peace dividends. For instance, efforts aimed at addressing contraband flows can 'play a pivotal role in addressing civil conflict, by removing the profit motive that keeps many antagonists armed and in the field. Put simply, reducing crime can help foster peace' (UNODC, 2010c: 272).

Efforts to counter organised crime and thus enhance stability will, however, require a co-ordinated global strategy focussed on crime prevention, tackling both supply and demand, as well as enhancing the capabilities of countries attractive to those involved in organised crime. The latter would involve supporting law enforcement efforts but also addressing governance and developmental weaknesses, which make the countries so attractive to those who want to evade detection by law enforcement officials or at least buy them off.

Conclusion

This chapter has discussed some of the core transnational threats commonly associated with armed conflict and often blamed upon conflict-affected environments. The main argument has been that these transnational threats are related to conflict, but there is more to it than the simple causal relationship often alluded to by policy-makers, politicians and media outlets. For instance, conflict-affected environments which lack state capacity may be less resilient to the operation of terrorists – but those who are most targeted by terrorist activity are those within conflict-affected environments, not those from more peaceful states who may fear the consequences of conflict elsewhere. While conflict-affected environments may enable terrorist activity (although they are not always the most conducive), triggers and drivers may, in fact, emanate from outside the conflict environment, including counter-terrorism and counter-insurgency efforts. Likewise, conflict-affected environments may lack state capacity and political will to combat the threat posed by piracy – but, as the Somalia example shows, piracy may in fact be a response to the activities of others, often from more peaceful and stable states, taking advantage of a weak state. In respect of organised crime, it is clear that it can grow in conflict-affected environments with limited rule of law, weak state security institutions and porous borders. Indeed, conflict-affected environments are often synonymous with organised crime, with the links between conflict-affected environments and organised crime much more pervasive and their effects much more penetrating than those between terrorism or piracy and conflict-affected environments. It is also evident that organised crime can get a stranglehold in conflict-affected environments and thereby increase insecurity and violence and undermine efforts to build peace. Scholars have also explored how organised crime can sustain armed conflict and undermine efforts to build peace, and have studied the relationship between conflict and organised crime in various conflict-affected environments, including Syria (Steenkamp, 2017), Mali (Lacher, 2012), Iraq (Williams, 2009), Afghanistan (Goodhand, 2008) and Colombia (Felbab-Brown, 2005; Garzón-Vergara, 2015). However, the role that other countries and other actors play in the relationship between organised crime and any particular conflict-affected environment also needs attending to if efforts to combat its threat are to be successful.

In short, there is a need to critically engage with discourses that associate conflict with terrorism, piracy and organised crime. There is also a need to understand the complex, context-specific causal factors and ever-changing socio-economic and political dynamics of terrorism, piracy, organised crime and other transnational security threats if those threats are to be effectively addressed. This chapter has also emphasised the need to critically reflect upon how and why concepts such as terrorism, piracy and crime are used, what explanations are given, what the policy implications are of the use of concepts and explanations, and ultimately who has the power to influence which concepts and explanations are used.

Summary of Key Issues

- There is a common perception that the global risks posed by countries in conflict, or at least vulnerable to it, are greater than the threats posed by stable countries.
- Even though the effects of conflict are felt beyond the borders of the conflict zone, it is important to remember that those most affected by conflict remain those in the midst of it.

- The effects of conflict can 'spill over' the borders of a state and potentially create regional instability.
- Lack of governance, security and the rule of law in conflict-affected or conflict-vulnerable states are widely considered to be conducive to transnational security threats such as terrorism, organised crime and piracy.
- It is important to be attentive to when labels such as terrorism and organised crime are used, by whom and what the policy implications might be.
- The complexity and context-specific nature of the causes, drivers and enablers of terrorism, piracy and organised crime need to inform efforts to counter these threats.
- Many of the countries most impacted by terrorism are affected by conflict, but not all conflict-affected places experience high levels of terrorist activity or become sanctuaries for terrorist groups, and many attacks have been planned from wealthy and stable countries.
- Likewise, while conflict-affected environments can be conducive to piracy which, in turn, feeds further insecurity, many places affected by conflict do not pose serious threats of piracy, and places where governance structures support piracy rather than are absent (as might be the case in conflict zones) appear to be more favourable to piracy.
- Organised crime fuels insecurity and can increase the risk of protracted or recurrent conflicts, while, conversely, conflict and, notably, post-conflict environments can be conducive to organised crime.
- While there is a relationship between conflict and organised crime, the biggest market for illicit goods are the richest countries, which is where transnational organised crime remains strong.

Reflective Question

How would more successful peacebuilding interventions contribute to addressing some of the transnational threats that exist today?

List of Core Resources

Transnational threats

Chomsky, N. (2017) *Prospects for Survival* (video). Available at www.youtube.com/watch?v=t0TE1Ib-O_M&list=RDt0TE1Ib-O_M&t=463.

De Maio, J. (2010) 'Is War Contagious? The Transnationalization of Conflict in Darfur', *African Studies Quarterly*, 11(4): 25–44.

Patrick, S. (2011) *Weak Links: Fragile States, Global Threats, and International Security* (New York: Oxford University Press).

The Stanley Foundation (2012) *Fragile States, Global Consequences* (video). Available at https://vimeo.com/26342266.

World Economic Forum (2017) *The Global Risks Report*, Geneva: World Economic Forum. Available at www3.weforum.org/docs/GRR17_Report_web.pdf.

Terrorism

Crenshaw, M. (2014) 'Terrorism Research: The Record', *International Interactions: Empirical and Theoretical Research in International Relations*, 40(4): 556–67.

Dim, E. (2017) 'An Integrated Theoretical Approach to the Persistence of Boko Haram Violent Extremism in Nigeria', *Journal of Peacebuilding and Development* 12(2): 36–50.

Glazzard, A. Jesperson, S., Maguire, T. and Winterbotham, E. (2017) 'Islamist Violent Extremism: A New Form of Conflict or Business as Usual?', *Stability: International Journal of Security and Development*, 6(1):13, 1–19.

Martin, G. and Prager, F. (2019) *Terrorism: An International Perspective* (Thousand Oaks: Sage).

Matfess, H. and Miklaucic, M. (eds.) (2016) *Beyond Convergence: World Without Order* (Washington DC: Center for Complex Operations Institute for National Strategic Studies National Defense University). Available at http://globalinitiative.net/wp-content/uploads/2016/10/beyond-convergence-world-without-order-.pdf.

Pollard, S., Poplack, D. and Kevin Carroll Casey, K. (2017) 'Understanding the Islamic State's competitive advantages: Remaking state and nationhood in the Middle East and North Africa', *Terrorism and Political Violence,* 29(6): 1045–65.

Richmond, O. and Tellidis, I. (2012) 'The Complex Relationship Between Peacebuilding and Terrorism Approaches: Towards Post-Terrorism and a Post-Liberal Peace?', *Terrorism and Political Violence*, 24 (1): 120–43.

Sandler, T. (2014), 'The Analaytical Study of Terrorism: Taking Stock', *Journal of Peace Research* 51(2): 257–71.

Schomerus, M. and El Taraboulsi-McCarthy, S. with Sandhar, J. (2017) *Countering violent extremism* (Topic Guide) (Birmingham, UK: GSDRC, University of Birmingham). Available at www.gsdrc.org/wp-content/uploads/2017/03/CVE.pdf.

Silke, A. (2018) *Routledge Handbook of Terrorism and Counterterrorism* (New York: Routledge).

Transnational Initiative Countering Violent Extremism (TICVE) (2015) *Countering Violent Extremism in the Wider Atlantic* (video). Available at www.youtube.com/watch?v=jsEzl4ZlfGo.

True, J. and Eddyono, S. (2017) *Preventing Violent Extremism: Gender Perspectives and Women's Roles* (Melbourne: Monash Gender, Peace and Security (GPS) Centre). Available at https://docs.wixstatic.com/ugd/b4aef1_5780b931ae164ace83e5377c490f05e1.pdf.

World Affairs Council of Greater Houston (WAC) (2016) *Exploiting Disorder: al-Qaeda and the Islamic State – International Crisis Group* (video). Available at www.youtube.com/watch?v=sVfIeWe2H7I&index=20&list=PLboAe3-SRewrm6HSWrq2a-cIdV8prcSah.

Zala, B. and Rogers, P. (2011) 'The "Other" Global Security Challenges: Socioeconomic and Environmental Realities after the War on Terror', *The RUSI Journal*, 156 (4): 26–33.

Piracy

Daxecker, U. and Prins, B. (2017) 'Financing rebellion: Using piracy to explain and predict conflict intensity in Africa and Southeast Asia', *Journal of Peace Research*, 54(2): 215–30.

Elmi, A. Ladan Affi, L., Knight, W. and Said Mohamed, S. (2015) 'Piracy in the Horn of Africa Waters: Definitions, History, and Modern Causes', *African Security*, 8(3): 147–65.

ISSAfrica (2017) *View on Africa: Is Piracy Back?* (video). Available at www.youtube.com/watch?v=iEKaua-Joq0.

Rohwerder, B. (2016) *Piracy in the Horn of Africa, West Africa and the Strait of Malacca* (GSDRC Rapid Literature Review). (Birmingham, UK: GSDRC, University of Birmingham). Available at www.gsdrc.org/wp-content/uploads/2016/09/piracy_rohwerder.pdf.

Sergi, B. and Giacomo Morabito, G. (2016) 'The Pirates' Curse: Economic Impacts of the Maritime Piracy', *Studies in Conflict and Terrorism*, 39(10): 935–52.

Shortland, A. and Varese, F. (2016) 'State-Building, Informal Governance and Organised Crime: The Case of Somali Piracy', *Political Studies*, 64(4): 811–31.

University of Chicago (2012) *Pirate State: Inside Somalia's Terrorism at Sea* (video). Available at www.youtube.com/watch?v=R5wVvZJf4b0.

Organised crime

Centre for Security Governance (CSG) (2017) *eSeminar – Organized Crime, Corruption & Peacebuilding* (video). Available at www.youtube.com/watch?v=8vZFk15EEF8.

Cockayne, J. (2013) 'Chasing Shadows: Strategic Responses to Organised Crime in Conflict-Affected Situations', *The RUSI Journal*, 158(2): 10–24.

Cockayne, J. and Lupel, A. (eds) (2011) *Peace Operations and Organized Crime: Enemies or Allies* (New York: Routledge).

De Boer, J. and Bosetti, L. (2017) *The Crime-Conflict Nexus: Assessing the Threat and Developing Solutions*, United Nations University (UNU) Centre for Policy Research, Crime-Conflict Nexus Series: No 1, May 2017 (Tokyo: UNU). Available at https://cpr.unu.edu/the-crime-conflict-nexus-assessing-the-threat-and-developing-solutions.html.

International Peace Institute (IPI) (2014) *Building Peace at the Nexus of Organized Crime, Conflict, and Extremism* (video). Available at www.youtube.com/watch?v=xXIOWue0Ir0.

McMullin, J. (2009) 'Organised Criminal Groups and Conflict: The Nature and Consequences of Interdependence', *Civil Wars*, 11(1): 75–102.

Miraglia, P., Ochoa, R. and Briscoe, I. (2012) *Transnational Organised Crime and Fragile States* (Paris: OECD). Available at www.oecd-ilibrary.org/docserver/download/5k49dfg88s40-en.pd?expires=1512903192&id=id&accname=guest&checksum=21F75184B2272220822D9DB5C0D9E078.

Rausch, C. (ed.) (2017) *Fighting Serious Crimes: Strategies and Tactics for Conflict-Affected Societies* (Washington DC: USIP).

Reitano, T., Jesperson, S., Bird Ruiz-Benitez de Lugo, L. (eds.) (2018) *Militarised Responses to Transnational Organised Crime: The War on Crime*, London: Palgrave Macmillan.

Rosato, V. (2016) '"Hybrid Orders" between Terrorism and Organized Crime: The Case of Al Qaeda in the Islamic Maghreb', *African Security*, 9(2): 110–35.

Sargent, K. (2014) *Re-thinking Post-Conflict State Building: Developing Better Governance and Fighting Corruption* (University of Leicester) (video). Available at www.youtube.com/watch?v=3dx6gq2IiMY&list=PLjQX5EXgm57S0L7nT-QMVhQLKi YNsSPxu.

Shaw, M. and Reitano, T. (2017) *Global Illicit Flows and Local Conflict Dynamics: The Case for Pre-Emptive Analysis and Experimental Policy Options*, United Nations University (UNU) Centre for Policy Research, Crime-Conflict Nexus Series: No 2, May 2017 (Tokyo: UNU). Available at https://i.unu.edu/media/cpr.unu.edu/attachment/2536/Synopsis-Crime-Conflict-FINAL.pdf.

Steenkamp, C. (2017) 'The Crime-Conflict Nexus and the Civil War in Syria', *Stability: International Journal of Security and Development*, 6(1):11, 1–18.

UN (2016a) *Security Sector Reform Integrated Technical Guidance Notes: Transnational Organised Crime and Security Sector Reform* (New York: UN). Available at www.unodc.org/documents/organized-crime/SSR_TOC_ITGN_2016_WEB.pdf.

UNODC (2018) *Global Report on Trafficking in Persons*, Vienna: UNODC. Available at: www.unodc.org/unodc/data-and-analysis/glotip.html. In particular, read 'Booklet 2 – Trafficking in Persons in the context of armed conflict'.

Conclusion

Understanding and Addressing the Challenges of Building Security and Justice After Conflict

The aim of this book has been to provide a basic overview of the ways in which security and justice are built in societies emerging from conflict, the challenges faced and ways in which those challenges can be addressed. The intention has been to provide a broad overview of the many actors and activities involved in building security and justice after conflict, and draw attention to the principles which guide – or should guide – this work. The book is designed to develop knowledge and understanding of the practical ways in which security and justice can be developed after conflict, as well as ways in which to address the broader international security risks posed by conflict-affected countries. Hopefully, in doing so this has enabled the development of the skills and knowledge to progress a career in international development – or its study – and, principally, to better respond to the security and justice challenges facing places as they emerge from conflict. The focus on the practical – as well as theoretical – aspects of peacebuilding draws from the author's engagement as a practitioner – as well as scholar – in peacebuilding, and finds expression in the number of practical examples and case studies, including historical cases, throughout each chapter. This concluding chapter will reflect upon some of the core challenges in building security and justice after conflict, and provide recommendations for ways in which to better understand and thereby address these challenges. Principal among these recommendations is the need to bridge the scholar–practitioner divide, engage in more critical and creative ways of thinking, promote inclusive approaches to study and to practice, and fundamentally ask whose security, whose justice and whose peace are we building.

Bridging The Scholar–Practitioner Divide

The practical is also elevated in recognition of the fact that there is often an unhelpful divide between the practical and the academic, conceptual or theoretical – and between practitioners and scholars. Practitioners and scholars rarely interact and often speak different languages, even though they sometimes share similar aims (ultimately to improve security and justice and contribute to paving the way towards more peaceful societies) and often can greatly benefit from each other (whether the practitioner's awareness of how things work in practice rather than in theory and the messiness of conflict and peacebuilding, or the scholar's research and critical thinking skills, and inclination to question dominant narratives and to self-reflect). It is hoped that by bridging the practical and theoretical in this book, the message is clear that neither theory ill-informed of practice nor practice not based upon critical refection and evidenced-based policies can effectively address the security and justice challenges of societies emerging from conflict (see Gordon, 2015). Put simply, there is a need to bridge the gap that often exists between practice and scholarship if there is to be a better understanding of and thus response to the challenges of conflict and peacebuilding.

The Need for Critical, Inclusive and Creative Ways of Thinking

There is an urgent need to better understand the challenges of conflict and peacebuilding because, despite the enormous investment of resources and time in addressing the security and justice challenges of countries emerging from conflict, we frequently see that such efforts fail to lead to long-term peace. Despite peacebuilding being big business today (if we consider the number of projects and people and the amount of investment that often follow conflict) and there being an increasing number of activities and actors engaged, conflicts continue to erupt, escalate and recur. Every year hundreds of thousands of people are killed as a result of conflict, millions are displaced and many more otherwise suffer the harmful effects of conflict. While there have been notable advances in addressing the causes of conflict and building sustainable peace, challenges remain and new threats arise. There is, therefore, a need to:

1. Engage in more critical reflection on lessons that can be learnt (from past successes and failures, including where lessons learnt have been applied without adequate consideration of context)
2. Broaden discussions on ways in which to build peace to include those voices that are often ignored or marginalised (including women, civil society actors, community representatives in conflict-affected environments, disabled people, the elderly, the displaced, children and youths)
3. Be more creative and innovative with ideas and methods of building security and justice after conflict (including broadening the scope of actors and disciplines beyond the political and the security sectors, and beyond the formal realm of international relations – to include artists, musicians, poets, those at the frontier of technological and scientific advancement, psychologists, caregivers and so on).

Asking Whose Security, Justice and Peace?

Building security and justice after conflict continues to attract significant investment and remains a core feature of peacebuilding because of a commonly held belief that security and justice are preconditions for sustainable peace and also, as a result, preconditions for broader international peace and security. Security and justice are also considered to be fundamental to the protection of human rights and to development. However, this book has endeavoured to show that security and justice (and even peace) are often highly politicised and contested terms. As scholars and practitioners, we always need to ask 'whose security?', 'whose justice?', 'whose peace?' and recognise that those who have power to determine what constitutes security and justice are also often able to determine what constitutes threats to security and justice and, furthermore, what should be mobilised to counter those threats. Indeed, we have seen throughout history, and as has been indicated in this book, deeming something to be a threat to security can often result in insecurity: it has been used to demonise minority groups, delegitimise claims for justice and justify hard security responses (including military intervention) and crimes (including, at its extreme, genocide). Oftentimes, the security and justice needs of the least powerful are overlooked in conflict-affected (and other) environments, while security threats and needs as determined by powerful groups are regarded as matters of fact. It is thus incumbent upon scholars and practitioners to listen for silence (as critical and feminist international relations scholars are prone to do) and to question the taken-for-granted.

Challenges in Building Security and Justice After Conflict

There are many challenges facing immediate post-conflict countries which complicate efforts to build security and justice. These are in addition to the challenges resulting from dealing with the politicised and contested terms which can thwart efforts to co-ordinate (if actors have different interpretations) and ensure that security and justice are equitable (if the security and justice needs of the marginalised do not find expression in policy or plans). Chief among these challenges is, of course, the nature of the conflict-affected environment itself. Most post-conflict societies are affected by continuing high levels of violence, including SGBV and possible revenge attacks; widespread human rights violations; widespread availability of SALW; a large mine problem with many areas remaining affected by landmines and other ERW; the presence of armed groups and/or organised criminal groups, which can become more active in jostles for power and in the absence of functioning state institutions; weak, dysfunctional, corrupt or non-existent security sector institutions and widespread impunity. A weak or non-existent government, damaged or destroyed physical infrastructure, widespread corruption, large numbers of internally displaced persons (IDPs) and a fractured civil society add to the challenges of restoring security and justice after conflict. Of course, these challenges are the focus of efforts to build security and justice after conflict. Were it not for these challenges, there would be little reason to engage in such efforts, but the complexity, context-specificity and dynamic character of these challenges is often underestimated.

Aside from these practical challenges, other challenges include structural, political, economic and psychosocial challenges. In the first instance, efforts to promote security and justice can threaten the interests of powerful groups and potential spoilers, involving as they often do the redistribution of power and efforts to promote accountability and limits to power. DDR, SSR, transitional justice, SALW control programmes, efforts to combat organised crime, efforts to promote gender equality or protect and promote human rights and so on are therefore often likely to promote hostile reactions and a balance may need to be secured between short- and long-term wins. This relates to the political will that is often wanting, but necessary if reform or peacebuilding efforts are to be successful. We must also acknowledge, of course, that there are many actors who have a vested interest in insecurity – both within and outside the conflict-affected environment.

Beyond the absence of political will and the drive of some actors to maintain insecurity, there are other economic and political challenges to building security and justice after conflict. Limited resources and competing priorities are common challenges, for instance, facing many peacebuilding and broader development activities. In terms of challenges which concern psychological factors, these can be critical but are often overlooked, at least by mainstream peacebuilding actors. The trauma, loss and grievance resulting from conflict, including how it can undermine trust in others and confidence in the peace process or prospects of the rule of law, can pose significant obstacles in the way of peacebuilding efforts. While it is, of course, much easier to do and much easier to quantify and evaluate, it always strikes me as strange that so much investment goes into repairing buildings and physical infrastructure, but so little into repairing the damage suffered by people. Attending to the psychological also reminds us that peacebuilding takes place at the micro level and not just the macro level, and that obstacles in the way of peace are just as likely to be found at the micro level (such as rivalry between colleagues in international organisations, or hostility between neighbours) as the macro level (such as deficiencies in structures, policies or institutions).

Limitations in Approaches to Building Security and Justice After Conflict

There are also inherent challenges or limitations associated with the way in which many formal peacebuilding programmes have been designed or implemented to date. There have been many critics that view peacebuilding as part of a neo-colonialist endeavour, legitimising intervention under the guise of assistance or aid but really in response to geostrategic or political self-interest on the part of the intervenors and can result in further insecurity (see Chapter 1 and Duffield, 2007). There has also been much criticism of the way in which western models have been transplanted onto conflict-affected societies with little regard for their relevance. Context-specificity, as has been discussed throughout this book, is essential if programmes are to be responsive to the specific context and thus be successful. As has been reflected upon throughout this book, there is a gap between the core principles which are generally agreed should inform peacebuilding practice – including context-specificity, local ownership, inclusion, gender equality, co-ordination and coherence of efforts – and practice. This gap between principle and practice is widely prevalent and this book has sought to argue that it is a core shortcoming and challenge facing efforts to build security and justice after conflict.

The Need for Inclusive Efforts to Build Peace

By focussing on external interventions to build security and justice after conflict, this book naturally focusses on top-down, state-centred approaches that have dominated programmes to date. However, throughout this book, the need to engage the non-state, the community level, the local and promote bottom-up or hybrid approaches to building peace has been emphasised. It has also been noted that the international community is also increasingly, but slowly, engaging non-state or informal security and justice providers as well as communities and civil society in efforts to rebuild security and justice, recognising the deficiencies of state-centred approaches which can compromise efforts to build inclusive and sustainable peace.

In essence, this book advocates an inclusive approach to building security and justice after conflict, recognising that effective programmes responsive to the security and justice needs of people affected by conflict can only be developed with their meaningful and active engagement. An inclusive approach also acknowledges that external intervenors may have subject-matter expertise, but those with the requisite expertise on the context to ensure that programmes are relevant and responsive are those from within those societies. It also acknowledges that those with security and justice expertise, and thus perceived as legitimately able to participate in discussions about building security and justice after conflict, are not just those with professional experience in the security and justice sectors but those with direct, and diverse, experiences of insecurity and injustice. Moreover, every effort should be made to ensure broad-based representation, particularly among the more marginalised groups, in decision-making about security and justice needs and responses. This is to ensure that future policies, structures and processes do not simply respond to the needs of dominant or elite groups, and that the dividends of peace are enjoyed equally.

This book has shown that it is often privileged, male, state-level representatives of the political administration and the security sector who tend to be consulted and engaged by external actors in security and justice programming. There are many reasons for this, including the time and cost constraints most international organisations operate under, which lend themselves to engaging only power brokers or those who speak the same language and have similar ideas. Consulting and engaging widely takes time, is costly and risks contention or compromise. It is, however, necessary if the needs of all are to be addressed, and security and justice are to be enjoyed equitably and sustainably. Contestation between different ideas and groups does not disappear if it is ignored; peacebuilding actually affords the possibility of groups discussing contesting ideas and negotiating an agreed set of shared principles and vision for the future. Acknowledging the complexity of peacebuilding can help manage expectations that efforts can only be successful with investment of considerable time and resources. Such investment can help build resilience against other security threats and prevent a recurrence of conflict, which would ultimately be much more costly in terms of financial expenditure and, of course, human life.

As has been referred to throughout this book, and was the focus of Chapter 9, there is a need to ensure that inclusive efforts to build security and justice after conflict attend to gender: to the gendered inequalities (including socio-economic and political inequalities) that sustain and are sustained by violence, including armed conflict; to the marginalisation of women in efforts to build peace, especially in the security sector; to the lack of attention paid to the security and justice needs of women and gendered harms, including SGBV and other forms of VAW in conflict-affected environments; and to the ways in which structures, processes and laws legitimise the marginalisation of women from decision-making and reaffirm gendered binaries which constrain and harm both men and women in society.

There is also a need to attend to power relations, and all processes and manifestations of exclusion and inequality, including those which are predicated upon race, ethnicity, class, indigeneity, religion, sexuality, physical ability and age as well as gender and other identifiers, such as whether someone is displaced, homeless, stateless or nomadic. There is a further need to attend to how these systems of power interact to compound insecurities and inequalities, as well as reinforce power relations and the propensity to conflict. In practice, this requires commitment to the principles of inclusion, equality and respect for others alongside a commitment to the protection of human rights and the advancement of social justice (see Held, 2010).

The Complexity of Conflict and Peacebuilding

This book has also shown that some of the challenges associated with building security and justice after conflict are as a result of the complex, interconnected nature of conflict dynamics and of peacebuilding activities. We began to refer to the links between conflict and post-conflict in the first chapter:

1. Challenging the usefulness of the 'curve of conflict' which suggests that there is linearity in the path between conflict and peace
2. Showing how violence, and the structures and dynamics which sustain it, can continue well into the post-conflict period
3. Arguing that there is a need to address the causes of conflict if peace is to be sustainable
4. Showing the missed opportunities of continuing to disproportionately invest in peacebuilding rather than conflict prevention.

The challenges associated with the complex, interconnected nature of conflict dynamics and of peacebuilding activities are also a result of the frequently huge number of activities and actors engaged. We have discussed the synergies and tensions between the different activities involved in building security and justice after conflict, and between short- and long-term security aims. We have also referred to the peace versus justice debate (Chapter 4) and the tensions that can arise between those engaged in human rights activities and those engaged in security activities. There is a huge and increasing number of actors; each have particular interests, perspectives and agendas, and each may have a different understanding of the conflict and how peace should be built. Expanding missions and mandates – and broad-based belief in the interdependence of security, human rights and development – brings actors together who would not have been previously, blurs areas of responsibility and can increase tension.

All of this necessitates considerable investment in co-ordination and communication, in part to manage expectations and ensure coherence of efforts. There is a need to recognise that activities in one area, such as DDR, directly impacts activities in another, whether SSR, transitional justice or SALW control as well as broader activities in the governance and economic sectors. Similarly, there is a need to recognise the complexity and interconnectedness of the global world:

1. The effects of conflict can sometimes have far-reaching effects (as can be seen if we consider the global migration crisis as millions of people flee conflict zones or other forms of insecurity and violence, or has been argued with respect to transnational security threats such as terrorism, piracy and organised crime)
2. The activities of those far removed from conflict can fuel or exacerbate conflict (as can be seen if we consider the global arms trade and the role of stable states in supplying arms and/or supporting one side or another)
3. Political drivers of insecurity intersect with the current political drivers of nationalism (secure borders, geostrategic interest or economic advantage) and, as Held (2010) says, prioritise the pursuit of national interest above the common good, overlooking what we have in common with others and how we depend upon each other for our well-being
4. The global political economy sustains (and is sustained by) violence and conflict, with the unequal distribution of wealth and power feeding inequalities and insecurities –
   a. Those who are socio-economically disadvantaged are more vulnerable to violence and other forms of insecurity
   b. Those countries that face development challenges are more prone to other forms of insecurity, including armed conflict and less resilient against their effects
   c. Inequalities can feed individual and group grievance, which can contribute to the outbreak, escalation or continuation of armed conflict
   d. Inequalities can lead to violence being meted out against the vulnerable, as part of the process of securitising inequality, blaming the poor for their own poverty as well as other social ills and thus legitimising inequalities and sustaining the unequal distribution of wealth, power and opportunity
5. We all have a moral responsibility to respond to injustices and insecurity – as Mac Ginty and Williams (2016: 240) have said: 'the problems of conflict and development are ones that affect all of us, wherever we live, and…there is a unity of the human spirit and of human suffering that makes us all morally responsible for each other's welfare'. Our action as well as our inaction determines what happens elsewhere, and we should not be deterred by the enormity of the task or calls that only those with specific roles or specific expertise have a role to play.

We can begin to fulfil this responsibility by equipping ourselves with knowledge – beyond sanitised versions of conflict and of peacebuilding, and beyond simplified accounts which erase people, ideas and events from history. We should question what is deemed to be official or legitimate, and ask for who and why certain narratives are elevated and others silenced. We can also begin to fulfil this responsibility by equipping ourselves with the skills required to gather information (from beyond official or widely available sources), to think critically and to analyse that information in a way that unpicks assumptions about cause or blame and that exposes binary distinctions (between good and evil, aggressive or protective man and passive or vulnerable woman) as limiting (in terms of their usefulness and basis in reality). As Mac Ginty and Williams (2016: 234) argue: 'Understanding requires empathy, and empathy requires a lot of contact with the real world'. This level of understanding generally demands extended periods of time living in conflict-affected environments (as an anthropologist might do or as the scholar–practitioner might have done) or at least privileging the voices of those who live or have lived in these environments. We can then ensure that our knowledge, our research, our analysis are put to good effect – whether as a student, scholar, practitioner or activist – by identifying ways in which it can inform policy and practice, whether through advocacy, awareness-raising or in the work we do to build security, justice and peace.

Working and Conducting Research in Post-Conflict Environments

In our studies, research and practice, we can learn from the challenges addressed in this book which face actors engaged with building security and justice after conflict. For instance, we can attend to the heightened security challenges including by:

1. Comprehensively researching and planning prior to engagement
2. Conducting conflict or security analyses and risk assessments, before and throughout our engagement, to ensure that we remain responsive to changing conflict dynamics
3. Remaining knowledgeable and vigilant, and have trusted local sources to rely on (and spend time building that mutual trust).

We can attend to heightened ethical challenges associated with working in insecure environments, often on sensitive topics and often with traumatised or vulnerable individuals, by ensuring that we endeavour to do no harm (a principle at least ostensibly at the heart of social science research as well as development practice) to others as well as to ourselves. We can do this by attending to the frequent imbalances of power between practitioner or scholar and those living in conflict-affected environments, and by ensuring that those living in conflict-affected environments are engaged in the design of the research or programmes and directly benefit from them. We can also ensure we do no harm to ourselves by looking after our physical and emotional health, by taking breaks, seeking support and recognising (and acting upon) the signs of stress, recognising that it poses harm to us and potentially to what we are working on and who we are working with. We can also respond to the dynamic nature of the conflict-affected environment by remaining flexible and ready to adapt plans to changing circumstances, and remain context-relevant, within ethical and security constraints. We can also develop humility, show respect for others and learn to listen: in conflict-affected environments especially, these skills will not only help build trusted relationships and facilitate our work, but will also keep us safe. Having respect for others means treating people as people and not simply as research subjects (or sources of data) or conflict actors (and potential brokers or spoilers of peace). These interpersonal skills are especially important when working in multicultural environments and where there are language barriers; respect for others and a willingness to listen and learn translate across cultures.

Knowledge and Power

It is not just in practice that we can contribute to building safer, more just societies. Through our scholarship and our research, we can effect change by equipping ourselves with knowledge and sharing what we have learnt. Specifically, we can effect change by analysing the complexities of peace and conflict, critically engaging with dominant discourses, questioning the taken-for-granted and identifying marginalised voices or approaches to building peace. These are particularly important activities, not just to lend a critical eye, or provide the evidence-base that policy needs, but because conflict and insecurity are often predicated upon silences, oppression, rumour, conspiracy, re-written histories and constructed narratives which serve to protect, defend, deny, deflect attention and justify actions and attitudes (Brun, 2013; Gordon, 2015). In conflict-affected environments, intrinsic links are evident between knowledge and power, truth and justice, and silence and suppression. In this context, the power and political nature of knowledge are clear, particularly the ability to present that knowledge as credible and authoritative to different audiences. This power also brings with it risk, particularly if certain actors want to prevent specific narratives or information from being communicated. Nonetheless, through navigating such risks, the potential is that, through scholarship and research, narratives which perpetuate conflict, harm and insecurity can be challenged, and a better understanding of, and thus response to, the challenges of conflict and peacebuilding can be developed (Gordon, 2015).

Conclusion

It is hoped that this book contributes to the discussion of ways in which to build security and justice after conflict, challenges often faced, and how to best overcome those challenges and contribute to building sustainable peace. This book has identified a number of principles that are critical to successful engagement and, while at the heart of peacebuilding policy, are infrequently adhered to in practice. These are the principles of inclusion, equality, local ownership, and co-ordination and coherence of efforts. In essence, this requires a deeper understanding of conflict-affected environments, and an acceptance of the complexity and dynamic nature of conflict and peacebuilding. It requires critical engagement with dominant discourses of security, justice and peace and self-reflection – asking ourselves for whom and for what we work or the research is for, and how we can ensure that it does not cause more harm than good. It requires more innovative and creative ways of addressing the challenges posed by conflict and peacebuilding. It also requires an acknowledgement that those who are best placed to inform peacebuilding processes include those who have suffered most and those who have most to gain, not least the more marginalised members of conflict-affected societies, and that neither international development nor scholarship should be exclusionary in its practices or language. Finally, it also requires a commitment to addressing the needs of those who continue to be exposed to insecurity and injustice whether during or in the aftermath of conflict or when societies are ostensibly at peace.

Bibliography

ABA (2018) 'Bosnia & Herzegovina Background', ABA website. Available at: www. americanbar.org/aba.html.

ABA (2019) American Bar Association (ABA) website. Available at: www.americanbar.org.

Abierta, V. (2016) '5 Challenges Criminal Economies Pose for Post-Conflict Colombia', *InSight Crime*, 15 February. Available online at: www.insightcrime.org/news-analysis/ five-challenges-criminal-economies-post-conflict-colombia.

ACCORD (2016) 'Understanding the Recruitment of Child Soldiers in Africa', Conflict Trends 2016/2, by Anne-Lynn Dudenhoefer, 16 August. Available at: www.accord.org.za/ conflict-trends/understanding-recruitment-child-soldiers-africa/.

Ackermann, A. (2003) 'The Idea and Practice of Conflict Prevention', *Journal of Peace Research*, 40(3): 339–47.

ACLED (2019) Armed Conflict Location & Event Data Project (ACLED) website. Available at: www.acleddata.com.

Adele, A. (2017) 'Land clashes test Côte d'Ivoire's fragile security', *IRIN*, 25 October. Available at: www.irinnews.org/news/2017/10/25/land-clashes-test-cote-d-ivoire-s-fragile-security.

Al Jazeera (2017) 'Inside Story – What happens to child soldiers when war ends?' (video). Available at: www.youtube.com/watch?v=9FISTRzjqXU.

Albrecht, P. and Jackson, P. (2014) 'State-Building through Security Sector Reform: The UK Intervention in Sierra Leone', *Peacebuilding*, 2(1): 83–99

Alda, E. and Mc Evoy, C. (2017) 'Beyond the Battlefield: Towards a Better Assessment of the Human Cost of Armed Conflict', Briefing Paper, Geneva: Small Arms Survey. Available at: www.smallarmssurvey.org/fileadmin/docs/T-Briefing-Papers/SAS-BP4-Beyond-battlefield.pdf.

AlertNet (2010) 'Conflict Resolution', AlertNet Crisis Centre. Available at: www.trust.org/ alertnet/crisis-centre/subtopic/conflict-resolution.

Alliance for Peacebuilding (2019) 'What is Peacebuilding', Alliance for Peacebuilding website. Available at: https://allianceforpeacebuilding.org/what-is-peacebuilding.

Alpert, M. (2016) 'To Be a Guerrilla, and a Woman, in Colombia', *The Atlantic*, 28 September. Available at: www.theatlantic.com/international/archive/2016/09/farc-deal-female-fighters/501644/.

Alusala (2016) 'Lessons from Small Arms and Weapons Control Initiatives in Africa', BICC Working Paper, January, Bonn: Bonn International Center for Conversion (BICC). Available at: www.bicc.de/uploads/tx_bicctools/wp_1_2016.pdf.

American Friends Service Committee (2014) 'Survivors Speak: Prisoner Testimonies of Torture in United States Prisons and Jails', A Shadow Report Submitted for the November 2014 Review of the United States by the Committee Against Torture, Washington, DC: American Friends Service Committee. Available at: www.afsc.org/document/ survivors-speak-prisoner-testimonies-torture-united-states-prisons-and-jails.

Amnesty International (1993) 'Violations of Human Rights in Armed Conflict: Proposals for Action', Statement by Amnesty International, 31 August. Available at: www.amnesty.org/ download/Documents/188000/ior300011993en.pdf.

Amnesty International (2014) *Ethnic cleansing on a historic scale: The Islamic State's systematic targeting of minorities in northern Iraq*, London: Amnesty International. Available at: www.amnesty.org/en/documents/MDE14/011/2014/en/.

Amnesty International (2017a) 'Human Slaughterhouse: Mass Hangings and Extermination at Saydnaya Prison, Syria', 07 February. Available at: www.amnesty.org/download/Documents/MDE2454152017ENGLISH.PDF.

Amnesty International (2017b) *Amnesty International Report 2016/2017: The State of the World's Rights*, London: Amnesty International. Available at: www.amnesty.org.au/wp-content/uploads/2017/02/air201617-english_2016-17.pdf.

Amnesty International (2018) 'Nigeria: Starving women raped by soldiers and militia who claim to be rescuing them', Amnesty International news, 24 May. Available at: www.amnesty.org/en/latest/news/2018/05/nigeria-starving-women-raped-by-soldiers-and-militia-who-claim-to-be-rescuing-them/.

Anderlini, S. (2007) *Women Building Peace: What They Do, Why It Matters*, Colorado: Lynne Rienner.

Anderlini, S. (2011) *World Development Report Background Paper*, Washington: World Bank. Available at: http://wdr2011.worldbank.org/sites/default/files/pdfs/WDR%20Background%20Paper_Anderlini.pdf?keepThis=true&TB_iframe=true&height=600&width=800.

Anderlini, S., Conaway, C. and Kays, L. (2007) 'Transitional Justice and Reconciliation' in International Alert/Women Waging Peace (eds) *Inclusive Security, Sustainable Peace: A Toolkit for Advocacy and Action*, London/Washington: International Alert/Women Waging Peace, 1-15. Available at: www.inclusivesecurity.org/wp-content/uploads/2013/05/101864251-Toolkit-for-Advocacy-and-Action.pdf.

Anderson, L. (2008) 'Analytical Inventory of Response by Peacekeeping Personnel to War Related Violence against Women', background paper for Wilton Park Conference, 'Women Targeted or Affected by Armed Conflict: What Role for Military Peacekeepers?', 27–29 May 2008.

Andrieu, K. (2010) Transitional Justice: A New Discipline in Human Rights, Online Encyclopedia of Mass Violence. Available at: www.massviolence.org/Article?id_article=359.

Annual Report of the Special Representative of the Secretary-General for Children and Armed Conflict, New York: UN. Available at: https://childrenandarmedconflict.un.org/virtual-library/documents/reports/.

Ansorg, N. and Gordon, G. (2019) 'Co-Operation, Contestation and Complexity in Post-Conflict Security Sector Reform', *Journal of Intervention and Statebuilding*, 13(1): 2–24.

ANU College of Law (2015) 'Professor Gerry Simpson The Annual Kirby Lecture on International Law 2015' (video). Available at: www.youtube.com/watch?v=bxzJK0nlNrY.

Arendt, H. (2006) *Eichmann in Jerusalem: A Report on the Banality of Evil*, London: Penguin.

Arnould, V. (2016) 'Transitional Justice in Peacebuilding: Dynamics of Contestation in the DRC', *Journal of Intervention and Statebuilding*, 10(3): 321–38.

Ashdown, P. (2002) 'What I Learned in Bosnia', New York Times, 28 October 2002.

Asmal, K., Asmal, L. and Roberts, R. (1997) *Reconciliation through Truth: A Reckoning of Apartheid's Criminal Governance* (2nd edn), London: Palgrave Macmillan.

Austrian Embassy (2019) 'Common European Security and Defence Policy (CSDP)', website of the Embassy of Austria in Washington DC. Available at: www.austria.org/common-european-security-and-defence-policy.

Autesserre, S. (2014) *Peacelands*, New York: Cambridge University Press.

Autesserre, S. (2018) 'Peacebuilding in Africa', Kujenga Amani podcast. Available at: http://apnpodcast.libsyn.com/sverine-autesserre.

Avoine, P. and Tillman, R. (2015) 'Demobilized Women in Colombia: Embodiment, Performativity and Social Reconciliation' in S. Shekhawat (ed.), *Female Combatants in Conflict and Peace: Challenging Gender in Violence and Post-Conflict Reintegration*, London: Palgrave Macmillan, 216–31.

Avruch, K. (2006) 'Culture, Relativism, and Human Rights' in J. Mertus and J. Helsing (eds), *Human Rights and Conflict: Exploring the Links between Rights, Law, and Peacebuilding*, Washington: USIP, 97–127.

Aydin, A. (2010) 'Where Do States Go? Strategy in Civil War Intervention', *Management and Peace Science*, 27(1): 47–66.

Azar, E. (1990) *The Management of Protracted Social Conflict: Theory and Cases*, Aldershot: Dartmouth.

Baaz, M. and Stern, M. (2013a) 'Fearless Fighters and Submissive Wives: Negotiating Identity among Women Soldiers in the Congo (DRC)', *Armed Forces and Society*, 39(4): 711–39.

Baaz, M. and Stern, M. (2013b) *Sexual Violence as a Weapon of War? Perceptions, Prescriptions, Problems in the Congo and Beyond*, London: Zed Books.

Baaz, M. and Utas, M. (2012) 'Beyond "Gender and Stir" in Baaz, M. and Utas, M. (eds), *Beyond 'Gender and Stir': Reflections on Gender and SSR in the Aftermath of African Conflicts*, Uppsala: The Nordic Africa Institute, 5–10. Available at: http://nai.diva-portal.org/smash/get/diva2:570724/FULLTEXT01.pdf.

Babayoko, N. (2017) 'Security and safety from the bottom up: hybrid security governance', prepared for the Learning Lab on Security Sector Governance in Africa – Dakar, 26–27 April 2016. Available at: https://issat.dcaf.ch/download/108726/1965079/Think%20Piece%20No%205_Hybrid%20Security.pdf.

Bacevich, A. (2015) *America's War for the Greater Middle East: A Military History*, New York: Random House.

Badescu, C. (2011) *Humanitarian Intervention and the Responsibility to Protect: Security and Human Rights*, Abingdon: Routledge.

Baker, B. (2010) 'The Future Is Non-State' in M. Sedra (ed.), The *Future of Security Sector Reform*, Waterloo: Centre for International Governance Innovation, 208–28. Available at: www.cigionline.org/sites/default/files/the_future_of_security_sector_reform.pdf.

Baker, B. (2017) 'Policing for Conflict Zones: What Have Local Policing Groups Taught Us?', *Stability: International Journal of Security and Development*, 6(1):9, 1–16.

Baker, C. and Obradovic-Wochnik, J. (2016) 'Mapping the Nexus of Transitional Justice and Peacebuilding', *Journal of Intervention and Statebuilding*, 10(3): 281–301.

Barnes, K. and Albrecht, P. (2008) *Civil Society Oversight of the Security Sector and Gender*, Geneva: DCAF. Available at: www.dcaf.ch/Publications/Civil-Society-Oversight-of-the-Security-Sector-and-Gender-Tool-9.

Barnett, M., Kim, H., O'Donnell, M. and Sitea, L. (2007) 'Peacebuilding: What Is in a Name?', *Global Governance*, 13: 35–58.

Barr, H. (2013) 'The long arc of justice in Afghanistan', *Foreign Policy*, 09 August. Available at: http://foreignpolicy.com/2013/08/09/the-long-arc-of-justice-in-afghanistan.

Basedau, M. and Lay, J. (2009) 'Resource Curse or Rentier Peace? The Ambiguous Effects of Oil Wealth and Oil Dependence on Violent Conflict', *Peace Research*, 46(6): 757–76.

Basoglu, M. (2017) 'Definition of Torture in US Law: Does It Provide Legal Cover for "Enhanced Interrogation Techniques"?' in M. Basolglu (ed) *Torture and Its Definition In International Law: An Interdisciplinary Approach*. Oxford: Oxford University Press.

Bassu, G. (2008) 'Law Overruled: Strengthening the Rule of Law in Postconflict States', *Global Governance*, 14: 21–38.

Bastick, M. (2010) *The Role of Penal Reform in Security Sector Reform*, Occasional Paper No. 18. Available at: www.dcaf.ch/role-penal-reform-security-sector-reform.

Bastick, M. (2017) 'Gender, Militaries and Security Sector Reform' in R. Woodward and C. Duncanson (eds), *The Palgrave International Handbook of Gender and the Military*, London: Palgrave, 387–402.

Bastick, M. and Valasek, K. (eds) (2008) *Gender and Security Sector Reform Toolkit*, Geneva: DCAF, OSCE/ ODIHR, UN-INSTRAW. Available at: www.dcaf.ch/gender-security-sector-reform-toolkit.

Bastick, M. and Whitman, T. (2013) *A Women's Guide to Security Sector Reform*, Geneva: DCAF. Available at: www.inclusivesecurity.org/wp-content/uploads/2013/02/WGTSSR-Web.pdf.

Batesmith, A. (2015) 'How 'International' Lawyers can Work More Effectively with their National Counterparts', (video) (University of Leicester). Available at: www.youtube.com/watch?v=ZwgZLSt8x_w&index=14&list=PLjQX5EXgm57STSvD19VcobrSyhF5pey-U.

Bauman, Z. (1989) *Modernity and the Holocaust*, Cambridge: Polity Press.

Baxell R. (2012) *Unlikely Warriors: The British in the Spanish Civil War and the Struggle against Fascism*, London: Aurum Press.

BBC (1999) *A Cry from the Grave* (video). Available at: www.youtube.com/watch?v=Fliw801iX84 (MySrebrenica, 2011).

BBC (2011a) 'Q&A: Somali Piracy', *BBC News Africa*, 21 January. Available at: www.bbc.co.uk/news/10349155.

BBC (2011b) 'Somali pirate attacks sharply down in November', *BBC News Africa*, 05 December. Available at: www.bbc.co.uk/news/world-africa-16040944.

BBC (2012) 'Q&A: DR Congo Conflict', *BBC News Africa*, 20 November. Available at: www.bbc.co.uk/news/world-africa-11108589.

BBC (2017) 'Islamic State and the crisis in Iraq and Syria in maps', *BBC News Middle East*, 28 November. Available at: www.bbc.com/news/world-middle-east-27838034.

Beaumont, P. (2018) 'Mass rape and killings in South Sudan may constitute war crimes, says UN', *The Guardian*, 10 July. Available at: www.theguardian.com/global-development/2018/jul/10/south-sudan-government-forces-accused-potential-war-crimes-horrific-acts.

Beban, P. (2010) *Can the UN Keep the Peace?* (video). Available at: https://vimeo.com/9157432.

Bell, C. (2006) 'Human Rights, Peace Agreements, and Conflict Resolution: Negotiating Justice in Northern Ireland' in J. Mertus and J. Helsing (eds), *Human Rights and Conflict: Exploring the Links between Rights, Law, and Peacebuilding*, Washington: USIP, 345–74.

Bell, D. and Carens, J. (2004) 'The Ethical Dilemmas of International Human Rights and Humanitarian NGOs: Reflections on a Dialogue between Practitioners and Theorists', *Human Rights Quarterly*, 26: 301–2.

Bell, D. and Coicaud, J.-M. (2006) 'The Ethical Challenges of International Human Rights NGOs', Policy Brief No. 9, 2006, Tokyo: UNU. Available at: http://i.unu.edu/media/publication/000/000/729/the-ethical-challenges-of-internationalhuman-rights-ngos-pb9-06.pdf.

Bellal, A. (2017) 'Non-State Armed Groups in Transitional Justice Processes: Adapting to New Realities of Conflict' in R. Duthie and P. Seils (eds), *Justice Mosaics: How Context Shapes Transitional Justice in Fractured Societies*, New York: International Centre for Transitional Justice (ICTJ).

Bellamy, A. (2010) 'The Responsibility to Protect: Five Years On', *Ethics and International Affairs*, 24(2): 143–69.

Bellamy, A. and Williams, P. (2010) *Understanding Peacekeeping*, Cambridge: Polity Press.

Bellamy, C. (2011) 'Maritime Piracy', *The RUSI Journal*, 156(6): 78–83.

Benedix, D. and Stanley, R. (2008) 'Deconstructing Local Ownership of Security Sector Reform: A Review of the Literature', *African Security Review*, 17(2): 93–104.

Bento, L. (2011) 'Toward an International Law of Piracy Sui Generis: How the Dual Nature of Maritime Piracy Law Enables Piracy to Flourish', *Berkeley J. Int'l Law*, 29(2): 399-455.

Berdal, M. (2009) 'Building Peace after War', *The Adelphi Papers*, 49: 407.

Berger, M. (2010) 'Sexual Violence Is Not "Collateral Damage"', *IPS Report*. Available at: http://ipsnews.net/news.asp?idnews=53459.

Beri, R. (2011) 'Piracy in Somalia: Addressing the Root Causes', *Strategic Analysis*, 35(3): 452-64.

Best, G. (1994) *War and Law since 1945*, Oxford: Clarendon Press.

Bhandari, C. (2015) 'The Reintegration of Maoist Ex-Combatants in Nepal', *Economic and Political Weekly*, 1(9): 63-8.

BICC (2017) *Keep The Safety On* (video). Available at: www.youtube.com/watch?v=gMKQWMLdcgg.

BICC (2008) *A Gun in Every Home* (video). Available at: www.youtube.com/watch?v=fUflPzT_QkY.

Bickford, L. (2014) 'Memoryworks/Memory Works' in C Ramírez-Barat (ed.), *Transitional Justice, Culture and Society: Beyond Outreach*, New York: ICTJ, 491–528.

Binkley, B. and Smith, L. (2012) 'Pirate Attacks', Pittsburgh: Matthew B. Ridgeway Center for International Studies, Pittsburgh University. Available at: http://research.ridgway.pitt.edu/blog/2012/05/15/pirate-attacks/#more-407.

Bjarnegård, E. and Erik Melander, E. (2011) 'Disentangling Gender, Peace and Democratization: The Negative Effects of Militarized Masculinity', *Journal of Gender Studies*, 20(2): 139–54.

Blair, D. (2016) 'The "Civilian Control of the Military" Fallacy', *The Atlantic*, 05 December. Available at: www.theatlantic.com/politics/archive/2016/12/democratic-political-control-of-the-armed-forces/509501/.

Blease, D. and Qehaja, F. (2013) 'The Conundrum of Local Ownership in Developing a Security Sector: The Case of Kosovo. New Balkan Politics', *Journal of Politics*, 1–21. Available at: www.newbalkanpolitics.org.mk/uploads/attachments/1._blease_and_qehaja.pdf.

Bøas, M. and Hatløy, A. (2008) 'Getting In, Getting Out: Militia Membership and Prospects for Re-Integration in Post-War Liberia', *The Journal of Modern African Studies*, 46(1): 33–55.

Boer, J. and Bosetti, L. (2015) 'The Crime-Conflict "Nexus": State of the Evidence', United Nations University Centre for Policy Research, Occasional Paper 5, July, Tokyo: United Nations University. Available at: http://collections.unu.edu/eserv/UNU:3134/unu_cpr_crime_conflict_nexus.pdf.

Boesten, J. and Fisher, M. (2012) 'Sexual Violence and Justice in Postconflict Peru', *USIP Special Report 310*, Washington: USIP. Available at: www.usip.org/files/resources/SR310.pdf.

Bogati, S. (2014) 'Assessing Inclusivity in the Post-War Army Integration Process in Nepal', *Inclusive Political Settlements Paper 11*, July, Berlin: Berghof Foundation. Available at: www.berghof-foundation.org/fileadmin/redaktion/Publications/Other_Resources/IPS/IPSPaper11-Assessing-Inclusivity-in-the-Post-War-Army-Integration-Process-in-Nepal_English.pdf.

Bojicic, V. and Kostovicova, D. (2011) 'Transnational networks and state-building in the Balkans', *openDemocracy*, 17 January. Available at: www.opendemocracy.net/vesna-bojicic-dzelilovicdenisa-kostovicova/transnational-networks-and-state-building-in-balkans.

Bolkovac, K. (2011) *The Whistleblower: Sex Trafficking, Military Contractors, and One Woman's Fight for Justice*, Basingstoke: Palgrave Macmillan.

Boraine, A. (2006) 'Transitional Justice: A Holistic Interpretation', *Journal of International Affairs*, 60(1): 17–27.

Bosco, D. (2014) *Rough Justice: The International Criminal Court's Battle to Fix the World, One Prosecution at a Time*, Oxford: Oxford University Press.

Bourne, M. (2018) 'Powers of the Gun: Process and Possibility in Global Small Arms Control', *International Politics*, 55: 441–61.

Bourne, M. and O. Greene (2012) 'Governance and Control of SALW after Armed Conflicts' in O. Greene and N. Marsh (eds), *Small Arms, Crime and Conflict: Global Governance and the Threat of Armed Violence*, London: Routledge, 183–206.

Bouvier, V. (2016) 'Gender and the Role of Women in Colombia's Peace Process', UN Women Background Paper, New York: UN Women. Available at: www.unwomen.org/-/media/headquarters/attachments/sections/library/publications/2017/women-colombia-peace-process-en.pdf?la=en&vs=17.

Božanić, D. (2016) *Gender and SALW in South East Europe*, Belgrade: South Eastern and Eastern Europe Clearinghouse for the Control of Small Arms and Light Weapons (SEESAC). Available at: www.seesac.org/f/docs/Armed-Violence/Gender_and_SALW_publication_eng-web.pdf.

Brahm, E. (2003) 'Conflict Stages' in G. Burgess and H. Burgess (eds), *Beyond Intractability*, Boulder: University of Colorado, Conflict Research Consortium. Available at: www.beyondintractability.org/essay/conflict_stages/.

Brecht, B. (1928) *The Threepenny Opera (Die Dreigroschenoper)*, opera, first staged in 1928 in Berlin.

Brett, J. (2009) 'Recent Experience with Comprehensive Civil and Military Approaches in International Operations', *DISS Report 2009:09*, Copenhagen: Danish Institute for International Studies (DIIS). Available at: www.isn.ethz.ch/isn/Digital-Library/Publications/Detail/?id=99488&lng=en.

Bridger, J. (2011) Somali Piracy and the World's Response, Toronto: The Atlantic Council of Canada. Available at: http://atlantic-council.ca/somali-piracy-and-the-worlds-response.

Brocklehurst, H. (2009) 'Childhood in Conflict: Can the Real Child Soldier Please Stand Up?' *Ethics, Law and Society: vol. 4*, Farnham: Ashgate Publishing, 259–70.

Bromley, M. (2016) 'The UN's Small Arms and Light Weapons Control Agenda Takes a (Very) Small Step Forward', Stockholm: SIPRI. Available at: www.sipri.org/commentary/blog/2016/uns-small-arms-and-light-weapons-control-agenda-takes-very-small-step-forward.

Brosig, M. (2010) 'The Multi-Actor Game of Peacekeeping in Africa', *International Peacekeeping*, 17(3): 327–42.

Brouneus, K. (2008) 'Truth-Telling as Talking Cure? Insecurity and Retraumatization in the Rwandan Gacaca Courts', *Security Dialogue*, 39(1): 55–76.

Brun, C. (2013) '"I Love My Soldier": Developing Responsible and Ethically Sound Research Strategies in a Militarized Society' in D. Mazurana, K. Jacobsen and L. Gale (eds), *Research Methods in Conflict Settings: A View from Below*, Cambridge: Cambridge University Press, 129–48.

Bryden, A. (2005) 'Optimising Mine Action Policies and Practices', in A. Bryden and H. Hänggi (eds), *Security Governance in Post-Conflict Peacebuilding*, Münster: Lit Verlag.

Bryden, A. and Olonisakin, F. (eds) (2010) *Security Sector Transformation in Africa*, Geneva: DCAF. Available at: www.dcaf.ch/DCAF/EZ/Publications/Security-Sector-Transformation-in-Africa.

Brzoska, M. (2006) 'Introduction: Criteria for Evaluating Post-Conflict Reconstruction and Security Sector Reform in Peace Support Operations', *International Peacekeeping*, 13(1): 1-13.

Brzoska, M. (2009) *Evaluating International Partnerships in Security Sector Reform in Post-Conflict Reconstruction and Peacemaking*, paper prepared for International Studies Association Annual Convention New York, Feb 15–18, 2009. Available at: https://ifsh.de/file-IFSH/IFSH/pdf/aktuelles/ISAPaper2009Brzoska.pdf.

Bull, C. (2007) 'Building the Rule of Law under UN Transitional Administration', Policy Brief No.7, Tokyo: UNU-Centre. Available at: http://unu.edu/publications/research-policy-briefs/2000-2010/building-the-rule-of-law-under-un-transitional-administration.

Bureau of the Commissioner General of Rehabilitation (BCGR) (2018) 'Programmes Conducted for Adults', BCGR website. Available at: http://bcgr.gov.lk/programs_adult.php.

Burgoon, B. (2006) 'On Welfare and Terror: Social Welfare Policies and Political-Economic Roots of Terrorism', *Journal of Conflict Resolution*, 50(2): 176–203.

Burian, A. (2017) 'Summary of Key SSR Developments and Trends 2005–2017', ISSAT Blog. Available at: http://issat.dcaf.ch/Share/Blogs/ISSAT-Blog/Summary-of-Key-SSR-Developments-and-Trends-2005-2017.

Burt, G. (2016) 'Security Sector Reform, Legitimate Politics and SDG 16', SSR 2.0 Brief, Issue No. 5, Ontario: Centre for Security Governance. Available at: http://secgovcentre.org/wp-content/uploads/2016/11/SSR-2.0-Brief-5_-_Burt_-_July_2016.pdf.

Burton, J. (1990) *Conflict: Resolution and Provention*, New York: St. Martin's Press.

Bush, K. (2011) 'How Can Research Contribute to Cross-Border Peacebuilding?', paper prepared for the Centre for Cross-Border Studies North/South Forum, Peacebuilding Across Borders. Derry/ Londonderry, 23 June (Draft). Available at: www.incore.ulst.ac.uk/pdfs/220311_Role_of_research.pdf.

Buzan, B., Wæver, O. and de Wilde, J. (1998) *Security: A New Framework for Analysis*, Boulder: Lynne Rienner.

Cahill-Ripley, A. (2016) 'Reclaiming the Peacebuilding Agenda: Economic and Social Rights as A Legal Framework for Building Positive Peace – A Human Security Plus Approach to Peacebuilding', *Human Rights Law Review*, 16(2): 223–46.

Call, C. (ed.) (2007) *Constructing Justice and Security after War*, Washington: USIP.

Call, C. (2008) 'The Fallacy of the "Failed State"', *Third World Quarterly*, 29(8): 1491–507.

Caparini, M. and Cole, E. (2008) 'The Case for Public Oversight of the Security Sector: Concepts and Strategies' in UNDP/DCAF (eds) *Public Oversight of the Security Sector: A Handbook for Civil Society Organisations*, New York: UNDP.

Caprioli, M. (2003) 'Gender Equality and Civil Wars', World Bank CPR Working Paper No. 8, Washington: World Bank.

Carpenter, C. (2006) 'Recognizing Gender Based Violence against Civilian Men and Boys in Conflict Situations', *Security Dialogue*, 37(1): 83–103.

Carroll, O. (2018) 'Brutal Video Exposes Torture in Russian Prisons', *Independent*, 20 July. Available at: www.independent.co.uk/news/world/europe/brutal-video-torture-makarov-putin-russian-prisons-a8456141.html.

Carter, S. and Clark, K. (2010) No Shortcut to Stability – Justice, Politics and Insurgency in Afghanistan, London: Chatham House. Available at: www.chathamhouse.org/sites/default/files/public/Research/Asia/1210pr_afghanjustice.pdf.

CASA (2017) 'Women, men and the gendered nature of small arms and light weapons', International Small Arms Control Standard 06.10. Available at: www.smallarmsstandards.org/isacs/0610-en.pdf.

Catani, C., Jacob, N., Schauer, E., Kohila, M. and Neuner, F. (2008) 'Family Violence, War, and Natural Disasters: A Study of the Effect of Extreme Stress on Children's Mental Health in Sri Lanka', *BMC Psychiatry*, 2 May 2008, 8: 33.

Center for Investigation and Documentation of the Association of Former Prison Camp Inmates of Bosnia-Herzegovina (2000), *I Begged Them to Kill Me – Crime against the Women of Bosnia-Herzegovina*, Sarajevo: CID.

Centre for International Governance Innovation (CIGI) (2010) 'Rule of Law and Justice Development in Post-Conflict with Jasteena Dhillon' (Video). Available at: www.youtube.com/watch?v=oAVcOua17S8.

Centre for Security Governance (CSG) (2016a) 'eSeminar: New Frontiers in Security Sector Reform' (video). Available at: www.youtube.com/watch?v=flqINeGsZBs.

Centre for Security Governance (CSG) (2016b) 'eSeminar: Is Peacebuilding Dying?' (video). Available at: www.youtube.com/watch?v=_pc2SgTob1g.

Centre for Security Governance (CSG) (2017) 'eSeminar - Organized Crime, Corruption & Peacebuilding' (video). Available at: www.youtube.com/watch?v=8vZFk15EEF8.

Chabal, P. (2009) *Africa: The Politics of Suffering and Smiling*, London and New York: Zed Books.

Chalk, P. (2008) *The Maritime Dimension of International Security Terrorism, Piracy, and Challenges for the United States*, Santa Monica: RAND. Available at: www.rand.org/pubs/monographs/2008/RAND_MG697.pdf.

Chandler, D. (2002) 'Introduction: Rethinking Human Rights' in D. Chandler (ed.), *Rethinking Human Rights: Critical Approaches to International Politics*, Basingstoke: Palgrave Macmillan.

Chandler, D. (2010) 'The Uncritical Critique of "Liberal Peace"', *Review of International Studies*, 36(1): 137–55.

Chandler, D. (2017) *Peacebuilding: The Twenty Year Crisis, 1997–2017*, London: Palgrave Macmillan.

Chandra, S. (2017) 'Beyond Transitional Justice: Peace, Governance, and Rule of Law', *International Studies Review*, 19(1): 53–69.

Chang, H.-J. (2007) *Bad Samaritans: Rich Nations, Poor Policies and the Threat to the Developing World*, New York: Random House.

Chang, H.-J. (2010) *23 Things They Don't Tell You About Capitalism*, London: Penguin.

Chappell, L. (2016) *The Politics of Gender Justice at the International Criminal Court: Legacies and Legitimacy*, New York: Oxford University Press.

Chappell, L. (2018) 'Gender Justice and Legitimacy at the International Criminal Court (ICC)', paper presented at the *International Political Science Association (IPSA) Conference*, 22 July, Brisbane, Australia.

Cheldelin, S. and Eliatamby, M. (eds) (2011) *Women Waging War and Peace: International Perspectives on Women's Roles in Conflict and Post-Conflict Reconstruction*, New York: Continuum International Publishing Group.

Cheng, C. (2012) 'Private and Public Interests: Informal Actors, Informal Influence, and Economic Order after War' in M. Berdal and D. Zaum (eds), *The Political Economy of Post Conflict Statebuilding*, London: Routledge.

Chesterman, S. (2004) *You, the People: The United Nations, Transitional Administration and State-Building*, Oxford: Oxford University Press.

Chetail, V. (ed.) (2009) *Post-Conflict Peacebuilding: A Lexicon*, New York: Oxford University Press.

Child Soldiers International (2018) 'A former child soldier at the ICC', Child Soldiers International website. Available at: www.child-soldiers.org/news/a-former-child-soldier-at-the-icc.

Child Soldiers International (2019) Child Soldiers International website. Available at: www.child-soldiers.org.

Children's Legal Centre (2011) Administrative Detention of Children: A Global Report, New York: UNICEF. Available at: www.unicef.org/protection/files/Administrative_detention_discussion_paper_April2011.pdf.

Chiyuki, A., de Coning, C. and Karlsrud, J. (2017) 'Introduction: Addressing the Emerging Gap between Concepts, Doctrine, and Practice in UN Peacekeeping Operations' in C. de Coning, C. Aoi and J. Karlsrud (eds), *UN Peacekeeping Doctrine in a New Era*, Abingdon and New York: Routledge.

Chomsky, N. (1994) *World Orders Old and New*, New York: Columbia University Press.

Chomsky, N. (2006) 'A Just War? Hardly', *Khaleej Times*, 09 May. Available at: www.khaleejtimes.com/editorials-columns/a-just-war-hardly.

Chomsky, N. (2017) *Prospects for Survival* (video). Available at: www.youtube.com/watch?v=t0TE1Ib-O_M&list=RDt0TE1Ib-O_M&t=463.

Chuter, D. (2003) *War Crimes: Confronting Atrocity in the Modern World*, Boulder: Lynne Reiner.

Chuter, D. (2006) 'Understanding Security Sector Reform', *Journal of Security Sector Management*, 4(2). Available at: www.davidchuter.com/Texts/jofssm_0402_chuter.pdf.

Chuter, D. (2011) *Governing and Managing the Defence Sector*, Pretoria: Institute for Security Studies. Available at: www.files.ethz.ch/isn/127832/GovManDefSec.pdf.

Chuter, D. (2012) 'The ICC: A Place for Africans or Africans in Their Place?' in V. Nmehielle (ed.), *Africa and the Future of International Criminal Justice*, The Hague: Eleven International Publishing, 161–184.

Chuter, D. (2014) 'Fighting for the Toolbox: Why Building Security and Justice Post-Conflict Is so Difficult' in E. Gordon (ed.), *Building Security and Justice in Post-Conflict Environments*, Leicester: University of Leicester, 9–25. Available at: https://uolscid.files.wordpress.com/2014/08/scid-reader-2014-bookmarked.pdf.

Chuter, D. (2015) *The Security Sector in a Law-based State: A Short Guide for Practitioners and Others*, pre-publication draft (may be cited). Available at: www.davidchuter.com/Texts/ChuterROLBook.pdf.

Chuter, D. (2017) personal correspondence with the author.

Chuter, D. (2018) 'African Solutions to Western Problems: Western-Sponsored Training Programmes for African Militaries: Impact on Peace and Democratic Consolidation' in D. Francis (ed.), *African Peace Militaries: War, Peace and Democratic Governance*, Abingdon: Routledge, 103–120.

CIGI (2010) *Child Soldiers in Uganda?* (video). Available at: www.youtube.com/watch?v=TLWpte-VRVY.

CIGI (2014) *Libya: Dealing with the Militias and Advancing Security Sector Reform*. Available at: http://secgovcentre.org/wp-content/uploads/2016/09/eSeminar-1-Summary-Report-08-Jan-14.pdf.

Clapham, A. (2017) 'Non-State Actors' in D. Moeckli, S. Shah, S. Sivakumaran, and D. Harris (eds), *International Human Rights Law* (3rd edn), Oxford: Oxford University Press.

Clapham, C. (1996) *Africa and the International System: The Politics of State Survival*, Cambridge: Cambridge University Press.

CMC International (2010) 'Impact of Mines/ERW on Women and Children', Landmine and Cluster Munition Monitor Factsheet, Geneva: CMC International. Available at: www.the-monitor.org/index.php/content/view/full/24507.

Coalition for the ICC (2018) 'Brigid Inder, WIGJ Executive Director', Coalition for the ICC website. Available at: http://coalitionfortheicc.org/brigid-inder.

Cockayne, J. (2011) *'State Fragility, Organised Crime and Peacebuilding: Towards a More Strategic Approach'*, Oslo: Norwegian Peacebuilding Resource Centre. Available at: www.peacebuilding.no/var/ezflow_site/storage/original/application/2af427c8039ed02db6fd29fab1144aa8.pdf.

Cockayne, J. (2013) 'Chasing Shadows: Strategic Responses to Organised Crime in Conflict-Affected Situations', *The RUSI Journal*, 158(2):10–24.

Cockayne, J. and Lupel, A. (eds) (2011) *Peace Operations and Organized Crime: Enemies or Allies*, New York: Routledge.

Cockayne, J. and O'Neil, S. (eds) (2015) *UN DDR in an Era of Violent Extremism: Is It Fit for Purpose?* Tokyo: UNU-CPR. Available at: https://peacekeeping.un.org/sites/default/files/un_ddr_in_an_era_of_violent_extremism.pdf.

Cockayne, J. and Pfister, D. (2008) 'Peace Operations and Organised Crime', *Geneva Papers 2*, Geneva: IPI. Available at: www.ipacademy.org/media/pdf/publications/geneva_paper_2.pdf.

Cockburn, C. (2010) 'Gender Relations as Causal in Militarization and War: A Feminist Standpoint', *International Feminist Journal of Politics*, 12(2): 139–57.

Cohen, D., Green, A., and Wood, E. (2013) 'Wartime Sexual Violence: Misconceptions, Implications, and Ways Forward', *USIP Special Report*, Washington: USIP. Available at: www.usip.org/files/resources/SR323.pdf.

Cohen, S. (2001) *States of Denial: Knowing about Atrocities and Suffering*, Cambridge: Polity Press.

Cohn, C. (2013) *Women and Wars: Contested Histories, Uncertain Futures*, Cambridge: Polity Press.

Colak, A. and Pearce, J. (2015) 'Securing the Global City?: An Analysis of the "Medellín Model" through Participatory Research', *Conflict, Security & Development*, 15(3): 197–228.

Colekessian, A. (2010) 'Reintegrating Gender: A Gendered Analysis of the Nepali Rehabilitation Process', Working Paper, UN International Research and Training Institute for the Advancement of Women (UN-INSTRAW). Available at: https://trainingcentre.unwomen.org/instraw-library/2010-R-PEA-NPL-GPS-WPS.pdf.

Collier, P. (2000) 'Doing Well Out of War: An Economic Perspective' in M. Berdal and D. Malone (eds), *Greed and Grievance: Economic Agendas in Civil War*, Boulder: Lynne Rienner, 91–112.

Collier, P. (2007) 'Economic Causes of Civil Conflict and Their Implications for Policy' in C. Crocker, F. Hampson and P. Aall (eds), *Leashing the Dogs of War*, Washington: USIP, 197–218.

Collier, P. and Hoeffler, A. (2000) *Greed and Grievance in Civil War*, World Bank Policy Research Working Paper, Washington, DC: World Bank. Available at: http://documents.worldbank.org/curated/en/359271468739530199/pdf/multi-page.pdf.

Collier, P., Hoeffler, A. and Söderbom, M. (2008) 'Post-Conflict Risks', *Journal of Peace Research*, 45: 461–78.

Collinson, S., Elhawary, S. and Muggah, R. (2010) 'States of fragility: stabilisation and its implication for humanitarian action', Humanitarian Policy Group (HPG) Working Paper, London: Overseas Development Institute (ODI). Available at: www.odi.org.uk/resources/download/4881.pdf.

Conflict Dynamics International (2015) *Children in Armed Conflict Accountability Framework: A Framework for Advancing Accountability for Serious Violations against Children in Armed Conflict*, Cambridge: Conflict Dynamics International. Available at: www.cdint.org/documents/CAC_Accountability_Framework-1.pdf.

The Conversation (2017) 'Bosnia's 25-year struggle with transitional justice' *The Conversation*, 05 April. Available at: https://theconversation.com/bosnias-25-year-struggle-with-transitional-justice-75517.

Cornish, P. (2007) 'No Room for Humanitarianism in 3D Policies: Have Forcible Humanitarian Interventions and Integrated Approaches Lost Their Way?', *Journal of Military and Strategic Studies*, 10(1): 139–48.

Correlates of War Project (2019) Correlates of War Project website. Available at: www.correlatesofwar.org.

Council on Foreign Relations (CFR) (2010) *Transnational Organized Crime as a Threat to Peace and Security*, New York: CFR. Available at: www.cfr.org/un/transnational-organized-crime-threat-peace-security/p22480.

Council on Foreign Relations (CFR) (2012) 'The Global Human Rights Regime', Issue Brief, Global Governance Monitor, Washington: CFR. Available at: www.cfr.org/humanrights/global-human-rights-regime/p27450.

Coventry University (2012) 'Reintegrating ex-combatants into civilian life: how not to do it! – Professorial Lecture: Alpaslan Özerdem' (video). Available at: www.youtube.com/watch?v=EE0FJNxMh0o.

CQ Researcher (ed.) (2011) *Issues in Peace and Conflict Studies: Selections from CQ Researcher*, Washington: Sage.

Cramer, C. (2006) *Civil War Is Not a Stupid Thing: Accounting for Violence in Developing Countries*, London: Hurst.

Crawford, T. (2001) 'Pivotal Deterrence and the Kosovo War: Why the Holbrooke Agreement Failed', *Political Science Quarterly*, 116(4): 499–523.

Crenshaw, M. (2007) 'Terrorism and Global Security' in C. Crocker, F. Hampson and P. Aall (eds), *Leashing the Dogs of War*, Washington: USIP, 401–24.

Crenshaw, M. (2014) 'Terrorism Research: The Record', *International Interactions: Empirical and Theoretical Research in International Relations*, 40(4): 556–67.

Crider, L. (2012) 'Rape as a War Crime and Crime against Humanity: The Effect of Rape in Bosnia-Herzegovina and Rwanda on International Law', paper prepared for the *Alabama Political Science Association Conference* held at Auburn University, 30-31 March. Available at: www.cla.auburn.edu/alapsa/assets/file/4ccrider.pdf.

Crocker, C., Hampson, F. and Aall, P. (eds) (2007) *Leashing the Dogs of War*, Washington, DC: USIP.

Crocker, C., Hampson, F. and Aall, P. (eds) (2015) *Managing Conflict in a World Adrift*, Washington, DC: USIP.

Csáky, C. (2008) *No One to Turn To: The Under-Reporting of Child Sexual Exploitation and Abuse by Aid Workers and Peacekeepers*, London: Save the Children. Available at: https://resourcecentre.savethechildren.net/library/no-one-turn-under-reporting-child-sexual-exploitation-and-abuse-aid-workers-and-peacekeepers.

Cubbon, J. (2014) 'International Criminal Justice in the Context of Conflict Prevention and the Promotion of Peace – John Cubbon', (video) (University of Leicester). Available at: www.youtube.com/watch?v=1Wz4P_KH_No&index=2&list=PLjQX5EXgm57S0L7nT-QMVhQLKiYNsSPxu.

Dahir, A. (2018) 'Piracy made a strong comeback in Somalia in 2017', *Quartz Africa*, 24 May. Available at: https://qz.com/africa/1287522/somali-piracy-and-armed-robbery-off-the-indian-ocean-doubled-in-2017/.

Daigle, M. and Myrttinen, H. (2018) 'Bringing Diverse Sexual Orientation and Gender Identity (SOGI) into Peacebuilding Policy and Practice', *Gender & Development*, 1(26): 103–20.

Dallaire, R. (2003) *Shake Hands with the Devil: The Failure of Humanity in Rwanda*, New York: Carroll & Graf.

Danticat, E. (2017) 'A New Chapter for the Disastrous United Nations Mission in Haiti?', *The New Yorker*, 19 October. Available at: www.newyorker.com/news/news-desk/a-new-chapter-for-the-disastrous-united-nations-mission-in-haiti.

Darcy, J. (2004) 'Human Rights and Humanitarian Action: A review of the issues', a background paper prepared for the workshop on Human Rights and Humanitarian Action convened by the IASC Sub-Working Group and co-hosted by UNICEF, the UN High Commission for Human Rights and ICVA, Geneva, April. Human Rights and Humanitarian Action – HPG Background Paper, London: Humanitarian Policy Group, Overseas Development Institute (ODI). Available at: www.odi.org/sites/odi.org.uk/files/odi-assets/publications-opinion-files/2311.pdf.

David, C. P. (1998) *La Guerre et la Paix: Approches Contemporaines de la Sécurite et de la Stratégie*, Paris: Presses de Sciences Po.

Davidson, B. (1992) *The Black Man's Burden: Africa and the Curse of the Nation-State*, New York: Three Rivers Press.

Davies, S. and True, J. (2015) 'Reframing conflict-related sexual and gender-based violence: Bringing gender analysis back in', *Security Dialogue*, 46(6): 495–512.

Davies, S. and True, J. (2017) 'When There Is No Justice: Gendered Violence and Harm in Post-Conflict Sri Lanka', *The International Journal of Human Rights*, 21(9): 1320–36.

Davies, S. and True, J. (2019) *The Oxford Handbook of Women, Peace, and Security*, Oxford: Oxford University Press.

Daxecker, U. and Prins, B. (2017) 'Financing Rebellion: Using Piracy to Explain and Predict Conflict Intensity in Africa and Southeast Asia', *Journal of Peace Research*, 54(2): 215–30.

DCAF (2007) *Trafficking in Human Beings*, Geneva: DCAF. Available at: www.dcaf.ch.

DCAF (2008) *Democratic Control of the Armed Forces*, DCAF Backgrounder Series, Geneva: DCAF. Available at: www.dcaf.ch/DCAF/EZ/Publications/Democratic-Control-of-Armed-Forces2.

DCAF (2009) *Security Sector Governance and Reform*, DCAF Backgrounder Series, Geneva: DCAF. Available at: http://dcafdev.ethz.ch/Publications/Publication-Detail?lng=en&id=99979.

DCAF (2015a) 'The Justice Sector', SSR Backgrounder Series. Available at: www.dcaf.ch/sites/default/files/publications/documents/DCAF_BG_6_The%20Justice%20Sector.11.15.pdf.

DCAF (2015b) 'Security Sector Governance: Applying the Principles of Good Governance to the Security Sector', *DCAF Backgrounder*, Geneva: DCAF. Available at: www.dcaf.ch/Publications/Security-Sector-Governance-Applying-the-principles-of-good-governance-to-the-security-sector.

DCAF/Atlantic Initiative (2017) *Gender Bias and the Law: Legal Frameworks and Practice from Bosnia & Herzegovina and Beyond*, Geneva: DCAF. Available at: www.dcaf.ch/gender-bias-and-law-legal-frameworks-and-practice-bosnia-herzegovina-and-beyond.

DCAF/ISSAT (2011) *SSR in a Nutshell: Manual for Introductory Training on Security Sector Reform*, Geneva: DCAF/ISSAT. Available at: http://issat.dcaf.ch/Home/Training-and-Capacity-Building/Training-Materials.

De Boer, J. and Bosetti, L. (2017) 'The Crime-Conflict Nexus: Assessing the Threat and Developing Solutions', United Nations University (UNU) Centre for Policy Research, Crime-Conflict Nexus Series: No 1, May 2017, Tokyo: UNU. Available at: https://cpr.unu.edu/the-crime-conflict-nexus-assessing-the-threat-and-developing-solutions.html.

de Coning, C. and Stamnes, E. (eds) (2016) *UN Peacebuilding Architecture: The First 10 Years*, Abingdon: Routledge.

De Maio, J. (2010) 'Is War Contagious? the Transnationalization of Conflict in Darfur', *African Studies Quarterly*, 11(4): 25–44.

de Watteville, N. (2002) 'Addressing Gender Issues in Demobilization and Reintegration Programs', Africa Region Working Paper Series No. 33, Washington: World Bank. Available at: http://pdf2.hegoa.efaber.net/entry/content/1505/DE_WATTEVILLE__Nathalie_de_2002_-_Addresing_Gender_Issues_in_Demobilization_and_Reintegration_Programs.pdf.

Deen, T. (2018) 'UN Cracks Down on Peacekeeping Troops over Human Rights Abuses, *IPS*, 13 April. Available at www.ipsnews.net/2018/04/un-cracks-peacekeeping-troops-human-rights-abuses.

Delcourt, B. (2016) 'The Rule of Law as a Vehicle for Intervention', *Journal of Intervention and Statebuilding*, 9(4): 471–94.

Department for Transport, UK Government (2012) opening remarks by the Rt Hon Justine Greening MP at the IMO high-level debate on armed guards to tackle piracy, London: UK Government. Available at: www.dft.gov.uk/news/speeches/greening-20120516a.

Derluyn, I., Vandenhole, W., Parmentier, S., and Mels, C. (2015) 'Victims And/Or Perpetra-tors? Towards an Interdisciplinary Dialogue on Child Soldiers', *BMC International Health and Human Rights*, 15.

DeWaal, A. (2013) 'Trans-national Organized Crime in Africa: Whose problem?', 23 April, Reinventing Peace, World Peace Foundations' Blog. Available at: https://sites.tufts.edu/reinventingpeace/2013/04/23/trans-national-organized-crime-in-africa-whose-problem/.

DFID (2010) Building Peaceful States and Societies, a DFID Practice Paper, London: DFID. Available at: www.gsdrc.org/docs/open/CON75.pdf.

Dharmapuri, S. (2011) 'Just Add Women and Stir'?, *Parameters*, 41(1): 56–70. Available at: www.carlisle.army.mil/usawc/parameters/Articles/2011spring/Dharmapuri.pdf.

Diaz, P. and Tordjman, S. (2012) *Women's Participation in Peace Negotiations: Connections between Presence and Influence*, New York: UN Women. Available at: www.unwomen.org/-/media/headquarters/attachments/sections/library/publications/2012/10/wpssourcebook-03a-womenpeacenegotiations-en.pdf?vs=1159.

Dim, E. (2017) 'An Integrated Theoretical Approach to the Persistence of Boko Haram Vio-lent Extremism in Nigeria', *Journal of Peacebuilding and Development*, 12(2): 36–50.

Dobbins, J., Seth, G., Keith, C. and DeGrasse, B. (2007) *The Beginner's Guide to Nation-Build-ing*, Santa Monica: Rand Corporation. Available at: www.rand.org/content/dam/rand/pubs/monographs/2007/RAND_MG557.pdf.

Dodge, T. (2009) 'What were the causes and consequences of Iraq's descent into violence after the initial invasion?' Written evidence submitted to the Iraq Inquiry. Available at: www.iiss.org/whats-new/iiss-in-the-press/press-coverage-2009/november-2009/what-werethe-causes-and-consequences-of-iraqs-descent-into-violence-after-the-initial-invasion/?locale=en.

Donais, T. (2009) 'Inclusion or Exclusion? Local Ownership and Security Sector Reform', *Studies in Social Justice*, 3(1): 117–31.

Donais, T. (2017) 'Engaging Non-State Security Providers: Whither the Rule of Law?', *Stabil-ity: International Journal of Security and Development*, 6(1): 7.

Donais, T. (2018) 'Security Sector Reform and the Challenge of Vertical Integration', *Journal of Intervention and Statebuilding*, 12(1): 31–47.

Donnelly, T., Nikolla, F., Poudel, A. and Chakraborty, B. (2013) *Community-Based Approaches to Safety and Security: Lessons from Kosovo, Nepal and Bang-ladesh*, London: Saferworld. Available at: www.saferworld.org.uk/resources/publications/741-community-based-approaches-to-safety-and-security.

Drumbl, M. (2012) *Reimagining Child Soldiers in International Law and Policy*, Oxford: Oxford University Press.

DuBois, M. (2018) 'The New Humanitarian Basics', Humanitarian Policy Group (HPG) Pol-icy Paper. Available at: www.odi.org/sites/odi.org.uk/files/resource-documents/12201.pdf.

Dudenhoefer, A.-L. (2016) 'Understanding the Recruitment of Child Soldiers in Africa', *Conflict Trends*, 16 August, African Centre for the Constructive Resolu-tion of Disputes (ACCORD). Available at: www.accord.org.za/conflict-trends/understanding-recruitment-child-soldiers-africa.

Dudouet, V. and Schmelzle, B. (eds) (2010) *Human Rights and Conflict Transformation: The Challenges of Just Peace*, Berlin: Berghof Conflict Research.

Duff, R. (2005) 'Notes on Punishment and Terrorism', *American Behavioral Scientist*, 48(6): 758–63.

Duffield, M. (2001) *Global Governance and the New Wars: The Merging of Development and Security*, London: Zed Books.

Duffield, M. (2007) *Development, Security and Unending War: Governing the World of Peoples*, Cambridge: Polity Press.

Dwarka, L. (2017) 'The African Standby Force: The African Union's Tool for the Maintenance of Peace and Security', *Contemporary Security Policy*, 38(3): 471–782.

Dyke, C. (2016) 'DDR and SSR in War-to-Peace Transition' SSR Paper 14, Geneva: DCAF. Available at: www.dcaf.ch/sites/default/files/publications/documents/ONLINE-DCAF-SSR-14-2016-12-21.pdf.

The Economist (2011) 'No Stopping Them', *The Economist*, 05 February, 60–62.

Eide, E., Kaspersen, A., Kent, R. and Hippel, K. (2005) *Report on Integrated Missions: Practical Perspectives and Recommendations*, Independent Study for the Expanded UN ECHA Core Group, New York: OCHA. Available at: http://ochanet.unocha.org/p/Documents/Report_on_Integrated_Missions_May_2005_Final.pdf.

ELAC, University of Oxford (2012) *The ICC at 10*, Panel Discussion (podcast). Available at: https://podcasts.ox.ac.uk/icc-10.

Elhawary, S. (2011) 'Is the UK Securitising Its Development Aid?', *ODI Blog*, 03 March, London: ODI. Available at: http://blogs.odi.org.uk/blogs/main/archive/2011/03/03/securitisation_aid_uk_multilateral_bilateral_aid_review_2011.aspx.

Eliatamby, M. (2011) 'Searching for Emancipation: Eritrea, Nepal, and Sri Lanka.' in S. Cheldelin and M. Eliatamby (eds), *Women Waging War and Peace: International Perspectives on Women's Roles in Conflict and Post-Conflict Reconstruction*, New York: Continuum International Publishing Group, 37–51.

Eliatamby, M. and Romanova, E. (2011) 'Dying for Identity: Chechnya and Sri Lanka' in S. Cheldelin and M. Eliatamby (eds), *Women Waging War and Peace: International Perspectives on Women's Roles in Conflict and Post-Conflict Reconstruction*, New York: Continuum International Publishing Group, 52–65.

Elmi, A. Ladan Affi, L., Knight, W. and Said Mohamed, S. (2015) 'Piracy in the Horn of Africa Waters: Definitions, History, and Modern Causes', *African Security*, 8(3): 147–65.

Enloe, C. (2000) *Maneuvers: The International Politics of Militarizing Women's Lives*, Berkeley: University of California Press.

Enloe, C. (2004) *The Curious Feminist; Searching for Women in a New Age of Empire*, Oakland, CA: University of California Press.

Ertman, T. (1997) *Birth of the Leviathan: Building States and Regimes in Medieval and Early Modern Europe*, Cambridge: Cambridge University Press.

Escola de Cultura de Pau (School for a Culture of Peace) (2009) *Alert 2009*, Barcelona: Escola de Cultura de Pau, Autonomous University of Barcelona. Available at: http://escolapau.uab.cat/img/programas/alerta/alerta/alerta09i.pdf.

Escribà-Folch, A. (2010) 'Economic Sanctions and the Duration of Civil Conflicts', *Journal of Peace Research*, 47(02 March): 129–41.

EU (2018) 'EU Missions and Operations', Brussels: EU. Available at: https://eeas.europa.eu/sites/eeas/files/factsheet-csdp_missions_and_operations_05-03-2018.pdf.

EU (2019) 'Rule of Law', EU website. Available at: http://ec.europa.eu/justice/effective-justice/rule-of-law/index_en.htm.

Europol (2017) *2017 EU Terrorism Situation and Trend Report*. The Hague: EUROPOL. Available at: www.europol.europa.eu/activities-services/main-reports/eu-terrorism-situation-and-trend-report-te-sat-2017.

Evans, G. (2005) 'The United Nations and Conflict Prevention'. *Address by Gareth Evans, President of the International Crisis Group, to the Dag Hammarskjöld Centenary Seminar co-hosted by IFRI and Swedish Embassy, Paris, 17 October*. Available at: www.crisisgroup.org/en/publication-type/speeches/2005/the-united-nations-and-conflict-prevention.aspx.

Evans, G. (2006) 'Conflict Prevention and Development Cooperation: From Crisis to Peaceful Governance'. *Keynote Address by Gareth Evans, President of the International Crisis Group, to Seminar on Channels of Influence in a Crisis Situation – How can Development*

Cooperation Support Conflict Resolution and Democracy? Sponsored by Crisis Management Initiative, Finnish Parliament and Foreign Ministry, and Democracy Cooperation Forum of Finnish Political Parties, Helsinki. Available at: www.gevans.org/speeches/speech208. html.

Evans, R. (2016) *The Pursuit of Power: Europe 1815–1914*, London: Viking.

FCO (2014) *Summit Report: The Global Summit To End Sexual Violence In Conflict*, London 2014, London: FCO. Available at: www.gov.uk/government/uploads/system/uploads/attachment_data/file/385811/FCO707_PSVI_post_summit_report_v10.pdf.

Fearon, J. and Laitin, D. (2003) 'Ethnicity, Insurgency, and Civil War', *American Political Science Review*, 97(1): 75–89.

Felbab-Brown, V. (2005) 'The Coca Connection: Conflict and Drugs in Colombia and Peru', *Journal of Conflict Studies*, 25(2): 104–28. Available at: https://journals.lib.unb.ca/index. php/JCS/article/view/489/823.

Fenton, S. (2017) 'UK prisons "holding child inmates in solitary confinement against UN torture rules"', *The Independent*, 21 February. Available at: www.independent.co.uk/news/uk/home-news/uk-prisons-child-inmates-solitary-confinement-un-torture-rules-young-offenders-institutes-break-jail-a7591781.html.

Ferris, E. (2007) 'Abuse of Power: Sexual Exploitation of Refugee Women and Girls', *Signs: Journal of Women in Culture and Society*, 32(3): 584–91.

Ferro, M. (2007) *Le Ressentiment Dans L'histoire*, Paris: Odile Jacob.

Ferstman, C. (2013) *Criminalizing Sexual Exploitation and Abuse by Peacekeepers*, Washington: USIP. Available at: www.usip.org/sites/default/files/SR335-Criminalizing%20Sexual%20 Exploitation%20and%20Abuse%20by%20Peacekeepers.pdf.

Finckenauer J. (2005) 'Problems of Definition: What Is Organized Crime?', *Trends in Organized Crime*, 8(5): 63–83.

FIP (2016) *Economías Criminales En Clave De Postconflicto: Tendencias Actuales Y Propuestas Para Hacerles Frente* (Criminal Economies in Light of the Post-Conflict: Current Trends and Proposals to Address Them). Bogotá: Fundación Ideas para la Paz (FIP). Available online at http://cdn.ideaspaz.org/media/website/document/56b8b198b6272.pdf.

Fischer, M. (2011) 'Transitional Justice and Reconciliation: Theory and Practice' in B. Austin, M. Fischer and J. Giessmann (eds), *The Berghof Handbook II*, Opladen: Barbara Budrich .

Flavin, W. (2003) 'Planning for Conflict Termination and Post-Conflict Success', *Parameters*, 23 (Autumn): 95–112. Available at: www.dtic.mil/cgi-bin/GetTRDo c?AD=ADA486290&Location=U2&doc=GetTRDoc.pdf.

Flint, J. and de Waal, A. (2009) 'Case Closed: A Prosecutor without Borders', *World Affairs*, 171(4): 23-38.

Flisi, I. (2017) 'The Reintegration of Former Combatants in Colombia', Inclusive Security Blog, Oxford Research Group, 13 February. Available at: https://sustainablesecurity. org/2017/02/13/the-reintegration-of-former-combatants-in-colombia/.

Ford, S. (2013) 'Fairness and Politics at the ICTY: Evidence from the Indictments', *North Carolina Journal of International Law and Commercial Regulation*, 39(1): 45–113.

Fortin, I. (2011) 'Security Sector Reform in Haiti: One Year after the Earthquake', *SSR Issues Papers No. 1*, Ontario: CIGI. Available at: www.cigionline.org/sites/default/files/SSR_Issue_no1.pdf.

Fortna, V. (2004) 'Does Peacekeeping Keep Peace? International Intervention and the Duration of Peace after Civil War', *International Studies Quarterly*, 48(2): 269–92.

Fragile States Index (2019) Fragile States Index website, Washington, DC: The Fund for Peace. Available at: http://fundforpeace.org/fsi/.

Frederickson, H. (2005) 'Whatever Happened to Public Administration? Governance, Governance Everywhere' in E. Ferlie, L. Lynn and C. Pollitt (eds), *Oxford Handbook of Public Administration*, Oxford: Oxford University Press.

Frei, N., Stahl, D. and Weinke, A. (2017) (eds) *Human Rights and Humanitarian Intervention: Legitimizing the Use of Force since the 1970s*, Göttingen: Wallstein Verlag.

Frey, B. (2004) 'Small Arms and Light Weapons: The Tools Used to Violate Human Rights', *Human Rights, Human Security, and Disarmament*, 3: 37–46.

Friesendorf, C. and Penksa, S. (2008) 'Militarized Law Enforcement in Peace Operations: EUFOR in Bosnia and Herzegovina', *International Peacekeeping*, 15(5): 677–94.

Front Line Defenders (2019) Front Line Defenders website. Available at: www.frontlinedefenders.org.

Galic, N. and Huhtanen, H. (2014) *Judicial Benchbook: Consideration of Domestic Violence Case Evaluation in Bosnia and Herzegovina*, Geneva: DCAF. Available at: www.dcaf.ch/judicial-benchbook-considerations-domestic-violence-case-evaluation-bosnia-and-herzegovina.

Galtung, J. (1964) 'An Editorial', *Journal of Peace Research*, 1(1): 1–4.

Galtung, J. (2013) 'Positive and Negative Peace' in G. Fischer and J. Galtung (eds), *John Galtung: Pioneer of Peace Research*, Berlin: Springer, 173–78.

Garcia, D. (2014) 'Global Norms on Arms: The Significance of the Arms Trade Treaty for Global Security in World Politics', *Global Policy*, 5(4): 425–32.

Garkawe, S. (2003) 'South African Truth and Reconciliation Commission: A Suitable Model to Enhance the Role and Rights of the Victims of Gross Violations of Human Rights?' *Melbourne University Law Review*, 27(2): 334

Garland, D. (1990) *Punishment and Modern Society: A Study in Social Theory*, Chicago: Chicago University Press.

Garzón-Vergara, J. (2015) 'Avoiding the Perfect Storm: Criminal Economies, Spoilers, and the Post-Conflict Phase in Colombia', *Stability: International Journal of Security and Development*, 4(1): 1–15.

Gearty, C. (2014) 'The State of Human Rights', *Global Policy*, 5(4): 391–400.

Gegout, C. (2013) 'The International Criminal Court: Limits, Potential and Conditions for the Promotion of Justice and Peace', *Third World Quarterly*, 34(5): 800–18.

Geneva International Centre for Humanitarian Demining (2019) website of the AP Mine Ban Convention Implementation Support Unit. Available at: www.apminebanconvention.org.

Geneva International Centre for International Humanitarian Demining (GICHD) (2016) *'Finishing the Job': An Independent Review of the Mine Action Sector in Cambodia*, Geneva: GICHD. Available at: www.gichd.org/fileadmin/GICHD-resources/rec-documents/Cambodia-Sector-Review-Final-Report-GICHD.pdf.

Gershenson, D. (2001) 'Sanctions and Civil Conflict', IMF Working Paper. Available at: www.imf.org/external/pubs/ft/wp/2001/wp0166.pdf.

Gerwarth, R. (2016) *The Vanquished: Why the First World War Failed to End, 1917–1923*, London: Allen Lane.

Gheciu, A. (2011) 'Divided Partners', *Global Governance*, 17(1): 95–113.

Gheciu, A. and Paris, R. (2011) 'NATO and the Challenge of Sustainable Peacebuilding', *Global Governance*, 17(1): 75–79.

Ghimire, S. (2018) *The Politics of Peacebuilding: Emerging Actors and Security Sector Reform in Conflict-Affected State*, Abingdon: Routledge.

Ghittoni, M. Lehouck, L. and Watson, C. (2018) *Elsie Initiative for Women in Peace Operations: Baseline Study*, Geneva: DCAF. Available at: https://dcaf.ch/sites/default/files/publications/documents/Elsie_Baseline_Report_2018.pdf.

Gibson, J. (2004) *Overcoming Apartheid: Can Truth Reconcile a Divided Nation?*, New York and Cape Town: Russell Sage Foundation and HSRC Press.

GICHD (2011) *Assisting Landmine and other ERW Survivors in the Context of Disarmament, Disability and Development*, Geneva: GICHD. Available at: www.gichd.org/fileadmin/ GICHD-resources/rec-documents/Brochure-Assisting-Survivors-June2011.pdf.

GICHD (2019) GICHD website. Available at: www.gichd.org.

GICHD and DCAF (2017) 'Seeking more coherent implementation in post-conflict security: Can we better align SSR, DDR, SALW and Mine Action?', Event Report, Geneva: GICHD and DCAF. Available at: www.gichd.org/fileadmin/GICHD-resources/rec-documents/ GICHD-DCAF-event-report-2017-05.pdf.

Girard R. (1972) *Le Violence Et Le Sacré*, Paris: Grasset.

Gizelis, T.-I. (2011) 'A Country of Their Own: Women and Peacebuilding', *Conflict Management and Peace Science*, 28(5): 522–42.

Glazzard, A., Jesperson, S., Maguire, T. and Winterbotham, E. (2017) 'Islamist Violent Extremism: A New Form of Conflict or Business as Usual?', *Stability: International Journal of Security and Development*, 6(1): 13, 1–19.

Gleditsch, N., Christiansen, L. and Havard, H. (2007) 'Democratic Jihad? Military Intervention and Democracy', *Policy Research Working Paper*, Washington: World Bank. Available at: http://ideas.repec.org/p/wbk/wbrwps/4242.html.

Glennie, A. (2010) *States of Conflict: Lessons in Conflict Prevention and Peacebuilding*, London: IPPR. Available at: www.ippr.org/files/images/media/files/publication/2011/12/states-of-conflict_lessons_Sep2010_1805.pdf?noredirect=1.

The Global Coalition Against Daesh (2018) website of the Global Coalition Against Daesh, 2018. Available at: http://theglobalcoalition.org.

Global Development (2015) 'What Causes Conflict and How It Can Be Resolved', *The Guardian's* Global Development podcast (2015). Available at: www.theguardian.com/ global-development/audio/2015/may/17/conflict-resolution.

Global Policy (2013) 'Chandra Lekha Sriram – Justice Programming in Conflict Affected and Transitioning Countries' (video). Available at: www.youtube.com/watch?v=pvB4jXnDIX8.

Goldstone, J. (2008) *Using Quantitative and Qualitative Models to Forecast Instability*, Washington: USIP. Available at: www.usip.org/files/resources/sr204.pdf.

Gomez, M. and Christensen, A. (2010) *The Impacts of Refugees on Neighboring Countries: A Development Challenges*, World Development Report 2011, Washington: World Bank. Available at: http://siteresources.worldbank.org/EXTSOCIALDEVELOPMENT/Resource s/244362-1265299949041/6766328-1265299960363/WDR_Background_Paper_ Refugees.pdf.

Goodhand, J. (2008) 'Corrupting or Consolidating the Peace? the Drugs Economy and Post-Conflict Peacebuilding in Afghanistan', *International Peacekeeping*, 15(3): 405–23.

Gordon, E. (ed.) (2014) *Building Justice and Security in Post-Conflict Environments: SCID Reader 2014*, Leicester: University of Leicester. Available at: https://uolscid.files. wordpress.com/2014/08/scid-reader-2014-bookmarked.pdf.

Gordon, E. (2014a) 'Security Sector Reform, Local Ownership and Community Engagement', *Stability: International Journal of Security and Development*, 3(1): 25, 1–18.

Gordon, E. (2014b) 'Security Sector Reform, Statebuilding and Local Ownership: Securing the State or Its People?', *Journal of Intervention and Statebuilding*, 8(2–3): 126–48.

Gordon, E. (2015) (ed.) *SCID Reader: Researching and Working in Conflict-Affected Environments*, Leicester: University of Leicester. Available at: http://tinyurl.com/pjfprek.

Gordon, E. (2017) 'Crimes of the Powerful in Conflict-Affected Environments: False Positives, Transitional Justice and the Prospects for Peace in Colombia', *State Crime Journal*, 6(1): 132–55.

Gordon, E. (2019) 'Gender and Defence Reform: Problematising the Place of Women in Conflict-Affected Environments', *Journal of Intervention and Statebuilding*, 13(1): 75–94.

Gordon, E., Sharma, S., Forbes, A. and Cave, R. (2011) *A Safer Future: Tracking Security Improvements in an Uncertain Context*, London and Kathmandu: Saferworld and Interdisciplinary analysts. Available at: www.saferworld.org.uk/downloads/pubdocs/A%20 safer%20future%20revised%20reduced.pdf.

Gordon, E., Welch, A. and Roos, E. (2015) 'Security Sector Reform and the Paradoxical Tension between Local Ownership and Gender Equality', *Stability: Journal of Security and Development*, 4(1): 53, 1–23.

Goswami, R. (2015) 'UNSCR 1325 and Female Ex-Combatants – Case Study of the Maoist Women of Nepal', Research Paper, UN Women. New York: UN Women. Available at: www. unwomen.org/-/media/headquarters/attachments/sections/library/publications/2017/ unscr1325-and-ex-combatants.pdf?la=en&vs=819.

Gowlland-Debbas, V. and Pergantis, V. (2009) 'Rule of Law' in V. Chetail (ed.), *Post-Conflict Peacebuilding: A Lexicon*, Oxford: Oxford University Press, 320–36.

Grady, K. (2010) 'Sexual Exploitation and Abuse by UN Peacekeepers: A Threat to Impartiality', *International Peacekeeping*, 17(2): 215–28.

Greenberg, M. and Zuckerman, E. (2009) 'The Gender Dimensions of Post-Conflict Reconstruction: The Challenges in Development Aid', in T. Addison and T. Brück (eds), *Making Peace Work: The Challenges of Social and Economic Reconstruction*, Basingstoke: Palgrave MacMillan.

Greene, O. and Marsh, N. (2013) *Small Arms, Crime and Conflict: Global Governance and the Threat of Armed Violence*, London: Routledge.

Greiff (De) P. (2010) Transitional Justice, Security, and Development, Security and Justice Thematic Paper, WDR Background Paper, Washington: WB. Available at: http://wdr2011. worldbank.org/sites/default/files/pdfs/WDR%20Background%20Paper_de%20Greiff_0. pdf?keepThis=true&TB_iframe=true&height=600&width=800.

Grillot, S. (2010) 'Guns in the Balkans: Controlling Small Arms and Light Weapons in Seven Western Balkan Countries', *Southeast European and Black Sea Studies*, 10(2): 147–71.

Grimm, S., Lemay-Hébert, N. and Nay, O. (2014) '"Fragile States": Introducing a Political Concept', *Third World Quarterly*, 35(2): 197–209.

Grono, N. (2009) 'The Role of International Justice Mechanisms in Fragile States', Speech by Nick Grono, Deputy President of the International Crisis Group (ICG) to the Overseas Development Institute, Peace Versus Justice? Understanding Transitional Justice in Fragile States, 09 October, Brussels: ICG. Available at: www.crisisgroup.org/global/ role-international-justice-mechanisms-fragile-states.

GSDRC (2016) 'Security and justice – Paul Jackson' (video). Available at: www.youtube.com/ watch?v=hwPYqmswbYg.

Gumede, W. (2018) 'The International Criminal Court and Accountability in Africa', WSG News, 31 January, website of the University of the Witwatersrand, Johannesburg. Available at: www.wits.ac.za/news/sources/wsg-news/2018/the-international-criminal-court-and-accountability-in-africa.html.

Habib, C. (2009) *Consociationalism and the Continuous Crisis in the Lebanese System*, Beirut: Majd.

Hafner-Burton, E. (2008) 'Sticks and Stones: Naming and Shaming the Human Rights Enforcement Problem', *International Organization*, 62: 689–716.

Hafner-Burton, E. and Ron, J. (2007) 'Human Rights Institutions: Rhetoric and Efficacy', *Journal of Peace Research*, 44(4): 379–84.

Haider, H. (2010) *Topic Guide Supplement on Statebuilding and Peacebuilding in Situations of Conflict and Fragility*, Governance and Social Development Research Centre (GSD-RC), October. Available at: www.gsdrc.org/docs/open/CON87.pdf.

Haider, H. (2014) *Conflict: Topic Guide*. Revised edition with B. Rohwerder. Birmingham: GSDRC, University of Birmingham. Available at: http://gsdrc.org/wp-content/uploads/2015/07/CON69.pdf.

Haider, H. (2016) 'Transitional justice: Topic guide', Birmingham, UK: GSDRC, University of Birmingham. Available at: www.gsdrc.org/wp-content/uploads/2016/08/TransitionalJustice_GSDRC.pdf.

Halilovic, M. (2015) *Survivors Speak: Reflections on Criminal Justice System Responses to Domestic Violence in Bosnia and Herzegovina*, Geneva: DCAF. Available at: www.dcaf.ch/survivors-speak-reflections-criminal-justice-system-responses-domestic-violence-bosnia-and.

Halilovic, M. and Huhtanen, H. (2014) *Gender and the Judiciary: The Implications of Gender within the Judiciary of Bosnia and Herzegovina*, Geneva: DCAF. Available at: www.dcaf.ch/sites/default/files/publications/documents/Gender_Judiciary_ENG%20FINAL.pdf.

Hall, E. (1977) *Beyond Culture*, New York: Anchor Books.

Hänggi, H. (2009) 'Security Sector Reform' in V. Chetail (ed.), *Post-Conflict Peacebuilding: A Lexicon*, Oxford: Oxford University Press, 337–49.

Hannan, S. (2012) 'Piracy Backgrounder', Pittsburgh: Matthew B. Ridgeway Center for International Studies, Pittsburgh University. Available at: http://research.ridgway.pitt.edu/blog/2012/05/15/piracy-backgrounder/.

Hanson, S. (2009) 'Backgrounder: Combating Maritime Piracy', The New York Times, 28 January. Available at: www.nytimes.com/cfr/world/slot1_20090127.html?pagewanted=all.

Happold, M. (2013) 'International Humanitarian Law and Human Rights Law' in N. White and C. Henderson (eds), *Research Handbook on International Conflict and Security Law*, Cheltenham: Edward Elgar Publishing, 1–20.

Harding, J. (2011) *The Doctrine of Humanitarian Intervention and the Neo-Colonial Implications of Its Revival in Our Unipolar World*, Information Clearing House. Available at: www.informationclearinghouse.info/article9280.htm.

Hardy, K. and Williams, G. (2014) 'What Is 'Cyberterrorism'? Computer and Internet Technology in Legal Definitions of Terrorism' in Chen, T., Jarvis, L. and Macdonald, S. (eds), *Cyberterrorism: Understanding, Assessment, and Response*, New York: Springer.

Harris, M. (2015) 'When a Child Goes to War' AEON, 01 June. Available at: https://aeon.co/essays/is-the-child-soldier-anything-more-than-a-tragic-victim.

Held, D. (2010) 'Cosmopolitanism after 9/11', *International Politics*, 47(1): 52–61.

Hendricks, C. (2012) 'Research on Gender and SSR in Africa' in: Baaz, M and Utas, M (eds), *Beyond 'Gender and Stir': Reflections on Gender and SSR in the Aftermath of African Conflicts*, Uppsala: The Nordic Africa Institute, 11–17. Available at: http://nai.diva-portal.org/smash/get/diva2:570724/FULLTEXT01.pdf.

Hendricks, C. and Hutton, L. (2008) 'Defence Reform and Gender' (Tool 3) in M. Bastick and K. Valasek (eds), *Gender and Security Sector Reform Toolkit*, Geneva: DCAF, OSCE/ODIHR,UN-INSTRAW. Available at: www.dcaf.ch/gender-security-sector-reform-toolkit.

Henshaw, A. (2016) 'Where Women Rebel: Patterns of Women's Participation in Armed Rebel Groups 1990–2008', *International Feminist Journal of Politics*, 18(1): 39–60.

Henshaw, A. (2017) *Why Women Rebel: Understanding Women's Participation in Armed Rebel Groups*, Abingdon: Routledge.

Herbst, J. (2000) *States and Power in Africa: Comparative Lessons in Authority and Control*, Princeton: Princeton University Press.

Herman, E. and N. Chomsky (1988) *Manufacturing Consent: The Political Economy of the Mass Media*, London: Vintage.

Hillenbrand, C. (2015) *Islam: A New Historical Introduction*, London: Thames & Hudson.

Hills, A. (2007) 'Democratic Control and Border Security in the Balkans', *Conflict, Security and Development*, 4(1): 97–107.

Hills, A. (2009) *Policing Post-Conflict Cities*, London and New York: Zed Books.

Hills, A. (2014) 'Security Sector or Security Arena? the Evidence from Somalia', *International Peacekeeping*, 21(2): 165–80.

HIPPO (2015) Report of the High-Level Independent Panel on Peace Operations (HIPPO). Available at: http://peaceoperationsreview.org/wp-content/uploads/2015/08/HIPPO_Report_1_June_2015.pdf.

Hofmann, H., Maspoli, G., Massleberg, A. and Rapillard, P. (2016) 'Linking Mine Action and SSR through Human Security' SSR Paper 15, Geneva: DCAF. Available at: www.dcaf.ch/sites/default/files/publications/documents/ONLINE-DCAF-SSR-15-2016-06-16.pdf.

Holmqvist, C. (2005) In 'Engaging Armed Non-State Actors in Post-Conflict Settings' in A. Bryden and H. Hänggi (eds), *Security Governance in Post-Conflict Peacebuilding*, Münster: LIT Verlag, 45–46.

Holt, M. (2014) *Women and Conflict in the Middle East: Palestinian Refugees and the Response to Violence*, London and New York: I.B. Tauris.

Holzer, G.-S. (2008) 'Somalia: Piracy and Politics', openDemocracy. Available at: www.opendemocracy.net/article/somalia-piracy-and-politics.

Houngbedji, M., Grace, R. and Brooks, J. (2012) 'The Impact of Gendered Misconceptions of Militarized Identities on Disarmament, Demobilization, Reintegration and Humanitarian Assistance in the Democratic Republic of the Congo', ATHA White Paper Series. Humanitarian Academy at Harvard, Cambridge: Harvard University. Available at: www.peacewomen.org/sites/default/files/impact_of_gendered_misconceptions_of_militarized_identities_on_disarmament_demobilization_reintegration_and_humanitarian_assistance_in_the_democratic_republic_of_the_congo_0.pdf.

Hourmat, M. (2016) 'Victim–Perpetrator Dichotomy in Transitional Justice: The Case of Post-Genocide Rwanda', *Narrative and Conflict: Explorations in Theory and Practice,* 4(1): 43–67. Retrieved from: http://journals.gmu.edu/NandC/issue/view/197.

House of Commons Foreign Affairs Committee (UK) (2011) 'Piracy off the Coast of Somalia', Tenth Report of Session 2010–12, London: The Stationery Office Ltd. Available at: www.publications.parliament.uk/pa/cm201012/cmselect/cmfaff/1318/1318.pdf.

House of Commons International Development Committee (UK) (2018) *Sexual Exploitation and Abuse in the Aid Sector*, London: HM Government. Available at: https://publications.parliament.uk/pa/cm201719/cmselect/cmintdev/840/84002.htm.

HRW (2009) Selling Justice Short: Why Accountability Matters for Peace, New York: HRW. Available at: www.hrw.org/sites/default/files/reports/ij0709webwcover_3.pdf.

HRW (2017) 'Colombia: Activists at Risk: Peace Promise Demands Guarantees for Rights Defenders', 24 April. Available at: www.hrw.org/news/2017/04/24/colombia-activists-risk.

HRW (2018) 'Statement on Compliance to the Intersessional Meetings of the Mine Ban Treaty, Geneva', Delivered by Steve Goose, Executive Director, Arms Division, 07 June, HRW website. Available at: www.hrw.org/news/2018/06/07/statement-compliance-intersessional-meetings-mine-ban-treaty-geneva.

Hubert, D. (2001) 'Small Arms Demand Reduction and Human Security: Towards a people-centred approach to small arms', Briefing Paper based on a paper presented by the author to the International Workshop on Small Arms Demand Reduction, Toronto, 14–17 March. Available at: www.ploughshares.ca/content/small-arms-demand-reduction-and-humansecurity-towards-people-centred-approach-small-arms.

Hudson, H. (2012) 'A Double-Edged Sword of Peace? Reflections on the Tension between Representation and Protection in Gendering Liberal Peacebuilding', *International Peacekeeping*, 19(4): 443–60.

Hudson, V. M., Caprioli, M., Ballif-Spanvill, B., McDermott, R., and Emmett, C. F. (2009) 'The Heart of the Matter: The Security of Women and the Security of States', *International Security*, 33(3): 7–45.

Huggins, M. (1998) *Political Policing: The United States and Latin America*, Durham NC: Duke University Press.

Hurwitz, A. (2008) 'Civil War and the Rule of Law: Toward Security, Development, and Human Rights', in A. Hurwitz and R. Huang (eds), *Civil War and the Rule of Law: Security, Development and Human Rights*, Boulder: Lynne Reinner, 1–18.

Huyse, L. and Salter, M. (eds) (2008) *Traditional Justice and Reconciliation after Violent Conflict: Learning from African Experiences*, Stockholm: International IDEA. Available at: www.idea.int/publications/traditional_justice/upload/traditional_justice_and_reconciliation_after_violent_conflict.pdf.

ICBL (2010) Landmine Monitor Report 2009: Toward a Mine-Free World Annual Report, Ottawa: Mines Action Canada. Available at: www.the-monitor.org/media/1641811/Landmine_Monitor_2010_lowres.pdf.

ICC (2014) *International Criminal Court (ICC-CPI) - Institutional Video* (video). Available at: www.youtube.com/watch?v=1K4Y8iqLzxQ.

ICC (2017) 'Remarks of ICC Prosecutor on future of international criminal justice' (video). Available at: www.youtube.com/watch?v=hhBm_CftY7o.

ICC (2019) ICC website. Available at: www.icc-cpi.int.

ICC IMB PRC (2017) *Piracy and Armed Robbery Against Ships*, Annual Report. London: ICC IMB. Available at: www.icc-ccs.org/reports/2017-Annual-IMB-Piracy-Report.pdf.

ICC IMB PRC (2019) website of the IMB Piracy Reporting Centre. Available at: www.icc-ccs.org/piracy-reporting-centre.

ICCLR (2001) *International Prison Policy Development Instrument*, Vancouver: ICCLR. Available at: www.icclr.law.ubc.ca/Site%20Map/Programs/Prison_Policy.htm.

Icelandic Human Rights Centre (2019) *The Human Rights Education Project*, Reykjavik: Icelandic Human Rights Centre. Available at: www.humanrights.is/en/human-rights-education-project/human-rights-concepts-ideas-and-fora/part-i-the-concept-of-human-rights/definitions-and-classifications.

ICG (2000) *War Criminals in Bosnia's Republika Srpska*, Brussels: ICG. Available at: https://d2071andvip0wj.cloudfront.net/103-war-criminals-in-bosnia-s-republika-srpska.pdf.

ICG (2010) 'Haiti: Stabilisation and Reconstruction After the Quake', *Latin America/Caribbean Report No. 32*, ICG: Port-au-Prince/Bogotá/Brussels. Available at: www.crisisgroup.org/~/media/Files/latin-america/haiti/32_haiti___stabilisation_and_reconstruction_after_the_quake.pdf.

ICG (2014) 'Bosnia's Future'. Available at: www.crisisgroup.org/europe-central-asia/balkans/bosnia-and-herzegovina/bosnia-s-future.

ICG (2015) 'Macedonia: Defusing the Bombs'. Available at: www.crisisgroup.org/europe-central-asia/balkans/macedonia/macedonia-defusing-bombs.

ICG Crisis Watch (2018) *CrisisWatch*, Brussels: International Crisis Group (ICG). Available at: www.crisisgroup.org/crisiswatch.

ICRC (2003) International Humanitarian Law and International Human Rights Law: Similarities and Differences, Geneva: ICRC. Available at: www.icrc.org/eng/assets/files/other/ihl_and_ihrl.pdf.

ICRC (2005a) *The Basics of International Humanitarian Law*, Geneva: ICRC. Available at: www.redcross.org.ph/pdfs/basics-of-international-humanitarian-law.pdf.

ICRC (2005b) *Water, Sanitation, Hygiene and Habitat in Prisons*, Geneva: ICRC. Available at: www.icrc.org/eng/assets/files/other/icrc_002_0823.pdf.

ICRC (2008) 'War Crimes under the Rome Statute of the International Criminal Court and their source in International Humanitarian Law: Comparative Table', ICRC Advisory Service on International Humanitarian Law, Geneva: ICRC. Available at: www.icrc.org/en/download/file/1093/war-crimes-comparative-table.pdf.

ICRC (2010a) IHL and Human Rights Law, Geneva: ICRC. Available at: www.icrc.org/eng/war-and-law/ihl-other-legal-regmies/ihl-human-rights/overview-ihland-human-rights.htm.

ICRC (2010b) *Respect for the Life and Dignity of the Detainees*, Geneva: ICRC. Available at: www.icrc.org/eng/what-we-do/visiting-detainees/overview-visiting-detainees.htm.

ICRC (2019) ICRC website. Available at: www.icrc.org.

ICTJ (2011) 'Peace versus Justice: A False Dilemma', ICTJ website. Available at: www.ictj.org/news/peace-versus-justice-false-dilemma.

ICTJ (video) (2011) *Peace and Justice*. Available at: www.youtube.com/watch?v=PWFpngEfu84.

ICTJ (2017) 'I Am Not Who They Think I Am | ICTJ' (video). Available at: www.youtube.com/watch?list=PLP8pOH5Q3gXU8a4qF6K9DuR9gGMy5tQi6&time_continue=54&v=GZz9TUVvnVk.

ICTJ (2019) ICTJ website. Available at: www.ictj.org.

ICTR (2018) 'Key Figures of Cases', ICTR website, updated 18 September. Available at: http://unictr.irmct.org/en/cases/key-figures-cases.

ICTR-TPIR (2014) '20 Years Challenging Impunity – United Nations International Criminal Tribunal for Rwanda' (video). Available at: www.youtube.com/watch?v=Q6nGK4A1UJ4.

ICTY (2010) *Voice of the Victims: Witness DD in the Krstić case* (video). Available at: www.youtube.com/watch?v=ZHnydxCvjKw.

ICTY (2012) 'Sexual Violence and the Triumph of Justice' (video). Available at: www.youtube.com/watch?time_continue=4&v=HZ4EM6iiq0k.

ICTY (2017) 'ICTY Facts and Figures', ICTY website, updated November 2017. Available at: www.icty.org/sites/icty.org/files/images/content/Infographic_facts_figures_en.pdf.

ICTY (2019) ICTY website. Available at: www.icty.org.

Idris, I. (2016) *Lessons from DDR programmes* (GSDRC Helpdesk Research Report 1368), Birmingham: GSDRC, University of Birmingham. Available at: www.gsdrc.org/wp-content/uploads/2016/06/HDQ1368.pdf.

Ignatieff, M. (2000) *Human Rights as Politics: Human Rights as Idolatry*, The Tanner Lectures on Human Values, delivered at Princeton University, 04–07 April. Available at: http://tannerlectures.utah.edu/lectures/documents/Ignatieff_01.pdf.

Ignatieff, M. (2001) *Human Rights as Politics and Idolatry*, Princeton: Princeton University Press.

IISS (2011) 'IISS Strategic Comments', Volume 17, Comment 40, London: IISS.

Ioannides, I. (2007) 'The European Union and Learning from Support for Post-Conflict Police Reform: A Critical Analysis of Macedonia (2001–2005)', PhD Thesis, Bradford: University of Bradford.

IMAS (2003) *Glossary of Mine Action Terms, Definitions and Abbreviations, International Mine Action Standards (IMAS) 04.10*. Available at: www.mineactionstandards.org/fileadmin/user_upload/MAS/documents/imasinternational-standards/english/series-04/IMAS-04-10-Ed2-Am4.pdf.

Inclusive Security and DCAF (2017) *A Women's Guide to Security Sector Reform: Training Curriculum*, Washington, DC: Inclusive Security and DCAF. Available at: www.dcaf.ch/womens-guide-security-sector-reform-training-curriculum.

Ingelaere, B. (2009) '"Does the Truth Pass across the Fire without Burning?" Locating the Short Circuit in Rwanda's Gacaca Courts', *The Journal of Modern African Studies*, 47(4): 507–28.

Institute for Economics & Peace (IEP) (2017) *Global Terrorism Index 2017*, Sydney: IEP. Available at: http://visionofhumanity.org/app/uploads/2017/11/Global-Terrorism-Index-2017.pdf.

Institute for Economics & Peace (IEP) (2018) *Global Terrorism Index 2018*, Sydney: IEP. Available at: http://visionofhumanity.org/app/uploads/2018/12/Global-Terrorism-Index-2018-1.pdf.

International Campaign to Ban Landmines – Cluster Munition Coalition (ICBL-CMC) (2016a) *Cluster Munition Monitor 2016*. Available at: www.the-monitor.org/media/2386748/Landmine-Monitor-2016-web.pdf.

International Campaign to Ban Landmines – Cluster Munition Coalition (ICBL-CMC) (2016b) *Landmine Monitor 2016*. Available at: www.the-monitor.org/media/2386748/Landmine-Monitor-2016-web.pdf.

International Campaign to Ban Landmines – Cluster Munition Coalition (ICBL-CMC) (2016c) *The Impact of Mines/ERW on Children*. Available at: www.the-monitor.org/media/2389719/MinesChildren2016Final.pdf.

International Campaign to Ban Landmines – Cluster Munition Coalition (ICBL-CMC) (2017a) *Cluster Munition Monitor*, ICBL-CMC. Available at: www.the-monitor.org/media/2582190/Cluster-Munition-Monitor-2017_web4.pdf.

International Campaign to Ban Landmines – Cluster Munition Coalition (ICBL-CMC) (2017b) *Landmine Monitor*, ICBL-CMC. Available at: www.the-monitor.org/media/2615219/Landmine-Monitor-2017_final.pdf.

International Campaign to Ban Landmines – Cluster Munition Coalition (ICBL-CMC) (2018) *Cluster Munition Monitor*, ICBL-CMC. Available at: http://the-monitor.org/media/2907293/Cluster-Munition-Monitor-2018_web_revised4Sep.pdf.

International Centre for Prison Studies (2008) 'Penal Reform and Gender', *Gender and Security Sector Reform Toolkit*, Geneva: DCAF. Available at: www.dcaf.ch/DCAF/EZ/Publications/Penal-Reform-and-Gender-Tool-5.

International Civil Society Action Network – ICAN (2017) 'ICAN's Gendered Transitional Justice Video' (video). Available at: www.youtube.com/watch?v=nAmWHdH0Doo.

International Forum for the Challenges of Peace Operations (2017) International Forum for the Challenges of Peace Operations website. Available at: www.challengesforum.org/en/.

International Labour Organization (ILO) (2006) *Red Shoes: Experiences of girl-combatants in Liberia*, Geneva: ILO, 10–14. Available at: www.ilo.org/wcmsp5/groups/public/---ed_emp/---emp_ent/--ifp_crisis/documents/publication/wcms_116435.pdf.

International Peace Institute (IPI) (2009) 'Global Terrorism: Task Forces on Strengthening Multilateral Security Capacity', IPI Blue Paper No. 4, New York: IPI. Available at: www.ipacademy.org/media/pdf/publications/global_terrorism_bluepaper.pdf.

International Peace Institute (IPI) (2014) 'Building Peace at the Nexus of Organized Crime, Conflict, and Extremism' (video). Available at: www.youtube.com/watch?v=xXIOWue0Ir0.

International Peace Institute (IPI) (2017) 'Peacemaking and Child Protection' (video). Available at: www.youtube.com/watch?v=E7Mj4dl6Vcg.

International Peace Institute (IPI) (2017) 'Local Peacebuilding Successes: Lessons for the International Community' (video). Available at: www.youtube.com/watch?v=dbmblrAilU0.

International Security Sector Advisory Team (ISSAT) (2015) 'Alwin van den Boogaard: Security Sector Development and Lessons from Burundi' (video). Available at: www.youtube.com/watch?v=t_EENdRB-1Q&list=PLVtNme7lSHM27k0-nvMKde7NBUBTCiyKt&index=3.

International Security Sector Advisory Team (ISSAT) (2015) 'Nicole Ball on democratic governance and SSR' (video). Available at: www.youtube.com/watch?v=P6rA4x-XFTg&list=PLVtNme7lSHM27k0-nvMKde7NBUBTCiyKt.

International Security Sector Advisory Team (ISSAT) (2015) 'Piet Biesheuvel on police and justice' (video). Available at: www.youtube.com/watch?v=bLL0MAjZnLo.

International Security Sector Advisory Team (ISSAT) (2015) 'Richard Monk on 'Police Reform and UN peacekeeping' (video). Available at: www.youtube.com/watch?v=kbQF5d7hxHI&list=PLVtNme7lSHM27k0-nvMKde7NBUBTCiyKt&index=5.

International Security Sector Advisory Team (ISSAT) (2015) 'When Everything is Broken – SSR in Libya: John Durance, former Director of the Security Sector Advisory and Coordination Division, UN Support Mission in Libya (UNSMIL)' (video). Available at: www.youtube.com/watch?v=V7jKtwfV8Fg.

Inter-Parliamentary Union (IPU-DCAF) (2003) *Parliamentary Oversight of the Security Sector: Principles, Mechanisms and Practises – Handbook for Parliamentarians*, Geneva: DCAF. Available at: www.ipu.org/english/handbks.htm#Decaf.

Interpeace (2010) 'Voices of Civil Society Organisations on Peacebuilding and Statebuilding', Background Paper, prepared as an input into the International Dialogue on Peacebuilding and Statebuilding, Geneva: Interpeace.

Iqbal, Z. and Starr, H. (2008) 'Bad Neighbours: Failed States and Their Consequences', *Conflict Management and Peace Science*, 25: 315–31.

IRIN (2006) 'Justice for a Lawless World? Rights and reconciliation in a new era of international law', IRIN News Report, Geneva: IRIN. Available at: www.irinnews.org/InDepthMain.aspx?InDepthId=7&ReportId=59464.

IRIN (2011) 'DRC-UGANDA: Male sexual abuse survivors living on the margins', IRIN News. Available at: www.irinnews.org/Report/93399/DRC-UGANDA-Male-sexual-abuse-survivors-living-on-the-margins.

ISS (2017) 'What is holding the African Standby Force back?', *On the Agenda*, 10 May. Available at: https://issafrica.org/pscreport/on-the-agenda/what-is-holding-the-african-standby-force-back.

ISSAfrica (2016) 'Making Peacebuilding More Effective' (video). Available at: www.youtube.com/watch?v=a1N9gQTPJCM.

ISSAfrica (2017) 'View on Africa: Is Piracy Back?' (video). Available at: www.youtube.com/watch?v=iEKaua-Joq0.

ISSAT (2010) *Defence Transformation*, ISSAT Operational Guidance Note. Available at: https://issat.dcaf.ch/download/2880/24592/ISSAT%20Programme%20Implementation%20OGN%20-%20Defence%20Transformation.pdf.

ISSAT (2015) *Reforming Security Sectors in Africa – Lessons from Burundi – Nicole Ball*. Available at: www.youtube.com/watch?v=_0-t5rhWGFU.

ISSR (2006) *Kosovo International Security Sector Review*, Pristina: ISSR.

Jackson, P. (2010) 'SSR and Post-Conflict Reconstruction: The Armed Wing of State Building?' in Sedra, M. (ed.), *The Future of Security Sector Reform*, Waterloo: Centre for International Governance Innovation [CIGI], 118–35. Available at: www.deslibris.ca/ID/225839.

Jackson, P. (2015) *Handbook of International Security and Development*, Cheltenham: Edward Elgar Publishing.

Jackson, P. (2017) 'Capacity Building and Security Sector Reform' in R. Dover, H. Dylan and M. Goodman (eds), *The Palgrave Handbook of Security, Risk and Intelligence*, London: Palgrave Macmillan, 281–96.

Jackson, P. (2018) 'Introduction: Second-Generation Security Sector Reform', *Journal of Intervention and Statebuilding*, 12(1): 1–10.

Jackson, P. and Bakrania, S. (2018) 'Is the Future of SSR non-linear?', *Journal of Intervention and Statebuilding*, 12(1): 11–30.

Jackson, P. and Beswick, D. (2018) *Conflict, Security and Development: An Introduction* (3rd edn), Abingdon: Routledge.

Jacobs, A. (2004) 'Prison Power Corrupts Absolutely: Exploring the Phenomenon of Prison Guard Brutality and the Need to Develop a System of Accountability', *California Western Law Review*, 41: 277–301.

Jacobs, J. (1961) *The Death and Life of Great American Cities*, New York: Vintage.

Jaye, T. (2006) *An Assessment Report on Security Sector Reform in Liberia*, Monrovia: Governance Reform Commission of Liberia.

Jenkins, K. and Plowden, W. (2006) *Governance and Nationbuilding: The Failure of International Intervention*, London: Edward Elgar.

Jennings, K. (2008) 'Unclear Ends, Unclear Means: Reintegration in Postwar Societies – The Case of Liberia', *Global Governance*, 14: 327–45.

Jennings, K. (2009) 'The Political Economy of DDR in Liberia: A Gendered Critique', *Conflict, Security and Development*, 9(4): 475–94.

Jeong, H. (2005) *Peacebuilding in Postconflict Societies – Strategy and Process*, Boulder: Lynne Reinner.

Jeong, H. (2017) *Peace and Conflict Studies: An Introduction*, London: Routledge.

Johnson, D. (2006) *The Root Causes of Sudan's Civil Wars* (3rd edn), New York: Three Rivers Press.

Jones, S., Wilson, J., Rathmell, A. and Riley, K. (2005) *Establishing Law and Order After Conflict*, Santa Monica: Rand Corporation. Available at: www.rand.org/pubs/monographs/2005/RAND_MG374.pdf.

Junger, S. (2016) *Tribe: On Homecoming and Belonging*, London: Fourth Estate.

JURIST (2018) 'Gender Equality', Judicial Reform and Institutional Strengthening (JURIST) Project website. Available at: www.juristproject.org/cct/gender-equality.

Kaldor, M. (2012) *New and Old Wars: Organized Violence in a Global Era*, Cambridge: Polity Press.

Kaldor, M. and Beebe, S. (2010) *The Ultimate Weapon Is No Weapon: Human Security and the New Rules of War and Peace*, New York: Public Affairs.

Kaldor, M. and Selchow, S. (2015) 'From Military to 'Security Interventions': An Alternative Approach to Contemporary Interventions, *Stability: International Journal of Security and Development*, 4(1): 32, 1–12.

Kalyvas, S. and Kocher, M. (2007) 'How 'Free' Is Free Riding in Civil Wars? Violence, Insurgency, and the Collective Action Problem', *World Politics*, 59(2): 177–216.

Kamau, M. (2018) 'Peacebuilding in Africa', Kujenga Amani podcast. Available at: http://apnpodcast.libsyn.com/episode-1.

Kaplan, O. and Nussio, E. (2018) 'Explaining Recidivism of Ex-Combatants in Colombia', *Journal of Conflict Resolution*, 62(1): 64–93.

Karlsrud, J. (2015) 'The UN at War: Examining the Consequences of Peace-Enforcement Mandates for the UN Peacekeeping Operations in the CAR, the DRC and Mali', *Third World Quarterly*, 36(1): 40–54.

Katz, L. (2011) 'World Peacekeeping: Do Nation-States Have a "Responsibility to Protect"?' in CQ Researcher (ed.), *Issues in Peace and Conflict Studies: Selections from CQ Researcher*, Washington, DC: Sage, 1–26.

Kaufman, J. and Williams, K. (eds) (2016) *Women, Gender Equality, and Post-Conflict Transformation: Lessons Learned, Implications for the Future*, Abingdon: Taylor and Francis.

Kaulemu, D. (2012) 'Culture, Customs, Tradition and Transitional Justice' in Okello, M.C., Dolan, C., Whande, U., Mncwabe, N., Onegi, L. and Oola, S. (eds), *Where Law Meets Reality: Forging African Transitional Justice*, Oxford: Pambazuka Press, Fahamu Books, 80–98.

Keen, D. (2012) *Useful Enemies: When Waging Wars Is More Important than Winning Them*, New Haven: Yale University Press.

Khakee, A. and Florquin, N. (2003) *Kosovo and the Gun: A Baseline Assessment of Small Arms and Light Weapons in Kosovo*, Geneva: UNDP and Small Arms Survey. Available at: .www.um.edu.mt/library/oar/bitstream/handle/123456789/16053/OA%20-%20Kosovo%20and%20the%20Gun.2-85.pdf?sequence=1&isAllowed=y.

Khattab, L. and Myrttinen, H. (2014) 'Gender, security and SSR in Lebanon', Background Paper, November. London: International Alert. Available at: www.international-alert.org/sites/default/files/Lebanon_SSRGenderSecurity_EN_2014.pdf.

Kiener, R. (2011) 'Dangerous War Debris: Who Should Clean Up After Conflicts End?' in CQ Researcher (ed.), *Issues in Peace and Conflict Studies: Selections from CQ Researcher*, Washington: Sage, 341–367.

Knight, C. and Wilson, K. (2016) *Lesbian, Gay, Bisexual and Trans People (LGBT) and the Criminal Justice System*, London: Palgrave Macmillan.

Knight, M. (2008) 'Expanding the DDR Model: Politics and Organisations', *Journal of Security Sector Management*, 6(1): 1–18.

Koning, R. (2008) 'Resource-Conflict Links in Sierra Leone and the Democratic Republic of the Congo', *SIPRI Insights on Peace and Security, No. 2008/2*. Available at: http://books.sipri.org/files/insight/SIPRIInsight0802.pdf.

Kort, M. (2007) 'A Conversation with Eve Ensler: Femicide in the Congo', Public Broadcasting Service, 17 September. Available at: www.pbs.org/pov/lumo/eve-ensler/.

Krause, K. (2007) *Small Arms and Light Weapons: Towards Global Public Policy*, Coping with Crisis Working Paper Series, New York: International Peace Academy (now International Peace Institute). Available at: www.files.ethz.ch/isn/126967/small_arms_light_weapons_03_2007.pdf.

Krause, J., Kraise, W. and Bränfors, P. (2018) 'Women's Participation in Peace Negotiations and the Durability of Peace', *International Interactions: Empirical and Theoretical Research in International Relations*, 44(6): 985–1016.

Kreutz, J. (2010) 'How and When Armed Conflicts End: Introducing the UCDP Conflict Termination Dataset', *Journal of Peace Research*, 47(2): 243–50.

Kuehnast, K., Oudraat, C. and Hernes, H. (2011) 'Introduction' in K. Kuehnast, C. Oudraat and H. Hernes (eds), *Women and War: Power and Protection in the 21st Century*, Washington: United States Institute of Peace.

Kunz, R. (2014) 'Gender and Security Sector Reform: Gendering Differently?', *International Peacekeeping*, 21(5): 604–22.

La Rosa, A.-M. and Philippe, X. (2009) 'Transitional Justice' in V. Chetail (2009) '*Post-Conflict Peacebuilding – A Lexicon*', New York: Oxford University Press.

Labuda, P. (2017) 'The Special Criminal Court in the Central African Republic: Failure or Vindication of Complementarity?', *Journal of International Criminal Justice*, 15(1): 175–206.

Lacher, W. (2012) *Organized Crime and Conflict in the Sahel-Sahara Region*, Washington, DC: Carnegie Endowment for International Peace.

Lacina, B. and Gleditsch, N. P. (2005) 'Monitoring Trends in Global Combat', *European Journal of Population*, 21(2–3): 145–66.

Lamb, G. and Stainer, T. (2018) 'The Conundrum of DDR Coordination: The Case of South Sudan', *Stability: International Journal of Security and Development*, 7(1): 9.

Lane, L. (2014) *Greek and Roman and Political Ideas*, London: Penguin.

Lauderdale, P. and Oliverio, A. (2005) 'Introduction: Critical Perspectives on Terrorism', *International Journal of Comparative Sociology*, 46(1–2): 3–10.

Laville, S (2015) 'French Wrote to Thank UN Worker for Disclosing Abuse by Troops', *The Guardian*, 01 May. Available at: www.theguardian.com/world/2015/may/01/french-letter-thanked-un-whistleblower-for-disclosing-abuse-by-troops.

Law, D. (2006) *The Post-Conflict Security Sector*. Policy Paper 14. Geneva: Geneva Centre for the Democratic Control of Armed Forces. Available at: www.files.ethz.ch/isn/18646/PP14_Law.pdf.

Lawrence, M. (2012) 'Towards a Non-State Security Sector Reform Strategy', SSR Issue Paper No. 8, Waterloo: Centre for International Governance Innovation (CIGI). Available at: www.cigionline.org/sites/default/files/ssr_no_8_0.pdf.

Laws, E. (2017) 'The impact of mines and explosive remnants of war on gender groups', K4D Helpdesk Report. Brighton, UK: Institute of Development Studies. Available at: https://assets.publishing.service.gov.uk/media/59844e0c40f0b61e4b00005c/149-the-impact-of-mines-and-explosive-remnants-of-war-on-gender-groups__1_.pdf.

Lederach, J. P. (1997) *Building Peace: Sustainable Reconciliation in Divided Societies*, Washington, DC: USIP.

Lederach, J. P. (2003) *Little Book of Conflict Transformation,* Intercourse, PA: Good Books.

Lederer, E. (2018) 'UN chief urges conflict prevention and "diplomacy for peace"', *Washington Post*, 29 August. Available at: www.washingtonpost.com/world/africa/un-chief-urges-conflict-prevention-and-diplomacy-for-peace/2018/08/29/a6703000-abf5-11e8-9a7d-cd30504ff902_story.html?noredirect=on&utm_term=.bea55c665cf0.

Ledwidge, F. (2011) *Losing Small Wars: British Military Failure in Iraq and Afghanistan*, New Haven: Yale University Press.

Lee-Koo, K. (2002) 'Confronting a Disciplinary Blindness: Women, War and Rape in the International Politics of Security', *Australian Journal of Political Science*, 37(3): 525–36.

Lee-Koo, K. (2018) '"The intolerable impact of armed conflict on children": The united nations security council and the protection of children in armed conflict', *Global Responsibility to Protect* 10(1–2): 57–74.

Lee-Koo, K., D'Costa, B. and Huynh, K. (2015) *Children and Global Conflict*, Cambridge: Cambridge University Press.

Levy, J. (2007) 'International Sources of Interstate and Intrastate War', in C. Crocker, F. Hampson and P. Aall (eds), *Leashing the Dogs of War*, Washington: USIP, 17–38.

Li, Q. (2005) 'Does Democracy Promote or Reduce Transnational Terrorist Incidents?', *Journal of Conflict Resolution*, 49(2): 278–97.

Liang, L. (2018) 'Beijing slams "Cold War, zero-sum mentality" of new strategy', *The Straits Times*, 21 January. Available at: www.straitstimes.com/world/us-defence-paper-rapped-for-labelling-china-russia-as-revisionist-powers.

Licklider, R. (1995) *Stopping the Killing: How Civil Wars End*, New York: New York University Press.

Lidauer, M. and Ngapna, H. (2009) *Report on the Pilot Course on Security Sector Reform*, ASSET. Available at: http://asset-ssr.org/images/pdf_file/english/ASPRReport.pdf.

Lieberfeld, D. (2005) 'Theories of Conflict and the Iraq War', *International Journal of Peace Studies*, 10(2): 1–21.

Livingston, S. (1997) 'Clarifying the CNN Effect: An Examination of Media Effects According to Type of Military Intervention', Research Paper R-18, June, Harvard: Shorenstein Center, Harvard University.

Llamazares, M. (2005) 'Post-War Peacebuilding Reviewed: A Critical Exploration of Generic Approaches to Post-War Reconstruction', Working Paper 14, Bradford: University of Bradford, Department of Peace Studies, Centre for Conflict Resolution.

Lord, J. and Stein, M. (2015) 'Peacebuilding and Reintegrating Ex-Combatants with Disabilities', *The International Journal of Human Rights*, 19(3): 277–92.

Lowe, K. (2012) *Savage Continent: Europe in the Aftermath of World War II*, London: Viking.

Löwenheim, O. (2008) 'Examining the State: A Foucauldian Perspective on International "Governance Indicators"', *Third World Quarterly*, 29(2): 255–74.

LSE (2010) *Human Rights in 21st Century* (video), lecture by Professor Noam Chomsky, MIT. Available at: www.youtube.com/watch?v=_AS34drNiOo.

LSE (2011) *Peace Vs. Women's Rights in Afghanistan: Compatible or Contradicting Concepts?* Presentation by Zainab Salbi, founder and CEO of Women for Women International (video). Available at: www.youtube.com/watch?v=F3PA0gjnChU.

LSE (2012) *The Burning Issue: The DNA of Human Rights* (video), lecture by Professor Conor Gearty, LSE. Available at: www.youtube.com/watch?v=U88_GY7uQwg.

LSE (2013) *Sri Lanka and the culture of impunity: human rights challenges in a post-war and post-conflict environment* (audio), panel discussion by Dr Paikiasothy Saravanamuttu, Dr Asanga Welikala, Uvindu Kurukulasuriya (Chair: Professor Chetan Bhatt). Available at: www.lse.ac.uk/website-archive/newsAndMedia/videoAndAudio/channels/publicLecturesAndEvents/player.aspx?id=1937.

LSE (2017) *Protecting Children in War and Conflict: European and global implications for child rights* (audio), lecture by Helle Thorning-Schmidt, Save the Children CEO, at the LSE, 12 January 2017, London: LSE. Available at: www.lse.ac.uk/website-archive/newsAndMedia/videoAndAudio/channels/publicLecturesAndEvents/player.aspx?id=3689.

LSE (2017) 'The Human Cost of Conflict: the search for dignity and rights of Palestine refugees' (video), presentation by Pierre Krähenbühl, UNRWA Commissioner-General. 04 December. Available at: www.lse.ac.uk/website-archive/newsAndMedia/videoAndAudio/channels/publicLecturesAndEvents/player.aspx?id=3949.

LSE (2017) 'Women, Peace and Security in the Global Arena' (video), Panel Discussion hosted by the LSE, 05 June, London: LSE. Available at: www.lse.ac.uk/website-archive/newsAndMedia/videoAndAudio/channels/publicLecturesAndEvents/player.aspx?id=3833.

Luban, D. (2014) *International and Transnational Criminal Law*, Frederick: Wolters Kluwer Law & Business.

Luccaro, T. (2016) 'Customary Justice: An Introduction to Basic Concepts, Strengths, and Weaknesses', International Network to Promote the Rule of Law (INPROL) Practitioner's Guide, September 2016. Available at: www.inprol.org/publications/15761/customary-justice-an-introduction-to-basic-concepts-strengths-and-weaknesses.

Luck, E. (2010) 'The Responsibility to Protect: Growing Pains or Early Promise?', *Ethics and International Affairs*, 24(4): 349–65.

Luckham, R. (2010) 'The Discordant Voices of "Security"' in A. Cornwall and D. Eade (eds), *Deconstructing Development Discourse – Buzzwords and Fuzzwords*, Rugby: Practical Action Publishing, 269–79.

Lumpe, L., Meek, S. and Naylor, R. (2000) 'Introduction to Gun-Running', in L. Lumpe (ed.), *Running Guns: The Global Black Market in Small Arms*, London: Zed Books, 1–10.

Lund, M. (1996) *Preventing Violent Conflicts*, Washington: USIP.

Lund, M. (2006) 'Human Rights: A Source of Conflict, State Making, and State Breaking' in J. Mertus and J. Helsing (eds), *Human Rights and Conflict: Exploring the Links between Rights, Law, and Peacebuilding*, Washington: USIP, 39–61.

Lund, M. (2009) 'Conflict Prevention: Theory in Pursuit of Policy and Practice' in J. Bercovitch, V. Kremenyuk, and I. Zartman (eds), *The SAGE Handbook of Conflict Resolution*, London: Sage, 287–308. Available at: www.wilsoncenter.org/sites/default/files/Conflict%20Prevention-%20Theory%20in%20Pursuit%20of%20Policy%20and%20Practice.pdf.

Lutz, E. (2006) 'Understanding Human Rights Violations in Armed Conflict', in J. Mertus and J. Helsing (eds), *Human Rights and Conflict: Exploring the Links between Rights, Law, and Peacebuilding*, Washington: USIP, 23–38.

Lyck, M. (2007) 'International Peace Enforcers and Indicted War Criminals: The Case of Ramush Haradinaj', *International Peacekeeping*, 14(3): 418–32.

McCullough, A. (2015) *The Legitimacy of States and Armed Non-State Actors: Topic Guide*, Birmingham: GSDRC, University of Birmingham.

Mc Evoy, C. and Hideg, G. (2017) *Global Violent Deaths 2017: Time to Decide*, Geneva: Small Arms Survey. Available at: www.smallarmssurvey.org/fileadmin/docs/U-Reports/SAS-Report-GVD2017.pdf.Mac.

Ginty, R. (2010) 'Hybrid Peace: The Interaction between Top-Down and Bottom-Up Peace', *Security Dialogue*, 41(4): 391–402.

McFate, S. (2010) 'The Link Between DDR and SSR in Conflict-Affected Countries', Washington: USIP. Available at: www.usip.org/files/resources/SR238McFate_DDR_SSR_Conflict.pdf.

Mac Ginty, R. (2011) *Peacebuilding by the International Community* (animation). Available at: www.youtube.com/watch?v=zN8rIxoXqWo&t=12s.

Mac Ginty R. and Richmond O. (2013) 'The Local Turn in Peacebuilding: A Critical Agenda for Peace', *Third World Quarterly*, 34(5): 763–83.

Mac Ginty, R. and Williams, A. (2016) *Conflict and Development* (2nd edn), Abingdon: Routledge.

Machel, G. (2010) 'Foreword' in S. Parmar, M. Roseman, S. Siegrist and T. Sowa (eds), *Children and Transitional Justice: Truth-Telling, Accountability, and Reconciliation*, New York: UNICEF, i–xiv.

MacKenzie, M. (2009) 'Securitization and Desecuritization: Female Soldiers and the Reconstruction of Women in Post-Conflict Sierra Leone', *Security Studies*, 18(2): 243.

McMullin, J. (2009) 'Organised Criminal Groups and Conflict: The Nature and Consequences of Interdependence', *Civil Wars*, 11(1): 75–102.

Mamdani, M. (2009) *Saviours and Survivors: Darfur, Politics and the War on Terror*, New York: Pantheon.

Mani, R. (2002) *Beyond Retribution: Seeking Justice in the Shadows of War*, Cambridge: Polity Press.

Mani, R. (2008) 'Exploring the Rule of Law in Theory and Practice', in A. Hurwitz and R. Huang (eds), *Civil War and the Rule of Law: Security, Development and Human Rights*, Boulder: Lynne Reinner, 21–45.

Marc, A., Willman, A., Aslam, G., Rebosio, M. with Balasuriya, K. (2013) *Societal Dynamics and Fragility: Engaging Societies in Responding to Fragile Situations*, Washington: World Bank.

Marenin, O. (2005) *Restoring Policing Systems in Conflict Torn Nations*, Geneva: DCAF. Available at: http://dcafdev.ethz.ch/Publications/Publication-Detail?lng=en&id=18349.

MAREX (The Maritime Executive) (2019) 'IMB: Gulf of Guinea Led the World for Piracy in 2018', *The Maritime Executive*, 16 January. Available at: www.maritime-executive.com/article/imb-gulf-of-guinea-led-the-world-for-piracy-in-2018.

Martin, G. (2017) *Understanding Terrorism*, Thousand Oaks: Sage.

Martin, G. and Prager, F. (2019) *Terrorism: An International Perspective*, Thousand Oaks: Sage.

Mashike, L. (2007) *'Former Combatants' Involvement in Crime and Crime Prevention' Research Report*, Johannesburg, South Africa: Centre for the Study of Violence and Reconciliation.

Mason, W. (2014) 'A Social Reconstruction Approach to Fostering Security & Justice After Conflict', video (University of Leicester). Available at: www.youtube.com/watch?v=gER3UI8AXaA&list=PLjQX5EXgm57S0L7nT-QMVhQLKiYNsSPxu&index=3.

Matfess, H. and Miklaucic, M. (eds) (2016) *Beyond Convergence: World Without Order*, Washington, DC: Center for Complex Operations Institute for National Strategic

Studies National Defense University. Available at: http://globalinitiative.net/wp-content/uploads/2016/10/beyond-convergence-world-without-order-.pdf.

Mazurana, D., Krystalli, R. and Baaré, A. (2018) 'Gender and Disarmament, Demobilization, and Reintegration: Reviewing and Advancing the Field' in Fionnuala Ní Aoláin, Naomi Cahn, Dina Francesca Haynes, and Nahla Valji (eds), *The Oxford Handbook of Gender and Conflict*, Oxford: Oxford University Press.

Mazurana, D. and Proctor, K. (2013) *Gender, Conflict and Peace*, Massachusetts: World Peace Foundation. Available at: http://fletcher.tufts.edu/~/media/Fletcher/Microsites/World%20Peace%20Foundation/Gender%20Conflict%20and%20Peace.pdf.

Mbadlanyana, T. and Onuoha, F. (2009) *Peacekeeping and post-conflict criminality – Challenges to the (re-)establishment of rule of law in Liberia*, Occasional Paper 190, South Africa: Institute for Security Studies. Available at: www.operationspaix.net/IMG/pdf/PAPER190.pdf.

Meernik, J. (2015) 'The International Criminal Court and the Deterrence of Human Rights Atrocities', *Civil Wars*, 17(3): 318–39.

Meharg, S., and Arnusch, A. (2010) *Security Sector Reform: A Case Study Approach to Transition and Capacity Building*, ed. Susan Merrill. PKSOI Papers. Carlisle, PA: Strategic Studies Institute, US Army War College.

Melander, E., Pettersson, T. and Themnér, L. (2016) 'Organized Violence, 1989–2015', *Journal of Peace Research*, 53(5): 727–42.

Menkhaus, K. (2004) 'Conflict Prevention and Human Security: Issues and Challenges', *Conflict, Security and Development*, 4(3): 419–63.

Menkhaus, K. (2009) 'Dangerous Waters', *Survival*, 51(1): 21–5.

Mertus, J. and Helsing, J. (2006) (eds), *Human Rights and Conflict: Exploring the Links between Rights, Law, and Peacebuilding*, Washington: USIP.

Mihr, A. and Sriram, C. (2018) 'Rule of Law, Security, and Transitional Justice in Fragile and Conflict-Affected Societies' in W. Durch, J. Larik, and R. Ponzio (eds), *Just Security in an Undergoverned World*, Oxford: Oxford University Press.

Ministry of Foreign Affairs, Sri Lanka (2017) 'Lecture on Transitional Justice by UN Special Rapporteur Pablo de Greiff' (video). Available at: www.youtube.com/watch?v=wHcb0wzCm1g.

Miraglia, P., Ochoa, R. and Briscoe, I. (2012) *Transnational Organised Crime and Fragile States*, Paris: OECD. Available at: www.oecd-ilibrary.org/docserver/download/5k49dfg88s40-en.pdf?expires=1512903192&id=id&accname=guest&checksum=21F75184B2272220822D9DB5C0D9E078.

Mobekk, E. (2005) 'Identifying Lessons in United Nations International Policing Missions', Policy Paper no. 9, Geneva: DCAF. Available at: http://dcafdev.ethz.ch/Publications/Publication-Detail?lng=en&id=18379.

Mobekk, E. (2010) 'Gender, Women and Security Sector Reform', *International Peacekeeping*, 17(2): 278–91.

Mobekk, E. (2010b) 'Security Sector Reform and the Challenges of Ownership', in M. Sedra (ed.) *The Future of Security Sector Reform*, Ontario: CIGI, 230–43. Available at: www.cigionline.org/sites/default/files/The%20Future%20of%20Security%20Sector%20Reform.pdf.

Monbiot, G. (2014) 'Orwell was hailed a hero for fighting in Spain. Today he'd be guilty of terrorism', *The Guardian*, 11 February. Available at: www.theguardian.com/commentisfree/2014/feb/10/orwell-hero-terrorism-syria-british-fighters-damned.

Moore, J. (2011) 'Truth Commissions: Can Countries Heal After Atrocities' in CQ Researcher (ed.), *Issues in Peace and Conflict Studies: Selections from CQ Researcher*, Washington: Sage, 317–40.

Moran, D. and Jewkes, Y. (2015) 'Linking the Carceral and the Punitive State: A Review of Research on Prison Architecture, Design, Technology and the Lived Experience of Carceral Space', *Annales De Géographie*, 2(702–703): 163–84.

Moratti, M. and Sabic-El-Rayess, A. (2009) *Transitional Justice and DDR: The Case of Bosnia and Herzegovina*, New York: International Center for Transitional Justice.

Mortimer, D. (1995) 'Integration, Demobilisation and Rationalisation', *African Security Review*, 4(6): 58–59.

Muggah, R. (2005) 'No Magic Bullet: A Critical Perspective on Disarmament, Demobilization and Reintegration (DDR) and Weapons Reduction in Post-Conflict Contexts', *The Round Table*, 94(379): 239–52.

Muggah, R. (2010) 'Rethinking Small Arms Control in Africa: It Is Time to Set an Armed Violence Reduction Agenda', *Conflict, Security and Development*, 10(2): 217–38.

Muggah, R. (2010a) 'Chapter Two: Stabilising Fragile States and the Humanitarian Space', *AdelphiPapers*, 50(412): 33–52.

Muggah, R. and O'Donnell, C. (2015) 'Next Generation Disarmament, Demobilisation and Reintegration', *Stability: International Journal of Security & Development*, 4(1): 30, 1–12.

Muižnieks, N. (2017) 'The Shrinking Space for Human Rights Organisations', Human Rights Comment, Strasbourg: Council of Europe, 04 April. Available at www.coe.int/hy/web/commissioner/blog/-/asset_publisher/xZ32OPEoxOkq/content/the-shrinking-space-for-human-rights-organisations.

Munala, J. (2007) 'Challenging Liberian Attitudes Towards Violence against Women,' *Forced Migration Review*, 27: 36–7. Available at: www.fmreview.org/FMRpdfs/FMR27/23.pdf.

Munive, J. (2014) 'Invisible Labour: The Political Economy of Reintegration in South Sudan', *Journal of Intervention and Statebuilding*, 8(4): 334–56.

Munive, J. and Stepputat, F. (2015) 'Rethinking Disarmament, Demobilization and Reintegration Programs', *Stability: International Journal of Security and Development*, 4(1): 48, 1–13.

Murithi, T. (2008) 'The African Union's Evolving Role in Peace Operations', *African Security Review*, 17(1): 70–82.

Murphy, C. (2005) 'Police Studies Go Global: In Eastern Kentucky?' *Police Quarterly*, 8(1): 137–145.

Murphy, C. (2017) *The Conceptual Foundations of Transitional Justice*, Cambridge: Cambridge University Press.

Murphy, M. (2007) 'Contemporary Piracy and Maritime Terrorism', *International Institute for Strategic Studies*, New York: Routledge.

Murphy, M. (2011) 'Somali Piracy', *The RUSI Journal*, 156(6): 4–11.

Naidoo, S. (2013) 'Mission Creep or Responding to Wider Security Needs? the Evolving Role of Mine Action Organisations in Armed Violence Reduction', *Stability: International Journal of Security and Development*, 2(1): 11, 1–8.

Narten, J. (2009) 'Dilemmas of Promoting "Local Ownership": The Case of Post War Kosovo' in R. Paris and T. Sisk (eds), *The Dilemmas of Statebuilding: Confronting the Contradictions of Post War Peace Operations*, Abingdon: Routledge, 252–86.

Nathan, L. (2007) *No Ownership, No Commitment: A Guide to Local Ownership of Security Sector Reform*, Birmingham: University of Birmingham.

NATO (2014) *Allied Joint Doctrine for the Military Contribution to Peace Support*, AJP-3.4.1. Brussels: NATO. Available at: https://assets.publishing.service.gov.uk/government/uploads/system/uploads/attachment_data/file/624153/doctrine_nato_peace_support_ajp_3_4_1.pdf.

NATO (2015) *Allied Joint Doctrine for the Military Contribution to Stabilisation and Reconstruction*, AJP-3.4.5(A). Brussels: NATO. Available at: www.gov.uk/government/publications/allied-joint-doctrine-for-the-military-contribution to-stabilization-and-reconstruction-ajp-345a.

NATO (2018) 'NATO-UN relations: looking ahead after 10 years of expanding cooperation', NATO website, 28 September. Available at: www.nato.int/docu/review/2018/Also-in-2018/NATO-UN-relations-looking-ahead-after-10-years-of-expanding-cooperation/EN/index.htm.

Nettlefield, L. (2010) 'From the Battlefield to the Barracks: The ICTY and the Armed Forces of Bosnia and Herzegovina', *International Journal of Transitional Justice*, 4(1): 87–109.

New York Times (2019) 'Syria – Uprising and Civil War', *NYT News*. Available at: http://topics.nytimes.com/top/news/international/countriesandterritories/syria/index.html.

Newman, E., Paris, R. and Richmond, O. (2009) *New Perspectives on Liberal Peacebuilding*, Tokyo: UNU Press.

Ní Aoláin, F. (2016) 'The Aftermath of War considering Gender in the Process of Disarmament, Demilitarization and Reintegration' in J. Kaufman and K. Williams (eds), *Women, Gender Equality, and Post-Conflict Transformation: Lessons Learned, Implications for the Future*, Abingdon: Taylor and Francis, 34–50.

Nickson, A. and Cutting, J. (2016) 'The Role of Decentralisation in Post-Conflict Reconstruction in Sierra Leone', *Third World Thematics: A TWQ Journal*, 1(6): 799–816.

Nietzsche, F. (2000) *Basic Writings of Nietzsche*, New York: Random House.

Niewyk, D. and Nicosia, F. (2000) *The Columbia Guide to the Holocaust*, New York: Columbia University Press.

Nobel Women's Initiative (2012) 'Women Forging a New Security: Ending Sexual Violence in Conflict', Conference Report 2011, Ottawa: Nobel Women's Initiative. Available at: http://issuu.com/nobelwomen/docs/forging-a-new-securityweb/5.

Nordås, R. (2011a) 'Sexual Violence in African Conflicts', *CSCW Policy Brief No. 1*, Oslo: CSCW/PRIO. Available at: www.prio.no/sptrans/-1653928576/SVAC-CSCW-Policy-Brief-01-2011.pdf.

Nordås, R. (2011b) 'What Do We Know about Sexual Violence in Conflict?' in L. Kvarving (ed.), *Sexual Violence, the Armed Forces and Military Operations*, Oslo: Norwegian Defence University College, 67–71. Available at: http://m.hogskolene.forsvaret.no/forsvarets-hogskole/forskning/publikasjoner/documents/skriftserie%203%20komplett.pdf.

Norville, V. (2010) *The Role of Women in Global Security*, Washington: USIP. Available at: www.usip.org/files/resources/SR264-The_role_of_Women_in_Global_Security.pdf.

Nosworthy, D. (2010) 'Children and Security Sector Reform in Post-Conflict Peace-Building', Innocenti Working Paper No. 2010-9, Florence: UNICEF Innocenti Research Centre.

Nygård, H. and Trappeniers, E. (2016) *'Conflict Recurrence'*, Oslo: PRIO. Available at: www.css.ethz.ch/en/services/digital-library/articles/article.html/196945/pdf.

O'Connor, V. (2015) 'Defining the Rule of Law and Related Concepts', INPROL Practitioner's Guide. Available at: www.inprol.org/publications/14549/defining-the-rule-of-law-and-related-concepts.

O'Connor, V. (2015) 'Mapping the Justice System and Legal Framework in a Conflict-Affected Country', INPROL Practitioner's Guide. Available at: www.inprol.org/publications/14887/mapping-the-justice-system-and-legal-framework-in-a-conflict-affected-country.

O'Connor, V. (2015) 'Understanding the International Rule of Law Community, Its History, and Its Practice', INPROL Practitioner's Guide. Available at: www.inprol.org/publications/14886/understanding-the-international-rule-of-law-community-its-history-and-its.

O'Neill, B. (2008) comment provided to Peace Building Initiative, Peace Building Initiative website. Available at: www.peacebuildinginitiative.org.

O'Reilly, M. (2016) 'Peace and Justice through a Feminist Lens: Gender Justice and the Women's Court for the Former Yugoslavia', *Journal of Intervention and Statebuilding*, 10(3): 419–45.

O'Reilly, M, Ó Súilleabháin, A. and Paffenholz, T. (2015) 'Reimagining Peacemaking: Women's Roles in Peace Processes', New York: International Peace Institute. Available at: www.ipinst.org/wp-content/uploads/2015/06/IPI-E-pub-Reimagining-Peacemaking.pdf.

OBP (2019) OBP website. Available at: http://oceansbeyondpiracy.org.

OECD (2005a) *Paris Declaration on Aid Effectiveness*, Paris: OECD. Available at www.oecd.org/dac/effectiveness/34428351.pdf.

OECD (2005b) *Security System Reform and Governance*, Paris: OECD. Available at: https://doi.org/10.1787/9789264007888-en.

OECD (2007a) *OECD DAC Handbook on Security System Reform – Supporting Security and Justice*, Paris: OECD. Available at: www.oecd.org/dataoecd/43/25/38406485.pdf.

OECD (2007b) *Principles for Good International Engagement in Fragile States and Situations*. Paris: OECD. Available at: www.oecd.org/countries/somalia/48697077.pdf (47–49).

OECD (2008) 'Concepts and Dilemmas of State Building in Fragile Situations: From Fragility to Resilience', OECD-DAC Discussion Paper. Available at: www.oecd.org/dataoecd/59/51/41100930.pdf.

OECD (2009) *Security System Reform: What Have We Learned? Results and Trends from the Publication and Dissemination of the OECD DAC Handbook on Security System Reform*, Paris: OECD. Available at: www.oecd.org/dac/incaf/44391867.pdf.

OECD (2010) *The State's Legitimacy in Fragile Situations: Unpacking Complexity*, Paris: OECD.

Ohlin, J. (2016) *Theoretical Boundaries of Armed Conflict and Human Rights*, New York: Cambridge University Press.

Oosterveld, W. and Galand, R. (2012) 'Justice Reform, Security Sector Reform and Local Ownership', *Hague Journal on the Rule of Law*, 4(1): 194–209.

The Open University (2016) 'Rights and Justice in International Relations', course materials, Milton Keynes: The Open University. Available at: www.open.edu/openlearn/people-politics-law/politics-policy-people/politics/rights-and-justice-international-relations/content-section-0.

Orifici, D. and Damman, S. (2009) 'Mine Action' in V. Chetail (ed.), *'Post-Conflict Peacebuilding – A Lexicon'*, New York: Oxford University Press.

Ormhaug, C., Meier, P. and Hernes, H. (2009) 'Armed Conflict Deaths Disaggregated by Gender', PRIO Paper, 23 November. Oslo: PRIO. Available at: http://citeseerx.ist.psu.edu/viewdoc/download?doi=10.1.1.613.9724&rep=rep1&type=pdf.

Ortega, L. (2015) 'Untapped Resources for Peace: A Comparative Study of Women's Organizations of Guerrilla Ex-Combatants in Colombia and El Salvador' in S. Shekhawat (ed.), *Female Combatants in Conflict and Peace: Challenging Gender in Violence and Post-Conflict Reintegration*, London: Palgrave Macmillan, 232–49.

OSCE (1994) *OSCE Code of Conduct on Politico-Military Aspects of Security*, adopted at the 91st Plenary Meeting of the Special Committee of the CSCE Forum for Security Co-operation in Budapest on 03 December 1994, Vienna: OSCE. Available at: www.osce.org/fsc/41355.

OSCE (2008) *Guidebook on Democratic Policing*, Vienna: OSCE. Available at: http://polis.osce.org/library/f/2658/2639/OSCE-AUS-SPM-2658-EN-Guidebook%20on%20Democratic%20Policing.pdf.

Ostojić, M. (2014) *Between Justice and Stability: The Politics of War Crimes Prosecutions in Post-Milosevic Serbia*, Farnham: Ashgate.

Oxfam (2014) 'UN Integrated Missions and Humanitarian Action', Oxfam Humanitarian Policy Note, updated August 2014. Available at www.oxfam.org/sites/www.oxfam.org/files/file_attachments/story/oi_hum_policy_integrated_missions_august2014.pdf.

Oxford Academic (2017) *What is the Arms Trade Treaty?* (video). Available at: www.youtube.com/watch?v=wasPiNwe6hQ.

Oxford Institute for Ethics, Law and Armed Conflict (ELAC), University of Oxford (2013) 'Order and the International Criminal Court: The Society of States and 'Humanitarian Pluralism', lecture by Dr Matthew Killingsworth (podcast). Available on iTunes.

Özerdem, A. (2015) 'Disarmament, Demobilization and Reintegration (DDR) of Ex-Combatants and Development with a Specific Reference to the Reintegration of the Taliban in Afghanistan' in P. Jackson (ed.), *Handbook of International Security and Development*, Cheltenham: Edward Elgar, 452–446.

Paffenholz, T., Ross, N., Dixon, S., Schluchter, A.-L. and True, J. (2016) *Making Women Count – Not Just Counting Women: Assessing Women's Inclusion and Influence on Peace Negotiations*, Geneva: Inclusive Peace and Transition Initiative (The Graduate Institute of International and Development Studies) and UN Women. Available at: www.inclusivepeace.org/sites/default/files/IPTI-UN-Women-Report-Making-Women-Count-60-Pages.pdf.

Paintin, K. (2009) *States on Conflict: A Case Study on Conflict Prevention in Macedonia*, London: IPPR. Available at: www.ippr.org.uk/publicationsandreports/publication.asp?id=691.

Palmer, D. (2017) 'The Framework Nations' Concept and NATO: Game-Changer for a New Strategic Era or Missed Opportunity?' NATO Defence College, Research Paper 132. Available at: www.ndc.nato.int/news/news.php?icode=965.

Pankhurst, D. (2007) 'Gender Issues in Post War Contexts: A Review of Analysis and Experience and Implications for Policy', *Working Paper No.9*, Bradford: Department of Peace Studies, University of Bradford (in conjunction with UNRISD).

Paris, R. (2001) 'Human Security – Paradigm Shift or Hot Air?', *International Security*, 26(2): 87–102.

Paris, R. (2002) 'Kosovo and the Metaphor War', *Political Science Quarterly*, 117(3): 423–50.

Paris, R. (2004) *At War's End: Building Peace After Civil Conflict*, New York: Cambridge University Press.

Paris, R. (2010) 'Saving Liberal Peacebuilding', *Review of International Studies*, 36(2): 337–65.

Paris, R. (2014) 'The "Responsibility to Protect" and the Structural Problems of Preventive Humanitarian Intervention', *International Peacekeeping*, 21(5): 569–603.

Paris, R. and Sisk, T. (2009) 'Conclusion: Confronting the Challenges' in R. Paris and T. Sisk (eds), *The Dilemmas of Statebuilding: Confronting the Contradictions of Postwar Peace Operations*, Abingdon: Routledge, 304–15.

Paris, R. and Sisk, T. (eds) (2009) *The Dilemmas of Statebuilding: Confronting the Contradictions of Postwar Peace Operations*, Abingdon: Routledge.

Pariyar, K. (2016) 'Women Promoted to Major for First Time in Nepal Army's Infantry', *Glocal Khabar*, 24 August. Available at: https://glocalkhabar.com/featured/women-promoted-to-major-for-first-time-in-nepal-armys-infantry/.

Parker, S. and Wilson, M. (2016) *A Guide to the UN Small Arms Process*, Geneva: Small Arms Survey. Available at: *www.smallarmssurvey.org/fileadmin/docs/Q-Handbooks/HB-02-Diplo-Guide/SAS-HB02-Guide-UN-Small-Arms-Process.pdf*.

Parlevliet, M. (2002) 'Bridging the Divide: Exploring the Relationship between Human Rights and Conflict Management', *Track Two*, 11(1). Available at: http://ccrweb.ccr.uct.ac.za/archive/two/11_1/bridging.html.

Parlevliet, M. (2010) 'Rethinking Conflict Transformation from a Human Rights Perspective, in V. Dudouet and B. Schmelzle (eds), *Human Rights and Conflict Transformation: The Challenges of Just Peace*, Berlin: Berghof Conflict Research. Available at: www.berghof-handbook.net/documents/publications/dialogue9_humanrights_complete.pdf, 15–46.

Parliamentary Assembly of the Council of Europe (2005) *Recommendation 1713 (2005) Democratic Oversight of the Security Sector in Member States*, Strasbourg, Council of Europe, adopted by the Assembly on 23 June 2005, Strasbourg: Council of Europe. Available at: http://assembly.coe.int/main.asp?Link=/documents/adoptedtext/ta05/erec1713.htm.

Pascucci, M. (2008) 'Efficacy of Private Military Contractors in Peace Operations', *Connections*, 05 December. Available at: www.oercommons.org/courses/efficacy-of-private-military-contractors-in-peace-operations/view.

Patrick, S. (2006) *Weak States and Global Threats: Assessing Evidence of "Spillovers"*, Center for Global Development, Working Paper No. 73. Available at: www.cgdev.org.

Patrick, S. (2011a) 'The Brutal Truth: Failed States are Mainly a Threat to Their Own Inhabitants. We Should Help Them Anyway', *Foreign Policy*, 187: 55–57.

Patrick, S. (2011b) *Weak Links: Fragile States, Global Threats, and International Security*, New York: Oxford University Press.

Peace Building Initiative (2009) Peace Building Initiative website. Available at: www.peacebuildinginitiative.org.

PeaceWomen (2018) 'The Resolutions', PeaceWomen website. Available at: www.peacewomen.org/why-WPS/solutions/resolutions.

Penal Reform (2019) Penal Reform website. Available at: www.penalreform.org.

Penal Reform International (2018) 'Global Prison Trends 2018', London: Penal Reform International. Available at: https://s16889.pcdn.co/wp-content/uploads/2018/04/PRI_Global-Prison-Trends-2018_EN_WEB.pdf.

Persio, S. (2017) 'After 13 Years and Several Scandals, U.N. Votes to End Mission in Haiti', *Newsweek*, 13 April. Available at: www.newsweek.com/minustah-mission-haiti-un-peacekeepers-scandal-583490.

Picciotto, R. (2010) 'Conflict Prevention and Development Co-Operation in Africa: An Introduction', *Conflict, Security and Development*, 10(1): 1–25.

Piedmont, D. (2015) *The Role of Disarmament, Demobilization & Reintegration in Countering Violent Extremism*, Ottawa: Centre for Security Governance.

Plumber, T. and Neumayer, E. (2006) 'The Unequal Burden of War: The Effect of Armed Conflict on the Gender Gap in Life Expectancy', *International Organization*, 60(3): 723–54.

Pollard, S., Poplack, D. and Kevin Carroll Casey, K. (2017) 'Understanding the Islamic State's Competitive Advantages: Remaking State and Nationhood in the Middle East and North Africa', *Terrorism and Political Violence*, 29(6): 1045–65.

Pouligny, B. (2004) *Ils Nous Avaient Promis La Paix: Opérations De l'ONU Et Populations Locales*, Paris: Sciences Po.

Pruitt, L. (2016) *The Women in Blue Helmets: Gender, Policing, and the UN's First All-Female Peacekeeping Unit*, Oakland: University of California Press.

Puechguirbal, N. (2012) 'The Cost of Ignoring Gender in Conflict and Post-Conflict Situations: A Feminist Perspective', *Amsterdam Law Forum*, 4(1): 4–19.

Puri, H. (2016) *Perilous Interventions: The Security Council and the Politics of Chaos*, New York HarperCollins Publishers India.

Putzell, J. (2007) 'Retaining Legitimacy in Fragile States', *id29 Insights*, Issue 66, Brighton: Institute of Development Studies, University of Sussex. Available at: https://assets.publishing.service.gov.uk/media/57a08c0540f0b64974000f3c/insights66.pdf.

Quaskenbush, S. and Venteicher, J. (2008) 'Settlements, Outcomes, and the Recurrence of Conflict', *Journal of Peace Research*, 45(6): 723–42.

Ramírez-Barat, C. (2014) 'Transitional Justice and the Public Sphere' in C. Ramírez-Barat (ed.), *Transitional Justice, Culture and Society: Beyond Outreach*, New York: ICTJ, 27–48.

Ramsbotham, O., Woodhouse, T. and Miall, H. (2016) *Contemporary Conflict Resolution* (4th edn), Cambridge: Polity Press.

Ramsey, A. (2011) 'Alternative Approaches: Land-Based Strategies to Countering Piracy off the Coast of Somalia', Brussels: NATO Civil-Military Fusion Centre. Available at: www.cimicweb.org/Documents/CFC%20Anti-Piracy%20Thematic%20Papers/CFC_Anti-Piracy_Report_Alternative%20Approaches_NOV_2011_FINAL.pdf.

Rausch, C. (ed.) (2017) *Fighting Serious Crimes: Strategies and Tactics for Conflict-Affected Societies*, Washington: DCL USIP.

Reed, P. (2015) 'Creating Strategies for Security Sector Reform in VUCA Operating Environments', video (University of Leicester). Available at: www.youtube.com/watch?v=L25OBjhWscs&list=PLjQX5EXgm57STSvD19VcobrSyhF5pey-U&index=4.

Rehn, E. and Sirleaf, E. (2002) 'Women, War and Peace: The Independent Experts' Assessment on the Impact of Armed Conflict on Women and Women's Role in Peacebuilding', New York: UNIFEM. Available at: www.unifem.org/materials/item_detail. php?ProductID=17.

Reitano, T.R., Jesperson, S., Bird Ruiz-Benitez de Lugo, L. (eds) (2018) *Militarised Responses to Transnational Organised Crime: The War on Crime*, London: Palgrave Macmillan.

Reliefweb (2006) 'Guatemalan blue helmet deaths stir Congo debate', 31 January. Available at: http://reliefweb.int/report/democratic-republic-congo/guatemalan-blue-helmet-deaths-stir-congo-debate.

Reno, W. (1998) *Warlord Politics and African States*, Boulder: Lynne Reiner.

Reno, W. (2011) *Warfare in Independent Africa*, Cambridge: Cambridge University Press.

Reuters (2017) 'Put Women at Center of Colombia Peacebuilding to Ensure Lasting Peace: Campaigners', 22 June. Available at: http://uk.reuters.com/article/us-colombia-peace-idUSKBN19C24L.

Rhodes, G. (2017) 'Improvised Explosive Devices and the International Mine Action Standards', *Journal of Conventional Weapons Destruction*, 21(3): Article 3.

Rice, C. (2008) remarks at the Launch of the Civilian Response Corps, Washington: US Department of State, 16 July, cited in Patrick, S. (2011b) *Weak Links: Fragile States, Global Threats, and International Security*, New York: Oxford University Press.

Richmond, O. (2009) 'Becoming Liberal, Unbecoming Liberalism: Liberal–Local Hybridity via the Everyday as a Response to the Paradoxes of Liberal Peacebuilding', *Journal of Intervention and Statebuilding*, 3(3): 324–344.

Richmond, O. (2014) 'The Impact of Socio-Economic Inequality on Peacebuilding and Statebuilding', *Civil Wars*, 16(4): 449–67.

Richmond, O. and Tellidis, I. (2012) 'The Complex Relationship between Peacebuilding and Terrorism Approaches: Towards Post-Terrorism and a Post-Liberal Peace?', *Terrorism and Political Violence*, 24(1): 120–43.

Rieff, D. (2018) 'The End of Human Rights? Learning from the failure of the Responsibility to Protect and the International Criminal Court', *Foreign Policy*, 09 April. Available at: https://foreignpolicy.com/2018/04/09/the-end-of-human-rights-genocide-united-nations-r2p-terrorism.

Rodríguez-Garavito, C. and Gomez, K. (2018) 'Rising to the Populist Challenge: A New Playbook for Human Rights Actors', Bogotá: Dejusticia. Available at: www.dejusticia.org/wp-content/uploads/2018/04/Rising-to-the-populist-challenge-VERSION-FINAL-PARA-WEB-1.pdf?x54537.

Rogers, P. (2009) 'Global Security after the War on Terror', London: Oxford Research Group. Available at: www.oxfordresearchgroup.org.uk/sites/default/files/GSAWTNov2009.pdf.

Rohwerder, B. (2016) *Piracy in the Horn of Africa, West Africa and the Strait of Malacca* (GSDRC Rapid Literature Review). Birmingham, UK: GSDRC, University of Birmingham. Available at: www.gsdrc.org/wp-content/uploads/2016/09/piracy_rohwerder.pdf.

Roll, K. (2015) 'Exploring the United Nations' Role in Disarmament, Demobilisation and Reinsertion, the Case of Timor Leste', University of Oxford podcast, 16 June. Available at: https://podcasts.ox.ac.uk/oxpeace-2015-mandates-and-majors-exploring-united-nations-role-disarmament-demobilisation.

Rosato, V. (2016) '"Hybrid Orders" between Terrorism and Organized Crime: The Case of Al Qaeda in the Islamic Maghreb', *African Security*, 9(2): 110–35.

Rosen, N. and Theros, M. (2011) 'Afghanistan: losing the Afghan people', openDemocracy, 16 January. Available at: www.opendemocracy.net/marika-theros-nir-rosen/afghanistan-losingafghan-people.

Rosendorff, B. and Sandler, T. (2005) 'The Political Economy of Transnational Terrorism', *Journal of Conflict Resolution*, 49(2): 171–82.

Rost, N. (2011) 'Human Rights Violations, Weak States, and Civil War', *Human Rights Review*, 12(4): 417–40.

Roth, K. (2017) 'The Dangerous Rise of Populism: Global Attacks on Human Rights Values', *Journal of International Affairs*, THE NEXT WORLD ORDER: Special 70th Anniversary Issue: 79–84.

Royal Commission into the Protection and Detention of Children in the Northern Territory (2017) *Final Report*, Canberra: Government of Australia, 17 November. Available at: https://childdetentionnt.royalcommission.gov.au/Pages/Report.aspx#_Read.

Royal United Services Institute for Defence and Security Studies (RUSI) and the Foreign Policy Research Institute (FPRI) (2009) *Reforming the Afghan National Police*, London and Philadelphia: RUSI and FPRI. Available at: www.fpri.org/research/nationalsecurity/afghanpolice/ReformingAfghanNationalPolice.pdf.

Ruggiero, V. (2007) 'War, Crime, Empire and Cosmopolitanism', *Critical Criminology*, 15(3): 211–21.

Rule of Law Legal Studies (2012) 'Video 1 – The Rule of Law' (video). Available at: www.youtube.com/watch?v=0Hubr8mZllc.

Rupesinghe, K. Sciarone, P. van de Goor, L. (eds) (2016) *Between Development and Destruction: An Enquiry into the Causes of Conflict*, Basingstoke and London: Palgrave Macmillan.

Saferworld (2010) *Common Ground? Gendered Assessment of the Needs and Concerns of Maoist Army Combatants for Rehabilitation and Integration*, London: Saferworld. Available at: www.saferworld.org.uk/oldsite/resources/view-resource/502-common-ground.

Saferworld (2011) *The Securitisation of Aid? Reclaiming Security to Meet Poor People's Needs*, London: Saferworld. Available at: www.saferworld.org.uk/resources/publications/505-the-securitisation-of-aid.

Saferworld (2013) We Have an Arms Trade Treaty – Now for the Real Work!, London: Saferworld. Available at: www.saferworld.org.uk/news-andviews/comment/81#.UVsd4Id17t4.twitter.

Saferworld (2014) *Community Security: A Vehicle for Peacebuilding and Statebuilding*. Briefing. London: Saferworld. Available at: www.saferworld.org.uk/resources/publications/833-community-security-a-vehicle-for-peacebuilding-and-statebuilding.

Saferworld (2014) *Masculinities, Conflict and Peacebuilding: Perspectives on Men through a Gender Lens*, London: Saferworld. Available at: www.saferworld.org.uk/resources/publications/862-masculinities-conflict-and-peacebuilding-perspectives-on-men-through-a-gender-lens.

Saferworld (2014) *Women and Security in Yemen* (video). Available at: www.youtube.com/watch?v=nPjclFe5Zsc.

Saferworld (2015) 'Saving lives: Improving community security through arms control in Kenya' (video). Available at: www.youtube.com/watch?v=Z6Jpq5N3N3U.

Saferworld (2019) website of Saferworld. Available at: www.saferworld.org.uk.

Saferworld and Nepal Institute for Policy Studies (2010) *Gender and Security Sector Reform*, London and Kathmandu: Saferworld and Nepal Institute for Policy Studies. Available at: www.saferworld.org.uk/Gender%20and%20Security%20Briefing%20Paper.pdf.

Saferworld/Forum for Civic Initiatives (2007) *Small Arms and Human Security in Kosovo: An Agenda for Action*, London/Pristina: Saferworld/Forum for Civic Initiatives. Available at: www.saferworld.org.uk/resources/publications/248-small-arms-and-human-security-in-kosovo-an-agenda-for-action.

Salahub, J., and Nerland, K. (2010) 'Just Add Gender? Challenges to Meaningful Integration of Gender in SSR Policy and Practice', in Sedra, M. (ed.), *The Future of Security Sector*

Reform, Waterloo: CIGI, 263–80. Available at: www.cigionline.org/sites/default/files/ The%20Future%20of%20Security%20Sector%20Reform.pdf.

Sambanis, N. (2007) *Short-Term and Long-Term Effects of United Nations Peace Operations*, Washington: World Bank. Available at: http://econ.worldbank.org/external/default/mai n?ImgPagePK=64202990&entityID=000016406_20070413150931&menuPK=64168 175&pagePK=64210502&theSitePK=477960&piPK=64210520.

Samuels, K. (2005) 'Sustainability and Peace Building: A Key Challenge', *Development in Practice*, 15(6): 728–36.

Sanchez, M. (2018) *United Nations International Police Officers in Peacekeeping Missions: A Phenomenological Exploration of Complex Acculturation*, Abingdon: Routledge.

Sánchez, F. Solimano, A. and Formisano, M. (2005) 'Conflict, Violence, and Crime in Colombia' in P. Collier and N. Sambanis (eds), *Understanding Civil War: Evidence and Analysis*, Washington, DC: World Bank, 119–59.

Sandel, M. (2009) *Justice: What's the Right Thing to Do?* New York: Farrar, Straus and Girroux.

Sandler, T. (2014) 'The Analytical Study of Terrorism: Taking Stock', *Journal of Peace Research*, 51(2): 257–71.

Sanin, F. (2010) 'Organizing Minors: The Case of Colombia' in S. Gates and S. Reich, (eds), *Child Soldiers in the Age of Fractured States*, Pittsburgh: University of Pittsburgh Press.

Sargent, K. (2014) 'Re-Thinking Post-Conflict State Building: Developing Better Governance and Fighting Corruption', (video) (University of Leicester). Available at: www.youtube. com/watch?v=3dx6gq2IiMY&list=PLjQX5EXgm57S0L7nT-QMVhQLKiYNsSPxu.

Sarosi, D. (2007) 'Human Security: Does Gender Matter', paper presented at Mainstreaming Human Security: The Asian Contribution Conference. 04–05 October, Bangkok. Available at: http://humansecurityconf.polsci.chula.ac.th/Documents/Presentations/Diana. pdf.

Sartre, P. (2011) 'Making UN Peacekeeping More Robust: Protecting the Mission, Persuading the Actors', New York: International Peace Institute. Available at: www.ipinst. org/2011/08/making-un-peacekeeping-more-robust-protecting-the-mission-persuading-the-actors.

Save The Children (2017) *Invisible Wounds: The Impact of Six Years of War on the Mental Health of Syria's Children*, London: Save The Children. Available at: www.savethechildren.org/ atf/cf/%7B9def2ebe-10ae-432c-9bd0-df91d2eba74a%7D/INVISIBLE%20WOUNDS%20 FINAL%20020317.PDF.

Save the Children UK (2009) 'Sexual Exploitation and Abuse by Aid Workers and Peacekeepers', Policy Brief, London: Save the Children UK. Available at: https://resourcecentre. savethechildren.net/node/2968/pdf/2968.pdf.

Scheffer, D. (1992) 'Towards a Modern Doctrine of Humanitarian Intervention', *University of Toledo Law Review*, 23: 253–274.

Scheye, E. (2009) '*State-Provided Service, Contracting Out, and Non-State Networks: Justice and Security as Public and Private Goods and Services*', Paris: Organisation for Economic Cooperation and Development (OECD).

Scheye, E. and Peake, G. (2005) 'Unknotting Local Ownership' in A. Ebnother and P. Fluri (eds), *After Intervention: Public Security in Post-Conflict Societies – From Intervention to Sustainable Local Ownership*, Geneva/Vienna: DCAF/PfP Consortium of Defence Academies and Security Studies Institutes, 235–260.

Schmeidl, S. and Piza-Lopez, E. (2002) *Gender and Conflict Early Warning: A Framework for Action*, London: International Alert.

Schmid, A. (2012) 'The Revised Academic Consensus Definition of Terrorism', *Perspectives on Terrorism*, 6(2): 158–59.

Schnabel, A. and Born, H. (2011) *Security Sector Reform Narrowing the Gap between Theory and Practice*, Geneva: DCAF. Available at: www.dcaf.ch/DCAF/EZ/Publications/Security-Sector-Reform-Narrowing-the-Gap-between-Theory-and-Practice.

Schomerus, M. and El Taraboulsi-McCarthy, S. with Sandhar, J. (2017) 'Countering violent extremism (Topic Guide)' Birmingham, UK: GSDRC, University of Birmingham. Available at: www.gsdrc.org/wp-content/uploads/2017/03/CVE.pdf.

Schreier, F. (2010) 'Trends and Challenges in International Security: An Inventory', Occasional Paper No. 19, DCAF, Geneva. Available at: www.dcaf.ch/Publications/Trends-and-Challenges-in-International-Security.

Scott, J. (1998) *Seeing like a State: How Certain Schemes to Improve the Human Condition Have Failed*, New Haven: Yale University Press.

Searle, A. (2003) *Wehrmacht Generals, West German Society, and the Debate on Rearmament, 1949–1959*, Westport, CT: Praeger Publishers.

Security Council Report (2011) 'Small Arms', Monthly Forecast, April. Available at: www.securitycouncilreport.org/monthly-forecast/2011-04/lookup_c_glKWLeMTIsG_b_6676145.php?print=true.

Sedra, M. (2010a) 'Introduction: The Future of Security Sector Reform', in M. Sedra (ed.), *The Future of Security Sector Reform*, Ontario: CIGI, 16–27. Available at: www.cigionline.org/sites/default/files/the_future_of_security_sector_reform.pdf.

Sedra, M. (2010b) *Security Sector Reform 101: Understanding the Concept, Charting Trends and Identifying Challenges*, Ontario: CIGI. Available at: www.cigionline.org/sites/default/files/SSR%20101%20Final%20%28April%2027%29.pdf.

Sedra, M. (ed.) (2010c) *The Future of Security Sector Reform*, Ontario: The Centre for International Governance Innovation (CIGI). Available at: www.cigionline.org/sites/default/files/The%20Future%20of%20Security%20Sector%20Reform.pdf.

Sedra, M. (2014) 'An Uncertain Future for Afghanistan's Security Sector', *Stability: International Journal of Security and Development*, 3(1): 1–16.

Sedra, M. (2017) *Security Sector Reform in Conflict-Affected Countries: The Evolution of a Model*, Abingdon: Routledge.

Sedra, M. (2018) 'Adapting Security Sector Reform to Ground-Level Realities: The Transition to a Second-Generation Model', *Journal of Intervention and Statebuilding*, 12(1): 48–63.

Sedra, M. and Burt, G. (2016) 'Integrating SSR and SALW Programming' SSR Paper 16, Geneva: DCAF. Available at: www.dcaf.ch/sites/default/files/publications/documents/ONLINE-DCAF-SSR-16-2016-06-16.pdf.

Selakovic-Bursic, S., Haramic, E. and Leenaars. A. (2006) 'The Balkan Piedmont: Male Suicide Rates Pre-War, Wartime, and Post-War in Serbia and Montenegro', *Archives of Suicide Research*, 10(3): 225–38.

Sergi, B. and Giacomo Morabito, G. (2016) 'The Pirates' Curse: Economic Impacts of the Maritime Piracy', *Studies in Conflict and Terrorism*, 39(10): 935–52.

Shanahan, T. (2016) 'The Definition of Terrorism' in R. Jackson (ed.), *Routledge Handbook of Critical Terrorism Studies*, Abingdon: Routledge.

Sharwood-Smith, C. (2014) 'The Structure and Activities of the UN Police Division', (video) (University of Leicester). Available at: www.youtube.com/watch?v=dYeGNmoO6oI&index=8&list=PLjQX5EXgm57S0L7nT-QMVhQLKiYNsSPxu.

Sharwood-Smith, C. (2015) 'Preparing Police Peacekeepers', (video) (University of Leicester). Available at: www.youtube.com/watch?v=YVZz6o9XUdU.

Shaw, M. (2011) '*Know Your Enemy: An Overview of Organized Crime Threat Assessments*', IPI Issue Brief, New York: IPI.

Shaw, M. and Reitano, T. (2017) 'Global Illicit Flows and Local Conflict Dynamics: The Case for Pre-Emptive Analysis and Experimental Policy Options', United Nations University

(UNU) Centre for Policy Research, Crime-Conflict Nexus Series: No 2, May 2017, Tokyo: UNU. Available at: https://i.unu.edu/media/cpr.unu.edu/attachment/2536/Synopsis-Crime-Conflict-FINAL.pdf.

Shaw, R. and Waldorf, L. (2010) 'Introduction: Localizing Transitional Justice' in Shaw, R. and Waldorf, L. (eds), *Localizing Transitional Justice: Interventions and Priorities after Mass Violence*, Stanford: Stanford University Press, 3–26.

Shestack, J. (1998) 'The Philosophic Foundations of Human Rights', *Human Rights Quarterly*, 20(2): 201–34.

Shortland, A. (2012) 'Treasure Mapped: Using Satellite Imagery to Track the Developmental Effects of Somali Piracy', London: Chatham House. Available at: www.chathamhouse.org/sites/default/files/public/Research/Africa/0112pp_shortland.

Shortland A. (2018) 'Dangers of Success: The Economics of Somali Piracy' in T. Reitano, S. Jesperson, L. Bird Ruiz-Benitez de Lugo (eds), *Militarised Responses to Transnational Organised Crime*. Gewerbestrasse: Springer Nature.

Shortland, A. and Varese, F. (2016) 'State-Building, Informal Governance and Organised Crime: The Case of Somali Piracy', *Political Studies*, 64(4): 811–31.

Silke, A. (2018) *Routledge Handbook of Terrorism and Counterterrorism*, New York: Routledge.

Simić, O. (2010) 'Does the Presence of Women Really Matter? Towards Combating Male Sexual Violence in Peacekeeping Operations', *International Peacekeeping*, 17(2): 188–99.

SIPRI (2017) 'Where Do We Go from Here? Conflict Prevention and New Multilateralism', video of panel discussion hosted by SIPRI. Available at: www.youtube.com/watch?v=vSYCdp3jPIc.

Sjoberg, L. (2014) *Gender, War, and Conflict*, Cambridge: Polity Press.

Sjoberg, L. (2016) *Women as Wartime Rapists: Beyond Sensation and Stereotyping*, New York: New York University Press.

Sjoberg, L. and C. Gentry (2007) *Mothers, Monsters, Whores: Women's Violence in Global Politics*, London and New York: Zed Books.

Small Arms Survey (2010) *Small Arms Survey 2010: Gangs, Groups, and Guns*, Geneva: Small Arms Survey. Available at: www.smallarmssurvey.org/publications/by-type/yearbook/small-arms-survey-2010.html.

Small Arms Survey (2011) *Small Arms Survey 2011: States of Security*, Geneva: Small Arms Survey. Available at *www.smallarmssurvey.org/publications/by-type/yearbook/small-arms-survey-2011.html*.

Small Arms Survey (2014) *Women and Guns*, Geneva: Small Arms Survey. Available at: www.smallarmssurvey.org/fileadmin/docs/A-Yearbook/2014/en/Small-Arms-Survey-2014-Highlights-EN.pdf.

Small Arms Survey (2016) 'The Online Trade of Light Weapons in Libya', Security Assessment in North Africa, Dispatch No. 6, Geneva: Small Arms Survey. Available at: www.smallarmssurvey.org/fileadmin/docs/R-SANA/SANA-Dispatch6-Online-trade.pdf.

Smith, D. (2004) *Trends and Causes of Armed Conflict*, Berlin: Berghof Research Centre for Constructive Conflict Management. Available at www.berghof-handbook.net/all.

Smith-Höhn, J. (2010) 'Transformation through Participation: Public Perceptions in Liberia and Sierra Leone' in A. Bryden and F. Olonisakin (eds), *Security Sector Transformation in Africa*, Geneva: DCAF, 89–110.

Snodderly, D. (ed.) (2011) *Peace Terms: A Glossary of Terms for Conflict Management and Peacebuilding*, Washington, DC: USIP. Available at www.usip.org/publications/usip-peace-terms-glossary.

Solomon, R. and Woocher, L. (2010) 'Confronting the Challenge of "Political Will"', *Prepared for the Instability Warning and Genocide Prevention Symposium, Vanderbilt*

University Law School, Washington: USIP. Available at: www.usip.org/publications/confronting-the-challenge-political-will.

South Eastern and Eastern Europe Clearinghouse for the Control of Small Arms and Light Weapons (SEESAC) (2006) *SALW Survey of Kosovo*, Belgrade: SEESAC. Available at: www.seesac.org/f/docs/SALW-Surveys/SALW-Survey-of-Kosovo-EN.pdf.

Soysa, I., Jackson, T. and Ormhaug, C. (2010) 'Tools of the Torturer? Small Arms Imports and Repression of Human Rights, 1992–2004', *The International Journal of Human Rights*, 14(3): 378–93.

Specht, I. (2010) 'Socio-Economic Reintegration of Combatants', London: International Alert. Available at: www.internationalalert.org/sites/default/files/publications/201009PracticeNote4SocioEconomicReintegration.pdf.

Spearin, C. (2011) 'UN Peacekeeping and the International Private Military and Security Industry', International Peacekeeping, 18(2): 196–209.

Sriram, C. (2008) 'Prevention and the Rule of Law: Rhetoric and Reality' in A. Hurwitz and R. Huang (eds), *Civil War and the Rule of Law: Security, Development, Human Rights*, Boulder: Lynne Reinner, 71–90.

Sriram, C. (2009) 'Justice as Peace? Liberal Peacebuilding and Strategies of Transitional Justice', *Global Society*, 21(4): 579–91.

Sriram, C. (2015) *Seminar on Mass Atrocities*, GSDRC podcast. Available at: www.gsdrc.org/professional-dev/mass-atrocities/.

Sriram, C., Martin-Ortega, O. and Herman, J. (2017) *War, Conflict and Human Rights: Theory and Practice* (3rd edn), Abingdon: Routledge.

Stabilisation Unit (2010) *Security Sector Reform and Rule of Law*, Stabilisation Issues Note, London: Stabilisation Unit. Available at: www.stabilisationunit.gov.uk/attachments/article/520/SIN%20Security%20Sector%20and%20Rule%20of%20law%2004102010.pdf.

Stabilisation Unit (2011) Website of the UK Government's Stabilisation Unit. Available at www.stabilisationunit.gov.uk/about-us/what-is-stabilisation.html.

Stabilisation Unit (2018) 'The UK Government's Approach to Stabilisation A guide for policy makers and practitioners', December, London: HMRC. Available at https://assets.publishing.service.gov.uk/government/uploads/system/uploads/attachment_data/file/767466/The_UK_Governments_Approach_to_Stabilisation_-_A_Guide__web_.pdf.

Stamnes, E. and Psland, K. (2016) 'Synthesis Report: Reviewing UN Peace Operations, the UN Peacebuilding Architecture and the Implementation of UNSCR 1325', Report No. 2, Oslo: Norwegian Institute of International Affairs. Available at www.un.org/pga/70/wp-content/uploads/sites/10/2016/01/NUPI_Report_2_16_Stamnes_Osland.pdf.

Stanford Center on Democracy, Development, and The Rule of Law (CDDRL) (2015) *Conflict and Crisis: Implications of Ongoing Human Rights Violations in Syria* (video), Stanford: Stanford CDDRL. Available at www.youtube.com/watch?v=XTF4sgIqc8I.

The Stanley Foundation (2012) *Fragile States, Global Consequences* (video). Available at https://vimeo.com/26342266.

Steenkamp, C., (2017) 'The Crime–Conflict Nexus and the Civil War in Syria', *Stability: International Journal of Security and Development*, 6(1): 11, 1–18.

Steinberg, D. (2008) *Women and Armed Conflict: Protection and Empowerment*. Brussels: ICG. Available at: www.crisisgroup.org/global/protection-and-participation-women-and-armed-conflict.

Steinberg, D. (2011) 'Women and War: An Agenda for Action' in K. Kuehnast, C. Oudraat and H. Hernes (eds), *Women and War: Power and Protection in the 21st Century*, Washington: USIP, 115–30.

Stepanova, E. (2010) 'Armed conflict, crime and criminal violence', SPIRI Yearbook 2010, Stockholm: SIPRI. Available at: www.sipri.org/yearbook/2010/02.

Stewart, F (2010) 'Horizontal Inequalities as a Cause of Conflict: A Review of CRISE Findings', *World Development Report 2011 Background Paper*, Washington: World Bank. Available at: http://siteresources.worldbank.org/EXTWDR2011/Resources/6406082-1283882418764/WDR_Background_Paper_Stewart.pdf.

Stewart, F. and Brown, G. (2007) 'Motivations for Conflict: Groups and Individuals' in C. Crocker, F. Hampson and P. Aall (eds) *Leashing the Dogs of War*, Washington: USIP, 219–241.

Stewart. T. (2018) 'Britain's Fight for Spain', Historic UK website. Available at: www.historic-uk.com/HistoryUK/HistoryofBritain/Britains-Fight-for-Spain/.

Stohl, R. and Hogendoorn, E.J. (2010) 'Stopping the Destructive Spread of Small Arms: How Small Arms and Light Weapons Proliferation Undermines Security and Development'. Available at: www.americanprogress.org/wp-content/uploads/issues/2010/03/pdf/small_arms.pdf.

Strachan, A. and Haider, H. (2015) *Gender and Conflict: Topic Guide*, Birmingham: GSDRC, University of Birmingham. Available at: http://gsdrc.org/wp-content/uploads/2015/07/gender_conflict.pdf.

Stroehlein, A. and Kroslak, D. (2008) *Somalia: "Oh My Gosh, Pirates!"*, Brussels: ICG. Available at: www.crisisgroup.org/en/regions/africa/horn-of-africa/somalia/op-eds/stroehlein-kroslak-somalia-oh-my-gosh-pirates.aspx.

Stuart, F and Brown, G (2007) 'Motivations for Conflict: Groups and Individuals' in C. Crocker, F. Hampson and P. Aall (eds), *Leashing the Dogs of War*, Washington: USIP, 219–41.

Swaine, A. (2018) *Conflict-Related Violence against Women: Transforming Transition*, Cambridge: Cambridge University Press.

Swanström, N. and Weissmann, M. (2005) 'Conflict, Conflict Prevention, Conflict Management and Beyond: A Conceptual Exploration', *A Concept Paper*, Washington and Sweden: Central AsiaCaucuses Institute and Silk Road Studies Program. Available at: www.silkroadstudies.org/new/docs/ConceptPapers/2005/concept_paper_ConfPrev.pdf

Tamanaha, B. (2004) *On the Rule of Law: History, Politics, Theory*, Cambridge: Cambridge University Press.

Tanner, F. (2010) 'Addressing the Perils of Peace Operations: Toward a Global Peacekeeping System', *Global Governance*, 16: 209–17.

Tarif, M. and Virculon, T. (2016) *Transitions Politiques: Les Déboires Du Modèle De Sortie De Crise En Afrique*, Paris: IFRI.

TEDx Talks (2017) *White Helmets: the power of trained volunteers* (video). Available at: www.youtube.com/watch?v=dpuny2eynIM.

Tennant, V., Doyle, B. and Mazou, R. (2010) *Safeguarding Humanitarian Space: A Review of Key Challenges for UNHCR*, Geneva: UNHCR.

Thapa, L. and Canyon, D. (2017) 'The Advancement of Women in Post-Conflict Nepal', Occasional Paper. Honolulu: Daniel K. Inouye Asia Pacific Center for Security Studies. Available at: http://apcss.org/the-advancement-of-women-in-post-conflict-nepal/.

Thoms, O. and Ron, J. (2007) 'Do Human Rights Violations Cause Internal Conflict?', *Human Rights Quarterly*, 29(3): 674–705.

Thoms, O. N. T., Ron, J., and Paris, R. (2010) 'State-Level Effects of Transitional Justice: What Do We Know?', *International Journal of Transitional Justice*, 4(3): 329–54.

Tilly, C. (1985) 'War Making and State Making as Organized Crime' in P. Evans, D. Rueschemeyer and T. Skocpol (eds), *Bringing the State Back In*, Cambridge: Cambridge University Press, 169–91.

Torjesen, S. (2009) 'New Avenues for Research in the Study of DDR', *Conflict, Security and Development*, 9(4): 411–23.

Transnational Initiative Countering Violent Extremism (TICVE) (2015) 'Countering Violent Extremism in the Wider Atlantic' (video). Available at: www.youtube.com/watch?v=jsEzl4ZlfGo.

Trefon, T. (2011) *Congo Masquerade: The Political Culture of Aid Inefficiency and Reform Failure*, London: Zed Books.

True, J. (2015) 'Winning the Battle but Losing the War on Violence: A Feminist Perspective on the Declining Global Violence Thesis', *International Feminist Journal of Politics*, 17(4): 554–72.

True, J. and Eddyono, S. (2017) 'Preventing Violent Extremism: Gender Perspectives and Women's Roles' Melbourne: Monash Gender, Peace and Security (GPS) Centre. Available at: http://docs.wixstatic.com/ugd/b4aef1_0f0e2df8aeb4448b806b7c59a5f4a4b0.pdf.

True, J. and Riveros-Morales, Y. (2019) 'Towards inclusive peace: Analysing gender-sensitive peace agreements 2000–2016', *International Political Science Review*, 40(1): 23–40.

Tryggestad, T. (2016) 'The Women, Peace and Security Agenda – 15 Years On', GS Policy Brief, PRIO. Available at: http://file.prio.no/publication_files/prio/Tryggestad%20-%20The%20Women%20Peace%20and%20Security%20Agenda,%20GPS%20Policy%20Brief%201-2016.pdf.

Turner, C. (2013) 'Deconstructing Transitional Justice', *Law Critique*, 24: 193–209.

UCDP (2019) Uppsala Conflict Data Program (UCDP) website, Uppsala: Uppsala University. Available at: http://ucdp.uu.se.

Uddin, K. (2014) 'Human Rights Violations by UN Peacekeepers', *Security and Human Rights* 25(1):130–144.

Uesugi, Y. (2014) *Peacebuilding and Security Sector Governance in Asia*, Münster: LIT Verlag. Available at: www.dcaf.ch/sites/default/files/publications/documents/FINAL_Pcbldng_SSG_Asia.pdf

UK Cabinet Office (2008) *The National Security Strategy of the United Kingdom: Security in an Interdependent World*, London: HMSO.

UK MoD (2009) 'Security and Stabilisation: The Military Contribution', *Joint Doctrine Publication 3–40*, London: MoD. Available at: www.mod.uk/NR/rdonlyres/A28A9419-9F11-4B3F-807B-D5B995BB7F69/0/securityStabilisation22032010v2A4web.pdf.

UN (1948) *Universal Declaration of Human Rights*, New York: UN. Available at: www.ohchr.org/EN/UDHR/Documents/UDHR_Translations/eng.pdf.

UN (1997a) 'ECOSOC Agreed Conclusions'. New York: UN. Available at: www.un.org/womenwatch/osagi/pdf/ECOSOCAC1997.2.PDF.

UN (1997b) 'Report of the Panel of Governmental Experts on Small Arms', A/52/298. Available at: www.securitycouncilreport.org/atf/cf/%7B65BFCF9B-6D27-4E9C-8CD3-CF6E4FF96FF9%7D/Arms%20A%2052%20298.pdf.

UN (2000a) 'Report of the Panel on United Nations Peace Operations' [the Brahimi Report], A/55/305 - S/2000/80, New York: UN. Available at: www.un.org/en/events/pastevents/brahimi_report.shtml.

UN (2000b) 'Secretary-General Salutes International Workshop on Human Security in Mongolia', Press Release, 08 May, SG/SM/7382. New York: UN. Available at: www.un.org/press/en/2000/20000508.sgsm7382.doc.html.

UN (2002) *Rome Statute of the International Criminal Court.* New York: UN, A/CONF.183/9. Available at: www.un.org/law/icc/index.html.

UN (2006) 'Report of the International Tribunal for the Prosecution of Persons Responsible for Serious Violations of International Humanitarian Law Committed in the Territory of the Former Yugoslavia since 1991', Note by the Secretary-General, A/61/271–S/2006/666. Available at: www.icty.org/x/file/About/Reports%20and%20Publications/AnnualReports/annual_report_2006_en.pdf.

UN (2010) 'Gender Guidelines for Mine Action Programmes', New York: UN. Available at: https://unmas.org/sites/default/files/ma-guidelines_0.pdf.

UN (2011) 'General Assembly Interactive Thematic Debate on the rule of law and global challenges', 11 April, New York: UN. Available at: www.un.org/en/ga/president/65/initiatives/ruleoflaw.shtml.

UN (2012) 'Women, Peace and Security: Conflict-Related Sexual Violence', Statement by the Special Representative of the Secretary-General on Sexual Violence in Conflict, Margot Wallström, *New York:* UN, 23 February 2012. Available at: www.un.org/sexualviolenceinconflict/wp-content/uploads/2012/07/SRSG-Statement-on-Women-Peace-Security-23-February-2012.pdf.

UN (2016a) 'Security Sector Reform Integrated Technical Guidance Notes: Transnational Organised Crime and Security Sector Reform', New York: UN. Available at: www.unodc.org/documents/organized-crime/SSR_TOC_ITGN_2016_WEB.pdf.

UN (2016b) 'The United Nations Policy on Victim Assistance in Mine Action', New York: UN. Available at: www.mineactionstandards.org/fileadmin/user_upload/images/publications/16-06-09_FINAL_UN_Policy_on_Victim_Assistance_in_Mine_Action.pdf.

UN (2017) 'Twenty Years for Children' (video), New York: UN. Available at: https://childrenandarmedconflict.un.org/video/twenty-years-for-children/.

UN (2018) 'Speakers Call for Addressing Causes of Conflict, Rather Than Investing in 'Bullets and Tanks', as General Assembly Continues High-Level Debate on Sustaining Peace', UN Meetings Coverage, General Assembly, Plenary, Seventy-Second Session, 85th & 86th Meetings (AM & PM), GA/12013, 25 APRIL 2018. Available at: Www.UN.ORG/PRESS/EN/2018/GA12013.DOC.HTM.

UN and World Bank (2018) *Pathways for Peace: Inclusive Approaches to Preventing Violent Conflict*, Washington, DC: World Bank. Available at: https://openknowledge.worldbank.org/handle/10986/28337.

UN High-Level Independent Panel on Peace Operations (HIPPO) (2015) 'Uniting Our Strengths for Peace: Politics, Partnership and People', Report of the UN High-Level Independent Panel on Peace Operations, 16 June. Available at: http://peaceoperationsreview.org/wp-content/uploads/2015/08/HIPPO_Report_1_June_2015.pdf.

UN Integrated Disarmament Demobilization and Reintegration Standards (IDDRS) (2006), *Integrated Disarmament Demobilization and Reintegration Standards (IDDRS)*, New York: UN. Available at: www.unddr.org/iddrs.aspx.

UN OCHA/IRIN (2005) *Broken Bodies, Broken Dreams: Violence against Women Exposed*, New York: UN OCHA/IRIN.

UN Office of Counter Terrorism (2019) website of UN Office of Counter Terrorism. Available at: www.un.org/terrorism.

UN Office of the Special Representative of the Secretary-General for Children and Armed Conflict (2012) 'Children and Justice During and in the Aftermath of Armed Conflict', Working Paper No. 3, New York: UN. Available at: www.un.org/children/conflict/_documents/Working%20Paper%20Number%203_Children%20and%20Justice.pdf.

UN Police (2019) UN Police website. Available at: https://police.un.org.

UN Rule of Law (2013) 'What is the Rule of Law?', UN Rule of Law website. Available at: www.un.org/ruleoflaw.

UN Rule of Law (2019) UN Rule of Law website. Available at: www.un.org/ruleoflaw.

UN Special Representative of the Secretary-General for Children and Armed Conflict (2017) *Promotion and Protection of the Rights of Children*, A/72/361–S/2017/821, 24 August, New York UN. Available at: http://undocs.org/en/S/2017/821.

UN Special Representative of the Secretary-General for Children and Armed Conflict (2018) *Promotion and Protection of the Rights of Children*, A/72/865–S/2018/465, 16 May, New York UN. Available at: http://undocs.org/en/S/2018/465.

UN Treaty Collection (2019) UN Treaty Collection website. Available at: https://treaties.un.org/Pages/ViewDetails.aspx?src=TREATY&mtdsg_no=XXVI-6&chapter=26&lang=en.

UN Women (2015) 'Women take the reins to build peace in Colombia', UN Women News, 28 May, New York: UN Women. Available at: www.unwomen.org/en/news/stories/2015/5/women-build-peace-in-colombia.

UN Women (2017a) 'Colombian women play central role in peace process', UN Women video, 18 January. Available at: www.youtube.com/watch?v=jhoYzh–tVw.

UN Women (2017b) 'Feminism in Times of War and Peace' (video). Available at: www.youtube.com/watch?v=mIP8XHi9938.

UN Women (2019) UN Women website. Available at: www.unwomen.org.

UNDDR (2019) UNDDR website. Available at: http://unddr.org.

UNDP (1994) *Human Development Report*, New York: UNDP. Available at: http://hdr.undp.org/en/reports/global/hdr1994/chapters/.

UNDP (2002) *Human Development Report 2002: Deepening Democracy in a Fragmented World*, New York: UNDP. Available at: http://hdr.undp.org/en/reports/global/hdr2002/chapters/.

UNDP (2005a) 'Disarmament, Demobilization and Reintegration of Ex-combatants', Practice Note, New York: UNDP. Available at: www.undp.org/cpr/documents/ddr/DDR_Practice_Note_English_PDF.pdf.

UNDP (2005b) *Programming for Justice: Access for All – A Practitioners Guide to A Human Rights-Based Approach to Access to Justice*, Thailand: UNDP Regional Centre. Available at: www.un.org/ruleoflaw/blog/document/programming-for-justice-access-for-all-a-practitioners-guide-to-a-human-rights-based-approach-to-access-to-justice/.

UNDP (2012) 'Sierra Leone: Saturday courts tackle gender-based violence', UNDP website, 07 March. Available at: www.undp.org/content/undp/en/home/presscenter/articles/2012/03/07/sierra-leone-saturday-courts-tackle-gender-based-violence-case-backlog-.html.

UNDP (2019) 'Human Development Index', UNDP website. Available at: http://hdr.undp.org/en/content/human-development-index-hdi.

UNDP/DCAF (2006) *Democratising Security in Transition* States – *Findings, Recommendations and Resources from the UNDP/DCAF Roundtable for CIS Parliamentarians*, Prague, New York: UNDP. Available at: www.undp.org/cpr/documents/sa_control/UNDP_DCAF_Democratising_Security.pdf.

UNDPKO (2008) *United Nations Peacekeeping Operations Principles and Guidelines*, 18 January, New York: UN. Available at: https://peacekeeping.un.org/sites/default/files/capstone_eng_0.pdf.

UNDPKO (2009) *Corrections Update*, Volume 1, October, New York: DPKO. Available at: www.un.org/en/peacekeeping/publications/cljas/corrections.pdf.

UNDPKO (2011) *Corrections Update*, Volume 3, September, New York: DPKO. Available at: www.un.org/en/peacekeeping/publications/cljas/corrections03.pdf.

UNDPKO (2018) 'Women in Peacekeeping', UNDPKO website, New York: UNDPKO. Available at: www.un.org/en/peacekeeping/issues/women/womeninpk.shtml.

UNEP (2005) *After the Tsunami: Rapid Environmental Assessment*, Geneva: UNEP. Available at: www.unep.org/tsunami/reports/TSUNAMI_report_complete.pdf.

UNESCO (2010) Guidebook for Planning Education in Emergencies and Reconstruction, Paris: UNESCO. Available at: www.iiep.unesco.org/fileadmin/user_upload/Cap_Dev_Technical_Assistance/pdf/Guidebook/Guideboook.pdf.

UNGA (2005a) 'In Larger Freedom: Towards Development, Security and Human Rights for All', A/59/2005, New York: UN. Available at: http://undocs.org/A/59/2005.

UNGA (2005b) 'Note to the General Assembly on the Administrative and Budgetary Aspects of the Financing of the United Nations Peacekeeping Operations', A/C.5/59/31, New York: UN.

UNGA (2011) 'Human Rights Council – Eighteenth session – Agenda item 3: Promotion and protection of all human rights, civil, political, economic, social and cultural rights, including the right to development', A/HRC/18/38, New York: UN. Available at: www2.ohchr. org/english/bodies/hrcouncil/docs/18session/A.HRC.18.38_en.pdf.

UNHCR (2019) UNHCR website. Available at: www.unhcr.org.

UNICEF (2014) *Hidden in Plain Sight: A Statistical Analysis of Violence against Children*, New York: UNICEF. Available at: http://files.unicef.org/publications/files/Hidden_in_plain_ sight_statistical_analysis_EN_3_Sept_2014.pdf.

UNICEF (2016) *Uprooted: The Growing Crisis for Refugee and Migrant Children*, New York: UNICEF. Available at: www.unicef.org/videoaudio/PDFs/Uprooted.pdf.

UNICEF (2019) UNICEF website. Available at: www.unicef.org.

United States Holocaust Memorial Museum (2018) *Holocaust* Encyclopedia. Available at: https://encyclopedia.ushmm.org/en.

Universal Rights Group (2017) 'Report of the Human Rights Council Strengthening Conference', held on 01 December in Geneva. Available at: www.universal-rights.org/ urg-policy-reports/human-rights-council-strengthening-conference.

University of Chicago (2012) *Pirate State: Inside Somalia's Terrorism at Sea* (video). Available at: www.youtube.com/watch?v=R5wVvZJf4b0.

UNMAS (2010) *UN Mine Action Service (UNMAS)* (video). Available at: www.youtube.com/ watch?v=qkCBfrTAT0Y.

UNMAS (2016) 'World Humanitarian Summit Opening Ceremony' (video). Available at: www.youtube.com/watch?v=ahgrJ7ram8M.

UNMAS (2019) UN Mine Action Service (UNMAS) website. Available at: www.mineaction. org/unmas.

UNODA (2019) UNODA website. Available at: www.un.org/disarmament/.

UNODC (2008a) *Handbook for Prison Managers and Policymakers on Women and Imprisonment*. Available at: www.unodc.org/documents/justice-and-prison-reform/women-and- imprisonment.pdf.

UNODC (2008b) *HIV and AIDS in Places of Detention: A Toolkit for Policymakers, Programme Managers, Prison Officers and Health Care Providers in Prison Settings*. Available at: www. unodc.org/documents/hiv-aids/HIV-toolkit-Dec08.pdf.

UNODC (2009) *Handbook on Prisoners with Special Needs*, Vienna: UNODC. Available at: www.unodc.org/pdf/criminal_justice/Handbook_on_Prisoners_with_Special_Needs.pdf

UNODC (2010a) *Crime and Instability: Case Studies of Transnational Threats*, Vienna: UNODC. Available at: www.unodc.org/documents/data-and-analysis/Studies/Crime_ and_instability_2010_final_26march.pdf.

UNODC (2010b) *Handbook for Prison Leaders: A Basic Training Tool and Curriculum for Prison Managers Based on International Standards and Norms*, Vienna: UNODC. Available at: www.unodc.org/documents/justice-and-prisonreform/UNODC_Handbook_for_Prison_ Leaders.pdf.

UNODC (2010c) *The Globalization of Crime: A Transnational Organized Crime Threat Assessment*, Vienna: UNODC. Available at: www.unodc.org/documents/data-and-analysis/ tocta/TOCTA_Report_2010_low_res.pdf.

UNODC (2010d) 'The Universal Legal Framework Against Terrorism', Counter-Terrorism Legal Training Curriculum, Module 2, Vienna; UNODC. Available at: www.unodc.org/ documents/terrorism/Publications/Training_Curriculum_Module2/English.pdf.

UNODC (2012) 'Yury Fedotov, Director General/Executive Director, Remarks at the Twenty-First Session of the Commission on Crime Prevention and Criminal Justice', Vienna: UNODC. Available at: www.unodc.org/unodc/en/speeches/remarks-at-21stccpcj.html.

UNODC (2013) 'Global Study on Homicide', Vienna: UNODC. Available at: www.unodc.org/gsh.

UNODC (2014) Human Trafficking Fund website. Available at: www.unodc.org/unodc/human-trafficking-fund.html.

UNODC (2016) *Global Report on Trafficking in Persons*, Vienna: UNODC. Available at: www.unodc.org/documents/data-and-analysis/glotip/2016_Global_Report_on_Trafficking_in_Persons.pdf.

UNODC (2017) *World Drug Report 2017*, Vienna: UNODC. Available at: www.unodc.org/wdr2017/index.html.

UNODC (2018) *Global Report on Trafficking in Persons*, Vienna: UNODC. Available at: www.unodc.org/unodc/data-and-analysis/glotip.html.

UNODC (2019) UNODC website. Available at: www.unodc.org.

UNODC and USIP (2011) *Criminal Justice Reform in Post-Conflict States: A Guide for Practitioners*, New York: UN. Available at: www.unodc.org/documents/justice-and-prison-reform/11-83015_Ebook.pdf.

UNODC Global Report on Trafficking in Persons (2009). Available at: www.unodc.org/unodc/en/data-and-analysis/glotip_2009.html.

UNOG (2018) 'The Convention on Certain Conventional Weapons', website of the United Nations Office at Geneva (UNOG), Geneva: UNOG. Available at: www.unog.ch/80256EE600585943/%28httpPages%29/4F0DEF093B4860B4C1257180004B1B30?OpenDocument.

UNOHCHR (2006) 'Mapping the Justice Sector', *Rule-of-Law Tools for Post-Conflict States*, New York and Geneva: UN. Available at: http://siteresources.worldbank.org/INTLAWJUSTINST/Resources/ruleoflaw-Mapping_en.pdf.

UNOHCHR (2009) 'Amnesties', Rule-Of-Law Tools for Post-Conflict States. New York: UN. Available at: www.ohchr.org/Documents/Publications/Amnesties_en.pdf.

UNOHCHR (2011) *International Legal Protection of Human Rights in Armed Conflict*, New York and Geneva: UN. Available at: www.ohchr.org/Documents/Publications/HR_in_armed_conflict.pdf.

UNOHCHR (2012) *The United Nations Human Rights Treaty System*, New York: UN. Available at: www.ohchr.org/Documents/Publications/FactSheet30Rev1.pdf.

UNOHCHR (2016) *Human Rights and Traditional Justice Systems in Africa*, New York: UN. Available at: www.ohchr.org/Documents/Publications/HR_PUB_16_2_HR_and_Traditional_Justice_Systems_in_Africa.pdf.

UNOHCHR (2017) 'End of mission statement by Dubravka Šimonović, United Nations Special Rapporteur on Violence against women, its causes and consequences, on her visit to Australia from 13 to 27 February 2017', Canberra, 27 February. New York: UNOHCHR. Available at: www.ohchr.org/EN/NewsEvents/Pages/DisplayNews.aspx?NewsID=21243&LangID=E.

UNOHCHR (2019) website of the OHCHR. Available at: www.ohchr.org.

UNOHCHR and UNMISS (2017) 'A Report on Violations and Abuses of International Human Rights Law and Violations of International Humanitarian Law in the Context of the Fighting in Juba, South Sudan, In July 2016', New York: UN. Available at: www.ohchr.org/Documents/Countries/SS/ReportJuba16Jan2017.pdf.

UNOHCHR and UNMISS (2018) 'Indiscriminate Attacks Against Civilians in Southern Unity April–May 2018', New York: UN. Available at: https://reliefweb.int/sites/reliefweb.int/files/resources/UNMISSReportApril_May2018.pdf.

UNSC (2000) UNSCR 1325. Available at: https://documents-dds-ny.un.org/doc/UNDOC/GEN/N00/720/18/PDF/N0072018.pdf?OpenElement.

UNSC (2008) UNSCR 1816. Available at: www.securitycouncilreport.org/atf/cf/%7B65BFCF9B-6D27-4E9C-8CD3-CF6E4FF96FF9%7D/Somalia%20S%20RES%201816.pdf.

UNSC (2010) Statement by the President of the Security Council, S/PRST/2010/4, New York: UN. Available at: www.securitycouncilreport.org/atf/cf/%7B65BFCF9B-6D27-4E9C-8CD3-CF6E4FF96FF9%7D/DT%20SPRST%202010%204.pdf.

UNSC (2012a) 'Delegations in Security Council Note Progress in Combating Piracy, but Warn 'Pirates Will Quickly Be Back in Their Skiffs' if Attention Diverted', Security Council: 6865th Meeting, New York: UN. Available at: www.un.org/News/Press/docs/2012/sc10820.doc.htm.

UNSG (1992) 'An Agenda for Peace: Preventive diplomacy, peacemaking and peace-keeping', Report of the Secretary-General pursuant to the statement adopted by the Summit Meeting of the Security Council on 31 January 1992, A/47/277 - S/24111, New York: UN. Available at: www.un.org/Docs/SG/agpeace.html.

UNSG (2001) 'Progress report on the prevention of armed conflict', Report of the Secretary-General, A/55/985-S/2001/574, New York: UN. Available at: www.undp.org/cpr/documents/prevention/SG%20report%20on%20prevention%20of%20armed%20conflict.pdf.

UNSG (2004a) 'A More Secure World: Our Shared Responsibility – Report of the Secretary-General's High-Level Panel on Threats, Challenges and Change', A/59/565, New York: UN. Available at: https://documents-dds-ny.un.org/doc/UNDOC/GEN/N04/602/31/PDF/N0460231.pdf?OpenElement.

UNSG (2004b) 'The rule of law and transitional justice in conflict and post-conflict societies', Report of the Secretary-General, S/2004/616, New York: UN. Available at: www.un.org/en/ga/search/view_doc.asp?symbol=S/2004/616.

UNSG (2006a) 'Disarmament, Demobilization and Reintegration', Report of the Secretary-General, A/60/705, New York: UN. www.undp.org/content/dam/undp/documents/cpr/documents/ddr/SG_Report_on_DDR_to_GA_s-60-705_March_2006.pdf.

UNSG (2006b) 'Progress report on the prevention of armed conflict', Report of the Secretary-General, A/60/891, New York: UN. Available at: https://undocs.org/A/60/891.

UNSG (2008a) 'Securing Peace and Development: The Role of the United Nations in Supporting Security Sector Reform', Report of the Secretary-General, *A/62/659-S/2008/39*. New York: UN. Available at: www.un.org/Docs/journal/asp/ws.asp?m=A/62/659.

UNSG (2008b) 'UN Approach to Rule of law Assistance', UN Secretary-General's Guidance Note. New York: UN. Available at: www.un.org/ruleoflaw/files/RoL%20Guidance%20Note%20UN%20Approach%20FINAL.pdf.

UNSG (2009) 'Report of the Secretary-General on peacebuilding in the immediate aftermath of conflict', A/63/881 – S/2009/304, New York: UN. Available at: www.unrol.org/files/pbf_090611_sg.pdf.

UNSG (2010) 'United Nations Approach to Transitional Justice', Guidance Note of the Secretary-General. New York: UN. Available at: www.un.org/ruleoflaw/files/TJ_Guidance_Note_March_2010FINAL.pdf.

UNSG (2012a) 'Conflict-related sexual violence', Report of the Secretary-General, A/66/657 – S/2012/33, New York: UN. Available at: www.peacewomen.org/assets/file/SecurityCouncilMonitor/Reports/sgreportcrsv_2012.pdf.

UNSG (2012b) 'Report of the Secretary-General on specialized anti-piracy courts in Somalia and other States in the region', S/2012/50, New York: UN.

UNSG (2012c) 'United Nations Global Counter-Terrorism Strategy: activities of the United Nations system in implementing the Strategy', Report of the Secretary-General,

A/66/762, New York: UN. Available at: www.un.org/en/terrorism/ctitf/pdfs/A%2066%20 762%20English.pdf.

UNSG (2013) 'Securing States and societies: strengthening the United Nations comprehensive support to security sector reform', Report of the Secretary-General, *A/67/970-S/2013/480*, New York: UN. Available at: www.securitycouncilreport.org/atf/ cf/%7B65BFCF9B-6D27-4E9C-8CD3-CF6E4FF96FF9%7D/s_2013_480.pdf.

UNSG (2014) 'Peacebuilding in the aftermath of conflict', Report of the Secretary-General, 23 September, *A/69/399–S/2014/694*, New York: UN. Available at: www.un.org/en/ peacebuilding/pbso/pdf/SG%20report%20OCT%202014%20EN69_399.pdf.

UNSG (2015) 'Report of the Secretary-General on Women and Peace and Security', *S/2015/716*, 16 September, New York: UN. Available at: www.un.org/ga/search/view_ doc.asp?symbol=S/2015/716&Lang=E.

UNSG (2017a) 'Report of the Secretary-General on Conflict-Related Sexual Violence', S/2017/249, 15 April. New York: UN. Available at: www.un.org/en/events/elimination-of-sexual-violence-in-conflict/pdf/1494280398.pdf.

UNSG (2017b) 'Special measures for protection from sexual exploitation and abuse: a new approach', Report of the Secretary-General, *A/71/818*, 28 February, New York: UN. Available at: https://conduct.unmissions.org/sites/default/files/a_71_818_1.pdf.

UNSG (2018) 'Report of the Secretary-General on Conflict-Related Sexual Violence', *S/2018/250*, 23 March, New York: UN. Available at: http://undocs.org/S/2018/250.

Uppsala Conflict Data Program (UCDP) (2019) UCDP website. Available at: http://ucdp. uu.se.

US Government (2002) *The National Security Strategy of the United States of America*, Washington: US Government. Available at: www.state.gov/documents/organization/63562. pdf.

USIP (2001) *Teaching Guide on International Terrorism: Definitions, Causes, and Responses*, Washington: USIP. Available at: www.usip.org/sites/default/files/terrorism.pdf.

USIP (2011) Truth Commission Digital Collection, Washington, DC: USIP. Available at: www. usip.org/publications/2011/03/truth-commission-digital-collection.

USIP (2013) *Men, Peace, and Security Symposium: Agents of Change – The Changing Nature of Conflict* (video). Available at: www.youtube.com/watch?v=LEAYxr8Xo7I.

USIP (2014) 'Female Soldiers and DDR: Sierra Leone, Nepal, and Colombia' (video). Available at: www.youtube.com/watch?v=exlyTT3t7lo.

USIP (2014) *Preventing and Mitigating Conflicts: Role of the International Courts* (video). Available at: www.youtube.com/watch?v=gz9zTbo_QI4.

USIP (2015) 'The Future of U.N. Peace Operations' (video). Available at: www.youtube.com/ watch?v=qZPqYNqsWNk.

USIP (2017) 'Demining War Zones: Opening Space for Building Peace' (video). Available at: www.youtube.com/watch?v=Y-UuIYgwctg.

USIP (2017) 'When Women in War Aren't Victims: A Security Blindspot' (video). Available at: www.youtube.com/watch?v=snXKuley0L4.

USIP/US Army Peacekeeping and Stability Operations Institute (2009) *Guiding Principles for Stabilization and Reconstruction*, Washington: USIP. Available at: www.usip.org/sites/default/files/guiding_principles_full.pdf.

van der Lijn, J. (2018) 'Multilateral Peace Operations and the Challenges of Organized Crime', SIPRI Background Paper, February. Stockholm: SIPRI. Available at www.sipri. org/sites/default/files/2018-02/multilateral_peace_operations_and_the_challenges_of_ organized_crime.pdf.

Van Buren, P. (2012) *We Meant Well: How I Helped Lose the Battle for the Hearts and Minds of the Iraqi People*, New York: Metropolitan Books.

Van Eekelen, W (2006) 'Civil-Military Relations and the Formulation of Security Policy', in W. Van Eekelen and P. Fluri (eds), *Defence Institution Building: A Sourcebook in Support of the Partnership Action Plan (PAP-DIB)* Vienna: LaVAK.

van Tongeren, P. (2013) 'Potential Cornerstone of Infrastructures for Peace? How Local Peace Committees Can Make a Difference', *Peacebuilding*, 1(1): 39–60.

Vasak, K. (1977) 'Human Rights: A Thirty-Year Struggle: The Sustained Efforts to Give Force of Law to the Universal Declaration of Human Rights', *UNESCO Courier*, 30(11), 28–29, Paris: UNESCO.

Venice Commission (European Commission for Democracy through Law) (2008) *Report on the Democratic Control of the Armed Forces*, adopted by the Venice Commission at its 74th Plenary Session, Venice, 14–15 March, Strasbourg: Council of Europe. Available at: www. venice.coe.int/docs/2008/CDL-AD(2008)004-e.asp.

Verkamp, B. (2006) *The Moral Treatment of Returning Warriors in Early Medieval and Modern Times*, Scranton: University of Scranton Press.

Vice News (2014) *After the Flood: Mines and Mass Graves in Bosnia* (video). Available at: www. youtube.com/watch?reload=9&v=Gy5hX267fi0.

Vinjamuri, L., and Snyder, J. (2015) 'Law and Politics in Transitional Justice', *Annual Review of Political Science*, 18: 303–27.

Visoko, G. (2017) *Shaping Peace in Kosovo: The Politics of Peacebuilding and Statehood*, London: Palgrave Macmillan.

Vlachova, M. and Biason, L. (2005) (eds), *Women in an Insecure World: Violence against Women, Facts, Figures and Analysis*, Geneva: DCAF.

Voeten, E. (2009) 'The Politics of International Judicial Appointments', *Chicago Journal of International Law*, 9(2): Article 3.

Voice of the Tribunal: UNICTR (2017) 'Symposium: Looking Back to Move Forward: Final Reflections on the ICTY' (video). Available at: www.youtube.com/watch?v=2tdKBHbZCnc.

Volkmer, I. (2014) *The Global Public Sphere: Public Communication in the Age of Reflective Interdependence*, Cambridge: Polity Press.

von Dyck, C. (2016) 'DDR and SSR in War-to-Peace Transition', SSR Paper 14, Geneva: DCAF. Available at: www.dcaf.ch/sites/default/files/publications/documents/ONLINE-DCAF-SSR-14-2016-12-21.pdf.

Walling, C. (2018) 'Insights on Victim Testimony and Transitional Justice: A Response to Angelina Snodgrass Godoy', *Journal of Human Rights*, 17(3): 384–91.

Walter, B. (2010) 'Conflict Relapse and the Sustainability of Post-Conflict Peace', background paper for WDR 2011, Washington: World Bank.

Waltz, K. (1979) *Theory of International Politics*, Reading: Addison-Wesley.

Ward, M., Greenhill, B. and Bakke, K. (2010) 'The Perils of Policy by P-Value: Predicting Civil Conflict', *Journal of Peace Research*, 47(4): 363–75.

Ward, J. and Marsh, M. (2006) 'Sexual Violence against Women and Girls in War and its Aftermath: Realities, Responses, and Required Resources', a briefing paper prepared for the Symposium on Sexual Violence in Conflict and Beyond, 21–23 June 2006, Brussels, Belgium, available at www.unfpa.org.

Waterfield, M. (2014) 'Conflict Assessments in the Planning of Stabilisation/Conflict Recovery Programmes', (video) (University of Leicester). Available at: www.youtube.com/watch?v=qXOPxV0FJcE&list=PLjQX5EXgm57S0L7nT-QMVhQLKiYNsSPxu&index=5.

Waters, T. and Waters, D. (eds) (2015) *Max Weber in Weber's Rationalism and Modern Society*. New York: Palgrave Books.

Watson, A. (2014) *Ring of Steel: Germany and Austria-Hungary at War, 1914–1918*, London: Allen Lane.

Weiss, T. (2012) *What's Wrong with the United Nations and How to Fix It*, Cambridge: Polity Press.

Weiss, T. and Collins, C. (2018) *Humanitarian Challenges and Intervention*, New York: Routledge.

Welch, A. (2014) 'Security Sector Management/ Development, Security and Local Ownership', (video) (University of Leicester). Available at: www.youtube.com/watch?v=C-ydEU2E6p8.

Welsh, J. (2010) 'Implementing the Responsibility to Protect: Where Expectations Meet Reality', *Ethics and International Affairs*, 24(4): 415–30.

Westendorf, J.-K. (2015) *Why Peace Processes Fail: Negotiating Insecurity After Civil War*, Boulder: Lynne Rienner.

Wezeman, P. (2010) *Arms flows and the conflict in Somalia*. Stockholm: SIPRI. Available at: www.sipri.org/sites/default/files/files/misc/SIPRIBP1010b.pdf.

Whittall, J. (2010) 'Humanitarian Early Warning Systems: Myth and Reality', *Third World Quarterly*, 31(8): 1237–50.

Whitworth, S. (2008) 'Militarized Masculinity and Post Traumatic Stress Disorder in J. Parpart and M. Zalewski (eds), *Rethinking the Wo/Man Question in International Relations*, London: Zed Books, 109–26.

Willems, R., Verkoren, W., Derks, M., Kleingeld, J., Frerks, G. and Rouw, H. (2009) 'Security Promotion in Fragile States: Can Local Meet National? Exploring the Connections between Community Security and Disarmament, Demobilization and Reintegration (DDR)', Human Security Gateway. Available at: www.humansecuritygateway.com/documents/CLINGENDAEL_SecurityPromotionFragileStates.pdf.

Willett, L. (2011) 'Pirates and Power Politics', *The RUSI Journal*, 156(6): 20–5.

Willett, S. (2010) 'Introduction: Security Council Resolution 1325: Assessing the Impact on Women, Peace and Security', *International Peacekeeping*, 17(2): 142–58.

Williams, M. (2011) '(Un)Sustainable Peacebuilding: NATO's Suitability for Postconflict Reconstruction in Multiactor Environments', *Global Governance*, 17(1): 115–34.

Williams, P (2009) *Criminals, militias, and insurgents: organized crime in Iraq*. US Army War College: Strategic Studies Institute. Available at: https://doi.org/10.21236/ADA504847.

Wilson, P. (2009) *The Thirty Years War: Europe's Tragedy*, Cambridge: Harvard University Press.

Wilson, R. (2001) *The Politics of Truth and Reconciliation in South Africa: Legitimizing the Post-Apartheid State*, Cambridge: Cambridge University Press.

Wilton Park (2014) *The UN in some of the toughest places in the world*, podcast. Available at: www.wiltonpark.org.uk/podcast/the-un-in-some-of-the-toughest-places-in-the-world/.

Wilton Park (2017) 'Effective IED clearance' (video). Available at: www.youtube.com/watch?v=gu-aqikxZ84.

Winfield, N. (1999) 'UN Failed Rwanda', 16 December, Global Policy Forum. Available at: www.globalpolicy.org/component/content/article/201-rwanda/39240.html.

Winslow, D. (2018) 'Strange Bedfellows in Humanitarian Crises: NGOs and the Military' in T. Shaw (ed) *Twisting arms and flexing muscles: Humanitarian Intervention and Peacebuilding in Perspective*, London: Routledge.

Wintour, P. (2016) 'Intelligence Files Support Claims Iraq Invasion Helped Spawn Isis', *The Guardian*, 07 July. Available at: www.theguardian.com/uk-news/2016/jul/06/intelligence-files-support-claims-iraq-invasion-helped-spawn-isis.

Wolf, A. (2002) *Does Education Matter? Myths about Education and Economic Growth*, London: Penguin.

Wood, E. (2014) 'Conflict-Related Sexual Violence and the Policy Implications of Recent Research', *International Review of the Red Cross*, 96(894): 457–78.

Woodhouse, T., Miall, H., Ramsbotham, O. and Mitchell, C. (2015) *The Contemporary Conflict Resolution Reader*, Cambridge: Polity Press.

Worcester, M. (2007) *The Threat of Transnational Crime*, Berlin: Institut für Strategie- Politik- Sicherheits- und Wirtschaftsberatung (ISPSW) Available at: www.isn.ethz.ch/isn/Digital-Library/Publications/Detail/?id=46129&lng=en.

World Affairs Council of Greater Houston (WAC) (2016) 'Exploiting Disorder: al-Qaeda and the Islamic State – International Crisis Group' (video). Available at: www.youtube.com/watch?v=sVfIeWe2H7I&index=20&list=PLboAe3-SRewrm6HSWrq2a-cIdV8prcSah.

World Bank (2011) *World Development Report 2011: Conflict, Security, and Development*. Washington DC: World Bank. Available at https://siteresources.worldbank.org/INTWDRS/Resources/WDR2011_Full_Text.pdf.

World Economic Forum (2017) *The Global Risks Report*, Geneva: World Economic Forum. Available at: www3.weforum.org/docs/GRR17_Report_web.pdf.

World Health Organisation (WHO) (2019) World Health Organisation website. Available at: www.who.int.

World Prison Brief (2017) 'Guidance Notes on Prison Reform', World Prison Brief online database. Available at: www.prisonstudies.org/research-publications?shs_term_node_tid_depth=29.

World Prison Brief (2019) World Prison Brief website. Available at: www.prisonstudies.org.

Wouters, J. (2005) 'The Obligation to Prosecute International Law Crimes'. Available at: www.law.kuleuven.be/iir/nl/onderzoek/opinies/obligationtoprosecute.pdf.

Wright, H. (2010) *Masculinities, Conflict and Peacebuilding: Perspectives on Men through a Gender Lens*, London: Saferworld. Available at: www.saferworld.org.uk/resources/publications/862-masculinities-conflict-and-peacebuilding-perspectives-on-men-through-a-gender-lens.

Xu, X. (2007) 'On Conflict of Human Rights', *Pierce Law Review*, 5(1): 31–57.

Yadav, P. (2016) *Social Transformation in Post-Conflict Nepal: A Gender Perspective*, Abingdon: Routledge.

Zala, B. and Rogers, P. (2011) 'The 'Other' Global Security Challenges: Socioeconomic and Environmental Realities after the War on Terror', *The RUSI Journal*, 156(4): 26–33.

Zartman, I. (2015) *Preventing Deadly Conflict*, Cambridge: Polity Press.

Zeigler, S. and Smith, M. (2017) 'Terrorism Before and During the War on Terror: A Look at the Numbers', *War on the Rocks*, 12 December. Available at: https://warontherocks.com/2017/12/terrorism-war-terror-look-numbers.

Zena, P. (2013) 'The Lessons and Limits of DDR in Africa', Africa Security Brief: A Publication of the Africa Center for Strategic Studies, No. 24. Available at: www.files.ethz.ch/isn/158581/AfricaBriefFinal_24.pdf.

Zoellick, R. (2009) 'Security Development', speech presented by the President of the World Bank Group at the United States Institute for Peace (USIP) 'Passing the Baton' Conference. Available at: http://siteresources.worldbank.org/NEWS/Resources/RBZUSIPSpeech010809.pdf.

Zyck, S. (2009) 'Former Combatant Reintegration and Fragmentation in Contemporary Afghanistan', *Conflict, Security and Development*, 9(1): 111–31.

Zyck, S. (2011) 'Review article: Explaining SSR's dearth of success stories', *Conflict, Security and Development*, 11(4): 497–507.

Index

Please note: page numbers in **bold type** indicate figures or illustrations, those in *italics* indicate tables or breakout boxes.

378   *Index*